LIVING IN AWE

ABUNDANCE · WELLNESS · EMPOWERMENT

*Creating a Thriving World from the
Inside-Out, Ground-Up & Top Down with Love*

MARK STEPHEN CHASAN

Living in AWE

Abundance • Wellness • Empowerment

Creating a Thriving World from the Inside-Out, Ground-Up & Top Down with Love

© 2010-2021 Mark Chasan

Print ISBN: 978-1-09838-5-132
eBook ISBN: 978-1-09838-5-149

ABOUT THE AUTHOR

Throughout history the two most impactful levers of influence on humankind have been (1) the environments in which we live and (2) innovation. By focusing on these levers of change, Mark seeks to accelerate and exponentiate the "Regenerative Economy" – an economy devoted to the thriving of people and planet.

Mark's track record includes being a lawyer; a serial entrepreneur with a public exit and two M&As; a renewable energy and structured finance executive; a financial advisor and innovator who has participated in over $500 million of financial transactions; and an intuitive healer.

As the CEO of Transformative, Inc. and AWE Global, Inc. ("AWE"), Mark is committed to the mission of creating an abundant, well and empowered society by focusing on (1) developing regenerative communities and environments, (2) advancing living systems innovation and eco-social entrepreneurship, and (3) fostering the "Regenerative Economy."

In *Living in AWE*, Mark brings a lifetime of valuable and inspiring experiences to provide holistic solutions to positively transform our world and increase the quality of our lives.

CONTENTS

INTRODUCTION

Creating a World of AWE

"In Abundance, poverty is alleviated
In Wellness, disease is healed
In Empowerment, limitation is superseded"

~Mark Stephen Chasan

When the Dalai Lama was asked what surprised him most, he said *"Man. Because he sacrifices his health in order to make money. Then he sacrifices money to recuperate his health. And then he is so anxious about the future that he does not enjoy the present; the result being that he does not live in the present or the future; he lives as if he is never going to die, and then dies having never really lived."*

As the Dalai Lama pointed out, we humans often engage in dichotomous, self-destructive and counter-intuitive behavior that is not beneficial to our health, happiness, fulfillment or survival. I find this behavior baffling considering our potential for love, beauty, kindness, creativity and brilliance. The desire for humankind to achieve its higher potential—to be more abundant, well, empowered, loving, and thriving—led me to ask the following questions:

- What are the root causes, beliefs and behaviors that perpetuate social dysfunction and activities destructive to our world?

- How can we shift our personal and collective consciousness, beliefs, behaviors and use of resources to serve the well-being of all humanity and the planet?

- How can we transform our current socio-political-economic system to reward conscious businesses and leaders devoted to human and planetary thriving rather than rewarding corrupt, greedy, polluting, exploitative and destructive businesses and leaders?

- How can we envision, design, build and manifest a regenerative Abundant, Well & Empowered world that elevates love, beauty, trust, respect and generosity over fear, greed, destruction, toxicity, divisiveness and war?

Living in AWE, was written to address the foregoing questions at this critical time in human history, with the intent of inspiring us to transform our individual beliefs and behaviors to take empowered action resulting in a civilization devoted to human and planetary thriving. This transformed civilization will be built upon each person's commitment to apply principles in their lives that foster abundance, wellness and empowerment, as well as an ever-deepening love, respect, and connection between each other and our planet. It is my hope that as more people adopt these principles, we can create a *"Regenerative Economy"* devoted to regenerating Earth's ecosystems so that current and future generations can flourish in a world of Abundance, Wellness & Empowerment.

THE PURPOSE OF LIVING IN AWE

As Buckminster Fuller said, *"In order to change an existing paradigm you do not struggle to try and change the problematic model. You create a new model and make the old one obsolete."*

My research and introspection have led me to the following conclusion: **The root causes of all social dysfunction are fear and disconnection. To heal this social dysfunction, it is essential that we create a new paradigm based upon loving and connecting with each other and our planet.**

The essential purpose of *Living in AWE* is to inspire a holistic paradigm shift in our perceptions, beliefs and behaviors to create a world of greater love, connection and "Ecosystemic Thriving."

The term "*Ecosystemic Thriving*" as used in this book, means a high degree of health, wellness, resilience, adaptability and evolutionary capacity of a living being or system and its environment in relationship to all other interconnected and interdepending beings. Thus, for humans to create Ecosystemic Thriving, we must go beyond our selfish desires, overconsumption and greed to consider the well-being of each other and our planet so we can transition from destructive industrialized practices to life-affirming regenerative practices.

Because the world is a reflection of the collective consciousness consisting of the beliefs and behaviors of each person, *Living in AWE* was written to help each of us make the personal changes to be more conscious, loving and supportive of the critical transformation needed. In this way, our individual contributions can incrementally transform the world. Transforming our world requires core systemic change. Rather than continuing to treat the symptoms, we need to cure the system. This transformation requires change from the <u>inside-out</u> (e.g., personal growth and belief change) <u>ground-up</u> (e.g., our individual and collective relationship with, and impact on, the earth and its ecosystems) and <u>top-down</u> (e.g., socio-political economic systems, governments, corporations and their leadership and governance).

Awe is state of amazement, wonder, love, reverence and gratitude for the miracles, big and small, that we, as humans, have the great fortune to experience. So many people in society have forgotten, or become numb to, the miracle of life. Each breath, the interactions of our cells, this beautiful planet and its complex ecosystems that give us life and sustain us are but a few of the amazing miracles we have been given. *Living in AWE* is being in a consistent state of awe and using our time, energy and resources to create an abundant, well and empowered world based upon love, connection and the creation of beauty devoted to thriving for people and planet. While it may take many generations, the time to start creating a world of AWE is now!

Living in AWE provides a roadmap of suggested fundamental principles, ideas and protocols to spark, inspire and empower the transformation we need to thrive as a species. Achieving the transformational goals for human and planetary thriving will require a change in beliefs and behaviors as well as mass adoption, implementation, dedication and collaboration.

It is my hope this book will inspire deeper research, collaboration, and commitment from impassioned people with brilliant minds, loving hearts, and expansive souls to manifest a reproducible template where the majority of human time, effort and resources are spent in support of planetary (including human) thriving. As this collaborative vision for a new and thriving paradigm gains momentum and becomes integrated into our daily lives, we will see a movement that transforms society and becomes a new way of life dedicated to the benefit of people and planet for generations to come.

THE INSPIRATION FOR LIVING IN AWE

The inspiration for this book started when my parents first took me to see the miracles of the tide pools at Abalone Cove when I was five years old. The sun shimmered on the ocean as a light breeze painted patterns on blue waters. Tide pools were teeming with life of all colors and shapes including orange and purple starfish, magical bobbing sea horses, iridescent abalone shells, sideways-walking black and orange crabs, and pulsing green sea anemones. It was the most wondrous sight I'd ever seen. I was in absolutely rapture and awe from the beauty, miracles and creativity of nature. I asked my parents to take me to the tide pools quite often, so I could re-experience the wonder and beauty of our planet.

Then something tragic happened. As a result of toxic chemicals and sewage dumped into the Santa Monica Bay, the marine life started to rapidly die. In just about 7 years after I had first seen the miracle of the tide pools teeming with life, the vitality and wonder of the tidepools was vanishing at an alarming rate. Moreover, the sky in Los Angeles had turned from blue to brown and smelled of petro-chemicals. There was often a toxic smog layer so thick that my eyes stung, my nostrils burned, and my lungs hurt, and visibility was often only 500 ft. In a few short years, through humankind's callous disregard for the environment, Los Angeles had become an ugly, toxic and unhealthy city with the ecosystems of the air and oceans polluted. At fourteen years old, I realized how fragile our ecosystem is and saw how our socio-economic-political system, based upon greed, hoarding and profit-at-all-costs, was creating great destruction to our beautiful planet and its life forms, including humans.

Now, in the 21st century, just a little over 250 years from the dawn of the industrial age, we face serious challenges to our health and survival, including climate change and natural disasters; bio-weapons and pandemics; toxicity in our air, water and food; widespread poverty; shortages of food and water; pervasive destruction of ecosystems; global economic collapse; and untenable levels of war and injustice.

We each have our unique perspective and experience of life and being human. Some believe that our world is working just fine the way it is, while others, including myself, believe our society has become largely dysfunctional and destructive to both humankind and nature and needs serious transformation.

There are significant facts demonstrating that our socio-economic-political system has become obsolete, destructive, dysfunctional and is displaying symptoms of sociopathy.

"Sociopathy" (now officially listed in the DSM as "Antisocial Personality Disorder") is characterized by **an abnormal lack of empathy** combined with **strongly amoral conduct** but masked by an ability to **appear outwardly normal**.

As will be discussed in greater detail, as a society, we spend substantial amounts of time, attention, money, resources and energy on endeavors that are destructive to humankind and the planet, with a general belief that such conduct is normal and somehow acceptable, rather than for the creation of regenerative abundance, beauty, wellness and joy for humankind and the health of our planet.

Here are a just few examples of such destructive behavior:

- Over the last 5 1/2 decades, the U.S. spent $5.5 trillion on production of nuclear weapons and an additional $13.2 trillion on other defense.[1] Global annual spending on defense is over $1.9 trillion per year according to Stockholm International Peace Research Institute (SIPRI).[2]

- Almost 9% of all annual country budgets are spent supporting oil, natural gas and coal industries through direct subsidies, consumer rebates and avoided taxes on pollution. The report published by The International Monetary Fund (IMF) estimates that annual worldwide subsidies to fossil fuels total $1.9 trillion.[3]

- An estimate of the global financial bailout that started in 2008 is $29 trillion, according to the Levy Economics Institute of Bard College.[4]

- According to the World Bank, 80% of humanity (nearly 5 billion people) live on less than $10/day. More astounding is that 8 of the wealthiest people control more resources than 3.6 billion of the poorest.[5]

- As a society, we can come up with trillions of dollars for war, unnecessary consumable products and bailing out financial institutions, but can't seem to provide $6 billion a year for healthy drinking water and $23 billion for sanitization to save the lives of the millions of people, including more than 800,000 children, that die each year from lack of potable water and sanitization.[6]

We, as a species, actively or tacitly participate in a sociopathic society that perpetrates inequitable and unethical conduct. The good news is that there are millions of people waking up and devoting themselves to building new systems and adopting new ways of living that will render the current system obsolete.

In truth, 99% of all species that have existed on the planet are now extinct. It's not a question of "if," but rather "when" and "how," humans will become extinct. It's my hope our extinction is not through our arrogance, neglect or apathy. It's also my hope we can take proactive steps to improve the quality and longevity of our lives while protecting the natural resources of our planet for future generations. The goal of *Living in AWE* is to offer a vision, blueprint and solutions for the transformation and evolution required for humankind and our planet to thrive for generations to come.

The Earth will be fine, maybe even better, without us. We do not need to "save the planet." We need to save ourselves by serving the planet! By caring for the planet in a way that promotes the health and thriving of ecosystems that support all life, we can save ourselves.

The health of our biosphere, from which we derive our next breath, our water, food, shelter, materials and economy, is key to our survival, health and happiness. Improving the quality and longevity of our lives will occur by proactively regenerating the health of our biosphere and deepening our connection, love, care and respect for each other and the Earth's ecosystems. As Margaret Mead said, *"We won't have a society if we destroy the environment."*

We are interconnected to each other and the biosphere. If our biosphere is not healthy, we are not healthy. For example, *"half of the world's oxygen is produced via phytoplankton photosynthesis. The other half is produced via photosynthesis on land by trees, shrubs, grasses, and other plants."*[7] As well, just about every living creature in the ocean and on land owes its existence to phytoplankton. If we destroy the phytoplankton by contaminating our oceans or increasing ocean temperature due to greenhouse gas emissions, we are likely to see accelerated rates of carbon dioxide coupled with a decrease of oxygen.

Because we are all interconnected, we are each affected when approximately 3 billion people are living in, or near, poverty. We are also affected by the inequitable distribution of wealth, war, pollution and destruction of our ecosystem. As a result of our interconnectedness, we each contribute to the creation of an energetic field of collective human consciousness. Thus, if humankind and our planet are suffering, we each experience a level of personal suffering, even if it is often at a subconscious or subtle level.

We have seen the warning signs of overconsumption, greed, waste and pollution of the environment for over 50 years, yet we arrogantly "steered the Titanic right into the iceberg of ecosystemic destruction." Now that the Titanic has likely hit the iceberg, I have found four primary coping strategies —1) party on the deck, 2) become immobilized by fear, 3) live in denial, or 4) build and deploy lifeboats.

I'm on the lifeboat team and devoted to accelerating the paradigm shift needed for the flourishing of humankind and the planet. As a small part of my contribution, I hope this book inspires the action and collaboration to co-create a new paradigm regenerative society devoted to abundance, wellness and empowerment in service to ecosystemic thriving, love and beauty.

THE GLOBAL HUMAN AGREEMENT

Our environment (including our conditioning, experiences and planetary condition) is the most influential impact on our consciousness, our beliefs and behaviors. Our beliefs and behaviors create a collective culture that influences our perception and experience of "reality." This collective culture and experience of "reality" manifests a "reinforcing feedback loop" that, in turn, affects the environment and human consciousness perpetuating the repetitive worldview and culture we accept as "reality."

Culture influences our perspective on such things as the following:

- Ideas of morality, ethics and judgment (e.g., right and wrong, good and bad, fair and unfair)

- Sense of beauty

- Dietary choices

- Way of relating to family, friends & society and our understanding of "appropriate" behavior

- Perceived need for money, jobs and stuff

- Desire for, and methods of obtaining, acknowledgment and recognition

- Our sexual, mating and reproductive patterns

In this book, the reinforcing circular feedback loop of environment, collective global consciousness, beliefs, behaviors and culture is referred to as "*The Global Human Agreement.*"

The Global Human Agreement creates and reinforces the macro experience of "reality" by humankind. While the current Global Human Agreement possesses a great deal of beauty, love, kindness, creativity and brilliance, it also consists of pervasive and untenable levels of fear, scarcity, toxicity, destruction, greed, poverty, cruelty, suffering and injustice. If we continue to perpetuate the current Global Human Agreement, there is a great likelihood that humankind will not survive as a species.

Each of us contributes to The Global Human Agreement in our thoughts, words and deeds, as well as our inaction. No matter what we do or don't do, we participate in, and influence the Global Human Agreement. We each possess the power and potential to change it. To the extent we change and empower ourselves, we incrementally change the Global Human Agreement. A critical step to transforming the Global Human Agreement and creating a "new reality," requires us each to consciously replace harmful and disempowering thoughts, beliefs, language, programs and behaviors with ones that are loving, life-enhancing, empowering, healthy and abundant. As we gain greater adoption of "new reality," we will see a tipping point where the late adopters and laggards become transformed.

THE POWER OF IMAGINATION AND EXPERIENTIAL REALITY

In the process of transforming our reality, the imagination plays a powerful and critical role. Literally, every creation and invention of humankind was borne in the imagination. Yet, imagination has frequently been relegated by our society to mere fantasy.

According to Albert Einstein, "*The true sign of intelligence is not knowledge but imagination.*" By continually challenging the status quo and using his imagination, Einstein came to defy the intellectual standard set by the scientific community since the time of Newton. He saw beyond what was considered commonly accepted and expanded the limits of human knowledge and potential. Einstein, who possessed great knowledge and imagination, said of the two, "*Imagination is more important than knowledge. For knowledge is limited to all we now know and understand, while imagination embraces the entire world, and all there ever will be to know and understand.*" Imagination is a vital component of the way we create our experiences and our world.

There is a thin veil between imagination and "physical reality." In our imagination, we are powerful and can create anything we desire with minimal effort. For example, we can imagine flying, telecommunicating, telekinesis, breathing under water and many other miracles. Many of these "miracles" have become reality with the advent of airplanes and spacecraft, submarines, mobile phones, and manufacturing processes that perform alchemy and reshape materials of all kinds into a vast array of products.

Our experience of physical "reality" is largely an imaginative process. In creating our "reality," our senses sample vibrations from the electro-magnetic spectrum. Once these vibrations are converted into sensory data our mind perceives the sensory data and our imagination creates the experience we call "reality." Our cognitive mind, through filters of beliefs and cultural programming, then interprets and assigns relationships and meaning to that which is sensed, perceived and created by our imagination. The interpretation of beliefs, culture, meaning and relationships is also an imaginative process. In this creative process, we literally imagine our world.

Using fMRI scans, researchers like V. S. Ramachandran, director of the Center for Brain and Cognition at the University of California, San Diego, have found that the same cells in the brain light up whether we perform an action ourselves, watch someone else do it, or when we simply imagine ourselves performing the action.[8]

The combined totality of our experience, (both our "real" and "imagined"), is referred to in this book as *"Experiential Reality."* Whether we experience a physical sensation, a thought that affects our emotional and physical state, a vivid dream, a mirage, or a belief that affects the way we relate to our world, all of these experiences form our view of the world and our "reality" causing profound impact in our lives and the lives of others.

For example, when you think of someone you love, what physiological changes occur, as opposed to thinking of someone who frustrates and angers you? Just thinking of different people and imagining different scenarios not only has a profound impact on our mental and emotional state, but also on our physical state, and therefore our physical reality.

Just as our eyes perceive visual objects by sensing vibrations from the visible electromagnetic spectrum, thoughts, beliefs and emotions have vibratory frequencies that impact our physical reality including our feelings, our bodies, our environment and our reality.

The way we imagine, perceive and believe the world to be, is generally the world we create. The creation of our reality is much like looking in a mirror—we instantaneously receive back whatever we project. Likewise, we're in a co-creative process with the universe in the creation of that which we experience as "reality." The universe instantaneously returns the vibrations, thoughts and emotions we transmit. If we experience anger and neediness, the universe returns anger and neediness, and we create our "reality" from that perspective. If, however, we are loving, joyful, trusting and abundant, the universe gives us love, joy, trust and abundance. We are literally creating our world each moment. And each moment, we have the power to choose how we perceive and create our world.

THE LANGUAGE OF AWE

Language is a powerful influence on our consciousness, beliefs and behavior. What we think, believe, and focus on shapes our perception, experience of life, and our "reality." A significant portion of our beliefs and thoughts arise in the form of language, and language and beliefs strongly influence how we behave. Our language, beliefs and behavior create culture.

When we think, or communicate, a thought in the form of a statement, we use language. Language is a cultural program taught to us by our society. We often believe when we think in a language, we're expressing our true selves and beliefs. We often forget that we're actually running a program we were taught by society.

For example, I wasn't born speaking English. I learned English because I was born in the U.S. When I think in English, I'm running a program—a program based upon the language, culture and belief systems of American society, my family, my friends, my teachers and media.

Behavior is often manipulated and motivated using language and propaganda that activates our sympathetic nervous system aka fight or flight mechanism. When we're in fight or flight, the executive decision-making ability of the pre-frontal cortex is taken over by the amygdala, which causes us to react rather than make well-considered decisions. Governments, advertisers and non-profits have used psychological manipulation to get the masses to take urgent action without significant cognitive appraisal for years by disseminating emotionally laden communications often using *"Survival Advantage"* language.

Survival Advantage language is often cloaked in double negative messaging such as "The War Against Terror", "The Fight Against Cancer," and "The End of

Poverty." Using Survival Advantage language creates a perception of urgency and importance that generates impulsive reactions rather than well considered responses.

Playing on our fear of such things as death, disease, injury, loss of wealth, damage to person or property, loss of freedom, being ostracized or inconvenienced, Survival Advantage is a potent tool. This is because we, as a species, put more emphasis on avoiding pain rather than moving toward pleasure. One bad incident (e.g., getting shot, falling from a cliff, contracting an incurable disease or losing one's wealth) can end, or cause serious harm to, one's life or enjoyment of life. Whereas many good incidents that enhance life (e.g., buying a house, taking a trip, getting a promotion, falling in love), to most of us, don't seem quite as urgent, important or motivating as avoiding something bad.

While Survival Advantage may be highly effective to remedy a real and imme-diate disaster (putting out a fire or avoiding immediate death or injury), it consis-tently fails when applied to long-term solutions that actually heal dysfunction and transform our world. Survival Advantage consciousness often keeps us focused on the symptom while perpetuating the system that caused the problem rather than creating new systems that will render the problem obsolete and improve human and planetary thriving. Because language is highly influential to the way we think, collaborate, plan, design and act, it's important we use language in alignment with the world we seek to create. By focusing on ending a problem rather than creating a better future, Survival Advantage consciousness perpetuates world's problems including war, disease, pollution, hunger, and injustice. After all the billions of dollars, time and effort that have gone into non-profits focused on ending and fighting against war, disease, poverty, environmental devastation, pollution, and social injustice, we still have just as much, if not more, of these challenges.

To transform our society, we need to replace dead-end, double-negative language with new creative, generative and evolutionary language. For example, rather than "The War on Terror," we can focus on "Creating Peace." The words "War" and "Terror" are Survival Advantage words with negative and harmful meanings. We will not create peace by waging war against terror. We only create more war and terror. However, war and terror become obsolete when we create and live in peace.

When Mother Theresa was asked why she didn't participate in anti-war demonstrations, she said, *"I will never do that, but as soon as you have a pro-peace rally, I'll be there."*

Rather than "Ending Poverty," what if we focused on the "Creating Global Abundance"? Currently poverty is defined as living on US $1.90 per day or less.[9] So using this metric, when we raise the standard of living of the billions of people living in poverty to US $1.91 per day, we can throw a big celebration for having achieved our goal of taking billions out of poverty. The reality is that these people will continue to live in poverty +$.01 without also factoring in inflation.

Instead of "Fighting Against Disease," what if we "Optimized Our Wellness" by building healthy immune systems? Spending on "healthcare" or more accurately, "sickcare," amounts to over $7 trillion per year.[10] If we "Optimize Our Wellness" rather than "Fight Against Disease" we could shift the massive amount of money spent on the "sickcare" system to increasing people's health through exercise, diet & nutrition, clean water and sanitation, outdoor activities, meditation, stress reduction and more vacation time, at a fraction of the cost of the sickcare system.

What if our thoughts, words and actions were motivated by an agenda to create peace and harmony rather than fight against and dominate other cultures to exploit their resources? What if the trillions of dollars, resources and energy currently spent on war and destruction were instead used to enhance quality-of-life and promote planetary thriving?

By spending time, energy and resources on developing local regenerative farms, we can give the world food security, materials to make homes, and agricultural jobs thereby rendering poverty and hunger conditions of the past. By then bringing renewable energy, computers, light manufacturing and regenerative applications to these communities along with a local exchange currency, we can then start creating abundance throughout the world.

I believe we can create a flourishing, abundant, well, empowered and beautiful world by devoting ourselves and our government spending to such endeavors as localized community regenerative farming, potable water infrastructure, healthy homes, renewable energy, biomimetic materials, waste upcycling, applied education, regenerative communities and optimal wellness systems while phasing out the effort, energy and money spent on extractive, exploitive and destructive industries (e.g., defense, oil, chemical, steel, GMO agriculture and a greenhouse gas belching supply chain).

LIVING IN AWE

"Awe" refers to an experiential state of perceptual vastness beyond the comprehension of our existing cognitive model. Awe is a state of wonder, reverence, admiration, respect and amazement. When we're in awe, the belief-filled, time-driven cognitive mind is overcome, and we find ourselves in a present state of openness to experiencing the miracles of life and the ineffable universe.

The acronym "AWE" and the words "*Abundance, Wellness & Empowerment*" were intentionally chosen to represent states of being for personal and societal transformation leading to planetary thriving.

In AWE, there is the perpetual ability to increase our quality of life and continually improve the way we serve each other and planet. The fundamental principles of AWE are as follows:

ABUNDANCE

"Abundance" is the state of being abundant. This state is experienced when we are fulfilled in the moment and have no perceived lack or need. In Abundance, we're overflowing, generous, collaborative, grateful, fulfilled and trusting.

We live in a universe of infinite possibilities, abundant resources, energy and opportunities. In fact, there are more opportunities to do good for each other and planet then there are people. Embracing these opportunities to create abundance will require deepening our gratitude, love, respect, connection and generosity for each other and our planet. Also, by applying regenerative principles—those seen in nature's ability to reproduce and perpetuate life—we can create an abundant world where such things as hunger, poverty, and scarcity consciousness are healed.

WELLNESS

"Wellness," as used in this book, is a whole and healthy balance of the mind, body, spirit and emotions resulting in an overall feeling of well-being and the ability to access massive amounts of energy available in the universe to create a powerful life experience. Wellness, like abundance, is a state of being. If we're willing to commit ourselves to the state of being optimally well, the quality of our lives and our powers of manifestation increase exponentially.

In Wellness, we focus on creating a state of optimal health, vitality and well-being in which disease ceases to exist. We can become healthy with strong immune systems and thrive in a symbiotic relationship with viruses and bacteria rather than trying to kill them with antibiotics.

The Wellness section contains a protocol for optimal wellness based upon the acronym **M.E.D.I.C.I.N.E.**, which stands for the following:

- **M**indfulness, Meditation & Optimized States of Being
- **E**xercise & Breath
- **D**iet & Nutrition
- **I**nternal Cleansing & Detoxification
- **C**ontentment, Calm, Rest, Sleep & Rejuvenation
- **I**ntimacy, Love & Connection
- **N**atural Connection & Environmental Thriving
- **E**pigenetics & Energetic Activation

When we possess optimal wellness, we experience greater vitality and energy, mental clarity and focus, stamina, emotional well-being and resilience, as well as greater spiritual connection and ability to manifest.

EMPOWERMENT

In this book, "Empowerment" refers to the ability, right and confidence to take autonomous and self-determined action that improves the quality of life and thriving for ourselves, humankind and the planet. The Empowerment section of this book provides suggestions and a roadmap to transforming ourselves and our world from its current states of dysfunction to function and thriving. In order to take the steps required to transform our world, we each need to understand our abilities and power to, as individuals, incrementally contribute to creating a new paradigm.

In Empowerment, we experience our individual power and collective will to change ourselves and transform the world. When we shift our perception of the world, the world changes. Our perceptions are often based upon conditioned and limiting beliefs, thoughts and feelings. When we question and shift our beliefs, thoughts and feelings, we create new awareness and potential. When we understand and act on our power to realize new potential, individually and collectively, we transform the world.

Each of us holds the power to transform not only our consciousness (e.g., perceptions, thoughts, beliefs and emotions), and our behaviors, but the world itself. This book provides a pathway for owning and expressing our power to create a new world—a world of AWE.

CREATING A NEW PARADIGM

In our society, many of us have been conditioned to elevate safety, security, comfort and convenience over love, freedom, adventure, and courage. We have been largely taught to fear the unknown, inconvenience, discomfort and embarrassment. As a result of this conditioning and fear, many of us have become complacent and satisfied with mediocrity. Ironically, in order to enjoy the convenience and security that we believe money will bring, we spend our time, energy and resources inconveniencing ourselves 40 hours a week in jobs that many of us don't enjoy. And many of the jobs perpetuate a society built upon extractive, exploitive, destructive and toxic industries that often threaten our health, safety and survival (e.g., fossil fuel, defense, chemical production, manufacturing and supply chain). We too often allow the economic imperative to trump the ethical imperative, resulting in the loss of our health, the diminution of our spirit and the destruction of nature and beauty.

Metaphorically, we're so busy, with our trillion-dollar rolls of duct tape, keeping the "old clunker" (belching out smoke and pollution) from falling apart, that we don't take time to explore new possibilities. If we just took our head out from under the old clunker's hood and looked up, we would see a brand-new Tesla with the keys and pink slip in it. In essence, by clinging to the existing system and attempting to fix it with the same tools that created the system, we move into our future facing backward, with disempowering beliefs in service to an obsolete and toxic system significantly dictating our future. By letting go of the past and focusing on creating a new future, unfettered by the thoughts, beliefs, conditioning and structures of the past, a wholly new future can be created.

Generally, if we are looking left, we are not looking right. If we're fixing problems with our left brain, we're not creating new potential with our whole brain. As Albert Einstein said, "We can't solve problems by using the same kind of thinking we used when we created them." In order to transform our world into an abundant, well and empowered world, new tools are needed.

This transformation starts with a change in the way we experience and view ourselves, each other and our world. This change starts with opening our minds to new possibilities giving rise to evolutionary consciousness and new beliefs from which we can build innovative regenerative environments that reshape our culture and socio-economic-political system from the ground up.

To positively transform our reality, it's important to do the foundational work of replacing limiting and harmful beliefs, systems, language and behaviors with empowering and life-enhancing beliefs, systems, behaviors and language that create our future (rather than fix our past).

Using an integrated whole-systems approach, *Living in AWE* provides a comprehensive guide and a tool chest to help us powerfully manifest our new realities in our lives and create a world of *AWE*, including:

- Consciously replacing harmful and disempowering beliefs and behavior patterns with those that are creative, life-enhancing, empowering, healthy and abundant

- Creating new realities using awareness, empowerment and manifestation tools included in this book (e.g., Experiential Reality, Quantum Manifestation, Vibrational and Emotional Mastery) and unlocking universal potential

- Transforming "The Global Human Agreement" by changing your beliefs and behaviors and your contributory effect on the collective reality

- Understanding and creating abundance both personally and globally

- Living in optimal health and wellness using the M.E.D.I.C.I.N.E. system

- Developing the Regenerative Economy (the largest and most robust economy in the history of humankind) that focuses human effort and resources on fostering planetary thriving, creating abundance and fulfilling humankind's potential for beauty and kindness

- Understanding and living in integrity with our values

- Transforming our organizations and organizational culture to be abundant, well and empowered

- Developing new models and metrics of success based upon qualitative and life-enhancing measurements

As will be discussed in this book, it's through the foregoing integrated whole-systems approaches and tools that we can shift our personal and collective consciousness to powerfully and positively transform our lives and create an Abundant, Well & Empowered world.

THE REGENERATIVE ECONOMY

For too long, we've attempted to cure the ills of society in the same way western medicine attempts to treat symptoms rather than cure the disease. We somehow believe we can solve our social and environmental issues with money, legislation and technology, while ignoring our conditioning and belief structures that created our current issues (e.g., fear and disconnection leading to overconsumption, greed, distrust, war, and environmental destruction). The current social and environmental issues we face require both personal and systemic change.

Leading physicists, such as Max Tegmark, Ph.D. and Fred Alan Wolf, Ph.D., support the idea that we live in a universe of infinite possibilities. I hold too that there is a possibility we can create a better world—a world in which we can live in abundance (rather than end poverty), increase wellness and thriving (rather than fight disease), and be empowered to courageously create a thriving, beautiful and regenerative world (rather than fearfully conforming to a world that is too often destructive, toxic and unjust).

This transformation starts with a change in the way we experience and view ourselves, each other and our world. This change starts with opening our minds to new possibilities giving rise to evolutionary consciousness and new beliefs from which we can build innovative regenerative environments that reshape our culture and socio-economic-political system from the ground up.

For a fraction of the money, effort, time and resources we spend on destruction, war, extractive industries and bailouts, we can create a multi-trillion-dollar *"Regenerative Economy"* dedicated to improving the quality of life globally. The Regenerative Economy has the potential of creating the most robust economy in the history of humankind and providing over a billion meaningful jobs in industries that serve human and planetary thriving such as (1) clean, affordable and abundant renewable energy; (2) pure water and aquatech; (3) fresh and nutritious food and agtech; (3) biomimetic renewable materials; (4) nature stewardship and resource management; (5) waste upcycling; (6) bio-energetic environmental remediation; (7) optimal wellness; and (8) wise, regenerative and resilient cities and communities.

Transforming our extractive world of scarcity to a regenerative world of abundance is critical for our continued survival and will lead to the thriving of humankind.

I was led to write this book to fulfill my longing, passion and dedication to transforming our world into one that is more loving, beautiful, abundant, well, empowered and ecosystemically thriving. However, *Living in AWE* represents just the tip of an iceberg for global transformation. I have learned much of what is in this book from observation, research and experience. I do hope that I can bring a holistic, integrated and innovative perspective to human potential and societal transformation in this book. In doing so, I realize that I, and my life, are a work-in-progress and I am humbled by the many people more knowledgeable than me on many subjects discussed in this book and the people who have committed their lives to the philosophies and practices herein. I do not hold myself out as an expert in many of the areas discussed in this book, however, where I lack expertise I have made considerable effort to gain knowledge, understanding and wisdom through research from, and conversations with, such experts. This book seeks to inspire the transformation we require to thrive as a species through consistent personal transformation work and the collaboration of impassioned individuals, experts, communities and organizations to further influence, evolve and execute the principals and blueprints of transformation articulated herein.

This is an opportunity to embark on an extraordinary journey that has the potential to positively transform our personal lives, humankind and the planet. Together we can create a world of AWE—Abundance, Wellness & Empowerment!

ACKNOWLEDGMENT

I give my deep love and appreciation for the amazing people that have supported and influenced my journey, who shaped who I am through their love, inspiration and encouragement. In particular, I want to thank those who have contributed to my growth and the desire, skill and passion to write this book including my mom (Roslyn Chasan) and dad (Fred Chasan) who have lovingly supported me from the time I was just an embryo to present; my brothers (Jeff Chasan and Paul Chasan) who have been my best friends for life, have challenged me and made me a better person. I also give many thanks to my AWEsome friends and advisors who helped me create the vision for AWE (Bill Reed, Dana Harrison, John Kinney, Jason Hobson, Neal Hoptman, Ted Lieser, Joyous Presence, Matt Lucas, Merrill Ward, Jacqueline Chan, Tony Greenberg, Stuart Ruddick, Graham Moles, Caitlyn Thomasson, Bonnie Adams and Hunter Lovins). I also want to thank the amazing women who loved me, expanded my heart and taught me how I am perceived and who've touched my soul deeply (Kim Chasan, Lisa Renee and Chandra Hines). I give deep gratitude to those who helped me evolve as a human and who also provided great support, input and editing to this book.

I also want to thank the many friends, colleagues, authors, speakers and teachers who have inspired me over the years with their commitment to transformation, their courage to speak the truth and the sacrifices they've made so others may live a higher quality of life.

I also give my deepest love, respect and gratitude for this wondrous planet that gives us life, nurturance and abundance. I have deep devotion and reverence to ineffable divine consciousness that lives me, breathes me and dances me, with its myriad of infinite possibilities, that miraculously combine to create the experience of my life and inspired me to author this book.

SECTION ONE –

AWE CONSCIOUSNESS

Consciousness and vibration are the basis of all life, as we know it.

Our experience of life is largely the process of imaginatively transforming vibrations into a sensate physical experience we call "reality."

This section is devoted to providing the foundational consciousness to create a world of AWE—Abundance, Wellness & Empowerment.

CHAPTER 1

Opening Our Eyes

When we "open our eyes" and consciously question our beliefs and behaviors, we let the light of possibility shine in so we may experience our limitless, free and creative power in a universe of infinite potential.

There was a boy named Ize (pronounced "eyes") born in a village where everyone was blind, except him. As he grew up, he tried to explain his experience to the others—things like the colors and shapes of the world, the brightness of the sun, the illumination of the moon and stars, and the vastness of earth and sky. No one in the village had ever had such an experience as Ize. The language of the village had no words or context to communicate about a world of light, color and visual space. Words like "green", "bright", "vastness", "stars" and "sky" didn't exist.

Ize tried to explain his wondrous experience to others, but the people in the village thought he was just a strange boy living in a fantasy world of imagination and dreams. As he grew up and insisted upon his world being real, the village completely ostracized Ize and considered him to be insane. They told their children not to go near Ize or talk to him because he was crazy. Ize grew up in isolation and loneliness. Even Ize's parents prohibited him from ever speaking of "seeing" things.

One day, Ize came upon a still pool. Looking at his reflection in the pool, he blinked and for the first time realized he was physically different from all the rest of the villagers. His eyes opened and closed, whereas the rest of the villagers' eyes were closed all the time. He wondered, "what would happen if I could get the villagers to open their eyes and see the world I experience?"

With this new knowledge, he went back to the village and tried to get people to open their eyes, but they refused to listen. The chief of the village, Djark, ordered that Ize be imprisoned so he wouldn't "infect" the community with his "insane" ideas.

Luckily for Ize, Djark's courageous son, Ogle, helped him escape. When Ogle opened the door to release Ize, Ize realized that Ogle's eyes were open too. Ogle had been listening to Ize. He was curious about the world Ize described and thus started experimenting with opening his eyes. When Ogle opened his eyes and saw the world that Ize had been describing to the village for so long, he couldn't wait to share his experiences with Ize.

Ogle took Ize to see Djark, who became outraged that his son's mind had been infected by the madness of Ize. Djark ordered Ize to be killed. However, Ogle pleaded with his father to give Ize a chance to redeem himself through a challenge: If Djark would agree to open his eyes and did not experience the new world of light and color that Ize and Ogle were describing, then Ize would be put to death. Djark loved his son greatly and knew his son was a trustworthy child. So, out of curiosity, and wanting to support Ogle, Djark acquiesced.

Ize and Ogle helped Djark open his eyes slowly. As he did so, light flooded in for the first time and it caused Djark physical pain, confusion and overwhelm. Djark immediately shut his eyes. He declared opening one's eyes dangerous to society and banned anyone from ever attempting to open their eyes under penalty of death. He then sentenced Ize to be stoned to death within one week's time.

During the ensuing days, Ogle pleaded with his father to change his mind regarding sentencing Ize to death. One day before Ize was to be stoned to death, Ogle implored his father to try to open his eyes again. Ogle argued with his father that, because of Ogle's ability to see, if he put Ize to death for seeing, he would also have to put Ogle to death. Because Djark loved his son so much and realized that his impulsive decision regarding stoning Ize to death would eventually require his son being put to death, Djark agreed to try opening his eyes again.

Fortunately, this time when Djark opened his eyes, it was dusk, and the light was not so bright. Therefore, Djark did not feel the pain he felt the first time he opened his eyes. This time, Djark saw color and the physical world around him. He was overwhelmed and amazed at all he had missed for so long. At once, he repealed his ruling, released Ize and made Ize the village's high "seer." As a result, the entire village learned how to open their eyes and experienced the miracle and magic of a "new world"—a world that was there the whole time but was never experienced due to the limiting belief systems and customs of the village that had gone on for generations.

Djark's experience was so profound, that he changed his name to Lyte, and that is how Djark became Lyte.

This story is meant to illustrate how many of us live limited, fearful and inhibited lives based upon disempowering and narrow-minded belief systems. This story also illustrates that when we question our old beliefs and act courageously to overcome our fears, we open ourselves to a world of possibilities allowing us to expand our consciousness and experience miracles in our life.

From the time we're infants, we're implanted with limiting generational belief systems and illusive reality structures that we complacently or unconsciously accept without question. When we're in our formative years, we're like open sponges absorbing information at a subconscious level without the benefit of a conscious filter. Much of this subconscious information forms our beliefs upon which we base our decisions and actions in life. Even though many of the beliefs we hold are untrue, limiting and/or detrimental, we often adhere to these beliefs because they have become intertwined with our identity.

Because of our strong desire to be loved and accepted by our family, friends and society, we often conform to and adopt the belief systems of others. Once we identify ourselves with these conditioned beliefs, we tend to defend these beliefs and attempt to get others to adopt them. We gain a sense of comfort, validation and belonging when we are in the company of those who share our belief systems. However, this process ultimately causes limitation, closed-mindedness and resistance to change. It also diminishes imagination and our ability to "open our eyes" to see new possibilities, adopt new beliefs, and experience outcomes and realities beyond those accepted within our social circles and culture.

The most insidious aspect of our programming is that we believe that we are our beliefs. Our identities are so intertwined with our beliefs, it is incredibly difficult to separate them. Most of us complacently accept societal belief systems without question. We don't usually ask how the beliefs got there or whether they align with who we are or would like to become. Many of the conditioned beliefs programmed from birth prevent us from experiencing our full potential, the miracles of life and living in AWE.

When we judge something as good, bad, right or wrong or believe something 100%, we close our minds to new possibilities and stop accessing consciousness. Robert Anton Wilson said of this, *"As soon as one believes a doctrine of any sort, or assumes certitude, one stops thinking about that aspect of existence."*

Personally, I only believe my most firm beliefs 80%. This allows me to consistently question my beliefs and use them as tools of evolutionary consciousness rather than letting my beliefs imprison me in rigidity. Like a tool, if one of my beliefs becomes dull and useless or fails to serve its purpose, I upgrade the tool or get a new tool that works. Inquiry of our belief systems allows new visions and possibilities to emerge. Shifting belief systems can enable us to illuminate our imaginations and empower new realities, awakening our divine nature within this universe of infinite potential.

Helen Keller, who was born blind and deaf and became a prolific author, had amazing inner vision, wisdom and profound lessons as evidenced by the following quotes:

"The most pathetic person in the world is someone who has sight, but has no vision."

"No pessimist ever discovered the secret of the stars, or sailed to an uncharted land, or opened a new doorway for the human spirit."

"Security is mostly a superstition. It does not exist in nature, nor do the children of men as a whole experience it. Avoiding danger is no safer in the long run than outright exposure. Life is either a daring adventure, or nothing."

So, where Helen Keller was blind but possessed vision, how is it that we see but often have no vision? I invite you to join me in "opening our eyes" and our minds to being visionaries with an optimistic mission to create a new and better world—a world of AWE.

CHAPTER 2

Paradox and Infinite Potential

We live in a universe of infinite potential, which includes the potential that there is no universe and no potential. Anything we imagine, no matter how far-fetched or diametrically opposed to another potential, exists in the universe beyond time, space and judgment in perfect harmony. . .(or not).

The concepts of timelessness, spacelessness and infinity are difficult for us to understand, discuss or resolve, thus creating paradox. This is because we experience our phenomenal "physical reality" in time and space. However, our physical reality arises through the conversion of vibration by our limited senses into a mental construct that we experience as reality. Also, a significant majority of our language and thought processes are based on space-time constructs.

A *paradox* is generally defined as a statement or group of statements that leads to a contradiction that defies reason. However, it's the application of our linear space-time-relative reasoning to a non-linear universe that creates paradox. This is largely due to an exclusive either/or mindset that's unaccepting of the **inclusive and/ all nature of universal consciousness**.

For example, when we attempt to describe that which is beyond time and space with words, it tends to lead to the paradox of making "something" out of "nothing." Also, we've been conditioned to fear the unknown, yet we know so little. We've been taught to desire predictability, security, safety and stability, yet live in a world and universe that contains significant chaos, unpredictability and instability. Moreover, the infinite universe in which we live contains and harmonizes love with fear, stillness with change, nothing with everything, and predictability with chaos.

We can become the creators of magic and miracles when we accept that 1) the paradox and the miracle of our infinite universe is beyond our reason and cognitive understanding; 2) we live in a universe of infinite possibilities, and 3) through vibration, we each are the co-creators of our own universe.

In support of this, Max Tegmark, Ph.D., a cosmologist and professor at MIT, states...

> *"In infinite space, even the most unlikely events must take place somewhere. There are infinitely many other inhabited planets, including not just one but infinitely many that have people with the same appearance, name and memories as you, who play out every possible permutation of your life choices."*

By *equanimously accepting infinite potential of the universe*, rather than trying to *rationally understand* the infinite possibilities of the universe, we can increase our access to consciousness to realize greater inspiration, joy, harmony and love in our lives and society. Equanimous acceptance entails an inclusive approach that simultaneously holds, as equal and without judgment, the "and/all," "either/or" and "not/nothing" characteristics of the universe. The universe and all of the diametrically opposed possibilities contained within it (e.g., light and darkness, positive and negative, love and fear, evolution and creation, stillness and motion, expansion and contraction) are held in perfect harmony by the universe without judgment (or not).

While we experience love, harmony and peace in the world, we also experience untenable amounts of fear, divisiveness, misunderstandings, conflicts and a pervasive inability to respectfully collaborate for the thriving of humankind and the planet. This is largely due to the application of an exclusive either/or mindset that views opposites and different perspectives through narrow, limited, linear, right-wrong reasoning and judgment. When we judge things as right or wrong, good or bad, or take exclusive either/or approaches, we isolate ourselves and close our access to consciousness. In this judgmental mindset, we tend to take a position that is unaccepting of others who disagree with our views, beliefs and positions.

This is a fundamental cause of separation, misunderstanding, closed-mindedness and disagreement. If allowed to fester, this leads to conflict, disrespect, hostility, violence, war and destruction.

By viewing the world through the lens of inclusivity, equanimity and infinite possibility, we become open to the co-existence of opposites in harmony. Even if our beliefs are diametrically opposed, we can still respect each other's right to exist and accept each other's view and experience as equal to our own. We then become open to "inclusive and/all (rather than either/or) consciousness" that allows new possibilities to emerge resulting in synergistic resolutions that lead to respectful, creative and life-enhancing decisions, beliefs and behaviors.

Accepting the infinite potential of the universe and each other opens our consciousness to new possibilities for collaboration, respect and harmonious acceptance of each other, even if we have opposing views.

The paradox of seemingly contradictory co-existing states is supported by the "wave-particle" work of Max Planck [11], Albert Einstein[12], Louis de Broglie[13], Arthur Compton[14], to name a few, which found that all particles simultaneously have a wave nature, and all waves simultaneously have a particle nature.

In essence, we are simultaneously the wave experiencing itself as a particle and a particle experiencing itself as a wave. The universe simultaneously holds the entire wave and all the particles. It does so in an inclusive and/all state of resolution that also includes the either/or and not/nothing possibilities of the universe. The unified consciousness represents the wave. The holographic matrix from which we receive our phenomenal experience of the physical universe is represented by, and experienced through, the particle.

In this quantum reality, we can be seen like raindrops that lose their separate form upon entering the ocean and return to form through the cycle of evaporation and condensation. When we're in universal consciousness, we are the timeless, spaceless wave. When we emerge from the wave into the perception of being an individual human in physical time and space, we are the particle. We experience the separateness of being as the particle and the wholeness of the universe as the wave.

By using our imagination, we can experience the particle and the wave simultaneously. The imagination is a powerful state of consciousness from which miracles and innovative ideas spring forth and manifest themselves in our physical reality. Imagination allows us the opportunity to connect with the creative processes of the universe and its resources.

It's long been accepted by science that the atom is the basic unit of all matter, consisting of 99.99% space and a few electrically charged particles. Since we humans are 99.99% space, what makes our "reality" seem so physical and material?

It could be that the physical world, as we know it, consists of 99.99% consciousness.

The foregoing is supported by the physicist, Dr. Fred Alan Wolf, Ph.D. in the following statement:

"From a scientific standpoint, it is difficult to say exactly what is going on. And the reason why we don't know is because we have no idea where the viewer is that sees this Light. As an example, right now, you have some sense of being present in your body looking out at the world. But according to what we know from physics, this is an illusion of perception: There is no place inside your body where "you" actually exist. You don't have a particular volume of space or spot that is "you." It is an illusion to think that everything outside that volume of space is "not you"—what you commonly say is "outside of you." The best description we can give for this sense of presence is that you "are everywhere."

The main reason that you have more awareness of being in a body is simply because the sensory apparatus of the body commands a great deal of your attention and that much of your attention is linked to your physical senses. We have the illusion that our human bodies are solid, but they are over 99.99% empty space.

If an atom is blown up to the size of an entire football stadium, the dense part of the atom would be comparable to the size of a single grain of rice placed on the 50-yard line. Now why is that important? Because in an atom, the nucleus accounts for 99.99% of all of the matter or mass, atoms are mostly made of space. So, although we experience ourselves as being these solid human bodies, it's more like "who we are" is an awareness or consciousness that lives in space."[15]

Our existence, our consciousness, our next breath and the arrangement of our atoms are all a miracle. Whether you believe in modern science and evolutionary theory or the religious ideology of creationism, we are each a miracle that demonstrates the infinite potential of the universe.

According to modern science, our atoms are not alive and do not hold consciousness. Yet here we are, each a living miracle made up of approximately 7,000,000,000,000,000,000,000,000,000 atoms that somehow spontaneously conspired to form the amino acids and proteins of our DNA, which led to the production of our cells to miraculously create our life form. Furthermore, each cell miraculously appears to possess some innate intelligence directing it to be an eyeball as opposed to a liver or a fingernail. Moreover, millions of cells die each second and almost all of the body's cells are replaced every year. Yet, somehow we retain our form, appearance and self-identity.

Whether we apply evolutionary theories or creationist theories, life is an amazing miracle!

According to George S. Fichter, author of *Endangered Animals*, 99% of the species that have existed on the planet for the last 4.5 billion years are now extinct. Applying evolutionary theory, some of the extinct species contributed along the evolutionary path to our existence and had to procreate, survive massive calamities, adapt to hostile environments and continue surviving and procreating in an unbroken chain for billions of years for you and me to exist. If the evolutionists are right, each of us is a miracle, existing against the most extreme evolutionary odds.

If we apply creationist theory, each of us is a divinely created miracle of "God" or a universal consciousness.

In a universe of infinite potential, all possibilities simultaneously exist and are held in perfect harmony (or not). For example, the positions of "Creationists" and "Evolutionists" would generally be perceived as diametrically opposing views. The Creationists believe man was created by God about 10,000 years ago. Evolutionists believe we evolved through genetic mutation, adaptation and transformation from a single-cell organism known as the "last universal ancestor (LUA)" that existed some 3.8 billion years ago. Using linear, either/or logic, only one or the other view can be right. However, in a universe of infinite potential, the creationists and evolutionists are simultaneously both right. There is the possibility that we were created and evolved. As well, in a universe of infinite potential, there also exists the possibilities that both are wrong, that neither are right nor wrong, one is right while the other is wrong, they are both partially right and wrong, there is no right or wrong, and there is no creationist and no evolutionist, plus every possible permutation and combination of the foregoing and beyond that which we know (or not).

The universe is timeless and boundless. However, we perceive the universe through a time/space consciousness and continually attempt to understand timelessness and boundlessness with our linear rational minds and limited sensory abilities. We attempt to explain the non-dualistic/always-never/infinite nature of the universe with limited dualistic language and a very limited knowledge of the universe.

For example, the standard big bang theory says the universe began with a massive explosion. However, recent theories are showing the universe is infinitely large and has no beginning or end.

Neil Turok, a world-renowned theoretical physicist at the University of Cambridge, explains the Big Bang represents just one stage in an infinitely repeated cycle of universal expansion and contraction. Turok theorizes that **neither time nor the universe has a beginning or end**:

> "There doesn't have to be a beginning of time. According to our theory, the universe may be infinitely old and infinitely large."

In a universe of infinite potential, there exists the potential that the universe does not exist. This begs the question of our own existence and the illusion/reality paradox from which we create our experience. The paradoxical and mysterious nature of the universe also provides significant evidence of how little we know, yet how potentially powerful we are as creators of infinite possibilities.

Assuming that we're creating our experience of "reality" from a universe of infinite possibilities that only exists in consciousness, by consistently questioning our belief systems by adding "or not" whenever we believe something must be a certain way, provides us the ability to expand our consciousness and cognitive neuroplasticity. Thus, in a universe of infinite possibility, anything we believe is true, the opposite is also potentially and simultaneously true somewhere else in the universe. These seemingly disparate and conflicting possibilities co-exist in complete harmony in the universe (or not). Using this form of inquiry, openness and non-attachment, we can powerfully create an optimal future from an abundant palette of choices and continue to recreate and optimize our future.

We've created a mental construct of "reality" based on our sensory perception of space and time as well as our conditioned beliefs. From this space/time perception and relative (subject-object) oriented consciousness, we tend to view our world as a set of linear time/space experiences and choices between "this" or "that." As a result of this mental construct, most of us live in an "either/or" reality rather than an "and/both/all" reality.

We experience each moment as one single possibility among an infinite number of possibilities happening in the universe at each moment. So, we perceive we exist in a specific location in the universe at a specific time. This is the center point of the universe we each perceive, and we create each moment through our perception.

In other words, as we move from one perceived position to another, our perception is that we are still the center, or zero point, of the universe. We contain infinitely smaller universes within us and are part of an infinitely larger universe. In essence, we're simultaneously the zero point and infinity of the universe consciously experiencing the possibility of our specific relative/time/space consciousness.

This notion is supported by the statement of astronomer, Jay Pasachoff, Ph.D. and astrophysicist, Alexi Filippenko, Ph.D. that *"In the inflationary theory, matter, antimatter, and photons were produced by the energy of the false vacuum, which was released following the phase transition. All of these particles consist of positive energy. This energy, however, is exactly balanced by the negative gravitational energy of everything pulling on everything else. In other words, the total energy of the universe is zero!"*

Each and every physical form, no matter how large or small (from an atom to the entire cosmos), whether we consider it "living" or "non-living" (e.g., a human, an extra-terrestrial, a molecule, a rock or an entire planet), plays its part as a manifest consciousness-energy placeholder at the center of an infinite web of holographic consciousness. In other words, each energetic placeholder expresses one in an infinite number of possibilities that arises into the illusion of form from consciousness. Concurrently, this placeholder is providing unique relative feedback to the whole of consciousness, due to its specific space-time coordinates in the matrix of infinite consciousness and possibility.

If the entire universe is consciousness, even inanimate objects hold, and are held within, consciousness. For example, let's pick one specific rock on a mountain out of billions of rocks in the world. This rock occupies a specific space and time in the entire universe. From its unique space/time coordinates, the consciousness creating and holding the rock's design, form and place in time and space, experiences what it is to be this specific rock and also what it is not to be the rock.

The rock, like every other manifest form, holds in its form universal and infinite potential and possibility. The rock can be part of a great mountain or used as material for sculpture, a "pet-rock," or as a nice place to sit and enjoy the view of the great mountain. It's easier to wrap our heads around these earthly possibilities where a rock is just a rock. However, when we use our imaginations and allow for the infinite possibilities of the rock, there exists the possibility the rock can transform into a human with wings who lives on sunlight and can fly to the moon back in a split second, or anything else your imagination can create.

In a universe of infinite possibilities, and according to quantum physicists, including Max Tegmark and Fred Wolf, the possibility of transformational creativity does exist. If quantum physics is taken literally, anything we think or imagine exists somewhere in the universe.

Once we understand that we each are infinite consciousness experiencing its potential through us, we're able to embrace, honor and appreciate the divinity, uniqueness and potential in each person and thing. We are then empowered to collaboratively co-create an inclusive, beautiful and loving world based upon divine experience inspired by a universe of infinite possibilities. . . (or not).

CHAPTER 3

Experiential Reality

─────────

The vast majority of what we experience as "reality" is imagined. Vibrations are converted into phenomenal sensory data that is interpreted by the imagination into the experience we call "physical reality." When we have an imaginative thought or other experience which can't be observed or verified by a third party, we often describe the experience with words such as "imagination," "fantasy," "dream" or "hallucination." Whether our experience is physical or etheric, "real" or "imagined," the totality of what we experience in the present moment is our "Experiential Reality."

Zhuangzi (396 BCE), the famous Chinese philosopher, tells a story where he dreamt he was a butterfly, flitting and fluttering around, happy with himself and doing as he pleased. He didn't know he was Zhuangzi. Suddenly he awakened and there he was, solid and unmistakably Zhuangzi. But he didn't know if he was Zhuangzi who had dreamt he was a butterfly, or a butterfly dreaming he was Zhuangzi.

Zhuangzi's perspective illustrates the thin veil between our "physical reality" and the world created in our imagination and dreams. In our physical reality, we receive data from our senses and create our experience of the world through synthesis of perception, imaginative construction and interpretation. Our experience of reality is largely an imaginative process of converting vibration and consciousness into a physical experience.

The totality of all we experience in the present moment, whether "real" or "imagined," or "physical" or "etheric" is referred to herein as *Experiential Reality.*" A mirage is not "real," but we see it as real. A dream is generally not considered real, yet we experience it as real while dreaming. A hologram looks 3D, while it's actually flat. A movie appears to be moving, yet it's a series of still photographs.

Some schools of thought in Buddhism (e.g., Dzogchen)[16], consider "perceived reality" literally unreal. As a prominent contemporary teacher, Chögyal Namkhai Norbu, puts it: "*In a real sense, all the visions that we see in our lifetime are like a big dream. . .*[17]" In this context, the term 'visions' denotes not only visual perceptions but appearances perceived through all senses, including sounds, smells, tastes, tactile sensations, and operations on received mental objects.[18] In the Buddhist view, the shared world of perceived and imagined realms are considered an illusion created by thought, whereas the non-dual, never changing, silence and stillness is the non-illusory state of being. However, "silence and stillness" as a concept is largely our imagination creating a conceptual state of being that is silent and still, in opposition and relation to, noisy and active. We humans are often in our minds chatting away and rarely experience true silence and stillness, however, when we do it is quite profound.

From the work of Piaget,[19] perceptions depend on the worldview of a person. The worldview is the result of arranging perceptions into context by imagination. It's also been proposed that the whole of human cognition is based upon imagination. That is, anything we cognitively perceive is a synthesis of sensory perception and imagination. In other words, nothing in our awareness exists without creative imagination.

The current experience of "reality" accepted by most of humankind is the phenomenal physical reality perceived by our five senses as evidenced by science, regulated by government and limited by societal belief systems.

"Reality" in everyday usage, means "the state of things as they actually exist." The term "Experiential Reality," as used in this book, includes everything that's experienced, whether or not it's imagined, visionary, dreamt, hallucinated, etheric, phenomenal, sensory, physical, verifiable, comprehensible or provable by science. If we experience it, it's Experiential Reality.

As mentioned before, it's widely accepted by science that we are 99.99% space. We are electromagnetic vibrations and consciousness filtered by sensations, perceptions, thoughts/beliefs, emotions, feelings, instinct and intuition filtered into our own imagined and interpreted "reality." Despite scientific evidence that our physical reality is an illusion produced by sensory input and interpretation, skeptical organizations (such as James Randi Educational Foundation and the Committee for Skeptical Inquiry) use the "scientific method" as a way of debunking evidence of exceptional human powers and natural unexplainable miracles in order to preserve the evidence-based status quo.

While science has contributed innumerable benefits to human life, in modern society, there is often a tendency to disregard as false or non-existent anything not scientifically proven.

However, **there are many things science cannot prove. . .**

- *Existential Truth*—Science can't prove that we actually exist or that our entire physical reality isn't just consciousness imagining itself.

- *Moral Truth*—Science can't prove the morality of any action, such as giving a donation to charity is good or that murder is evil.

- *Logical Truth*—Science can't prove "truth" because it relies upon the systems, tools and logic of humans and upon the assumption that our logic is the truth while not accounting for human error.

- *Experiential Truth*—Science can't prove that anyone loves another. There is no scientific test confirming a subjective experience of emotion.

There are many aspects of life we experience that are far beyond our knowledge and the evidentiary methods of science. For example, most of us have experienced love, yet science can't prove love exists.

Carl Sagan said, "*We live in a society exquisitely dependent on science and technology, in which hardly anyone knows anything about science and technology.*"

According to Albert Einstein, "*The true sign of intelligence is not knowledge but imagination.*" By continually challenging the status quo and using his imagination, Einstein came to defy the intellectual standard set by the scientific and academic communities of his time. He often questioned existing realities and theories. By doing so, he was able to see beyond what was considered commonly accepted and expand the limits of human knowledge.

Einstein, who possessed great knowledge and imagination, said of the two, *"Imagination is more important than knowledge. For knowledge is limited to all we now know and understand, while imagination embraces the entire world, and all there ever will be to know and understand."*

I have realized that the more I know, the more I don't know. I created the following scale to remind me how little I know, so I can remain open to questioning reality, the possibilities of the universe, changing my beliefs and valuing my imagination:

"What I know is the size of me. What I know I don't know is the size of planet earth. What I don't know, I don't know is the size of the universe. What I can imagine is infinite."

Imagination is the window into the infinite possibilities of the universe. Free from the boundaries of linear space and time, cause and effect, imagination provides us the power to create "realities" where anything is possible. Aside from the creation of non-physical "realities," imagination is responsible for just about every invention, technology, design, piece of art or music and manufactured product, we have in our world, including such things as a simple bowl, the printing press, Beethoven's 5th, the space shuttle and the Internet. In fact, every original invention in the myriad of inventions started with imagination and was then manifest into physical reality. When we look at our world and notice all the inventions, designs, systems and behaviors arising from imagination, we can see the miraculous power of Experiential Reality in action.

When we allow the imagination to become a real and powerful force in our life, we enter the realm of "Experiential Reality." It's here where the perceptive veils of separation between the worlds of physical "reality" and imagination dissolve, and the potential of unlimited powers of manifestation and performance are unleashed.

Most of us have been taught to minimize, as mere fantasy, the imaginative experiences we have. However, these experiences are often every bit as real as those considered "real" in our daily lives. In our dreams and imaginations, many of us have experienced flying, shape-shifting, lifting massive weights and doing all kinds of super-human acts. Some of us have also experimented with psychoactive substances that provided experiences far beyond commonly defined boundaries of "physical reality" but were nonetheless very real experiences in the moment. For example, when a meditating Buddhist dissolves into non-dualistic stillness, an entheogenic journeyer becomes the Mandelbrot pattern, the dreamer dreams he's a butterfly, or a visionary envisions a future and it manifests, these experiences are very real to the experiencer, yet cannot be proven by science.

In our Experiential Reality, we experience flying, but in our physical reality, we believe we need a mechanical device to fly, so from our imagination, we invent airplanes as the physical manifestation of our Experiential Reality. In Experiential Reality, we can do telekinesis, but believe we need machines, heat and chemicals to transform and shape materials, so we invent manufacturing processes and facilities. Aborigines are adept at telepathic communication, but we believe we need devices, such as cell phones, to communicate over long distances and invent them using our imagination.

When we live in Experiential Reality, we can transcend the conditioned limitations of our existing reality and create miracles. Below are a few examples of humans pushing the limits of accepted reality to demonstrate the power of human potential...

- *Going extended periods without air, food or water...*
  - Yogi Satyamurti spent 8 days in an underground pit
  - Michael Werner lived 9 years on sunshine with occasional fruit juice and coffee
  - Hira Ratan Manek lived after a 411 day fast
  - Prahlad Jani went years without food or water, plus a 10-day controlled observation without food or water
  - On April 30, 2008, David Blaine spent 17 minutes and 4 seconds underwater, and on September 5, 2003, Blaine survived 44 days sealed inside a suspended transparent Plexiglas case without any food or nutrients and just 4.5 liters of water per day
- *Levitation and Psychokinesis...*
  - Yogi Subbayah Pullavar, was reported to have levitated into the air for four minutes in front of a crowd of 150 witnesses on June 6, 1936.[20]

- In 2012, researchers at the U.S. Department of Energy's Argonne National Laboratory in Illinois proved levitation using sound waves emitted by an acoustic levitator — an instrument designed by NASA for simulating microgravity.[21]

- Matthew Manning of the UK could "bend metal paranormally, affect electrical equipment, move compass needles, and make medical diagnoses. He was tested by psychologist, William Braud of the Mind Science Foundation in the late 1970s, with results that, according to Braud and coauthors in a research paper published in 1979, were better than chance. The events of his childhood and later investigations by George Owen of the Cambridge Psychical Research Society were published in a 1974 book entitled The Link.[22]

- Uri Geller was famous for bending spoons and moving objects with his mind. In 1975, Uri Geller was tested at the Stanford Research Institute by two scientists, Russell Targ and Harold Puthoff, who said they were convinced that Geller's demonstrations were genuine.[23]

- Saint Francis of Assisi is recorded as having been "suspended above the earth at a height of up to 1.8 meters."[24]

- Nina Kulagina (1926–1990) was filmed performing telekinesis while seated in numerous black-and-white short films mentioned in the U.S. Defense Intelligence Agency report from 1978.[25]

- Swami Rama (1925–1996)—a yoga skilled in controlling his heart functions, was studied at the Menninger Foundation in 1970, and was found to have telekinetically moved a knitting needle twice from a distance of five feet. During the study, Swami Rama wore a facemask and gown to prevent allegations that he moved the needle with his breath or body movements, and air vents in the room had been covered.[26]

- *Spiritual healing powers*

  - Edgar Cayce—A clairvoyant known, as "The Sleeping Prophet" for his trance states, over thirty years, is reputed to have healed tens of thousands of people using psychic energy known as "trance healing." Today there are many people who consider him one of the founders of both holistic medicine and the New Age movement.[27]

- Morris Goodman—Involved in an airplane crash which resulted in his neck being broken at C1 and C2, his spinal cord crushed, and every major muscle in his body virtually destroyed. Morris was no longer able to perform any bodily function except blinking his eyes. Morris was told by doctors that his injuries were too severe for him to survive, and he would be a "vegetable" until he died. Against all odds, he survived, learned to talk and walk and became a highly sought-after speaker known as "The Miracle Man" who travels the world sharing his story with millions of people and teaching his philosophy on goal setting and personal growth and development.[28]

- Judith Orloff, an Intuitive Medicine practitioner, has authored numerous books on the power of intuition to guide the body in healing where traditional medicine has failed. She is a practicing intuitive who guides individuals to a greater understanding of their own body's healing signals, enabling them to reach a breakthrough that goes beyond traditional western medicine's painkillers to holistic healing from within. This intuitive healing harnesses the powerful healing capacity of your own body to overcome emotional blockage that can cause physical damage.[29]

- Barbara Brennan was a physicist for NASA for several years before she began studying biometric energy fields after receiving acupuncture treatments following a severe accident. Brennan is a medical intuitive who can interpret medical and psychological conditions by reading the auras of individuals. She can sense the auras of her patients with all five senses as well as see into the past traumas. Working closely with her patients, she clears and balances their energy fields to bring them back into harmony with the Divine. Today Brennan focuses on teaching others her healing techniques and doing research into ways that integrate traditional medical science with the empowered techniques of her Energy Consciousness System.[30]

- Lisa Renee, an energetic intuitive, author and leader of ascension, spontaneously healed my Dad of a potentially fatal staph infection heading toward his weakened heart that his doctors couldn't cure. They told him he had two weeks to live. After one week of focused quantum healing by Lisa his staph infection disappeared. My Dad, who was an M.D., described it as a miracle.

- *Extreme physical performance*

  - Roger Bannister, an English athlete, was the first person to run under a 4-minute mile, in 1954, when it was believed an impossible feat that would explode one's heart.[31]

  - Mrs. Angela Cavallo lifted a car, under which her son, Tony Covallo, was trapped, high enough and long enough for two neighbors to replace the jacks and pull her son Tony from beneath the car.[32]

  - Lydia Angiyou, 41, fought a polar bear long enough for hunters to arrive, and saved her 7-year-old son, and two other children.[33]

  - Teenage daughters, Hanna (age 16) & Haylee (age 14) lifted a tractor to save their dad pinned underneath.[34]

We each possess the powers of manifestation and can actually alter our physical reality by using our will and imagination. The world we encounter with "Experiential Reality" is every bit as real and as much of an illusion as our "physical reality."

For instance, when we have sexual fantasies, our bodies become aroused from our thoughts—we experience stimulation in our bodies even though we're not actually having sex. The somatic-mental-energetic feedback loop enhances the reality of the experience. As our minds become more excited, our bodies become more aroused, building the sexual energy and tension through our imagination.

Even though a scenario is imagined, we experience the emotions and feelings resulting from our imagined reality in our body as if the scenario were happening right now. Our bodies experience bio-chemical-energetic shifts in the present time that are perceptively real even though they are produced by our imagination.

Let's imagine a future circumstance, such as asking a wealthy friend to invest in a company you want to start. If you imagine your friend giving you the money, telling you what a great idea you have and showing real enthusiasm for the success of your company, you would likely experience the emotions of happiness, excitement and courage. You'd then be motivated to ask your friend for the money. However, if you imagine your friend being dismissive and telling you that your idea is foolish, your present emotional state is likely to be a combination of disappointment, rejection, fear and anxiety. In this case, you'd be more reluctant to contact your friend and ask him to invest.

The way you imagine your life impacts your reality and the physical world. The imagination is very powerful in creating our reality. When we're in fear and limitation, we use our imagination in a manner that creates more fear and limitation. When we're in love and abundance, we create more love and abundance. The mind is like a fertile garden. If we plant seeds of poison, poisonous plants will grow. If we plant nutritious and beautiful seeds, nutritious and beautiful plants will grow. Therefore, it is important to use the power and impact of our imagination in a disciplined manner that turns our visions into physical realities that enhance the quality of life for people and planet.

Imagination is the window into universal/divine consciousness and the key to unlimited creative potential and power. One of the greatest gifts we can give ourselves and humanity is to fully embrace our imagination and use it to create an improved world.

What if we are infinite creative consciousness slowed down to a physically dense vibration that allows creative consciousness to subjectively experience itself?

What if we're here to experience the magic and exquisite sensuality of being human, remember our divinity and transcend the illusion of limitation to create at will from infinite potential?

Through imagination, we have direct access to the infinite creative potential of the universe allowing us to freely, easily and instantaneously create any experience we choose.

Governments and corporate sponsored media use pervasive images and stories of war, violence, crime, hatred and peril to instill fear and beliefs that the world is unsafe, hostile and dangerous. To save ourselves from this "unsafe, hostile and dangerous world," society has been conditioned to imagine the worst, live in fear, and conform to systemic status quo to live a "safe and secure life." In exchange for the illusory assurance of "safety," "security," "jobs," and "stability" from our corporations and governments, we're asked to give up our freedom, time, independence, brilliance, imagination, creativity, joy and power to live regulated lives within systems that don't serve us or the planet.

Using our imaginations to create Experiential Reality, we become co-creators of our experience with the universe. We transform ourselves from enslaved physical machines to creative geniuses in charge of our own destiny. When our imagination becomes embodied as Experiential Reality, the divide between imagination and physical reality dissolves and we gain a very powerful tool for manifesting the life of our dreams. By expressing embodied Experiential Reality as our physical reality through visualization, declaration and consistent action, our Experiential Reality starts manifesting into physical reality. Then our physical reality aligns with our Experiential Reality and a feedback loop is created that exponentially accelerates our creative abilities. This is where we begin living our dreams.

Napoleon Hill, author of "Think and Grow Rich," interviewed many famous people to find a common thread or simple formula for wealth and success. Those interviewed included Thomas Edison, Alexander Graham Bell, George Eastman, Henry Ford, Elmer Gates, John D. Rockefeller, Sr., Charles M. Schwab, F.W. Woolworth, William Wrigley Jr., John Wanamaker, William Jennings Bryan, Theodore Roosevelt, William H. Taft and Jennings Randolph.

Hill found that using one's imagination, focusing the mind, having a definite meaningful purpose and taking action were the most basic and shared fundamentals of success. According to Hill:

> "All the breaks you need in life wait within your imagination; Imagination is the workshop of your mind, capable of turning mind energy into accomplishment and wealth."

> "Cherish your visions and your dreams as they are the children of your soul, the blueprints of your ultimate achievements."

The more we practice manifesting our Experiential Reality with imagination, the more powerful and rapid our ability to manifest our physical reality becomes. In accordance with the saying "be careful what you wish for," the rapid and powerful manifestation through Experiential Reality is an awesome power that requires awesome responsibility, discipline, clarity of thought, depth of understanding the effect of our actions, and a high-degree of integrity.

When engaging in Experiential Reality, it's important to allow the mind to open to the potential implications that will unfold from bringing our visions into reality. Once we understand the impacts of our visions and ideas, we can create a full sensory experience of the reality we want to manifest. We see, hear, smell, taste and feel our visions in deep and vivid detail. This takes discipline. However, when our visions and imagined reality become embodied, physical manifestation can happen very quickly.

One of the greatest gifts we can give ourselves and humanity is to fully embrace our imagination and create a new Experiential Reality for humankind. Because we are interconnected with each other, our planet, and the entire cosmos as divine creators of our own reality, what we experience has an incremental rippling effect throughout the perceived physical universe. The more we are able to master our Experiential Reality and the awesome power and responsibility of manifestation resulting therefrom, the more rapidly and powerfully we can use our divine creative abilities to transform our world.

CHAPTER 4

Creating Reality from Vibration

"Everything in life is vibration."

~Albert Einstein

As comedian and philosopher, Bill Hicks, so eloquently said, *"All matter is merely energy condensed to a slow vibration, that we are all one consciousness experiencing itself subjectively. There is no such thing as death—life is only a dream—and we are the imagination of ourselves."*

The essence of the universe we perceive as "reality" is consciousness and vibration. Whether consciousness creates vibration or vibration creates consciousness is paradoxical and is more likely co-creative, concurrent and interactive. As written by Deepak Chopra, *"The universe doesn't contain consciousness, since "contain" implies a closed space. Consciousness is unbounded; it is one."* While, from a universal perspective, we are one consciousness, our experience of reality as humans is mostly subjective and dualistic.

It is apparent that we experience and "co-create" our "reality" through a concurrent feedback loop of receiving, processing, interpreting and transmitting vibration with cosmic consciousness. As renowned quantum physicist, Michio Kaku, stated, *"the "Mind of God," is cosmic music resonating throughout hyperspace."* I refer to this co-creative interplay between consciousness and vibration as the *"Cosmic Jam Session."* The Cosmic Jam Session refers to the method by which infinite creative consciousness emerges and experiences itself by converting vibrations into an infinite number of subjective realities. When we become adept at engaging in the Cosmic Jam Session, we exponentially increase our power to manifest that which we envision. In order to become adept in the Cosmic Jam Session, we first need to understand how we create "reality" from vibration and how to utilize our creative power for the thriving of self, humanity, the earth and the universe.

All things in our universe are constantly in vibrating and in motion. All life, our senses, our consciousness and everything we experience in the universe consists of vibration, including the interactions between atoms, senses, thoughts, emotions and feelings. Even our consciousness involves the emergent process of awareness, perception, imagination and interpretation of universal vibration.[35]

All our sensory inputs of sight, sound, touch, smell and taste are transmitted through our nervous system to our brains using a combination of electro-vibrational impulses. Our minds interpret this vibrational sensory data to create our subjective "reality."

For example, the light and colors we see are converted by our mind from portions of the electromagnetic spectrum visible to the human eye known as "the visible spectrum" with vibrational wavelengths from about 390 to 700 nanometers. Our ears allow us to hear vibrations in the form of sound waves generally between 20 hertz and 20,000 hertz. Our olfactory sense of smell relies on vibrational energy as an odor's character is encoded in the ratio of activities of receptors tuned to different vibrational frequencies. As well, our taste buds rely on the interpretation of vibration, as demonstrated by neuroscientist, Paul Bach-y-Rita's device that allows blind people to see with their tongue using electro-vibration. Our ability to feel depends upon the neuro-somatic interpretation of vibration and electronic impulses.

Energy and consciousness have frequency and vibration, some of which are measurable by the devices we have created. For example, our brain waves and neural responses can be measured by electroencephalogram (EEG), our heartbeats by electrocardiogram (ECG), and our muscle action by electromyograph (EMG). Spectrophotometry is used to measure the vibrational frequencies of light and materials. Also, devices such as Magnetic Resonance Imaging (MRI), Positron Emission

Tomography (PET), Magnetoencephalography (MEG) have been used to map the brain's electrical activity and frequencies.

According to Michio Kaku, a leading physicist and co-founder of String Field Theory...

> *"The latest version of String Theory is called M-Theory, "M" for membrane. So we now realize that strings can coexist with membranes. So the subatomic particles we see in nature, the quartz, the electrons are nothing but musical notes on a tiny vibrating string.*
>
> *What is physics? Physics is nothing but the laws of harmony that you can write on vibrating strings. What is chemistry? Chemistry is nothing but the melodies you can play on interacting vibrating strings. What is the universe? The universe is a symphony of vibrating strings. And then what is the mind of God that Albert Einstein eloquently wrote about for the last 30 years of his life? We now, for the first time in history, have a candidate for the mind of God. It is cosmic music resonating through 11- dimensional hyperspace.*
>
> *So first of all, we are nothing but melodies. We are nothing but cosmic music played out on vibrating strings and membranes. Obeying the laws of physics, which is nothing but the laws of harmony of vibrating strings."*

As Kaku indicates, our entire experience of reality is principally a vibrational jam session with the universe. Whether the vibrations are of light (by which we see) or sound (by which we hear and speak) or the vibrations of our thoughts and feelings, we're constantly receiving, processing and transmitting vibrations in a Cosmic Jam Session with universe. Our individual experience of universal vibrations creates our unique individual reality, and our individual reality affects collective and cosmic reality.

We are essentially an imagined body of vibrations creating our reality by sampling a limited set of data particles through our senses from an infinite wave of vibrations. We then convert this data into meaning and subjective reality in a co-creative Cosmic Jam Session with universal consciousness. Much like musicians who master their instrument, the more we **practice vibratory awareness and**

manifestation, the more powerful we become at **co-creating with the universe to realize profound miracles** in our lives.

Similar to great jazz musicians jamming together, instantaneously hearing, playing and co-creating with each other in the moment, we're in a constant co-creative emergent "jam session" with the universe. Whatever we receive from, and transmit to, the universe (e.g., sense, perceive, think, emote, feel, and express) has a vibration. The vibrational stimulus we receive from the universe is interpreted and responded to at levels of unconsciousness, subconsciousness, consciousness and super-consciousness. When we interpret and transmit the universe's vibrational information, the universe instantaneously receives our vibrational frequency transmission and returns complementary vibrations back to us. We then receive the vibratory transmission of the universe and immediately transmit back to the universe our interpretation of the universal vibration. This *"Vibratory Feedback Loop"* is what perpetuates the states of being that form our "reality."

If we want to create a new reality, we need to change our consciousness and vibrational state. If we are unaware of our Vibrational Feedback Loops, there's a tendency to perpetuate states of being that do not serve our potential or the reality we wish to create. By increasing our awareness and mastery of our vibrational states, we can transform the *Vibratory Feedback Loops* that influence our consciousness, our states of being, our relationship with the universe and our co-creative process of manifestation.

To illustrate the practical application of vibrational consciousness, as an entrepreneur, I've experienced numerous challenges in my endeavors, including obtaining resources, inspiring my team, creating market adoption, gaining customer loyalty and procuring financing. I often found myself worrying and forecasting the worst-case scenario. When I was in this state of being, I experienced feeling disempowered, overwhelmed and ineffective. I also felt my body constrict, my energy levels decrease and my ability to derive joy and enthusiasm from my activities diminish.

When in this state of low vibration, my abilities to inspire my team, get investors to commit their money and muster the courage and tenacity necessary to succeed were compromised. While in this state, a feedback loop was created where the universe reinforced my vibrational state by sending back the vibrational frequencies I was transmitting to the universe.

When I raised my vibrational state with the tools I'll be sharing in this book, I became a much more inspiring leader, and attracted investment and powerful relationships. Moreover, my energy level was much higher, my focus and abilities to execute increased exponentially and I had a lot more fun in my work and life. I acted in a manner aligned to a powerful and creative vibrational state and the universe responded by providing amazing synchronicities that matched the best possible outcomes I envisioned.

When we can intentionally transform our Vibratory Feedback Loops, we become vibrationally literate energy virtuosos adept at utilizing the infinite, miraculous, reflexive and imaginative nature of the universe to create new and inspiring realities in our lives. We then can powerfully engage in an inspiring and conscious Cosmic Jam Session with the universe, joyously playing in harmonic resonance and coherence with those vibrations that serve our highest vision, nature and potential.

The universe contains all possible vibrational frequencies. When we sense, choose, amplify and integrally align with the vibrational frequencies that are the most expansive, life-enhancing and supportive to our growth and state of being, our lives become miraculous. This takes skill and sensitivity. Like learning to play a musical instrument, the more we practice, the more our skill at jamming with the universe increases and the more reflexive the co-creative process becomes. With sufficient discipline and repetition, we can become virtuosos with the instrument of vibrational coherence to create the life we desire.

As mentioned, the combination of our vibrational frequencies attracts similar frequencies from the universe and sets up feedback loops. Like attracts like. However, with sensitivity and intention, we can turn repetitive limiting feedback loops into expansive spirals that change the frequency and amplitude of our vibrations, allowing us to break free of limiting recurring patterns. For example, we can shift the frequency of anger into passion, passion into inspiration and inspiration into love.

CREATING "REALITY" FROM VIBRATIONS

This section provides details on (1) how our 3 *"Vibratory Consciousness Centers"* (*Body, Mind and Soul*) interact with our 7 *"Vibratory Receptors & Transmitters"* (*Sensations, Perceptions, Thoughts, Emotions, Feeling, Instinct and Intuition*) to create our reality from vibration; (2) what each of the Vibratory Consciousness Centers and Vibratory Receptors and Transmitters do and how they interact with each other in the Cosmic Jam Session; and (3) how to use the vibratory tools to become a Maestro in the Cosmic Jam Session of your life.

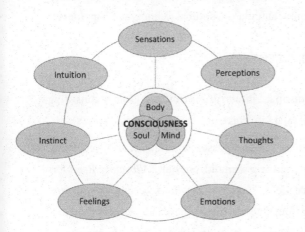

The *Vibratory Consciousness Centers* interpret the inputs from the *Vibratory Receptors & Transmitters* to create consciousness, meaning, and experience; the totality of which is referred to herein as "Experiential Reality." *Vibratory Consciousness Centers* transmit these reconstructed vibrations simultaneously to the universe and the *Vibratory Receptors & Transmitters*. The *Vibratory Receptors & Transmitters*, the *Vibratory Consciousness Centers* and cosmic consciousness are in a continual and concurrent co-creative process that generate *Vibratory Feedback Loops* in the *Cosmic Jam Session*. The processing of the *Vibratory Feedback Loops* happens so rapidly that we often are unaware of the process by which "reality" is created and experienced.

Using the experience of music as an analogy to help explain the Cosmic Jam Session, when most people hear a symphony, they can't generally distinguish between the instruments (e.g., the brass from the woodwinds), understand the harmonic progression and the rhythmic relationship between the parts being played. However, trained musicians, hear and understand music in a unique way—their training allows them to distinguish various instruments, the key, the chord changes, and the interweaving complexities of the composition. The most complete and inspiring musicians have the ability to compose, perform, co-create, collaborate and improvise music, giving these musicians a deeper understanding of music and an increased ability to create and influence music.

Similarly, when we become adept at understanding and utilizing the 7 *Vibratory Receptors & Transmitters (Sensations, Perceptions, Thoughts, Emotions, Feeling, Instinct and Intuition)* with the 3 *Vibratory Consciousness Centers (Body, Mind and Soul)* in the Cosmic Jam Session of our life, we can increase our vibrational and emotional intelligence to powerfully create the symphony of our lives and manifest such things as greater love, fulfilling relationships, abundance, optimal wellness and happiness.

VIBRATORY CONSCIOUSNESS CENTERS.

As mentioned above, there are 3 distinct *Vibratory Consciousness Centers* consisting of **1) Body, 2) Mind, and 3) Soul** (aka Life Force or Energetic Consciousness).

The 3 *Vibratory Consciousness Centers* possess a unique way of receiving, processing, interpreting and experiencing stimuli from our 7 *Vibratory Receptors & Transmitters (Sensations, Perceptions, Thoughts, Emotions, Feeling, Instinct and Intuition)*. Each of the 3 *Vibratory Consciousness Centers* have independent functions and yet are interconnected and interdependent in providing us with the experience we call "reality" as discussed in greater detail below:

1. **Body**—The body has a unique consciousness known as "*Somatic Consciousness.*" Somatic Consciousness is experienced through the instruments of sensations, perceptions, feelings and *Instinctual Emotions*. Somatic Consciousness represents a combination of non-conscious, sub-conscious and autonomic functions, as well as data and information being processed without the direct cognitive appraisal and awareness.

    The body, with an estimated 100 trillion cells,[36] is an amazing genius capable of handling trillions of transactions per second. Our body connects to, receives and filters massive amounts of stimuli. With the faculties of the brain such as the amygdala, hippocampus and caudate nucleus in the brain stem, our body has the innate intelligence to keep us breathing, keep our cells regenerating, our heart beating, our food digesting, our energy converting, our senses receiving and our brains performing, among many other functions.

The body is interconnected to the entire universe and our *Somatic Consciousness* is always in the present moment of now. The body processes information in a non-linear parallel manner and is far more powerful in influencing our reality than the cognitive mind. Thus, by being sensitive to our *Somatic Consciousness*, we can become more acutely aware of the present moment. We can also become aware of the plethora of data inputs from the universe allowing us to distinguish *"Somatic Consciousness"* from the past-future linear rationalization of the mind's *"Cognitive Consciousness."*

The body is a unified, living system of consciousness. The most influential systems of body consciousness are the brain, nervous system, heart, stomach and sensory organs. These systems not only play a critical role in our somatic consciousness, but also in the way we create and perceive our experience of life and "reality."

a.   *The Brain*—Our remarkable and complex brain (as an organ of the body distinguished from "the mind") contains a network of about 100,000 miles of blood vessels[37] and 100 billion neurons.[38] Each of the 100 billion neurons has on average 7,000 synaptic connections to other neurons[39] with the capacity to perform an estimated 38 quadrillion operations per second.[40] Even though the brain is credited with cognitive consciousness, the majority of its function is processing our environment and keeping our body alive.

The brain functions as a whole interconnected organ in, and with, the body, and even though the body has a high degree of somatic awareness, the fields of science and psychology have segmented and modularized the brain map into conscious, preconscious and unconscious functions. It has also labeled areas of the brain as reptilian, mammalian and neo-mammalian.

1. The **"Reptilian Brain"** or **Archipallium** is responsible for basic physical, autonomic, sensory and motor functions, including the following:

Structure	Function
Brain Stem	Autonomic functions such as heart rate, blood pressure, breathing and digestion. The Reticular Activating System (RAS) in the brain stem controls consciousness, sleeping, dreaming and habituation. Motor and sensory neurons pass through the brain stem and connect the Peripheral Nervous System from the body and Central Nervous System of the spine and brain where it's processed by the RAS. The RAS processes 400 billion bits of information per second and filters it down to 2000 bits of information per second for the cognitive brain to process.[41]
Cerebellum	Aids in the coordination of movement and balance.
Basal Nuclei	The basal ganglia are associated with a variety of functions, including voluntary motor control, procedural learning relating to routine behaviors or "habits" such as eye movements, cognitive, and basic emotional functions.
Olfactory Bulbs	Sense of smell.

2. The "**Old Mammalian Brain**," also referred to as the **Limbic System** or **Paleomammalian Cortex**, is primarily responsible for our emotional life, filtering sensory data and formation of memories as well as supporting a variety of functions, including emotion, behavior, motivation long-term memory and olfaction. The Limbic System includes the following:

Structure	Function
Hippocampus	Processes new memories for long-term storage, as well as cognition and spacial memory. If you didn't have it, you couldn't live in the present, you'd be stuck in the past of old memories. It is among the first functions to falter in Alzheimer's
Amygdala	Emotional integration of sensory input and memories and signaling the cortex of motivationally significant stimuli. When stimulated, the amygdala emphasizes emotions of fear, anger and anxiety. The memory function tends to be more autobiographical rather than spacial, contributing to self-identification. Also, the amygdala is responsible for social processing such as face identification as well as influencing social functions such mating.
Thalamus	Acts as a sensory (i.e., sight, sound, hearing, taste and touch, but not smell) relay system from the spinal cord and brainstem to the cerebral cortex.
Hypothalamus	Monitors numerous bodily functions including blood pressure and body temperature, as well as controlling body weight and appetite, sex drive and fight and flight impulses through the regulation of adrenaline. The Mammillary Bodies in the Hypothalamus also contribute the processing of recognition memory.
Entorhinal Cortex	The main interface between the hippocampus and neocortex has an important role in autobiographical, declarative, episodic and spacial memories, and memory optimization during sleep.

3.   The "**New Mammalian Brain**" is associated with "higher functioning" mammals, including the primates and humans and comprises almost the whole of the hemispheres of the brain, made up of the Cerebrum. The **Neocortex,** often referred to as the **Neopallium**, is the largest part of the cerebral cortex, which is the outer layer of the Cerebrum. The Neocortex is involved in higher-order brain functions including sensory perception, cognition, motor commands, spatial reasoning and language. The Cerebrum is the largest brain structure in humans and accounts for about two-thirds of the brain's mass. It is divided into two sides — the left and right hemispheres—that are separated by a deep groove down the center from the back of the brain to the forehead. These two halves are connected by long neuron branches called the Corpus Callosum, which is relatively larger in women's brains than in men's brains. The Cerebrum is divided into four sections, called "lobes", as follows:

Structure	Function
Frontal Lobe	Associated with reasoning, planning, parts of speech, movement, emotions, and problem solving, including judgment, abstraction, and motivation. The basic activity of this brain region is considered to be orchestration of thoughts and actions in accordance with internal goals and has been implicated in planning complex cognitive behavior, personality expression, decision-making, and moderating social behavior, as well as managing emotional impulses including empathy, altruism and interpretation of facial expressions. The frontal lobe contains the pre-frontal cortex, which is responsible for "executive function." Executive function relates to the ability to (a) differentiate among conflicting thoughts, (b) determine good and bad, better and best, same and different, (c) analyze future consequences, work toward a defined goal and predict of outcomes, and (d) engage in social "control" (the ability to suppress urges that, if not suppressed, could lead to socially unacceptable outcomes).[42]
Parietal Lobe	Receives and processes sensory information from the body with an emphasis on touch and the use of vision for calculating the location and speed of objects.

Occipital Lobe	Responsible for processing, interpreting and routing visual data.
Temporal Lobe	Controls memory storage area, emotion, hearing, and, on the left side, language.

Many believe conscious awareness originates in the brain alone. However, research suggests consciousness emerges from the brain and body acting together. A growing body of evidence suggests the heart and stomach play particularly significant roles in our consciousness.

The cognitive functions of the brain, that lead to self-awareness, rational thought, planning, problem solving, judgment and achieving goals are referred to herein as *"The Cognitive Brain."*

The collective and interconnected brain-body processes (e.g., respiratory, cardiovascular, nervous, digestive, endocrine, reproductive, integumentary, muscular, skeletal, immune, lymphatic) will be referred to as *"The Somatic Brain."*

While our society puts great emphasis on the Cognitive Brain, it's the Somatic Brain that's the real genius.

The Cognitive Brain occupies only 17% of the brain's total mass and controls only 2-5% of what we actually perceive and how we behave. The "Somatic Brain" represents 83% of the brain's mass and processes the other 95-98% of all somatic, subconscious and non-conscious functions, perceptions and behavior.[43]

The Cognitive Brain can only process serially (one thought at a time), whereas the Somatic Brain processes in parallel (multiple inputs and processes simultaneously).

While the study of the brain's actual processing capacity is subject to various measurements and approaches, there is support showing the Somatic Brain can perform 38 quadrillion operations per second[44] whereas the Cognitive Brain only processes 2,000 bits of information per second.[45] Moreover, the Reticular Activating System ("RAS"), a neural network in the brain stem, processes about 400 billion bits of information per second and filters out most of the sensory data and somatic information to deliver only information relevant to self-aware consciousness created in the Cognitive Brain. In essence, the Somatic Brain turns vibration into a perceived physical reality and our cognitive input is selected and modified by the RAS in our brain stem.

b. *The Gastrointestinal Tract aka "the Gut"*—Most of us have had "gut feelings" or "butterflies" in our stomach and/or intestines. The gut, especially from the stomach, large and small intestines provides us an ancient wisdom that is instinctual and intuitive.

The gastrointestinal tract consists of the mouth, salivary glands, esophagus, stomach, liver, gallbladder, pancreas, large intestine, small intestine, appendix, rectum and anus. The **enteric nervous system ("ENS")** is embedded in the lining of the gastrointestinal tract or gut. The ENS, often referred to as the "second brain" consists of sheaths of neurons embedded in the walls of the alimentary canal, which measures about nine meters end to end from the mouth to the anus. The ENS contains some 100 million neurons, more than in either the spinal cord or the peripheral nervous system.

The main role of the ENS is controlling digestion, swallowing, the release of enzymes to break down food, the control of blood flow promoting nutrient absorption and elimination. The ENS also provides regulation of microbes and health of our gut biome. Our gut, along with the microbes that live our gut biome, influences our consciousness, often having a significant effect on our energy level, our mood and our cravings.

Michael Gershon, Chairman of the Department of Anatomy and Cell Biology at New York—Presbyterian Hospital/Columbia University Medical Center, and author of the *"The Second Brain"*, validates the enteric nervous system is our second brain. According to Gershon, *"Structurally and neurochemically, the enteric nervous system (ENS) is a brain unto itself. Within those yards of tubing lies a complex web of microcircuitry driven by more neurotransmitters and neuromodulators than can be found anywhere else in the peripheral nervous system."*

Gershon estimates about 90% of the fibers in the vagus nerve carry information from the gut to the brain rather than from the brain to the gut. The vagus nerve interfaces with the parasympathetic control of the heart, lungs, and digestive tract.

In Leo Galland's article published in the Journal of Medicinal Food, entitled the *"The Gut Microbiome and the Brain,"* Galland writes:

"The human gut microbiome impacts human brain health in numerous ways: (1) Structural bacterial components such as lipopolysaccharides provide low-grade tonic stimulation of the innate immune system. Excessive stimulation due to bacterial dysbiosis, small intestinal bacterial overgrowth, or increased intestinal permeability may produce systemic and/or central nervous system inflammation. (2) Bacterial proteins may cross-react with human antigens to stimulate dysfunctional responses of the adaptive immune system. (3) Bacterial enzymes may produce neurotoxic metabolites such as D-lactic acid and ammonia. Even beneficial metabolites such as short-chain fatty acids may exert neurotoxicity. (4) Gut microbes can produce hormones and neurotransmitters that are identical to those produced by humans. Bacterial receptors for these hormones influence microbial growth and virulence. (5) Gut bacteria directly stimulate afferent neurons of the enteric nervous system to send signals to the brain via the vagus nerve. Through these varied mechanisms, gut microbes shape the architecture of sleep and stress reactivity of the hypothalamic-pituitary-adrenal axis. They influence memory, mood, and cognition and are clinically and therapeutically relevant to a range of disorders, including alcoholism, chronic fatigue syndrome, fibromyalgia, and restless legs syndrome. Their role in multiple sclerosis and the neurologic manifestations of celiac disease is being studied. Nutritional tools for altering the gut microbiome therapeutically include changes in diet, probiotics, and prebiotics."[46]

In addition to the scientific support above, I once asked a Zen monk, "Where is the central source of consciousness in your being?" He put his hands on his gut. When I inquired as to why he believed his consciousness center was his gut, he replied, "Consciousness is everywhere in the body, and the center that is nearest to the original source of our physical being is the navel. The heart is next closest, and the brain is furthest away from the original source. Presence and truth emerge closest to original source."

c.   *The Heart*—Research in the new discipline of neurocardiology conducted at the Institute of HeartMath shows that the heart is a sensory organ and a sophisticated center for receiving and processing information through its nervous system. The heart can function like the brain. It has the ability to learn, remember, and make functional decisions independent of the brain's cerebral cortex.

Moreover, numerous experiments demonstrate the heart continuously sends signals to the brain, influencing the function of higher brain centers involved in perception, cognition, and emotional processing.[47] The heart generates the body's most powerful and most extensive rhythmic electromagnetic field. Compared to the electromagnetic field produced by the brain, the electrical component of the heart's field is about 60 times greater in amplitude and permeates every cell in the body.[48] The magnetic component is approximately 5000 times stronger than the brain's magnetic field and can be detected several feet away from the body with sensitive magnetometers.[49] As amazing as the brain is, the heart may even be more so.

Research at the Institute of HeartMath shows that information pertaining to a person's emotional state is communicated throughout the body via the heart's electromagnetic field. The rhythmic beating patterns of the heart change significantly as we experience different emotions.

Constrictive emotions, such as anger or frustration, are associated with an erratic, disordered, incoherent pattern in the heart's rhythms. In contrast, expansive emotions, such as love or appreciation, are associated with a smooth, ordered, coherent pattern in the heart's rhythmic activity. In turn, these changes in the heart's beating patterns create corresponding changes in the structure of the electromagnetic field radiated by the heart, measurable by a technique called spectral analysis.[50]

The heart has a powerful influence on the brain. This could explain why when we're caught up in romantic love our brain function is altered, and we often make seemingly irrational and/or emotional decisions. However, it could be argued that decisions made in love, from the heart, even though often impractical or irrational, intuitively provide some of the most amazing experiences in our lives.

According to HeartMath, the human heart emits a measurable electromagnetic field that surrounds the body and extends in every direction several feet away from the body. The human heart and its field interacts with the electromagnetic fields of all living things, the planet and even the universe. Also, the human heart has both long and short term memory which affect our emotional experiences.

The heart has a different intelligence than the mind in that it understands "feelings" and "connection" in the present moment. The heart intuitively understands the unified, interconnected creative energy and life force in each of us that we often refer to as "Love."

d. *The Nervous System*—The human nervous system provides the highway by which all sensory data travels to the consciousness centers of the body, mind and energetic consciousness. The nervous system is a network of cells called neurons. Neurons are electrically excitable and transmit information in the form of electrical and chemical signals and vibrations. Your brain has around 100 billion neurons. Each neuron communicates with thousands of other neurons through synapses—special junctions where chemicals help bridge the gap between one neuron and the next. The nervous system is amazingly vast, with each of us having as many neural connections as the Milky Way Galaxy has stars.

Neurons are the core components of the nervous system, which includes the brain, spinal cord, and peripheral ganglia.

A number of specialized types of neurons exist:

- *Sensory neurons* that respond to touch, sound, light and numerous other stimuli affecting cells of the sensory organs that then send signals to the spinal cord and brain.[51]

- *Motor neurons* that receive signals from the brain and spinal cord, cause muscle contractions, and affect the glands.

- *Interneurons* that connect neurons to other neurons within the same region of the brain or spinal cord.

A typical neuron possesses a **cell body, dendrites,** and an **axon.** Dendrites are the branched projections of a neuron that act to conduct the electrochemical stimulation received from other neural cells to the cell body of the neuron from which the dendrites project.[52] An **axon,** also known as a nerve fibre, is a long, slender projection of a neuron that transmits electrical impulses and information to different neurons, muscles and glands.

The way the nervous system works is via electrochemical signals received on the dendrites of a neuron and passed on thru an axon. The electrical signal in axons is a brief voltage change called an action potential, or nerve impulse, which can travel long distances, sometimes at high speeds, without changing size or shape. When an action potential arrives at the ends of the axon, it interacts with up to thousands of neighboring cells across synapses. The electrochemical interactions at these synapses modify the intensity of the signals as they pass from cell to cell.

The nervous system is divided into the *central nervous system* and the *peripheral nervous system.* The central nervous system contains the brain and spinal cord. The peripheral nervous system contains the rest of the nervous system. One division of the peripheral nervous system is the autonomic nervous system. The autonomic nervous system controls the automatic activities in the body. For instance, our heartbeat, breathing, senses, and digestion happen all without our conscious involvement.

The autonomic nervous system is divided into two branches; one contains sympathetic nerves and the other the parasympathetic nerves. The sympathetic nervous system is responsible for the body's reaction to stress; this is the 'fight or flight' response. The parasympathetic nervous system supports the vegetative bodily functions such as digestion, rest and sleep.

All we sense, perceive and think happens through vibro-electrical impulses. Essentially, we are containers of electrochemical vibrations experiencing electro-vibrational stimuli from the universe and creating meaning from these stimuli.

e.   **_Senses_**—A broadly acceptable definition of a sense would be "*A system that consists of a group of sensory cell types that responds to a specific physical phenomenon (stimulus), and that corresponds to a particular group of regions within the brain where the signals are received and interpreted*."[53]

There are a number of differing definitions of what constitutes a sense. However, there's general agreement on the *five traditionally recognized human senses* of **sight, hearing, taste, smell** and **touch**. We also have the ability to detect other sensorial stimuli associated with "feeling" including temperature and kinesthetic sense. Kinesthetic sense has 3 components: 1) *Proprioception* or the sense of the relative position of neighboring parts of the body and strength of effort being employed in movement; 2) *Exteroception* by which one perceives the outside world; and 3) *Interoception* by which one perceives such things as pleasure, pain, hunger, sexual arousal and the movement of internal organs. As well, we have a *sixth sense or the power to perceive intuitively* beyond the five senses and the kinesthetic senses.

The five phenomenal senses of sight, hearing, smell, touch and taste provide us with the ability to sample particles from the wave of universal stimuli, while at the same time filtering stimuli and limiting our experience of perceptive dimensional "reality." Our limited dimensional reality is constrained by the small sampling of stimuli received by our senses and our ability to utilize the stimuli in creating our experiential reality.

As shown by the Electromagnetic Spectrum chart below, we receive through our senses and cognitively process a very small part of the electromagnetic spectrum.[54]

The Electromagnetic Spectrum

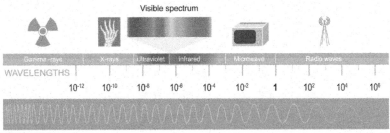

For example, sight signals take 50 milliseconds to zip from eye to brain for the brain to perceive sight. Only about 10% of the available light makes it to the retina and much of the information received is decoded and rearranged by the brain. A typical human eye will respond to wavelengths from about 380 to 750 nm (nanometers—1 millionth of a meter) known as the visible spectrum.[55] Humans generally cannot see infrared above 750 nm or ultraviolet below 200 nm, whereas bees and many other insects can see light in the ultraviolet spectrum, which helps them find nectar in flowers.

Another example is our hearing. Hearing occurs when vibrations are detected by the ear and transduced into nerve impulses perceived by the brain (primarily in the temporal lobe). The vibrations are characterized in frequency ranges measured with hertz (Hz) or vibrations per second. 1hz is equal to one vibration per second. The average human range of hearing is from 15Hz to 20kHz, whereas dogs can hear from 40Hz to 60kHz. This explains why the high frequencies generated above 20kHz are not generally heard or perceived by humans (e.g., a dog whistle of 22 kHz can be heard by dogs, but not by many humans).

Our bodies are continually receiving a wave of vibrational stimuli. The wave of vibrational stimuli is received and sampled through our senses and nervous system where the vibrational stimuli is "particalized" into data packets. These data packets can be then processed by the Cognitive Brain to create the experience we call "reality."

2. *Mind*—While the brain is an organ that provides somatic and cognitive functions that keep us alive and allow us to process the human experience, the "mind" is not a physical organ. The mind refers to our state of self-awareness and the ability to make conscious choices, including the elements of thought, imagination, memory, will, reasoning, cognitive emotion, perception, identity, individuation, space/time consciousness, navigation, logic and planning. Often the two are made synonymous with one another, but they are very different. Where the brain is material, the mind is ethereal. The mind, however, is interconnected and interdependent with the brain and somatic functions.[56]

The bodily organs and systems described above are responsible for providing the sensory input required to create and maintain our perception of reality from vibrations. The sensory organs and nervous system deliver data. The Somatic Brain perceives and filters the data, but assigns no meaning or importance to it, except as is necessary to protect the survival of the body. **The "mind" processes data into meaningful and subjective information from which self-awareness, imagination and meaning emerge creating the experience we call "reality."**

Unlike Somatic Consciousness, which is servile, Cognitive Consciousness of the mind is volitional. In Cognitive Consciousness, we observe ourselves, control our mind, change our mind, set goals, make plans, judge results, as well as create future and past scenarios. We often act as if these imagined and creative future or past scenarios are real and present, when generally, they're not. For example, when we worry over some future event, even though we're projecting or imagining the event, we feel symptoms of fear, anxiety and worry (e.g., racing heart, tightening of the body, shallow breath) in the present, even though the event has not occurred and may not occur.

Unlike Cognitive Consciousness that shifts between past and future with occasional moments in the present, Somatic Consciousness is always in a state of present awareness. Somatic Consciousness sets no goals, makes no plans and does not engage in judgments of right or wrong, good or bad, true or false. Somatic Consciousness doesn't realize the mind is in an almost constant state of imagining and interpreting present sensations and perceptions into past-future meaning not bound by space-time physicality. **Somatic Consciousness accepts whatever the mind is thinking as if it is real, true and present.**[57]

To illustrate this interaction, while I was boarding a plane, I was informed I'd have to check my carry-on bag. When I sat down in my seat, I put my hands in my pockets and realized I'd left my keys in my bag. My mind immediately started spinning out an imagined scenario in the future where the airline had lost my bag and keys. I envisioned all the inconveniences I would experience from my lost bag and keys, such as not getting my car out of the parking garage, having to spend additional money for a cab and parking, not being able to get into my house and the expense of sleeping in a hotel. I started to experience the emotions of anxiety and even mild fear. Even though the scenario and emotions were not true and were not actually happening, my body responded as if the scenario was actually happening—my breath became shallow, my heart rate increased, my chest got tight and my palms started sweating slightly.

I became aware of my runaway mind and its impact on my body. I thought to myself, "We live in a universe of infinite possibilities. Choose the scenario you most desire." I then created the scenario where my bag was the first one off the baggage carousel and that everything was completely fine.

My Somatic Consciousness adapted to this new scenario and my heart rate decreased, my breathing relaxed and deepened, my chest expanded, and I dosed off for a comfortable nap. When I arrived at baggage claim, my bag was there waiting.

I reflected that I was conditioned to fear inconvenience and the expenditure of money. I realized how often I entered into states of fear when nothing was real or threatening to my well-being. Whether or not the thoughts of the future scenario influence future outcomes, they absolutely have an impact on our bodies current state of being.

This illustrates how our Mind influences our body and the feedback loops of Cognitive Consciousness and Somatic Consciousness work in tandem to not only create our present experience, but also the likelihood of future outcomes.

The mind is indeed a powerful instrument of manifestation. With its capacity to self-realize, ability to imagine, potential to transcend linear thought, and overcome programmed limitations, the mind is the powerhouse of creativity that effects physical reality.

Within our mind, we imagine and create our reality moment to moment. The brain turns vibrational stimulus into physical reality and the mind imagines and interprets the stimuli perceived by the brain into "cognitive reality."

According to Deepak Chopra, *"The human brain gives physical expression to the mind. As different as a thought and a neuron are, they run on parallel tracks. They are complementary; therefore, it isn't necessary to argue which came first. This isn't a chicken-or-the-egg problem. Mind and brain occupy their own levels of reality simultaneously. They form a feedback loop that passes from the mental to the physical domain while never losing sight of either one."*[58] The material neuron and the energetic thought run parallel. They exist together and separate at the same time.

All consciousness we experience already exists in universal consciousness in parallel. However, in our conscious mind, we tend to be linear. The "supermind" of imagination and transcendence provides us the ability to transcend linear reality; to access and create from infinite consciousness. Whereas our self-aware and emergent experience of mind is, in essence, consciousness experiencing itself as a vibrational physical hologram.[59]

3. ***Soul (Life Force or Energetic Consciousness)***—Plato considered the soul the essence of a person. He described this essence as an incorporeal, eternal occupant of our temporary human form continually reborn in subsequent bodies.

Elaborating on the soul, Plato said, *"The soul takes flight to the world that is invisible but there arriving she is sure of bliss and forever dwells in paradise."* .

There's been a great deal of research, discourse and conjecture over millennia concerning "the soul," largely because it's difficult to prove or disprove immaterial, nonphysical entities. In his discussions of rational psychology, Immanuel Kant said, *"We cannot prove a priori the immateriality of the soul, but rather only so much: that all properties and actions of the soul cannot be cognized from materiality."* In Kant's summation, the soul cannot be defined in physical, material terms; it dwells in the realm of immateriality not in the physical world of materiality.

Advances made in neuroscience have shown that areas of the brain, when stimulated or damaged, can cause spiritual and transcendental experiences. Neuroscience has not presently answered the question regarding our existence, our consciousness and the life force that keeps us breathing. This potentially begs the question; what and/or who is living and breathing us?

The Bahá'í Faith affirms that the soul continues to live after physical death and is immortal. This belief is also supported by the Christian faith, as well as many other religions. In many ancient cultures (e.g., Hebrew, Egyptian, Greek, Hawaiian), the word "soul" often has a meaning equivalent to "life," "vital breath" and/or "consciousness."

The *"Soul,"* as used herein, is *the energetic consciousness and life force unconstrained by physicality, space and time.*

The light of universal consciousness shines through the projector of our soul, illuminating the film strip of human consciousness that is projected by our mind onto the screen of our interpreted "physical reality."

In my experience, the human soul often consists of a collection of archetypical personalities. These archetypes combine in unique ways to give expression and singularity to each human experience. Examples of soul archetypes include King-Father, Queen-Mother, Child-Prince-Princess,

The Healer, The Hero-Knight, The Wisdom Holder, The Witch-Sorceress, The Earth Mother, The Trickster-Joker, The Creator-Artist-Musician, The Lover(s) and The Magician. Archetypes may also include animals, celestial bodies, shapes, symbols and numbers.

The collection of certain soul archetypes combine to create the unique and individual essence of each person. Some of the archetypes are dominant, while others are subservient. Also, some archetypes are subtle and opaque while others are more apparent. An awareness of the complex interplay between the archetypes provides us with an amazing ability to co-create with our archetypes utilizing their unique, special and powerful gifts to manifest our lives. However, as our soul evolves, the archetypes, and our need to archetypically identify ourselves, drop away until only pure unified (un)consciousness remains.

It is the soul's energetic, timeless, spaceless and selfless essence that allows us to experience a direct connection with the pure potential of infinite possibility while being in the experience of human consciousness. The soul provides divine guidance, the capacity to self-realize and experience our full divine potential as vibrant living beings. An awareness of the soul's infinite connection to the power of all possibility is precious. Through our souls, we can ascend beyond the physical into the spiritual realm of divine inspiration and quantum creation.

As discussed above, the 3 *Vibratory Consciousness Centers of Body, Mind and Soul* are interconnected and constantly interacting and influencing each other as well as the 7 *Vibratory Receptors and Transmitters* discussed below. Much like the neural networks in our bodies that are receiving and transmitting data, information and moving the life force that keeps us alive, our *Vibratory Consciousness Centers* and *Vibratory Receptors and Transmitters* are connected to each other and all consciousness in the universe in a constant jam session of transmitting, receiving, communicating and creating experiential reality.

<u>*Vibratory Receptors & Transmitters.*</u> Below are the *7 Vibratory Receptors & Transmitters* and the corresponding *Vibratory Consciousness Centers*:

7 Vibratory Receptor & Transmitters	Corresponding Vibratory Consciousness Centers
1. Sensation	Body
2. Perception	Body-Mind
3. Thought	Mind
4. Emotions	Mind-Body
5. Feelings	Body-Mind
6. Instinct	Body-Soul
7. Intuition	Soul-Mind-Body

We create our experience of "reality" through the receipt and transmission of vibrations to and from our *Vibratory Receptors & Transmitters* and converting those vibrations into experience through our *Vibratory Consciousness Centers*. For clarity, each of the *Vibratory Receptors & Transmitters* possesses distinct vibratory characteristics, much like the difference between the characteristics of a violin, a saxophone or a piano. Also, each of the *Vibratory Receptors & Transmitters* uniquely and collectively influence and resonate with the *Vibratory Consciousness Centers*. The unique characteristics, vibrations and patterns of the *Vibratory Receptors & Transmitters* interact with each other and the *Vibratory Consciousness Centers*, much like musicians jamming together.

By being sensitive to the subtleties and interactions of the *Vibratory Receptors & Transmitters* and *Vibratory Consciousness Centers*, we can powerfully increase and improve our (i) mental, physical, emotional and spiritual states of being, (ii) awareness, emotional intelligence and response-ability, (iii) relationships to each other and our environment, (iv) health and vitality, and (v) ability to manifest desired outcomes.

Like becoming a virtuoso of a musical instrument, mastery of the *Vibratory Receptors & Transmitters* and *Vibratory Consciousness Centers* can be honed through attention and practice as tools to express and create the life of your dreams.

The following provides a summary of the *Vibratory Receptors & Transmitters*:

1. Sensation

Sensation is the first stage in the biochemical and neurologic process that begins with a stimulus impinging upon the receptor cells of a sensory organ, such as light upon the eyes, sound in the ears, taste on our tongue, smell in our nose, air on our skin. Our five phenomenal senses of sight, hearing, smell, taste and touch, limit and filter the massive wave of data we receive each moment, and thus constrain and limit the experience of our "phenomenal reality."[60]

Our senses receive raw data from our environment and create information that is transmitted throughout somatic pathways in the form of sensation prior to reaching the mind for processing.

A "tree" at the sensation stage may just appear as light waves and patterns. The image would be upside down and the light waves in the pattern of the tree would be missing the color green on the leaves and the color brown on the trunk and branches. Until the wave data is (i) sampled and filtered by our senses, (ii) reconstructed in the perception of our brain, and (iii) identified by our mind as a tree, we have not yet turned this light wave data into information we use and understand in the context of our dimensional reality.

In addition to outside stimulus, we also receive internal stimuli from our bodies. Although our bodies sometimes make sounds and give off odors, the primary sensation relevant to our internal stimulus is touch and feel.

For the purposes of distinction in this book, "sensation" is based upon raw sensory data, whereas "feelings" are based upon the cognitive awareness of our physical sensations.

2. Perception

Perception is the process of attaining awareness of sensory information. When sensory data reaches our mind, it's generally filtered into a perception that fits our contextual worldview. For example, when our eyes sample and filter the light waves of a tree, we filter, connect and contextualize these shapes in a story that fits our basic view of the world. At this point, we perceive the object (tree) without any knowledge, labeling or identification as to what it is. We have not yet added thought (e.g., "that's a tree," "it is a plant that provides fruit, timber and shade") or emotion to our perception of the tree, (e.g., "the tree is beautiful," or "I feel peaceful when I look at the tree").

Our minds instantaneously filter and reorganize our *Basic Perception* into *Cognitive Perception*. *Cognitive Perception* is the result of interplay between one's perceived sensations and their experiences, including one's culture, beliefs and the interpretation of data being perceived. Sometimes, because of our cultural belief systems and/or limited experiences, we don't have the contextual frame of reference to understand or perceive sensory data. In these instances, we experience what is referred to by science as "perceptual blindness."

For example, if a driver focused on texting and not on the road, fails to notice the bicyclist he almost hit, that would be a form of perceptual blindness or "inattentional blindness."

The best-known study demonstrating "inattentional blindness" is the "Invisible Gorilla Test," conducted by Daniel Simon at the University of Illinois and Christopher Chabris of Harvard University. This study asked subjects to watch a short video of two groups of people (wearing black and white t-shirts) pass a basketball around. The subjects were told to either count the number of passes made by one of the teams or keep count of bounce passes vs. aerial passes. In the video, a person wearing a full gorilla suit walks through the scene. After watching the video, the subjects were asked if they saw anything out of the ordinary take place. In most groups, 50% of the subjects did not report seeing the gorilla. These results indicate the relationship between what's in one's visual field and perception is based on attention.

In an account published in *Trends in Cognitive Sciences*, Richard Nisbett and Takuhisa Masuda made the case for "cultural" influences on perception. The crux of the argument is that visual perception in Americans is more analytical, while in Asians, it's more holistic. Americans pay attention to details, Asians to the larger picture. Americans examine objects in isolation, whereas Asians are more sensitive to context.[61]

Perceptual blindness occurs when our senses receive data, but our minds are not processing the data into conscious and useable information. It's true if we don't have a context for something, it's difficult to understand it. For example, when we're infants, we perceive our environment, but don't yet comprehend our environment. For example, a baby will hear an alarming noise, but not understand it's a fire truck siren.

Likewise, there's a metaphorical story about Peruvian Indians being perceptually blind to the arrival of Spanish ships. As the story goes, these Peruvian Indians had never seen large ships. While the Peruvian Indians perceived objects, they didn't have any context to understand the cloth and wood structures floating on the ocean were ships carrying Spaniard Conquistadors. As well, when the Spanish Conquistadors were first seen riding horses, the indigenous Indians believed the man and horse were a single "Manimal." The Indians had never seen a horse before and never thought of the concept of riding an animal. It was the Shaman, who was open to other-worldly possibilities that was first able to more fully see and contextualize the ships, their purpose, as well as the men on horses.

The Shaman had a more expanded consciousness of reality and could understand the significance of the Spanish ships. The more we expand our consciousness to include a universe of infinite possibility, the more we increase our awareness and the scope of our perception, the more we can understand our lives and environment.

3. Thoughts

Thought consists of mental forms and processes that allow us to model the phenomenal world of space and time, as well as our interconnected world beyond space and time (e.g., imagination, instinct, intuition, emotion) to create, react and respond to our experiences according to our conscious objectives, plans, ends and desires. Thought generally refers to any mental or intellectual activity involving an individual's subjective consciousness. It can refer either to the act of thinking, imagining, believing or the resulting ideas or arrangements of ideas. Thought includes cognition, sentience, self-consciousness, beliefs and imagination. Thought is the consciousness of "mind" and the mind's primary function is to provide meaning, navigation, order, filtering, individuation, planning and understanding of the human experience. Thought also provides us the ability to be self-aware and have past and future experiences in the realm of mind. Thoughts can be expansive (e.g., open to inquiry and infinite possibilities) or constrictive (e.g., limited, linear, conforming).

Beliefs are often conditioned thought forms, the truth of which may come from facts and experiences, but often rely on conviction, trust and faith rather than fact or truth. Beliefs have a profound impact on our reality and are a powerful influence on our thoughts. Beliefs can be empowering (e.g., I believe I am the creator of my universe and all that experience I create) or disempowering (e.g., I believe I am only one little powerless person and can't do anything to make the world a better place). Empowering beliefs can have disempowering impacts and results (e.g., arrogance, rigidity, spiritual and emotional bypass, judgmental, closed-mindedness) and disempowering beliefs can sometimes have empowering impacts and results (e.g., empathy, compassion, kindness). Beliefs, when held with 100% conviction, can reduce our ability to access the infinite potential of universal consciousness and evolve new beliefs.

At the higher level of functioning, thought ascends into the super-conscious state of imagination. Imagination provides us the ability to form mental images, sensations and concepts, without the need for sensory involvement, although our senses do influence our imagination. Imagination is a fundamental facility that helps us create and understand our world. Imagination is the faculty through which we encounter everything. The things we touch, see, smell and hear, all coalesce into a "picture" in our imagination and then become experienced as "reality." Furthermore, anything we visualize, whether past, present or future accesses our imagination.

4. Emotions.

Emotions are energy in motion generally derived from a reaction, response and relationship to one's instinctual nature, beliefs, circumstances, and/or environment.[62] In psychology and philosophy, emotion is often defined as *a subjective, conscious experience characterized primarily by psycho-physiological experiences that include mental and physical states of being leading to biological and neurological responses to stimuli.*[63] Emotions are associated and considered reciprocally influential with mood, temperament, personality, motivation and behavior.

Because emotions are essentially vibrational and energetic states, they can arise from a wide variety of stimuli, including thoughts, beliefs, events, sensations, perceptions, feelings, our environment and even other emotions. In addition, emotions are influenced by hormones and neurotransmitters, such as serotonin, oxytocin, dopamine, adrenaline, cortisol and GABA.

Alternatively, emotions are often defined as a *"positive or negative experience associated with a particular pattern of energetic and psycho-somatic activity."*[64] When we judge our emotions as negative or positive, there's a tendency to disconnect from, or bypass, the emotional experiences we believe are "negative." This can result in missing the messages, lessons and growth opportunities that exist from fully experiencing our emotions and not judging them. Emotions often arise as a result of a belief or expectation interacting with a circumstance. For example, if I believe making money is good and losing money is bad, when I make money, I may experience the emotion of happiness, and when I lose money, I may experience the emotion of anger. In this example, my emotional state is conditioned upon making money. When we become aware of the conditionality of emotion, we can gain incredible power to unconditionally experience the emotions we desire, such as unconditional happiness, love and joy.

Emotions are wonderful teachers that make us aware of our beliefs and perception of circumstances, giving us an opportunity to change our beliefs and the way we view life. When we become aware of our beliefs and perceptions, we can begin to consciously choose our beliefs and emotions to optimize our states of being and change our experience of the world.

The intensity and experience of each emotion can shift subjectively from person-to-person and circumstance-to-circumstance depending upon factors such as one's beliefs, conditioning, sensitivity and experiences. For instance, one person (John) may experience the fear of skydiving with emotions of passion and exhilaration, while another person (Jane) might consider such an activity absolutely terrifying. While both people would feel fear, the vibration and intensity of the fear would be experienced differently by these two people. Jane would likely never even consider skydiving due to her beliefs about skydiving and safety, while John would overcome his fear with a courageous jump and a Woohoo! However, being terrified of public speaking, John would not likely engage in public speaking due to his fear, whereas Jane loves public speaking and even though she gets "butterflies" before speaking, Jane courageously overcomes her fear and finds public speaking exhilarating. The intensity and effect of emotion is subjectively experienced by each person under different circumstances based upon their beliefs, conditioning, sensitivity and experiences.

The Frequencies of Emotion. Each emotion has a vibrational frequency signature that causes a resonant field that is often experienced as differing levels of expansive or constrictive states of being (e.g., physical, mental, energetic).

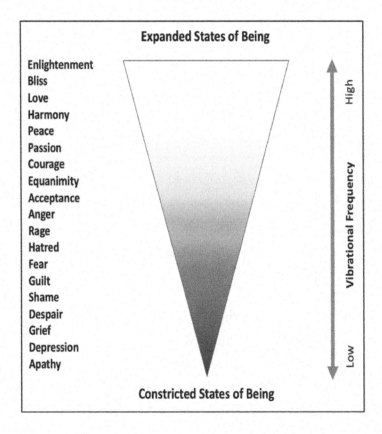

The body resonates with the energy signature/vibrational frequency of each emotion. This has a profound influence on our state of being by either expanding or contracting our energy field and somatic sensation. An expansive emotion triggers parasympathetic states of being, typically experienced as openness and relaxation, whereas a constrictive emotion causes sympathetic states often experienced as tightness and tension.[65]

As shown in the illustration, which provides examples of different emotions on the frequency scale, love, bliss and empowerment are very high energy emotions associated with expanded states of being, whereas apathy, depression and grief are very low energy emotions leading to constricted states of being. Emotions with an expansive resonance activate the parasympathetic nervous system resulting in the release of serotonin and the body becoming relaxed and feeling open. Emotions with both low energy and constrictive resonance can cause either a lack of energy and motivation while emotions that are higher energy but are still constrictive typically activate the sympathetic nervous system resulting in the release of neurotransmitters such as adrenaline and cortisol readying the body for fight-or flight. For example, anger typically causes the body to become tight and constricted, but unlike apathy, anger has sufficient energy and frequency to motivate action. The energy from anger can be used to spiral the emotion of anger into more expanded emotional states such as courage, passion and love.[66]

The energetic and vibrational frequency signature of each emotion creates a feedback loop that affects our mental, physical, energetic and emotional states of being. According to Harvard Medical School, *"When someone experiences a stressful event, the amygdala, an area of the brain that contributes to emotional processing, sends a distress signal to the hypothalamus. This area of the brain functions like a command center, communicating with the rest of the body through the nervous system so that the person has the energy to fight or flee."*[67] The mind, for instance, may imagine a mere inconvenience in the future and intensify it into a horrible emergency. Even though this event occurs in the imagination at some time in the future, the body, being in an always-present state of awareness, resonates with the frequency and amplitude of emotion experienced from the imagined scenario, which causes a shift in the physical state. The body doesn't know we are imagining some future event and thus when we imagine a circumstance that causes us to experience constrictive emotions, especially those having to do with survival, the body enters into the "fight-flight" state of the sympathetic nervous system. The body tightens resulting in the mind perceiving some emergency at the physical level. This leads to greater intensity of the emotion at the mental, energetic and physical level, creating a perpetuating Vibratory Feedback Loop. This will typically continue until there is new stimulus to break the pattern of the Vibratory Feedback Loop. Those that are unaware of their Vibratory Feedback Loops, can live in a chronic fight-flight condition. By being aware of our Vibratory Feedback Loops, we can consciously provide new circumstantial, belief and/or mental stimulus to break the pattern.

To gain vibrational/emotional mastery, it's important to increase our understanding and experience of vibrations and emotions, including their character, the way they arise, their expression and their impact on our lives.

So how do emotions arise and how do we become more aware of the emotions we are experiencing?

Any one, or a combination of, the *Vibratory Receptors & Transmitters* and *Vibratory Consciousness Centers* can start a sequence and feedback loop that triggers an emotion. This can be linear, parallel, random, independent and/or collective. To provide more clarity, below are *6 Elements of Emotion* that individually, or in combination, contribute to the existence and experience of emotion:

1. *Environmental-Sensory Stimulus*—An outer stimulus, such as a vibration, event or object, triggers sensory signals to the brain and body (e.g., a rattlesnake or coiled piece of rope).

2. *Perceptive Awareness*—Perception of the Environmental-Sensory Stimulus (e.g., awareness of an object that is not yet identified as a rattlesnake or a coiled-up piece of rope).

3. *Physiological Arousal*—Instinctual reaction to the Environmental-Sensory Stimulus and Perceptive Awareness (e.g., the somatic wisdom preparing the body subconsciously by engaging the sympathetic nervous system if the object is a rattlesnake)

4. *Cognitive Appraisal & Beliefs*—Represents the subjective thought and interpretation of the events, objects and stimulus (e.g., "The object is a rattlesnake and could potentially kill me if it bites me—run away!" or "The object is a rattlesnake. They are fairly non-aggressive snakes. Walk around it and I'll be

fine"). I could also just imagine a rattlesnake without any outside stimulus and still create a chain of elements leading to the experience of emotion.

5. *Feelings*—Subjective awareness of a physical experience (e.g., feeling high energy or low energy, tight or relaxed) juxtaposed on the experience of Environmental Sensory Stimulus, Perceptive Awareness, Physiological Arousal, and Cognitive Appraisal & Beliefs). However, feelings can be instinctual and jump from Perceptive Awareness to Feelings.

6. *Expression & Motivation*—Emotional energy being manifest into mental action (e.g., inspiration, creativity, will-won't decision, withdrawal, suppression), physical action and body language (e.g., running, smiling, staring, fighting), verbal language (e.g., talking, yelling, arguing), and/or energetic action (e.g., increased/expanded or decreased/contracted energy).

Klaus Scherer, a Professor of Psychology at the Swiss Center for Affective Sciences, specializing in the psychology of emotion, developed the Component Process Model (CPM), consisting of 5 components of emotion, similar to the 6 *Elements of Emotion* listed above. Scherer stated that these components did not work independently of each other but were part of a collective-collaborative process. Subjective feelings influenced and were influenced by other components such as physiological arousal being driven by cognitive appraisal. [68]

Other leading emotional theorists have posited differing views on whether an emotion arises by itself or from an event, a physical state, cognitive appraisal or beliefs. Using the example of a rattlesnake as the event stimulus, below is a brief summary of other theories of emotion[69]:

- *Walter Cannon*—rattlesnake (event) → fear (emotion) → fight or flight (physical response)

- *James–Lange*—rattlesnake (event) → fight or flight (physical response) → fear (emotion)

- *Richard Lazarus*—rattlesnake (event) → rattlesnakes can kill me (cognitive appraisal) → fear (emotion) → fight or flight (physical action)

- *Singer-Schachter*—rattlesnake (event) → fight or flight (physical action) → rattlesnakes can kill me (cognitive appraisal) → fear (emotion)

The foregoing, like so many scientific theories, are based upon a fairly linear and analytical framework. However, our experience of life, including our emotions, can be serial or parallel as well as partial or whole. There is likely no one-size-fits-all linear way to experience life or an emotion, so each of the above theorists are right some of the time, partially right some of the time and wrong some of the time. For example, if I experience a purely instinctual emotion such as fear and react physically without thinking and cognitive appraisal, then Cannon and James-Lange would be correct in that circumstance. However, if I engage in cognitive appraisal, then the emotional theorists who excluded cognitive appraisal (e.g., Cannon, James-Lange), would not be correct in that situation and Lazarus and Singer-Schachter would be correct.

Like an improvisational jam session, there's no one way to write a song or to improvise music. Any one, or a combination, of the foregoing *6 Elements of Emotion* can trigger an emotion. Similarly, an emotion can trigger any other *Vibratory Receptors & Transmitters* and/or *Vibratory Consciousness Centers*, individually or in combination, to initiate a sequence that results in an experience of "reality." Like emotions, there are times when music just pours out and is expressed spontaneously without much involvement from the analytical mind while other times it is carefully and thoughtfully composed and performed using primarily cognitive functions.

It is clear, from my observation and experience, that emotions can trigger or be triggered by any other stimulus or concurrent stimuli of the *Vibratory Receptors and Transmitters* and/or the *Vibratory Consciousness Centers*.

Emotions can be classified as **Instinctual Emotions** and **Cognitive Emotions**. Joseph LeDoux, Ph.D., professor of neuroscience and psychology at New York University, posits that automatic physiological responses to danger and issues of survival are hard-wired in the brain and cognitive appraisal is irrelevant to these physical responses to threats. LeDoux argues, and I agree, that people are not born with phobias and that conscious emotions are learned through experience or programming. I also agree with Lazarus, professor in the Department of Psychology at University of California, Berkeley, that cognitive appraisal often creates and contributes to our emotional state.

- **Instinctual Emotions** are generally associated with survival and protection of one's life and well-being (e.g., fight, flight, food, mating). Generated from a combination of somatic consciousness, the sympathetic nervous system and the amygdala, Instinctual Emotions arise somatically and bypass cognitive appraisal. Because **the body is always in the state of present awareness**, Instinctual Emotions tend to be felt somatically in the "moment of now." Thus, Instinctual Emotions are generally more immediate and present than Cognitive Emotions (discussed below).

Somatic theories of emotion claim that bodily responses, rather than judgments, are essential to emotions. The first modern version of somatic emotion theories came from William James in the 1880s. This theory has been supported with modern neurological evidence by theorists such as John Cacioppo[70], António Damásio[71], Joseph E. LeDoux[72], and Robert Zajonc[73].

To illustrate the functioning of Instinctual Emotions, if I imagine having amazing sex and my body has no response, the emotions that arise from physical arousal would not emerge. However, if I become aroused physically, the body-mind feedback loop becomes engaged, creating "reality" through the embodiment of my imagination, thereby intensifying the feelings of arousal as my somatic feelings and emotions become engaged with my imagination. Another example would be, if I am standing on the edge of a cliff and I feel someone approaching from behind me, I will somatically react in a way to preserve my safety to avoid falling off the cliff. These are just a couple of examples that demonstrate the body's profound instinctual involvement and influence on our emotional, mental and energetic states of being.

Other emotional theorists believe that emotions happen in the mind, which leads us to the discussion about Cognitive Emotions below. In reality, we are energetic creatures and emotions, being energy in motion, affect our being at all levels, including mental, physical and energetic.

Because of the subconscious/somatic nature of Instinctual Emotions, there has been a great deal of behavioral programming focused on the Instinctual Emotions in our society. Examples include attaching our survival instincts to generating money and our mating instincts to purchasing products. When we become aware of the relationship between Instinctual Emotions and Cognitive Emotions, we gain emotional proficiency and awareness giving us the ability to respond to, rather than be manipulated by, programming and artificial survival-based stimuli.

- *Cognitive Emotions* tend to be based in the mind rather than the natural and present Instinctual Emotions of the body. Cognitive Emotions are triggered by thought and generally involve the prefrontal cortex. This brain region has been implicated in planning complex cognitive behaviors, personality expression, decision-making and moderating correct social behavior. The most typical function carried out by the pre-frontal cortex area is "executive function" which provides the ability to differentiate between conflicting thoughts, make judgments (e.g., good or bad, true or false), distinguish between same or different pattern recognition, future consequences of current activities, prediction of outcomes, and social "control" (suppression of socially-unacceptable behavior).

  Richard Lazarus, Ph.D., posited that cognitive activities such as judgments, evaluations, beliefs, or thoughts, are necessary for an emotion to occur. This cognitive activity may be conscious or unconscious and may or may not take the form of conceptual processing.

  Cognitive Emotions tend to arise from dualistic, polarized, future or past thinking and a plethora of conditioned emotional triggers. Unlike the present-moment Instinctual Emotions, Cognitive Emotions are often based upon future projection, past experiences, imagination, interpretation, falsity, rationalization, manipulation, mistaken assumptions and conditioned beliefs.

  For example, according to currently accepted authority, we are born with only two fears: 1) the fear of falling and 2) the fear of loud noises.[74] However, the Diagnostic and Statistical Manual of Mental Disorders (DSM) published by the American Psychiatric Association lists over 150 phobias. Most of the phobias listed in the DSM are cognitive, which indicates they are generally learned or conditioned.

Utilizing the tools of mindfulness, equanimity, inquiry and breath-work, we can powerfully guide and optimize our Cognitive Emotional states to be more pure and present so as to align with our desired states of being and free ourselves from conditioned beliefs and emotional manipulation that often negatively affect our states of being.

- ***Basic and Complex Emotions.*** In addition to being Instinctual or Cognitive, emotions can be *Basic* or *Complex*. An example of a *"Basic Emotion"* is the fear of falling from a great height. Fear of falling from a great height is singular, simple and can save our life. Love, on the other hand, is a *"Complex Emotion"* as it contains many different emotions and vibrations combined together for multiple reasons (e.g., bonding, comfort, mating, community, collaboration, support, safety, skill set diversity, intimacy), but not a singular reason.

  Also, emotions can be of varying duration with some emotions occurring over a period of seconds (e.g., embarrassment) while others can last years (e.g., love).

  As will be further explored in the chapter on *Emotional Intelligence*, we can utilize the energy from all our emotions to fuel the fulfillment of our dreams.

5. Feelings.[75]

From my experience and observation, "feelings" are often confused with emotions. For the purposes of distinguishing between feelings and emotions in this book, *"Feelings"* are embodied emotions experienced as physical states of being with somatic consciousness.[76]

Feelings and emotions are often used interchangeably in our communication without much thought to their differences. By distinguishing between feelings and emotions, we can exponentially increase our emotional intelligence, cognitive abilities and health, as well as help prevent our bodies from being ravaged by stress and constrictive emotions. Engaging in emotional intelligence, we can activate our pre-frontal cortex rather than the amygdala, allowing us to intentionally and mindfully express our emotions to create the life and outcomes we desire. In my experience, those that have a deeper understanding of their emotions and feelings tend to be more evolved as humans and consistently experience more expanded and states of being that serve their ability to manifest a more loving, thriving and abundant life and world.

Unlike "emotions" which consist of energetic charge often resulting from thoughts, beliefs and circumstances, **"feelings" are embodied present somatic states of being such as hungry, sexually aroused, hot, warm, cold, relaxed, tired, tense, excited, vital, strong, expanded, contracted, tingly, calm, comfortable, heavy, lite, tight, open and loose.** The body does not concern itself with conditionalities of the mind like whether you'll get a promotion or get married to your lover or become a billionaire. The body's consciousness is largely concerned with such things as present safety, well-being, comfort and the preservation of life. The body's consciousness is also concerned with avoiding threats to safety, life, well-being and comfort.

The body responds to the stimulus from our internal and external experiences in real-time. Because of the body's present state of awareness, it is susceptible to, and interconnected with, our thoughts, emotions and imagination and doesn't differentiate between real and present emotions and those that are imagined past or future projections. When we imagine an unpleasant circumstance, we often experience associated constrictive emotions (e.g., fear, anxiety, shame, guilt, anger). For example, if we imagine ourselves in a war zone, the brain is likely to create the emotion of fear. Resonating with the frequency of fear, the body becomes tight, tense and constricted and the hormones and neurotransmitters related to fear get released to activate the sympathetic nervous system in readiness for fight or flight. When the mind perceives the tightness of the body and the readiness for fight or flight, the mind perpetuates the state of fear until the body relaxes. The body won't relax until the mind is out of a state of fear. This feedback loop can result in chronic states of fear and sympathetic nervous system states. If, however, I imagine myself laying in the sun on a beach in Hawaii and take some nice deep relaxing breaths, my mind becomes peaceful, my body becomes relaxed, and I experience an emotional state of calm and serenity. My body and mind can then both relax and enter the parasympathetic nervous system state, thereby shifting the feedback loop of fear to a feedback loop of calm, serenity and joy.

The feedback loops happen so rapidly that often the physical sensation and the emotion are perceived as happening concurrently. As provided in the example above, we can reset the feedback loops and allow both the body and mind to relax, by (1) taking a deep conscious breath, (2) being objective about our thoughts, emotions and feelings/somatic experience, and (3) replacing non-serving thoughts and imagined scenarios with those that are pleasurable and serve our highest state of being. When we imagine a scenario that we find pleasurable (e.g., taking a wonderful vacation, making love, fulfilling a goal), we are likely to experience expansive emotions (e.g., happiness, love, joy and bliss) that activates our parasympathetic nervous system giving the body the ability to relax, the organs to efficiently function, our bodies to heal, and our pre-frontal cortex to be more fully engaged. We can also engage in immersive physical activities that cause our bodies to relax (e.g., massage, lovemaking, yin yoga, cuddling, walking, stretching).

To help further clarify the distinction between feelings and emotions, we often hear people say, "*I feel angry.*" This is generally not an accurate statement because the body does not "feel angry," but rather the mind experiences the emotion of anger, often as a result of a *Cognitive Emotion* caused by a belief intersecting with a circumstance (e.g., unmet expectations, feeling wronged). The body responds to the emotional charge and vibrations in the form of somatic "feelings" that match the emotional vibration of anger. The body doesn't "feel angry," but may feel tight, constricted, tense or charged. A more accurate description would be, "*I'm experiencing the emotion of anger which is causing my body to feel tightness and constriction.*"

The body generally responds to emotion by activating either the sympathetic or parasympathetic nervous system in a way that corresponds with the intensity and frequency of the emotional charge. For example, anger is an emotion with a vibration that generally causes the body to activate the sympathetic nervous system. The sympathetic nervous system prepares the body for fight or flight, which causes tension and constriction. The power or amplitude of the emotional charge determines the intensity of the body's response (e.g., mild, moderate, and extreme).

When entering the sympathetic nervous system mode, "excitatory neurotransmitters," such as norepinephrine, epinephrine (aka adrenaline) and cortisol, flood our body resulting in a "fight or flight" response. This process happens without cognitive thought; it's a somatic reaction to the scenarios we create in our minds and the resulting emotional frequency and amplitude.

When we experience expansive emotions such as love, peace and joy, the parasympathetic nervous system is activated in resonance with the emotional frequencies and "inhibitory neurotransmitters" are released, such as serotonin and GABA. The chemicals tend to relax, open and expand the way the body feels.

Dopamine is a dual-purpose neurotransmitter, as it can be both excitatory and inhibitory. Dopamine elevates mood, focus and motivation and is linked with the feeling of inspiration. States of inspiration and enlightenment access the whole nervous system as the body is concurrently relaxed, expanded and energized. I refer to this state of being as the *"Awesympathetic"* state due to the experience of being concurrently relaxed while also being energized, activated, creative, focused and cognitively high functioning. In my practice of living in AWE, I try to maintain the Awesympathetic state during my waking hours and enter the parasympathetic state for breaks during the day and when winding down for the night.

As mentioned, feelings can come from internal and environmental stimuli as well as from thoughts and emotions. To help distinguish between physiologically and cognitively created feelings, I have categorized feelings into two separate classes:

- *"Somatic-Instinctual Feelings"* arise from original somatic awareness, experiences of the body and/or instinctual coding without being initiated or filtered by cognitive emotion or rational thought. Examples include somatic pleasure and pain such as cold, hot, hungry, sexual arousal, falling, tight and loose. For instance, if I grab a hot pan, my body immediately and directly experiences the heat and I release the pan as a protective measure to prevent myself from getting burned. Because the feeling is experienced directly by my body in the present moment, it is a Somatic/Instinctual Feeling.

   The body is amazingly aware and present. It's constantly adjusting to keep us alive and in a state of healthy homeostasis and comfort. Most of this happens autonomically without any cognitive awareness.

   Somatic-Instinctual Feelings are generally felt directly when we're immersed in physical survival or physical activity such as eating, breathing, sex, falling, walking, defending ourselves or fleeing from immediate bodily harm. Somatic-Instinctual Feelings can also come from thermal regulation, heart rates, breathing, digestion, hydration, metabolism, resting, dreaming and engaging in immersive or passive "mindless" experiences that allow us to feel and deep and present awareness of embodiment.

Barring physiological or neurological disorder, our Somatic-Instinctual Feelings are generally more accurate, present and trustworthy than Derivative-Cognitive Feelings. Because our Derivative-Cognitive Feelings are generally initiated by cognitive thought and imagination based upon subjective beliefs, conditioning and future-past imagined events, our Derivative-Cognitive Feelings are generally less trustworthy than our Somatic-Instinctual Feelings. Our Derivative-Cognitive Feelings are nonetheless highly valuable in understanding and guiding the body-mind-emotional feedback loops.

It often becomes difficult to discern between Derivative-Cognitive Feelings and Somatic-Instinctual Feelings when we're unaware of our thoughts, conditioning or imagined events and their impact on our state of being.

The somatic consciousness of the body, being in the present moment, reacts immediately to stimuli including our environment, thoughts, beliefs, emotions and imagined events. Even if the stimuli is imagined, the body reacts to imagined events as real and present. The body's state and response to stimuli activates mental awareness of the state, of the body, creating a feedback loop of thought, emotion and imagined events. If we lack aware-ness and discernment of the initiating consciousness, stimuli, emotions and feelings creating the mind-body feedback loop, a perpetuating feed-back loop can be created leading to chronic non-serving states of being. However, the more we practice being aware of the stimulus-response and causal feedback loops between our body, mind and emotions, the more we can engage our objective higher consciousness to gain greater awareness and mastery over our emotions, feelings, beliefs and state of being.

- *"Derivative-Cognitive Feelings"* occur when our somatic state of being is triggered by thought, cognitive emotion or imagined stimuli. In other words, when we have a thought, Cognitive Emotion or imagined event, the body responds. Once the mind becomes aware of the body's physiological condition, it then interprets the condition of the body and generates a Cognitive Emotional state from the physical stimuli of the body. The Cognitive Emotions then create an energetic stimulus which the body senses and responds by generating Derivative-Cognitive Feelings. The mind then perceives the physiological state of the body and interprets the somatic physical stimulus into cognitive appraisal that generates a cognitive emotional state. This is the manner in which a cognitive feedback loop is typically created between the mind, emotions and body.

For example, after I picked up and dropped the hot pan, I judge myself as being stupid for picking up the hot pan and experience the emotion of anger toward myself. Resonating with the frequency of anger, my body constricts, and I experience the Derivative-Cognitive Feelings of tightness and increased heart rate as I enter the sympathetic nervous system state. Even though the danger of getting burned by the hot pan is no longer present, because of the feedback loop of Cognitive Emotions and Derivative Cognitive Feelings, I perpetuate the experience of grabbing the hot pan and my judgement about myself for doing so long after the actual event has passed.

While we experience Derivative-Cognitive Feelings as real, they are often not based upon truth or actual facts. The greater the involvement and influence of our mind's interpretation and story machine, the further away from the truth our feelings get. Derivative-Cognitive Feelings feel real because the body responds in the present moment to thought, emotion and imagination without filtering the truth or veracity thereof. The embodiment of emotional energy is what makes Cognitive Emotions, future-past thought and imagined scenarios feel so real.

In order to more effectively discern our Somatic-Instinctual Feelings from our Derivative-Cognitive Feelings, if we are driving down the road and someone driving the opposite direction suddenly swerves into our lane and we automatically steer away to avoid the immediate and present danger of the collision, we would generally have an experience of Somatic-Instinctual Feelings. We experience the immediate burst of intense energy for fight or flight along with heightened awareness and alertness. We then reflect that the person's inattention to his driving nearly killed us. We may scream "Idiot!" and get angry. We may think about how the "jerk" almost killed us. At this point, we've switched from Somatic-Instinctual Feelings to Derivative-Cognitive Feelings and our body feels tension, agitation, nervousness, increased heart rate, trembling and constriction caused by the cognitively created emotions of fear and anger over a situation that is no longer real, immediate or present.

While we experience Derivative-Cognitive Feelings as real, they are often not based upon truth. Whereas, Somatic-Instinctual Feelings are both embodied in "physical reality" and closer to the truth because they generally happen in the present moment without the mind's interpretation. The greater the involvement and influence of our mind's interpretation, meaning and story machine, the further away from the truth our feelings get.

If we allow our thoughts, beliefs and imaginations to consistently trigger constrictive emotions, such as fear and anxiety, that activate our sympathetic nervous system, we're likely to live in a prolonged *Constricted State of Being* causing us to suffer from stress and stress-related illnesses, such as heart disease, cancer and neural disorders.

If we want to have optimal health and vitality, it's important not only to include healthy diet and exercise in our routines and practices, but also healthy thoughts, serving emotions and optimal imagined outcomes that stimulate our expanded parasympathetic and/or our *Awesympathetic* states of being. The parasympathetic state of being leads to relaxation, healing, rejuvenation, emergence and increased immune system functioning. The *Awesympathetic* state of being promotes flow, focus, happiness, inspiration, motivation, achievement and fulfillment of our goals. The more we live in an *Expanded State of Being*, the more likely we'll have a healthier and happier life.

When we are aware of the parts that contribute to the symphony of our thoughts, emotions, imagined outcomes and feelings, we can make conscious and discerning choices as to the truth, value and integrity of our thoughts, beliefs, emotions, imagined outcomes and feelings. With this greater awareness, we can create the reality we desire by (1) consciously distinguishing between that which is real, immediate and present and that which is imagined, (2) directing our mind to imagine the most desirable outcome, (3) mindfully guiding the physical-mental-emotional feedback loops to create circumstances and environments that nurture our potential, and (4) utilizing the power of our imagination to create the reality we desire.

6. Instinct.

Instinct is defined as (1) a natural or inherent aptitude, impulse, or capacity, (2) a largely inheritable and fixed tendency of an organism to make a complex and specific response to environmental stimuli without involving reason, or (3) behavior that is mediated by reactions below the conscious level.[77]

From the discussion on feelings above, there is a fine-line distinction between *Somatic-Instinctual Feelings* and *Instinct*. *Somatic-Instinctual Feelings* are a hybrid of somatic feelings and instinct. Instinct is primarily a somatic impulse based upon ancient genetic memory and connection to the present vibrational state that influences *Somatic Consciousness*. Instinct influences and creates behavior without cognitive filtering or restriction. *Instinct* is an innate cellular knowing and connection with one's outer environment and the inner life force that drives somatic behavior. Metaphorically, *Instinct* is the driver of the "somatic car" and *Somatic Feeling* is how the car responds to *Instinct's* driving and the environment.

Examples of instinctual action patterns can be observed in the behavior of animals, such as (a) reproduction and feeding among insects, (b) the automatic movement toward the ocean of sea turtles hatched on a beach, (c) the communication of honeybees dancing in the direction of a food source without formal instruction, (d) birds flying south, (e) animal fighting and courtship, (f) internal escape functions, and (g) nesting.

Much of the inherited patterning and cellular memory of our past evolution instinctually drives our behavior. Although modern humans (homo sapiens sapiens) have "evolved" in thought, culture and society over some 200,000 years, our somatic awareness and instinct are products of planetary evolution going back 4.5 billion years. The evolutionary survival instincts and patterns are imprinted into our genes driving the way we relate to the planet and each other.

As well, societal survival instincts also dominate our beliefs and behaviors. For example, in his book *"Germs, Guns and Steel,"* Jared Diamond argues that the gaps in power and technology between human societies originate in environmental differences, which are amplified by various positive feedback loops. Eurasian nations conquered populations of other areas and maintained their dominance, through (1) superior weapons (guns); (2) virulent diseases to which Eurasian conquerors had developed immunities, but the conquered populations were susceptible (germs) and (3) centralized government that promoted nationalism and powerful military organizations (steel). Eurasia was also the beneficiary of favorable geographic, climatic and environmental characteristics after the last Ice Age about 13,000-15,000 years ago. As a result of this combination of advantages, the Eurasian gene pool and culture proliferated and had a profound influence on our culture, beliefs, behaviors and instincts, much of which has found its way into our cellular memory.

Our instinct is embedded in our somatic wisdom and provides us the ability to connect deeply with the wisdom of the earth and nature. Our modern-conditioned minds tend to be disconnected from nature, the planet and each other. It's this disconnection that has led to so many of the imbalances created by humankind. By becoming more keenly aware of, and integrated with, our instinctual wisdom, we can access a great deal of understanding and awareness to guide us toward optimal and life-affirming experiences.

The language of instinct is spoken in vibrations that are understood by the body in the form of sensations and feelings. By listening to the body and trusting its instinctual wisdom, we can use this incredible genius to improve the quality and experience of our lives, as well as our well-being and thriveability.

Instinct is an inner sense of somatic knowing, beyond the bounds of cognitive or rational thought, about how to optimally interact and respond to our environment. Unlike intuition, instinct generally doesn't use words or visual messaging, but rather somatic feelings, urges and vibrations to deliver its messages and drive behavior, often resulting in expansion or contraction of the body. For instance, when the body feels tight or constricted, it's often warning us of a circumstance that should be avoided such as impending danger that threatens our well-being, whereas when the body is open and expansive, it's telling us that a circumstance is safe and/or favorable for our well-being.

By listening to the language of our instinct, feeling the expansion or contraction of our body, and trusting our "gut feeling" provides us with an innate genius to guide us to deeper wisdom in relationships with each other, our environment and our planet.

7. Intuition.

Intuition is the ability to acquire knowledge, a sense of knowing and universal guidance without inference from, or the use of, reason. Intuition generally appears as flashes of insight that are beyond logic. Operating through a super-conscious or unconscious connection between the universe and our soul-mind-body *Vibratory Consciousness Centers*, Intuition is often received through visual, auditory and kinesthetic communication channels. The channels are generally referred to as clairvoyance, clairaudience and clairsentience. Although Intuition is often referred to in terms of visual, auditory and/or kinesthetic sensory awareness, Intuition doesn't generally communicate through the normal physical sensory channels. Intuition generally uses an inner vision, voice or feeling that provides an internal sense of knowing, often referred to as "sixth sense."

For Rudolf Steiner, Intuition is the third of three stages of higher knowledge, coming after imagination and inspiration, and is characterized by a state of immediate and complete experience of, or even union with, the object of knowledge without loss of the subject's individual ego. *"Just as in the body, eye and ear develop as organs of perception, as senses for bodily processes, so does a man develop in himself soul and spiritual organs of perception through which the soul and spiritual worlds are opened to him. For those who do not have such higher senses, these worlds are dark and silent, just as the bodily world is dark and silent for a being without eyes and ears."*[78] Intuition is the sense of the spiritual world, the world of our soul's understanding.

Intuition arises when thought ascends the boundaries and constraints of limited, linear thought processes and expands into the realm of non-linear/non-rational super-consciousness.

Most of us have had the experience where our *Intuition* gives us guidance and direction. When we listen to our Intuition, things generally go well. When we don't listen, the opposite tends to happen. It is from having these experiences that we learn and gain the wisdom of listening to our Intuition. On occasion, however, Intuition guides us to take risks and exposes us to unpleasant challenges so that we may gain experience, strength, courage and wisdom.

Our Intuition is, in essence, like an intelligent radio tuner that is capable of playing multiple channels, but automatically tunes into the strongest station that will provide us with the experience most aligned with our "higher self."

However, sometimes our Intuition gives us guidance and then shifts guidance. I have often found this both unsettling and irritating. This is because our intuition is already tuned into parallel possibilities and their outcomes. Sometimes our intuition guides us into situations for the benefit of others rather than ourselves and/or to achieve positive planetary outcomes. In these situations, there is generally a gift in the challenge and an opportunity to learn valuable lessons necessary for us to achieve our life's purpose.

Our intuition allows us to "feel, hear and/or see" the unfolding outcomes of our choices and be magnetized toward choices that will yield the maximum fulfillment of our highest life's purpose and most positive collective outcome.

THE SONG OF LIFE AND CREATION

We each are given the gift of co-creating the experience of an entire universe from vibration resulting in a cosmic symphonic jam session!

The *Vibratory Receptors & Transmitters* and *Vibratory Consciousness Centers* discussed above are interconnected to each other and contribute to our integrated and unique human experience. Any *Vibratory Receptor & Transmitter* and/or

Vibratory Consciousness Center, singularly or in combination, can initiate an experiential sequence.

To explain this, let's use the metaphor of a song. The components of a song are melody, harmony, rhythm and lyrics. When writing a song, any one part (harmony, melody, rhythm or lyrics) may be the initial creative spark upon which the rest of a song is created. For example, a singer may start humming a melody, which is the initial creative spark that inspires the guitarist to play the chords (harmony), and the drummer and bassist then lay down the groove (rhythm) to fit the harmony and melody. The singer then starts singing lyrics and modifies the melody based upon the music being played. The guitarist then finds new inspiration from the melody and lyrics and changes the rhythm and voicing of the chords, and so on. The initial creative spark could have just as easily been the drummer laying down a beat, the bass following the drummer, the guitarist playing chords over the rhythm and then the singer joining in.

As is often the case, a combination of two or more components synchronistically combine to create the music we experience (e.g., improvisational jam sessions). Musicians, when improvising, are concurrently hearing, interpreting, imagining and playing the music. From a purely mechanical perspective, there should be time delays between the hearing, interpretation, imagination and playing of improvised music. These delays would make playing improvised music as a group theoretically impossible, yet the miracle of playing simultaneous and synchronous music happens because our reality is based upon far more than mechanics, chemistry and science. The musicians are accessing and playing with universal vibration and consciousness, creating and sharing a miraculous reality in the present moment.

The ability to "hear" the whole song, each part individually and understand how each part contributes to the whole, is the way a trained musician listens to music. When listening to a song, the untrained ear generally hears the music as the sum of its parts. However, when we focus our listening to one part of the song, our attention shifts to the component upon which we are focusing. So, if we are singing along with a song, the lyrics and melody become dominant in our field of attention. If we are drumming with the song, the rhythm and groove become dominant.

Similarly, any one, or a combination, of the *Vibratory Receptors & Transmitters* may trigger any, or a combination, of the *Vibratory Receptors & Transmitters* that creates our experience of reality. Like engaging in an improvisational jam session, the more we become aware of the contribution and interaction of each of the *Vibratory Receptors & Transmitters* and *Vibratory Consciousness Centers* to the whole of our experience, the greater our ability to intentionally, joyfully and masterfully create our reality. For example, a sensation may initiate a perception, which generates a thought that triggers an emotion, or intuition may trigger a feeling which leads to a thought. The triggering sequence happens so quickly that, unless we focus our attention on the sequence of events, the separate contribution of each of the *Vibratory Receptor & Transmitters* and *Vibratory Consciousness Centers* is experienced as a simultaneous and unified event.

Our *Vibratory Receptor & Transmitters* and *Vibratory Consciousness Centers* are constantly jamming with each other to create our experience of a universal reality, similar to how musicians concurrently hear, perform, and extemporaneously compose music in an improvisational jam session.

By increasing our awareness and mastery of the interaction of our *Vibratory Receptors & Transmitters* and/or *Vibratory Consciousness Centers*, we can more easily and joyfully create our lives, much like virtuosic musicians joyfully and easily create music. The ability to master the *"Cosmic Jam Session"* gives us the power to consciously create and guide our reality rather than unconsciously being controlled by subconscious beliefs, urges and programs.

BECOMING A COSMIC JAM SESSION VIRTUOSO

Our ability to powerfully co-create our world is directly related to the vibrational states we transmit and receive from the universe. When we consciously focus our *Vibratory Receptors & Transmitters* and *Vibratory Consciousness Centers* on living in our *highest expression* (e.g., expansive, life-enhancing, inspiring, awe) resulting in the most *beneficial behavior*, we can create and live the life of our dreams.

The universe is very virtuosic and plays an infinite number of songs at once. It is adaptable, resilient and able to immediately play along with whatever tune we are playing.

For example, if we want to realize abundance in our life, it's vital we bring our *Vibratory Receptors & Transmitters* and *Vibratory Consciousness Centers* into alignment with the state of being abundant. This will send a vibration of abundance to the universe. In turn, the universe sends us vibrations matching the state of our abundance. Because we are in abundance consciousness, we resonate with and are open to receiving these vibrations. This creates a feedback loop of abundance vibrations. As the internal and universal vibrations of abundance increase, it leads to the energetic state of being abundant. When the abundant state of being is outwardly expressed as behavior, we attract abundance into our life.

The *Vibratory Receptors & Transmitters* most in alignment with receiving universal wisdom are *Intuition* and *Instinct*. When we're focused on "listening" to, and being guided by, our intuition and instinct, we connect directly into universal and natural wisdom, uncluttered by space/time perception, reason, rationalization, interpretation and duality. When we're guided by our intuition and instinct, we naturally align to the vibrational song being played by the universe for our optimal experience. Often our optimal experience comes in the form of challenges that help us grow. It's important to recognize and be grateful for the gifts given by the universe in the form of challenges.

Our intuition and instinct are often blocked by mind chatter and conditioned beliefs, especially when we're guided to engage in something challenging. This is largely due to our preponderantly mind-based society that conditions us for safety, comfort and convenience rather than living full, fearless, expansive lives based upon intuition, instinct and imagination. As a result, we frequently override strong messages from our intuition and instinct with rationalization—in essence, we often turn our "mind amp" up to level 10 and blare a solo to a different tune than the one being played by universe for our benefit. This "rationalization" and mind chatter prevents us from intuitively and instinctually listening to the wisdom of the universe. When we override universal and natural wisdom, the results are often an experience that's unpleasant, painful or disastrous.

If we insist on playing a song based upon fear, destruction, toxicity, separation and war, the universe will oblige by jamming with us, and we get to live with the undesired results. However, if we listen carefully, we can play a song for our optimal well-being and thriving—possibly the song of love, peace, beauty, joy and AWE.

When we listen to the wisdom of the universe through our intuitive and instinctual channels as well as the other *Vibratory Receptors and Transmitters* and *Vibratory Consciousness Centers*, we align with the vibration, consciousness and creative power of the universe in an optimal co-creative jam session.

The foregoing illustrates how *Vibratory Receptors & Transmitters* and *Vibratory Consciousness Centers* interconnect, trigger and influence our daily lives. When we are not conscious of this process, we are prone to unconscious reactions, expressions and behaviors that have undesirable impacts in our lives. By being aware of our *Vibratory Receptors & Transmitters* and *Vibratory Consciousness Centers*, we can consciously guide and use them as tools to manifest expression and behavior that is in alignment with our creative aspirations and highest potential.

We are always in a co-creative jam session with the universe. Each moment, we have the opportunity and choice to create and play the song of life and plant the seeds in the quantum field that manifest our dreams leading to the most amazing symphony of our lives.

CHAPTER 5

Emotional Intelligence

(Understanding Feelings, Beliefs and Behaviors)

Emotional intelligence is the ability to sense, understand, and effectively apply the power and acumen of emotions as a source of human energy, information, connection, and influence.

—Robert K. Cooper, PhD

Our emotions, feelings, beliefs and behaviors are powerful factors in our lives. They significantly influence our state of being, our perception of the world, how we interact with each other and build culture. *Emotional Intelligence* provides us the ability to *mindfully harness the power of our emotions, feelings and beliefs* with *situational awareness,* leading to *positive behaviors* that can profoundly *improve our lives, our relationships and the way we experience our world.*

As was discussed in the previous chapter, a great deal of what we experience as reality is influenced by our emotions, feelings, beliefs and behaviors. In our society, however, we are generally not taught Emotional Intelligence. As a result of this, many people don't have the tools to (1) understand how conditioned beliefs effect their emotions, (2) distinguish between their emotions and feelings, and (3) use their emotions and feelings to guide positive and serving behaviors.

The following definitions are provided to help give greater understanding of the essential differences between emotions, feelings, beliefs, behaviors and culture:

1. *"Emotions"* are energy in motion derived from a reaction or response to one's instinctual nature, beliefs, circumstances, and/or relationship with one's environment;[79]

2. *"Feelings"* are embodied emotions and energy experienced as somatic consciousness and physical states of being and experiences;[80]

3. *"Beliefs"* are attitudes or states of trust, faith or confidence that some idea or principle is true;[81]

4. *"Behavior"* is the expression of thoughts, beliefs, emotions and feelings.[82]

5. *"Culture"* represents the behaviors of individuals in a group including their practices, beliefs, knowledge, arts, laws, customs, capabilities, and habits.[83] When behaviors reach certain levels of adoption and consistent practice, they become "Culture." Culture creates a feedback loop that perpetuates the environmental adaptation, thoughts, beliefs, emotions and behaviors that created it.

Rather than suppressing, bypassing or restraining our emotional energy and feelings, we can fully express them in positive ways with behavior that serves individual, societal and planetary thriving. As we become more aware and Emotionally Intelligent, we are able to guide constrictive energetic charges of emotion and resulting somatic responses/feelings to be expressed as loving, expansive and positive behavior.

There is a critical distinction between fully and presently experiencing our emotions and feelings and the expression of emotion and feelings as behavior. Behavior is often believed to be the expression of emotion, thoughts, beliefs and feelings, however, behavior can be based upon inaction and indecision. For example, when we fail to take action required for positive transformation of ourselves and society, the failure to act is behavior that influences our culture. Culture often creates a feedback loop that perpetuates the environment, thought, beliefs, emotions and behaviors that created it. This explains why "culture" is often so difficult to change. To change culture requires personal transformation that influences widespread adoption of new thoughts, beliefs, emotions and behaviors.

To gain Emotional Intelligence, it's important to understand and master the instruments of our beliefs, emotions and feelings to powerfully align them with our behaviors and intentions to create the life of our dreams. Rather than thinking, feeling and behaving like an automaton, mindlessly following societal conditioning, we can become powerful, free and sovereign beings capable of transforming the world. The greater our Emotional Intelligence, the more we can consciously express our behavior in positive ways that manifest our intentions, transform our culture and create a thriving world. In order to increase our Emotional Intelligence, it's important that we express our emotions and feelings with behaviors that result in life affirming and beneficial outcomes.

Our "*Internal Experience*" is the combination of beliefs, thoughts, emotions, and feelings filtered through our perception of "reality." Utilizing Emotional Intelligence increases our awareness and conscious expression of our Internal Experience leading to behavior that enhances our lives and our world. The following example illustrates how our *Internal Experience* leads to behavior and how important it is to be aware of both our *Internal Experience* and our behavior so that we can behave in ways that transform our culture:

As I'm driving down the road, I put my signal on to change to the left lane. The car in the left lane behind me accelerates to prevent me from entering the lane. Based upon my beliefs and conditioning, I say to myself "what a jerk—how discourteous." I then experience the emotion of anger from my beliefs coupled with this circumstance. The energetic charge and vibration of anger causes my body to tense in preparation for fight or flight. The blood drains from my prefrontal cortex into my amygdala. This is followed by a decrease in my IQ and rational functioning. The emotional state of anger coupled with the tension in body causes the Internal Experience of anger. Without tools to shift the expression of anger into positive behavior, I'm likely to express my Internal Experience with behavior like honking my horn and giving "the jerk" a stiff middle finger. My behavior then may trigger behavior in "the jerk" that escalates into road rage.

Alternatively, I could have consciously changed my behavior by flipping him the peace sign and smiling. I also could have said to myself, "he must be in a big hurry" or "he needs this space more than I do" and laughed and went on without expressing anger or behaving in an aggressive manner.

Emotions can provide a powerful energetic charge that can be intentionally expressed and manifest into constructive behavior and outcomes. One of the major challenges we face in mastering our emotions is the judgment of emotions as good or bad. We often feel guilt, denial, conflict or resistance to certain emotions we believe are "bad." For instance, most of us would consider emotions such as anger and fear to be "bad" emotions. Truly, all emotions can be utilized for positive experience. For example, fear can protect us from harm and anger can drive us to create amazing change in our lives. As well, we can experience expansive emotions more exquisitely because of the opposite constrictive emotions. For example, we experience the expansiveness of love much more deeply, because we also experience the constriction of fear.

Emotions can be suppressed, denied or limited. Emotions can also be expressed, guided, directed and when released through conscious and healthy behavior can energize and improve our lives and the lives of others. Until emotions are expressed and released, they tend to build up and can cause damage to ourselves and others. To be Emotionally Intelligent in the expression of our emotions and feelings can allow us to release the energetic charge of emotions and feelings through behaviors that positively transform our world.

Much like how an artist uses colors to create a painting, we can use emotions as tools to create and manifest fulfilling lives. Just like colors, emotions are neither good nor bad—they can be blended and used to create a desired outcome. Rather than seeing emotions as good or bad, positive or negative, higher or lower, I invite you to experience emotions as expansive or constrictive. For if we fear "negative" emotions, we tend to live in fear. If we strive hard to experience only "positive" emotions, then we create stress and rigidity about negative emotions in our lives. For example, I've seen many people in the "Love & Light" community living in perpetual levels of fear resulting from the denial of their darkness or their shadow. Fear contracts and works adversely to the expansive emotion of love. By embracing and loving the darkness and our shadow, we can more fully experience the expansive state of love. By fully embracing and presently experiencing our emotional states without judgment, rather than disconnecting, bypassing or avoiding them, we gain the power of Emotional Intelligence.

We can create amazing lives and a beautiful loving world by mindfully utilizing emotions and feelings as creative tools for conscious expression and behavior in alignment with our highest life-affirming potential. We can, for instance, turn fear into anger, anger into passion, passion into inspiration and inspiration into love, and thereby create a world of extraordinary beauty, brilliance, love and kindness from fear.

For example, my father was a World War II Drill Sergeant and "Depression Baby" with a fairly violent temper who hated hippies. Since I was a young hippie, the verbal and physical abuse from my father caused me to experience a great deal of anger and frustration. This, however, turned out to be an amazing gift as my anger and frustration gave me a great deal of energy. I directed and expressed my emotional energy from anger to the behavior of playing drums. I found myself spending many hours pounding my Dad's imaginary face on my drumheads. This opportunity became a gift that taught me how to channel my ostensibly "negative" emotions and express them in a way that had a positive effect on my life. As a result of the "negative emotions," I became an accomplished professional drummer and musician. Thanks for the gift, Dad! We each have an opportunity to turn challenges and constrictive emotions into gifts and growth experiences.

BEHAVIOR—THE EXPRESSION OF BELIEFS, THOUGHTS, EMOTIONS AND FEELINGS

Our beliefs, thoughts, emotions, and feelings have a profound impact on our *Internal Experience*. When our *Internal Experience* is expressed as behavior, it not only profoundly affects our own lives, but the lives of those around us as well as our culture, society and environment. If we want to profoundly shift ourselves and our world, it is critical that we increase our awareness of how circumstances and conditioned beliefs trigger thoughts, emotions and feelings. With this awareness, we can shift our emotional states, somatic responses and behavior.

As mentioned, when my physically and verbally abusive, WWII drill sergeant father often frustrated and angered me, rather than punching a wall, I hit my drums. I redirected the expression of my Internal Experience of frustration, anger and tightness in my body into behavior that had a creative and positive effect on my life rather than a negative impact. Also, through my music, I was able to bring joy and inspiration to others and make a living.

Much of our behavior has been conditioned or learned from influences such as parents, friends and media. Upon the occurrence of a circumstance, we often react with behavior learned from our influences. For example, when people get mad (experience the emotion of anger), they often express the conditioned behavior of yelling, screaming, aggressive body language, hitting something and/or throwing objects. When we become conscious of our beliefs, emotions and feelings, we can then consciously choose to either adopt or release a belief and choose the "highest expression" of our emotions and feelings, as well as the resulting behavior.

The "**highest expression**," of an emotion, thought, feeling or vibration, as used in this book, means the **most present and aware expression resulting in behavior that creates the greatest benefit for all stakeholders**. Stakeholders include one's self, those impacted by the behavior, as well as society and the environment.

Most people in the world today have not been taught to express their emotions and feelings with awareness in a beneficial and responsive manner. Instead, the expression of emotions and feelings in our society is often reactive and irresponsible, based upon unconscious or subconscious programming and beliefs. Additionally, our subconscious and habitual behaviors often override our rational mind.

To illustrate this point, John is walking down the street and smells a sweet aroma in the air. He perceives the smell of chocolate chip cookies baking. He remembers his Mom baking chocolate chip cookies for him. The memory of Mom baking chocolate chip cookies triggers emotions associated with John's love of his Mom and her love for him. The emotion of love grows into feelings of warmth and gratitude. John then starts missing his Mom who lives far away. He then experiences the emotion of sadness and gets a sensation of emptiness in his stomach. He perceives this feeling as hunger, which leads to the thought that he should go into the bakery and buy some cookies. John isn't hungry and is also a bit overweight, so the thought of eating cookies leads to feelings of guilt and shame. The vibrations of guilt and shame cause constriction and his amygdala takes over. The guilt and shame, in combination with deeply missing his Mom, generates cognitive feelings of emptiness and hunger.

The cognitive feelings lead to a subconscious survival urge to eat the cookies and move from feeling unfulfilled to feeling fulfilled. John goes into the bakery and buys three chocolate chip cookies. As he eats the cookies, John's subconscious and emotional cravings are temporarily satisfied with the taste, smell and feel associated with eating cookies and thoughts of his Mom. This leads to momentary emotions of happiness and love, and he begins to feel warm, fulfilled and grateful. As John walks out of the bakery, he reflects on his impulsivity of eating three cookies when he is trying to lose weight. John starts feeling guilt and shame again for giving into his urges, which triggers yet another Vibratory Feedback Loop. If we are to achieve the life we desire, we need to be ever vigilant of the manner in which subconscious, emotional and habitual stimuli can derail us.

The vibrational field of the universe is like rich soil growing whatever we plant in it. The seeds of our thoughts, emotions and behaviors that we plant in the vibrational field grow into the crop that becomes the reality of our lives. Our thoughts, beliefs, emotions, expressions and behaviors are all forms of energetic charge and vibration seeking expression. With awareness and practice, we get to choose a *responsive expression* that is conscious, responsible and supportive of our potential rather than unconscious and potentially destructive *reactive expression*.

The three following examples illustrate the difference between consciously processing and expressing our beliefs, thoughts, emotions and feelings as beneficial behavior versus unconsciously reacting to conditioned beliefs, thoughts and emotions.

1. Reactive Behavior Caused by Subconscious Beliefs & Emotions. In this example, emotions are triggered subconsciously resulting in expression and behavior that is **unconscious** and/or **reactive**. This has a significant likelihood of creating unintended and harmful results.

Trigger Circumstance	Your spouse asks for a divorce because he/she is in love with someone else.
Belief	Marriage is "until death do you part."
Emotions Triggered	• Anger • Insecurity/Loss • Jealousy • Revenge
Reactive Expression & Behavior	• *Anger*—Yell, Scream, Physical Abuse • *Insecurity/Loss*—Cry, Plead, Manipulate • *Jealousy*—Yell, Scream, Manipulate, Violation of Privacy and Physical Violence • *Revenge*—Mental and Physical Abuse, Lawsuits, Harassment, Infliction of Emotional Distress

2. Conscious Responsive Behavior after Mindful Inquiry and Validation of
Beliefs and Emotions. In this example, the **underlying belief** leading to the emotions is **consciously questioned**, but is **affirmed, adopted** and **remains unchanged**. Thus, the belief triggers the same emotions that one associates with the beliefs above. However, in this example, **the emotions are examined and understood as energetic charge and are consciously expressed as beneficial behavior.**

Trigger Circumstance	Your spouse asks for a divorce because they are in love with someone else.
Belief	Marriage is "until death do you part."
Conscious Belief Questions and Answers	Q: Is this belief about marriage really my belief? • Yes. Q: Where did I get this belief? • My parents, friends, and society. Q: Is this belief true to me? • Yes. I want to stay married and took the vow seriously. I believe in marriage for life. Q: Is my belief empowering? • Yes, I believe the institution of marriage provides strength, consistency and the needed foundation to raise a family. Q: Do I want my freedom, as well? • No, I am happy in a marital relationship and do not have a desire for another partner or multiple partners.
Emotions Triggered	• Anger • Insecurity/Loss • Jealousy • Revenge

Conscious *Emotion* *Questions* *and Answers:*	Q: What is the message from my emotions? • I am experiencing anger resulting from a perceived lack of appreciation and disrespect. • I feel empty, hurt and shut down. I don't want to love and trust anymore, as I want to avoid feeling hurt. • I fear being on my own. My life will change and so much is unknown. I'm scared of the unknown. • Divorce is very expensive, and I will lose much of the wealth I worked so hard to create. • I hope that my spouse's relationship fails, and he/she ends up as hurt and unhappy as I am. Q: What is to be learned? What are the gifts? Where is my growth lesson in this? How am I responsible for creating the current circumstances? • I need to learn to love myself. • I need to love and trust even when I am feeling hurt. • I need to be whole in myself and the independence will help me grow stronger. • Change creates growth. The unknown provides the desire to know and I will learn valuable lessons from this experience. • There are things much more important than money, such as finding true reciprocal love, health and freedom. I am grateful. • I will not take my relationship for granted in the future and will strive to create more romance, adventure and intimate communication. • If I truly love my wife/husband, then her/his happiness is important to me. If she/he is not happy in our relationship, we can't be happy as a couple. I accept that, although I am feeling many unsettling emotions now, in time this is likely to be the best for both of us. Q: What is the highest and most evolved expression of my emotions that will create the greatest good? • Love and understanding. • Open and honest communication. • Introspection and determining what I want to do in my life and using this as an energetic catalyst to achieve my independent goals. • Peaceful and compassionate resolution. • Gratitude for time we shared and for the new opportunities that lay ahead.

Conscious Expression & Behavior	• My emotions are energetic and I can use this energy to create and manifest much good in my life and my spouse's life.
	• I choose to express my emotions in a manner that fosters beneficial behavior such as compassionate acts of kindness and support.
	• I will utilize my anger for motivating me to reach goals that improve my life like getting in great shape and learning a new language.
	• I will use my insecurity to go deeper into loving and healing myself and sharing that love with others.
	• I will use the energetic charge of my jealousy and anger to consciously spiral it into a creative expression (e.g., music, poetry, art, writing, exercise) and express gratitude for the love we shared, as well as the freedom and happiness that is now mine to experience.
	• I will bring my greater understanding, the personal growth and a deeper love into my next relationship and it will be even better than my current and past relationships.

3. Conscious Responsive Behavior after Mindful Inquiry and Change of Beliefs and Emotions.

In this example, the **belief is consciously questioned** and is found **not true** or **empowering**. As a result, the **emotions shift with the belief system from disempowering constrictive/repelling emotions to empowering expansive/attractive emotions. The emotions are expressed for the highest good with beneficial behavior.**

Trigger Circumstance	Your spouse asks for a divorce because they are in love with someone else.
Belief	Marriage is "until death do you part."
Conscious Belief Questions and Answers	Q: Is this belief about marriage really my belief? • No, not on deeper inquiry. Q: Where did I get this belief? • My parents, friends, society and some Disney movies. Q: Is this my truth? • No. I truly believe that we should each live our lives in the most fulfilling way that brings us the most joy. Q: Is my belief empowering? • While for some societal/religious belief of about marriage for life can be empowering, it's more important for my spouse and I to be fulfilled rather than be unhappy and obey dogmatic beliefs. Marriage can be wonderful under the right conditions for many people. I enjoyed our marriage, but I really don't want the church and state in my relationship. I would rather consciously create my relationship. We each evolved as people during our marriage and the constraints of our marriage weren't serving us. I believe we will find greater love and joy with other partners and in other relationship structures. Q: Do I want my freedom as well? • Yes. Although I am grateful for, and enjoy, our relationship, both of us should feel happy and inspired for the relationship to be truly fulfilling. I really have wanted greater freedom and the time is here for me to embrace it.

	Q: Can we still love each other? • Yes, I believe love transcends the physical realm and intimacy. I understand that if I truly love someone, I need to support them in living a happy and fulfilling life. Q: What is the highest and most evolved expression of my emotions that will create the greatest good? • Love and understanding. • Open and honest communication. • Introspection and determining what I want to do in my life and using this as an energetic catalyst to achieve my goals. • Peaceful and compassionate resolution. • Gratitude for time we shared and for the new opportunities that lay ahead. • A life-long loving friendship with mutual support for each other's growth and happiness.
Emotions with the Triggering Belief Consciously Diffused	• Acceptance • Openness • Gratitude • Love • Compassion

| *Conscious Emotion Questions and Answers:* | Q: What is the message from my emotions?
• Accept the circumstances with grace as a sign that it is time to have independence so my spouse and I can evolve and grow.
• It is time to be open to freedom, new opportunities and growth.
• Feel gratitude that the truth has been revealed and for the experiences the two of us shared together that led me to who I am at this moment.
• Love myself—be whole. Show my spouse love and compassion.
• There is much that is unknown and will be revealed. There are many different outcomes. I desire to create a more fulfilling future and must be conscious in my actions. I understand that my thoughts, words and deeds greatly influence on my life, and I accept my responsibility for the highest expression and most integral behavior.

Q: What is to be learned? What are the gifts? Where is my growth lesson in this?
• To understand and express my true self and be transparent in my relationships.
• Even though change can be challenging, change allows for growth and receiving new opportunities.
• Remain open, grateful and loving. Be courageous in my vulnerability so that my heart can give and receive love deeply. Keep my vibration high and the universe will return what I transmit.
• I want my spouse/beloved and I to live happy and healthy lives that fulfill our potential. I accept that this is in the highest good and will help support this transition with behavior that is kind, loving and compassionate.

Q: What are the highest emotions and most evolved behavior that will create the greatest benefit?
• Love and understanding.
• Acceptance, empathy and compassion.
• Joy and happiness.
• Vulnerable and real introspection
• Enthusiastically and courageously embrace the unknown and the opportunities for growth, evolution and freedom that lay ahead |

Conscious Expression & Behavior	• Demonstrate in thoughts, words and deeds, love and gratitude for time we shared, and for the new opportunities that lay ahead. I will create more romance, adventure, presence, and a higher expression in my future relationships. • I will appreciate my current and future relationships and not take them for granted. • I will be more present, listen more deeply and be more compassionate in my communication to support my loved ones. • I will create a safe container and an environment of nurturance for love to grow. • I will be open and honest in my communication and impeccable with my word to grow trust in my relationships. • My emotions are energy that I can use to achieve my goals and manifest great benefits for myself and the world. I choose to express my emotions in a manner that fosters the highest good. • My commitment to growth, openness and vulnerability will attract even greater love and more inspiring opportunities for me. • My love and gratitude will be used to foster open, compassionate and heart-based communication and resolution. • Although there is much that isn't known, I have the power and sovereignty to experience and respond to circumstances and choose my wholeness, abundance and the best outcomes. • My love can now expand and be freely shared with and expressed to others.

As demonstrated in the foregoing examples, by applying conscious questioning, awareness and listening at the belief and emotion stage, we can raise the vibrational frequency of our *Vibratory Receptors & Transmitters* and *Vibratory Consciousness Centers* to create a sequence leading to the highest expression and beneficial behavior for mutual good and value.

MIND/FUTURE EVENT TRIGGERING

About 75,000 years ago, our minds and bodies worked as one in the present moment, but then we started developing the neo-cortex which led to the growth of the ego and our ability to plan for the future and reflect on the past as well as modern capacity for novelty and invention.[84] Now, in the 21st century, our minds are often "disconnected" from our present reality and unaware of our somatic consciousness and our mind-body-nature connection.

Because we live in a predominantly mind-oriented and information-based society, we generally have a great deal of our attention on the *Vibratory Receptor & Transmitter* of **Thought** and the *Vibratory Consciousness Center* of **Mind**. As a result, we tend to experience an inordinate amount of mind-thought generated *Cognitive Emotions* and *Derivative-Cognitive Feelings* rather than *Instinctual Emotions* and *Somatic-Instinctual Feelings*. The *Cognitive Emotions* and *Derivative-Cognitive Feelings* are often triggered by our thinking about fictitious scenarios that might happen in the future, or reflecting on the past, rather than an actual present occurrence.

For example, John boards an aircraft from Los Angeles to Maui. Upon takeoff, he starts thinking about the plane crashing into the Pacific Ocean. He creates this whole scenario in his head as if it were real. From his thoughts of the plane crashing, John experiences fear and anxiety. John's breathing grows shallow, a feeling of tension wells up inside him, his heart starts racing, his palms get sweaty, his glands start pumping out adrenaline and cortisol and he becomes intensely contracted and stressed. Five hours later, the plane arrives safely in Maui. During the entire flight, John is having a real somatic experience of stress involving the *Cognitive Emotions* of fear and anxiety along with the associated physical symptoms of *Derivative-Cognitive Feelings*, all based upon an imagined and fictitious scenario. John's imagined scenario created feedback loops that caused his flight to be unpleasant and stressful. With greater awareness and *Emotional Intelligence*, John could have objectively shifted his imaginative scenario to seeing the plane land safely and him relaxing in the sun on a beautiful beach. His flight experience would have been relaxed and wonderful. How often do we, in our journey of life, imagine the worst case scenario and create feedback loops that make our lives unnecessarily stressful and unpleasant?

As we increase our awareness of the *Vibratory Receptor & Transmitters* and *Vibratory Consciousness Center*, we improve our abilities to objectively view our emotional, physical and environmental states of being, hold the best outcome in our minds and break free of non-serving patterns and feedback loops in order to experience states of being that serve our higher nature, potential and life-experience.

EMOTIONAL INTELLIGENCE EXERCISE

The mind is like a garden of fertile soil. The seeds of thought we plant in the garden of our mind grow into the crops that we harvest as reality in our lives. If we plant toxic seeds, we're likely to experience toxic lives. If we plant the beautiful and healthy seeds, we're likely to experience wellness and beauty in our lives. As mentioned, our thoughts and imagination effect or emotional state, our physical state and energetic state. In order to become more aware of the seeds we're planting, I invite you to engage in the *Emotional Intelligence* exercise below to experience greater *Emotional Intelligence* and power to transform, increase your ability to consistently plant the seed that serve your higher self and improve your state of being.

- Sit comfortably and center yourself by focusing your breath at the 3rd eye between and slightly above your eyebrows. Breathe fully in a relaxed manner. Take at least 10 conscious deep and relaxed breaths. Allow your body and mind to relax more deeply with each breath. Become aware of your thoughts as well as your mental, physical, energetic and emotional states. Take an inventory of the following states of being ("*States of Being Inventory*"). Take as much time as you require to fully experience each of the 7 steps. While the *States of Being Inventory* can be done in less time, it is recommended that at least 2 minutes is given to each of the 7 steps.

  1. What are the thoughts I'm thinking? First, allow yourself to just objectively view your thoughts without judgement. Then ask are they empowering, disempowering or neutral?

  2. What is my present mental state? Is it clear, aware, distracted or dull?

  3. What sensations am I feeling in my body and where am I feeling them? Are my sensations comfortable and open or constricted, uncomfortable and/or painful? Where in my body am I feeling these sensations? How does my breath and focus clear or enhance these sensations?

  4. What is my energetic state? Is it high, average or low? How do my breath, focus and thoughts affect my energetic state?

5. How is energy moving through my body? Where does it seem slow, constrictive or blocked? How do my breath, focus, thoughts and/or movement affect the flow of energy?

6. What is my emotional state? (e.g., inspired, empowered, awesome, equanimous, angry, depressed, apathetic)?

7. What is the vibrational quality of each of my states of being (mental, physical, energetic and emotional)? What is the frequency and strength of the vibrations I feel and how are they affecting my state of being?

- After completing the foregoing *States of Being Inventory*, focus on your breath and third eye for 10 breaths, returning to a space of centeredness and equanimity. Find and hold the space in between your thoughts. If a thought comes up, let it go and return to empty space between your thoughts without any attachment or judgment about your thoughts or the space between them. Take at least 5 minutes to just observe any thoughts that may arise without any attachment or judgment and return to the space in between thoughts. If you can hold the space between thoughts for 5 minutes, you have arrived at a level a mastery most humans never achieve. So, if thoughts arise, just relax, let go of any judgments and "shoulds" and return to the space between your thoughts.

- After 5 minutes redo the *States of Being Inventory* questions above. Make a mental note of shifts in your states of being and how they may have shifted from the first session of the *States of Being Inventory* and then ask the following questions and be open to hearing/receiving the answers from source:

  1. Are my thoughts and beliefs empowering the outcomes I desire to create in my life, and if not, what thoughts and beliefs would be most empowering?

  2. Are the emotions I'm experiencing empowering and expansive (e.g., courage, love, joy, inspiration and bliss) or disempowering and constrictive (e.g., apathy, grief, shame or fear)? How can acknowledge and guide my emotions to being more empowering and expansive?

3. Is my body feeling open, comfortable, vital, healthy and energized? If not, how can I enhance my energetic and physical states of being to support that which I seek to manifest?

4. Do my desires only benefit myself or do they create value for people and planet? What specifically is the benefit for people and planet created by my desires?

5. Are my states of being optimally functioning to provide the support to manifest my dreams and how can I express myself to behave in ways that exponentially increase the manifestation of my dreams?

By doing the foregoing centering and inquiry exercise on a regular basis, we exponentially increase Emotional Intelligence, the awareness of our states of being and our ability to shift our states of being to align to support our higher creative purpose and potential.

Emotional Intelligence can be cultivated by (i) directing our thoughts, (ii) evaluating and changing our beliefs, (iii) consciously experiencing our emotions without polarized judgment, and (iv) expressing our state of being with behavior that aligns to the highest benefit to ourselves and others. With Emotional Intelligence we can produce the highest vibrational feedback loop with the universe to attract and manifest remarkable results that positively transform our lives, our relationships and the world.

CHAPTER 6

The Global Human Agreement

We are each interconnected with, and a product of, our environment. The environments in which we were born and live possess unique characteristics from which beliefs and agreements arise. Our beliefs and agreements when expressed become behavior. Collective behavior creates culture. Culture often becomes a perpetuating influence our environment, beliefs, agreements and behaviors forming the basis of an interconnected, collective and imagined agreement of "reality" referred to herein as the "Global Human Agreement."

We each were born into an environment with pre-existing and unique characteristics that shape our view of the world. These characteristics are largely environmental and cultural and include geography, climate, language, beliefs, behaviors, agreements and customs. Culture arises from our environment and has a profound influence on creating our "reality" and our identity, including our belief systems, worldview, emotions, behavior and impact on the ecosystem.

"*Culture*" can be defined as *an integrated system of behavioral patterns of the members in society or group*. In terms of humanity, "culture" refers to the evolved human capacity to classify and represent experiences with symbols, enter into agreements and use imagination to transform reality.

From the time of our birth, we are conditioned and indoctrinated into a culture that, both consciously and subconsciously, influences our way of thinking, expressing, doing and being, including our...

Ideas of morality, ethics and judgment (e.g., right and wrong, good and bad, fair and unfair)

- Sense of beauty
- Dietary choices
- Ways of relating to family, friends and society
- Perceived need for money, jobs, material items and possessions
- Desire for, and methods of obtaining, acknowledgment and recognition
- Sexual, mating and reproductive patterns
- Religious, celebratory and ritualistic practices

To provide a few examples of how conditioning and ethnocentricity in culture impacts us, the Inuit/Eskimos find whale blubber appetizing and the Chinese eat monkey brains and ox penises. Polynesians have hundreds of words to describe ocean conditions, whereas in the U.S., there are hundreds of words for money and genitals. Haitian Voodoo practitioners journey to the waterfalls of Saut d'Eau in the summer to worship the goddess of love by getting publicly naked and wiggling around in mud mixed with the blood and heads of sacrificed animals. The Kayan women of Burma use brass rings that deforms the clavicle and rib cage to create the appearance of a beautiful, stretched neck, whereas in the U.S., women wear makeup, high heels, padded bras and often get breast implants, collagen injections and Botox to make themselves more attractive.

"Ethnocentrism" is a term used to describe the phenomenon of judging another culture solely by the values and standards of one's own culture.[85] Ethnocentric individuals judge other groups relative to their own ethnic group or culture, especially with concern for language, behavior, beliefs, customs, and religion. Often ethnocentric individuals believe themselves to be right and superior and others with different cultures to be wrong or strange. By viewing the world through the lens of our culture and belief systems as superior to others, we perpetuate disconnection, separation, divisiveness and intolerance. To move toward love, connection and inclusion, a shift to acceptance and respect of other cultures and beliefs needs to occur as we evolve to a higher planetary culture.

The "Father of American Anthropology," Franz Uri Boas, wrote, "*If we were to select the most intelligent, imaginative, energetic and emotionally stable third of mankind, all races would be present.*" As humans, we are an interconnected and interdependent species living on planet Earth. The way we treat each other and the planet has a profound impact on our lives and ability to thrive. Because we are all interconnected to each other and our ecosystem, a unified human and planetary consciousness exists, referred to herein as the *"Global Human Agreement."*

The Global Human Agreement creates, defines, impacts and reinforces our experience of "reality" resulting in the manifestation of a "Planetary Culture." Planetary Culture not only influences our beliefs, thoughts, emotions, feelings, behavior and environment, but also causes feedback loops that reinforce and perpetuate the existing Global Human Agreement. In modern society, many of us have been conditioned to identify, define and value ourselves based on material, external and/or conditioned criteria, such as the following:

- Our physical appearance—our gender, race, size, coloring, body type and attractiveness

- Our possessions—our possessions such as homes, cars, boats, planes, toys, businesses, money, stocks and bonds

- Our social environment and connections—our family, friends and Circle of Influence (sometimes also thought of as possessions, such my wife, my kids, my friends)

- Our work and activities—our accomplishments, education, jobs, sports, entertainment, hobbies and ways we occupy our time

- Our environment—where we live, our community, state, country, the climate, geography, socio-economic status, culture and connection to nature

- Our ideology—our perceptions, thoughts, beliefs, emotions, feelings, ideas, principles, religion and language, much of which is programmed by society

What we find beautiful, what we deem important, and how we treat each other are largely conditioned agreements. Our monetary system is a conditioned agreement to exchange our time, effort, services and goods largely for paper that is worthless except for our agreement that it has value. Additionally, our economic system, our political systems and legal systems are, in essence, just agreements, as well as the use of Gross Domestic Product as a quantitative measurement of "success."

All of us, with very few exceptions, are born into environments with systemic and cultural agreements in place. We're often conditioned from the time of birth to unwittingly and subconsciously adopt these agreements through our parents, friends, educational institutions/teachers, government/leaders/elders and media/storytellers. These agreements form the basis of our beliefs, behaviors and identity. Becoming aware of, and questioning, these agreements, gives us the ability to clear and transcend the conditioned, and often limiting and antiquated, beliefs and behaviors caused by living in these conditioned agreements. When we question and transcend limiting and antiquated agreements, we can transform ourselves and the world.

While there are examples of beauty, love, kindness, creativity and brilliance in the current Global Human Agreement, it also contains pervasive and untenable levels of fear, scarcity, toxicity, destruction, greed, poverty, cruelty, suffering and injustice. If we continue to perpetuate the current Global Human Agreement, there is a great likelihood that humankind will not survive as a species. Overall, the current Global Human Agreement is not serving humankind and the planet and is in need of serious transformation. In order to thrive as a species, it is critical that we create a new life-affirming Global Human Agreement and Planetary Culture that unifies and serves humankind and the planet.

Each of us contributes to The Global Human Agreement in our thoughts, words and deeds. As well, our inaction (e.g., not thinking, not speaking, not being responsible, conformity and/or not taking action), also influences the Global Human Agreement. For example, when we see injustice, suffering and destruction in our world, or when we elevate the economic imperative over the ethical imperative, and do nothing to change it, by our inaction, we perpetuate these things in our world. No matter what we do or don't do, we participate in, and influence the Global Human Agreement.

Because each of us contributes to the collective Global Human Agreement, we each possess the power and ability to change the Global Human Agreement. **If we want to change the Global Human Agreement, we must change ourselves and evolve beyond the current Global Human Agreement.**

Making this change in ourselves requires deep inquiry into our conditioned self-identity and the replacement of limiting/non-serving patterns, thoughts, beliefs, perceptions and behaviors with those that are creative, life-enhancing, empowering, healthy and abundant. As we make this change we concurrently improve the human and planetary ethos.

Activating the individual transformation necessary to make significant impact to the Global Human Agreement requires courage, commitment and empowerment. Transformation rarely happens in our comfort zone. The transformative process often necessitates questioning one's own reality, challenging the status quo, and enduring inconvenience, expense and discomfort. Courageously committing to transform the feedback loop of the destructive, fear-based aspects of the Global Human Agreement will set us free to powerfully manifest new realities and fulfill our potential as empowered creators of our reality. This takes awareness, inquiry, observation and consistent reinforcement.

Buddha is attributed with saying, *"Do not believe in anything simply because you have heard it. Do not believe in anything simply because it is spoken and rumored by many. Do not believe in anything simply because it is found written in your religious books. Do not believe in anything merely on the authority of your teachers and elders. Do not believe in traditions because they have been handed down for many generations. But after observation and analysis, when you find that anything agrees with reason and is conducive to the good and benefit of one and all, then accept it and live up to it."* As Buddha suggests, we can consciously evaluate our belief systems and adopt that which serves one and all.

By taking the following steps, we can move from disempowering thoughts, views, beliefs, emotions and judgments to powerfully creating our future and influencing the transformation of the Global Human Agreement in which we participate:

1. Become aware that our language, programs and beliefs were largely learned from society (e.g., our families, friends, education system) and develop a consistent practice of using language that's affirmative, loving, compassionate and expansive;

2. Consistently engage in empowered inquiry to question our beliefs and "reality;"

3. Practice objectivity, equanimity and non-attachment to our beliefs to allow our beliefs to serve us rather than imprison us;

4. Consciously replace limiting beliefs (e.g., disempowering, divisive and destructive) with empowering beliefs (e.g., inspiring, unifying, motivating, loving and life-enhancing) that benefit people and planet;

5. Practice expressing empowering beliefs in acts of love, respect, generosity, compassion, beauty, and kindness; and

6. Create environments, support groups, communities and cultures that consciously support serving empowering beliefs.

In alignment with Buckminster Fuller's personal challenge to future world visionaries, let's create *"a world that works for 100% of humanity, in the shortest possible time, through spontaneous cooperation, without ecological offense, or the disadvantage of anyone."*

Fortunately, there's a groundswell of people awakening from a mass slumber and challenging the current Global Human Agreement, who desire to build a "new civilization" and global community. This global community will be built upon whole systems dynamics, environmental consciousness, regenerability, living systems innovation, equitability, social responsibility, life-affirming values and creative empowerment.

When we transcend our ethnocentric arrogance and embrace the notion that we are all interconnected to, and interdependent upon, each other and our ecosystem, we start embracing human and planetary unity, acceptance, love and respect.

This new and empowered Planetary Culture will recognize the interconnection of all things and ultimately provide the planet and all living beings with the ability to thrive. Action-oriented, conscious and responsible individuals

that have a passionate desire to improve life on this planet will create this new civilization and culture. This new civilization and culture will start individually, take root locally with abundant, well and empowered communities and naturally grow globally as the existing Global Human Agreement is rendered obsolete by this transformation.

By being the change we want to see and respecting the value, rights and interconnectivity of all life, we can create a Global Human Agreement based upon beauty, love, kindness, creativity, respect and brilliance. With this new Global Human Agreement, humankind can manifest a world that is Abundant, Well & Empowered.

CHAPTER 7

A Vision of AWE

(Creating an Abundant, Well & Empowered World)

"All our dreams can come true, if we have the courage to pursue them."

~ Walt Disney

W hat if we could create an Abundant, Well & Empowered world that fosters humankind's potential for love, brilliance, beauty and kindness to be equitably enjoyed in harmony by all people and life on the planet?

I and many others believe we can create a better world. However, much of society has been conditioned to believe that a world of love, beauty, abundance, wellness and empowerment is just an unpragmatic, woo-woo utopian dream. There are many in society that don't question our current "reality" or give thought to its impacts. They continue to perpetuate the current Global Human Agreement with its obsession for maximizing profits from endless growth and consumption, extraction, and exploitation resulting in scarcity, toxicity, war, injustice and destruction of the biosphere. A significant percentage of the world's population has been conditioned to believe that our current society and economy is based on pragmatism and that our destructive behavior is somehow justified.

Pragmatism is defined as *a practical and logical approach based upon reality rather than ideological and theoretical considerations.* Your next breath, water, food and shelter are pragmatic because they are real. Our monetary system is an ideological and theoretical construct based upon an agreement that relatively worthless paper has value. You can't breathe, drink, eat, or live in your dollar bills. For example, if a billionaire were about to drop dead of dehydration, he would give you every dollar he has for a glass of water.

We are the only species that think we need money and we lived approximately 200,000 years without it. Governments, central banks and corporations have privatized of our commons (e.g., public water, food, lands and materials), thereby requiring money for us to meet our physical needs. We now are conditioned to believe that we need money to live. By creating local, living, self-sufficient economies that provide water, food and shelter afforded by the regenerative abundance of the planet, the money required for the purchase of physical necessities diminishes. The foregoing begs the following questions:

- Is it pragmatic to destroy the biosphere that provides the air, water, food and materials that keep us alive?

- Is it pragmatic to eat food, drink water and breathe air full of toxic chemicals that compromises our health?

- Is it pragmatic to suffer from rampant avoidable diseases (e.g., cancer, heart disease, obesity, diabetes and depression) caused by a toxic, stressful and sedentary society?

- Is it pragmatic to utilize extractive and depleted materials when renewable materials and waste can be used?

- Is it pragmatic to elevate the economic imperative over the ethical imperative leading to war, exploitation, injustice, poverty and eco-social destruction?

- Is it pragmatic to devote the time, energy and resources of humankind to jobs contributing to environmental destruction (e.g., making obsolete weapons and junk products and supporting the fossil fuel burning supply chain) when meaningful jobs can be created to increase the health, harmony and thriving of people and planet?"

The "economic pragmatists" consider money to be practical and real. Yet, money is an illusory agreement that a piece of paper has far more value than its intrinsic worth. For example, a piece of paper with Benjamin Franklin's picture on it is worth 100 times more than a similar piece of paper with George Washington's picture on it.

I posit that real pragmatism is creating a world that is Abundant, Well & Empowered—a world where our air is clean, water is pure, the food we eat is nutritious, the homes we live in are healthy and safe, the energy we consume is renewable and the work we do is meaningful and beneficial to the planet and our species.

Real pragmatism is based upon that which sustains and enhances the quality of life. Moreover, without the planet we have no life and no economy. All we have is provided by the planet. "Natural capital" (the work, services, processes and goods provided by the Earth for free) is estimated at $72 trillion per year[86] and is being eroded through human activities at a rate of $7.3 trillion per year.[87] Based upon this math, we have ten years before humankind reaches the point of no return. And yet, despite this math, is there really any price tag we can put on the air, water, food, shelter and energy that the planet gives us to sustain all life on this planet?

No matter what our race, origin, religion, gender, age, economic status or ideology, we all need air, food and water to live and we are all miraculously sustained by a life force beyond our comprehension. In this regard, **"ethical good" can be defined as that which sustains life and develops mutually beneficial value-adding relationships between all living entities that result in "*Ecosystemic Thriving.*"** For humans to create Ecosystemic Thriving and ethical good, we must go beyond our selfish desires, overconsumption and greed to consider the well-being of each other and our planet and transition from destructive industrialized practices to life-affirming regenerative practices. The Earth is naturally abundant and has generously given us all we need to live abundant and high-quality lives. If we care for our planet and regenerate her natural systems, we will all have sufficient water, food, energy and shelter. We produce enough food for 10 billion people, but 50% of it goes to waste largely because of greed, fear and failure to democratize resources.[88] It is largely this greed and fear that perpetuates a centralized supply chain that is belching out greenhouse gasses, causing massive amounts of waste pollution and keeping about half of humankind in or near poverty.

The so-called "pragmatic" version of the "real world" is rooted in fear. Fear has a constrictive quality and often causes disconnection leading to distrust, greed, scarcity, competition and destruction. A society built upon fear, control and scarcity is doomed to fail. Love is expansive and creative. Love is the miraculous energy and life force that creates and sustains life. Love connects us and leads to real abundance, trust, generosity, collaboration and compassion. By shifting the essential nature of our society to love from fear, we have the opportunity to thrive.

Most of us have witnessed the great love, brilliance, beauty, compassion, generosity and creativity of which we humans are capable. We are powerful beyond measure to create a world that works for the benefit of all life—a thriving and regenerative world where our time, energy and resources are focused on loving and caring for each other and the planet. A world abundantly supporting the well-being of all life is both pragmatic and essential for us to thrive as a species.

Based upon my experience and knowledge of the amazing potential of humankind, I dream and hold vision for an Abundant, Well & Empowered world in my lifetime. Fortunately I, and a rapidly growing number of people, are devoting themselves to making this dream and vision a reality.

A **dream** is essentially a succession of images, ideas, emotions, and sensations that generally occur involuntarily during certain stages of sleep, but also can happen during waking hours, such as a daydream.[89] A dream can stimulate and catalyze new ideas, visions and action, leading to new realities. However, a dream is not necessarily grounded in reality.

A **vision** is a clear and prescient construct of the future that is generally capable of becoming a reality. A vision is usually connected with increasing the quality of life and/or advancing technology, society, politics, economics and resource practices.

A **visionary** is a person with a clear, distinctive, and specific vision of the future.

As a visionary and innovator, Steve Jobs, is credited with saying, *"Here's to the crazy ones, the misfits, the rebels, the troublemakers, the round pegs in the square holes... the ones who see things differently—they're not fond of rules... You can quote them, disagree with them, glorify or vilify them, but the only thing you can't do is ignore them because they change things... they push the human race forward, and while some may see them as the crazy ones, we see genius, because the ones who are crazy enough to think that they can change the world, are the ones who do."*

It's the dreamers and visionaries that awaken us to new possibilities and change the world. For example, the dreams and visions of Martin Luther King for a fair and just world; Thomas Edison for electric light, recorded sound and motion pictures; The Wright Brothers for powered flight; Rachel Carson for a world that is beautiful, natural, healthy and awe-inspiring; Mother Teresa for a world of love, compassion in which hunger, suffering and disease are healed; Buckminster Fuller for *"a world that works for 100% of humanity, in the shortest possible time, through spontaneous cooperation, without ecological offense, or the disadvantage of anyone."* Each of these dreamers and visionaries, through their tenacity, courage and passion had a significant impact on our "reality."

I also have a dream that we can create a world of AWE (Abundant, Well & Empowered) and a vision for a world where we all can thrive and have access to pure water, healthy food, secure & safe shelter and the freedom to be inspired, engage in life-long learning and fully express our love, brilliance, beauty and kindness, with harmony and respect for all life.

THE CRYSTALLIZATION OF THE DREAM INTO A VISION

The dream of AWE crystallized into a vision on January 1, 2010. I was meditating on top of a hill overlooking a beautiful valley. I was in a present, peaceful and spacious state of being, feeling the sunlight and fresh breeze on my skin. I became one with nature and then started letting go of my external awareness and dissolving into the infinite and silent space inside of me. I was deep in mediation, when all of sudden, gunshots went off in the valley below me. This surprised me and brought me back into my cognitive processes, yet I still maintained a meditative state. I asked Higher Consciousness, "How can we transform this world of guns, war, toxicity, destruction and injustice into a world that is loving, compassionate and thriving?" I then was "downloaded" with two versions of our future—the first was a dystopian, sociopathic, fascist plutocracy and the second a world of AWE.

In the first version of our future, the industrialized war complex and society's consumptive addictions had led to the destruction of our biosphere. The soil was depleted of nutrients from destructive agricultural practices. Our rivers, oceans and wetlands had been destroyed by the dumping of chemicals, industrial waste, sewage and overfishing. There were massive food & water shortages resulting from abuse of the planet's resources, as well as climate change causing widespread desertification, natural disasters and starvation. The toxicity levels in our air, food & water were leading to widespread disease and virulent pandemics causing suffering and death. The global financial systems had failed due to abuse of power and corruption, leading to massive global inflation and poverty. The oligarchs including the central bankers, ultra-wealthy insiders and power elite took control of countries, governments and resources using bioweapons to create a pandemic as a rationale to deploy mandatory weaponized vaccines and microchipping (with digital identity, medical, banking and personal records, digital currency, proof of vaccinations, proof of compliance and geotracking) as condition to public access, passports, driver's licenses, currency transactions, and other privileges. With the power of the military and government, the plutocratic oligarchs took control of the world's water, agriculture, energy, manufacturing, education, media and healthcare creating a global police state. The microchipping coupled with weaponized vaccines gave governments the ability to remotely administer pain using the 5G grid frequencies to activate nanoparticles from the vaccines, as well as photonic and sonic weapons. Additionally, with the advent of a centralized digital global currency and digital bank accounts coupled with privatization of virtually all natural resources, the oligarchs, through the governments and military they controlled, determined whether people ate or starved and whether they lived or died, at the press of button. The oligarchs gained complete power and control over the masses while providing advantageous access, rights, wealth and freedom to themselves, other privileged plutocrats and their insiders, while the masses fought over the crumbs. The chasm between the rights and access of rich and poor caused great inequities, suffering and poverty.

I asked, *"How can we stop the corrupt plutocracy and dystopian fascism, the industrialized war machine, the overconsumption, the injustice and the suffering that will destroy our world?"*

Higher Consciousness answered with, *"You can't stop it. In this version of Earth, humanity and its systems are out of control. The current socio-economic-political system is unsustainable and will eventually destroy itself and most of humankind." You can't fight against it because it is too powerful. You can't escape it because the Matrix is so pervasive. It's like a runaway train that cannot stop and will soon go off the rails"*

I said, *"In a universe of infinite possibilities, there must be something we can do to transform the world. What can we do? What can I do?"*

Higher Consciousness responded with, *"Create a new world rather than stop the old one. Be a functional virus in a dysfunctional system. The change needs to come from the inside-out, ground-up and top-down."*

I inquired, *"What do you mean by that?"*

Higher Consciousness said, ***"The key to transformation is to embrace and work within the current system rather than fight against it. Love in the face of hate. Create in the face of destruction. Be generous in the face of greed. And be compassionate in the face of cruelty."***

"Continually question all you believe and have been told about the world and life. You must focus on loving, creating and demonstrating new systems rather than fighting the old ones. The process of inquiry is what opens up consciousness and imagination that allows the creative power of love to blossom."

"You need to internally transform yourself by abundantly filling yourself with love, compassion, healing life-force and generosity and being a living example, through your being and behavior. Continuously express and share this abundant, loving, joyful and compassionate state of being (inside-out). Your being and doing will heal the environment (ground-up) by demonstrating a harmonious and thriving relationship between people and planet that will transform the current destructive socio-economic-political system (top-down) to one that is regenerative, loving and equitable. As you create and live in this new world, where your environment and everyone in it is abundantly sharing love, compassion, laughter, optimal wellness and unity, expansive and exponential change will happen—like a functional virus in a dysfunctional system."

I said, *"I am just one guy and this vision is so big and audacious. While I am creative and passionate about making the world a better place, how can I accomplish this?"*

Higher Consciousness replied, ***"You are not alone. There are millions of people tapping into this consciousness and wanting to live in a world that is abundant, thriving, loving and connected. Trust me. You have my support and the support of millions of collaborators. Throughout your life, you have been trained for this. Realize that you and I are creating this version of the world together. I also co-create with every human being, every life form and "non-living" forms. Your world is the manifestation of divine consciousness and vibration. It is your purpose in life to manifest this exemplary vision that will start with a demonstration, become a movement and eventually a way of life. Devote your life to this and I will show you, guide you and support you. Here is a new vision of the world. . ."***

I then received a profound download showing me the World of AWE. . .

A VISION OF AN ABUNDANT, WELL & EMPOWERED WORLD

I was given a vision of a thriving world where our air, water and food are clean and free of toxins and where all people have access to these basic necessities as well as shelter, energy, education and healthcare. The world is powered by 100% renewable, clean and inexpensive energy sources. With these energy sources and new desalinization, atmospheric water and agricultural technologies, everyone on the planet has access to pure water, nutritious food and renewable materials for building shelters.

Spending on the industrialized and military economy has shifted to the Regenerative Economy with the majority of humankind engaging in meaningful work in service to planetary thriving (e.g., regenerative agroforestry, conservation and healing of natural habitats, biomimetic innovation, eco-art, bioenergetic technologies, clean energy, renewables). People are being paid in an ethical decentralized currency and only purchasing products and services from conscious corporations that are committed to eco-social responsibility. The destructive unethical corporations of the industrial age have gone out of business and no longer exist. The entire world is experiencing the most abundant, healthy and peaceful economy in history. The large defense and military budgets have been shifted to creating armies that serve peace, humankind and the environment. Desertification is being reversed by regenerative land management programs that include planting forests and crops and promoting natural animal habitats. These land management programs are creating healthy soil that sequesters carbon and creates new abundant grass lands, arable land, forests, farms and fruit orchards. The wetlands, rivers, oceans, reefs and forests are seeing renewal due to new ecological and conservation regulations and commitment of resources.

The cities are full of lush green rooftops and hanging gardens as well as prolific edible landscaping. There is an abundance of food and nobody is begging or hungry. Those with criminal tendencies, addictions and mental illness are being lovingly treated, cared for and rehabilitated rather than being punished and imprisoned. Concrete, asphalt, high-rises and density have given way to open spaces, recreational areas, gardens and local farms. There are mixed-use plazas where families and friends gather to enjoy and socialize. Children are completely safe to play and enjoy the outdoors.

Due to the pervasive availability of the Internet and the vast knowledge of humankind accessible in the cloud, libraries and schools have been converted into centers for innovation, applied learning, personal development, optimal wellness and creative expression. The education system integrates children, families, community and nature to inspire children in learning practical, creative and social skills to enhance their life and the lives of future generations. In this way, today's children will be able to foster a world of healthy, beautiful and thriving world and the most robust economy in the history of humankind—an economy based upon love, respect, inclusivity, regenerability and ecosystemic thriving.

Based upon experiential and applied learning, the education system integrates earth-wisdom from ancient cultures and biomimicry with modern technology. Using cloud-based learning technologies with wearable devices, the world becomes the classroom and students can learn at their own pace, from anywhere and find that which inspires them. With support from peers, family, community and teachers in applied learning environments, students have the opportunity to learn real and valuable skills that support the thriving of people and planet. For example, children can learn such subjects as biology, geometry and art in nature and on the farm;

chemistry in the biofuels lab and the teaching kitchen; math in the computer and design lab, as well as through music and working on construction projects; and business/economics by helping run a business in which they have interest and aptitude.

The "inspired learning system," will focus on building skills and capacity in service to the thriving of people and planet with an emphasis on earth and natural resource regeneration and stewardship; living, renewable and clean technologies that enhance life, health and beauty; emotional intelligence; collaboration; and community well-being.

Education has been transformed into lifelong learning rich in art, music, collaborative connection, emotional intelligence, philosophy and appreciation of cultural inclusivity. To strengthen their body, mind, soul and collaboration, students learn about healing practices, with classes in nutrition, massage, energy-work, tai chi, meditation and yoga, as well as participating in physical conditioning and sports.

By the time kids are 18, they have real-world proficiency and skills in all of these areas and the ability to choose that which is of the greatest inspiration to them and value to society.

With smart and mixed-use city and community design, more people walk and ride bikes. The crowded freeways and roads with cars spewing fossil fuel emissions have been replaced with smart public transportation and personal vehicles made of bio-resins running on maglev tracks and hyperloops powered by renewable energy sources with beautiful median landscaping. Utilizing computer piloted highly safe drone technologies, transportation has also moved into the airways. Vehicles with new propulsion systems and clean fuels have made transportation and travel beneficial for the planet by releasing oxygen and water vapor into the atmosphere. Moreover, holographic communications systems have minimized the need for business travel and driving to the office.

Because communities and cities provide clean environments where people are eating healthy foods, drinking pure water, getting regular exercise and doing meaningful and environmentally conscious work. The population has a high degree of health and happiness. Diseases caused by sedentary, stress-filled work and junk food consumption, such as obesity, heart disease, mental illness, diabetes, osteoporosis and cancer, are a thing of the past. The "sickcare" system has been replaced with the new "optimal wellness system" where profits are aligned to increasing health rather than sickness and treating the symptoms of unhealthy patients.

Our communities (cities, suburbs and rural areas) have been transformed into "Regenerative Communities" using whole systems planning and design, smart-growth, collaborative consumption, local economies, living microgrids and onsite self-sufficiency for water, food and power. These Regenerative Communities integrate residential, retail, entertainment, office, food production, water catchment and con-servation, energy production, waste upcycling, education, community facilities, light industrial and open spaces in a walkable/bikeable footprint. The demand for living in Regenerative Communities has grown exponentially and these communities have proliferated creating a robust multi-trillion-dollar construction industry, creating millions of jobs and abundance around the globe.

In these Regenerative Communities, people share resources and live high-qual-ity, amenity-rich lives. These shared resources include community farms, kitchens, dining halls, laundry facilities, transportation fleets, media & arts centers, technology & science centers, and optimal wellness centers, birthing and hospice centers, as well as spaces for connecting and engaging in community projects that feed, nourish, enlighten and create beauty for the community.

Combining collaborative consumption, well-being, energy and supply chain efficiency with consciously designed and built whole-systems environments for living, working, learning and playing, Regenerative Communities reduce con-sumption, waste, greenhouse gasses and pollution. The focus of these communities is developing technologies, services, products and businesses that enhance life and the health of our ecosystem. The most valuable intellectual property is that which is the most life enhancing.

With automation and robots, people have more quality free time to enjoy their family, friends, well-being, passions, hobbies, innovation and the fulfillment of their dreams, as well as life-affirming pursuits.

Principles, transparent agreements and incentives for cooperation form the pri-mary basis of governance and social conduct rather than rules, regulations, penalties and punishment. The corrupt financial and economic model based upon scarcity run by the central bank has been replaced with a "living value" reputation-based, zero-balance economic system owned by the people. Reputation is the new form of credit and currency based upon the consistency of value creation, integrity, service, generosity, compassion, eco-social contribution and wisdom. The currency of "living value" is based upon one's contribution to ecosystemic health and social well-being with life-enhancing innovation, products and services being of the greatest value.

Because our culture and environments support human potential for love, respect and life-affirming action, our consciousness is shifting and we are creating a world of Abundance, Wellness & Empowerment from the inside-out, ground-up and top-down. And as future generations are born into this world they evolve it and create an even more abundant, well, empowered, loving and beautiful world for themselves and future generations.

PRAGMATISM AND AN AMBITIOUS GOAL

The Vision of creating an Abundant, Well & Empowered world is admittedly an ambitious goal. It will initially take the collaboration of thousands of pioneers to build the first demonstrations of Regenerative Communities based upon living innovation and biomimetic technologies, optimal wellness and deep love for each other and our planet. As these exemplary beacons of a higher quality of life shine their light onto the world, hundreds of thousands of early adopters will create the demand to develop additional Regenerative Communities. Then, over time, millions will embrace regenerative living and a world of AWE will become a way of life.

There are many people who fear change and attempt to ostracize those seeking to make change. And yet, there is a groundswell of people everywhere embracing the transformation of our world.

In every major evolutionary change in human history, some brave pioneers had enough courage and tenacity to overcome ridicule, ostracism, discomfort and threats to their person and freedoms. The transformation necessary for the survival and thriving of humankind will not be made in our comfort zone or with the same tools and mindset that created the systemic dysfunction we now face in our world."

Einstein said, *"Great spirits have always encountered violent opposition from mediocre minds."*

Contributing to human evolution and transformation is a "choiceless choice" for me—it is my path.

If we're going to survive and potentially thrive as a species, we need to urgently make critical changes in ourselves and our world. Now is the time to be lovingly and ethically ambitious.

We're all interconnected, yet many of us seem to have forgotten this. None of us are immune from human suffering and ecosystemic destruction. When the biosphere and people suffer, we each are impacted. We can try to ignore it, desensitize ourselves and become callous, but no matter how hard we try, we feel it in our hearts and in our guts; we smell it in the air we breathe; we taste it in our water; and we see it in the eyes of the homeless and hungry.

I can't, in good conscious, bring children into the current world and raise them to be functional cogs in a dysfunctional socio-economic-political system that is built upon extraction and exploitation, resulting in unsustainable levels of poverty, injustice, war, toxicity, pollution and destruction of our biosphere.

I am devoting myself to creating a world where future generations won't suffer from starvation, poverty, desertification, war and pollution. I want to leave a legacy of an Abundant, Well & Empowered world for the children of today and for future generations. If I can make even an incremental difference, the world will have been a better place for me being here. If I try, I may succeed. If I don't try, I will definitely fail.

Let's talk about ambition. I can think of no greater ambition than to do great things that are beneficial to the thriving humankind and the planet.

We seem to have forgotten that just over 400 years ago, the United States of America was a dream. People from many different cultures and social-economic strata started journeying to America to fulfill a dream of life, liberty and the pursuit of happiness incorporated into the Declaration of Independence.

When the first immigrants came to the U.S., they knew very little about this "new land," but courageously packed up their families and sailed on boats for weeks, suffering nausea, vomiting, fever, rodents, no sleeping quarters, bathrooms or showers. These people had ambition, courage and a dream of a better life—a life of abundance, freedom and self-sufficiency; the promise of being rewarded for hard work, innovation and courage; and the potential to enjoy a life of liberty, self-expression and happiness.

At the time of signing the Declaration of Independence in 1776, no major metropolitan city existed—the U.S. was almost entirely raw natural land. There were only 13 States and the entire United States had a population of approximately 2.5 million colonists (less than the current number of employees in the Federal Government). The city of New York occupied only the lower portion of Manhattan island and had a population of approximately 25,000.

Look what has happened since the Declaration of Independence was signed (just a little over 350 years ago). With the advances in technology and innovation, just imagine what we could do in the next 100 years. I am convinced that if we apply new conscious, ethical and regenerative constraints to our ambitions, and focus our resources on ecosystemic thriving, we can create a world where humankind and our planet are thriving, abundant, well and empowered.

MANIFESTING THE DREAM AND VISION

Dreaming is powerful! When we dream about creating a new world, it is critical that we dream consciously and consider the impact of our dreams on each other and the planet. In our modern world, we often dream about having more money, more stuff, more power, more control, more popularity, more privileges, without regard to the affect our dreams have on others, and often to the exclusion of others (also known as "exclusivity").

Creating a new unified global reality can be quite challenging due to the disparity and divisiveness that arises from the unique perspectives, cultural conditioning, belief systems, and experiences of each individual. Despite this, we have some things in common—we are all human, we all depend on the planet and each other for our survival, we breath the same air, and we need water, food and shelter. We are also, at our core, a tribal species that thrives with collaboration, love and touch.

I have not met many people that want polluted air, poisoned water, toxic food, extractive and dirty energy, unhealthy live/work environments, poor health, broken education systems, ecological destruction, poverty, war or social injustice. However, there are many people that will allow such conditions to be perpetuated if doing so creates jobs, makes or saves money, increases their power and control, and doesn't cause to much inconvenience.

We are the planet! There is no separation. Each breath, drop of water and the nutrients that sustain our lives are gifts from the planet. The planet does not need us. We need the planet. It will heal itself and be just fine without us; however, we have an opportunity to thrive, if we serve the planet and each other and choose unity, love and synergistic resolution over selfish hoarding, scarcity, fear and compromise.

Consider the trillions of dollars, jobs and economic growth that will result from healing the Earth's ecosystems; developing living technologies; building/rebuilding regenerative communities and cities; evolving our energy, food, water and transportation systems and infrastructure; and transforming healthcare, education, business and government. A living Regenerative Economy benefits all people, regardless of race, religion, country, age, political affiliation or ideology.

Living in AWE was written with the intent of turning the vision of AWE into a reality. To become a reality, it requires the application of new tools, beliefs and methods, rather than attempting to fix the existing and obsolete paradigm with the same mindset, tools and behaviors that created the existing paradigm. It also requires the commitment of time, energy, money and resources aligned with developing a world of Abundance, Wellness & Empowerment.

If we are to create a world where future generations can thrive, we need to transform our world from the 1) **inside-out,** 2) **ground up**, and 3) **top-down.** Below are some examples of the actions we can take to evolve and expand human consciousness, culture and systems to create a Regenerative Economy and an Abundant, Well & Empowered world.

"Inside-out" includes replacing old beliefs, perceptions, emotions, priorities and experiences ("ways of being") with those that are loving, compassionate, healthy, as well as outwardly expressing these new ways of being to create new behavior and culture. Keys to shifting our personal beliefs and behaviors leading to the transformation of our current social-economic-political system, beliefs, conditioning and program ("the Matrix") include the following:

- Filling our minds, hearts and being with abundant love, respect, compassion and generosity for each other and the planet, and generously expressing this new way of being to create a culture of love, respect, compassion and generosity;

- Focusing our words, thoughts and deeds on what we want to create rather than focusing on what we want to avoid such as elevating love over fear, peace over war, generosity over hoarding, respect over disregard, oneness over separation, and collaboration over competition;

- Understanding that each of us is powerful beyond measure and we are each and collectively interconnected with and interdependent upon all creation;

- Exploring new possibilities (in a universe of infinite possibilities) that fulfill our potential for brilliance, beauty, love and compassion, and expanding our consciousness through inquiry, imagination, dreaming and visioning;

- Finding love for each person and all things and respecting the uniqueness of each other's experience as equal to our own;

- Respect our body by increasing our health, wellness and vitality through highly nutritious foods, pure water, clean air, healthy built environments and the integration of mindfulness and movement in our daily lives;

- Consistently go beyond our comfort zone to courageously be the change you want to see;

- Practicing mindfulness and recognizing that each moment is an opportunity to express love, compassion and generosity; to connect deeply; to be courageously vulnerable; to be grateful; and to be joyous.

- Boldly envisioning and creating an Abundant, Well & Empowered world.

"Ground up" refers to transforming the environments in which we live, work, learn and play to be ecologically conscious, energy-efficient, sustainable, Abundant, Well & Empowered. Our environment is the most impactful influence on our lives—it creates beliefs, behaviors, culture and feedback loops that reinforce are ways of being. To transform our environment requires the proactive commitment of energy, effort and resources to rebuild our environments, infrastructure and culture including:

- Employing collaborative consumption and effective utilization;

- Replacing fossil fuels and other extractive energy and materials with renewable energy and materials;

- Developing "*Wise, Regenerative and Resilient Cities and Communities*" that are self-sufficient, healthy and based upon living systems wisdom with planning, design and engineering processes that include localized conservative water security (catchment, wells, recycling), clean energy generation, building healthy soil, nutritious food production and waste upcycling to increase regenerative abundance, efficiency, decrease waste and minimize the centralized supply chain carbon footprint;

- Restoration of the Earth's ecosystems and preserving Earth wisdom cultures;

- Converting and upcycling waste into valuable energy and products;

- New transportation with the proliferation of renewably powered public and transportation solutions with increased walkable & bikeable live-work logistics;

- Balancing population growth and increasing carrying capacity with abundant food, water, energy and renewable materials; and

- Developing a regenerative infrastructure serving ecosystemic thriving and providing meaningful work including planting trees & reforestation, regenerative agriculture, replenishing our fisheries, developing regenerative communities, as well as regenerative technologies deployment including agtech, aquatech, biomimetic materials renewable energy and waste upcycling.

"**Top-down**" involves we, the people, 1) using our economic influence and power ("economic vote") to support conscious companies committed to eco-social responsibility while unethical companies that pollute and cause destruction go bankrupt, 2) exercising the power of collective voice (e.g., internet and social media) to influence change in government, corporate leadership and the regulatory environment so that government, business and regulations support people and planet, and 3) accelerating and supporting regenerative businesses, transformational educational institutions, ethical financial institutions and regenerative resource/ infrastructure solutions. Actions that will transform the authority, control and power structures of business, financial and government institutions include the following:

- Implementing new regulatory systems and long-term planning that promote and incentivize ethical business and government;

- New metrics for qualitative, ethical and sustainable business practices, manufacturing processes and government and elevating ethical and qualitative imperatives over economic and quantitative imperatives knowing that ultimately what is good for life is good for business;

- Having the courage and heart to stand for the greatness of humankind, empowering and encouraging people to take risks, make mistakes, lose money, innovate, laugh, learn and evolve in the face of adversity, criticism and ostracism from mediocre minds;

- Increasing innovation over standardization, collaboration over competition, transparency over secrecy, wholeness over divisiveness, health over disease and function over dysfunction;

- Developing new organizational structures and governance that are nimble, adaptable and resilient, and can rapidly respond to change to implement new innovation and functions for the benefit of people and planet;

- Economic, political and social reform that supports a Regenerative Economy and creates meaningful work for humankind in service to people and planet;

- Transforming political systems so that they empower ethical leadership and governments to serve the best interests and thriving humankind and the planet; and

- Implementation of a decentralized, people-owned, ethical zero balance economy based upon contribution of value, collaboration and reputation rather than debt.

This transformation will require immediately embracing new opportunities for ethical life-enhancing and regenerative practices, as well as transforming beliefs and behaviors that increase our ability to live in love, unity and harmony with each other and nature.

Each of us has an imagination and the ability to dream, express and create. It is from imagination, collective dreaming and expression that the world in which we live has been created and is being created in each moment.

By serving the thriving of people and planet, I believe that we can create a society with the most robust economy we have ever seen—The *"Regenerative Economy."*

The "Regenerative Economy" will result in a higher quality of life that includes economic abundance; greater freedom; optimal well-being; clean energy and infrastructure; healthier and happier homes, workplaces and schools; effective and inspiring education; unity, a thriving biosphere, and world peace.

By imagining and clearly envisioning the world we want to create and focusing our time, effort, energy and resources on creating a world in alignment with our vision, we can realize our vision.

In the words of Marianne Williamson, *"We are powerful beyond measure."* As co-creative dreamers and visionaries of our "reality," we, individually and collectively, possess immeasurable power to transform our world and create a new reality.

Imagine the world you would like to create. What does this new world look like and how would you create it? Does your dream increase the quality of life— does your dream provide benefits for humankind and planet, or just yourself? Are you willing to be the change you would like to see? What personal changes are required and will you make in order for you to be in alignment with the change you wish to create?

Experiencing your imaginative vision as reality is the first step to manifesting a vision for a new world.

We live in a universe of infinite possibilities, yet most of us live lives of such limited possibilities. There are energies, forces and consciousness in the universe that support human thriving, yet most of us are "perceptually blind" to it. Let us open our eyes, minds and hearts to new possibilities that are life-enhancing and expansive for humankind so that it may thrive by expressing its potential for love, brilliance, beauty and kindness, to create a world of AWE.

SECTION TWO –

ABUNDANCE

_____

While many of us have been conditioned to believe that abundance is a state of having, it is actually state of being—A state in which we are sufficient, fulfilled, healthy and thriving in the present moment. More money and material possessions do not create abundance. It is state of being unconditionally abundant that brings us abundance. Abundance often arises from acceptance, contentment and gratitude and is expressed in the practice of love, service and generosity.

CHAPTER 8

River of Abundance

(Being Abundant and the Expansive Current of Abundance)

"The miracle is this—the more we share, the more we have."

~Leonard Nimoy

My inner journey to the River of Abundance brought me to the understanding that "Abundance" is simply the state of being abundant. The River of Abundance increases in size and flow the more abundant we are and the more we share our abundance.

In my desire to be a more evolved, spiritual and ethical human, I became aware of a conflict in my beliefs regarding spirituality and materiality. While I enjoy the options and convenience of money and material wealth, my beliefs around money seemed misaligned with my spiritual beliefs. I started asking myself why I believed spiritual leaders with great wealth were hypocrites, or why I believed ultra-wealthy individuals were less spiritual. Where did I get these beliefs? Are they true?

I asked myself, "Why should spiritual leaders be deprived of material wealth in order to be spiritual? Does wealth make one less spiritual and poverty make one more spiritual? Is money inherently evil? Does our monetary system create inequity and competition or is our monetary system an expression of our inner nature and/ or conditioning?"

In order to reconcile my conflict between materiality and spirituality and gain greater insight into true abundance, I approached my teacher, Gurmukh Kuar Khalsa, who embodies a balance between spirituality and physical abundance. She recommended a 48-day program of cleansing, Kundalini yoga exercises and an hour of meditation upon waking and before going to sleep. My conflict between spirituality and materiality was reconciled coincidentally on the 48th day when I received the following vision in my meditation:

I was traveling through a lush emerald forest and came over a hill to witness the most beautiful waterfall and river of flowing liquid golden light. As I approached the river, many people were on the banks of the river warning me not to go any closer to the river. "It's a trap," they said, "don't go in." I looked in their eyes and saw fear. I continued walking toward the river.

Happily splashing in the river of golden light were people inviting me to jump in and join them in their celebration. I saw happiness, abundance, love and joy in their eyes. They explained that the river was the "River of Abundance." They explained that the river contained an infinite supply of life affirming energy and expanded in size and energy each time a new person jumped in. They also told me that in order for the river to keep flowing and increasing in size, the secrets of the river had to be shared with others.

I jumped into the river and immersed myself in its golden liquid light. I played and splashed joyously, drinking in the river's energy to my heart's content, feeling my vitality, clarity, love, joy and abundance increasing. As others along the banks saw that I wasn't harmed and was actually being filled—growing healthier, stronger, and more abundant—they too jumped in. The river expanded for them, and more and more followed. We invited more people to jump in and the river kept expanding, with each person receiving and sharing their abundance.

I came to understand that in my vision, the river is a metaphor for the abundance of our universe, nature and the life force that fuels our human experience. The state of abundance is expansive, plentiful, nurturing, healing and regenerative. When we are in abundance, we become free of constrictive states of being, such as fear, scarcity, stinginess and resistance, which lead to overconsumption, hoarding, inequity, competition and war. To receive abundance from the universe, it's vital that we pay it forward by first being in the internal state of abundance and then sharing that abundance outwardly with others.

Abundance, as a natural state of being, is evidenced by the planet's ability to heal, restore and regenerate ecosystems that sustain life on Earth, as well as the potential for infinite energy, matter and consciousness contained in the universe.

I have found it helpful to use happiness as an analogy to help more people understand and experience abundance. **Abundance is the state of being abundant**. Abundance is much like happiness in that they're both internal states of being. Most of us have experienced happiness and can recall moments of being happy. If we experience enough happiness in our life, we gain the ability to guide ourselves from less desirable emotions to the state of happiness. However, how many of us have experienced true abundance?

To be truly happy and abundant, it is essential that our happiness and abundance are unconditional. Our belief systems, however, often keep us in the pursuit of conditional happiness or abundance, dependent upon external prerequisites and conditions prior to us experiencing the desired states of being (e.g., money, possessions, relationships, social status and influence), rather than the immediate and unconditional experience of being happy and living in abundance for no reason and without condition. It's simple to be happy and abundant, by just being so. While simple, it's not always easy to experience unconditional happiness and abundance. This is largely because we have been conditioned to believe that our internal states of happiness and abundance are dependent upon the fulfillment of some external circumstance (e.g., "I'll be happy when I meet the love of my life" or "I will be abundant when I have $20 million in my bank account").

Having material wealth and being abundant can and do exist concurrently. The internal state of abundance doesn't come from external conditions, however, external conditions do influence internal states of being. I have known plenty of unfulfilled centi-millionaires and billionaires who actually believe they don't have enough money and possessions, and despite their large material wealth, they live in non-abundant states of ego gratification, incessantly desiring more possessions, wealth and power with only fleeting moments of satisfaction from having their addictive cravings temporarily filled by compulsive consumption and "winning the game." The inner world of fear, scarcity, insecurity and ego gratification create the physical environment that generates the feedback loop perpetuating non-abundance.

The following story by Buddhist teacher, Kyabje Kalu, illustrates the distinction between material riches and abundance:

> "At the time of Buddha Sakyamuni, a monk found himself in possession of a marvelous jewel that granted any wish—all the gold, silver, and precious stones you could ask for. The lucky owner thought: 'I am a monk and have no need of all these riches. Better to give this jewel to a poor person. But there are so many of them, why favor one over another? Buddha is omniscient. He will tell me whom to give it to.' So, going to Buddha, he explained his difficulty and asked him to designate a fitting recipient. Buddha Sakyamuni recommended that he give it to the king of that area, a very wealthy and powerful monarch. The monk made the offering, and the king accepted it, inquiring about the reason for the gift. The monk explained, 'I thought I should give this gem to a poor person, but not knowing whom to choose, I asked Buddha Sakyamuni. He advised me to bring it to you.'
>
> The king thought that was quite strange, since there probably was no one on earth richer than he. So he went to Buddha Sakyamuni for an explanation. The king asked why Buddha had chosen him when the monk had asked which poor person would best be provided for with the gem.
>
> 'It's true,' Buddha said. 'Without a doubt, there is no one wealthier than you in the world; but there is also no doubt that there is no need as great as yours. That is why I told the monk to give you the gem.' "

No jewel or amount of unlimited wealth could fill the hole of unfulfilled need in the king's life, because no matter how much the king possessed, he always desired more.

As simply illustrated in this story, "Abundance" is a state of "Being", not a state of *"having."* The monk who was willing to give away the jewel, was more abundant than the king. When we are in the state of abundance, we have all we need in the moment and are not in pursuit of having more.

Upon deeper inquiry and experience, I came to understand that abundance, not scarcity, is a more powerful and expanded spiritual state. I repeatedly found that those who are more in alignment with their divine nature are naturally more abundant and able to rapidly manifest their desires with greater ease.

While some spiritual renunciants live in a state of abundance without material conditionality, many spiritual renunciants live unsustainable and non-abundant lives, constantly seeking donations, begging for support or living in subsistence without experiencing true abundance, joy, bliss and love. By contrast, there are quite a few individuals that are not considered "spiritual" leaders, but who have demonstrated the ability to draw upon universal energy and consciousness to hold a vision and synchronously attract the resources to manifest their vision into highly impactful companies. Individuals such as Pierre Omidyar, Bill and Melinda Gates, Warren Buffet, Elon Musk, Richard Branson, Marc Benioff, Michael Bloomberg, Sergey Brin, Larry Page and Oprah Winfrey have created massive economic abundance for themselves and many others, not only with their businesses, but also with their philanthropic donations. While these individuals may not often be thought of as spiritual or enlightened leaders, their transformative impact on society is significant. As well, many less wealthy renunciants have demonstrated the ability to live in greater states of internal abundance and bliss than some of the most rich and powerful people in the world, having helped millions of people achieve spiritual growth, and transforming the world with their love, light, wisdom and good deeds (e.g., the Dalai Lama, J. Krishnamurti, Sri Aurobindo, Meher Baba, Joseph Campbell, Thich Nhat Hanh, Martin Luther King, Jr., Mother Teresa, and Amma).

It doesn't matter how spiritual, rich, powerful or philanthropic an individual may be, if their internal state of being is not abundant, they, and what they create, are not likely to be abundant, even if they manage to amass significant physical wealth. This is because *abundance is an internal state of being expressed in acts of love, gratitude and generosity. True abundance is not conditioned upon external circumstances, possessions or demonstrations. When we create from abundance and engage in conduct from an internal state of abundance, the world we create becomes abundant.*

While it's difficult to objectively see or measure the impact of the non-physical energy fields created by those persons meditating in temples, ashrams and caves around the world, my experience has shown that truly abundant spiritual leaders and teachers generally have much greater impact in the world, than do the "spiritual renunciants" living in poverty. Abundant spiritual masters possess internal abundance and are also able to manifest external abundance with ease—they generously create, give, share and support higher levels of joy, bliss, harmony, wellness, abundance and peace in the world. These abundant spiritual masters, intuitively and instinctually understand the laws of sufficiency and balance. They don't need, pursue or have an addiction to material wealth or money. They manifest what they need with ease to achieve benevolent purposes that raise consciousness, improve lives and advance the human condition.

When we are in a state of poverty or non-abundant consciousness, our inner scarcity and limitation creates the need to hoard, overconsume and compete. These states of being often lead to a culture of lack, scarcity, poverty, cruelty and disease. We have the choice to be in abundance in any given moment. Although many of us feel constrained in our freedom of expression by conditioning, governmental regulation and societal pressures, we do have the ultimate choice of what we think, what we believe and how we perceive the world. Since we have the choice to view life in the most inspiring and fulfilling ways, we can, at any time, think fulfilling and positive thoughts. Achieving a consistent state of abundance requires reprogramming ourselves—a process to free ourselves of disempowering belief systems and re-pattern ourselves into a continual state of abundance including the following:

- Being ever vigilant and conscious of our mental, emotional, energetic and physical states of being;

- Continually questioning any and all beliefs;

- Consciously and immediately shifting from non-abundant states of being and thoughts to abundant states of being and thoughts. For example, taking a conscious breath and being grateful for the miracle of your breath. Find something beautiful in and/or around you to be grateful for; and

- Using the massive abundance of energy, brainpower, effort and resources of humankind in service to people and planet leading to a regenerative and abundant world that supports thriving for all life.

We can transform into the state of abundance by simply feeling grateful for our next breath. Inhale and feel yourself being filled with new energy, life and potential. Feel the exquisiteness of this moment, the ability to imagine and the freedom to choose your next thought. Feel the abundance in your mind, heart, soul and every cell of your body. Realize the abundant power of creation we each hold and the miraculous gifts bestowed upon us. Take a moment to open yourself to the infinite energy and potential in the universe around you and inside you, as well as the myriad of ecosystemic interactions on planet Earth that create and sustain the miracle of life, including yours. Feel yourself in a state of abundance overflowing with the potential for goodness, vitality, thriving and unlimited opportunity in the world. Welcome to the state of abundance—enjoy your stay!

While abundance is a state of *being*, it's also expressed in behavior as a state of *doing*. The expression of abundance starts with an internal state of being abundant emanating from the inside-out with the expression of behavior demonstrating abundant qualities, such as gratitude, generosity, sharing, trust and love. When we're in "abundance consciousness," we're able to access the abundant energy and consciousness of the universe to create a world that allows all life to thrive. For example, Mother Earth, in her regenerative and abundant capacity, gives us life, air, water, food, materials and everything we need to thrive and doesn't ask for money. All she asks is that we give her love, respect and care in return, but because our society is conditioned to live in fear and scarcity, we rape Mother Earth, steal from her and destroy her living and regenerative systems.

Visualize yourself in a world where everyone has clean air, pure drinking water and fresh nutritious food. See a world where people deeply understand their connection to each other and nature and honor this connection with acts of beauty and kindness. Picture a society engaged in meaningful work that contributes to the beauty and well-being of people and planet; a society with spacious free time to enjoy our families and friends, commune with nature, pursue our passions and hobbies, engage in activities for health, and inspired self-development.

Now feel and visualize the opposite—a world of lack, poverty, cruelty, war, injustice, pollution and disease. Feel discontent for what you don't have, jealousy for those who have more, anger for your mistakes, fear of your future and the guilt for taking and hoarding more than is sufficient for your needs, causing others to starve and live in pain. The air you breath is polluted with smog and radioactive isotopes, your water has toxic chemicals including the film of oil and heavy metals such as lead, mercury and asbestos, your food consists of irradiated and heavily processed fast foods and you live in unsustainable cities with noise pollution and the constant threat of war, terrorist attacks, climate disasters and pandemics.

This is rhetorical, but in which scenario would you rather live? How would living in a continual state of abundance transform your thoughts, emotions, well-being and actions? How could you positively transform yourself and our world? How would this affect others and contribute to greater love, abundance, wellness & empowerment in our world?

As we create ever greater abundance internally and in our physical world, we expand our River of Abundance and create a culture of abundance. Physical abundance stems from the regeneration of ecosystems. By engaging in "Regenerative Practices" such as living systems principles, biomimicry, and living in service to the thriving of people and planet, we can create a regenerative and abundant world. This creates the feedback loop of abundance between our internal states of being and our environment, thus exponentially increasing and perpetuating inner and outer abundance.

The more we develop regenerative practices, the more abundance and resources we have, and the easier it becomes to generously create and share value. The more we share value, the more abundance we create and receive, and the more abundant the world becomes.

Value and abundance can come in many forms, such as love, friendship, well-being, service, emotional support, guidance, money, real estate, personal property, intellectual property, acknowledgment and validation. Thus, a person who provides great value by living abundantly and helping to awaken others to their abundance is likely to receive great value in many forms, and therefore increase his or her abundance.

It has been my experience that when I'm in the state of abundance, I become so positively charged and full of universal energy, my human container overflows with inspiration and abundance. This energy expands beyond me and creates synergistic attraction. People and opportunities start magically showing up to support me in expanding my abundance and fulfilling my purpose. While the state of abundance can be chosen at any moment, for no reason or condition, the support the universe provides increases or decreases based upon my level of inspiration, passion and commitment to my purpose, as well as the degree of alignment to the laws of universal abundance (e.g., life affirming, expansive and generously given for the benefit of others).

So long as my purpose and actions are in alignment with the laws of universal abundance, amazing synchronous metaphysical manifestation occurs. When I'm on my path and integrally aligned to my core purpose in life, the universe, throughout my life, has consistently aligned with me to attract great opportunities, friends, connections, love and wealth to help me manifest the vision I serve. In these moments of full internal abundance, I also have been blessed with greater creativity, passion, humor, inspiration, health and energy. The universe keeps giving as long as I keep giving. The opportunities I receive expand as I generously share opportunities with others.

I invite you to try this approach to creating abundance in your life for 30-days and observe what shows up. I am confident that, at the very least, you will notice being happier and more fulfilled, and as you increase your internal abundance, your relationship with the world will improve in remarkable ways.

When we internally experience the vast abundance of the universe and express that abundance in our daily lives, it creates a transformative field of copious energy. As we access, share and expand this field of energy, it exponentially increases the volume and flow of the River of Abundance, creating a culture of abundance that ultimately leads to a world of AWE.

The spiritual nature of abundance encourages (i) generous giving and service, (ii) engaging in kind and loving thoughts, words and deeds that are life-enhancing, (iii) creating a beautiful and healthy environment in which all life can thrive in the balance of inclusivity, (iv) generously transferring knowledge, inspiration and imparting wisdom, and (v) voluntarily acknowledging and rewarding value when received from others.

The potential of humankind, and the opportunities for beauty, kindness and equitability in this world, are truly abundant. There are more opportunities to heal each other and the planet than people can fulfill in the next 500 years. Let's seize these opportunities to create lives with meaningful, joyful and inspired work in service to the thriving of people and planet rather than jobs!

To create an abundant world, it takes the courage to jump into the River of Abundance in the face of those who perpetuate fear, cynicism and conformity to mediocrity, while leveling their criticism against the "unrealistic dreamers" that seek to create an abundant and beautiful world. So let us dream of an abundant world, love our critics and hold deep trust that we are internally abundant, and the universe will perpetuate abundance for us and others. Generously sharing our abundance expands abundance and our giving increases the ability to receive.

The key to abundance is being in a state of abundance for no reason or condition whatsoever in every moment. In other words, abundance is created being fulfilled and grateful for the experience of each moment and being free of needs—even the need to live, the need to strive, the need to be a self. It's the consciousness of "need" that leads to a perception of lack or incompleteness. Conditionality and the perception of lack are antithetical to abundance consciousness.

Sometimes we need a little help breaking through or dissolving our present state of being. Acceptance, surrender, gratitude and fulfillment are the cornerstones of abundance. These characteristics are not conditions of abundance, but rather tools that help us to experience abundance.

When we're in a truly abundant state, we become open to allowing the infinite energy and creative consciousness of the universe to stream through us, generating such an overflow of energy and inspiration that complacency is rarely the result. In this state, it's more likely we'll become a wellspring of goodness, love, sharing, inspiration and creativity.

As we transform ourselves and express our abundance, we transform our world. As we live in abundance, our behavior shifts and influences the behavior of others. For example, as we become more abundant, we might find that we (i) desire less and share more, (ii) engage in acts of beauty and kindness, (iii) voluntarily create, recognize and exchange value, (iii) create greater abundance, peace, wellness and equitability in our lives and those whose lives we touch, and (iv) shift our consumptive habits to support the health of people and planet.

Moreover, as the viral nature of abundance consciousness expands to include a significant percentage of the population, it's foreseeable our measurement and beliefs of "success" will shift from quantitative (e.g., gross domestic product and profits) to qualitative (e.g., health, beauty, love and connection).

Being in abundance provides us with profound powers of manifestation. Once we experience the flow of limitless energy through us, we shift to bountiful states of being. By continually monitoring our state of being and consciously opening ourselves to receive abundance, we can consciously increase the volume and frequency of cosmic energy and consciousness that overflows our ability to contain it.

Once our thoughts, perceptions, emotions and beliefs are in alignment with abundance consciousness so that the cells and fiber of our being resonate and overflow with abundance, the following becomes our truth:

- I am abundant in each moment.

- I am one with the universe and create abundantly with universal consciousness.

- There are no limitations or blockages—I openly receive the abundance of the universe.

- I am totally fulfilled and nourished in the present moment, experiencing exactly what I am meant to experience.

- I accept and surrender to the unfolding experience of each moment with gratitude.

- I am totally fulfilled at all moments and surrender to each moment as it unfolds.

- I attract abundance and have all that I need at each moment.

- The universe infinitely supports me with all I need to live in abundance, joy, bliss, harmony and love.

- The universe exponentially increases my manifestations and attracts all I need to realize my dreams.

- Life and death are merely holographic experiences, I hold no fear and release all lack and neediness, including the need for my next breath.

- I recognize and voluntarily reward value to create personal and global abundance.

As we consistently apply this discipline, we find we're increasingly able to guide ourselves into desired and abundant states of being. Each time we do this, we create new patterns and reinforce our desired states of being, thereby making it easier to be in these desired states. Eventually, the state of abundance becomes the natural, automatic and continual state of our being.

When we're in the state of abundance, we have amazing, miraculous and limitless power to create a bountiful world of joy, inspiration, health, harmony, love, respect, beauty and wisdom.

CHAPTER 9

Law of AttrAction

"I have brought myself, by long meditation, to the conviction that a human being with a settled purpose must accomplish it, and that nothing can resist a will which will stake even existence upon its fulfillment."

~ Benjamin Disraeli

The "Law of Attraction" provides that what you focus on is what you receive from life. However, some new-age gurus and practitioners have forgotten that half of "Attr**Action**" is *Action*. They guide you to say affirmations, focus your mind, and write down your desires, which will magically make all your dreams come true. While imagination and visualization are highly influential and powerful in creating our physical reality, to manifest our vision and dreams into physical reality, it's important we also take embodied action that aligns with our vision and dreams.

For example, if I envision being a great surfer, it's not likely to happen by me sitting on a pillow repeating the affirmation "I am a great surfer", writing my desire to be a great surfer on a sacred scroll and putting it at the base of my alter, or "surfing" the Internet. If I want to be a great surfer, I'll need to get a board, go to the beach, get lessons, paddle out and dedicate myself consistently to mastering the sport. If I have a natural ability, get great coaching, do a great deal of visualization, dedicate myself to the sport, and spend about 10,000 hours surfing, I have the likelihood of becoming good enough to become a professional surfer. Visualization can improve self-confidence, desire and dedication to powerfully accelerate my learning, increase my performance and make surfing more fun. Also, visualization can help attract the opportunities and people that will increase the likelihood of achieving my dream.

A practice that employs a combination of mental focus, affirmations, visualization and declarations in conjunction with consistent, dedicated and aligned **action** has been proven for centuries to yield exponentially greater results than just visualization, affirmations or action alone.

For example, aside from hours of disciplined training, many Olympic athletes have achieved exponentially improved performance by focusing their minds on peak performance by utilizing visualization and affirmations. Studies conducted at The Cleveland Clinic, concluded that mental training and visualization "enhances the cortical output signal, which drives activation level and increases strength." As well, according to Dr. Charles Garfield, in his indispensable book _Peak Performance_, Eastern European sports scientists, coaches and athletes found that mental training and visualization were the single most powerful tools in enhancing optimal levels of performance for athletes.

In his book, _Karate of Okinawa_, William Cummins supports the ancient practice of visualization with scientific studies by Russian scientists, who compared four groups of Olympic athletes in terms of their training schedules, as follows:

- Group 1 = 100% physical training;
- Group 2 = 75% physical training with 25% mental training;
- Group 3 = 50% physical training with 50% mental training;
- Group 4 = 25% physical training with 75% mental training.

I was surprised when I found that Group 4, with 75% of their time devoted to mental training, demonstrated the best performance. Bear in mind, that the subjects were already Olympic athletes with years of dedicated training, coaching and support with highly developed neuro-muscular memory and peak physical condition.

Proponents of The Law of Attraction and Creative Visualization include Gandhi, Martin Luther King, Jr., Oprah Winfrey, Will Smith, Eckhart Tolle, Louis Hay, Arnold Schwarzenegger, Anthony Robbins, Bill Gates, Jim Carey, Lance

Armstrong and Tiger Woods. All of these individuals credit mental training, visualization and focus in conjunction with aligned action to their success.

The Law of Attraction and Creative Visualization isn't just reserved for celebrities and exceptional achievers. Attraction and visualization expert, Natalie Ledwell, stresses that people from all walks of life can benefit from visualizing the achievement of their goals. *"The secret to using the Law of Attraction is to not only visualize the goals or results you want to manifest, but to fully experience and embody how it will feel when you get there,"* said Ledwell.

About 10% of the population claim they can't visualize. However, as long as we have an imagination, we can visualize. For example, if you've ever felt stress, worry or excitement about some future or past event (e.g., the feeling of anticipation and excitement on a first date, or the feeling of anxiety when you forecast not having enough money to pay your bills) you've visualized. Just about everyone can visualize anything because everyone has an imagination and we often use our imaginations to reconstruct our past or visualize our future.

For those who have difficulty with visualization, think about an image of a big yellow lemon. You take it out the refrigerator. It feels cold. You cut the lemon in half with a knife. The fresh aroma of lemon fills the air. You squeeze the lemon and its cool juice squirts on your hand. You lick the juice off your hand and experience the salivary glands excreting saliva at the thought of tasting the sour lemon juice. If you experienced any part of the foregoing, you can visualize.

The mind is like a muscle. If you don't exercise it, the mind becomes less effective. When you discipline your mind to focus on, and envision in exquisite detail that which you want, somatic and cognitive consciousness work together to attract the information and resources you need to support the reality created by the conscious mind. Of specific importance in attracting and creating the life you desire is the **Reticular Activating System ("RAS").**

The RAS is a network of neural pathways that processes about 400 billion bits of information per second and filters this massive amount of information to deliver 2,000 bits of information per second to the cognitive brain, based largely upon what the cognitive brain and mind deem important. The amount of domain-specific information that can be processed during a certain period of time has an estimated capacity ranging from 2 to 60 bits per second (bps) for attention, decision-making, perception, motion, and language, and up to 1 million bps for sensory processing.[90] This means that over 99.99% of all the information that we receive goes unnoticed by our *cognitive brain*.

The RAS is critical in delivering that small amount of information necessary to fulfill the orders our brain deems important. If our brain orders information that supports limiting beliefs, the RAS will deliver information in support of those limiting beliefs. If we discipline our brain and develop neural networks and belief systems that support our desires, the RAS will deliver the information that serves our desires.[91] A good example of this is when a woman can sleep through loud traffic and noise in a large city but is awakened promptly due to the sound of her baby crying.

While the RAS is also responsible for keeping us alive by controlling cardio-vascular functions, breathing, the transmission of sensations from the eyes and ears, sleep, consciousness and pain modulation, **the most relevant function of the RAS, as it relates to the Law of *AttrAction*, is habituation**.

The cognitive brain builds neural networks over time through the repetitive patterns of habituation. These neural networks hold memories and beliefs about our identity, our relationship to our environment and the reinforcement of our created reality. Unless the cognitive brain is consciously disciplined, it will instruct the RAS to filter 400 billion bits of information it receives into just 2,000 bits of information the cognitive brain has habitually deemed important and relevant to perpetuating its reality. Thus, it is important to program the RAS to deliver the 2,000 bits of information that is important to us and aligns with what we seek to attract. This programming often requires a change in habitual thought patterns.

The RAS attempts to regulate our autonomic system to keep us in a state of comfort. Many of us have been conditioned to experience fear, caution and/or discomfort from unknown circumstances, unfamiliar beliefs and new ways of being. In order to maintain a state of comfort, the RAS provides us information that supports our existing beliefs, habits and reality. This explains why our beliefs and habits are often stronger than our desires.

When we try to change a belief, habit or way of being to fulfill our desires, the RAS does not respond until we have arrived at a level of comfort, confidence and knowing in our beliefs by creating the neural networks to embed the desire as a habitual belief. Fortunately, the RAS can be reprogrammed to deliver the information and resources you desire.

In order to get the RAS to use its vast power to fulfill that which you desire, it's important to reprogram the brain's belief systems and habitual ways of thinking. This can be accomplished through visualization exercises that include emotional and somatic embodiment of desired experiences (i.e., seeing, hearing, smelling, tasting and feeling the experience).[92] Also, by being vigilant of our thoughts and changing limiting and sabotaging thoughts to ones that are optimistic, positive and encouraging, we can shift the way the RAS delivers information to the cognitive brain.

As the RAS and *Somatic Brain* do not differentiate between truth or falsity of an imaginative vision and physical reality, they are both reality to the RAS and *Somatic Brain*. Thus, when you persistently hold a detailed embodied vision and take consistent actions in alignment with that vision, you send the message to the subconscious Somatic Brain and the RAS that the vision is real, relevant and important. While building this internal reality, you need to discipline the mind to immediately shift from any negative or detracting thoughts and visualizations to the thoughts and visualizations that support your desires.

The evidentiary basis and comfort level to support the RAS happens internally. Thus, if you want to increase your wealth, health and improve the quality of your life, you would visualize in great detail living a life of wealth, health and leisure. Most people would visualize making a certain the amount of money (e.g., $1 million per year), however, money doesn't truly buy love, freedom and health. While money can be tool of convenience that can lead to a higher quality of life, it's critical to see beyond the short-sighted belief that money will give you the lifestyle you desire. It is important that you build beliefs and an internal reality that you are actually living a lifestyle of wealth (not just making money), by visualizing your life in detail. For example, (1) see your environment (e.g., where you live, work, learn, play and engage in activities), (2) picture your interaction of love, trust, laughter and mutual admiration with friends, family, colleagues and acquaintances, (3) visualize how you spend your time from when you wake up to when you go to sleep, (4) experience the value you're creating in the world and the improvement you're making in your and other's lives, (5) see your workplace (e.g., the office, your colleagues, the happy customers; the amazing products and/or services you are selling) or your retirement; (6) experience the money flowing into your bank account, the account balance increasing and the feeling of complete financial security, (7) envisage your freedom and leisure time (e.g., travel, adventure, health, learning, dining at fine restaurants, time with loved ones), (8) picture owning your dream home, and (9) visualize generously sharing your wealth with those you love and enjoy, while improving the quality of life on this planet.

In programming our RAS, we may fall into the trap of envisioning material things that we have been conditioned to desire, (e.g., house, cars, toys, clothes and money), rather than what we really need to live a truly fulfilling high-quality of life. Be careful what you envision. It is vital that we visualize the non-material physical, mental, emotional and spiritual needs that will bring more love, connection, health, happiness and fulfillment into our lives rather than just the material aspects of wealth.

Because the RAS does not distinguish between the world of *Experiential Reality* created by imagination and the perceived physical world, to activate the highly valuable and miraculous RAS to enhance your life and achieve your dreams, it's vital to:

1. Observe, discipline and guide your mind to consistently focus on the outcomes you desire;

2. Visualize your desires in great detail to embody them and make them real to the RAS and Somatic Mind. Put yourself completely in the scene of that which you desire—see it, hear it, feel it, smell it and taste your visual world and experience it as real;

3. Experience the emotions and feelings associated with living the life of your dreams;

4. Take consistent action in alignment with your values and desires; and

5. Create value. You will find the greater the benefit and value your vision provides to people and planet, the greater benefit and resources you will receive.

The famous motivational speaker, Earl Nightingale, said *"Success is the progressive realization of a worthy ideal."* When we focus our thoughts on the realization of a worthy ideal, and progressively and consistently take action to realize that goal, the universe provides us support, attracting the resources we need to realize our goal.

The mind is like fertile soil and our thoughts are like seeds. The thoughts we plant in our mind will grow. When we are unaware of our thoughts, it's likely we'll plant unwanted and potentially poisonous seeds, which will grow and become part of our reality. When we are aware and mindful of our thoughts, we can discipline ourselves to plant wholesome, beautiful and nutritious seeds in our mind that will be expressed outwardly in our lives. Either way, the seeds will grow, reproduce and manifest. We have a choice to either plant poisonous or nourishing mental seeds.

Why, with the power of choice, do we so often tend to imagine negative outcomes rather than positive ones?

This is because many of us are implanted with fear, apathy and other limiting programs that continually pull our minds into thoughts and visions of failure and defeat before we even try. Failure is easy—do nothing, risk nothing, begin nothing and you are likely to fail for having never tried. Failure is easy to imagine and takes very little risk or exposure to the unknown. On the other hand, success often takes vision, action, courage, commitment and discipline. Success has its risks, mistakes, failures, and unknowns, as well as its sweet victory. Almost everything we learned, we failed at before we learned it (e.g., learning to walk, ride a bike, swim, a language).

As Mark Twain wrote, *"I am an old man and have known a great many troubles, but most of them never happened."* Like Mark Twain, most of us worry about negative outcomes and most of the worry is wasted energy. Furthermore, the time and energy devoted to self-defeating visualization is time and energy taken away from visualizing and manifesting your most desired outcomes. It's important to note negative visualization will program the RAS to deliver that which we don't want.

Negative thoughts are a waste of imagination. It is important to become conscious of our limiting programs and thoughts when they arise and focus our mind on planting seeds that bear nourishing and beautiful fruits, such as the fruits of love, abundance, wellness and empowerment. In a universe of infinite possibility, we can choose the possibility most aligned with the achievement of our vision and program our minds and the RAS to fulfill our desires.

We are either focusing on what we want or what we don't want. Our minds generally cannot focus on both at the same time. What we feel, believe, take action upon and experience comes right back to us from the universe. We reap what we sow. If we're loving, we receive more love. If we're hateful, we receive more hate. If we're needy, we receive more need. If we're abundant, we receive more abundance.

By focusing our thoughts and energy on positive outcomes, the likelihood of manifesting positive outcomes dramatically increases. In order to create the life we desire and attract the resources we need, we must first use our imagination and the power of conscious choice to create our internal state of being. Embodying our imagination (feeling the imagined vision in our bodies) is the start of the process whereby vision becomes physical reality. As mentioned previously, the combination of imagination and physical reality is referred to as "Experiential Reality."

Since there is a thin veil between our imagination and our physical reality, the conscious and disciplined visualization of positive outcomes supported by a present state of gratitude results in real life experiences. These experiences increase our optimism, inspiration, joy and abundance. When we're in elevated and expanded states of being, we're much more able to attract and magnetize resources.

As soon as we imagine our desires and visions in detail, we have an internal cognitive experience that affects our vibration, life force and state of being (mental, emotional, physical, and energetic). Our subconscious and somatic consciousness accepts our visualizations as real experiences and supports us in turning our state of being into physical reality.

When we focus on a specific outcome and communicate that vision to the universe in the language of vibration through our *Vibratory Consciousness Centers* (body, mind, soul) and *Vibratory Receptors & Transmitters* (sensation, perception, thought, emotion, feeling, intuition and instinct), we energetically empower the field of infinite possibility to collapse possibilities into Experiential Reality. This, in turn, creates physical probabilities that, with consistent action, accelerate and exponentially increase the likelihood of a vision becoming a manifest physical reality. When we articulate our desired outcome and purpose outwardly to others and take actions consistent with our desired outcomes, the probability of successfully achieving our desired outcome again increases exponentially.

Since our vibratory states create feedback loops in concert with the universe, it's important to be conscious of our *Vibratory Receptors & Transmitters* and *Vibratory Consciousness Centers*. By choosing, for no reason whatsoever, to be unconditionally optimistic, joyful, abundant, loving, inspired and confident, we dramatically raise our emotional and spiritual vibration while exponentially increasing the likelihood of attracting people, resources and opportunities into our lives to help us manifest our vision.

Visualization + Positive Thought + Declaration + Aligned Consistent Action = Success

Since our external physical reality is a reflection of our internal reality, it's vital to discipline our mind and imagination in great detail and with caution, much like an engineer designing a rocket ship. We are the engineers of our lives and the more detail we envision, the greater the likelihood that our vision will manifest into a reality that aligns with our desires.

However, be careful what you ask for. We often adopt the conditioned Western capitalist version of "success" and "achievement" like making lots of money and own-ing lots of "stuff" (e.g., big homes, yachts, planes, fast cars, etc.). Still it's been proven, over and over again, that money and "stuff" doesn't create fulfillment or happiness. In fact, the acquisition of "stuff" often comes with debt, obligation and lack of freedom.

While money can provide convenience, sense of security and a degree of freedom, it can also become an addictive trap, (e.g. obsessing over money and allowing it to create fear and insecurity in our life). Most people want what money represents (e.g., love, connection, a safe and comfortable home, optimal health, true abundance, freedom, adventure, respect and admiration), rather than printed paper notes (money).

When envisioning your desires, it's important to listen to, and follow, your internal instinct, intuition and universal guidance to ensure that this powerful tool of manifestation is used in alignment with your core purpose, rather than one that's conditioned. When you visualize that which you want to attract, I invite you to go beyond the symbolism of money and "stuff," to that which you actually desire. Take into account how the manifestation of your desires will impact you, your family, friends, community and the world. Take a moment to go beyond the material definition of "success" in capitalist society and ask some deeper more human, qualitative and emotional questions:

- How does the fulfillment of my desires affect my relationships? Are they more loving and fulfilling? How does the fulfillment of my desires improve the quality of life beyond my own?

- What am I doing? How am I living? How am I being? What emotions am I feeling?

- What value am I creating for people and planet and how does it feel to be appreciated and acknowledged with equitable exchange for the value I am creating?

- How do I employ ethics and integrity in my dealings?

- Do I feel inspired, passionate, loving, joyful and expanded when I visualize manifesting my desires?

- Am I just collecting physical wealth or is there a deeper purpose to my desires? What good am I doing with my wealth? What purpose am I serving with my wealth? Is my wealth emotionally fulfilling? Am I hoarding my wealth at the expense of others or am I giving back in service to humanity?

In this journey, what we focus on is so important. While the acquisition of wealth, power and material possessions may be something you desire, it is vital to remember that what we experience is more important than what we have and our self-worth is more valuable than our net worth. Be clear on what you desire and how achieving your desires impacts the rest of the world. While focusing our thoughts on desired outcomes and engaging in creating an embodied Experiential Reality, programming the mind and RAS, it is vital that we take consistent action in alignment with our visions and desires. It's when we are in action, that we courageously improve ourselves, grow, gain wisdom and realize our dreams.

It is also important to understand that the universe requires us to "pay it forward" by first being internally abundant before we receive physical abundance. In other words, we need to be happy before the universe gives us happiness and we need to be abundant before the universe gives us abundance. We need to experience our wealth before it appears in physical form and to create value before we receive value. The beauty of paying it forward is that even if things don't work out exactly as we envision, we still increase the quality of our lives in each moment through experiencing states of optimism, joy, abundance, love, happiness, inspiration and confidence, as well as developing deep friendships. Moreover, if we trust in, and co-create with, the universe, we often receive much more than we envisioned.

True abundance and success arise when we follow our hearts, declare our purpose and take action consistent with our declared purposes. It's when we embody our purpose that we no longer pursue it. We become our purpose in action and get to experience the great passion, inspiration and growth that living a life of deep meaning and purpose has to offer.

CHAPTER 10

Quantum Multi-Dimensional Manifestation

"Choice, is what presents us with a multitude of paths, because choice creates a flow of electrons through the brain in a manner that inexorably leads to quantum superposition, and the many-worlds that are the inevitable result."

~Kevin Michel, Author of *Moving Through Parallel Worlds to Achieve Your Dreams*

Quantum **Multi-Dimensional Manifestation ("QMM")** is a powerful manifestation "technology" that goes beyond the "Law of AttrAction" to exponentially increase and accelerate your ability to create the life you desire, whether it be increasing your wealth, finding the love of your life, possessing optimal health, improving your communication, or creating a better world.

Utilizing QMM provides us with the ability to:

- Exponentially expand our awareness

- Increase intuition and make conscious choices in life

- Increase the power of imagination and manifestation

- Deepen our awareness of potential outcomes that exist simultaneously in parallel universes

- Tap into "future" outcomes and receive "blueprints" for achieving the highest potential from our future self

- Manifest "Experiential Realities" into physical realities with greater ease and clarity

- Live in synchronicity, flow and abundance

- Enter into a co-creative partnership with the universe

This chapter will provide a deeper understanding of the infinite potential of the universe and our power as co-creators of reality. The concepts discussed in this chapter include the following:

1. Expanded Multi-Dimensional Awareness

2. The Multiverse, Parallel Universes and Infinite Possibilities

3. Quantum Multi-Dimensional Manifestation

While these concepts are not mainstream and may appear esoteric, imaginative and futuristic, significant scientific research supports that these concepts are as real as the physical world we perceive. The universe is infinite, timeless and spaceless while also concurrently holding infinite physical and spatial realities.

According to Amedeo Balbi, cosmologist and author, *"In an infinite universe, every possible event does happen. Not just that: it happens an infinite number of times."* Quantum physicist, Brian Green, wrote, *"And in each universe, there's a copy of you witnessing one or the other outcome, thinking—incorrectly—that your reality is the only reality."*

Based upon the principles of quantum physics, QMM allows us to expand our beliefs and consciousness to include infinite parallel realities and possibilities. In this expanded state, we can directly access the power of visualization, imagination and manifestation used by billionaires, inventors and luminaries such as Albert Einstein, Michelangelo, Nikola Tesla, Isaac Newton, Alexander G. Bell, Oprah Winfrey and George Lucas.

For example, the great inventor, Nikola Tesla, would often have spontaneous visions for an invention or a solution to a particular problem he'd encountered. After receiving these visions, Tesla would visualize an invention in his mind with extreme precision, including all dimensions, from which his inventions were constructed.

Oprah, another luminary that utilizes visioning and co-creating with God, wrote:

> "Everyone has the power for greatness—not for fame but greatness, because greatness is determined by service." Even before I first heard my all-time favorite quote from Dr. Martin Luther King Jr., I knew in my heart that the message was true. As far back as I can recall, my prayer has been the same: "Use me, God. Show me how to take who I am, who I want to be, and what I can do, and use it for a purpose greater than myself."

> "All of us need a vision for our lives and even as we work to achieve the vision, we must surrender it to the power that is greater than we know. It's one of the defining principles of my life that I love to share: God can dream a bigger dream for you than you could ever dream for yourself. Success comes when you surrender to that dream—and let it lead you to the next best place."[93]

QMM engages the universe in co-creative collaboration with us to unlock the infinite possibilities and potential of parallel quantum realities concurrently existing in the universe at the present moment.

Kevin Michel, Author of _Moving Through Parallel Worlds to Achieve Your Dreams,_ articulates the concept of using parallel realities to create a desired future:

> "The 'Many-Worlds Interpretation of Quantum Mechanics' speaks to possibility and it speaks to opportunity. By appreciating its existence and adopting the paradigm of its existence, we start to realize that our future has infinite potentiality, and we realize that the 'Ideal Parallel World' of our dreams already exists along one path of our potential future; therefore our behaviors in the present can guide us to that Ideal Parallel World."

Michel's definition of "Many-Worlds Interpretation of Quantum Mechanics" opens up various possible outcomes as QMM aligns the creative power, consciousness and wisdom of the universe with our vision. **By trusting and surrendering to the universe and being fully open to receiving the infinite potential and miracles the universe offers, we enter into a co-creative relationship with the universe to synchronistically manifest existent parallel possibilities into this reality.**

Through QMM, we can tap into multi-dimensional realities by 1) utilizing imagination (the portal of cosmic consciousness) to access the parallel possibilities;

2) vividly experiencing the parallel possibilities as reality in the present dimension; 3) connecting with the version of the parallel "you" desired; 4) surrendering to the belief in potential infinite possibility; and 5) taking action based upon divine guidance in alignment with the present-future version of you.

Bill Bryson, author of _A Short History of Nearly Everything_, said, "_Energy is liberated matter, matter is energy waiting to happen._" QMM liberates the constructs of mind, body, space and time so the quantum energy of the universe can stop waiting and perform magic in our holographic physical world.

The "magic" of QMM is activated by the following 4 steps:

1. **Tap into the quantum field of infinite possibilities and parallel realities by opening to your imagination and allowing your imagination the freedom to guide you;**

2. **Clearly visualize the quantum reality most aligned with your soul and which feels the most energetically expansive and life-affirming (e.g., enthusiasm, inspiration, joy and bliss);**

3. **Embody the quantum multi-dimensional reality as an existent physical reality;**

4. **Fully surrender yourself to the co-creative relationship with the universe; and**

5. **Take action in alignment with universal/divine guidance to powerfully manifest your co-created reality.**

Once we free ourselves from the belief of a singular rigid physical "reality," we start to experience a world of infinite possibilities—a world that's inspiring, fun and creative. Through the dedicated use of QMM, we can experience a phenomenal playground to express ourselves as divinely creative humans—humans who can reach their highest potential.

As a foundation to exponentially increasing our power of manifestation with QMM, it's important to expand our consciousness beyond time and space to include Quantum Multi-Dimensional awareness and access to the infinite possibilities of the Multiverse and Parallel Universes.

1. EXPANDED MULTI-DIMENSIONAL AWARENESS

> *"The atoms or elementary particles themselves are not real; they form a*
> *world of potentialities or possibilities rather than one of things or facts."*
>
> ~Werner Heisenberg, Ph.D.

Luminaries of new physics, such as Albert Einstein, Max Tegmark, Michio Kaku, Stephen Hawking, Brian Greene, David Bohm, Ervin Laszlo, Werner Heisenberg and Fred Alan Wolf support that human potential goes far beyond the three-dimensional realities of space and the fourth dimension of time.

In order to expand our power of manifestation to a quantum co-creative relationship with the universe, it's foundational that we to expand our awareness beyond the four-dimensions of the phenomenally perceived physical world.

The term "dimension" is generally used to describe the parameters and characteristics of an experience that defines a condition, realm, form, environment or universe. "Dimension" as used in this chapter, refers to parameters and characteristics of our individual and collective experience of human reality in a universe of infinite possibilities and parallel realities.

Although mainstream consciousness supports that we live in a world of four-dimensions, including the three dimensions of **space** (height, width, depth) and the non-space fourth dimension of **time**, there are numerous dimensions and sub-dimensions influencing our human experience. Each of our five senses interacts and integrates with multiple dimensions (e.g., environmental, vibrational, conceptual, quantum and unknown) in creating our experience of physical reality. In order to expand our dimensional awareness, an overview of other dimensions to consider follows:

- **Sensory Dimensions** include the five senses of sight, hearing, smell, touch and taste. Instinct and intuition are often lumped together into the sixth sense. However, I posit that instinct and intuition can be categorized as two different senses as they each provide different sensing mechanisms. As well, each sensory dimension contains sub-dimensions.

Sensory Dimensions	
Sense	**Examples of Sensory Sub-Dimensions**
1 Sight	Height, Width, Depth, Brightness, Color, Hue
2 Hearing	Volume, Pitch, Brightness, Rhythm, Tone, Harmonics, Percussion
3 Smell	Flowery, Foul, Fruity, Burnt, Resinous, Spicy
4 Touch	Temperature, Pressure, Movement
5 Taste	Sweet, Salty, Umami, Bitter, Sour
6 Instinct	Feeling, Inner Knowing, Connectedness, Somatic Awareness, Empathy, Natural Guidance
7 Intuition	Energetic Consciousness, Divine Connection, Vibratory Feedback, Super-Consciousness, Universal Guidance, Clairvoyance, Clairaudience, Clairsentience and Multi-Dimensional Awareness

- **Environmental Dimensions** include those forces that effect our environmental experience of reality (e.g., gravity, air, water, earth, sunshine, barometric pressure).

- **Vibrational Dimensions** comprise all vibrations and movement in the universe from which we sense, perceive and create reality (e.g., energy, magnetism, sound waves, light waves, microwaves, neural transmission, energetic resonance).

- **Conceptual Dimensions** consist of those things perceived, conceived, thought, dreamt or imagined. Conceptual dimensions transcend the agreed and provable phenomenal "reality" of space and time (e.g., cosmic consciousness, imagination, dreams, visions, thoughts and emotions).

- **Quantum Dimensions** are those dimensions that convert potential into vibrations, waves, particles, forces and matter and vice versa. (e.g., supergravity, strings, zero-point, infinity, potential, the paradox of the simultaneous wave and particle, and entanglement)

- **Unknown Dimensions** include the many undiscovered and incomprehensible dimensions affecting our reality that aren't understood or described at present.

The foregoing dimensions concurrently interact with each other to create our holographic reality. Many of these dimensions are beyond the realm of the consciousness, cognitive understanding, the perception of our senses, and our language to communicate. Yet we can, and often do, experience these dimensions as we create our perceived Experiential Reality. Carl Jung said, *"The unconscious has no time. There is no trouble about time in the unconscious. Part of our psyche is not in time and not in space. They are only an illusion, time and space, and so in a certain part of our psyche time does not exist at all."*

We often mistakenly believe that our mind's interpretation of our phenomenal sensory data and linear experience of time accurately reflects physical "reality." However, our senses limit the full dimensional experience of the perceived physical world. Our entire physical being, including our brain, processes an estimated 38 quadrillion bits of information per second.[94] Even as large as this stream of information sounds, it's a small sampling of all the information existing in our environment that doesn't make it past the limitations of our sensory filters. And as discussed previously, this seemingly massive amount of information is further limited and constrained to 400 billion bits of information per second by the Reticular Activating System (RAS) before this information is processed by the brain. Remember, the amount of information that makes it to our cognitive awareness is only 2000 bits of information per second.[95]

One of the most notable concepts of quantum physics is the *"Wave-Particle Duality,"* which holds that all elemental particles (e.g., electrons, protons, neutrons, atoms, and molecules) exhibit the properties of both particles and waves. They behave like waves when they're not observed, and like particles when observed. When an observation is made, the wave state changes from a vibratory wave state into a physical particle state. Thus, our observation and intention create our physical reality.[96]

As we create our physical reality, we perceptually filter "the wave" of information flowing from the universe by sensorially sampling packets of data as "particles." The particles are "extracted" from the massive wave of infinite vibration and consciousness, and transformed into electrical impulses. From here, they are further filtered and then rearranged, fabricated and imagined into the "reality" we each experience.

Much like a film, where still photo frames are rolled through a projector at 24 frames per second and appear to depict the fluid motion of life, we capture momentary particle samples from a cosmic wave of information through our senses. From these limited momentary particle samples, we create what appears to be a fluid human reality—"*the holographic projection of our life.*"

Our perceptive and cognitive filters shape our "reality" by influencing which information gets through to the perceiving mind. When we filter out information that doesn't fit into our conditioned experience of life, it's called "perceptual blindness."[97] Perceptual blindness is largely due to societal and self-imposed belief systems and conditioning that limit our experience of reality and our capacity for expanded consciousness. The artificial filters of consciousness that limit expanded possibilities include conditioning, beliefs, culture, environment and the Global Human Agreement.

Humankind has largely been conditioned to perceive the physical world (e.g., people, animals, plants, physical structures, Earth's elements) as real and existent, while the etheric world (e.g., aliens, spirits, psychic powers, dreams, visions, energetic beings and divine forces) is often considered imaginary, non-existent, strange, "woo-woo," unpragmatic and/or abnormal. These limiting beliefs and perceptions of reality suppress our ability to be divine creators of an expanded reality in a universe of infinite possibility.

In a quantum world of infinite possibility, we are, in essence, a wave of infinite consciousness and potential subjectively experiencing itself as a particle of collapsed experiential reality in space and time. In other words, while having our phenomenal human experience, we are also simultaneously infinite consciousness and potential. **When the particle of human experience dissolves into the infinite wave, we have access to anything and everything we can imagine, as well as that beyond our imagination and cognitive awareness.**

By expanding our multi-dimensional awareness beyond societal conditioning and the mainstream limited view of reality, we can exponentially increase our possibilities, creative abilities, access to consciousness and powers to manifest a life beyond our dreams.

In addition to expanding our dimensional awareness, QMM can be used expand our awareness to infinite quantum realities taking place within and beyond space and time. This brings us to the subject of *"The Multiverse, Parallel Universes and Infinite Possibilities."*

2. THE MULTIVERSE, PARALLEL UNIVERSES AND INFINITE POSSIBILITIES

In his Scientific American article entitled *Parallel Universes*, Dr. Max Tegmark wrote, *"In infinite space, even the most unlikely events must take place somewhere. There are infinitely many other inhabited planets, including not just one but infinitely many that have people with the same appearance, name and memories as you, who play out every possible permutation of your life choices."*

The effectiveness of QMM is directly proportional to the expansion of our dimensional awareness and openness to unlimited potential. If it can be imagined, it exists in a parallel dimension. For example, in less than ten seconds, I can imagine growing wings, flying to the sun and back, transforming into a unicorn and exploding into a galaxy. While this imaginative scenario seems impossible in our linear and physical reality, that set of events just happened in the dimension of my imaginative universe, and, according to Tegmark, actually took place somewhere in the universe of infinite possibility. The universe is like an always-on and ever-adjusting combination of possibilities. Our consciousness is a product of our experiences and perceptions, as limited or expanded by our belief systems, thoughts and transcendent ability. The key to increasing the effectiveness of QMM is to consistently remove limitations, expand our experience of reality, increase multi-dimensional awareness, trust our intuition, free our imaginations, and align with divine guidance.

In our dimensional experience, every thought, choice and action causes the collapse of infinite possibilities into a set of seemingly finite probabilities we experience as a singular linear dimensional reality. However, all the thoughts, choices and actions we didn't experience in this reality are experienced in other simultaneous parallel universes at different space-time coordinates. Our limited mind-synthesized reality creates the illusion of a single linear time-space life that has a beginning, middle and end. However, in addition to the perceived beginning, middle and end, there exists infinite, parallel permutations of our life occurring simultaneously in *Parallel Universes*, all of which are contained in a single *Multiverse*.

The term *"Multiverse"* refers to the infinite possible universes that comprise all that potentially exists. The various universes within the Multiverse are referred to as "*Parallel Universes*."[98]

According to the *Multiverse* theory, each moment, an identical "you" exists in a parallel universe. For example, in a parallel universe, there is another "you" reading this paragraph—this person is an exact replica of you living on an exact replica of our planet.[99] The life of this person has been identical to your life in every aspect up to this moment, when he or she decides to stop reading the rest of this chapter while you read on. The moment that exact replica thinks a different thought, makes a different decision or takes a different action, another version of you continues to experience the reality of that version of you.

There is not just one copy of you in a single parallel universe, but rather an infinite number of copies of you in an infinite number of parallel universes. Each parallel universe contains one possible permutation of you among an infinite number of permutations of you. Now expand the possibilities beyond the mechanical laws of physics governing our reality into infinite possibilities and combinations. We currently have an estimated 7.5 billion people on this planet, with each person creating an infinite number of permutations and combinations each moment in a universe of infinite possibilities. Now take each permutation and put it in its own parallel universe. Then take the permutations just from our own little planet Earth and multiply that by an estimated 20 billion earth-like planets in the Milky Way galaxy, which is one of 100 billion galaxies. My mind just blew a fuse!

Perhaps in order to keep us from blowing a fuse in our futile attempt to cognitively grasp the infinite combinations and permutations of the ineffable universe, we experience only one version of ourselves at a time. This one version provides our limited minds with one "reality" that appears linear, stable and predictable. The universe, however, is simultaneously linear and non-linear, stable and unstable as well as chaotic and ordered.

Although we understand that anything is possible, we live in a "reality" largely focused on what is probable rather than what is possible. These probabilities are based upon our evolutionary path, our conditioning, and the self-imposed linearity of our lives. The universe, however, is more like our imagination and operates outside of space and time, where any combination of events is possible. Moreover, in a "universe of infinite possibilities," there is also the possibility that there is no universe, no infinity and/or no possibility.

All possibilities relating to each form, exist in a timeless, spaceless, non-form-based consciousness and fold into a perceived "reality" of time and space as a result of the self-aware and fractalized consciousness in the process of self-realization.

The dimension representing the current human experience of planet Earth, occurs at a specific space-time-frequency vector defined by the "holographic matrix," which contains the information, parameters and principals upon which we create our dimensional reality. The holographic matrix defines the parameters of our perceived world and also contains infinite stacks of different parallel universes concurrently co-existing at different frequencies, but conforming to the same dimensional parameters and principles. In addition to our holographic matrix, there are an infinite number of dimensional realities with different frequencies, principles and parameters.

All these possibilities and permutations exist simultaneously, and yet we experience our physical existence as a linear space-time reality within the limitations of our (1) phenomenal senses, which are set to receive stimuli within a limited a range in accordance with our dimensional container, (2) our perception, and (3) our intellectual and imaginative capacity as constrained by our beliefs, context, culture and consciousness.

Nobel laureate Steven Weinberg likens this multiple universe theory to a radio where different stations are being broadcast simultaneously on different frequencies, but we only hear the station to which our radio dial is tuned. In this radio analogy, we concurrently share space and time with an infinite number of parallel realities broadcasting at their own frequency. All of these frequencies are stacked within the planet Earth frequency band and each of us is tuned into the radio station experience broadcasting on the frequency our individual tuner is set to receive. When we expand our consciousness to include infinite possibilities and apply QMM, we access our ability to increase our frequency range and the bands in which those frequencies operate, thereby enhancing the ability of our receiver to pick up more stations. We also increase our power of quantum awareness and expression (e.g., amplitude), thereby expanding our consciousness, creativity, possibilities and power of manifestation.

QMM works in a similar manner to "*Quantum Entanglement*." Quantum Entanglement holds that if two electrons were created at the same time and you jiggle an electron on one side of the universe, an invisible force instantaneously traverses millions of light-years and sets another electron into a resonant jiggling motion. Since all electrons were theoretically created simultaneously in the "big bang" or the "*Big Divine Awakening*", the entire universe emanated from the same original source and there's interconnectivity and among all things in the universe.[100] Just like Quantum Entanglement, when we tap into the unified quantum "field" our influence and choices affect and shape the entire universe.

Another widely adopted quantum experiment relevant to QMM is known as "*The Copenhagen Interpretation*." Using the Double Slit Experiment, The Copenhagen Interpretation holds that all particles exist as waves of probability. The Double Slit Experiment shows that a photon, fired at a plate with two slits in it, when observed will sometimes go through the right slit, sometimes through the left slit. However, if nobody is observing, the photon goes through both slits simultaneously (meaning, a single thing will be in two places at once). It's from the cloud of non-observing possibility that, through our perceptions, observations and beliefs, we create our reality.[101]

Additionally, the infamous *Schrodinger's Cat* experiment posits that if you put a cat in a box, then press a button that has a 50% chance of filling the box with poison gas, the cat exists as a "cat-cloud" simultaneously both alive and dead until you look in the box. In summary, this means that if everything exists as a probability wave, then anything possible could happen at any time and our desire and creative consciousness effects the outcome we experience.[102]

Furthermore, the *Many Worlds Theory* introduced by Hugh Everett III replaces *The Copenhagen Interpretation's* theory that particles can change their behavior seemingly at will with a bit more esoteric idea. Under *The Copenhagen Interpretation*, the reason we think particles are changing their behavior is because we're only seeing that particle's action in one universe, rather than the infinite number of universes. So an observed particle with two options—for instance going through the right slit or the left slit can also go through both slits and actually does all three.

The Many-Worlds Theory implies that the universal wavefunction is objectively real and that all possible alternative histories and futures are real—each representing an actual "world" (or "universe"). This implication of this theory is that there is no wave function collapse and that all possible outcomes of quantum measurements are physically realized in some "world" or universe.

A simple explanation of the implications of The Many Worlds Theory is that for every action you've ever taken, every thought you have had, down to the movement of every atom in your being, there's a parallel universe where an infinite number of your doppelgangers did something else instead.[103]

Another theory relevant to QMM is the *Many Minds Interpretation*. According to H. Dieter Zeh, Professor Emeritus and theoretical physicist of the University of Heidelberg, the Many Minds Interpretation posits that we have many minds and the moment our brain makes an observation, an infinite number of parallel brains observe every possible outcome.[104] The Many Minds Interpretation distinguishes itself from Everett's Many Worlds Interpretation upon the theory that it is observer's mind that is branching rather than many worlds branching at each quantum decision point.[105] It is likely that both (1) infinite worlds exist concurrently, and (2) the mind, upon choosing an outcome or world, creates the existence of a singular Experiential Reality in the linear human and individual timeline of this dimension.

Quantum physics supports that we live in a Multiverse of infinite possibility. Using QMM, we can powerfully tap into this infinite creative power of the universe to affect our potential outcomes and exponentially, synchronously and synergistically increase the manifestation of our visions.

3. QUANTUM MULTI-DIMENSIONAL MANIFESTATION

"If you obsess over whether you are making the right decision, you are basically assuming that the universe will reward you for one thing and punish you for another.

The universe has no fixed agenda. Once you make any decision, it works around that decision. There is no right or wrong, only a series of possibilities that shift with each thought, feeling, and action that you experience.

If this sounds too mystical, refer again to the body. Every significant vital sign— body temperature, heart rate, oxygen consumption, hormone level, brain activity, and so on- alters the moment you decide to do anything... decisions are signals telling your body, mind, and environment to move in a certain direction."

~Deepak Chopra

As Chopra suggests, the universe is much like an infinite combination generator that changes as you change—creating new combinations and realities based upon each decision you make and action you take.

QMM is a powerful manifestation "technology" that utilizes our co-creative abilities with infinite possibilities in a way that exponentially increases our ability to create the life we desire now and in our perceived future.

Computer scientist, Alan Kay, said, *"The best way to predict the future is to invent it."*

The conscious, integral and powerful approach to manifestation using QMM provides us with the greatest potential for "inventing our future," living the life of our dreams and experiencing great fulfillment. However, many people lack the tools to tap into multi-dimensional reality and receive the divine guidance to powerfully co-create their lives in alignment with their higher, most life-fulfilling purpose.

Most of us have been conditioned to accept a limited reality in our lives based upon such things as going to school, getting a job, earning money, buying a car, buying a house, buying stuff to fill our house, getting married, having kids, retiring and dying. While these things may be in alignment with the highest expression of many humans in this dimension, many of us are unaware of other options and don't question this limited reality or seek our true and highest expression. Most of us, including me, were not trained to be "quantum manifesters," but rather were taught to conform to a limited reality, using linear approaches of achieving our goals in the physical world such as intention, will, cognitive intelligence and brute force. While these linear approaches can potentially lead to the outcome you desire (or were conditioned to believe you desire), it's often a slow, inefficient and uncreative process. Using QMM accelerates the process of creative and quantum manifestation. I'm still a student of QMM and still get caught in my conditioning. However, when I consistently practice QMM on a daily basis, magic happens and my ability to practice and expand beyond my conditioned limitation increases exponentially.

As we practice QMM, the following will help us to dismantle our limited and linear conditioning to learn new ways of being and creating:

- Use the imagination and reflexive nature of the universe to create from infinite possibility and potential
- Clearly visualize, embrace and embody creative potential and miracles as realities
- Be in inquiry and at peace with the unknown rather than requiring the answer
- Align with, listen to, trust and follow universal wisdom and guidance
- Be present and in this moment embody the state of being you seek to experience (e.g., enthusiastic, grateful, joyful, fulfilled, inspired)
- Elevate love, courage and creativity over fear, limitation and conformity
- Practice equanimity rather than attachment to a specific outcome
- Embrace the challenges that make us more loving, compassionate, grateful, wise and able to receive the gifts of quantum universal co-creation
- Possess a deep knowing and certainty that the universe is working in powerful ways beyond our linear comprehension to create that which we truly desire
- Accept and surrender to what is while allowing for miracles and transformation

In order to communicate this new way of manifesting with QMM, I use the analogy of raising your arm. Unless you're suffering from neuromuscular or other impairment, when you intend to raise your arm, you merely intend it, and your arm raises easily and naturally. It doesn't take a great deal of cognitive mental focus and affirmations. You don't concentrate your mind on the numerous tiny linear neuromuscular and other systemic functions that must happen, nor do you say repetitive affirmations or pray to get your arm to raise. There's a certain knowing that your arm will raise *reflexively* just by your intending to do so.

While the neuromuscular memory required to raise your arm was learned over a period of time, when each of us were born, we came equipped with a universal memory embedded in our *Vibratory Receptors & Transmitters* and *Vibratory Consciousness Centers* that represents the "*Quantum Neuromuscular System*" of the universe. Using the *Quantum Neuromuscular System* we can reflexively manifest our desires with ease like raising our arm. While simple, it's not necessarily easy to do, especially given our conditioning. Just like walking or riding a bike, using QMM generally takes learning, discipline and practice. The primary tools of universal co-creation and communication are intuition, instinct and imagination. To access our intuition, instinct and imagination, we need to breathe, become present, quiet our mind chatter, conditioning and self-limiting beliefs, and dissolve into the creative universal oneness. When accessing our intuition, instinct and imagination, we open up a direct communication pipeline with the "*Quantum Neuromuscular System*" leading to much greater ease in engaging in co-creative manifestation.

QMM provides us with a miraculous vehicle powered by universal energy, infinite possibility and a highly effective navigation system guided by divine wisdom. Manifestations arise from using QMM through trust that the universe is working to provide each of us with the most fulfilling experiences in life. Sometimes these experiences show up as challenges that help us grow stronger, wiser, more compassionate and loving. This requires joyful surrender, acceptance and gratitude. When we're in the present state of joyful surrender, acceptance and gratitude, we're able to more effectively embrace the playful, creative and divine nature of our being and more easily access the *Quantum Neuromuscular System*.

Each of us has the potential to live this human experience as fully realized divine beings. This is done by dissolving the veils and limitations of linear physical reality and living in an expanded multi-dimensional reality that gives us the ability to create with much greater ease and agility. This again is often simple, but not easy, as dissolving the layers of ego, conditioning, beliefs and habits can be quite challenging.

As mentioned, every form is unified and one within the cosmic consciousness of all possibility and holds the potential of all possibility. In the state of QMM, we align our consciousness with eternal cosmic consciousness. This expands our horizon beyond our belief systems, opening us to a world of astounding new and expanded multi-dimensional realities and powers of manifestation.

Unlocking the power QMM requires the following fundamentals:

- Tapping into infinite possibilities parallel universal realities
- Establishing a co-creative relationship with the universe
- Utilizing the power of imagination and visualization
- Surrendering to universal guidance and following intuition and instinct
- Dissolving egoic limitations to access universal co-creative consciousness and utilize the reflexivity of the *Quantum Neuromuscular System*.

I've used QMM many times in my life with astounding results. These results include, creating the first company in history to sell digital music files online and taking it public; visualizing and attracting amazing soul mates into my life; synchronously manifesting collaborators and investors for projects; instantaneously healing myself; and creating surfing waves in fairly flat ocean conditions.

QMM is a state of being where creation occurs without striving, doubt, pursuing or even trying, just as easy as raising your arm, taking a breath or the next thought entering your mind.

As mentioned, I'm still a student of QMM and have found it to be both magical and illusive. It is simple, but often not easy. There is a certain state of being and consciousness in which QMM operates. The more I practice QMM, the greater its effectiveness and results. QMM is somewhat paradoxical as commitment to the practice and the guidance takes discipline, consistency and action. Somewhat ironically, the practice itself is about releasing anything resembling discipline, consistency and action by surrendering to the emergence of, and becoming, that which you embody. In essence, QMM is a state of oneness with the universe, and a knowing beyond all doubt that, without striving, pursuing, intent or attachment to an outcome, what you envision has already happened, is happening and will happen, beyond any sense of time or spatial physicality. It is simple, easy and reflexive when you are in the zone. Getting into "the zone" is the challenging part.

The following is a protocol that can be used to guide us into "the zone" of QMM:

1. Surrender into a state of pure imagination. Let go of any and all limitations and restricting beliefs, including your physical form and identity.

The imagination is the portal to infinite possibility. Just about every invention of humankind was originated in the imagination. By entering the state of pure imagination and letting go of all limitations and conditions, you can create anything you desire in your imagination. If you want to create it, just imagine it.

The first step of QMM is to dissolve and let go of limiting and conditional beliefs. Next, let go of all attachment to your identity—your body and its needs, your possessions, your job, your family, looking good, what others think of you, and your inner critic's self-defeating chatter. Let your imagination run completely wild. See how effortlessly and quickly you can create in your imagination—you can instantly become or do anything or be anywhere in the universe or beyond. Allow yourself to be silly and have fun by creating the most unusual combinations you can imagine. Play with this a bit. Stay in this state of pure unlimited imagination for at least five minutes. The longer the better. By putting ourselves into the state of unlimited possibility, we exponentially expand our consciousness and creativity to invite new opportunities into our lives. In this state of imaginative consciousness and creativity, we have amazing powers of attraction and manifestation.

2. Guide your awareness to objectively observe and embody the myriad versions of you as a human on Earth and become aware of the attributes, characteristics and experiences of each.

This is much like trying on clothes. You slip into and out of different forms and versions of you in parallel universes. While slipping into and out of versions of you, experience yourself as having the unlimited potential to observe, occupy, manifest and experience form without attachment, identification or judgment. There are versions of you that made different choices and ended up with different lives. What are these versions of you doing with their lives? What activities are they engaged in? What are you, as another version, seeing, smelling, hearing, feeling and tasting? What thoughts are you thinking? Who are you spending time with? Where and how are you living? What emotions are you feeling? Objectively take in all the details and experience Can you equanimously hold and accept these experiences objectively without attachment or judgment?

3. Become aware of the shift in your consciousness and body as you try on different forms of yourself.

Notice, as you "try on" different forms of you, that certain versions of you are experiencing expansiveness, connectedness, inspiration, bliss, love and co-creation with the universe, while other versions of you are contracted, limited, struggling and disconnected. As you experience each form of you going about his or her activities, become aware of the vibrational experience of the *Vibratory Receptors & Transmitters* and *Vibratory Consciousness Centers* of each version of you. What sympathetic and resonant vibrations occur in you as the observer and experiencer of these different forms? What feelings arise in your body? Does your body expand or contract in the form you're experiencing? What emotions are you experiencing? Is the experience increasing energy or sucking energy? What thoughts arise? When you experience the version of you that expands and inspires you the most, merge with that version of you and take on the personality, characteristics and experiences of this version of you. You may also find attributes and qualities (e.g., personalities, experiences, characteristics, wisdom) you desire in several versions of you. Take note of these.

There is a version of you that embodies and aggregates the attributes you desire in a single version of you.

4. Choose and embody the version of you that holds the most expansive, highest and resonant vibration. This is your "Highest Potential Self." Trust completely in the guidance of, and merger with, your Highest Potential Human Self.

As you experience the different versions of you, you'll develop an intuitive knowing and recognize that a version of you contains the most expansive, resonant, highest and life-enhancing attributes for your human experience and thriving. This is known as your *"Highest Potential Self."* When you merge with your *Highest Potential Self,* you then are able to embody attributes and qualities of your *Highest Potential Self.* Take time to allow the merging your *Highest Potential Self* to saturate your being.

After merging with your Highest Potential Self in the realm of imagination and Experiential Reality, you may experience a shift from limitless and formless imagination back into physical density as you return to your accustomed physical human form. You may find that you revert to your genetic coding, space-time reality, conditioning, and habitual ways of being. Nonetheless, you will also notice a transformative and evolutionary shift. As you consistently devote yourself to the practice of embodying your Highest Potential Self, the more profound, rapid and permanent the shifts become, until we are consistently living as our Highest Potential Self.

To merge with your Highest Potential Self requires an unwavering commitment to following the path of your Highest Potential Human Self. This takes a great deal of awareness, discipline and consistent practice. When you consistently and impeccably follow and adopt the "blueprint" and attributes of your Highest Potential Self, you start to merge with your Highest Potential Self. In order to manifest your Highest Potential Self into this physical reality requires sensitivity to, and awareness of, the experiences and attributes of your Highest Potential Self. Use this awareness to shift your Vibratory Receptors & Transmitters and Vibratory Consciousness Centers and reprogram your RAS and your quantum field to align with the attributes of the Highest Potential Self.

The practice of being our Highest Potential Self requires that we release our minds and every cell in our body from negativity, doubt, limitations, conditions, phobias and fears, such as the fear of being ostracized by our friends, family and society, fear of failure and fear of death. Once we're no longer shackled by the confines of generational conditioning, fear and limitations, we achieve another level of freedom and mastery in embodying our Highest Potential Self.

5. Manifest your reality in alignment with your Highest Potential Human Self using the reflexive nature of the universe.

We are simultaneously the creator, as well as the "experiencer" of all reality we create. By regularly taking time to remind ourselves that we are the creator of our reality, we can powerfully align our human experience with universal forces to create the life of our dreams in integrity with, and as the expression of, our Highest Potential Self.

When we use QMM to manifest from an unlimited place of creativity and feel our timeline and reality merging with that of our Highest Potential Self, the universe aligns to create the environment, circumstances, people and resources required for us to realize living as our Highest Potential Self.

Once we fully embody the Highest Potential Self and utilize QMM, we become able to make clear decisions based upon our experience and understanding of future occurrences in existence in other dimensions that already exist and how we, as our Highest Potential Self, manifested and achieved these outcomes. Our abilities to manifest these already existing futures are accelerated and exponentiated as a result of using QMM.

Using QMM, we then let go of the struggle, the mental concentration, the attachment to outcomes and just reflexively manifest our highest desires at will.

SECTION THREE –

WELLNESS

Wellness is the experience of optimal physical, mental, emotional, spiritual/energetic and social/fiscal health. Our wellness is one of our most precious gifts. When we are well, we can thrive and experience a full and vital life and yet so many of us don't appreciate the gift until it is gone. By integrating a wellness practice into our daily lives, we can increase our vitality and thriving.

CHAPTER 11

M.E.D.I.C.I.N.E.

(The New Prescription for Wellness)

We are a miraculous and complex species whose health and wellness is depen-
dent upon a myriad of interconnected and interdependent ecosystemic
dynamics. These dynamics include our environment; our genes; microbes;
our diet; our beliefs; our relationships with each other and our planet; as
well as our physical, emotional, mental and energetic states of being. Thus,
if we are to possess optimal health and wellness, we must embrace a life-
style and practice that holistically integrates and enhances the ecosystemic
factors that promote our individual, societal and planetary well-being.

The miracle of life goes on inside and around us—energizing, breathing and living us. We have little cognitive awareness of the seven octillion (billion-billion-billion) atoms and the 37 trillion cells engaging in about 6 trillion transactions per second that sustain each of our human lives.[106]

Our DNA and RNA transform amino acids into chains of positively and negatively charged proteins that animate life to create living cells. During our lives, we are in a constant process of change, adaptation, resilience and regeneration. For example, we regenerate a new stomach lining every four days, our skin every five weeks and our livers every six weeks. We rebuild our entire skeletal structure every three months and recreate our entire body, down to the last atom, every five to seven years. When we inhale, the oxygen that autonomically flows into our lungs is absorbed by the bloodstream and the cells. When we exhale, carbon dioxide from our cells is processed through the bloodstream and released into the atmosphere. We convert food into glucose and electrical energy through the digestive process and the Krebs cycle. Our immune and endocrine systems defend our bodies against dangerous bacteria, viruses, fungus, parasites and microbes, eliminate toxins and repair damage from electromagnetic bombardment and radiation.[107]

Among the myriad of miraculous interactions and interconnections happening each second, upon which we rely for our life, health and thriving, here are just a few examples:

- The breath and air that keeps us alive is largely due to phytoplankton. Often referred to as "the planet's most important organism," phytoplankton is a one-celled photosynthetic plant that produces 50% of the Earth's oxygen and an efficient storage sink for carbon dioxide. It is also the main source of food for herbivorous marine creatures and 16% of animal protein consumption by humans comes from fish. Our lives and health depend on phytoplankton, yet human activities causing climate change and ocean acidification are destroying phytoplankton.[108]

- The mitochondria in our cells convert glucose to adenosine triphosphate ("ATP"), a source of chemical energy. Without mitochondria, an organelle strikingly similar to bacteria, we would die.[109]

- Honeybees don't just make honey. They pollinate more than 90% of flowering food crops, including most fruits, nuts, avocados, soybeans, asparagus, broccoli, celery, squash and cucumbers.[110] In fact, about one-third of the human diet comes from insect-pollinated plants, and the honeybee is responsible for 80 percent of that pollination, according to the U.S. Department of Agriculture. Colony Collapse Disorder, that has wiped out 10 million honey bee hives, was caused primarily by the use of insecticides, pesticides and fungicides.[111] It's predicted the lack of honeybees will result in a massive food crisis. Greenpeace estimates the natural work done by honeybees is worth $300 billion annually. Preserving and sustaining the life of bees is of tantamount importance to our species.

- The life-giving interconnection between gravitational forces of the universe keeping our planet in orbit; the warmth and energy of the sun; the abundance of the Earth's oceans, watersheds and soil; and the air we breathe; and regeneration of our biosphere.

- The experience of life and self-awareness that converts consciousness and vibrations into an experiential phenomenal reality we call "life."

We are part of a larger "ecosystem" that includes not only our planet and its myriad of interconnected cellular and non-cellular organisms, elements, molecules, and atoms, but also the moon, sun, stars and the cosmos. We are also dependent upon the vibrational quantum energy field and consciousness aka "life force" that keeps the universe spinning and miraculously generates, animates and maintains all life within it. Concurrently, we each are an ever-changing, self-aware universe of cells, energy, consciousness, atoms and bio-energetic systems, as well as a habitat for bacteria, viruses, parasites, fungus and other microbes. In fact, the ratio for the average human is 1.3 microbes to every 1 human cell.[112] Our society is essentially a collection of individuals living in relationship to each other, the planet and the cosmos in an interconnected and interdependent ecosystem.

The ecosystem contains the potential to synergistically optimize or compromise our health, adaptability, resilience and regenerability. Our health and thriving is directly proportional to the quality of the interconnected and symbiotic relationship with the ecosystem. Thus, improving the health of the ecosystem improves our health.

The complex interactions, interconnections and systems that support our ecosystem and the miracle of life are beyond our cognitive comprehension. While there is only one whole (the entire universe), from our anthropocentric perspective, we tend to view life as compartmentalized interconnected *"Nested Wholes."* For example, we have a tendency to divide the universe into galaxies, solar systems and planets. We then divide our planet into continents, countries and states. We separate ourselves from nature (e.g., "people and planet") and further separate ourselves from each other with the *Nested Wholes* of culture, race, religion, gender, age, geography and ideology. We further divide ourselves into biomechanical systems (e.g., cardiovascular, digestive, immune, skeletal) and then into cells, elements, molecules and atoms.

While using *Nested Wholes* to help us perceive, understand and order our world into a reality that is assimilable, *Nested Wholes* can also lead to non-integrated, exclusionary or anthropocentric arrogance. For example, the exclusionary and reductionist approach used by allopathic medicine often sees humans and life on this planet as biomechanical-chemical systems rather than as unique bioenergetic miracles interconnected with, and interdependent on, each other, this planet and the universe. In the Oxford Medical Journal article entitled *Medical reductionism: lessons of great philosophers,*[113] Mark Beresford writes:

> *"It is not only in the laboratory where reductionism pervades. The evidence-based medicine (EBM) movement has effectively taken over as the dominant force in medical research, from the design and reporting of trials, through the development of treatment guidelines to the funding and commissioning of new drugs. However, the generally accepted universality and objectivity of EBM comes at a cost—clinical problems must be defined in heavily simplified terms to enable randomized controlled trials and meta-analyses. This reductionism requires complex entities to be simplified as quantitative units to which statistical methods can be applied. Clinical researchers constantly strive to subdivide patients into defined groups in order to test which will benefit most from a particular treatment option. The uniformity of practice that ensues might be too crude to apply to an individual patient's experience."*

The evidence-based reductionist method, as applied in allopathic medicine, too often excludes the emotional, natural, environmental, experiential, energetic, and ecosystemic aspects of health. While scientific method has its benefits, it has its limitations. For example, science has yet to prove love or the quality of emotion, but has proven that those who receive positive mental, emotional and spiritual support have greater health and heal more quickly. According to Dr. Bruce Lipton, author of *The Biology of Belief: Unleashing the Power of Consciousness, Matter and Miracles,*

> *"A renaissance in cellular biology has recently revealed the molecular mechanisms by which thoughts and perceptions directly influence gene activity and cell behavior...Energy psychology, through its ability to rapidly identify and reprogram*

limiting misconceptions, represents the most powerful and effective process to enhance physical and emotional well-being."

As is supported by Dr. Bruce Lipton, in our journey to possessing optimal wellness, **it's important to be inclusive and holistic—integrating science and technology into a framework that includes the miracles, beliefs, environment, emotions, energy, ecosystemic interconnection and the qualitative aspects of life.**

Our experience and quality of life is largely dependent upon our present state of being. Our state of being is directly related to, and influences, our wellness. The most direct and profound impact on our wellness include our **physical, mental, emotional, environmental, spiritual/energetic and social/fiscal** states of being (hereinafter *"Foundational States of Well-being").*

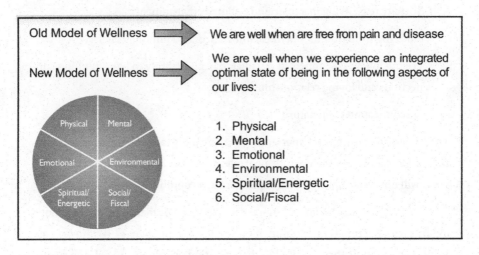

Our current healthcare system tends to focus on a myopic biomechanical and physical approach to health rather than an integrated holistic approach to optimal wellness.

Optimal wellness requires a holistic approach that integrates and consistently elevates our *"Foundational States of Well-being."* For example, if we exercise, eat well and meditate, but breathe polluted air, drink toxic water and spend our days sitting indoors under fluorescent lights at a stressful job, our wellness will likely be compromised and not optimal.

The following are ten examples of factors that often degrade and impede optimal wellness:

1. Stress, fear, anxiety, and constrictive emotions

2. Poor diet and nutrition

3. Sedentary lifestyle and lack of exercise

4. Lack of sleep, rest and rejuvenation

5. Resistance, constriction, and blockages that slow and limit access to abundant flows of energy and vitality

6. Feeling unfulfilled, failing to realize your potential and living out of alignment with purpose, by working a job you dislike

7. Toxicity (e.g., living in a toxic and polluted environment)

8. Suffering from trauma, chemical imbalances and limiting beliefs

9. Feeling lonely, disconnected or isolated (e.g., Inability to have fulfilling connections and loving relationships)

10. Disconnection from nature

A person consistently experiencing the foregoing is not likely to possess optimal wellness and all of the doctors, pharmaceuticals, scalpels and radiation in the world will not create optimal wellness under such conditions.

Optimal wellness requires a commitment to a lifestyle that holistically promotes and integrates optimal functioning of our *Foundational States of Well-being* with positive ecosystemic thriving. Rather than focusing on killing and fighting against bacteria, fungus and viruses, optimal wellness focuses on strengthening our immune systems, improving the quality of our lives and the thriving of our ecosystem.

Unfortunately, our society and the western healthcare system have largely disconnected from nature and arrogantly ignored the ecosystemic wisdom of our planet and ancient health practices. Rather than promoting the holistic thriving of all life and optimal human wellness, our industrialized society and healthcare system have too often attempted to fight against, control, eradicate and destroy earth's natural systems and species with such things as antibiotics, antivirals, antihelminthics, pesticides, insecticides, herbicides and fungicides. Although there is a rational basis for utilizing these toxic and "anti-life" approaches to save lives and rebalance human health, frequently these approaches that "fight against," "war against," "eradicate," and "kill" life are often short-sited and cause more damage to human health and Earth's ecosystemic than good (e.g., the prevalence of more virulent and resistant bacteria, viruses and parasites). This, however, gives drug companies the ability to patent and sell stronger drugs to kill the new and more resistant strains of bacteria, viruses and parasites. We have become too dependent on "anti-life" and "anti-sickness" approaches to health. We could instead be focused on creating optimal wellness and thriving lives.

There are many health practitioners, scientists and researchers in the medical field that are truly committed to helping people, improving health and minimizing suffering. However, the healthcare system (or more appropriately *"sickcare system"*) has largely become a multi-trillion-dollar industry whose economic benefits and motivation are out of alignment with promoting the health and wellness of the people it supposedly serves. There is little money in healthy people and cures. The big money received by the sickcare system is made in treating unhealthy people.

While the western healthcare system has developed amazing diagnostic tools and treatment regimens that have saved many lives and prevented much suffering, the "healthcare" system has essentially become neither healthy nor caring. Global annual health spending is estimated at over $8 trillion per year.[114] The U.S. healthcare system, alone generates approximately $4 trillion per year, representing over 20% of the GDP of the United States. Although the U.S. has the most expensive healthcare system in the world, it's ranked number 37 out of 191 countries by the World Health Organization as to the overall efficiency and quality of care.[115] Also troubling is the misinformation and misaligned lobbying in the name of healthcare which continues to "infect" and influence the U.S. and most of the world. This lobbying and misinformation, in truth, has very little to do with healthcare and much to do with financial gain and power. OpenSecrets.org, a research group analyzing money in politics, has been tracking spending on lobbyists. Health Care (including pharmaceutical and health, health products, hospitals/nursing homes, health professionals and health services/HMOs) consistently spends more on lobbying than any other industry.

Between 2000-2019, the Health industry spent over $8.7 billion on lobbying, compared to Oil and Gas at over $2.1B and Defense at over $2.3B.[116] The big spenders in healthcare are the American Medical Association, American Hospital Association, the Pharmaceutical Research and Manufacturers of America, AARP and Blue Cross/Blue Shield.

While many people in the healthcare industry provide ethical care and improve the comfort and quality of people's lives, the health care industry often appears to have a greater interest in making money than preventing and curing disease. The *"industrialized medical complex"* has a distinction of being:

- **The third largest cause of death** in the U.S. after heart disease and cancer[117], and

- **The leading cause of bankruptcy** in the U.S.[118]

According to Dr. Barbara Starfield of the Johns Hopkins School of Hygiene and Public Health, **225,000 Americans die each year**[119] as a result of medical treatments:

- 12,000 deaths per year due to unnecessary surgery

- 7,000 deaths per year due to medication errors in hospitals

- 20,000 deaths per year due to other errors in hospitals

- 80,000 deaths per year due to infections in hospitals

- 106,000 deaths per year due to negative effects of drugs

In addition to the deaths caused by the healthcare system, there are an estimated **7.5 million unnecessary medical and surgical procedures performed each year.**[120] Gary Null, PhD., in his book "Death by Medicine," writes, *"Rather than reverse the problems they purport to fix, these unwarranted procedures can often lead to greater health problems and death."*

Out of 37 million hospital admissions per year, the Institute for Healthcare Improvement (IHI) estimates that approximately 40% of the admissions, or nearly **15 million people, suffer from occurrences of medical harm in the U.S. each year.**[121]

While the long and expensive double-blind studies and clinical trials required by the FDA have created standardization and enhanced product safety, there are hundreds of FDA approved drugs that have been taken off the market as a result of horrible side effects, including heart, liver and renal damage, blood toxicity, cancer, depression and death.[122] Moreover, cures have been delayed or prevented from being marketed. Likewise, practitioners who use safe, effective and non-invasive alternative treatments, cures and preventative measures are often raided, shut down, fined and/ or incarcerated by the FDA.[123]

Many diseases that conventional western medicine "attempts" to treat are potentially avoidable through the application of a holistic, integrative, regenerative and intuitive medicine. According to the Center for Disease Control and Prevention, chronic diseases and conditions, such as heart disease, stroke, cancer, diabetes, obesity, and arthritis, are among the most common, costly, and preventable of all health problems.[124]

Jack Anderson, a Pulitzer Prize winner for national reporting and a renowned investigative journalist, said, *"The incestuous relationship between government and big business thrives in the dark."* The incestuous control of healthcare by the FDA, AMA and pharmaceutical industry has resulted in regulations that protect the monopoly of the *industrialized medical complex*. The FDA, with its overreaching and massively expensive regulatory framework and unreasonable enforcement against alternative health practitioners, serves to protect the fiefdom of the industrialized medical complex. Republican congressman, Ron Paul, opined: *"But the FDA and the drug companies are in bed together and they squeeze out competitors and build up their monopolies and they love government medicine because they make more money."*[125]

Eric G. Campbell, director of research at the Mongan Institute for Health Policy at Massachusetts General Hospital and an associate professor at Harvard Medical School led a survey in 2007 of department chairs at 125 U.S. medical schools and the 15 largest independent teaching hospitals. Approximately 460 department chairs completed the survey published in the New England Journal of Medicine. The results showed an astounding 67% of departments and 60% of department chairs either received payments from drug companies for consulting, research grants, or funding to support continuing medical education. In addition to the manipulation by phar-maceutical companies of medical schools and research, according to the survey, 94% of the 3,167 doctors responding admitted receiving from the drug industry, food or drug samples, reimbursement for continuing medical education expenses and/or attendance at professional meetings (generally sponsored by the drug industry), as well as payments for consulting, lecturing, and enrolling patients in clinical trials.[126]

Western medicine has virtually created a regulatory monopoly on healthcare through their propaganda and lobbying efforts. The current regulatory environment not only effectively thwarts smaller companies and alternative health providers from selling their products and services (often with real cures and less harmful treatments),[127] it also creates significant liability and risk to M.D.s seeking to utilize alternative modalities to benefit their patients.[128] Practitioners and M.D.'s providing alternative treatments, cures, disease prevention optimal wellness practices are often targets of the government and industrial medical complex.[129]

What if we aligned the economic interests of health practitioners with our health? What if doctors made more money and had more free time by fostering the health of their patients? What if doctors were able to utilize "alternative" and holistic approaches without being exposed to liability for utilizing approaches outside the "standard of care" (e.g., scalpels, radiation and pharmaceuticals)?

It's clear that massive regulatory and economic reform is required to align the healthcare system with health and care for our well-being. However, for the time being, we need to take personal responsibility for our health with a lifestyle that includes, at a minimum, exercise, nutritious food, relaxation and rejuvenation, improved states of being and more connection with each other and nature rather than blindly relying on the authority of the current *sickcare system*.

Afterall, the therapeutic approach of Hippocrates, known as "The Father of Medicine," was based on "the healing power of nature." Hippocrates is famous for his quotes on health and the practice of medicine including:

"Let food be thy medicine and let medicine be thy food."

"The Natural forces within us are the healers of disease."

The following is a popular modern version of the Hippocratic Oath taken by M.D.s when admitted to practice:

"I swear to fulfill, to the best of my ability and judgment, this covenant:

I will respect the hard-won scientific gains of those physicians in whose steps I walk, and gladly share such knowledge as is mine with those who are to follow.

I will apply, for the benefit of the sick, all measures that are required, avoiding those twin traps of overtreatment and therapeutic nihilism.

I will remember that there is art to medicine as well as science, and that warmth, sympathy, and understanding may outweigh the surgeon's knife or the chemist's drug.

I will not be ashamed to say, "I know not," nor will I fail to call in my colleagues when the skills of another are needed for a patient's recovery.

I will respect the privacy of my patients, for their problems are not disclosed to me that the world may know. Most especially must I tread with care in matters of life and death. If it is given me to save a life, all thanks. But it may also be within my power to take a life; this awesome responsibility must be faced with great humbleness and awareness of my own frailty. Above all, I must not play at God.

I will remember that I do not treat a fever chart, a cancerous growth, but a sick human being, whose illness may affect the person's family and economic stability. My responsibility includes these related problems, if I am to care adequately for the sick.

I will prevent disease whenever I can, for prevention is preferable to cure.

I will remember that I remain a member of society, with special obligations to all my fellow human beings, those sound of mind and body as well as the infirm.

If I do not violate this oath, may I enjoy life and art, respected while I live and remembered with affection thereafter. May I always act so as to preserve the finest traditions of my calling and may I long experience the joy of healing those who seek my help."

The foregoing Oath provides sound and ethical principles for the practice of medicine and healing arts. Yet our government and the industrialized medical complex have often declared war on alternative and natural medicine.

With the deaths, unnecessary surgeries, bankruptcies, side effects, addictions and industry-induced illnesses, combined with the corrupt practices of the "sickcare" system, it appears the medical industrial complex has failed to honor the Hippocratic Oath.

Unfortunately our "sickcare" system is misaligned with our health and best interests because it makes money on sickness rather than wellness. The more sick people there are, the more money the system makes. At present, financial gain, not wellness, could be said to be the primary motivation of the medical industrial complex.

I respect, admire and appreciate the men and women that have chosen professions in healthcare with the noble intention of helping people live healthier lives. However, many healthcare practitioners tend to work very long hours with a great deal of stress and an incredible amount of regulatory restriction. They don't often have time to engage in independent research and a high percentage of doctors and conventional healthcare providers rely on medical training, literature and research provided and sponsored by the pharmaceutical and medical industry.[130] As a result, most western medical doctors and conventional healthcare practitioners get training in diagnosing and treating symptoms within the protocols of the industrialized medical complex, (e.g., pharmaceutical drugs, surgery and radiation), but have little training in achieving optimal wellness, disease prevention or curing/treating disease with safe, non-invasive modalities (e.g., nutrition, supplements, homeopathy, Chinese medicine, hydrotherapy, energy medicine, internal cleansing, massage, exercise, meditation and lifestyle change).

My critique of the medical system is based, in part, on my father's experiences with the medical system. My dad was an M.D. that fully believed in, and supported, the practice of evidence-based medicine promulgated by the AMA, FDA and big pharma. In accordance with his training and conditioning as an M.D., he really believed that he was offering the best healthcare to his patients. As part of his training, my dad was conditioned to believe that allopathic medicine was superior to all other types of health disciplines for all situations.

Although as an M.D., my dad was considered by society an authority on healthcare, he had no training in nutrition, natural medicine, alternative medicine or preventative medicine. He was of the opinion that nutritionists, doctors of Oriental

Medicine, chiropractors, energy workers, massage therapists, naturopaths, homeopaths and other complementary health providers were all "quacks."

When I was young, I asked my dad, "*Why don't we eat vitamins?*" His response (based upon his training as an M.D.) was, "*Vitamins are unnecessary—just expensive piss. Just follow the FDA nutritional guidelines and you'll be fine.*" When asked, "*Why don't we eat organic food?*" my dad told me, "*Your stomach doesn't know the difference. Neither the AMA nor the FDA says there is any benefit to eating organic food.*"

When my Dad turned 50, he started suffering from heart disease that required several angioplasties. At 60, he started his journey down the slippery slope of industrialized medicine resulting in a septuple bypass, two heart valve replacements, osteoporosis, diabetes, loss of hearing, loss of libido, a weakened immune system, numerous staph infections, about fourteen different prescription medications per day, and dialysis three times per week. The more pharmaceuticals he took, the weaker his immune system became, making him more susceptible to illness. The dialysis was necessitated by renal failure caused by numerous staph infections resulting from hospital stays, medical negligence and the side effects of his fourteen daily pharmaceutical medications.

When he turned 70, he realized the medical system couldn't be trusted and realized that the system was misaligned with his health interests, and changed his lifestyle. Although it was too late to prevent the existing diseases and damage to his health, he started taking vitamins, eating organic food, exercising and opening his mind to complementary medicine and energy healing. As a direct result of these lifestyle changes, he was able to improve his health and vitality for many years.

I am not suggesting that we throw the baby out with the bathwater, but rather that western medicine include holistic, inclusive and integrative approaches to healing. I, and many others, are confident that for diagnostics, emergency care and treatment of acute injuries, conventional western medicine is vastly superior to just about any other medicine practices in the world. For example, if I am in an accident with arterial hemorrhaging or suffering from a heart attack, I would much rather have an M.D. than a Shaman with a rattle. However, if I were seeking advice and protocols for achieving optimal wellness, living a healthy lifestyle or preventing disease, I would much rather see an integrative or regenerative health practitioner or team of practitioners with holistic expertise in areas such as nutrition, exercise, mindfulness, emotional healing, herbal remedies, energetic healing and bodywork. For my well-being, I would much prefer a holistic practitioner for whom promoting health is more important than treating disease, and who doesn't have a vested economic interest, like most conventional medical doctors, in cutting me open with a scalpel, pouring pharmaceuticals down my throat and irradiating me.

With evidence-based medicine's obsession with standardization and regulation of systems, processes, protocols and licensing, the *industrialized medical complex* has taken a mechanical, chemical and biological approach to medicine while largely abandoning the natural healing arts successfully used for millennia to prevent, treat and cure disease, as well as promote optimal wellness in humans as complex interconnected organisms.

There is ample evidence that most disease is largely psychosomatic and that we are directly responsible for our health or illness.[131] The term psychosomatic means that emotional, mental, and behavioral habits play a subtle but critical role in determining health.

This said, it's critical that a system designed to foster optimal wellness include holistic, ecosystemic, integrated and regenerative approaches supported by open-minded and collaborative practitioners who utilize the most natural and beneficial health solutions. I call this system of fostering holistic wellness *"Ecosystemic Medicine."*

"Ecosystemic Medicine" consists of healing practices that use living, energetic and whole systems approaches based upon observing and imitating nature's wisdom and integrating the natural and holistic wellness wisdom of indigenous and ancient cultures with modern technology and evidence-based medicine. Many health practices of indigenous cultures have evolved over thousands of years and are proven by continued use. If they weren't effective, they generally wouldn't have lasted through the millennia.

Indigenous medicine utilized plants, animals, water, hot-cold therapy, minerals, soil, sound, light and energy. These early healing methods were further based upon observation and integration of interconnected relationships between living systems and energies of the earth, sun, moon and stars, the tribal community and the individual.[132] As can be observed, our planet gives, sustains and regenerates life and health. Observation of nature clearly demonstrates that healthy cells and systems are those that are the most adaptable, resilient and able to regenerate life. Ancient healers learned from and understood connection with nature as the source of life and well-being.

By mimicking nature and its regenerative processes to increase the adaptability, resilience and health of humankind in a value-adding relationship with our ecosystem, we can more effectively create and maintain an optimal state of wellness.

Ecosystemic Medicine holistically integrates and includes many healing systems and modalities (e.g., ancient, modern, natural, evidence-based, technological) and provides a tool chest of applications to promote health and wellness. The practitioners of *Ecosystemic Medicine* can choose the most appropriate tools from a tool chest of protocols and applications to maintain and increase wellness and optimize the *Foundational States of Well-being* (e.g., physical, mental, emotional, environmental, spiritual/energetic and social/fiscal).

Rather than preventing, fighting, and treating disease, *Ecosystemic Medicine* focuses on fostering optimal wellness through ecosystemic (inner and outer) balance and thriving. Ecosystemic balance and thriving is accomplished by seeing the individual as an interconnected and interdependent being in relationship with the whole of creation. This holistic approach integrates the miracle of life and regenerative quality of nature with a lifestyle that optimizes the *Foundational States of Well-being*. For example, rather than using antibiotics that kill bacteria, *Ecosystemic Medicine* focuses on optimizing immune system functions so that a symbiotic relationship is formed with bacteria creating immunity and resiliency from exposure to bacteria rather illness and disease. Rather than giving a patient anti-inflammatories and anxiety medications, *Ecosystemic Medicine* practitioners would seek to cure the root cause of inflammation and stress, which is often resistance.

Many diseases that conventional western medicine attempts to treat are preventable through the application of *Ecosystemic Medicine's* natural, integrated and proactive approach to wellness. *Ecosystemic Medicine* holistically incorporates the best and most effective approaches, diagnostic tools, prevention protocols, treatments and curative tools from a wealth of health systems (e.g., Ancient/Earth, Allopathic, Chiropractic, Oriental Medicine, Ayurvedic, Homeopathic, Naturopathic, Energetic, Spiritual, Emotional, Psychological and Nutritional). The use of natural, non-toxic and non-invasive approaches should, in most instances, be the primary choice for creating optimal health as well as preventing, treating and curing disease.

The practice and protocols of *Ecosystemic Medicine* are built upon the following tenets:

1. Evaluate all possibilities and treat the person, not a symptom;

2. Provide optimal wellness rather than prevent disease, prevent disease rather than cure it, cure disease rather than treat it;

3. Increase the number of tools for health and openly collaborate with others who possess synergistic and complementary tools;

4. Remain open-minded to new possibilities and evolving health practices;

5. Engage in the most effective applications with the least amount of damage, side effects, time and cost to the patient;

6. Use non-invasive and non-toxic procedures whenever possible;

7. Elevate achieving optimal results for the patient over profits;

8. Utilize intuitive, energetic, instinctual and qualitative practices to promote healing;

9. Collaborate with other practitioners; and

10. Empower the patient to take responsibility and proactively engage in their health decisions and protocols.

The most valuable health practitioner for your life and well-being is you. By educating yourself, taking responsibility for your health and committing to a healthy lifestyle, you can possess a life of optimal wellness. It's quite alright to question authority, evaluate your doctor's advice and do research. Some of the greatest healers, ethical thinkers and technologists in history were self-taught. For example, Buddha did not possess a Ph.D. in philosophy or healing. Thomas Edison, one of the greatest inventors of all time, did not have a formal science education or degree. Abraham Lincoln, one of the finest ethical and legal minds in American history, did not have a law degree or pass a bar exam. Even Hippocrates, known as the "Father of Medicine," did not possess a degree or license as an M.D.

Ecosystemic Medicine addresses and holistically integrates the complex, interconnected and interdependent systems vital to our well-being, which include nature's ecosystems. Moreover, because our bodies are constantly in a state of change, adaptation and regeneration, *Ecosystemic Medicine* incorporates qualitative, adaptable and self-evolving approaches addressing the physical, mental, emotional, spiritual, fiscal, social, occupational and environmental aspects contributing to an individual's wellness.

While exercise, nutrition, genetics and environment play a massive role in wellness, it's important to be 1) aware of our current states of being; 2) energetically robust; 3) emotionally conscious; 4) mentally present; and, 5) clear of blockages, trauma, toxins and pain. It's also essential for optimal wellness to live in expansive and healthy states of being, engage in loving connection with each other and nature, as well as balance work with play, rest and rejuvenation. In order to possess optimal wellness, we need a system that is integrated, whole and regenerative.

The "**M.E.D.I.C.I.N.E.**" protocol described below and in the following chapters is an integrated, holistic and regenerative system for optimal wellness that includes the following:

- **M**indfulness, Meditation & Optimized States of Being
- **E**xercise & Breath
- **D**iet & Nutrition
- **I**nternal Cleansing & Detoxification
- **C**ontentment, Calm, Rest, Sleep & Rejuvenation
- **I**ntimacy, Love & Connection
- **N**atural Connection, Environmental & Ecosystemic Thriving
- **E**pigenetics & Energetic Activation

The foundation of optimal wellness depends upon holistic and integrated approaches resulting in open flow of vital energy in our body, mind and soul in relationship to our environment. In my healing practice, I've seen many people who take great care of their bodies by exercising regularly, eating organic foods and vitamins, but still have a great deal of stored pain and resistance in their bodies. Stored pain, resistance, trauma and constrictions whether in our bodies, minds, emotions or energy field drain life force and vitality.

We are much like electrical circuits. When a resistor is put in an electrical circuit it causes slowing or blockage of the current. This resistance creates heat and if the resistance or heat is too great, it damages the entire circuit board. Therefore, it is critical to our well-being that energy is flowing in and through our bodies without resistance, constriction or blockage.

Resistance, limitation, and blockage can result from emotional, mental, physical trauma, stress, stagnant energy or toxicity from our environment creating a persistent feedback loop. Resistance, in my experience, is the root cause of congestion, inflammation, stress, discomfort, pain, disease and death. It is therefore important to be fully present and conscious of resistance and its symptoms in our body, mind, emotional and energy fields. We can then utilize the practice and protocols of M.E.D.I.C.I.N.E. to consciously clear and remove resistance and its related symptoms.

The M.E.D.I.C.I.N.E. program is designed for optimal regenerative wellness, increased vitality, harmonious living and increased energetic flow. The integrated and holistic nature of M.E.D.I.C.I.N.E. optimizes our *Foundational States of Wellbeing* while increasing our ability to receive universal abundance that supports our full creative expression and manifestation. In the following chapters, we will explore M.E.D.I.C.I.N.E. in greater detail.

CHAPTER 12

Mindfulness, Meditation & Optimizing States of Being

Mindfulness is the objective and non-judgmental present awareness of our State of Being in relationship to our environment. Using meditation as a foundational tool for achieving mindfulness, we can consciously choose to optimize our State of Being.

What we experience, whether real or imagined is our *Experiential Reality*. Experiential Reality has real impact on our lives in the present moment and is a significant influence on future outcomes. By using mindfulness and meditation, we can consciously shift our Experiential Reality and optimize our states of being.

Rather than consistently holding optimized states of being, many of us experience consistent levels of anxiety, stress and fear that negatively affect our health and state of well-being. Whether its worrying about paying bills, keeping or finding a job, finding and/or keeping the love of your life, or meeting the expectations of family, friends and colleagues, a majority of the things that create worry, anxiety, stress and fear in our society are neither immediate nor life threatening. Rather the fear we experience is often based upon some future imagined event or some past circumstance we regret. Even the fear of serious threats such as pandemics, climate disasters and terrorist attacks that urgently need to be solved, are typically not immediately threatening to our life. The state of being in consistent fear and anxiety wreaks havoc on our health and reduces our quality of life. We were not meant to be in constant anxiety and fear leading to constricted sympathetic nervous system states of fight or flight. The sympathetic nervous system was meant to be activated only during extreme conditions (e.g., when we were hunting or being hunted or faced with immediate threats to life and limb). Moreover, when we are in fight-or-flight, our ability to make sound decisions and solve problems is compromised.

In order to optimize our health, it's critical that we **optimize our states of being** and **enhance our Experiential Reality**. By being more equanimous and consciously shifting our state of being to hold the best outcome rather than the worst, we can dramatically and immediately improve the quality of our life and our ability to respond to challenges. Mindfulness and mediation are tools that allow us to consciously shift our states of being to optimize our lives and our wellness.

MINDFULNESS & MEDITATION

Numerous scientific studies have linked mindfulness and positive emotions with better health, longer life, and greater well-being.[133] Despite substantial evidence supporting the benefits of mindfulness, meditation and positive emotional states, many people haven't been exposed to, nor embraced, mindfulness, meditation and the ability to use the power of these tools to consciously optimize their lives and well-being.

Thich Nhat Hanh, a revered Buddhist monk, states, *"I define mindfulness as the practice of being fully present and alive, body and mind united. Mindfulness is the energy that helps us to know what is going on in the present moment."*

In my experience, *mindfulness is the equanimous, direct and present awareness of our State of Being in relationship to our environment.*

Meditation is a foundational tool for achieving mindfulness. Meditation can be defined as *the mindful service of self-inquiry, observation and realization in the here and now*. Meditation is a mental discipline to quiet and create greater awareness in the reflexive, "thinking" mind that is incessantly processing stimulus, generating meaning and creating the interpretative story of our subjective "reality." Mindfulness and meditation have been proven to provide the following benefits:[134]

• Reduction of stress & anxiety	• Enhances self-awareness and memory
• Increased concentration and mental clarity	• Improved sleep
• Improved ability to experience calm and relaxation	• Balancing and increasing efficiency of the endocrine system
• Overcoming depression, addiction and improving mood and self-esteem	• Improving physical, emotional and energetic well-being
• Transcending ego and increasing objectivity	• Pain relief
• Accessing the creative mind and expanded consciousness	• Increased ability to manifest one's visions

While meditation and mindfulness are often recognized as a component of eastern religions, just about every religion or spiritual practice uses some form a meditation (e.g., prayer, chanting, movement, conscious breathing, focusing on a symbol). Meditation and mindfulness have been practiced for thousands of years starting with the Hindus (1500 BCE). However, meditation and mindfulness have been incorporated by Daoists (600 BCE), Buddhists (535 BCE), Christians (530 CE), Muslims (9th century CE) and Jews (10th century CE) as well.[135]

When we allow a circumstance to trigger a constrictive state of being, mindfulness allows us to objectively observe, experience and shift our state of being and our perception of the triggering event(s). This empowered state of observation allows us to shift from being in reactive constricted emotional states (e.g., fear, anxiety, anger, shame) to being in responsive parasympathetic expanded states (e.g., courage, compassion, inspiration, empathy, love).

In the parasympathetic expanded states of mindfulness, our mind and organs work more effectively, we think and communicate more clearly and our overall state of wellness increases (e.g., reducing blood pressure, strengthening the immune system, and emotional state).[136] Additionally, when we are mindful, our ability to be responsive and proactive vastly improves. This enhances the way we relate to ourselves, others and our environment.

Entering a mindful state that increases awareness and quiets the mind can be accomplished through the following:

- Concentrating the mind by focusing on object (e.g., a candle, statue of Buddha, a cross) or engaging in a repetitive mantra

- Equanimous observation of one's thoughts

- Immersion into activities that bring us into present somatic awareness such as intentional breathing, yoga, extreme sports and divine sexual union

- Energetic resonance with the modalities of sound, light or vibration

- Acceptance, surrender and letting go of all concentration and observation to dissolve into stillness, silence and emptiness.

By either being fully absorbed in one or more of the foregoing activities or dissolving into silence and stillness, we can increase present awareness, reduce stress, become more objective, optimize our state of being or quiet the mind, or drop into oneness, much like a raindrop dissolving into the ocean.

Although there are numerous variations, there are 3 main disciplines of meditation: *Mindfulness, Concentration* and *Immersive*. Because we expend a lot of time and energy in our mind, I add a **4th discipline** I affectionately call "*Mindless Meditation.*" With the mind-chatter and distractions that are so prevalent and often overwhelming in modern society, many of us have become disconnected from nature, our breath, life-energy, our heart's desire to give and receive love, stillness and silence. The following are brief summaries of 4 disciplines of meditation that can help us reconnect with what's important in our lives:

1. *Mindfulness Meditation* is a flowing and objective discipline that allows the meditator to objectively view one's thoughts and environment from the perspective of an observer.

   In *Mindfulness Meditation*, the meditator may start by centering attention on a process (e.g., breathing, a sound or a mantra), an object (e.g., a tree, photograph, statue of Buddha or mala beads) or an activity (a yoga posture or repetitive movement). Although the meditation process begins with a focus (often with focus on breath), in *Mindfulness* Meditation, the meditator lets go of focus and freely observes his or her mind. No thought, image or sensation is considered a distraction or creates any stress. The meditator stays in the present moment by remaining in observer-consciousness without cognitive analysis, judgment, fantasy or subjectivism regarding the contents of awareness. If the meditator is drawn back into subjective thought, the meditator merely shifts back to observation of thoughts or reengages in centering to start the process over.

2. _Concentration Meditation_ is a discipline that generally requires the meditator to focus on a singular process, object or activity and quiet the mind through disciplined attention.

In _Concentration Meditation_, the meditator holds attention on a particular process, object or activity (e.g.,, mantra, concentrated gazing, breath) while minimizing distractions; bringing the mind back to concentrate on the chosen process, object or activity. Much like the centering described above in _Mindfulness Meditation_, _Concentration Meditation_ requires a greater degree of discipline as thoughts, images or sensations, other than the singular focus, are generally regarded as unwanted. So rather than just letting go and mindfully observing one's thoughts, _Concentration Meditation_ requires a return to the singular focus until such time as the meditator can master holding the focus for long periods of time. Generally, the longer one can hold attention on the chosen singular focus, the deeper the meditation and the greater the mastery.

3. _Immersive Meditation_ utilizes immersive action and attention to bring about a present flow and a state of unity between doing and being.

Immersive Meditation centers on an activity that is physically or mentally challenging so that the meditator is completely immersed and focused in the activity in the present moment so that no other thoughts, whether analytical, past or future, enter the consciousness. There is total presence and immersion in the here and now through the activity. Examples of immersive activities include music, art, sports and athletic activities, yoga, dancing, laughing and tantric sex.

4. <u>*Mindless Meditation*</u> is the natural dissolution of thought and sensory overwhelm into the silence, stillness and emptiness that is eternal and a natural part of our being.

    The silence, stillness and emptiness that the meditator dissolves into exists between thoughts. In order to experience the space between all things, it requires losing one's mind and entering into a state of "mindlessness." Paradoxically entering into a state of "mindlessness" often requires mindfulness as an entry point. This is done by being the observer of our minds and shifting our conscious awareness from mindfully observing our thoughts to holding the space between thoughts. Many believe that when they're in observer consciousness, they have achieved an egoless and empowered state. However, the trap here is the ego becomes the observer. In other words, the objective ego of the observer is observing the subjective ego mind. So we need to go a step further. Once we have entered into "observer consciousness," we can become aware of the still point between the last thought and the next thought. We can hold that still point and dissolve into emptiness by passively releasing observation of the still point. When the awareness of self, space and time vanishes, we merge into the void.

TRANSCENDENCE, ASCENDANCE & INSCENDANCE

In addition to the forms and techniques of mediation mentioned above, the intent of the meditation yields different results and experiences that can enhance our lives.

- *"Transcendence"* has an outward focus of going beyond the body and mind and dissolving into the infinity of space or divine light. Transcendence generally means to rise above, exceed or go beyond. Many spiritual and meditation techniques deal with the transcendence of mind and human suffering in order to experience unity, stillness and present state consciousness.

    The transcendence of mind, as generally taught, is dependent upon some action such as (i) focusing one's thoughts on a repetitive activity (e.g., repeating a mantra) or an object (e.g., statue of Buddha), or (ii) mindfully observing one's thoughts and becoming the observer of the observer. These techniques are used to transcend the subjective body-mind experience to arrive at the stillness, silence and peace of unity. The act of transcendence requires going beyond our sensory phenomenal reality. As our attention transcends the body, our somatic consciousness often becomes more sensitive and acute (e.g., noises become louder, our skin starts tingling), keeping us at phenomenal consciousness. It can take significant discipline to transcend mind chatter and physical stimuli. However, as we move our consciousness to more objective levels of observation (e.g., when we observe ourselves as the observer of the observer of the phenomenal stimuli) or go so deeply into focus, we start to transcend the physical gravity that holds us in our body and the associated time-space subjective mind chatter.

"Transcendental Meditation opens the awareness to the infinite reservoir of energy, creativity, and intelligence that lies deep within everyone. The goal of the Transcendental Meditation technique is the state of enlightenment. This means we experience that inner calmness, that quiet state of least excitation, even when we are dynamically busy."~ Maharishi Mahesh Yogi

- *"Ascendance"* is an outward to inward focus that seeks the embodiment of infinite consciousness in human body-mind consciousness. Using ascendant meditation, we access and ground cosmic consciousness and universal possibilities into our physical reality. By expanding our awareness of infinite possibilities, we increase access to imagination and our ability to manifest our creative potential. Oneness is achieved through the unified embodiment of divine consciousness.

Lisa Renee, a highly respected expert on *Ascension*, describes the *Ascension* process as follows . .

"The Ascension process is about moving the consciousness from one reality to another and the awareness of possible multiple realities existing simultaneously. Since a "reality" is a dimension, what we are undertaking is, in essence, a complete dimensional shift. A dimensional reality is held in place by a complex layer of coded energetic grids to create the illusion of time and space for the consciousness to perceive and to participate in its own experience within the broadband widths of that particular range of frequency. As the

dimensional grid shifts its frequency and its magnetic attributes change, all things existing within that "broadband" reality will also shift and change in a myriad of ways. The "natural" laws governing time and space as we know them will change. This also means the perception of our spatial awareness, our relationship to time and space will also change rather dramatically." This definition of the ascension process aligns with many of the discoveries in the science of quantum physics.

- *"Inscendence"* is an inward focus using the phenomenal sensory mechanism of the body to dissolve into the infinity and zero-point that already exists in each of us. The body's consciousness is always in present state awareness. Since most meditation seeks to bring us into the present state of awareness, to still the mind and experience oneness, the body is our portal into present state consciousness. We create each moment of reality through sensory stimuli received through the body and interpreted by the mind. By *dissolving into* our somatic consciousness, we become one with our body and the present environment we are creating. Through this inward journey, we can experience a very natural dissolution into the stillness and zero-point that exists within us.

  Inscendence requires no *focusing, separating, rising above, exceeding, bringing in, grounding or going beyond* associated with transcendence or ascendance. *Inscendence* is the natural dissolution into stillness and silence that already exists naturally within us (e.g., the space between thoughts, the space between the in-breath and the out-breath, the space in our cellular and atomic structure).

  Our sensory and somatic awareness is always present in the here and now. As long as we are sensually aware of our phenomenal physical world through sight, hearing, touch, taste and smell, we continually experience stimulus-response feedback loops. Even with sensory deprivation techniques such as floatation tanks and anechoic chambers, disconnection from the somatic awareness can be difficult.

  By trying to disconnect from our senses, we actually create greater awareness of the senses and a greater sense of separation. Many transcendent meditation practices ask us to focus on breath or mantra. While conscious breathing may still the mind, breathing activates the sense of touch and feel as the breath moves through the nose and throat and into the lungs. As the lungs expand and contract, we feel pressure. If we breathe through our nose, we are apt to smell. If we breathe through our mouth, we are apt to taste. If we use a vocally expressed mantra, it adds the additional layers of sound and hearing. As we sit or lay down, we feel pressure on our bodies. Even with our eyes closed, we may experience shifting color and light, and although we may be in a silent room, there is ambient noise and the sounds of our own hearts.

The more we try to separate from, transcend or turn off, our senses, typically the more accentuated our senses become and the more we reinforce our separateness from the world around us.

Every day we breathe and experience the space between the in-breath and the out-breath that is neither in nor out. Every day we experience a space between our thoughts that is not a thought. These things are simple, natural and occur without thought. Moreover, just like the universe, we are made of almost entirely of space.

With *Inscendance*, acceptance and surrender in the here and now allows us to deepen into oneness with the natural space existing in our body and between thoughts and then *dissolve into stillness and "   "*. *Dissolving into stillness and "   "* can happen very naturally when our consciousness dissolves into the space between phenomenal existence.

By becoming completely one with our senses and the environment we are sensing and perceiving, we can effortlessly merge and dissolve into " " like a raindrop dissolving into the ocean. There is no focus or observation, nowhere to go, nothing to be or do, no achievement or pursuing. Just allow yourself to effortlessly dissolve deeply into your senses, the core of your physical being, and the **silence, stillness and "   " that is already "within" you. You are already 99.99% space, just leave the .01% behind as you dissolve into that which you already are.** Dissolve into the experience of oneness that already exists in you, until there is no "you" and no experience.

When we "drop in" to our soma and allow the natural patterns of universal flow to carry us to the silence, stillness and " " within us, we release the phenomenal world of sensory stimulus, resistance, attachment, agendas, manipulation and illusion of "I." The silence, stillness and " " that exists within allows us to dissolve naturally into the unmanifest beyond symbolic universal oneness and nothingness.

Meditation can be practiced while doing any activity such as driving your car, walking, working and engaging in sports. By merely focusing on one's breath and becoming aware of one's present state of being, a working meditative state can be achieved. To go deeper often requires quiet time to focus or immerse oneself completely in an activity.

Each of us has the ability to engage in meditation. As we practice meditation, we increase our ability to remain in the present state of consciousness for extended periods of time. As we extend our present state of awareness, we increase the benefits that meditation brings to optimize our states of being.

OPTIMIZING STATES OF BEING

Optimizing States of Being involves the act of consciously feeling, scanning and becoming aware of our physical, mental, emotional, energetic and spiritual states of being. Our states of being are interdependent, interconnected and influence our overall state of being and wellness.

Examples of these States of Being include the following:

- **Physical State** consists of the cellular, sensory, neural and somatic states of being as they relate to our internal and external environment.

- **Mental State** comprises thoughts, beliefs, imagination and subconscious conditioning.

- **Emotional State** contains the full spectrum of emotions, (e.g., love, hate, joy, sorrow, anger, calmness, fear and courage) and their related frequencies and charge, which have an expansive or constrictive effect on the other states of being.

- **Energetic State** includes energetic awareness, electromagnetic field, auric field, vibrational frequencies, quantum field and the morphogenetic field.

- **Spiritual State** embraces soul consciousness, super-consciousness, Divine connection, oneness and enlightenment

Dr. Candice Pert's book *Molecules of Emotion*, informs us that the "mind" is not focused exclusively in the head, but rather distributed throughout the whole body via signal molecules. Through mindfulness, we can influence the vibratory molecular signals and change our entire state of being.

Conscious monitoring can be done anywhere and is recommended throughout the day. The most powerful results, however, are generally achieved when sitting or lying quietly without interruption.

The purpose of conscious monitoring is to mindfully observe our state of being so that we can proactively shift or clear limiting mental, emotional, physical, energetic and spiritual states of being and replace them with optimal states of being.

Conscious monitoring, clearing and optimizing states of being help us to:

- Possess optimal states of health

- Experience unconditional love

- Experience great clarity, vitality and abundant energy

- Manifest abundance in our lives

- Develop inspired and deeply loving relationships and communication

- Embody sexual wellness, potency, connection and passion

- Optimize systemic functioning, especially the immune, digestive, nervous, reproductive and endocrine systems

- Provide clear, flowing and vital energy necessary to activate quantum optimization (See "Energetic and Epigenetics" below)

- Eliminate *"Constrictive States of Being"* and shift to *"Expansive & Optimal States of Being"* including the following:

State of Being	Constrictive States	Expansive & Optimized States
Physical	Restricted, Congested, Tight, Inflamed, Painful, Diseased	Healthy, Vital, Energized, Open, Powerful, Comfortable
Mental	Dull, Depressed, Sluggish, Unclear, Insecure, Low Esteem	Clear, Confident, Courageous, Coherent, Creative, Inspired
Emotional	Fear, Apathy, Depression, Guilt, Shame, Anger	Love, Awe, Inspiration, Joy, Compassion, Passion
Energetic	Blocked, Resistant, Constricted	Flowing, Pure, Expansive
Spiritual	Disconnected, Isolated, Misaligned, Incoherent	Empowered, Unified, Interconnected, Harmonious, Abundant, Infinite

When we are objectively aware of our states of being, we can clear and transform Constrictive States of Being to Expansive and Optimized States of Being. This can be accomplished by scanning the subtle energy systems interacting with our body, mind, emotions and energy field and then consciously responding to, removing, dissolving or replacing Constrictive States of Being. We then can transform to Expansive States of Being and access maximal energetic current to allow us to optimize our state of being and powerfully manifest miracles in our lives.

By engaging in conscious monitoring, clearing and shifting our states of being using the process described below, we can optimize our mental, emotional, physical, energetic and spiritual states of being. For example, anger is often considered a "negative" emotion by our society. However, anger can often contain a valuable message and significant energy that can propel us to achieve our goals. Anger often causes constriction and tightness in our body giving us a feeling of discomfort. When we become objectively aware of anger and hear its message, we can guide the energy and experience of anger into passion. We can then transform passion into love, and love into bliss thereby transforming the experience of anger into emotional states that provide powerful and positive outcomes in our lives.

By paying attention to the valuable messages of our thoughts, beliefs and emotions, we can then take action to release the emotion(s) and transform limiting thoughts and beliefs along with any associated constriction, discomfort and trauma. If we hear the message from the emotion(s) but fail to take action, the thoughts, emotions and resulting symptoms are likely to continue. To heal constriction, discomfort and trauma, we must take healing action. This can occur by changing the beliefs, thoughts, emotions or circumstances that are triggering constrictive emotions and discomfort. This process allows us to guide and express the charge of an emotion in an optimal way.

Provided below are two sections: 1) The Full Protocol for Optimizing States of Being; and, 2) Condensed Protocols for Optimizing States of Being

The Full Protocol is a deep and thorough process to scan, clear and transform Constrictive States of Being and to Optimize States of Being. The Full Protocol generally takes between 30 to 60 minutes. However, you may wish to go longer depending upon the amount of clearing you need. As you do the work, trust your intuition and guidance to know when and if you are complete.

The Condensed Protocol is used to engage in specific rapid clearing, optimization and maintenance. The Condensed Protocol can be done quickly and easily so that you can consistently clear and optimize states of being throughout the day. The Condensed Protocol can be done in as little as 3 minutes, but averages 5-10 minutes. For those who perceive themselves as "too busy to breathe," at least take a conscious breath once an hour and mindfully check your state of being. You can do this with a packed schedule of work and responsibilities. Just devoting a few seconds of your day to a conscious breath each hour, and monitoring your states of being, will improve the quality of your life and health.

I recommend practicing the Full Protocol at least once a week and the Condensed Protocol each day and throughout the day as needed. Doing the Condensed Protocol first thing in the morning right upon awakening for about 10 minutes adds amazing positivity, productivity, synchronicity and inspiration to my day. I also find that doing the Condensed Protocol before I go to sleep for 5 minutes is highly effective for deeper sleep, optimal dream states and rejuvenation.

Also, throughout the day, I drop into conscious breath, move my body and consciously monitor my state of being. When I become aware of constrictive or limited states of being, I often optimize my states of being using the Condensed Protocol. This can be done either holistically or with a specific focus on my body, mind, emotions, energy or spiritual field. Other times, I just focus on and optimize the thought, belief, emotion, body sensation or stuck energy that is creating an undesirable state of being. This often takes less than a minute and can be done during a phone call, while reading, writing or even in meetings.

Monitoring, clearing and optimization is much like riding a bike. At first, it takes time practicing and after enough practice, it becomes easy and natural. In the beginning, I highly recommend doing the Full Protocol as often as possible, no less than every other day and the Condensed Protocol daily.

The more time you spend in equanimous observation, the faster you increase your awareness and ability to optimize your thoughts, beliefs, emotions, feelings and your energy field. After sufficient practice in building present state awareness, clearing and optimization happen more quickly, automatically and powerfully. If you stick with this practice consistently for 30-days, profound transformation and miracles will start happening in your life.

FULL PROTOCOL FOR OPTIMIZING STATES OF BEING

The following is a two-part process for observing, clearing and optimizing states of being.

- Part 1 provides instruction on objectively observing and monitoring our thoughts, emotions, bodies, energy fields, and spiritual state.

- Part 2 focuses on clearing *Constrictive States of Being* and achieving *Expansive & Optimal States of Being.*

Much of this protocol relies upon visualization and a foundational belief that what we "see" and experience in our visualizations is as real as anything we experience with our five senses (see chapter on "Experiential Reality"). We each have the gift of intuition (e.g., a sense of knowing not based upon logic), instinct (e.g., a "gut feeling" and somatic awareness), imagination (e.g., the ability to dream and visualize) and the ability to experience the vibrational energy field (e.g. feeling the sun's rays on your skin or the vibration of music at a concert). However, many of us have never practiced using these gifts or hold beliefs that limit sensitivity and openness to our power of intuition, instinct, imagination and energetic mastery. The key to mastery is replacing limiting beliefs and skepticism with trust and inner-knowing of your abilities to see, feel and clear your thoughts, physical, emotional, energetic and spiritual fields to achieve clarity of flow and optimal well-being.

Part 1: Conscious Observation of States of Being

1. *Conscious Breath*. Start by focusing on your breath. Start slow, deep, relaxed and rhythmic breathing. Observe how your breath moves your body and fills it with enriching oxygen and energy. Focus your breath at your third eye about one-half inch above the center of your eyebrows. Breathe, relax and let go.

2. *Observe Your Mind and Thought Process*. Equanimously observe each thought and vision that enters your mind without judgment, attachment, interference or subjective involvement. Relax even more deeply into being the observer of your thoughts and become aware of the space between each conscious thought. When you have arrived at a steady state of relaxed equanimous observation, start noticing the object of each thought (e.g., person, place, thing, emotion, environment, condition).

   No matter what comes to mind (e.g., relationships, business, finances, health, romance, sex), stay in the relaxed equanimous state of observation. If you get sucked back into subjective thought, don't judge yourself, just return to being the equanimous observer by becoming aware, relaxing and shifting back to observing your thoughts and visions. Relax, accept, surrender.

3. *Observe the Interplay Between Thoughts, Beliefs and Emotions*. Thoughts and beliefs often lead to an emotional response. When this occurs, observe any emotions that arise from your thoughts and beliefs. Observe the interplay between each thought and belief entering your mind and the emotional state that is connected to each thought and belief. Without judgment, notice which thoughts and beliefs trigger emotions such as fear, anger, anxiety, apathy and which initiate emotions such as joy, bliss, love, confidence and passion. Also,

observe how each emotion can trigger certain thoughts and beliefs and the feedback loops that are at play.

Also, without judging yourself, observe how circumstances, whether real or imagined, affect the interplay of thoughts, beliefs and emotions. Inquire into your beliefs: How did you come to learn or acquire the triggering belief? Is this belief serving your optimal state of being? In a universe of infinite possibilities, what other beliefs are possible? How would an alternative belief better serve you? What other possible outcomes exist?

4. *Observe the Interplay Between Thoughts, Beliefs, Emotions and Feelings.* As thoughts, beliefs and/or emotions arise, observe, without judgment, the effect that they have in your body and its feelings. Do you feel your body opening/expanding or closing/contracting? Does your body feel strong or weak? When you experience a thought, belief or emotion in your body, does it increase energy, vitality, lightness and openness or does it create physical conditions such as restriction, congestion, darkness, sluggishness, discomfort, pain or illness? What part of the body feels the thought, belief or emotion? Is the thought, belief or emotion moving in and through the body or is it being stored in the body (e.g., in the neck, back, heart or stomach)? Does the thought, belief or emotion have a shape or color? What feelings are arising in your body and how do those feelings trigger various thoughts, beliefs and emotions?

5. *Observe the Interplay Between Thoughts, Beliefs, Emotions, Feelings and Your Energy Field.* As we observe our energy fields, we "see" not with our eyes but with our internal vision. When using internal vision to scan our energy field, each of us has a unique way of "seeing" and experiencing our energy field. Experiencing our energy field may include (a) different color combinations (e.g., bright greens, blues, purples and golds or black, red, burnt orange and brown), (b) shapes (e.g., spheres, squares, blobs, tentacles), textures (e.g., thick tar, gravel, pure water, or light particles), and feelings (e.g., expanded, constricted, tight, loose, light, heavy, empty, full) that correspond with, and indicate the health and flow of, our energy field. We also may see our energy field expanding and flowing or contracting and congested. The energy field relates to, and effects, all of our states of being. What effect do the colors, shapes,

textures, feelings of expansion or contraction have on our states of being and our energy field?

If we allow ourselves to trust our intuition and instinct, the colors, shapes, textures, feelings and flow of our energetic field provides messages and meaning about our energetic state of being as well as our overall states of being. Healthy energy fields are generally flowing, expansive and clear. They often have bright colors such as white, light purple, bright green, bright blue or gold with textures that are transparent and moving, while areas that are unhealthy, out of alignment, constrictive or blocked will generally possess darker non-vibrant colors such as dark brown, burnt red, burnt orange or black and solid textures like tar, glue, mucus, or concrete. As well, when we focus on an area in our energy field that is unhealthy, the body will often contract and when we focus on a healthy area, the body will expand.

Here, without judgment, observe the interplay between thoughts, beliefs, emotions, feelings and your energy field. Do you visualize or "see" your energy field expanding or contracting? Do the thoughts, beliefs, emotions or feelings constrict, slow or thicken your energy field or do they expand, open and increase flow to your energy field? Observe your thoughts, beliefs, emotions and feelings as energy fields and notice their colors, textures, shapes and how they interact with each other. Without judgement or attachment, make note of the shapes, textures, feelings and states of expansion that most support your highest states of being.

6. *Observing the Observer.* When we equanimously observe our thoughts, emotions, beliefs, feelings and energy field, we enter into "universal consciousness." By engaging in observing the observer, we become aware of messages and guidance that arise from universal consciousness regarding our soul's path, seeing our alignment with divine co-creation. We can then observe our soul observing us and merge into unity consciousness. Our soul is our direct connection to universal consciousness. When we observe our soul, we become aware of our alignment and connection to universal oneness. It often takes several levels of observation to reach unity consciousness (e.g., observing self → observing

the observer observing self → observing the observer observing the observer observing self → observing the observer observing the observer observing the observer observing self).

PART 2: CLEARING AND OPTIMIZING STATES OF BEING

After you have completed the observation process above, it's now time to clear and optimize our mental, emotional, physical, energetic and spiritual states of being, as well as optimize our integrated state of being.

1. *Clear and Optimize Thoughts, Beliefs and Emotions.* Return to relaxed conscious breathing and observing your thought process and allow thoughts to bubble into conscious awareness. As thoughts come into awareness that align with your desires, energize you and expand you, give thanks, love and energy for those thoughts. Anchor those thoughts into your mind and physical state of being. Feel the sensations of each of those thoughts in every cell of your body. Let the sensation grow and expand beyond your body reaching into the energetic field and attracting experiences from the field that align with the frequency and expansive nature of your state of being with each expansive thought.

    If a thought or emotion comes into awareness that appears dark, constrictive, self-defeating, uncomfortable or otherwise out of alignment with your optimal state of being, focus on that thought and observe its effect on, and interplay with, your emotions, feelings, body and energy field. Determine the root and catalyst for that thought. Why are you thinking that thought and what value and lessons does it bring you? Is this a new thought or is it a repetitive thought? If it is repetitive, it is likely that either the thought needs attention (e.g., acknowledgment, action and resolution), or the thought is habitual and needs to be cleared and replaced with more expansive thoughts.

    Often the thoughts that trigger discomfort or constrictive emotions and feelings are those that most need our attention. They are often messengers of issues needing resolution. Sometimes these are traumas that need to be cleared, or situations that need to be addressed before we can move to the next level of manifesting the life we desire. Engage in a dialogue with the thought, belief or emotion and ask its purpose, origin and message. Hold equanimous space for the thought, belief or emotion to complete the explanation of its purpose, provide you with its origin, and communicate its message to you. Let it move through you without restriction—let it flow. Once the message is clearly communicated, give thanks and love to the thought or emotion. Actually let it know its message has been heard, received, understood and appreciated. By doing this, the thought or emotion has served its purpose and doesn't keep repeating itself. It can leave your energetic, physical, mental and emotional fields. However, if the message requires attention or action, the emotion, belief and/ or thought may continue to arise until required attention or action is fulfilled.

The origin of a thought, belief or emotion may be a circumstance, a story, an experience or a sensation or another thought, belief or emotion. For instance, the origin of a thought may be an emotional trauma from a relationship where there your love broke up with you creating a villain-victim story. This circumstance and its interpretation can lead to a story of being "dumped" or having your "heart broken." Carrying this story over a significant period of time can result in the physical manifestation of the emotional trauma, such as constrictive psycho-somatic feedback loops that manifests into symptoms of a tight chest, shallow breath, heart issues and disease. Behavioral symptoms such as depression, unworthiness, lack of trust and reluctance to love can also become habitual.

Another example could be anxiety over whether we will make enough money to pay our bills and have enough financial security. Our anxiety causes constriction in the body and, if allowed to become repetitive, can lead to an unhealthy psycho-somatic feedback loop that often causes symptoms such as tightness, fatigue, nervousness, inability to focus, headaches, neckaches and backaches. This is where we are likely to experience repetitive thoughts, beliefs and emotions become habitual.

Using the foregoing example about financial security, we might find that we believe that we 1) need money to survive, and 2) need a job to make money. By shifting these two beliefs, we can also shift the emotions related to the belief and circumstances. Maybe we could survive without money by providing an exchange of service that fulfills our needs and desires. Maybe we could start our own business and don't need a job. Possibly, the universe is giving us an opportunity for personal growth (like shifting and clearing your states of being, aligning with your soul path, clearing fear and limitation, or learning some new skills) that will provide greater abundance and alignment with our higher purpose. It might also be that we have to shift a limiting belief about money (e.g., belief that money is evil) that is not aligned with our desire for wealth, financial security and freedom.

If lack of money is causing a feedback loop of stress, anxiety and fear that controls our thoughts and actions, our ability to attract abundance is marginalized. Rather than focusing on the lack of money, focus on creative solutions to either obtain abundance and the things you desire.

If a thought, emotion or belief is not serving you, clear it and replace it with a belief or thought that serves you (e.g., "Money provides convenience, comfort, options and adventures and allows me to buy things I want." "I easily attract and generate abundance and vast sums of money"). By being grateful and fulfilled for what we have, we start creating from a place of abundance. We then can transform our thoughts, beliefs, emotions and circumstances.

When a belief or belief system is causing the disempowering thoughts, emotions and circumstances, examine the belief. . . Where did you acquire the belief ? Is the belief one you gained through experience or one you acquired from your parents, friends, a teacher, media or society? Is the belief empowering or disempowering? Is the belief expansive and energizing or constrictive and draining? Question the belief. Is the belief valid and true for me? Are there exceptions to the belief? What other beliefs are available that will more effectively serve me?

It may be said we repeat the same stories, thoughts and emotions until we don't. By becoming aware of our habitual patterns and stories and taking committed action we can transform our habitual psycho-somatic feedback loops. Consciously clearing old anxiety-ridden thoughts, stories and emotions from the repetitive feedback loops gives us the opportunity to transform constrictive states of being to optimized states of being. When we shift our thoughts, beliefs and emotions from those that cause constriction, fear, anxiety and stress to those that create expansiveness, calm, courageousness and inspiration, we can transform our state of being into expansive abundance, allowing us to effectively attract money and abundance in our lives. This can be done by (1) replacing a thought or belief like "I am not good enough" with "I am amazing and have unique and valuable gifts," (2) visualizing yourself living the life you desire (e.g., being happy, abundant, wealthy, in a beautiful relationship and doing the things you love), and (3) opening up to creative and imaginative solutions. As mentioned in the chapter on the *Law of AttrAction*, a very powerful tool is taking action in support of your empowering thoughts, beliefs and emotions.

As we shift our beliefs, thoughts and emotions, our world also shifts. Shifting our beliefs from limiting to empowering, and from constrictive to expansive, our emotional state and thoughts shift as a result, empowering us to create our lives in alignment with our highest potential.

2. *Clear and Optimize Physical States of Being.* As we shift from constrictive and limiting emotions, beliefs and thoughts to empowering and expansive emotions, beliefs and thoughts, observe how this new state affects your physical being. You may find that your physical state of being shifts from being heavy, constrictive, sluggish and/or tight to being light, energized, vital and/or expansive.

Start mindfully moving and stretching your body. Breath, move through, shake out and release any remaining constrictive physical states of being. Start the movement from the toes, feet and ankles, through the calves and knees, up through the thighs and hamstrings, to the pelvis, hip and buttocks, into the lower back and abdomen, to the mid-back and chest, to the upper back shoulders, arms, wrists and hands, up to the neck, jaw, nose, eyes, ears, temples, forehead and scalp. Sometimes you may find fear in moving through an area that is stuck or uncomfortable. Be courageous and gently move through the full range of motion of such areas in your body. Courageously and gently moving through stuck and constricted areas will release the fear, anxiety, anger and other constricting emotional states. If the movement causes physical pain, as opposed to tolerable discomfort, see a health care professional to help you with the process of moving from pain to comfort by healing or clearing the root cause of the pain.

3. *Scan and Optimize Your Energy Field.* Return to conscious breathing and close your eyes. Relax and observe your energy field. Do you see any spots in your energy field where energy is slow, stuck or blocked? Ideally, we want to see pure white light flowing through your inner and outer body and a clear and expansive energy field surrounding you. In my experience, energy that is blocked often appears as black or dark brown and has a solid consistency. Burnt red or burnt orange generally indicates energy that is moving slowly as a result of trauma, pain, conflict or misalignment that has not yet become a blockage. Slow or stuck energy often appears in the form of a syrupy or tar-like substance rather than pure energy. Healthy energy is generally clear, flowing and transparent. As we monitor our energy field, we become more experienced at "seeing" and clearing our field. Each person is likely to have a somewhat unique experience is "seeing" and clearing their energy field.

Clearing the energy field can be done by flooding white light through the energy field with each inhale and releasing blockages, congestion, trauma, restriction, toxins and stuck energy with each exhale. In order to do this, return your focus to breath and feel the life force your breath provides. Feel the life force moving throughout your entire body. Breathe into the areas that are blocked, stuck or slow and expand the breath to envelop your entire body and being.

With each inhale, visualize abundant clear universal light energy flowing through the crown chakra in the top of your head and washing through your mind, body and energy field—enveloping you and flowing through you completely from head to toe.

With each exhale, see the white light energy clearing, removing and washing away any dark spots or congested energy in your field and releasing toxins in your body. Bathe and immerse yourself in this light allowing it to permeate your field and every cell of your body, so that there is no distinction between the light and you. Now feel the power of life force breathing life and energy into your mind, body and soul. Feel the cleansing light washing through you and removing all things that do not serve you (e.g., blockage, restrictions, beliefs, emotions, trauma, toxins and limitations), leaving only pure white, freely flowing, and expansive energy full of healing life force.

4.   *Alignment of Soul Path with Divine Consciousness.* Return to observing the observer observing self and the observer observing the observer observing self and repair any disconnection, misalignment or conflict between you, your soul and universal consciousness. This is done by intuitive and trusting visualization, dialogue and feeling. When you are making choices out of alignment with universal guidance and your highest soul-purpose, universal energy and support is reduced. Universal guidance speaks to us through our intuition and instinct. When we align with universal guidance, we feel our state of being lighten and expand. By allowing ourselves to visualize, feel and/or hear universal guidance with full trust in our intuition and instinct, we increase our energy and focus to synchronistically co-create with the universe.

5.   *Gratitude.* Consciously feel the new clear and expansive life force, thoughts, beliefs, emotions, energy and somatic feelings that are now serving you and your optimal state of well-being. Feel this deeply; memorize this feeling as your new standard. Give gratitude to yourself, the universe and divine consciousness for co-creating this new state of well-being.

CONDENSED PROTOCOLS FOR INTEGRATIVE OPTIMIZATION

This Condensed Protocol is an expedited process of scanning and clearing the body, mind, emotions and energy field. Sometimes the Condensed Protocol raises awareness of issues needing additional attention, so feel free to utilize parts of the Full Protocol.

1.   *Rapid Scanning, Clearing and Optimizing States of Being.* Focus your attention on your breath and relax into slow, deep and easy breaths. Notice and feel how your body expands and contracts with each breath and how your breath moves throughout your body. With each inhale, feel the life force of breath filling your

entire body with clear energy and life force, moving and dissolving constrictive thoughts, emotions and blockages. With each exhale, move through, release and eliminate constrictive thoughts, emotions and blockages.

Start mindfully moving your body, paying attention to constrictive physical conditions that arise as you move. Start the movement from the toes, feet and ankles, through the calves and knees, up through the thighs and hamstrings, to the pelvis, hip and buttocks, into the lower back and abdomen, to the mid-back and chest, to the upper back shoulders, arms, wrists and hands, up to the neck, jaw, nose, eyes, ears, temples, forehead and scalp. As you move your body, shake out and release all constrictive physical conditions, thoughts or emotions through breath. If you come across restriction or limitation, courageously and gently move through the restriction or limitation. In this process, you may notice your physical being move from dark, heavy, drained and constrictive to light, tingly, open, and vital. Here your mind becomes more aware, inspired and innovative and your emotional state expand.

2.   *Scan and Clear Stuck "Constrictive States of Being" from Your Energy Field.* After clearing your physical, mental and emotional states of being, return to conscious breathing. See the pure energy in your breath bringing light into your energy field. Scan your energy field. Do you see any spots in your energy field where energy is slow, stuck, restricted or blocked?

With each inhale, visualize abundant clear universal light energy flowing through the crown chakra in the top of your head and washing through your mind, body and energy field. See this energy surrounding you, enveloping you and flowing through you completely from head to toe.

With each exhale, see white light energy clearing, removing and washing away any dark spots or congested energy, restriction, limitation, toxins or congestion in your field. Bathe and immerse yourself in this light and allow it to permeate your field and every cell of your body, so that there is no distinction between the light and you. Now feel the power of life force breathing life and energy into your mind, body and soul. Feel the cleansing light of spirit washing through you and removing all things that do not serve you, including dark spots, blockage, restriction and congestion in your energy field, leaving only pure white expansive flowing energy.

Inhale deeply and hold this feeling of pure flowing energy while you open your eyes and exhale. Now breathe deeply and slowly while integrating this feeling into your physical, mental, emotional and energetic being.

3. *Gratitude.* Allow the expansive life force, clarity and improved states of being to fill every cell of your body, to inhabit your thoughts, to raise your emotional state and charge your being with vitality. Feel this deeply, memorize your states of being and your integrated state of being as your new standard and give gratitude to yourself and the Divine.

CHAPTER 13

Exercise & Breath

"Those who think they have no time for exercise will
sooner or later have to find time for illness."

~Edward Stanle

E xercise is of key importance to a state of well-being and breath is of key importance to our ability to stay alive. Although some of us need to be more creative
about making time to exercise, such as exercising while working, with family, on
the computer or watching television, we can easily take time to breathe more consciously throughout our day. Both exercise and breath provide benefits including
stress reduction, improved posture, greater energy, increased metabolism, weight
control, improved mood and enhanced sexual performance.

In this chapter, we will explore various exercise and breath modalities to help
increase your wellness and quality of life.

EXERCISE

A multitude of reasons exist for engaging in regular physical exercise, including
the following:

Increased energy	Healthy bone density
Improving cardiovascular system function	Fortifying immune system function
Burning fat	Joint flexibility
Strengthening muscles	Balancing the endocrine system
Boosting mental acuity, cognition and awareness	Enhancing positive emotional states
Toning the body	Improved digestion
Stress release	Honing athletic performance
Improved nervous system functioning	Improved immune system functioning
Enhanced sexual performance	Weight control

Given all of the benefits above, it's highly recommended that everyone incorporate some form of exercise into their daily routine.

Exercises are generally grouped into three categories depending on the overall effect they have on the human body:

1. **Flexibility & Balance** exercises such as yoga, Pilates and stretching improve the range of motion of muscles and joints.

2. **Aerobic & Cardiovascular** such as cycling, aerobics, martial arts, walking, running, hiking, swimming and playing tennis, basketball and other participatory sports increase cardiovascular health, endurance, increase oxygen and provide overall system benefits and health.

3. **High Intensity Interval Training, Anaerobic & Strength Training** such as weight/strength training, isometrics, functional training, jumping, sprinting and/or high-intensity-interval-training to build muscle, increase muscle and tendon strength, bone density and metabolic rate.

A balanced exercise regimen should consist of a combination of all three exercise groups. Flexibility exercises should be done daily for at least 15 minutes; Aerobic exercise should be done at least 3 to 4 days per week for at least 30 minutes; and Anaerobic exercise should be done at least 3 days per week for at least 15 minutes. It's important to select an activity from each group that appeals most to you. It is essential for exercise to be fun. Below are some activity options along with a list of the calories burned.[137] Please note, that the following chart is general and that actual calories burned depend upon many factors including gender, weight, age, metabolic rate, muscle mass, intensity level, temperature and nutrition.

Calories Burned in 30-Minute Activities

Activity	125 lb. Person	155 lb. Person	185 lb. Person
Aerobic dancing (low impact)	115	172	230
Aerobic dancing (low impact)	115	172	230
Aerobics step training, (4" step)	145	218	290
Aerobics, slide training (basic)	150	225	300
Backpacking with 10 lb. load	180	270	360
Backpacking with 20 lb. load	200	300	400
Badminton	150	225	300
Basketball (game)	220	330	440
Basketball (leisurely, nongame)	130	195	260
Bicycling, 10 mph	125	188	250
Bicycling, 13 mph	200	300	400
Billiards	45	68	90
Bowling	55	82	110
Canoeing, 2.5 mph	70	105	140
Canoeing, 4.0 mph	135	202	270
Croquet	60	90	120
Cross country snow skiing, intense	330	495	660
Cross country snow skiing, moderate	220	330	440
Dancing (noncontact)	100	150	200
Dancing (slow)	55	82	110
Gardening, moderate	90	135	180
Golfing (walking, w/o cart)	100	150	200
Golfing (with a cart)	70	105	140
Handball	230	345	460
Hiking with a 10 lb. load	180	270	360
Hiking with a 30 lb. load	235	352	470
Hiking, no load	155	232	310

Housework	90	135	180
Jogging, 5 mph (12 minutes/mile)	185	278	370
Mowing	135	202	270
Ping Pong	90	135	180
Raking	75	112	150
Racquetball	205	308	410
Rowing (leisurely)	75	112	150
Rowing machine	180	270	360
Running, (7.5 minutes/mile)	305	458	610
Running, (6 minutes/mile)	350	525	700
Scrubbing the floor	140	210	280
Scuba diving	190	285	380
Sex	100	150	200
Skipping rope	285	428	570
Snow shoveling	195	292	390
Snow skiing, downhill	130	195	260
Soccer	195	292	390
Squash	205	308	410
Stair climbing	140	210	280
Surfing	133	210	278
Swimming (50 yards/minute)	225	338	450
Table Tennis	90	135	180
Tennis	160	240	320
Tennis (doubles)	110	165	220
Trimming hedges	105	158	210
Vacuuming	75	112	150
Volleyball (game)	120	180	240
Walking, 4 mph	100	150	200
Washing the car	75	112	150
Waterskiing	160	240	320
Weeding	100	150	200
Weight training (40 sec. bet. sets)	255	382	510
Weight training (60 sec. bet. sets)	190	285	380
Weight training (90 sec. bet. sets)	125	188	250

In order to get the maximum benefits in the least amount of time, add bursts in intervals that increase your heart rate to any fitness activity. For example, when walking or hiking, sprint for 30 seconds every 5 minutes. If doing balancing exercises, incorporate jumping. If lifting weights, do more reps until you can't lift anymore and intersperse some cardio in between (e.g., 30-60 seconds of jump rope).

It's also better to do 5 minutes of exercise than nothing at all. However, to obtain observable benefits from your exercise routine in a reasonable period of time, it's recommended that the <u>minimum</u> exercise times (in minutes) outlined in the chart below be implemented.

Beneficial Health Program

	Monday	Tuesday	Wednesday	Thursday	Friday	Saturday	Sunday
Flexibility/Balance	15	15	15	15	15	15	15
Aerobics/Cardio	25		25		25		
HIIT/Anaerobics/ Strength/Core		15		15		15	
TOTAL	**40**	**30**	**40**	**30**	**40**	**30**	**15**

If you are seeking to possess <u>optimal</u> health and an amazing body, it's advised that you implement the following exercise schedule:

Optimal Health Program

	Monday	Tuesday	Wednesday	Thursday	Friday	Saturday	Sunday
Flexibility/Balance	30	20	30	20	30	20	20
Aerobics/Cardio	45		45		45	30	
HIIT/Anaerobics/ Strength/Core		30		30		30	
TOTAL	**75**	**50**	**75**	**50**	**75**	**80**	**20**

The programs above are general in nature and each person, depending, upon their current condition, their wellness goals and their enthusiasm for exercise can do more than the foregoing. It's also recommended that you select several different activities to keep your exercise fun, interesting and spontaneous rather than routine.

For example:

- Flexibility & Balance training one day may consist of yoga and the following day is alignment, balance or Pilates

- Aerobics & Cardio training may alternate between cycling, martial arts, running, swimming, tennis or basketball

- High Intensity Interval Training, Anaerobics, Strength & Core may alternate between weight lifting, isometric/calisthenics and high intensity bursts for 1-3 minutes such as sprinting, jumping rope, punching a heavy bag.

We have a choice to go through life in great health and vitality or not. Many people I talk to about exercise tell me how busy they are—they just don't have the time between their families, work and friends to exercise regularly. I respond by asking them, "What good will you be to your family, work and friends if you're lying in a hospital bed, or have so little vitality that you can no longer meaningfully engage with your family, business and social relationships?

Much like a car, we can either change the oil or pay for a transmission. So either "change your oil" regularly with exercise and good nutrition or pay the expense of "changing the transmission" with a hospital, a doctor and a lifelong prescription of expensive medications and sliding down the slippery slope of pharmaceutical drugs and the sickcare system.

"I gotta work out. I keep saying it all the time. I keep saying I gotta start working out. It's been about two months since I've worked out. And I just don't have the time. Which is odd. Because I have the time to go out to dinner. And watch TV. And get a bone density test. And try to figure out what my phone number spells in words." ~Ellen DeGeneres

Here are solutions for those that have the "limited time" excuse for their failure to exercise.

- *TV Time*—If you really feel TV is worth your time and brain cells, instead of being a couch potato watching TV, stretch, ride a stationary and/or lift weights while watching TV.

- *Work Time*—Get up and stretch. Do leg lifts at your desk. Do push-ups. Do deep knee bends. Do ab crunches and core contractions while sitting at your desk. Take a break and go for a walk—use the stairs. Instead of having a lunch meeting at a restaurant, go for a walk together and have a picnic. Stand up and stretch while taking phone calls. Take your call on your cell phone and go for a walk outside.

- *Family Time*—If you want to spend time with your family, rather than watching TV, try something healthy and interactive together (e.g., go for a walk, take a bike ride, do some yoga, play basketball or frisbee). Actually talk and interact with each other rather than staring blankly at a screen. Spend the weekends engaging in activities together (e.g., hiking, yoga, martial arts, swimming, surfing, skiing, tennis, tai-chi, running, biking, baseball, basketball). Your family will love you for it and you will find yourself having a great time contributing to your and your family's health.

If you are just plain lazy and don't like exercise, at least you're honest with yourself, but then, unless you are genetically blessed, at some time in your life, the sedentary nature of your existence is likely to create undesired circumstances in your life. Most of us have to choose between exercise or being out of shape, overweight, unhealthy and possibly suffering from diseases like obesity, diabetes and cardiovascular disease.

A balanced exercise regimen of about 30-45 minutes per day can help prevent many of these devastating conditions, while providing you with a sense of health, vitality, energy, mental acuity, enhanced self-image and heightened emotional states. There are even some new exercise technologies, such as whole-body vibration, that deliver remarkable fitness results in about 15 minutes per day.

The beauty of exercise is that not only do we reduce the likelihood of disease, but we also feel better and receive many great positive benefits. One of the primary cornerstones of wellness is exercise. So please give yourself the gift of great health and find time to make exercise an important part of your daily life.

BREATH

Even more important than exercise is breath. Once you stop breathing, you die. Luckily for us, breathing is an autonomic function. There is a big difference between ordinary autonomic breathing, stress constricted breathing and conscious breathing.

Autonomic breath happens unconsciously and represents the survival impulse that keeps us alive. Constricted breathing results from such things as fear, anger, anxiety and stress, and is often unconscious. Due to our artificially stressful lives, we frequently find ourselves inhibiting our autonomic breath by holding our breath or engaging in shallow and constricted breathing. By practicing conscious deep and relaxed breathing, we can expand and exercise our lungs, increase the flow of life-giving energy and oxygen, and can help facilitate stress reduction and removal of toxins.

One of the great advantages to exercise is that, when done vigorously, it generally requires us to breathe more fully, which has a positive effect on the cardiovascular, pulmonary and respiratory systems, expands our lungs and oxygen intake, and can enhance mindfulness and elevate mood.

Conscious breath alone, without exercise, can provide the following benefits:[138]

Increased energy	Mental acuity and clarity
Improved cardiovascular system function	Fortifying immune system function
Enhanced endocrine system functioning	Enhanced sexual performance
Weight control	Improved posture
Boosted mental cognition and awareness	Enhanced positive emotional states
Improved digestion	Improved digestion
Increased respiratory system function	Enhanced athletic performance
Improved nervous system functioning	Stress release
Mood stabilization	Increased metabolism

Oxygen is vital to the process of creating energy and fueling your body and mind. Unlike food, there are no calories in oxygen. You can breathe in all you want for as long as you want and still no calories! The extra oxygen intake will raise metabolism, thus helping burn calories at a faster rate. The tightening and strengthening of core muscle groups while breathing helps posture, strength and overall physical energy. As well, by engaging in conscious breathwork, we train our autonomic breathing function to work more efficiently, thus exponentially increasing the benefits of conscious breathing throughout the day.

According to many spiritual and healing practices, breath contains the energy of life. The Indians refer to the life-giving energy of breath as **Prana** and have elevated the art of breathing to a healing science. One of the major schools of Indian breathing tradition is **Pranayama**. Pranayama consists of Prana and Ayana. "Prana" represents the breath and vital energy source behind all life activities. "Ayama" means control. Thus, Pranayama could be translated as "the control of the vital energy."

Pranayama is more than simple breathing exercises, but rather techniques that increase the quantity and quality of Prana in the body. Thus, while doing the breathing exercises outlined below, it is also helpful to visualize the effect of the breath on the body.

There are many different breathing practices in Pranayama, but below are some core breathing techniques I have found incredible for my wellness on many levels.

- **_Deep Breathing_**—The practice of deep breathing consists of a conscious long and deep breathing. (Recommended time is at least 15-20 minutes using a combination of the techniques below with a minimum of 3 minutes each, but even a few conscious breaths throughout the day can create remarkable shifts in one's state of being)

  - _Technique 1—Diaphragmatic Breathing with Inhale Focus_:

    The technique has a relaxing and soothing effect on your mind, aids the body in detoxification, and provides a natural increase in energy.

    1. Inhale deeply through the nose into the belly so that your belly expands, but your chest does not. Exhale through the nose.

    2. Each inhale should be twice as long as the exhale. To more accurately measure the time of your breaths, practice with an 8-second-count inhalation and a 4-second-count exhalation.

- _Technique 2—Diaphragmatic Breathing with Exhale Focus_:

  The technique has a relaxing and soothing effect on your body and mind and provides a calm and centered state of being.

  1. This is essentially the same as Technique 1, except the exhale is twice as long as the inhale. By switching the count so that the exhale count is 8 seconds and inhale count is a 4 seconds, this breath provides a detoxifying effect, can eliminate stress and provide a calming effect.

- _Technique 3—Full Inhale with Explosive Exhale_:

  This technique is amazing for bringing great amounts of energy into the body while ridding the body of toxins and stored emotional residue.

  1. Start with a deep diaphragmatic breath through the nose and allow the breath to continue to fill the chest.

  2. Keep inhaling until you feel you can't inhale any more. Hold the breath and attempt to take an additional 3 inhales.

  3. Explosively exhale through the mouth with an exclamation of Paaahhhhh!

  4. Empty all the air from the lungs until there is no additional air left in the lungs.

- _Technique 4—Full Lung and Activated Core_:

  This breath increases metabolism and helps in weight reduction, core muscle control and posture.

  1. Pull in the stomach and tighten the core, also contract the region of your anus and sex organs.

  2. Breathe deeply into the chest and lungs so that the chest and rib case expand, but not the abdominals.

  3. The in-breath and the out-breath are equal with a count of 4 seconds each.

- _Technique 5—Alternating Nostril Breathing_:

  This Pranayama provides energy, removes stagnation and helps remove laziness and procrastination. This Pranayama also helps promote weight loss.

  1. Close the right nostril with your right thumb and inhale through the left nostril. Do this to the count of 4 seconds.

  2. Immediately close the left nostril with your right ring finger, and at the same time remove your thumb from the right nostril, and exhale through the right nostril. Do this to the count of 8 seconds. This completes a half round.

  3. Hold the ring finger of the right hand on the left nostril and inhale through the right nostril for a count of four seconds. Close the right nostril with your right thumb and exhale through the left nostril to the count of 8 seconds. This completes one full round.

- **_Breath of Fire_**—To do this technique, first imitate a dog panting. Then close your mouth and do this breath through your nose. This technique can cause dizziness and is best performed lying down. Once you have become experienced at this breath, it can be utilized in any position, posture or exercise to exponentiate the activity being done. This breath detoxifies the body, lungs and bloodstream and strengthens nervous, digestive, endocrine and immune systems. Start with 100 breaths of fire and work up to a number that gives a sensation of clarity and ecstasy.

- **_Cooling Breath_**—This Pranayama is accomplished by sucking in the breath through a rolled tongue or closed teeth and exhaling through the nose. This Pranayama cools the body, reduces fever and improves the function of the endocrine glands. Repeat until your body feels cool and comfortable.

- **_Chakra Column Breath_**—This breath activates and balances the chakra energy centers and moves Kundalini energy from the coccyx (root chakra) up the spine through the top of the head (crown chakra). To do this breath, take a full and deep inhale through the nose for a count of 8-seconds. Hold the breath for a count of 8-seconds and immediately tighten the anus, sex organs, abdomen, chest, throat, jaw, forehead and head, so that your entire body is tight while you are holding your breath. Exhale forcefully through the nose and release all the energy upward through the top of the head. This breath gives you clarity, motivation, balance and emotional stability. Repeat at least 10 times.

- *Calming Breath*—Inhale and exhale through the nose in a relaxed manner with a 4-second count on the inhale, hold for a 4-second count, exhale for a 4-second count and hold for 4-second count. Repeat at least 10 times.

- *Focused Breath*—Inhale deeply into areas of the body that need release or healing. Take a full deep breath driving the breath into the focus area and bring light and powerful healing energy into that part of the body. Hold the breath for between 4-second to 10-second counts. Powerfully exhale and release all tension from that area and visualize all toxins, blockages, limitations and resistance leaving with the exhale. Repeat at least 10 times.

INTEGRATED EXERCISE, MOVEMENT, BREATH, INTENTION & MEDITATION

In my experimentation with various exercise regimens, I found most regimens lacked the holism for a deeply fulfilling and highly beneficial practice. It was challenging to find a practice that was truly integrated—yoga didn't really work cardio or dynamic strength; HIIT didn't provide cardio, or the flexibility and balance of yoga; running and biking didn't provide flexibility, balance or strength training. I created *AWEbunDance* as a holistic wellness practice that integrates flexibility, balance, strength, core, cardio with energetic clearing, intention, breath and meditation. This is accomplished through a mixture of Kundalini Yoga, Ashtanga Yoga, Mixed Martial Arts, Ecstatic Dance, Calisthenics, Isometrics, Energetic Clearing, Intentional Movement & Breathing and Mindfulness practices.

Below is an example of a 45-minute AWEbunDance practice I developed to help promote optimal wellness:

Instruction	Time/ Mins
Spinal Stretch: Minute 1: Come sitting with your legs crossed. Grab the ankles and with arms straight. Inhale into the chest. Push the chest out and pull the shoulder blades together in back. Exhale and keeping the arms straight, let the stomach and diaphragm collapse, the back round and neck fall forward. Focus on breath—with each inhale feel the chest, lungs and heart expanding. Feel the pranic energy flowing through and filling the body. With each exhale eliminate any toxins, blockage, congestion, fear or other limitation. With each in-breath, breathe more deeply and fully. With each out-breath release more. Minute 2: Increase tempo and pace of breathing and grab the knees Minute 3: Continue motion but grab the shoulders.	3
Spinal Twist: Transition: Inhale through your nose and hold for ten seconds Start twisting from side to side, exhaling through your nose on each side. Keep twisting and let your neck also turn from side to side. Transition: After one minute while keeping the breath and twisting motion do your best to transition from seated to standing.	1
Squat Twist: Come into a squat and hold the squat structure while continuing to turn from side to side with hands on your shoulders for 1 minute. Focus on the root chakra and bringing energy into the root. Experience your connection to the planet, to primal life force and build the natural, primal life force within you.	1
Standing Twist: Minute 1—Come to standing with the legs about 6 inches outside the hips. Let the arms come off the shoulders and swing around you so that they hit you in the butt. Minute 2 Minute 2—Start rotating the hips and pelvis. Feel the energy coming through the second chakra about two inches below the naval. Focus on diaphragmatic breathing into the solarplexis with firm core. On the exhale crunch the abdomen toward the lower back and the lower back toward the abdomen to work the core.	2

Neck Rotation: Transition—Take deep breath and hold it for 5 seconds. Let the breath drive the movement. Inhale and let the head tilt back (6 o'clock). Exhale and let the chin drop forward (12 o'clock). Starting with your head dropped at 12 o'clock, inhale as slowly as you can and circle the head & neck counterclockwise until it comes back to 12 o'clock. Relax and exhale. Now reverse direction by rolling the head and neck clockwise using the same breathing pattern. Try to make the breathing and motion slower with each new rotation	1
Hip Rotation: Transition—Take a deep breath and hold it for five seconds. Start rotating the hips in a figure 8 pattern and exhale at the zero point for 30 seconds Change direction for 30 seconds	1
Full Body Scan and Release: Transition—Take deep breath and hold it for 5 seconds. Move your toes and feet and breathe into and clear any pain, discomfort, limitation or resistance. Now focus on your calves, then your thighs, then your pelvis, hips and buttocks, then your abdomen and lower back, then your chest and mid-back, then your neck, then your head and face.	1
Shake it Loose: Start shaking your hands, then add arms and shoulders. Then start shaking your feet and add your legs. Then start shaking your hips, pelvis and buttocks. Then start shaking your torso and finally shake your neck and head. Your entire body should be shaking ecstatically at this point. Now start dancing around while shaking and intensify the shaking. Build the energy and bring overflowing energy, joy, love and gratitude.	1
Abundance: Transition: Let the body come to rest and become still, breathing in a deep and relaxed manner. Now transition into big expansive movements of opening your arms wide at the chest and breathing deeply and powerfully. Expand your chest. Open your heart. Feel the pranic energy of each breath filling you with abundant love. With each exhale, eliminate fear, pain and blockage, while giving yourself a hug and loving yourself just as you are. Allow your entire being to fill with abundant love and possibility. Start moving around the room dancing and playing with the Abundant Love practice. Try different angles (e.g., up high, down low, diagonal)	1

Infinity: Minute 1: Start standing with your hands in front of you with the index fingers pointing away from your body and touching together. Throughout this exercise, keep your index fingers together. Make a horizontal figure 8 starting with the outer edge of the left-hand chopping downward through the zero-point coming up and then the outer edge of the right-hand chopping down. Exhale on the downward motion and inhale on the upward motion. Start exaggerating the figure 8 making it bigger and coming around your back so that your body twists. Minute 2: Reverse the motion and breath, exhaling on the upward motion and inhaling on the downward motion. Minute 3. Start bringing the hips and pelvis into the figure 8. For an extra challenge, stand on one foot while the other foot does a figure 8 and alternate.	3
Martial Arts Integration: Transition from Infinity by punching or kicking on each exhale in the following pattern: 1-right arm punches straight, 2-left arm punches straight, 3-right arm cross body punch, 4-left arm cross body punch, 5-right front kick, 6-left front kick, 7-right side kick, 8-left side kick, 9-right back kick, 10-left back kick (repeat)	2
Martial Arts Balance and Hip Stretch: Lift your right leg straight out in front of you (at 12 o'clock with the knee locked as high as you can up to being parallel with the floor. While standing on your left leg, slowly move the right leg parallel to the floor like a hand on a clock until it is at 6 o'clock behind you and bring it back to 12 o'clock (approximately 10 seconds each way). Without letting the right leg down when the leg has returned to 12 o'clock bend the knee and place the outside of the right ankle just above the left knee. Squat back into a one-legged chair pose. You should feel a stretch in the right hip. Put the hands overhead sink down. Hold for 10 breaths. Do the opposite side.	1
Surf-Dog-Asana: From standing, put the hands flat on the floor (bend the knees if necessary). Come into downward dog. Stand on the tiptoes, push the ankles back with the calves attempting to place the heels flat on the floor. Inhale into the chest, arch the back, push the chest out, push forward into flat hands. Exhale into plank. Inhale into upward dog. Exhale and jump the right foot to meet the outside of the right hand (like getting up on a surfboard). Come into warrior 2 and raise the hands overhead and then into warrior 1 and then reverse warrior. Bring the hands back to the flow, jump back into plank and come into downward dog. Repeat above except jump the left foot forward (the surfboard pose).	1

Frog Pose: From downward dog jump both feet up to meet your hands in a squat with your knees facing out, heals touching and on your tip toes. All ten fingertips are touching the floor in front of your feet. With the neck back (6 o'clock), look up. This is the exhale position. Keeping the fingers on the floor throughout this exercise, inhale powerfully through the nose and bring the heels to the floor and straighten the legs as much as possible while keeping the heels and fingers on the floor.	1
Lateral Isometrics: Lock the fingers of the right hand over the left and pull the hands apart while keeping them locked. Keep the torso straight and pull back with the right arm while resisting with the left. Then pull with the left arm while resisting with the right. Repeat 10 times on each side. Now freeform (e.g., low, high, diagonal, behind the head, etc.)	1
Dance Your Infinitely Abundant Yoga and Martial Arts: Throw on some good dance music and integrate into a free form dance, the Abundance, Infinity, Martial Arts and Yoga moves from above.	10
Hamstring & Lower Back Stretch: Sit with your legs fully extended in front of you, suck in your abs, straighten your spine and stick your chest out. While holding this posture, bend forward and touch your toes or as far as you can go with straining. Breathe into chest and hold for 30 seconds. Repeat.	1
Bridge Pose: Lay flat with knees bent and heels flat on the floor. Lift the pelvis toward the ceiling with your weight on the shoulders. Put the palms on floor just outside the shoulders with fingers point toward the top of your head and raise yourself on your hands arching your back. Hold for 10 seconds. Lower and straighten the legs and arms overhead for 10 seconds. Repeat.	1
Bow Pose: Roll to the right onto your belly. Reach back and grab your ankles, push the ankles back with the legs while pulling them toward your head with your arms and bringing the back into an accentuated arch. Hold for 10 seconds and put lower the feet and put the arms overhead and roll to the left. For increase the challenge of this posture, rock back and forth. Repeat.	1
Stretch Pose with Breath of Fire: Lay flat on your back. Arms at your side. Raise your feet 6 inches off the ground with straight legs. Raise your arms off the ground with palms in. Look at your feet and do 100 breaths of fire.	1

Relaxation, Meditation and Integration: Allow the body to fully relax and melt into the floor. Let all tension drain from the body. Feel the new energy and vitality swirling through your open body. Relax more deeply and allow the body and energy to integrate. Scan your body and become objective about any thoughts moving through your mind like watching a movie. Set intentions that you would like to manifest (e.g., health, love, abundance, developing virtues and/or overcoming shadow).	10
TOTAL MINUTES	**45**

Exercise and breathwork are critical to optimal health. Using exercise and breathwork together powerfully increases the benefits of each to improve the functioning of all the body's systems, increasing life force, vitality, health and efficiency. Moreover, by integrating exercise and breathwork with the other protocols of M.E.D.I.C.I.N.E. exponentially increases the quality and wellness in all aspects of your life.

CHAPTER 14

Diet and Nutrition

"The food you eat can be either the safest and most power-
ful form of medicine or the slowest form of poison."

~Dr. Ann Wigmore

Diet and nutrition are of supreme importance to personal, societal and environmental wellness. The way we eat has a massive impact on not only our health,
but our economy and our environment. The agriculture and food industries have a
huge impact on our society, our economy and our environment. Unfortunately the
impact of the food and agriculture industries are often very harmful to the health
and thriving of humankind and our planet. By eating more consciously, we can
transform the destructive practices of the agriculture and food industries, while
drastically improving our health.

While volumes of research and books have been written on the subject of
diet and nutrition, most research and books advocate for a myopic or silver-bullet
solution to health (e.g., take vitamins, eat raw, be vegan or vegetarian, the Atkins
Diet, the Zone Diet, the Paleo Diet or the Keto Diet). It is the intent of this chapter
to provide the reader with a spectrum of information to empower the reader to
(1) make conscious choices that best suit the reader's lifestyle and wellness goals,
and (2) understand the planetary impact of the reader's food choices and to make
choices that are good for both the reader and the planet. In this chapter, we will
cover the following:

A.   ***The Basic Conscious Diet***. This part focuses on eating a healthy diet that consciously takes into account our personal wellness and our impact on the planet, including the following:

   1.   *The Impact of our Diet Choices on our Health, Environment, Economy and Society*

   2.   *The Benefits of Local and Organic Foods*

   3.   *Top 10 Conscious & Healthy Eating Guidelines*

B.   ***The Supercharged Diet for Optimal Health and, Wellness***. This part goes into a deeper discussion providing the reader with specific information, protocols and benefits for achieving optimal wellness through diet, nutrition and hydration including the following:

   1.   *The Nutritional Building Blocks* (Proteins, Carbohydrates & Fats)

   2.   *Essentials of a Healthy Diet* (Vitamins, Minerals & Enzymes)

   3.   *Supplementing Your Diet* (Herbs, Superfoods & Antioxidants)

   4.   *Optimizing Your Diet* (Portioning, Ketogenics, Alkalizing Diet, Hydration, Food-combining, Blood Type & Optimizing Mitochondrial Health)

A. BASIC DIETARY CONSCIOUSNESS

1. The Impact of our Diet Choices on our Health, Environment, Economy and Society

Many of the foods consumed in the world today contain harmful and toxic ingredients that have been processed, artificially preserved, pasteurized, homogenized, artificially flavored, artificially colored, frozen, irradiated, and/or canned. Much of our fruit and vegetables have been grown in depleted, toxic soil and sprayed with petro-chemicals, pesticides, herbicides and other toxins, and a large proportion of our animals have been inhumanely treated, stuffed into small pens, fed toxic unnatural foods, hormones, antibiotics, and painfully slaughtered in unsanitary facilities. Food is energy and the way it's grown and raised has an impact on our health and the energy we receive into our bodies.

It takes a conscious effort to find and consume healthy, nutritious and whole-some foods. The choices we make in our diet have a direct impact on our personal health and the health of the planet and society.

Diet can be somewhat subjective—some people do well on a high protein diet that may include eating foods such as meats, dairy and seafood, while others do just fine on a vegan diet. When considering our food choices, it is important to be mindful of not only our own health, but our impact on others and the environment. The food we choose has personal health, humanitarian, environmental, cultural, ethical and spiritual impacts.

Additionally, much of what we prefer to eat depends upon cultural orientation, genetics, belief systems and conditioning. For example, about 40% of the population of India is vegetarian and don't eat cows because Hindus consider cows sacred. In the U.S., however, only about 3.2% of the population identifies as vegan or vegetarian.[139] As one of the largest consumers of meat in the world, the U.S. alone is responsible for billions of animals being inhumanely raised and slaughtered as well as millions of acres of forests and other lands destroyed each year to satisfy the American craving for meat. In 2017, the U.S. meat industry alone processed 9 billion chickens, 32 million cattle and calves, 241 million turkeys, 121 million hogs and 2 million sheep/lambs into over 100 billion lbs. of meat.[140] Moreover, industrial meat production is a major cause of greenhouse gases contributing to global warming, waste and water pollution, with industrial grain-fed cattle topping the chart.

What and how we consume sends an economic message that either supports or opposes animal cruelty, destruction of the environment, wasteful resource usage, disease, social injustice and the unhealthy practices of commercial growing and ranching various foods. According to sources including United States EPA, and the Food and Agriculture Organization of the United Nations[141]:

- The livestock industry not only uses more land than any other human activity or industry; it's also one of the largest contributors to water pollution and a bigger source of greenhouse-gas emissions than all the world's trains, planes, and automobiles combined.

- The steady growth of global meat production comes at considerable cost. Industrial methods in the livestock sector result in cutting down forests to expand grazing lands and the use of large quantities of water and land for growing grains, such as corn or soybeans, for animal feed. Production also relies on heavy doses of antibiotics and hormones for livestock animals.

- Close to 70 percent of the planet's agricultural land is used for animal pasture. Another 10 percent is used to grow grains to feed livestock (for meat and dairy). Producing beef is much more resource-intensive than producing pork or chicken, requiring roughly three to five times as much land to generate the same amount of protein. Beef production alone uses about three-fifths of global farmland but yields less than 5 percent of the world's protein.

- Agriculture uses about 70 percent of the world's available freshwater, and one-third of that is used to grow the grain-fed to livestock. Beef is by far the most water-intensive of all meats. The more than 15,000 liters of water used per kilogram is far more than is required by a number of staple foods, such as rice (3,400 liters per kg), eggs (3,300 liters), milk (1,000 liters), or potatoes (255 liters).

- Worldwide, more than 40 percent of wheat, rye, oats, and corn production is fed to animals, along with 250 million tons of soybeans and other oilseeds. Feeding grain to livestock improves their fertility and growth, but it sets up a de facto competition for food between cattle and people.

- If the 670 million tons of the world's grain used for livestock feed were reduced by just 10 percent, this would free up 67 million tons of grain, enough to sustain 225 million people or keep up with world population growth for the next three years. If each American reduced his or her meat consumption by only 5 percent, roughly equivalent to eating one less dish of meat each weak, 7.5 million tons of grain would be saved, enough to feed 25 million people, or the approximate number of people going hungry in the United States each day.

- Meat production also has a growing impact on nations facing water scarcity, from the North China Plain to the Middle East, from sub-Saharan Africa to northern India to the Southwest United States. For example, shifting from pork to chicken requires half the grain, and hence half as much water.

- The massive quantities of waste produced by livestock and poultry threaten rivers, lakes and other waterways. In the United States, the waste generated by livestock is 130 times that produced by humans. Livestock wastes are implicated in waterway pollution, toxic algal blooms and massive fish kills.

- The world's livestock herds account for roughly 25 percent of anthropogenic emissions of methane—a potent greenhouse gas contributing to climate change. The current scale of meat production wreaks havoc on the environment and threatens human health.

- A rich body of medical and epidemiological literature implicates excessive meat consumption as the principal risk factor in the development of a variety of lifestyle diseases, ranging from cardiovascular deterioration to many types of cancer. The healthiest humans are not those who eat high on the food chain, nor those who obtain insufficient nutrition at the absolute bottom. People who consume a diverse, plant-based diet, rich in whole grains, vegetables and fruits are by far the healthiest individuals. Plant-based diets are associated with lowering overall mortality and ischemic heart disease mortality; reducing medication needs; supporting sustainable weight management; reducing incidence and severity of high-risk conditions, such as obesity and obesity-related inflammatory markers, hyperglycemia, hypertension, and hyperlipidemia; and even reversing advanced cardiovascular disease and type 2 diabetes.[142]

In addition to the above issues, we are faced with a water crisis that, according to Water.org, is currently killing 3.6 million people each year from water-related diseases with children accounting for 84% of water-related deaths.[143] The water and sanitation crisis claims more lives through disease than any war claims through guns. With desertification from global warming, privatization of water, increasing water shortages and a broken water infrastructure, eating foods that conserve this precious resource is of the utmost importance.

As mentioned above, meat production uses massive amounts of water that could be used to grow other more ecological, sustainable and healthy foods, thereby simultaneously preserving water, promoting health and helping to end hunger. In fact, in the United States, meat consumption alone accounts for 30% of our water footprint.

UNESCO's research states, "*Global freshwater withdrawal has increased nearly seven-fold in the past century (Gleick, 2000). With a growing population, coupled with changing diet preferences, water withdrawals are expected to continue to increase in the coming decades (Rosegrant and Rigler, 2000). With increasing withdrawals, also consumptive water use is likely to increase. Consumptive water use in a certain period in a certain river basin refers to water that after use is no longer available for other purposes, because it evaporated (Perry, 2007). Currently, the agricultural sector accounts for about 85% of global freshwater consumption (Shiklomanov, 2000; Hoekstra and Chapagain, 2007).*"[144]

Here is a list of the water required to produce certain foods:[145]

Description	Gallons of Water per Pound of Food
Lettuce	23
Tomatoes	26
Wheat	25
Carrots	33
Broccoli	34
Cauliflower	34
Brussel Sprouts	34
Cantaloupe	40
Eggplant	43
Apples	49
Strawberries	50
Grapefruit	61
Oranges	67
Lemons	77
Dairy Milk	90
Bananas	100
Soybean Tofu	220
Asparagus	256
Plums	261
Raisins	273
Dates	292
Corn Oil	309
Chicken Egg	477
Sunflower Oil	814
Chicken	815
Walnuts	1,112
Lamb	1,248
Pork	1,630
Olive Oil	1,729
Beef	1,847
Almonds	1,929

In addition to the environmental impact and resource consumption associated with producing food, the packaging, shipping and storage of food create a significant carbon footprint that contributes to greenhouse gas emissions. Michael Pollan, author of *Omnivore's Dilemma,* suggested that if Americans went meatless one night a week, it would be equivalent to taking "30 to 40 million cars off the road for a year."

There is also significant research, supporting that regeneratively pasture-raised grass-fed and grass-finished ruminants (e.g., beef, sheep and bison) can have a positive impact on our environment and our health.

Allan Savory, a Zimbabwean ecologist, livestock farmer, and President of the Savory Institute, originated "Holistic management" a whole-systems approach to managing resources. Savory advocates using bunched and moving livestock to what he claims mimics nature, as a means to heal the environment. Savory states that *"Only livestock can reverse desertification. There is no other known tool available to humans with which to address desertification that is contributing not only to climate change but also to much of the poverty, emigration, violence, etc. in the seriously affected regions of the world."* Savory, who has been praised by both cattle farmers and environmentalists, believes grasslands hold the potential to sequester enough atmospheric carbon dioxide to reverse climate change.[146]

Savory's research supports that replacing industrial grain-fed beef with regeneratively grown grass-fed beef, could be a significant contributor to both human health and our environment. Grass-fed and grass-finished beef comes from cows that graze on pasture and consume their natural diet of grass, as opposed to industrial beef, which comes from cows raised in concentrated animal feeding operations and are fed a diet containing grains and often growth hormones and anti-biotics.

Also, according to Dr. Joseph Mercola, grass-fed beef is significantly healthier than industrial grain-fed beef due to higher healthy fatty acids including Omega 3, lower bacteria, lower industrial toxins, healthier more humanely raised animals and higher quality meat.

There is evidence that by eliminating consumption of industrial beef and lamb and consuming only regeneratively raised grass-fed/grass-finished beef and lamb, we can increase both the health of our planet and ourselves.

Consciously choosing foods that minimize use of water, land, transport, packaging, petroleum, chemicals and greenhouse gas emissions can provide both greater health for humans and our planet. When you do decide to eat meat, you can make a difference by making more responsible selections such as regeneratively raised and/or produced pasture raised chicken, eggs, grass-fed/grass-finished beef, lamb and bison while eliminating industrially raised grain-fed meats and choosing meats that use less water per pound. Also, when you decide to eat veggies and fruits, make organic and less water-intensive choices such as lettuce, carrots, broccoli and Brussels sprouts over tofu or asparagus and cantaloupe, apples, grapefruit, oranges and strawberries instead of plums, raisins and dates.

2. The Benefits of Local and Organic Foods

By choosing fresh and local foods, we can reduce our carbon footprint and get better tasting, fresher and more nutritious food. Aside from disintermediating a toxic centralized supply chain that burns greenhouse-gas-emitting fossil fuel, purchasing from local farmers also promotes a healthy local economy.

Many small organic farms use conscious practices that build high-quality soil that yields more nutritious food, as opposed to the destructive commercial farming practices that deplete and toxify soil and crops. Local farmers' markets are great places to get wholesome, nutritious, fresh, organic foods at reasonable prices. If there are no farmers' markets in your area, health food stores and organic grocers are the next best option. If you live in a "food desert," online stores such as ThriveMarket.com and Amazon.com provide great services for the delivery of fresh, organic foods and products to your doorstep.

The organic certification is not perfect, but does provide a reasonable degree of assurance that the food was produced with higher organic standards and without harmful synthetic pesticides. While ethical organic farmers may have their crops contaminated by neighboring commercial farm crop dusting, the concentrations of harmful agricultural chemicals is generally much lower than commercially grown crops. As well, certain countries with corrupt regulatory practices may provide "organic" certifications to farmers that are not organic. While these corrupt practices do exist, it has been my experience that the quality and taste of organic food is generally much higher than commercially grown agriculture.

Aside from reasonable assurances of higher quality food and better health, when you buy organic, you are voting with your dollars. This creates market demand that incentivizes the agricultural industry to adopt ethical and responsible farming practices and for the grocery industry to carry organic products.

It is important to determine not only the ingredients of your food, but also the origin of your food, the methods by which it was produced, its sustainability and potential toxicity. Claims like "natural" or "pesticide free" are not regulated and do not provide significant assurances of quality.

This section is not about dictating a myopic system or dietary limitations, but rather about raising awareness so that we can make conscious choices in our diet and nutrition. Many people do not understand the choices they have or the impact of the choices they make. Most people have been culturally and unconsciously conditioned to eat foods that their parents and society taught them to eat. In many cultures, especially the U.S., these foods are not nutritious, healthy, natural or energetically aligned with their well-being.

People often tell me that eating healthy, fresh and organic foods costs too much money and takes too much time. That's like saying, *"Getting oil changes cost too much money and are inconvenient, I'd rather wait and replace the transmission."* If we truly make our health a priority, we will make diet and nutrition a priority.

As Michael Pollan, author of *In Defense of Food: An Eater's Manifesto,* points out...

"While it is true that many people simply can't afford to pay more for food, either in money or time or both, many more of us can. After all, just in the last decade or two we've somehow found the time in the day to spend several hours on the internet and the money in the budget not only to pay for broadband service, but to cover a second phone bill and a new monthly bill for television, formerly free. For the majority of Americans, spending more for better food is less a matter of ability than priority.

A Big Mac currently costs about $5 and weighs about ½ pound. The salad bar at Whole Foods is currently $8.99 per pound. A ½ pound of the salad bar at Whole Foods costs less than a ½ pound Big Mac.

What we eat not only impacts our health, but it also impacts society, the economy and the environment. The global food and grocery retail industry is estimated to be over $12 trillion per year.[147] When we buy groceries, we vote with our dollars and $12 trillion has a lot of influence on our economy, corporations and governments. If we are looking to improve the health and the well-being of ourselves and our world, it's important that our diet choices balance not only personal health, but also the health of the planet and society. For example, if we choose to eat animal flesh as a protein source, eating chicken instead of beef, would carry a lower environmental impact, but also may not provide the level of environmental repair of regeneratively pasture-raised, grass-fed, grass-finished beef. Savory's regenerative system of Holistic management, mentioned above, also recommends pasture raised chickens as part of the ecosystem for rebuilding grasslands and soil. Therefore, eating chicken that is organic, pasture-raised and humanely-raised, slaughtered and processed, is a conscious choice that is healthier, energetically cleaner and better tasting. Moreover, the animal has not suffered undue cruelty nor was it pumped full of hormones and antibiotics.

Fish and seafood also provide a more conscious choice than beef, but many fish are caught using trawlers and other environmentally harmful commercial fishing means. Also, many commercial species have been fished so heavily that they are currently on the endangered species list. These include Bluefin Tuna, Atlantic Halibut, Atlantic Cod, Chilean Sea Bass, Spiny Lobster, Shark, and Orange Roughy."[148]

Moreover, several species of fish contain high mercury levels, which can create toxicity if eaten too frequently. The following is a partial list of fish and seafood mercury levels:

High Mercury	Moderate Mercury	Low Mercury
Swordfish, Shark, King Mackerel, Tuna, Chilean Sea Bass	Striped Bass, Grouper, Halibut, Anchovies, Butterfish, Snapper	Salmon, Sardine, Tilapia, Trout, Whitefish, Cod, Herring, Shrimp, Crab, Scallops, Clams and Oysters

Furthermore, certain seafood taken from polluted waters may contain other toxins, such as polychlorinated biphenyl ("PCB"), hydrocarbons and pesticides. Farmed fish, although a conscious choice from the standpoint of renewability and conservation, are often raised in overcrowded and polluted ponds and forced to live in unnatural conditions in their own waste. Moreover, many farmed fish, especially farmed salmon, are fed unnatural and unhealthy diets and given antibiotics, resulting in unhealthy, nutritionally obsolete and energetically damaged fish. There are, however, some open ocean and sustainable fish farms that produce healthy fish with conscious methods. Oysters, shrimp, tilapia, sturgeon and catfish have been successfully and environmentally farmed, but it's important to do the research on the source of your seafood.

Clearly, certain food choices provide higher nutrition, enhanced assimilation, greater energy and are consciously and spiritually more evolved. But not all people thrive on the same diet. Some people are genetically predisposed to a higher protein diet. For example, the Eskimos would not do to well on a low-fat vegetarian diet—they need a high-fat diet to survive in their environment and have become genetically predisposed to a high-fat diet.

As well, lifestyle plays a big part in dietary requirements. Someone who is a long-distance runner will generally need greater amounts of carbohydrates, whereas a body builder will require greater amounts of protein. A swami, who spends much of his day sitting in meditation, can do very well on a vegetarian diet.

Many societies on the planet have become addicted to white flour, refined sugar, caffeine and trans-fat, all of which promote microbial growth and disease. By eliminating or minimizing these products from our diet, we can make substantial gains in our wellness.

3. Top 10 Conscious Eating Guidelines

Below is a list to help you make more conscious and healthy choices regarding your diet and nutrition.

1. Make conscious lifestyle choices that provide the highest nutritional value and health benefits while balancing environmental, social and spiritual concerns with the following guidelines:

    - *Real* rather than processed

    - *Raw* rather than cooked whenever possible and safe

- *Fresh* rather than packaged

- *Organic* rather than conventional

- *Alkaline/Alkalizing* rather than acidic and acid producing

- *Nutrient rich* rather than empty calories

- *Locally grown* and sourced rather than shipped from miles away

2. Read the labels of the food you purchase. If the food has artificial colors, preservatives, artificial flavors, refined sugar, refined flour, corn syrup and a whole bunch of chemicals that you cannot pronounce, put the product back.

3. Eat densely nutritious "Superfoods," consisting of fresh vegetables, low glycemic fruits, and foods high in antioxidants. (see below information on "Superfoods")

4. Engage in basic food-combining including

- Eat fresh low glycemic fruits by themselves and preferably in the morning.

- Eat proteins with vegetables

- Eat starch with vegetables

- Avoid mixing proteins with starches.

5. Eat for nutritional purposes rather than psycho-emotional purposes. If you are eating when you are not hungry or eating to mask an emotional craving (e.g., eating food when you are feeling lonely, bored, frustrated or angry), there is a strong indication that you're eating is psycho-emotional.

6. Cut down on, or cut out red meat, pork, sugar, grains, desserts, soda, alcohol, and tobacco, as well as processed and fried foods, particularly those that contain partially hydrogenated oils (trans fats) and refined sugar.

7. Substitute healthier choices for the foods you like. Here are some examples:

- Instead of drinking soft drinks full of caffeine and sugar, drink carbonated drinks that are organic and contain low glycemic sweeteners such as agave or stevia, or just drink carbonated mineral water with lemon, lime, ginger or other natural flavoring added. As well, coconut water is a healthy substitute for soft drinks.

- Rather than buying frozen or canned vegetables buy fresh vegetables.

- Eat fish low in mercury such as salmon rather than high mercury fish such as swordfish or tuna, as well as non-threatened renewable seafood such as shrimp and oysters.

- Substitute poached eggs, turkey bacon and an organic mixed green salad (or baked potatoes if you must) for the traditional fried eggs, bacon and hash browns for breakfast.

- Eat an ostrich burger, turkey burger, bison burger or veggie burger, or eat only pasture-raised, grass-fed and grass-finished beef burger instead of an industrial grain-fed beef burger.

- If you desire baked goods, eat whole grain (or preferably non-grain) gluten-free baked goods rather than refined flour baked goods.

- Eat only non-GMO foods.

8. Engage in a cleanse at least quarterly (see Section on Internal Cleansing).

9. Graze throughout the day or eat 5 small ("portion-controlled") meals rather than 2 or 3 larger meals. The lighter you eat the more easily your body can digest your food and convert it into useable energy.

10. Chew your food slowly and thoroughly. Enjoy every bite.

By following the foregoing basic guidelines, you will receive amazing payoffs in your overall health, energy, vitality, mental acuity, endurance and libido.

Also, there is an incredible variety of foods that fit the foregoing guidelines. Once you find the combination of foods and supplements that agree with your dietary preferences and provide you with optimal health benefits, it becomes very easy to continue in a lifestyle of healthy diet and nutrition.

Creating a healthy diet and nutrition lifestyle does take research and experimentation. However, the research and experimentation can be very fun and interesting and will yield permanent lifelong benefits. Fortunately, this chapter provides greater depth, research and facts to help you benefit from a lifestyle of health and nutrition. Again, it is important to not only do your own research, but also to consult with experienced health professionals. Journaling and various mobile and biometric apps can also provide you with meaningful feedback about the efficacy of your diet and nutrition choices.

B. SUPERCHARGED DIET AND NUTRITION FOR ACHIEVING OPTIMAL WELLNESS

This section is written for those that want to supercharge their health, possess amazing vitality and increase systemic functionality (i.e., immune, endocrine, cardiovascular, nervous, muscular, skeletal, reproductive, digestive, excretory and integumentary). This section covers the keys to supercharging your diet and includes the following:

1. *The Nutritional Building Blocks* (Proteins, Carbohydrates & Fats)

2. *Essentials of a Healthy Diet* (Vitamins, Minerals & Enzymes)

3. *Supercharging Your Diet* (Herbs, Superfoods & Antioxidants)

4. *Optimizing Your Diet* (Portioning, Ketogenics, Alkalizing Diet, Hydration, Food-combining, Blood Type & Optimizing Mitochondrial Health)

While achieving optimal wellness requires additional levels of awareness, discipline, time, attention and money, health is one of the greatest gifts we can give our loved ones and ourselves. And in the long run, having optimal health has remarkable returns on investment, not only in improving the quality of our lives, but in the time and money we save by avoiding the healthcare system and its expenses.

1. The Nutritional Building Blocks (Proteins, Carbohydrates & Fats)

Understanding the nutritional building blocks is important to a conscious approach to a nutritional and optimized diet. The nutritional building blocks are 1) **Proteins**, 2) **Carbohydrates** and 3) **Fats** and it's important to have a daily balance of each.

a. *Proteins*[149]

Proteins are essential for human life and are the building blocks of tissue, bones, muscle, blood and cartilage, as well as cellular function.

Proteins are organic compounds made of amino acids chains and joined together by peptide bonds. A peptide is defined as two or more bonded amino acids. Peptides are precursors to proteins, which require at least 50 bonded amino acids.

When you eat foods containing protein, the protein is broken down by the stomach into basic units called amino acids. The amino acids then can be reused to make the proteins your body needs to maintain muscles, bones, blood, and body organs.

Protein is 90% of the dry weight of blood, 80% of muscles, and 70% of the skin. Proteins provide the building blocks for connective tissue and are the primary constituents of enzymes, hormones and antibodies. They encompass many important chemicals including immunoglobulins and enzymes. In short, protein forms the foundation of muscles, skin, bones, hair, heart, teeth, blood, and brain and the billions of biochemical activities going on in our bodies every minute. Proteins are used by our bodies for many specific functions including:

- Making hemoglobin, the part of red blood cells that carries oxygen to every part of your body.
- Building bone, muscle, tissue, cartilage and internal organs
- Metabolic functions
- Energy production
- Enzyme production and digestion
- Maintains pH
- Maintains fluid balance
- Bolsters immune system function
- Stores nutrients

Depending upon your spiritual beliefs, diet, allergies, gut biome health, enzymatic function, geography, customs and preferences, the most complete and easiest protein sources for a majority of people to assimilate are animal protein sources, such as fish, meat and dairy.

However, protein requires enzymes to break it down and vitamins to assimilate it. The protein-dense sources are beef, chicken, lamb, fish, milk and eggs. Another great source of protein is whey, considered the gold standard of protein powder, is a complete protein containing all 9 essential amino acids, but low in fat and lactose. In most cooked meats and pasteurized dairy products, enzymes have been destroyed, which makes digestion more difficult. Many meats and dairy products should not be eaten raw due to questionable processing and distribution practices in the commercial meat and dairy industries. However, extremely fresh, grass-fed, grass-finished, organic, pasture-raised and source verified meats and dairy may be eaten raw with excellent results.

Not all proteins are created equally. There is a significant difference in the digestibility, bioavailability and ability to assimilate different proteins. The Digestible Indispensable Amino Acid Score ("DIAAS") is used to determine the digestibility and bioavailability of proteins. DIASS scores over 100 are considered high-quality protein sources, between 75-99 are considered good protein quality sources, and below 75 are considered low quality protein sources.[150]

DIAAS Chart

Protein Source	DIAAS	Protein Source	DIAAS
Milk Protein Concentrate	118	Chickpeas	83
Whole Cow's Milk	114	Pea Protein Concentrate	82
Pork	114	Quinoa	67
Egg	113	Hemp	61
Beef	111	Rice	59
Whey Protein Isolate	109	Kidney Beans	59
Chicken Breast	108	Peas	58
Fish	100	Oat	54
Spirulina	100	Roasted Peanuts	43
Mycoprotein	99	Wheat	40
Soy Protein Isolate	90	Almonds	40

Vegans will obviously not choose animal proteins in their diet and must be more creative. Often soy or seitan are used, but are typically low in one or more of the essential amino acids even though the overall protein content is high. There is also some controversy regarding the safety of soy. Soy protein is thought by some researchers to be high in mineral-blocking phytates and thyroid-depressing phytoestrogen and is often highly processed and GMO. If you desire to use soy, organic, non-GMO, soy is recommended. Seitan is made from wheat gluten, which has serious health impacts to those with celiac disease or gluten sensitivity. Wheat gluten has been implicated in causing inflammation, poor digestion, damage to the lining of the small intestine, memory loss, Alzheimer's and dementia.[151]

Pea protein is gaining popularity as great protein sources for vegans and vegetarians and has an 82 DIAAS. Pea protein is a complete protein, containing all nine essential amino acids and including branched-chain amino acids ("BCAAs") and is especially high in arginine, which promotes healthy blood flow and heart health. Also, pea protein contains isoleucine, leucine and valine, which promote muscle growth. Pea protein is easily digestible and more bio-available than other plant-based proteins.

Hemp protein is also gaining traction with vegans and vegetarians. Hemp contains vitamins (particularly the tocopherols and tocotrienols of the Vitamin E complex), phytosterols and trace minerals. Like other oil seeds, the hemp nut consists mainly of oil but has a high protein content of approximately 33%. Although hemp does not presently have a DIAAS, hemp does have a *Protein Digestibility-Corrected Amino Acid Score* ("PDCAAS"). The PDCAAS values for hemp include 84.1-86.2 (49-53%) for whole hemp seed, 90.8-97.5 (46-51%) for hemp seed meal, and 83.5-92.1 (63-66%) for dehulled hemp seed.[152] Overall, hemp's main nutritional advantage over other seeds lies in the composition of its fatty acid profile and in its protein, which contains all of the essential amino acids in nutritionally significant amounts and in a desirable ratio.

Also, spirulina (a blue-green algae) has a DIAAS of 100 and is considered a whole superfood and containing an average of 60% protein. Spirulina also contains beneficial fatty acids and is a powerful antioxidant.[153]

Additional sources of plant-based protein include brown rice protein, legumes (e.g., lentils, black beans, chickpeas, pinto beans, lima beans), quinoa, oats, peas, nuts (e.g., sunflower seeds, pistachios, almonds, cashews) and guava.

Since proteins are made of amino acid chains and joined together by peptide bonds, understanding and supplementing our diet with amino acids can dramatically improve our health. Also, utilizing collagen peptides can reduce the symptoms of aging and promote healthy hair, skin, nails, bones and joints. As well, L-cysteine, glutathione (a linear tripeptide of L-glutamine), and glycine (considered the body's master antioxidant), improve insulin resistance; increases cellular functioning; assist in removal of heavy metals; helps detoxify the liver; reduces oxidative stress, cell damage; and diminish symptoms of Parkinson's disease and autism.

When we consume protein, our digestive systems break down the protein into its various amino acids, and our cells use free-floating amino acids to build new protein molecules pursuant to our genetic instructions in our DNA to RNA, which then sequence the amino acids into a polypeptide protein chain. This process, called *protein synthesis*, is critical to maintaining and growing muscles, improving brain function, strengthening the immune system, elevating mood, raising metabolism or help us sleep.

There are 3 different types of amino acids: (1) Essential Amino Acids; (2) Non-Essential Amino Acids; and Conditional Amino Acids, described below:[154]

1. **Essential Amino Acids** are the following 9 amino acids that our bodies cannot produce on their own and must be consumed:

Histidine	Has been found to improve rheumatoid arthritis, allergies, ulcers, anemia and kidney disease.
Isoleucine	Consider the "Endurance Amino Acid, Isoleucine helps to efficiently turn calories into energy and maintain energy levels. It helps regulate blood sugar, boosts energy, promotes healing and repair damaged muscle.
Leucine	Playing an essential role in protein production, Leucine promotes stronger and bigger muscles while reducing muscle degradation and improving workouts.
Lysine	Help prevent cold sores and other forms of the herpes simplex virus as well as improving athletic performance.
Methionine	Aids the liver health in fighting viral infections and healing damaged tissue. As an antioxidant, it also reduces damage done by free radicals.
Phenylalanine	There are three types of phenylalanine. There's D-phenylalanine, L-phenylalanine, and DL-phenylalanine. L-phenylalanine is the version that's considered an essential amino acid. Phenylalanine helps treat various skin diseases, improves focus, reduces pain, and helps with weight loss.
Threonine	Used for treating a variety of nervous system disorders including multiple sclerosis and ALS. Threonine is converted into glycine in the body, which helps the brain reduce muscle spasms. These spasms would happen constantly but for the threonine.
Tryptophan	There are two types of tryptophan: L-tryptophan and D-tryptophan. L-tryptophan helps create 5-HTP, serotonin, melatonin, and vitamin B6, and effectively improves mood, increases brain function and helps depression and insomnia.
Valine·	Prevents muscle breakdown and promotes nervous system, brain function. coordination and. It also boosts workout recovery times.

2. **Non-Essential Amino Acids** are those that our bodies can produce on their own. Even though our bodies make these amino acids, supplementation can provide significant health benefits:

Alanine	Assists the body in sugar and acid metabolism and improves energy levels and the functioning of the immune and nervous systems.
Asparagine	Plays an important role in the biosynthesis of glycoproteins and protein synthesis. Asparagine helps transport nitrogen throughout the body and decreases fatigue.
Aspartic Acid	Plays an important role in hormone production and release and normal nervous system function.
Glutamic Acid	Important to cellular metabolism, L-Glutamic Acid is stored in the cells and is one of the most abundant sources of excitatory neurotransmitters in the body, helping increase focus, alertness, and energy.
Serine	Plays a critical role in the metabolism of fats, fatty acids, and cell membranes. It also supports immune system efficiency and muscle growth.
Selenocysteine	Has been used to decrease incidence of cancer, cardiovascular diseases and muscle disorders.

3. **Conditional Amino Acids** are produced by the body and are generally non-essential. However, when the body is operating at a less than optimal fashion, these non-essential amino acids become essential and require supplementation. They also can be consumed to promote greater health.

Arginine	Promotes heart and artery health, removal waste from the kidneys, healthy immune system function, and regulation of hormone production.
Cysteine	Essential for making the powerful antioxidant glutathione. Supports protein synthesis, metabolic functions, and detoxification of the body. Also, Cysteine has been used to improve respiratory condition, brain function, mood disorders and addictive behavior.
Glutamine	As one of the most important nutrients for digestive health and immune system function, L-Glutamine helps reduce the symptoms of diseases like Crohn's disease, colitis, and ulcers. It's also popular with athletes and bodybuilders for its ability to reduce muscle breakdown, improve muscle growth and improve protein metabolism. Glutamine is the most common amino acid in the muscles.
Glycine	Main amino acid in collagen and required for the production of glutathione. Glycine promotes healthy liver function, prevents muscle loss, protect against heart disease, increase insulin response, and improve sleep quality.
Tyrosine	Tyrosine is made from another amino acid called phenylalanine. It's involved primarily to help improve memory, learning, alertness, and focus.
Ornithine	Aids athletic performance by speeding up recovery and maintaining glutamine and ammonia levels.
Proline	Found mostly in the skin's collagen. Collagen is the skin's supportive protein that prevents skin damage and wrinkling. Proline helps improve tendon, bone, and connective tissue health.
Tyrosine	Helps improve alertness, attention and focus, strengthens nervous system functioning and regulates mood.

b. **Carbohydrates**[155]

Carbohydrates ("Carbs") supply the body with the energy it needs to function. Carbs are found almost exclusively in plant foods, such as fruits, vegetables, peas, beans and grains. Milk and milk products are the only foods derived from animals that contain a significant amount of carbohydrates.

Carbohydrates are divided into two groups:

1.   **Simple Carbs** that include fructose (fruit sugar), sucrose (table sugar), glucose (dextrose) and lactose (milk sugar), and honey, as well as other **sugars**. Fruits are one of the richest natural sources of Simple Carbs. Simple Carbs or simple sugars (except fructose) are typically high on the glycemic index, so they tend to cause a rapid rise in blood sugar. Simple Carbs are good for immediate energy, but not so good for sustained energy, appetite management and blood glucose control.

2.   **Complex Carbs** are also made up of sugars, but the sugar molecules are strung together to form longer, more complex chains. Complex Carbs include fiber and starches. Foods rich in Complex Carbs include **vegetables, potatoes, whole grains, peas, and beans**.

Carbohydrates are the main source of blood glucose, which is a major fuel for all of the body's cells and the only source of energy for the brain and red blood cells. Except for fiber, which cannot be digested, both simple and complex carbohydrates are converted into glucose. The glucose is then either used directly to provide energy for the body, or stored in the liver for future use.

It's also important to be **aware** of the differences between **Refined Carbs** and **Unrefined Carbs**, which generally refers to starches and grains.

1.   **Refined Carbs** refers to foods where machinery has been used to remove the high fiber (the bran and the germ) from the grain. Examples include white rice, white bread, processed cereals, and pasta/noodles made from white flour.

2.   **Unrefined Carbs** contain the whole grain, including the bran and the germ, so they are higher in fiber, convert into glucose at a slower rate and avoid the sugar rush/crash syndrome found in Refined Carbs. Examples include quinoa, whole grain rice, whole oats and whole wheat pasta.

Refined Carbs may be complex carbohydrates, but because of the refining and processing, many of the health benefits of being Complex Carbs have been lost and the body digests these carbs more rapidly thereby creating a glucose conversion and release pattern similar to that of Simple Carbs.

Besides being the most easily accessible energy source for muscles and organs of the body, carbohydrates play an important role in the construction and maintenance of the body's tissues, organs and cells, including nerve cells. Also, many of the foods rich in Carbs, such as fruits and vegetables, provide fiber which aids in healthy digestion.

When a person consumes more carbohydrate calories than the body can readily use, the **excess carbohydrates** are generally stored in the body as **fat**. When eating meals high in carbohydrates or sugars, the body converts useable sugars from carbohydrates to energy while excess sugars are either stored for near-term energy or converted to fat.

The sugar-to-fat conversion occurs in two ways—an immediate response, where enzymes are mobilized to rapidly convert sugars into fat; and a slower response, in which several different genes are turned on and off, creating more enzymes that can also turn sugar into fat.

Thus, eating carbohydrates sufficient for your body's needs is essential for a healthy diet and well-being. However, eating too many carbohydrates, especially refined and simple carbohydrates, can lead to obesity and diseases such as diabetes, chronic yeast and microbial infections. Therefore, the following guidelines should be utilized when consuming carbohydrates:

1.   Eat unrefined complex carbohydrates.

2.   Eat fruit as the only simple carbohydrate. Fruit should be eaten separately (See section on Food-combining). Fruits are important to

nutrition and wellness, however, because many fruits contain high levels of fructose, it is advisable to choose low glycemic fruits such as cherries, grapefruit, apples, pears, plums, blueberries, blackberries, raspberries, strawberries, peaches and lemons.

3. Simple carbs, whether unrefined or refined, should not be eaten, except for fruit. But if you feel you must, eat only limited amounts occasionally.

4. Eat carbs in portions that can be efficiently and immediately utilized by the body.

5. Eat carbs in smaller portions throughout the day to keep the metabolic rate high and consistent while avoiding glycemic spikes and storage of unused carbs as fat.

6. Eat a high fiber diet including such foods as oat bran, hemp seeds, flax seeds, chia seeds, psyllium seed husk, legumes (especially green peas, lentils and black beans), artichokes, broccoli, Brussels sprouts, pears and raspberries. A high fiber diet helps normalize bowel movements, support intestinal health, lower cholesterol levels, and maintain blood sugar level, as well as promoting healthy weight and longevity.

c. **Fats**[156]

The most misunderstood nutrient is fat. Many people believe fats are bad and should be avoided. While too much of anything can be dangerous, certain fats are required for a healthy and nutritional diet.

Fat is an essential nutrient for proper body function. It provides energy for the body and is used in the production of cell membranes and in compounds called eicosanoids. These compounds are similar to hormones and help regulate blood pressure, blood vessel constriction, blood clotting, heart rate and the nervous system. Fat also helps transport fat-soluble vitamins, such as A, D, E and K, from food into the body. Moreover, fat promotes healthy hair and skin, protects vital organs, and insulates the body.

Fats are made up of glycerol (three-carbon atoms that form the backbone of fatty acids) and fatty acids (chains of carbon, hydrogen and oxygen). They are stored in the body as triglycerides, which also circulate in the blood.

All fats and oils contain both saturated and unsaturated fatty acids. Fats are classified as either saturated or unsaturated depending on the percentage of fat that is dominant. For example, butter contains mostly saturated fat as well as lesser amounts of unsaturated fat. As a result, it is classified as a saturated fat. Meanwhile, canola oil has a high percentage of monounsaturated fat, as well as smaller amounts of polyunsaturated fats and saturated fats. It is classified as a monounsaturated fat.

Fats are divided into three main categories: 1) **Unsaturated Fats**, 2) **Saturated Fats**, and 3) **Trans Fats**.

1.   **Unsaturated fats** include *polyunsaturated fats* and *monounsaturated fats*. The difference between the two are that polyunsaturated fats are simply fats that have more than one double-bonded (unsaturated) carbon in the molecule.

      • *Polyunsaturated fats* are found primarily in foods from plant origin and from fish. Polyunsaturated fats are found primarily in oils from plants, including sesame and sunflower seeds, corn and soybeans, many nuts and seeds and their oils, as well as fatty fish such as salmon.

      Polyunsaturated fats can be further divided into two subgroups: 1) **Omega-6 fatty acids** and **Omega-3 fatty acids**. Omega 3 (linolenic acid), primarily derived from fish oils, and Omega 6 (linoleic acid), primarily derived from plant sources such as flax and hemp seeds and nuts, are known and understood to be **Essential Fatty Acids ("EFA's")** since they are generally obtained by ingesting foods. The body needs EFA's to help synthesize certain hormones and hormone-like substances, provide structure for cell membranes, keep the brain and nerves healthy, and support natural growth.

Omega-3 and Omega—6 fatty acids have been demonstrated to reduce the risk of cardiovascular disease, increase cellular efficiency and ability to retain nutrients, boost immune system, increase brain function, enhance kidney function, reduce blood pressure, reduce swelling, inflammation and pain and promote gastrointestinal function.

Again, hemp nut and **hemp oil** offers vegetarians high concentrations of EFA's and an omega-6/omega-3 ratio of approximately 3:1., which is a very desirable omega-6/omega-3 ratio. Hemp oil also provides significant amounts of rare 'super' polyunsaturated fatty acids, notably gamma-linolenic acid (GLA) and stearidonic acid (SDA), which have been found to be very good for the skin.

- *Monounsaturated fats* are found mostly in foods from plant origin, have a lower melting point and are usually liquid at room temperature, but start to solidify at refrigerator temperatures. Monounsaturated fats not only lower levels of "bad" cholesterol, but also raise the levels of high-density lipoprotein (HDL) cholesterol, which has health benefits. Sources of monounsaturated fats include **canola, olive and peanut oils**, and **avocados**. Monounsaturated fats provide omega-9 fatty acids, with oleic acid being the most common monounsaturated fatty acid. Although omega-9 fatty acids are not considered essential (because they can be produced by the body), they have many health benefits including increasing "good" high-density lipoproteins and lowering "bad" low-density-lipoproteins ("LDL") cholesterol, as well as eliminating arterial plaque, which has been implicated in heart attack and stroke.

2. **Saturated fats** are found mainly in *animal fats* (e.g., butter, lard) and certain *plant* fats (e.g., coconut oil, palm oil, cocoa butter). They typically have a high melting temperature because of their chemical structure and are solid or hard at room temperature. There is,

however, a difference between plant derived saturated fatty acids and animal derived fatty acids. Distinguishing between animal and plant saturated fatty acids is important. As an example, two Superfoods, Coconut and Cacao contain high amounts of saturated fats, but have important functional attributes.

Coconut has proven to be a valuable superfood even though it is a source of saturated fats and was originally criticized by the medical establishment. Coconut contains a very healthy form of fat called medium-chain triglycerides (MCTs). Although MCTs are a form of saturated fat, MCTs are very digestible and possess antiviral and antimicrobal properties. Specifically, coconut and coconut oil contain a fatty acid called lauric acid, which is effective in fighting a number of bacteria and supporting the immune system.

Some older research performed in the 1950's and 1960's in the U.S., utilized hydrogenated coconut oil, in which the essential fatty acids were removed, showed hydrogenated coconut oil performs much like animal saturated fats in raising serum cholesterol. However, when *virgin coconut oil*, which is a significant source of lauric acid, is used, it has been shown to lower serum cholesterol as well as providing strong anti-microbial, anti-viral and anti-obesity benefits. Lauric acid in diets in the western hemisphere tends to be low to practically non-existent. The lauric acid in coconut oil is used by the body to make the same disease-fighting fatty acid derivative monolaurin that babies make from the lauric acid they get from their mothers' milk. The monoglyceride monolaurin is the substance that keeps infants from getting viral or bacterial or protozoal infections.[157] Until just recently, this important benefit has been largely overlooked by the medical and nutrition community.

Cacao has been shown to be an incredibly powerful antioxidant with benefits including appetite suppression, anti-aging, lower blood pressure and cough suppression. Additionally, cacao is a source of (1) *theobromine*, which invigorates and stimulates phenylethylamine, the touted "love chemical" that increases happiness, alertness and well-being, (2) *tryptophan,* which helps increase and stabilize mood, and (3) *anandamide,* the "bliss chemical" which relaxes body and mind, magnesium for a healthy heart and muscle relaxation, Cacao also contains *iron, folic acid and vitamins A, E, K.*

3. **Trans fats** are a form of unsaturated fat in which hydrogen atoms are added during a process called hydrogenation. Trans fatty acids are mainly manufactured fats that are stable and solid at room temperature. Trans fats are found in deep-fried foods, margarines, baked goods and other processed foods made with "hydrogenated" or "partially hydrogenated vegetable oils." Some trans-fat is found naturally in small amounts in various meat and dairy products. Trans fats should be avoided as they have been found to be a major contributor to obesity, cardiovascular disease, cancer, diabetes and birth defects.

In addition to the foregoing, humans and other mammals have two types of fat: 1) Brown Adipose Tissue ("BAT"), often referred to as *"Brown Fat"*; and 2) White Adipose Tissue ("WAT") or *"White Fat."* Brown Fat's primary function is to turn food into body heat. Brown Fat has more capillaries than White Fat, as well as a high number of iron containing mitochondria. Unlike White Fat which primarily stores calories as triglycerides, Brown Fat burns calories by dissipating chemical energy as heat.

White Fat generally builds up around the waist, thighs and abdomen, whereas Brown Fat accumulates around the neck, shoulders and upper chest. White Fat around the abdomen is associated with a higher risk of metabolic disease, whereas White Fat around the hips does not. When we consume excess calories, the body converts them into White Fat.

Brown Fat helps maintain metabolism and is used for regulating body temperature. It also contributes to energy expenditure. Studies show that those with more Brown Fat than White Fat burn more calories and tend to be less prone to obesity and related diseases such as diabetes, cardiovascular disease, hypertension, stroke, arthritis and various types of cancer.[158]

Brown Fat can be activated by exposure to cold temperature, which can be done by turning down your thermostat, or more effectively through whole-body cryotherapy treatments. Also, stimulating melatonin production can increase Brown Fat. This can be done by getting sunlight exposure and avoiding nighttime exposure to TVs, computer and other screens, as well as eating melatonin-rich foods such as almonds, tart cherries, cardamom and coriander. Also, intermittent fasting has been found to stimulate trans-forming White Fat into Brown Fat.[159]

The Digestion and Use of Proteins, Carbs and Fats

The following provides information on how our bodies process food containing proteins, carbs and fats:

Saliva contains enzymes that break any starch in the food down to sugar. This, along with any fat and water in the food, travel to the stomach, where the contents get churned up. Pepsin, an enzyme that digests protein, and hydrochloric acid further break down the food, turning it into a substance called chyme.

The mixture enters the duodenum—the place where the gall bladder secretes its bile. This bile dissolves the fat in water, thinning it out and making it easier to absorb. Enzymes from the pancreas enter the duodenum and further break down the sugar, fat and protein. Now everything is dissolved and is in fluid form, so it is absorbed through the lining of the small bowel. Fat, sugar and protein now go their separate ways.

- *What happens to the sugar?*

  It goes directly into the bloodstream, and several different organs take the sugar they need as it passes by. Some is stored in the liver as glycogen and whatever remains is converted to fat and stored in fat cells.

- *What happens to the fat?*

  First, it goes into the bloodstream and travels to the liver. The liver burns some of the fat, converts some to substances like cholesterol and sends the balance to fat cells, where they are stored until needed. By eating a low carbohydrate, *ketonic* diet, the body will use fat as an energy source when insufficient glucose from carbohydrates exist.

- *What happens to the protein?*

  It is broken down into building blocks known as peptides. It is then further broken down and becomes amino acids. The amino acids are absorbed through the small intestine's lining and enter the bloodstream. Some of the amino acids build the body's protein stores, while excess amino acids are converted to fats and sugars and follow the paths described above. Although protein does go through additional processes that give the body greater ability to utilize protein, consuming excessive amounts of protein gets stored as fat.

A main cause of weight gain is overeating. Dietary fat is the substance most often stored as fat in the end. No matter what you eat, your body typically takes whatever it can't use and sends it to fat cells. Fat cells also store toxins. Thus, there is high likelihood that the more excess fat you store, the more toxins you carry in your body.

2. Essentials of a Healthy Diet (Vitamins, Minerals and Enzymes)

According to Dr. James B. Sumner, Professor of Biochemistry, Cornell University, 3 classes of elements are essential for good health: 1) **Vitamins**, 2) **Minerals** and 3) **Enzymes**.

a.   *Vitamins*[160]

Vitamins are necessary for human life and health. With the exception of Vitamin B12, vitamins aren't manufactured in our bodies. These organic compounds need to be obtained from diet and external sources. If we are deprived of a particular vitamin, we will generally suffer a symptom or disease related to the deficiency. With low levels of nutrients remaining in many of the foods we eat, it has become necessary for optimal health to supplement our food intake with vitamins, minerals and enzymes.

More people are waking up and taking back responsibility for their wellness from a corrupt and broken health care system. Increasing numbers of people are turning to nutritional, dietary and herbal supplements to prevent diseases and promote general good health. Vitamin supplements are taken by more than 75% of the world's population and the pharmaceutical companies and medical establishment don't like it, because people are getting healthy without their expensive services, pharmaceutical drugs and other sickcare products. As we eat healthier, we eat into the profits of the corrupt medical establishment.

Our health care system is not the only thing toxic in our modern lifestyle, we can also include processed and toxic food, polluted air, poisoned water, and chemicals in our homes, cars and workplaces, all of which contribute to diminishing our health. Our bodies are continuously under attack from all kinds of factors that threaten to damage our health. Aside from the toxic lifestyles to which we are exposed, the lack of nutrients in our food makes it more difficult to resist, defend and repair the onslaught of our contaminated environment.

Therefore, our bodies struggle to get all the basic elements we need to function properly. Nutritional supplements can provide the essential elements our bodies need to thrive, and to achieve optimum health.

Although dietary supplements are necessary to complement our diet, they are not a replacement for healthy eating. Quality and efficacious dietary supplements taken in appropriate doses will help improve health regardless of eating habits, but taken in combination with a conscious and nutritious diet, dietary supplements can help us achieve higher levels of health and well-being.

Vitamins are classified into two main categories:

1. *Water Soluble Vitamins*—*Vitamins that dissolve in water include the B complex, C and P.*

2. *Fat Soluble Vitamins*—*Vitamins that require fats/lipids to be dissolved and are absorbed through the intestinal tract include A, D, E, F and K.*

The term "Vitamin" does not include other essential nutrients, such as minerals, enzymes, essential fatty acids, essential amino acids or other nutrients that promote well-being. There are additional nutritional supplements that are important for health that have been referred to as "vitamins," but have not been accepted or been reclassified by mainstream science. These include Choline (B-4), Inositol (B-8 or Bh), Paba (Bx), Essential Fatty Acids (F), Flavinoids (P) and S-Methylmethionine (U). They are listed below because of the important contribution to one's health and because they are often considered as vitamins.

Vitamins	
Vitamin A **(Retinol)**	**Recommended Daily Dosage:** Men : 3,000 IU Women: 2,700 IU
Natural food sources:	**Indication/Benefits:**
Eggs, fish liver oils, beef, chicken, carrots, squash, sweet potatoes, broccoli, green leafy vegetables	Essential for eyes; healthy formation of bones, teeth, skin; maintenance of outer layer of many tissues & organs; promotes growth & lactation; necessary for night vision; good for growth & repair of body tissues; good for health of hair and eyes.
Deficiency:	**Overdose:**
Night blindness; reduced hair growth in children; loss of appetite; dry, rough skin; lowered resistance to infection; dry eyes.	Headaches; fatigue; blurred vision; diarrhea; vomiting; irregular periods; joint and bone pain; dry, cracked skin; rashes; loss of hair; liver damage.

Beta Carotene	**Recommended Daily Dosage:** Men :10,000 IU Women: 8,000 IU
Natural food sources:	**Indication/Benefits:**
Orange and red colored vegetables, eggs, fish liver oils, beef, chicken, carrots, squash, sweet potatoes, broccoli, green leafy vegetables, mangos, papayas	Converted to Vitamin A in the body. Antioxidant. (See Vitamin A—Retinol)
Deficiency:	**Overdose:**
See Vitamin A (Retinol)	See Vitamin A (Retinol)

Vitamin B Complex	
B-1 *(Thiamine)*	**Recommended Daily Dosage:** Men: 1.3 mg Women: .8 mg
Natural food sources:	**Indication/Benefits:**
Nuts, wheat germ, poultry, fish, brown rice, egg yolks, legumes, whole grains, blackstrap molasses, brewer's yeast, whole wheat, seafood, potatoes, pork, sunflower seeds.	Necessary for carbohydrate metabolism and muscle coordination. Promotes proper nerve function. Maintains health of skin, mouth, eyes, hair; stabilizes appetite. Essential for normal functioning of heart, nerve tissues, muscles, digestion, learning capacity and growth.
Deficiency:	**Overdose:**
Anxiety; depression; hysteria; muscle cramps; loss of appetite; in extreme cases beriberi (mostly in alcoholics).	Unknown, although excess of one B vitamin may cause deficiency of others.
B-2 *(Riboflavin)*	**Recommended Daily Dosage:** Men: 1.6 mg Women: 1.1 mg
Natural food sources:	**Indication/Benefits:**
Nuts, whole grains, blackstrap molasses, yogurt, poultry, mushrooms, oysters, green vegetables, spinach, milk, cheese, eggs, liver, brewer's yeast.	Needed for metabolism of all foods and the release of energy to cells. Essential to the functioning of Vitamin B6 and Niacin.
Deficiency:	**Overdose:**
Cracks and sores around the mouth and nose; visual problems.	See Vitamin B1.
B-3 *(Niacin)* (Niacin is converted to niacinamide in the body)	**Recommended Daily Dosage:** Men: 23 mg Women 16 mg
Natural food sources:	**Indication/Benefits:**
Beans, green vegetables, rice, bran, whole wheat, nuts, brewer's yeast, fish, dairy products, poultry, lean meats, milk, eggs, cheese, peas, mushrooms, tuna.	Needed in many enzymes that convert food to energy. Helps maintain a healthy digestive tract and nervous system. In very large doses, lower cholesterol (large doses should only be taken under the advice of a physician).
Deficiency:	**Overdose:**
In extreme cases, pellagra, a disease characterized by dermatitis, diarrhea and mouth sores.	Hot flashes; ulcers; liver disorders; high blood sugar and uric acid; cardiac arrhythmias.

Choline (sometimes referred to as B-4) is grouped with the B complex vitamins as a necessary source of methyl groups (B6, B12 and Folic Acid) for methyl group transfer.	**Recommended Daily Dosage:** Men: 1000mg Women: 1000mg
Natural food sources: Leafy green vegetables, lecithin, egg yolks, brewer's yeast, fish, legumes, soybeans, wheat germ.	**Indication/Benefits:** Weight and cholesterol level control, cell membranes health, prevention of gallstones, maintenance of the nervous system, assisting memory and learning, resistance to stress. Choline is critical for normal membrane structure and function.
Deficiency: Raised cholesterol levels, high blood pressure as well as kidney problems, digestive problems such as vomiting, inability to digest fats, stunted growth and fatty buildup in the liver.	**Overdose:** Fishy body odor, low blood pressure and diarrhea.
Pantothenic Acid (often referred to as B-5)	**Recommended Daily Dosage:** Men: 100mg Women: 100mg
Natural food sources: Fish, meat, poultry, eggs, legumes, mushrooms, avocados, broccoli and sweet potatoes.	**Indication/Benefits:** Weight and cholesterol level control, cell membrane health, prevention of gallstones, maintenance of the nervous system, assisting memory and learning, resistance to stress. Choline is critical for normal membrane structure and function.
Deficiency: Fatigue, insomnia, depression, irritability, upper respiratory infections.	**Overdose:** Diarrhea, heartburn, nausea and joint pain.

B-6 *(Pyridoxine)*	**Recommended Daily Dosage:** Men: 1.8mg Women: 1.5mg
Natural food sources:	**Indication/Benefits:**
Spinach, broccoli, bananas, milk, cabbage, cantaloupe, legumes, black-strap molasses, peas, wheat germ, whole grains, brown rice, prunes, fish, leafy green, vegetables, brewer's yeast, prunes, soya beans, Animal protein foods.	Needed for protein metabolism and absorption, carbohydrate metabolism. Helps form red blood cells. Promotes nerve and brain function, weight control, healthy skin, nerves, muscles, antibody formation and digestion.
Deficiency:	**Overdose:**
Anemia, convulsions, nervousness, dermatitis, insulin, sensitivity, hair loss, mouth disorders, acne, irritability, muscular weakness, depression, learning disabilities, arthritis.	Nerve damage.
B-7 *(Also known as Biotin; Vitamin H; Coenzyme R; Biopeiderm)*	**Recommended Daily Dosage:** Men: 60mcg Women: 60mcg
Natural food sources:	**Indication/Benefits:**
Sardines, legumes, egg yolks, unpolished rice, lentils, mung bean sprouts, whole grains, brewer's yeast, oats, nuts, wheat germ, peanut butter and liver.	Essential for proper body chemistry including growth-promoting factor; fatty acid production; carbohydrate-fat-protein metabolism, glucose metabolism. Good for healthy hair, skin and muscles.
Deficiency:	**Overdose:**
Extreme exhaustion, loss of appetite, impairment of fat metabolism, muscle pain, depression, grayish skin color, dermatitis.	See Vitamin B1.

Inositol *(Sometimes known as Vitamin Bh or B-8), was reclassified as an essential eukaryotic metabolite that is a component of a major class of membrane phospholipids)*	**Recommended Daily Dosage:** Men: 1000mg Women: 1000mg
Natural food sources: Citrus fruits, nut, milk, meat brewer's yeast, blackstrap molasses, whole grains, vegetables.	**Indication/Benefits:** A fundamental ingredient of cell membranes and is necessary for proper function of nerves, brain, and muscles. Vital for hair growth, metabolism of fats and cholesterol; formation of lecithin; good for vital organs, reduction of anxiety, mood enhancement.
Deficiency: Eczema, hair loss, constipation, and abnormalities of the eyes and raised cholesterol	**Overdose:** Unknown
B-12 *(Cyanocobalamin)*	**Recommended Daily Dosage:** Men: 2 mcg Women: 2 mcg
Natural food sources: Found almost exclusively in animal products such a fish, meat, poultry and eggs	**Indication/Benefits:** Builds genetic material. Helps form red blood cells.
Deficiency: Pernicious anemia; nerve damage	**Overdose:** See Vitamin B-1
Folate *(Folic Acid)*	**Recommended Daily Dosage:** Men: 400 mcg Women: 400 mcg
Natural food sources: Citrus fruits (e.g., grapefruit, oranges, lemons and strawberries), papaya, cantaloupe, broccoli, green peppers, tomatoes, sprouted alfalfa seeds, peppers, citrus fruits, papaya, potatoes, cantaloupe, strawberries, chilies.	**Indication/Benefits:** Folic acid is an important B Vitamin for DAN production, cell growth, and metabolism. It also reduces the risk for high blood pressure as well as brain and spine birth defects.
Deficiency: Fatigue, macrocytic anemia, and lethargy	**Overdose:** Nausea, sleeplessness, gas, depression

PABA *(Para-Aminobenzoic Acid and sometimes referred to as Vitamin Bx)*	Recommended Daily Dosage: Men: 500 mg Women: 500mg
Natural food sources:	**Indication/Benefits:**
Citrus fruits (e.g., grapefruit, oranges, lemons and strawberries), papaya, cantaloupe, broccoli, green peppers, tomatoes, sprouted alfalfa seeds, peppers, citrus fruits, papaya, potatoes, cantaloupe, strawberries, chilies.	Growth-promoting factor; sunscreen; acts as coenzyme in breakdown and referable of protein; formation of red blood cells; color restoration; aids bacteria in producing folic acid; maintains healthy skin, hair.
Deficiency:	**Overdose:**
Fatigue, irritability, nervousness and depression might manifest itself as well as constipation.	Nausea, skin rashes and vomiting

Vitamin C (Ascorbic Acid)	Recommended Daily Dosage: Men: 50 mg Women: 50 mg
Natural food sources:	**Indication/Benefits:**
Leafy green vegetables, yogurt, wheat germ, blackstrap molasses, brewer's yeast.	Antioxidant. Helps bind cells together and strengthens blood vessel walls. Helps maintain healthy gums. Supports immune system. Aids in the absorption of iron.
Deficiency:	**Overdose:**
Muscle weakness, bleeding gums; easy bruising. In extreme cases, scurvy.	Unknown

Vitamin D (Caliciferol)	Recommended Daily Dosage: Men: 200 IU Women: 200 IU
Natural food sources:	**Indication/Benefits:**
Egg yolk, milk, fish liver oil, sardines, salmon and tuna. Exposure to sun enables body to make its own Vitamin D.	Helps build and maintain teeth and bones. Enhances calcium absorption.
Deficiency:	**Overdose:**
Rickets in children; bone softening in adults; osteoporosis.	Calcium deposits in organs; fragile bones; renal and cardiovascular damage.

Vitamin E (Tocopherol)	Recommended Daily Dosage: Men: 400 IU Women: 400 IU
Natural food sources: Brown rice, vegetable oils such as corn, soy or cottonseed, nuts, wheat germ, sweet potatoes, eggs and oatmeal.	**Indication/Benefits:** Antioxidant. Helps form red blood cells, muscles and other tissues. Preserves fatty acids.
Deficiency: Fragility of red blood cells, dry dull hair, sterility, impotency, miscarriages, gastro-intestinal problems, heart disease, enlarged prostate.	**Overdose:** Unknown

Essential Fatty Acids (There are two families of EFAs—omega-3 and omega-6. Omega-9 is necessary but not considered essential as the body can manufacture Omega-9. EFA's were originally classified as **Vitamin F** but were later reclassified as fats rather vitamins).	Recommended Daily Dosage: Fish Oil 1200 mg DHA 400 mg EPA 800 mg
Natural food sources: Flaxseed oil, grapeseed oil, fish oils, hemp seeds, salmon, sardines, avocados, almonds, peanuts, macadamias.	**Indication/Benefits:** Supports cardiovascular, reproductive, immune, and nervous systems. Formation of cell walls, making them supple and flexible, and improving circulation and oxygen uptake with proper red blood cell flexibility and function.
Deficiency: Acne, dandruff, dry hair, eczema, varicose veins, weak nails, gallstones, cardiovascular disease, insulin resistance, depression, accelerated aging, stroke, obesity, diabetes, arthritis, ADHD, and Alzheimer's Disease.	**Overdose:** Hardening of arteries and weakening of bones.

Vitamin K (Phylloquinone)	Recommended Daily Dosage: Men: 80 mg Women: 80 mg
Natural food sources:	**Indication/Benefits:**
Cauliflower, soybeans, polyunsaturated oils, fish liver oils, egg yolks, yogurt, kelp, cow's milk, alfalfa, leafy green vegetables, blackstrap molasses.	Needed for normal blood clotting. Helps promote bone health.
Deficiency:	**Overdose:**
Defective blood coagulation.	Jaundice in infants

Flavinoids (AKA Vitamin P)	Recommended Daily Dosage: Men: 500 mg Women: 500 mg
Natural food sources:	**Indication/Benefits:**
Citrus fruits, green tea, wine, dark chocolate, pine bark, onions, garlic.	Flavonoids have been referred to as "nature's biological response modifiers" because of strong experimental evidence of their inherent ability to modify the body's reaction to allergens, viruses, and carcinogens. They show anti-allergic, anti-inflammatory, anti-microbial and anti-cancer activity. as well as cardiovascular disease.
Deficiency:	**Overdose:**
Bruising	Diarrhea

S-Methylmethionine (Vitamin U)	Recommended Daily Dosage: 4 glasses of fresh raw cabbage juice
Natural food sources:	**Indication/Benefits:**
Cabbage, Cabbage Juice	Helps digestion and gastro-intestinal problems, including ulcerative colitis.
Deficiency:	**Overdose:**
Unknown	Unknown

b. *Minerals*[161]

Minerals are very similar to vitamins in that they function in the body as co-enzymes. Minerals are essential for good health. Minerals are needed to help keep the blood and body fluids in their proper state. They are also needed to help form bone, proper muscle function and support the nervous system.

The body utilizes over 80 minerals for maximum function. Because our plants and soils are so nutrient-depleted, we are not getting all the minerals we need. Evidence of mineral malnutrition include such conditions such as energy loss, premature aging, diminished senses, and degenerative diseases like osteoporosis, heart disease, and cancer.

There are two types of minerals:

1. *Trace Minerals*, of which cobalt, copper, chromium, fluorine, iron, iodine, manganese, molybdenum, selenium and zinc are considered necessary micronutrients.

2. *Bulk Minerals*, of which calcium, chloride, magnesium, phosphorus, potassium, sodium and sulfur are essential.

Trace Minerals are also known as micronutrients and are found only in minute quantities in the body, yet are vitally important. The quantities in which they are found are so small they can only be detected by spectrographic methods or by using radioactive elements. Our diets of refined foods are generally deficient in trace elements and should be supplemented.

Bulk Minerals are found and needed in larger amounts by the body than trace minerals to carry on body functions. There are 3 basic classifications of minerals:

1. *Elemental Minerals* found in their pure elemental form or as salts such as calcium, magnesium, potassium, chromium, sodium, iron, copper, silver, gold and zinc. They are the most commonly used form in nutritional supplements, especially for the essential minerals, because larger amounts are indicated. They are generally the least expensive form of minerals but their primary disadvantage is that their degree of absorption is the least of all 3 forms.

2. _Chelated Minerals_ are easier to assimilate. In the process of chelation, be it either in the laboratory or in nature itself, the amino acid surrounds the mineral and thereby helps to solubilize it, making the "mineral chelate" more bioavailable or useful to the body. Examples of chelated minerals are the magnesium aspartate (magnesium chelated with the natural aspartic acid) and chromium picolinate (chromium chelated with picolinic acid). In many cases, chelated minerals are about 40% more efficient in regard to absorption and assimilation into the body than metallic minerals.

3. _Colloidal Minerals_ are minute particles that either are, or can be, easily dispersed in a medium such as water. Because the minerals are made up of such small particles, there is greater exposure to the liquid or solvent they are to be distributed in. This results in increased solubility, bioavailability, absorption, and usefulness to the body.

Because minerals are stored mostly in bone and muscle tissue, overdose is uncommon, but when mega doses are taken over an extended period of time, toxic amounts can accumulate in the body and result in the symptoms indicated below.

Minerals	
Boron	**Recommended Daily Dosage:** Men: 3 mg Women: 3 mg
Natural food sources: Prunes, dates, raisins, grapes, pears, green leafy vegetables, nuts and beans	**Indication/Benefits:** Helps build strong bones and teeth, anti-parasitic, increased sex drive, helps relieve symptoms of menopause and vaginitis, anti-aging qualities
Deficiency: Depressed growth, osteoporosis	**Overdose:** Skin dryness, digestive upsets

Chromium	Recommended Daily Dosage: Men: 200 mcg Women: 200 mcg
Natural food sources:	**Indication/Benefits:**
Eggs, beef, whole grains, brewer's yeast as well as molasses	Increases effectiveness of insulin, healthy blood circulatory system; synthesis of fatty acids, cholesterol and protein
Deficiency:	**Overdose:**
Depressed growth rate, atherosclerosis, intolerance in diabetics, may cause irritability, confusion, weakness, depression	Skin dryness, digestive upsets, not recommended for diabetics

Chloride	Recommended Daily Dosage: Men: 750 mg Women: 750 mg
Natural food sources:	**Indication/Benefits:**
Unprocessed natural foods, salt.	A natural salt of the mineral chlorine, chloride works with sodium and potassium to help maintain the proper distribution and pH of all bodily fluids and encourages healthy nerve and muscle function. Independently, chloride contributes to digestion and waste elimination. It is a key component of hydrochloric acid, one of the gastric juices that digest foods.
Deficiency:	**Overdose:**
Chloride deficiency is extremely rare and is usually due to illness such as excessive vomiting.	Although toxic in large amounts, excess chloride is excreted in urine, preventing potentially dangerous accumulation.

Cobalt	Recommended Daily Dosage: Men: .2 mg Women: .2 mg
Natural food sources:	**Indication/Benefits:**
Eggs, beef, whole grains, brewer's yeast and molasses.	Increases effectiveness of insulin, healthy blood circulatory system; synthesis of fatty acids, cholesterol and protein.
Deficiency:	**Overdose:**
Depressed growth rate, atherosclerosis, intolerance in diabetics, may cause irritability, confusion, weakness, depression.	Skin dryness, digestive upsets, not recommended for diabetics.1

Copper	Recommended Daily Dosage: Men: .2 mg Women: .2 mg
Natural food sources:	**Indication/Benefits:**
The richest sources of copper in the diet are Liver and other organ Meats, Seafoods, Nuts and Seeds.	Component of several enzymes, needed to make skin, hair and other pigments. Stimulates iron absorption. Needed to make red blood cells, connective tissue and nerve fibers.
Deficiency:	**Overdose:**
Rare in adults. Infants may develop a type of anemia marked by abnormal development of bones, nerve tissue and lungs.	Liver disease; vomiting; diarrhea.

Iodine	Recommended Daily Dosage: Men: 150 mcg Women: 150 mcg
Natural food sources:	**Indication/Benefits:**
Mushrooms, kelp, fresh vegetables, fish and seafood	Regulates energy production and rate of metabolism, enhances thyroid function, stabilizes body weight, needed for prevention of goiter, good for healthy hair, skin, nails, and teeth .
Deficiency:	**Overdose:**
Obesity, irritably, dry hair, nervousness, cold hands and feet, refer	Toxic buildup in the liver and in rare instances the heart.

Iron	Recommended Daily Dosage: Men: 150 mcg Women: 150 mcg
Essential for making hemoglobin, the red substance in blood that carries oxygen to body cells.	Essential for making hemoglobin, the red substance in blood that carries oxygen to body cells.
Deficiency:	**Overdose:**
Skin pallor; weakness; fatigue; headaches; shortness of breath (all signs of iron-deficiency anemia)	Toxic buildup in liver and in rare instances the heart

Magnesium	Recommended Daily Dosage: Men: 1000 mg Women: 850 mg
Natural food sources:	**Indication/Benefits:**
Spinach, Beef Greens, Broccoli, Tofu, Popcorn, Cashews, Wheat Bran	Activates enzymes needed to release energy in body. Needed by cells for genetic material and bone growth.
Deficiency:	**Overdose:**
Nausea, irritability, muscle weakness; twitching; cramps, cardiac arrhythmias.	Nausea, vomiting, low blood pressure, nervous system disorders. Warning: Overdose can be fatal to people with kidney disease.

Molybdenum	Recommended Daily Dosage: Men: 250 mcg Women: 250 mcg
Natural food sources:	**Indication/Benefits:**
The concentration in food varies depending on the environment in which the food was grown. Milk, Beans, Breads and Cereals contribute the highest amounts.	Component of enzymes needed in metabolism. Helps regulate iron storage.
Deficiency:	**Overdose:**
Unknown	Gout-like joint pain.

Phosphorus	Recommended Daily Dosage: Men: 250 mg Women: 210 mg
Natural food sources:	**Indication/Benefits:**
Chicken Breast, Milk, Lentils, Egg Yolks, Nuts, Cheese	With calcium builds bones and teeth. Needed for metabolism, body chemistry, nerve and muscle function.
Deficiency:	**Overdose:**
Weakness; bone pain; Anorexia.	Hinders body's absorption of calcium.

Potassium	Recommended Daily Dosage: Men: 4,000 mg Women: 4,000 mg
Natural food sources: Bananas, almonds, orange juice, prune juice, raisins, lima beans, acorn squash, sunflower seeds, molasses	**Indication/Benefits:** Helps maintain regular fluid balance. Needed for nerve and muscle function. Lowers blood pressure. Helps bone mineral density.
Deficiency: Nausea, anorexia, muscle weakness, irritability. (Occurs most often in persons with prolonged diarrhea.)	**Overdose:** Symptoms of hyperkalemia may include tingling of the hands and feet, muscular weakness, and temporary paralysis. The most serious complication of hyperkalemia is the development of cardiac arrhythmia, which can lead to cardiac arrest. Warning: Overdose can be fatal to people with kidney disease.

Sodium	Recommended Daily Dosage: Men: 2,400 mg Women: 2,400 mg
Natural food sources: Salt, anchovies, bacon, kelp, soy sauce	**Indication/Benefits:** Sodium is an electrolyte in the body and is required in the manufacture of hydrochloric acid in the stomach, which protects the body from any infections that may be present in food.
Deficiency: A deficiency is rare, but can easily happen with diarrhea, vomiting or excessive sweating, and a shortage may lead to nausea, dizziness, poor concentration and muscle weakness.	**Overdose:** Excessive sodium may cause high blood pressure, which may lead to a host of health problems. Excessive long-term use of sodium may also cause a loss of calcium from your body.

Sulfur	Recommended Daily Dosage: Men: 2,000 mg Women: 2,000 mg
Natural food sources:	**Indication/Benefits:**
Meat, fish, poultry, eggs, dairy products, peas, and beans	Accounting for some 10% of the body's mineral content, sulfur is part of every cell, and supports protein-rich tissues of hair, nails, muscle, and skin. It helps regulate blood sugar levels, blood clotting, antibacterial treats poisoning from aluminum, cadmium, lead, and mercury.
Deficiency:	**Overdose:**
A deficiency is rare, but can happen with diarrhea, vomiting or excessive sweating, and a shortage may lead to nausea, dizziness, poor concentration and muscle weakness.	Unknown

Zinc	Recommended Daily Dosage: Men: 12 mg Women: 9 mg
Natural food sources:	**Indication/Benefits:**
Oysters, shrimp, crab, beef, turkey, whole grains, peanuts, pumpkin seeds and beans.	Necessary element in more than 100 enzymes that are essential to digestion and metabolism. Zinc is needed to manufacture testosterone and for prostate health. Zinc is lost on ejaculation, since sperm needs this mineral to swim towards the egg. All vegans and vegetarians should also consider their zinc intake, as well as people suffering from psoriasis and women while pregnant or lactating.
Deficiency:	**Overdose:**
A shortage of zinc is common since zinc is lost in the milling process and cooking. A deficiency will result in an under-performing immune system, open to infections, allergies, night blindness, loss of smell, falling hair, white spots under finger nails, skin problems and sleep disturbances. Men with zinc shortage may have a problem with fertility, low sperm count and low libido, while women may experience irregular periods.	Elevated intake of zinc (1- 2 gram per day) over an extended period can actually harm your immune system instead of assisting it. Intake of zinc should be kept to under 100 mg per day as larger amounts may result in nausea, diarrhea, dizziness, drowsiness and hallucinations.

c.   *Enzymes*[162]

Enzymes are part of a group of organic proteins known as amino acids found in all living things. Without enzymes, life would cease. Seeds could not sprout, the soil could not produce, and fruits and crops would not ripen or grow. Moreover, the cells of any cellular entity could not conduct the transactions necessary to sustain life.

Based upon the work Dr. Edward Howell and Arlene Bushard[163], enzymes are required for life, as they are needed for every chemical reaction that takes place in the human body.

There are a great variety of enzymes. However, they can be categorized in 3 major classes: 1) Digestive Enzymes; 2) Metabolic Enzymes, and 3) Food Enzymes. Our body produces digestive and metabolic enzymes. These are known as "endogenous enzymes." Food enzymes, however, are not produced by our bodies and can only be consumed orally. These are known as "exogenous enzymes."

1.   **Digestive enzymes** allow us to properly digest foods, breaking down the nutrients so that they are able to pass through the minute pores of the intestine wall and into the bloodstream. This allows nutrients to be absorbed into the bloodstream and the waste to be discarded. Human digestive enzymes include ptyalin, pepsin, trypsin, lipase, protease, and amylase. The body does not make cellulase, an enzyme necessary for proper digestion of fiber, so it must be introduced through the raw foods we eat.

2.   **Metabolic Enzymes** speed up the chemical reaction within the cells for detoxification and energy production. They enable us to see, hear, feel, move and think. Every organ, every tissue, and all 100 trillion cells in our body depend upon the reaction of metabolic enzymes and their energy factor. Metabolic enzymes are produced by every living cell. However, the liver, pancreas, gallbladder and other organs play a vital role in their production. Metabolic enzymes contribute to rebuilding the glands, nerves, muscles and bones; fixing of iron into the red blood cells and coagulation

of the blood. Metabolic enzymes also aid in the elimination of carbon dioxide from the lungs and many other vital functions.

3. **Food Enzymes** are introduced to the body through the consumption of raw foods and supplemental enzyme fortifiers. Raw foods naturally contain enzymes, providing a source of digestive enzymes when ingested. However, raw food manifests only enough enzymes to digest that particular food, not enough to have any support systemically. The cooking and processing of food generally destroys its enzymes. Since most of the foods we eat are cooked or processed in some way and since the raw foods we do eat contain only enough enzymes to process that particular food, our bodies must produce the majority of the digestive enzymes we require. For these reasons, it's recommended that we supplement our diet with enzymes.

Enzymes can turn protein into fat or sugar, while others change carbohydrates into fat and others can change fat into carbohydrates. Other enzymes attack waste material in the blood and tissues, turning it into urea and uric acid, which are easily eliminated from the body.

All the starches and sugars are changed by enzyme action into dextrose, a simple sugar. After absorption, some of the dextrose remains in the blood; some of it is changed into glycogen by enzyme action and is stored in the liver and muscles; and some goes directly to the cells to be oxidized by enzymes, furnishing heat and energy to the tissues. The spent substances being eliminated as carbon dioxide are burned by the enzyme action to form heat and energy and some is stored as fatty tissue.

When we are young, the body's enzyme-creating mechanism functions satisfactorily, but as we grow older, enzymatic function tends to falter, contributing to the signs of aging and age-related diseases set in. It has been scientifically established that the body's ability to function properly is contingent on its supply of enzymes. Researchers at Michael Reese Hospital in Chicago discovered that when undergoing a saliva test, older people were found to have only 1/30 the number of enzymes contained in the saliva of young people.

When the supply of enzymes begins to run low, a withering process begins to set in on humans, animals and even insects. Scientists have long been wondering if premature cellular exhaustion is the basic cause of many of our health problems. It is suggested by many authorities that some people age early due to enzyme exhaustion and that others remain young at 80 because of the abundance of enzymes. Therefore, not only are enzymes needed for present health and functionality, but also are key to anti-aging.[164]

Enzymes are sensitive to heat and pH. If enzymes are not exposed to heat and other destructive forces, they can remain intact for virtually thousands of years. A small increase of heat will increase the catalysis potential. A large increase of heat will "denature" the enzymatic protein structure causing the enzyme to lose its 3-dimensional configuration. It is this structure that allows the enzyme to function in it specific catalytic action. Changes in an enzyme's optimal pH could denature it by changing the charge about the amino acids that make up the functional shape. Most of the shape is determined by ionic bonding within the protein itself.

According to Dr. Edward Howell in his book Enzyme Nutrition, prolonged temperatures over 118°F will destroy enzymes, the enzyme amylase can still convert starch to sugar at air temperatures up to 160°F but will wear out after thirty minutes, and the optimum temperatures for enzymes are 45°F to 140°F. Dr. John Whitaker, world-renowned enzymologist, and former Dean of the Department of Nutrition and Food Science at U.C. Davis, states that every enzyme is different and some are more stable at higher temperatures than others, but most enzymes will not become completely inactive until food temperatures (as opposed to air temperatures) exceed 140°F to 158°F. As well, many raw foodists put the bar at 108°F. As a guideline, if the temperature of the food would cause significant discomfort to your hand, the enzymes are in danger of being destroyed. As well, food heated between 108°F to 118°F would generally maintain enzymatic integrity.

Thus, the more raw and unprocessed food we eat, the greater likelihood of providing ourselves with the needed enzymes to aid our digestion and systemic functions. Below are a few examples of food comparisons relating to enzymatic content:

- Raw milk contains enzymes, pasteurized milk does not. Similarly, butter made from pasteurized cream contains no enzymes.

- Wheat kernels contain the enzymes, amylase and protease. Enzymes generally remain intact after the grinding process, however, baking destroys the enzymes. Most baked goods, including breads and breakfast cereals, are devoid of enzymes because of the various processes used in their manufacture.

- White sugar contains no enzymes because of the heat required in its processing, but the original cane contains its full quota of enzymes.

- Most canned vegetables, fruits and juices contain no enzymes because the heat utilized in the canning process.

- Many vitamin supplements generally are processed using heat which effectively leaves them devoid of enzymes.

The human body, through the pancreas, spleen and other organs produces many endogenous enzymes to provide the function of enzymes that were originally contained in our food. All bodily processes take energy. Digestion is one of the most energy-intensive bodily process. Thus, if the bulk of our diet is processed and heated foods devoid of enzymes, our body has to work harder to create enzymes to digest our food. When we eat a raw and unprocessed diet rich in enzymes, the body does not need to expend as much energy in the digestion process. This leaves us with greater energy to detoxify and repair our bodies, and to utilize for thought and physical activities.

Although the importance of ubiquitous functioning of enzymes is key to health and life itself, this section on diet and nutrition will focus on digestive enzymes. Digestive enzymes start working when food enters the mouth and come in contact with saliva. The enzymes amylase and lipase present in saliva start the breakdown of carbohydrates and fats, while the chewing of food stimulates the production of digestive enzymes in the stomach. The stomach produces hydrochloric acid and various digestive enzymes that break down proteins, fats and carbohydrates in preparation for absorption.

The bulk of digestion and absorption takes place in the small intestine. Additional digestive enzymes (trypsin, chymotrypsin, pancreatin and papain) produced either by the lining of the intestines or by the pancreas continue the breakdown of fats, carbohydrates and proteins. Bile, produced by the liver, helps with the digestion and absorption of fats. The result of this process is that the food is reduced to molecules of sugars, amino acids and fatty acids, which are then absorbed through the wall of the small intestine. The following are the essential digestive enzymes:

Oral Cavity	
Bromelaine	Tenderizes meat and acts as an anti-inflammatory agent.
Betaine	Effects cell fluid balance as osmolytes.
Salivary Amylase (also known as Ptyalin	Produced by salivary glands breaks down starch into sugar.
Stomach	
Pepsin	The main gastric enzyme secreted by the gastric glands. It breaks proteins into smaller peptide fragments.
Gelatinase	Degrades type I and type V gelatin and type IV and V collagen, which are proteoglycans in meat.
Gastric Amylase	Degrades starch.
Gastric Lipase	A tributyrase by its biochemical activity, as it acts almost exclusively on tributyrin, a butter fat enzyme.
Renin	Digests milk proteins and turn them into peptides.

Pancreas, Liver & Gallbladder—The pancreas makes pancreatic juices and hormones, including the hormone, insulin. The pancreatic juices are enzymes that help digest food in the small intestine. They flow into the main pancreatic duct. This duct joins the common bile duct, which connects the pancreas to the liver and the gallbladder. The common bile duct, which carries bile (a fluid that helps digest fat), connects to the small intestine near the stomach.

Trypsin	A protease that cleaves proteins at the basic amino acids.
Chymotrypsin	A protease that cleaves proteins at the aromatic amino acids.
Steapsin	Degrades triglycerides into fatty acids and glycerol.
Carboxypeptidase	A protease that takes off the terminal acid group from a protein.
Elastase	Degrades the protein elastin and some other proteins.
Lipase	Breaks down fats and converts triglycerides to mono-glycerides and free fatty acids.
Nucleases	Degrades nucleic acids, like DNAase and RNAase.
Pancreatic Amylase	Degrades most carbohydrates including starch, glycogen and cellulose.
Bile	Produced by the liver, emulsifies fat, allowing more efficient use of lipase in the duodenum and converting lipids to smaller and more manageable size.

Jejunum and Ileum—The jejunum and ileum of the small intestine secretes a juice called succuss entericus which contains the five **following** enzymes that degrade disaccharides into monosaccharides.

Sucrase	Breaks down sugars turning sucrose into glucose and fructose.
Maltase	Breaks down grains and turns sucrose into maltose and glucose.
Isomaltase	Breaks down sucrose into maltose and isomaltose.
Lactase	Breaks down sucrose into lactose, glucose and galactose.
Intestinal Lipase	Breaks down fatty acids.

Essential Exogenous Enzyme

Cellulase	Breaks down plant fiber (e.g. fruits, vegetables) and is not produced by the body.

To maximize enzymatic efficiency, be aware that raw seeds and nuts often contain enzyme inhibitors that neutralize some of the enzymes produced by the body and can cause swelling of the pancreas. In addition, peas, beans and lentils contain some inhibitors. Sprouting and fermentation can help remove enzyme inhibitors from food without cooking the food.

In summary, enzymes are essential to your life and health. Ensure you are eating a diet rich in enzymes with a high percentage of raw low glycemic fruits and vegetables. When safe, and if part of your dietary choice, raw dairy and meats can be included. Also, using a dietary enzyme supplement containing the foregoing enzymes can be used to support a healthy diet.

The best source for healthy vitamins, minerals and enzymes is fresh, raw, nutritious and organic foods. In addition, eating herbs, high antioxidant foods and Superfoods (described below) will minimize the need for vitamin, mineral and enzyme supplements. However, due to widespread depleted soil conditions, it's recommended that you supplement your diet with formulations of essential vitamins, minerals and enzymes.

3. Supercharging Your Diet (Herbs, Antioxidants and Superfoods)

In addition to the vitamins, minerals and enzymes essential for optimal health, we can optimize our health with 1) **Herbs,** 2) **Antioxidants**, and 3) **Superfoods.** Although herbs, antioxidants and Superfoods are not considered "essential" by the western medical or scientific community, they are important for disease prevention and optimal health. Including herbs, antioxidants, and superfoods in your diet, increases vitality, mental acuity, endurance, longevity, and libido, as well as contributing to mood enhancement and improved body system functions (e.g., immune, cardiovascular, digestive, reproductive, nervous, endocrine).

a.   *Herbs*[165]

Medicinal herbs have been effectively used for centuries in prevention and treatment of illness, for culinary ingredients and in spiritual practices. Medicinal herbs are gaining popularity as an alternative to pharmaceutical drugs due to their very gentle and natural healing properties and lack of side negative effects. The following is by no means an exhaustive list of herbs, but does provide a summary of some of the most popular and useful herbs.

Astragalus	Promotes resistance against disease by activating immune system, reduces blood pressure, helps treat heart disease and diabetes and increases energy and stamina.
Avena Sativa (Oats)	Soothes nervous system and performance anxiety; boosts fertility, strengthens heart, good for urinary organs, reduces nicotine craving and helps with detoxification.
Billberry	Can inhibit or reverse eye disorders and improves night vision.
Bladderwrack	Has natural iodine to promote a healthy thyroid; encourages good circulation and eases obesity; gently stimulates the metabolism.
Cat's Claw	An immune system builder, cat's claw cleanses and detoxifies the entire digestive system by scrubbing the intestinal walls and increasing the absorption of nutrients.
Celery Seed Extract	Reduces joint and urinary tract inflammations, such as rheumatoid arthritis, cystitis or urethritis, and is also used for weak conditions, pain relief and nervous exhaustion.
Cinnamon/ Cassia	In oil form, Cinnamon and Cassia are very high in antioxidants and anti-microbial properties earning it a reputation as a cure for colds. It has also been used to treat diarrhea and other problems of the digestive system. Also, Cinnamon and Cassia have been reported to have remarkable pharmacological effects in the treatment of type II diabetes.
Coriander/ Cilantro	Coriander/Cilantro has a long history as a digestive aid. The herb contains an antioxidant that helps prevent animal fats from turning rancid. It also contains substances that kill meat-spoiling bacteria and fungi. These same substances also prevent infection in wounds. Additionally, this herb is an effective agent for heavy metal detoxification.
Damiana	Sexual stimulant that enhances sexual performance; tonic to improve overall body function; helps relieve anxiety and promotes a feeling of well-being
Don Quai	Stimulates circulation to purify and cleanse blood; nourishes brain cells; soothes central nervous system; helps relieve menopause and menstrual problems; fights colds, fever and anemia.
Echinacea	An immuno-stimulator that stimulates the body's immune system, warding off infections, particularly the common cold. Also, has been utilized in treatment of AIDS and cancer to help boost immune system function.

Fenugreek	A seed used to boost testosterone, treat skin conditions, stabilize sugar absorption, alleviate menstrual cramps and lower cholesterol.
Fo-Ti	Promotes anti-aging effects of hair and muscle loss; an anti-toxic and anti-cancer tonic for the liver and blood to restore vigor and energy; anti-swelling effects ease pain, backache and constipation; tranquilizing properties aid insomnia.
Garcinia Cambogia	A natural and generally safe weight loss aid that helps stop and reduce production and storage of fat; inhibits conversion of carbohydrates into fat; works in conjunction with a low-fat diet; suppresses the appetite; and acts as an antibacterial.
Garlic	Improves immune system function, helps prevent heart disease by reducing high blood pressure and lowering cholesterol, fights infections and is an anti-inflammatory.
Ginger Root	Promotes endurance and increases stamina; eases cold symptoms; soothes and promotes healing of minor burns and skin inflammations; digestive aid for nausea, vomiting, cramps and motion sickness.
Ginkgo Biloba	Improves blood circulation to the brain and other organs; aids memory loss and depression; improves short term memory and mental clarity; great antioxidant to fight free radicals and slow aging process; improves nervous system function; reduces frequency of asthma and allergy attacks; fights heart disease.
Ginseng	Energizes and rejuvenates; increases energy and endurance and promotes mental and physical vigor; fights stress; increases brain and memory center function; helps relieve menopause and menstrual problems; stimulates circulatory system; boosts immune system function; lowers cholesterol; helps prevent heart disease; and raises sexual potency and vitality.
Goldenseal	Goldenseal is an excellent antibiotic which has for various treatments equaled or outperformed allopathic antibiotics, but without the side effects. It is known to destroy harmful bacteria and germs and is very helpful against staph and strep. It is very potent for intestinal, antibacterial activity. This herb helps eliminate infection in the body and destroys many types of bacterial and viral infections and stimulates the kidney function for urinary infections.

Gota Kola	Nerve tonic to promote relaxation; enhances memory; has calming effect on body; improves circulation by strengthening veins and capillaries; reduces pain and swelling; eliminates excess fluids; relieves congestion due to cold and upper respiratory infections; lowers fever.
Grape Seed	A strong antioxidant; a natural diuretic; builds immune system; helps skin wounds heal faster; promotes healthy circulation; improves skin tone and elasticity.
Green Tea	Powerful antioxidant; protects against digestive and respiratory infections; anti-cancer and heart disease properties; reduces cholesterol and triglycerides; enhances immune function; increases energy; enhances weight loss by reducing appetite and fat tissue accumulation.
Guarana	An energizer; increases mental alertness and fights fatigue; increases stamina and physical endurance; high energy source; helps diminish appetite.
Hawthorn	Has been demonstrated to support overall heart health, digestion, sleep disorder from nervous tensions and sore throats.
Hydrangea	Hydrangea root has been most promising in the treatment of an inflamed or enlarged prostate gland. It is also used for urinary stones associated with urinary infections.
Juniper Berry	The traditional use of juniper is as a diuretic and to treat conditions of the bladder or kidneys by washing out the offending bacteria in urinary tract infections. The diuretic action is well established and attributed to terpinene-4-ol, which increases the filtration rate of the kidney.
Kava	Provides a calming effect that relieves anxiety, restlessness, sleeplessness, and stress-related symptoms such as muscle tension or spasm.
Licorice Root	Lowers cholesterol; reduces pain and stiffness from arthritis; reduces fever and inflammation; promotes healing of wounds; prevents tooth decay; soothes stomach aches, ulcers, bladder, kidney and urinary tract ailments; cleanses colon; good for sore throats and cough; breaks up congestion.
Maca	Regulation of hormones, heightened libido, improved semen quality in men and improved vaginal moistness in women.
Marshmallow Root	Used in treating irritated tissues in urinary tract infections such as cystitis, colitis, and diverticulitis.

Muira Puama	A sexual stimulant and potent aphrodisiac; used as a stomach tonic and treatment for rheumatism; improves sexual desire and libido; improves circulation to prostate; helps with menstrual problems.
Parsley Root	Parsley root flushes out the urinary tract and helps prevent and treat kidney stones. Also, this herb alleviates intestinal and menstrual cramps and flatulence.
Rehmannia Glutinosa	Replenishes vital force; helps with diabetes, urinary tract problems, anemia and regulating menstrual flow; beneficial for hypoglycemia and liver protection; helps reduce blood pressure and increase circulation; blood tonic; alleviates night sweats and fever.
Reishi Mushroom	For heart health including normal cholesterol, blood pressure and circulatory system support; helps with normal sleep; promotes immune system health; cardiac and liver tonic.
Saw Palmetto	Beneficial for the reproductive organs of both sexes; works as an aphrodisiac and tonic; used to ease swelling of the prostate and excessive urination.
Schizandra	An antioxidant; protects against free radicals, infections and stress; an energizer; helps fight fatigue and lung disease; a digestive aid; improves vision; stimulates circulation of blood; normalizes blood sugar and blood pressure.
Shitake Mushroom	Enhances the immune system's ability to fight against infection; provides nutrients to cleanse and heal; aids mineral absorption; lowers blood sugar; helps prevent high blood pressure and heart disease; cancer-fighting agent; aids depression and fatigue; promotes vitality and longevity.
Suma	Builds and protects the immune system by fighting free radicals, slows aging process; boosts energy; relieves stress; regulates blood sugar; promotes new cell growth and healing of wounds; enhances sexual functions; fights viral infections.
St. Johns Wart	A mood stabilizer that reduces depression and anxiety disorders.
Turmeric	Used in India use it as an antiseptic for cuts and burns. It is also used as an anti-bacterial and anti-tumoral agent that has been shown to help melanoma and cystic fibrosis. It is taken in some Asian countries as a dietary supplement to help stomach problem liver function and brain function.

Uva Ursi	Contains powerful phytochemicals such as volatile oils, arbutin, quercetin, and mallic and gallic acids. Arbutin is highly antibacterial and destroys bacteria and fungus that infect the urinary system such as E. coli, Candida albicans and Staphylococcus. One of the ways arbutin does this is by releasing aglycone hydroquinone and other phytochemicals into the urine. Quercetin is a capillary protectant, protecting the literally trillions of capillaries existing as part of the delicate kidney filtering system. Mallic and gallic acids, the same as found in apples and apple cider vinegar, have long been used for kidney and bladder infections.
White Willow Bark	Soothes headaches; helps insomnia; relieves pain; reduces inflammation in arthritic and rheumatic joints; good for neuralgia; contains tannins which are good for the digestive system.
Yohimbe	An aphrodisiac; dilates the blood vessels and brings the blood closer to the surface of the sex organs; lowers blood pressure; increases the reflex excitability of the lower region of the body.
Zhi Shi (Bitter Orange)	Increases metabolism and caloric expenditure; fat burner by stimulating breakdown of fat; promotes weight loss; increases energy; improves circulation and liver function; aids in relief of chest congestion, bronchitis and indigestion.

b. *Antioxidants*[166]

Antioxidants are substances that protect cells from the damage caused by unstable free radical molecules. An antioxidant is a molecule capable of slowing or preventing the oxidation of other molecules. Oxidation reactions can produce free radicals (highly reactive, high-energy particles) that ricochet wildly throughout the body starting chain reactions that damage cells. Antioxidants terminate these chain reactions by removing free radical intermediates and inhibiting other oxidation reactions by being oxidized themselves.

Free radicals can be produced within the body by natural biological processes or introduced from outside via tobacco smoke, toxins, pollutants in air, water and food and sub-optimal eating habits. Free radicals are believed to accelerate the progression of cancer, cardiovascular disease, rheumatoid arthritis, chronic fatigue, and age-related diseases. Antioxidants found in superfoods and traditional fruits and vegetables help to neutralize free radicals in our bodies.

The standardized measurement of the total antioxidant power of a substance is ORAC, short for Oxygen Radical Absorbance Capacity. Antioxidant power is the ability to neutralize oxygen free radicals. The more free radicals a substance can absorb, the higher it's ORAC score. Traditional nutritionists and M.D.'s recommend that we consume around 5000 ORAC units per day to significantly impact antioxidant activity in the body and reduce free radical damage. One serving (half a cup) of widely available fruits or vegetables provides approximately 500 ORAC units.

Most of us do not eat 10 servings of fruits and vegetables a day, and therefore require antioxidant supplements and/or high antioxidant Superfoods in order to get the recommended amount of ORAC units necessary to offset the damage caused by free radicals in our body. Therefore it's essential to our health that we enhance our diet with antioxidant foods and supplements. Examples of supplements include beta-carotene, lycopene, vitamins C, E, and A, CoQ10, resveratrol, pycnogenol, glutathione, lipoic acid, melatonin, uric acid and astaxanthin. Also, the enzymes, superoxide dismutase, catalase and preoxiredoxins are catalytics that help reduce free radicals.

In addition to the vitamins A, C and E, below is a list of the antioxidants that are considered the most effective.

Glutathione	Glutathione, a tripeptide found in every cell in the body, is considered to be one of the most powerful antioxidants. This is largely because of its unique ability to exponentiate the performance of all the other antioxidants and its key role in energy utilization, detoxification and cellular protection.
Alpha-Lipoic Acid	Alpha-Lipoic Acid helps reduce inflammation, chelate heavy metal and help increase the effects of, and regenerate, other antioxidants.
CoQ10	CoQ10 provides protection from free radicals, helps increase cellular energy, supports heart health, improves immune system function, helps reduce signs of aging, regulates blood pressure and increases nervous system function.
Resveratrol	Resveratrol is an antioxidant that is effective in warding off symptoms of aging. Resveratrol can cross the blood-brain barrier and is known for its anti-aging properties including protecting the brain and nervous system, reducing risk of Alzheimer's, inhibiting cancer, lowering blood pressure, as well as improving heart health and blood vessel elasticity.
Astaxanthin	Astaxanthin, produced by microalgae, is a highly powerful carotenoid reputed to be 65 times more powerful than vitamin C, 54 times more powerful than beta-carotene and 14 times more powerful than vitamin E. Benefits attributed to Astaxanthin include improved immune system function and cardiovascular health, protection of eyes and skin from ultraviolet radiation, reduction of risk of Alzheimer's and dementia, greater endurance, blood sugar stabilization, increased sperm count, relieving indigestion and reducing oxidative damage to DNA.

A recommended supplement would include a blend of the foregoing plus a phyto-medicine formulation utilizing the high antioxidant foods and spices listed in the table below. If you already take a vitamin supplement, then it's recommended that you purchase a pure antioxidant supplement rather than spending your money on duplicating antioxidants and vitamins. If you consciously and regularly eat the Superfoods and high antioxidant foods listed below, additional antioxidant supplements may be less important.

Below are two tables. The first shows the "**Top 50 Antioxidant Foods**" and the second shows the "**Top 15 Antioxidant Spices**."

Top 50 Antioxidant Foods

ORAC UNITS PER 100 GRAMS (about 3.5 ounces)					
RANK	FOOD	ORAC	RANK	FOOD	ORAC
1	Raw Cacao Powder	95,500	26	Brussels Sprouts	980
2	Raw Cacao Nibs	62,100	27	Plums	949
3	Maqui Berry Powder	75,000	28	Alfalfa Sprouts	930
4	Acerola	70,000	29	Broccoli Florets	890
5	Maqui Berry Juice	40,000	30	Beets	840
6	Tibetan Goji Berries	25,300	31	Avocado	782
7	Acai	18,500	32	Oranges	750
8	Elderberry	14,600	33	Red Bell Peppers	710
9	Dark Chocolate	13,120	34	Red Grapes	739
10	Black Current	8,000	35	Cherries	670
11	Milk Chocolate	6,740	36	Kiwi Fruit	610
12	Prunes	5,770	37	Grapefruit, pink	483
13	Cabernet Sauvignon	5,000	38	Grapes, White	460
14	Pomegranates	3,307	39	Onion	450
15	Raisins/Dark Grapes	2,830	40	Corn	400
16	Blueberries	2,400	41	Egg Plant	390
17	Blackberries	2,036	42	Cauliflower	385
18	Garlic	1,939	43	Peas, Frozen	375
19	Kale	1,770	44	Potato	300
20	Cranberries	1,750	45	Cabbage	295
21	Strawberries	1,540	46	Leaf Lettuce	265
22	Noni Fruit Juice (pure)	1,506	47	Cantaloupe	250
23	Spinach	1,260	48	Banana	210
24	Lemon Juice	1,225	49	Apple	207
25	Raspberries	1,220	50	Tofu	205

Top 15 Antioxidant Spices

RANK	SPICES	ORAC
1	Cloves, ground	314,446
2	Sumac, bran, raw	312,400
3	Cinnamon, ground	267,516
4	Oregano, dried	200,129
5	Turmeric, ground	159,277
6	Cumin Seed	76,800
7	Parsley, dried	74,349
8	Basil, dried	67,553
9	Curry Powder	48,504
10	Sage, fresh	40,000
11	Mustard Seed	29,257
12	Ginger, ground	28,811
13	Black Pepper	27,618
14	Thyme, fresh	27,426
15	Marjoram, fresh	27,297

c.   *Superfoods*[167]

In making conscious choices in our diets for optimal wellness, it is important to also include a diet rich in "Superfoods." According to nutritional expert, David Wolfe, *"Superfoods are the most powerful, nutritious, mineral-rich plant foods on Earth."*

Superfoods are defined as foods with high phytonutrient content that function to improve health if consumed regularly and contain a full spectrum of high-density nutrition and are generally high in antioxidants. Superfoods represent a superior natural source of protein, vitamins, minerals, enzymes, co-enzymes, antioxidants, beneficial fats, essential fatty acids, essential amino acids, fiber, and polysaccharides.

Unlike vitamins or dietary supplements taken in isolation, Superfoods generally provide a naturally balanced spectrum of many nutrients that support each other and prevent the kind of imbalances that often occur when vitamins are taken alone. Superfoods immediately help nourish our brain, bones, muscles, skin, hair, nails, cardiovascular system, endocrine system, immune system, nervous system and reproductive system.

Eating Superfoods for extended periods of time can correct imbalances from missing nutrients in our food and replace empty bulk calories with nutritionally dense foods. When we eat a diet rich in Superfoods, we eat less bulk and get more nutrition. Thus, less energy is spent on digestion thereby allowing the additional energy to be used to detoxify and repair the body promoting optimal weight, increased mental acuity, greater sexual vitality, increased overall energy, enhanced athletic performance with rapid recovery times, and strengthening the systems of the body.

According to my research synthesized from sources including David Wolfe, the NIH, Dr. Mercola, and Dr. Jacqueline Chan, as well as many years of personal experimentation, research and experience, **The Top 20 Superfoods** that provide the greatest nutritional value and benefits include the following:

1. Maqui	Maqui is a tiny and deep purple color fruit from Chile. Maqui has the highest antioxidant value of any known superfruit. Maqui is also an excellent source of Vitamin C, iron and potassium. Its reputed benefits include promoting healthy immune system, stamina, increased strength, longevity, cardiovascular health.
2. Coconut	Coconut is highly nutritious and rich in fiber, vitamins, and minerals. It is classified as a "functional food" because it provides many health benefits beyond its nutritional content. Coconut oil is known to possess healing properties beyond that of any other dietary oil. In traditional (non-western) medicine around the world, coconut is used to treat a wide variety of health problems including the following: abscesses, asthma, baldness, bronchitis, bruises, burns, colds, constipation, cough, dropsy, dysentery, earache, fever, flu, gingivitis, gonorrhea, irregular or painful menstruation, jaundice, kidney stones, lice, malnutrition, nausea, rash, scabies, scurvy, skin infections, sore throat, swelling, syphilis, toothache, tuberculosis, tumors, typhoid, ulcers, upset stomach, weakness, and wounds. Modern medical science is now confirming the use of coconut in treating many of the above conditions. Published studies in medical journals show that coconut, in one form or another, may provide a wide range of believed health benefits including antiviral (e.g., influenza, herpes, measles, hepatitis C, SARS), antibacterial (e.g., throat infections, ulcerative bacterium, urinary tract infections, gum disease and cavities, pneumonia, and gonorrhea), antifungal (e.g., candidiasis, ringworm, athlete's foot, thrush, diaper rash), antiparasitic (e.g., . tapeworms, lice, giardia), and antioxidant. Also, coconut has been shown to boost energy, endurance, enhance athletic performance, improve digestion and absorption of nutrients, support endocrine, cardiovascular and immune system function. Furthermore, coconut is amazing for supporting healthy skin and preventing skin diseases and symptoms.[168]
3. Goji Berries	Goji berries are a sweet red nutrient-dense fruit native to Asia that serves as both a botanical medicine and a food. It has been used as a medicinal food for thousands of years with over 15% protein, 21 essential minerals, and 18 amino acids, as well as lycium barbarum polysaccharides (LBP). Benefits appear to include strengthening the immune system, antioxidant and anti-aging, protection of the liver, cardiovascular health, optical health and enhancement and stimulation of HGH.

4. Cacao	Cacao beans and powder in their raw, unprocessed and unadulterated state are rich in nutrients and beneficial to health and contains high amounts of antioxidants, neurotransmitters, essential minerals and EFA's. Cacao has acknowledged benefits including increased vitality, mental acuity, energy and mood; healthy skin, strong bones and lower blood pressure.
5. Maca	Maca is a nutrition-packed root vegetable, also known as "Peruvian ginseng," that grows in the mountain plateaus of the Peruvian Andes. Maca contains numerous trace minerals (including iodine), B vitamins, linoleic and oleic oils (essential fatty acids), and 18 amino acids, including 7 of the 9 essential amino acids. Maca is also rich in sugar, proteins, starches, and important minerals, such as iron, magnesium, calcium, and phosphorous. Maca has been used to support the immune and endocrine systems, regulation of hormones, heightened libido, improved semen quality in men and improved vaginal moistness in women.
6. Bee Pollen	Bee pollen is more rich in proteins than any animal source. It contains more amino acids than beef, eggs, or cheese of equal weight. Royal Jelly also has significant 12% protein. These Superfoods are particularly concentrated in all elements necessary for life including Vitamins A, B complex, C, D and E, as well as rutin, RNA and DNA. Beneficial uses include weight loss, enhanced immune function, increased libido and fertility, increased energy, as well as an effective antioxidant, antimicrobial and anti-aging remedy.
7. Chlorella	Chlorella is a single-celled alga. Throughout its two-billion-year history on this planet, it has survived because it's tough outer shell protected its genetic integrity, and it is one of the most efficient foods on earth in using and concentrating sunshine, as shown by its high chlorophyll content and rapid reproduction. Chlorella is a natural, pure, whole food with all the materials to support life. Cracked cell wall Chlorella provides a tremendous source of concentrated nutrition. Chlorella is the best known source of chlorophyll, with nearly 10 times the amount of chlorophyll found in alfalfa, from which most commercial chlorophyll is extracted. With 58% protein, a full spectrum of amino acids, vitamins including A, B complex (including B-12), C and E, and minerals including calcium, iodine, iron, magnesium, phosphorous and zinc. Chlorella's reputed benefits include digestive health, liver function, detoxification, immune system support, normalization of blood sugar, healing wounds, normalize blood pressure.

8. Blue-green Algae (Hawaiian Spirulina & Klamath Lake Blue-greenAlgae) and Marine Phytoplankton	Hawaiian Spirulina is an ocean algae that has both green and blue pigments and is distinct from the fresh water "blue-green algae." Spirulina contains over 60% complete protein (almost three times as much as that found in beef). It has high concentrations of B complex vitamins, vitamin E, carotenoids, iron, manganese, zinc, essential fatty acids such as gamma linolenic acid (which is only otherwise found in mother's milk), and more beta carotene than you can find in carrots. Spirulina is also one of the few plant sources of vitamin B12, which is essential for healthy nerves and tissues. Spirulina can help stimulate the immune system, increase production of antibodies, and promote a healthy response to allergens. It may also help reverse age-related declines in memory and learning, help maintain healthy cholesterol and blood pressure levels, and promote the development of red blood cells, and promote the growth of probiotics to help maintain intestinal health.

Like Spirulina, Klamath Lake Blue-green Algae provides one of the most balanced and complete sources of vitamins, minerals, trace elements, nucleic acids, essential fatty acids, phytonutrients and antioxidants, including beta-carotene, on the planet. With almost 70% complete protein and no cholesterol, Blue-green Algae is a great source of protein for vegans. Klamath Lake algae's unique growing environment endows it with valuable attributes not found in other algae. Because Klamath Lake rests in an ancient, mineral-rich volcanic bed, the algae grown in it is a superior source of naturally occurring minerals. Of particular value are the distinctive peptide molecules which act as precursors to two important brain foods: glycogen and neuropeptides. Benefits include increased mental clarity, energy, respiratory and cardiovascular health, endurance, immune system functions.

Phytoplanktons are microscopic plants and bacteria, which are ocean-bound and can provide us with an awesome amount of nutrition. Phytoplankton provide most of the trace elements we need, Vitamins B12, C and E, magnesium, chlorophyll, potassium and numerous other vitamins and minerals. Beneficial uses include enhanced brain function, cardiovascular health, cholesterol reduction, stabilization of blood sugar, joint pain relief, prevents psoriasis and dermatitis and enhanced vision. |

9. Sea Vegetables (Nori, Kelp & Dulse)	Kelp and Sea Vegetables contains 10 to 20 times the minerals and vitamins of land vegetables. These vitamins include A, B complex including B12, C, and E. The mineral content of sea vegetables is extraordinary and includes all 56 minerals and trace minerals with high concentrations of calcium, magnesium, potassium, calcium, sodium, chloride and iodine. Sea vegetables contain significant amounts of protein, sometimes as much as 48%. Sea plants are also a rich sources of both soluble and insoluble dietary fiber. The large brown seaweeds known as the "kelps" contain algonic acid. Studies have shown that algonic acid removes heavy metals and radioactive isotopes from the digestive tract, as well as strontium 90 from the bones. Sea vegetables have traditionally been used in Asia for heart disease, hypertension, cancer, and thyroid problems.
10. Turmeric	Turmeric is a plant related to ginger, which was originally from India, and used as a spice and for its medicinal benefits. Curcumin is the active compound in turmeric with benefits including reduction of inflammation, antioxidant, prevention of diseases including heart disease, diabetes and cancer. Turmeric may also be used to aid wound healing and pain reduction. The absorption and effects of curcumin can be enhanced by combining it with black pepper.
11. Aloe Vera	Aloe is considered an herb superfood due to its seventy-five healing compounds including natural steroids, antibiotic agents, amino acids, minerals and enzymes." In addition to its nutritional benefits, aloe vera gel can be used topically on burns, sunburns, cuts, scrapes, eczema and acne. Aloe contains vitamins A, B12, C, and E, the minerals sulfur, calcium, magnesium, zinc, selenium, and chromium, as well as antioxidants, fiber, amino acids, enzymes, sterols, lignins, essential fatty acids and polysaccharides. Aloe helps lubricate joints, stimulate the brain and nervous system and improve the health of skin, promote digestion, weight loss and muscle gain. Moreover, aloe vera has been used to fight chronic viral, nanobacteria, and fungal infections, promote digestive wellness, (antimicrobial properties), reduce inflammation, boost the immune system, hydrate cells, prevent radiation sickness, cancer, heart disease, diabetes and premature aging.

12. Hemp Seeds	The hemp seed is approximately 40% oil and 30% protein. Hemp protein contains all the essential amino acids needed by humans and is considered a "high-quality" and highly digestible vegan protein source. Hemp is high in omega 3 and omega 6 fatty acids, which strengthen the immune system and nourish the brain, skin, and virtually every system in the body. Hemp is high in antioxidants, vitamins and minerals. Food grade hemp contains little to no THC and food crops are regularly tested before being sold. The seeds can be eaten raw or lightly cooked. They have a light, nutty flavor and can be easily incorporated into salads, cereal, or trail mix.
13. Acai	Acai is a small berry from the Amazon known for its high levels of antioxidants and anthocyanins. Nearly 50% of the Acai berry is fat with 74% of the fat coming from healthy unsaturated fats such as Omega 3, Omega 6 and Omega 9. 7.59% of the weight of the Acai pulp is from amino acids with 19 different amino acids. Three Phytosterols have also been identified in Acai (B-sitosterol, campesterol and sigmastero) have been shown to have numerous health benefits for maintaining healthy heart and digestive function. Acai also contains vitamins A, B1, B2, B3, C and E, potassium, calcium, magnesium, copper and zinc. Acai has been found to help maintain the healthy function of the endocrine, immune and cardiovascular system, increase energy, libido and stamina, promote healthy skin and hair, deeper sleep, and rejuvenation. Also, acai is known to be powerful anti-inflammatory that can help promote healing and reduce pain and soreness from inflammation.
14. Camu Camu	The Camu Camu berry is a native vegetation of the Amazon rainforest of Peru. This fruit is rich in phytonutrients that have health benefits such as leucine, amino acids, valine, serine and is known as the highest natural source of vitamin C. If compared to an orange, this fruit contains 30 times more vitamin C, 10 times more iron, 3 times more niacin, 5% more phosphorus and 2 times the amount of riboflavin. Camu Camu has antibacterial, antiviral and antioxidant properties. Camu Camu helps weight loss and building lean muscle mass, mood enhancement, mental acuity and focus, and provides nervous system, immune system and endocrine system support.

15. Inca Berry	Inca Berries grow wildly in mineral-rich soils all over the Peruvian Andes. They contain 16% protein on average as compared to goji berries' 13-14%. This is an extraordinary level of protein for a fruit. Inca berries are an excellent source of beta carotene, vitamin C, thiamine, niacin, phosphorous, bioflavinoids, and protein. This fruit has anti-sclerotic, antiviral, anti-carcinogenic, anti-inflammatory, antihistamine, and antioxidant properties that promote intestinal health and regularity, immune system, cardiovascular system, endocrine system, reproductive system, brain function and eye health.
16. Noni	The noni fruit contains a nutrient rich cocktail of vitamins, minerals, phytochemicals, amino acids and antioxidants. Noni fruit powder contains 71% carbohydrate, 36% fiber, 5.2% protein and 1.2% fat. Noni is high in vitamins A, B3 and C. Also, iron, potassium, calcium and sodium are present in moderate amounts. Noni fruit's health benefit and superfood classification result from the number of phytochemicals, including lignans, polysaccharides, flavonoids, iridoids, fatty acids, scopoletin, catechin, beta-sitosterol, damnacanthal and alkaloids. It has been widely reported that Noni stabilizes cholesterol at normal levels, increases energy when consumed over a period of time, delivers abundant antioxidants to scavenge free radicals, helps maintain the immune, endocrine and cardiovascular systems, reduces inflammation and enhances energy and well-being.
17. Mangosteen	Mangosteen is a fruit that comes from a tropical evergreen tree of southeast Asia. The primary active components of the mangosteen fruit are called xanthones. Xanthones are a class of polyphenolic compounds that are biologically active and structurally similar to bioflavanoids. Xanthones occur rarely in nature, however, 40 of the 200 Xanthones are contained in Mangosteen. Mangosteen also contains polysaccharides, sterols, proanthocyanidins and catechins and has very high ORAC properties making it a very powerful "anti" superfood with reputed benefits including antioxidant, anti-inflammatory, anticonvulsant, antiaging, antiviral, antimicrobial, antifungal and analgesic. Mangosteen also supports cardiovascular health, oral health, eye health, weight regulation, nervous system, endocrine system and immune system.

18. Sacha Inchi	Sacha Inchi is a rich and natural legacy from the ancient civilizations of Peru culminating with the Incas. The sacha inchi oil displays a very high content of Omega-3 (48%) and Omega-6 (35%) fatty acids. It is therefore an ideal ingredient in anti-aging products, moisturizers or products for dry and sensitive skin. Sacha Inchi also has been known to help lower LDL cholesterol levels and supports a healthy cardiovascular system, aids with the treatment of hypertension, diabetes, weight loss and depression.
19. Shilajit	The origins of Shilajit are fascinating. Two hundred million years ago, during the time of drifting tectonic plates, the Indian subcontinent collided with the landmass of Eurasia. This impact caused entire rain forests to crumple and become trapped between and below the two land masses. Buried under the Himalayas and subjected to millions of tons of pressure, the rainforests, once teeming with plant and animal life became transformed into the nutrient-rich substance, Shilajit. During the hot Indian summer months, Shilajit becomes liquified and the ancient substance rises to the surface oozing through cracks in Himalayan mountains. Appearing first as a thick, gooey liquid, Shilajit quickly dries and can be powdered and purified for use as a human medicine and food supplement. The high mineral content of 84 organic minerals and adaptogens of Shilajit is reputed to be excellent for preventing and treating conditions such as diabetes, fibromyalgia, neurological damage, nutritional deficiencies, calcification of tissues and glands, heavy metal toxicity, immune suppression, attention deficiencies, impotence, depression, arthritis, irregular blood pressure, kidney stones, aging and obesity.
20. Avocado	One of the most nutrient-dense foods, avocados are high in fiber and, ounce for ounce, top the charts among all fruits for folate, potassium, vitamin E, and magnesium. The delicious healthy monounsaturated fat in the avocado is one of its biggest benefits. The only other fruit with a comparable amount of monounsaturated fat is the olive. The monounsaturated fat in avocados is oleic acid, which may help lower LDL cholesterol while increasing good HDL cholesterol. Avocado also is gaining support for prevention of breast and prostate cancer, and promoting healthy skin, digestion, blood regulation.

4. Optimizing Your Diet (Alkanilization, Portioning, Food-combining, Ketogenics, Blood Type & Optimizing Mitochondrial Function)

Now that we have learned what to put in our mouths, let's explore *when, how much* and the *best combinations* to put in our mouths to get optimal results. In this section, we'll explore (a) **Portioning,** (b) **Ketogenics,** (c) **Hydration,** (d) **Alkalizing Diet,** (e) **Food-Combining,** (f) **Blood Type Diet,** and (g) **Optimizing Mitochondrial Health** to provide the following benefits:

• Maintain optimal weight (including weight loss and gain)	• Build lean muscle mass and reduce fat
• Increase digestive efficiency	• Strengthen the nervous system
• Maintain optimum alkalinity for optimum health	• Neutralize harmful acids that lead to illness
• Cleanse the kidneys, intestines and liver	• Protect your body from free radical damage
• Maintain stronger bones and healthier teeth	• Control digestive problems
• Alleviate insomnia	• Increase muscle and joint mobility
• Regulate blood sugar levels and blood pressure	• Combat arthritic conditions and heart disease
• Breakdown and eliminate heavy metals, drug residues and other toxins	• Improve overall systemic health
• Help regulate metabolism	• Strengthen immune system function
	• Increase energy and stamina
	• Keep your heart beating regularly

a.   *Portioning*[169]

Portioning is discipline of balancing energy intake with energy output to achieve a desired result. The desired result can include losing, maintaining, or gaining weight, building lean muscle mass, increasing energy, increasing endurance and/or increasing strength.

The relevant unit measure of the energy required to turn food into energy is the "**calorie**." In nutrition, calories are calculated from food composition. Such calculations use internationally agreed conventional conversion factors, which are rounded values that roughly approximate the average energy density of a large number of different food samples. Not all foods within each category are created equally, however, the table below shows a basic consensus and understanding of the energy provided by various nutrients and the amount of energy required to consume the nutrients.

Nutrient	Calories per gram
Carbohydrate	4 kcal
Protein	4 kcal
Fat	9 kcal
Alcohol	7 kcal

Thus, from the chart above, fat contains the most calories and therefore requires the greatest amount of metabolic energy to consume. Because unused carbohydrates are stored as fat, high carbohydrate diets, even if they contain no fat, will be stored as fat, thus requiring greater metabolic energy to burn the fat from stored carbohydrates.

The ideal caloric intake is different for everyone. Caloric needs depend on factors such as age, gender, height, weight, body frame, physical activities, hormones, genetics, metabolism and environment. An intake between 1200 and 1400 calories per day is considered a low intake called basal metabolic needs, or the calories needed to keep the heart beating and all the internal organs working. Calorie levels below 1200 per day should generally be avoided, because they may decrease metabolism, are usually nutrient deficient and hard to follow for any length of time.

The Daily Values (DVs) used on the new food labels are based upon an intake of 2000 calorie per day diet (the average amount needed for adults of "average" size who engage in moderate physical activities). The average caloric intake per person in Ethiopia is 1,667, Western Europe is 3,400 and the U.S. is 3,666. The optimal average daily caloric range is about 1600-2400 calories per day.

Weight will increase with caloric intake exceeding output and decrease with output exceeding caloric intake. Below are Input and Output Tables. The Input Tables show the average caloric content of various foods by average portion and per 100 grams based upon preparations which are raw, steamed, boiled or baked, not fried. The Output Table of shows the average calories burned for various activities for 30 minutes based upon individuals weighing 100, 150 and 200 lbs.

Caloric Input Table Based Upon 6 Food Groups

Fruits & Vegetables	Calories per Avg. Serving	Calories per 100 grams
Apple	44	44
Banana	107	65
Baked Beans	170	80
Blackberries	25	25
Broccoli	27	32
Cabbage	15	20
Carrot	16	25
Cauliflower	20	30
Cucumber	3	10
Grapefruit	32	32
Lettuce	4	15
Mushrooms	3	15
Olives	50	80
Onions	49	33
Orange	40	30
Peach	35	30
Spinach	8	8
Strawberries	10	20
Tomato	30	20

Meats & Seafood	Calories per Avg. Serving	Calories per 100 grams
Anchovies Tinned	300	300
Bacon	300	500
Beef	320	280
Chicken	220	200
Cod	150	100
Crab	200	110
Duck	400	110
Halibut	220	125
Lamb	300	300
Lobster	200	100
Mussels	90	90
Pheasant	200	200
Prawns	180	100

Pork	320	290
Salmon	250	320
Sausage Pork	200	120
Trout	100	100
Tuna Canned	200	160
Turkey	80	80

Dairy	Calories per Avg. Serving	Calories per 100 grams
Cheese (avg.)	110	440
Cottage cheese	49	80
Cream Cheese	128	160
Cream	160	200
Eggs	90	150
Ice Cream	200	190
Milk (whole)	175	70
Milk (skimmed)	95	38
Yogurt (whole)	90	60
Yogurt (skimmed)	95	38

Breads, Starches & Grains	Calories per Avg. Serving	Calories per 100 grams
Bagel	140	310
Bread (white)	96	240
Bread (wheat)	88	220
Cereal (avg.)	130	370
Naan Bread	300	320
Pasta	330	110
Porridge	193	55
Potatoes	210	70
Rice	420	140
Spaghetti	303	101

Fats	Calories per Avg. Serving	Calories per 100 grams
Butter	112	500
Cooking Oils	135	900
Cod Liver Oil	135	900
Margarine	50	750
Butter	112	500

Sugars	Calories per Avg. Serving	Calories per 100 grams
Honey	42	280
Maple Syrup	15	300
Jam	38	250
Chocolate	200	500
Honey	42	280

By subtracting 500 calories from your daily intake value you will lose around 1 pound per week. This is based upon the fact that one pound of fat is equal to 3500 calories. 7-days x 500 calories per day is equal to 3500 calories per week. As well, by increasing output by the same amount can also create the same result. However, some exercises have an exponential affect by raising metabolism and increasing muscle mass.

Calories burned from activity is based upon many factors, including body weight, intensity of activity, conditioning level and metabolism. The chart below shows the calories burned doing different activities for an average time of 30 minutes based upon the weight of the individual.

Caloric Output Table Based Upon 30 Minutes of Activity[170]

Activity	125 lb. Person	155 lb. Person	185 lb. Person
Aerobic dancing (low impact)	115	172	230
Aerobic dancing (low impact)	115	172	230
Aerobics step training, (4" step)	145	218	290
Aerobics, slide training (basic)	150	225	300
Backpacking with 10 lb. load	180	270	360
Backpacking with 20 lb. load	200	300	400
Badminton	150	225	300
Basketball (game)	220	330	440
Basketball (leisurely, nongame)	130	195	260
Bicycling, 10 mph	125	188	250
Bicycling, 13 mph	200	300	400
Billiards	45	68	90
Bowling	55	82	110
Canoeing, 2.5 mph	70	105	140
Canoeing, 4.0 mph	135	202	270
Croquet	60	90	120
Cross country snow skiing, intense	330	495	660
Cross country snow skiing, moderate	220	330	440
Dancing (noncontact)	100	150	200
Dancing (slow)	55	82	110
Gardening, moderate	90	135	180
Golfing (walking, w/o cart)	100	150	200
Golfing (with a cart)	70	105	140
Handball	230	345	460
Hiking with a 10 lb. load	180	270	360
Hiking with a 30 lb. load	235	352	470
Hiking, no load	155	232	310
Housework	90	135	180
Jogging, 5 mph (12 minutes/mile)	185	278	370
Mowing	135	202	270
Ping Pong	90	135	180
Raking	75	112	150

Racquetball	205	308	410
Rowing (leisurely)	75	112	150
Rowing machine	180	270	360
Running, (7.5 minutes/mile)	305	458	610
Running, (6 minutes/mile)	350	525	700
Scrubbing the floor	140	210	280
Scuba diving	190	285	380
Sex	100	150	200
Skipping rope	285	428	570
Snow shoveling	195	292	390
Snow skiing, downhill	130	195	260
Soccer	195	292	390
Squash	205	308	410
Stair climbing	140	210	280
Surfing	133	210	278
Swimming (50 yards/minute)	225	338	450
Table Tennis	90	135	180
Tennis	160	240	320
Tennis (doubles)	110	165	220
Trimming hedges	105	158	210
Vacuuming	75	112	150
Volleyball (game)	120	180	240
Walking, 4 mph	100	150	200
Washing the car	75	112	150
Waterskiing	160	240	320
Weeding	100	150	200
Weight training (40 sec. bet. sets)	255	382	510
Weight training (60 sec. bet. sets)	190	285	380
Weight training (90 sec. bet. sets)	125	188	250

The foregoing caloric input and energy output charts evidence that a significant amount of exercise is required to burn our caloric intake. In addition to optimizing caloric intake and energy output, "grazing" throughout the day or eating 5 small meals instead of 3 medium to large meals helps maintain metabolism, enhances digestion and increases useable energy. This type of eating also reduces the storing of carbs and fats as body fat.

Also, by choosing highly nutritious foods, such as the Superfoods mentioned above, we can lower our food intake while providing our bodies the nutrition and energy it needs to optimally perform. Moreover, it is recommended to eat with intention and for purpose. For example, for instant energy, eat carbs; for sustained energy, eat fats; and for building lean muscle mass, eat protein.

Using your hands as a guide is another way to estimate appropriate portion size. Although each person is different and has individual portion requirements based upon such factors as age, gender, activity levels, metabolism and body mass, the following is a general guide:*

Description	Women	Men
Vegetables & Salads	1 fist / 1 cup	2 fists / 2 cups
Fruits	1 fist / 1 cup	1 fists/ 1 cup
Proteins	1/2 fist	1 fist
Grains & Starches	1/2 fist	1/2 fist
Nuts	1/4 fist	1/2 fist
Oils & Butters	1/4 fist	1/4 fist

*It is recommend that you consult an experienced healthcare provider to get tested for food allergies and intolerances as well as choosing the most nutritious and beneficial foods for you along with determining the most optimal portions for you.

Again, the foregoing chart is not personalized, however, when choosing from the foregoing chart, the portion for an entire meal should be limited, generally, to no more than 1.5 fists of food for women and 3 fists of food for men per meal, but no one constituent portion exceeding the portion above. For example, if you are a man, do not eat 3 fists of protein, but rather 2 fists of protein and 1 fist of vegetables. If you are woman, do not eat 1.5 fists of grains, but rather ½ a fist of grains, ½ a fist of vegetables and ½ a fist of proteins.

By combining (1) portion-control, (2) food-combining, (3) choosing complex and low glycemic carbs over simple and high glycemic carbs, and (4) eating highly nutritious foods, we can exponentiate the value and beneficial effects of our meals by getting more nutrition with less calories.

b. **Ketogenics**[171]

The ketogenic diet is a high-fat, adequate-protein, low-carbohydrate diet that forces the body to burn fat rather than carbohydrates. Carbohydrates are the first source the body uses for conversion into glucose, which fuels energy and brain function. When there are insufficient carbohydrates in the diet, the liver converts fat into fatty acids and ketones. In this case, ketones replace glucose as an energy source. Ketosis occurs when there is an elevated level of ketones in the blood.

The benefits of a ketogenic diet, include weight loss, reduction of inflammation, lower risk of cancer, increased muscle mass, reduction of appetite and lower insulin levels.

Harvard University's, School of Public Health reports:[172]

"There is not one "standard" ketogenic diet with a specific ratio of mac-ronutrients (carbohydrates, protein, fat). The ketogenic diet typically reduces total carbohydrate intake to less than 50 grams a day—less than the amount found in a medium plain bagel—and can be as low as 20 grams a day. Generally, popular ketogenic resources suggest an average of 70-80% fat from total daily calories, 5-10% carbohydrate, and 10-20% protein. For a 2000-calorie diet, this translates to about 165 grams fat, 40 grams carbohydrate, and 75 grams protein. The protein amount on the ketogenic diet is kept moderate in comparison with other low-carb high-protein diets, because eating too much protein can prevent ketosis. The amino acids in protein can be converted to glucose, so a ketogenic diet specifies enough protein to preserve lean body mass including muscle, but that will still cause ketosis.

Many versions of ketogenic diets exist, but all ban carb-rich foods. Some of these foods may be obvious: starches from both refined and whole grains like breads, cereals, pasta, rice, and cookies; potatoes, corn, and other starchy vegetables; and fruit juices. Some that may not be so obvious are beans, legumes, and most fruits. Most ketogenic plans allow foods high in saturated fat, such as fatty cuts of meat, processed meats, lard, and butter, as well as sources of unsaturated fats, such as nuts, seeds, avocados, plant oils, and oily fish. Depending on your source of information, ketogenic food lists may vary and even conflict."

Dr. Mercola provides additional details into the various types of Keto, stating, *"There are several variations of the ketogenic diet based on specific needs:*

- *Standard Ketogenic Diet (SKD)*

    SKD is the type I typically recommend for most people, because it is very effective. It focuses on high consumption of healthy fats (70 percent of your diet), moderate protein (25 percent) and very little carbohydrates (5 percent).

    Keep in mind there's no set limit to the fat, because energy requirements vary from person to person, depending on their daily physical activities.

    However, majority of your calories still need to come from fats, and you still need to limit your consumption of carbohydrates and protein for it to become a standard ketogenic diet.

- *Targeted Ketogenic Diet (TKD)*

    TKD is generally geared towards fitness enthusiasts. In this approach, you eat the entirety of your allocated carbs for the day in one meal, 30 to 60 minutes before exercise. The idea here is to use the energy provided by the carbs effectively before it disrupts ketosis.

    If you're following this approach, eat carbs that are easily digestible with a high glycemic index to avoid upsetting your stomach. Then, when you're done exercising, increase your intake of protein to help with muscle recovery, then continue consuming your fats afterwards.

- *Cyclic Ketogenic Diet (CKD)*

    Whereas TKD is focused on fitness enthusiasts, CKD is focused more on athletes and bodybuilders. In CKD, you cycle between a normal ketogenic diet, followed by a set number of days of high carb consumption, also known as "carb-loading."

The idea here is to take advantage of the carbohydrates to replenish the glycogen lost from your muscles during athletic activity or working out.

If you're a high-level athlete or bodybuilder, CKD may be a viable method for you. It usually consists of five days of SKD, followed by two days of carb-loading. During the ketogenic cycle, carb consumption is around 50 grams, but when you get to the carb-loading cycle, the amount jumps to 450 to 600 grams. Again, this method isn't recommended for most people who don't have a high rate of physical activity.

- *High-Protein Ketogenic Diet*

  This method is a variant of the SKD. In a high-protein diet, you increase the ratio of protein consumption to ten percent and reduce your healthy fat consumption by ten percent. In a study involving obese men, researchers noted that it helped reduce their hunger and lowered their food intake significantly, resulting in weight loss. If you're overweight or obese, this may help you at first, then you can transition to SKD after you normalize your weight.

- *Restricted Ketogenic Diet*

  As mentioned earlier, a ketogenic diet can be an effective weapon against cancer. To do this, you need to be on a restricted ketogenic diet. By restricting your carbohydrate and calorie intake, your body loses glycogen and starts producing ketones that your healthy cells can use as energy. Because cancer cells cannot use these ketones, they starve to death." [173]

Before committing to a Ketogenic Diet, it is important to consult with an experienced healthcare provider who make informed recommendations based upon your health, medical conditions and goals. When committing to a ketogenic diet, **remove** foods containing sugars, sweeteners, starches, milk, flour and grains, and **include** the following organic foods:

Recommended Foods for Ketogenic Diet		
Coconut Oil	Fish (e.g., Wild-Caught Salmon, Sardines & Anchovies)	Raw Nuts (Almonds, Macadamias & Pecans)
Olive Oil	Shellfish (e.g., Scallops, Oysters, Clams, Lobster, Crab)	Seeds (e.g., Pumpkin, Flax, Sesame, Chia)
Raw Grass-fed Butter	Bone Broth	Avocados
Ghee	Arugula	Kale
Raw Cacao Butter	Broccoli	Spinach
Pastured Eggs	Zucchini	Cilantro
Grass-fed Meats	Brussels sprouts	Low Quantities of Low Glycemic Fruit (e.g., Blackberries, Blueberries, Cranberries, Limes, Lemons and Grapefruit)
Stevia as an acceptable sweetener	Black Coffee	Teas

c.   *Alkalizing Diet[174]*

We are 70% water and the health of our cells is directly related to, and dependent upon, the quality and pH balance of the water in and around them. It's scientifically proven that maintaining an alkaline pH state in and around our cells helps the body ward off attacks from microbes, bacteria, viruses and cancer. Moreover, proper pH is critical to proper body functioning including optimal immune system performance and assimilation of vitamins, minerals and food.

The pH scale is from 0—14

(0-6.9 = acidic, 7.0 = neutral, 7.1-14 = alkaline)

Acid 0 - 6.9	Neutral 7	Alkaline 7.1-14

| 0 | 1 | 2 | 3 | 4 | 5 | 6 | 7 | 8 | 9 | 10 | 11 | 12 | 13 | 14 |

7.35-7.45.
Ideal Blood pH

The abbreviation "pH" stands for potential hydrogen. The pH of any solution is the measure of its hydrogen ion concentration. The higher the pH reading, the more alkaline and oxygen rich the fluid is. The lower the pH reading, the more acidic and oxygen deprived the fluid is. The pH range is from 0 to 14, with 7.0 being neutral. Anything above 7.0 is alkaline, anything below 7.0 is considered acidic.

Life on earth depends on appropriate pH levels in and around living organisms and cells. Human life requires a tightly controlled pH level in the blood serum in slightly alkaline range between 7.35 to 7.45 to survive. Urine and saliva pH tends to be more acidic than blood. Healthy ranges for saliva and urine can range from 4.5 to 8.0, but a more optimal range is 6.5 to 7.2.[175]

Fortunately, our lungs and kidneys regulate pH by eliminating carbon dioxide (CO_2), the most common acid in our bodies. By consuming alkalizing beverages and foods, we increase antioxidant consumption and can help the body more effectively eliminate acids and free radicals.

The pH number is an exponent number of 10. Thus, a small difference in pH translates to a big difference in the number of oxygen or OH-ions. A difference of 1 in a pH value means ten times the difference in the number of OH-ions, a difference of 2 means one hundred times the difference in the number of OH-ions. In other words, blood with a pH value of 7.45 contains 64.9% more oxygen than blood with a pH value of 7.30.

While oxygen and an optimal alkaline pH balance may help keep the body healthy and bolster immune system function to prevent cancer, viruses and anaerobic microbes, alkalizing is really about keeping an optimal balance. While higher pH balance indicates that the cellular fluid is more oxygen rich, over-alkalization can be detrimental to health.

The normal human cell has a lot of molecular oxygen and a slightly alkaline pH, whereas cancer cells generally have an acid pH and lack of oxygen. At a pH slightly above 7.4, most cancer cells become dormant which allows healthy cells to proliferate.[176] However, above 7.45, healthy cellular functioning becomes impaired. Once cancer cells overcome the immune system and proliferate, alkalinity is generally not considered an effective treatment. For example, according to Dr. Robert Gilles, Ph.D. who has studied tumor formation and acidity, tumors make themselves acidic, even in an alkaline cellular structure, and that acidic therapies are often more effective than alkaline therapies.[177]

Cancer needs an acid and low oxygen environment to survive and flourish. An acidic balance generally:

- decreases the body's ability to absorb minerals and other nutrients

- reduces the energy production in the cells

- diminishes ability to repair damaged cells

- decreases ability to detoxify heavy metals

- reduces immune system function

- increases susceptibility to fatigue and illness

- provides an environment for cancer and virus to thrive

An extended time in the acid pH state ("Acidosis"), can lead to rheumatoid arthritis, diabetes, lupus, tuberculosis, osteoporosis, high blood pressure, cancer and many other undesirable diseases.

Testing your pH level:

It's easy to test your pH level using litmus paper and doing the two following tests:

1. *Salivary pH Test:* Simply wet a piece of Litmus Paper with your saliva two hours after a meal. This will give a reflection of your state of health. The optimal pH for saliva is 6.4 to 6.8. A reading lower than 6.4 is indicative of insufficient alkaline reserves. Immediately after eating, the saliva pH should rise to 7.8 or higher. Unless this occurs, the body likely has alkaline deficiencies and will not assimilate food very well.

2. *Urinary pH Test:* The pH of the urine indicates how the body is working to maintain the proper pH of the blood. The urine reveals the alkaline building (anabolic) and acid tearing down (catabolic) cycles. The pH of urine indicates the functioning of the kidneys, adrenals, lungs and gonads to regulate pH through the buffer salts and hormones. Urine

can provide a fairly accurate picture of body chemistry, because the kidneys filter out the buffer salts of pH regulation and provide values the body elimination. Healthy urine pH can vary from around 4.5 to 8.0 for its extremes, but the ideal range is 6.5 to 7.2, with the higher end preferred.

While alkaline diets are still considered controversial by some, alkalizing foods generally provide higher antioxidants that help the body remove toxins, free radicals and acids. Having said this, the National Health Institute reported that alkaline diets may have the following benefits:[178]

1. *Increased fruits and vegetables in an alkaline diet would improve the K/Na ratio and may benefit bone health, reduce muscle wasting, as well as mitigate other chronic diseases such as hypertension and strokes.*

2. *The resultant increase in growth hormone with an alkaline diet may improve many outcomes from cardiovascular health to memory and cognition.*

3. *An increase in intracellular magnesium, which is required for the function of many enzyme systems, is another added benefit of the alkaline diet. Available magnesium, which is required to activate vitamin D, would result in numerous added benefits in the vitamin D apocrine/exocrine systems.*

4. *Alkalinity may result in added benefit for some chemotherapeutic agents that require a higher pH.*

The 3 following suggestions are the most natural and powerful way to raise alkalinity.

1. *Coral Minerals*—A powerful supplement that works very well to rapidly alkalize bodily fluids is coral minerals with a significant calcium content. Coral calcium has a very high alkaline pH, which means it can help offset the acid in your body and help return your body to the normal/slightly alkaline level.

2. *Baking Soda*—Research has shown that baking soda (sodium bicarbonate) has alkalizing, antacid and electrolyte replacement properties, as well as enhancing immune system and anti-inflammatory response. Long

distance runners and swimmer have used baking soda to enhance performance and offset acid build up in the muscles.[179]

3. *Alkalizing Foods*—There is a general consensus that diet can markedly affect the pH of person's acid load. Eating 75% alkalizing foods and 25% or less acid forming foods can help increase alkalinity and optimal health. The Superfoods mentioned above, generally fall into the category of alkalizing foods. As a rule of thumb, vegetables and fruits are alkalizing foods, whereas, flesh meats, coffee, sugar, artificial sweeteners, alcohol, soft drinks, tobacco, cheese, beans, antibiotics, white flour products and refined salt are acid forming foods.

Please note that an *alkaline* pH in foods or beverages doesn't mean the food or beverage is *alkalizing*. To determine which foods are alkalizing, scientists utilize pH measurement system known as the Potential Renal Acid Load (PRAL). PRAL can be used to determine which foods are acid-forming and which foods are alkalizing by providing an estimate of the production of endogenous acid that exceeds the level of alkali produced by the kidneys after the body metabolizes that food. This method of calculation was experimentally validated in healthy adults, and it showed that, under controlled conditions, acid loads and renal net acid excretion (NAE) can be reliably estimated from diet composition.

For example, lemon juice has a pH of approximately 2.5, but despite its high acidity, is actually alkalizing. This is because fruits and vegetables are generally high in alkaline nutrients such as *potassium, calcium* and *magnesium*. These minerals ultimately reduce the amount of acid that the kidneys will need to filter out and are therefore given a PRAL score demonstrating that these foods are alkalizing. Conversely, acidic nutrients such as *protein, phosphorus* and *sulfur* increase the amount of acid the kidneys must filter out. Meats, nuts and grains, which typically contain these nutrients, generally receive a PRAL score showing that these foods are acidifying.[180]

To help you determine which foods to eat for optimal alkalization, the following chart contains a list of several different alkalizing and acidifying foods:

Alkalizing Foods and Acidifying Foods

Alkalizing Foods		
Vegetables	**Fruits**	**Proteins**
• Alfalfa	• Apple	• Chicken Breast
• Asparagus	• Apricot	• Eggs
• Barley Grass	• Avocado	• Flax Seeds
• Fermented Veggies	• Banana (high glycemic)	• Hemp Protein
• Watercress	• Cantaloup	• Pea Protein
• Beets	• Cherries	• Pumpkin Seeds
• Broccoli	• Currants	• Pumpkin Seeds
• Brussel Sprouts	• Dates	• Sunflower Seeds
• Cabbage	• Figs	• Tempeh (fermented)
• Carrots	• Grapes	• Tofu (fermented)
• Cauliflower	• Grapefruit	• Whey Protein
• Celery	• Honeydew Melon	• Yogurt
• Chard	• Lemon	**Nuts**
• Chlorella	• Lime	• Almonds
• Collard Greens	• Nectarine	• Chestnuts
• Cucumber	• Orange	
• Daikon	• Peach	**Beverages**
• Dulce	• Pear	• Almond Milk
• Dandelions	• Pineapple	• Coconut Water
• Edible Flowers	• Berries	• Grapefruit Juice
• Eggplant	• Tangerine	• Green & Veggie Juices
• Garlic	• Tomato	• Green Teas
• Kale	• Tropical Fruits	• Herbal Teas
• Kohlrabi	• Watermelon	• Kombucha
• Lettuce & Leafy Greens		• Lemon Juice
• Mushrooms	**Spices**	• Vegetable Juices
• Mustard Greens	• Cinnamon	
• Nightshade Veggies	• Curry	**Other**
• Onions	• Ginger	• Apple Cider Vinegar
• Parsnips	• Mustard	• Bee Pollen
• Peas	• Chili Peppers	• Lecithin Granules
• Peppers	• Sea Salt	• Probiotic Cultures
• Pumpkin	• Miso	• Aloe Vera
• Rutabaga	• Tamari	
• Sea Vegetables	• All Herbs	
• Spirulina		
• Sprouts	**Sweeteners**	
• Squash	• Honey	
• Wheat Grass	• Stevia	

Acidifying Foods		
Fats & Oils	**Grains & Starches**	**Proteins**
• Avocado Oil	• Amaranth	• Chicken Breast
• Canola Oil	• Barley	• Eggs
• Corn Oil	• Buckwheat	• Flax Seeds
• Hemp Seed Oil	• Corn	• Hemp Protein
• Flax Oil	• Kamut	• Pea Protein
• Lard	• Hemp Seed Flour Oats	• Pumpkin Seeds
• Olive Oil	(rolled) Quinoa	• Pumpkin Seeds
• Safflower Oil	• Pasta & Noodles	• Sunflower Seeds
• Sesame Oil	• Potatoes	• Tempeh (fermented)
• Sunflower Oil	• Rice (all)	• Tofu (fermented)
	• Rye Spelt	• Whey Protein
Animal Proteins	• Wheat	• Yogurt
• Beef	• Wheat Germ	
• Carp		**Sweeteners**
• Clams	**Beans & Legumes**	• Sugar
• Fish	• Black Beans	• Agave
• Lamb	• Chick Peas	• Corn Syrup
• Lobster	• Green Peas	
• Mussels	• Kidney Beans	**Alcohol & Beverages**
• Oyster	• Lentils	• Beer
• Pork	• Lima Beans	• Coffee
• Rabbit	• Pinto Beans	• Hard Liquor
• Salmon	• Red Beans	• Rice Milk
• Shrimp	• Soy Beans	• Soft Drinks
• Scallops	• White Beans	• Soy Milk
• Tuna		• Wine
• Turkey	**Nuts**	
• Venison	• Cashews	**Drugs & Chemicals**
	• Brazil Nuts	• Petrochemicals
Fruits	• Macadamias	• Antibiotics
• Cranberries	• Peanuts	Psychedelics
	• Pecans	• Pesticides
Dairy	• Tahini	• Herbicides
• Cheese	• Walnuts	• Cigarettes
• Milk		
• Butter		

d. Hydration[181]

Water is essential to life and our health. Drinking pure, clean water in its natural state with (e.g., spring, glacier, deep aquifer water) is generally much healthier than filtered waters (e.g., reverse osmosis) and tap water. Proper hydration from healthy water sources help maintain body weight, improve the health of skin, decrease muscle and joint inflammation and cramping, improve circulation, detox the body and aid digestion.

While some sources, such as the NRDC and the EPA, state that tap water is safe drink, the truth is that tap water is generally treated with a number of chemicals most often to kill bacteria and other microorganisms, including chlorine, fluoride, aluminum sulfate, calcium hydroxide and sodium silico-fluoride.[182] As well, it is fairly common to find lead, aluminum, hormones, prescription drugs and agricultural chemicals in the public water supply. The Environmental Working Group ("EWG") analyzed data from almost 50,000 U.S. public water utilities nationwide, tested for 500 contaminants and found 267. EWG's analysis revealed that the 267 contaminants had the following associated health risks:[183]

- *93 linked to an increased risk of cancer. More than 40,000 systems had detections of known or likely carcinogens exceeding established federal or state health guidelines—levels that pose only negligible health risks, but are not legally enforceable.*

- *78 associated with brain and nervous system damage.*

- *63 connected to developmental harm to children or fetuses.*

- *38 that may cause fertility problems.*

- *45 linked to hormonal disruption.*

According to the EWG, *"The vast majority of the nation's drinking water supplies get a passing grade from federal and state regulatory agencies. However, many of the 250-plus contaminants detected through water sampling and testing are at levels that are perfectly legal under the Safe Drinking Water Act or state regulations, but well above levels authoritative scientific studies have found to pose health risks."*

While there are opposing views and data, I prefer to err on the side of health and scientific data. I would, therefore, support and act upon the data from EWG rather than the government agencies.

Moreover, even if we drink water that is "clean and filtered," not all water is equal for proper hydration and health. According to Dr. Joseph Mercola, 40% of the bottled water is tap water and that drinking from plastic bottles could lead to BPA exposure. BPA is a synthetic hormone disruptor linked to learning and behavioral disorders, altered immune system function, prostate and breast cancer, risk of obesity and early puberty. Additionally, plastic bottle waste represents a significant environmental issue.[184]

I prefer, and recommend, spring water bottled at the source in glass from companies that provide for recycling of the glass bottles. Mountain spring water generally has the ideal pH range of 6.5-7.5 and contains a natural complement of minerals and healthy organic compounds. While I prefer mountain spring water, there are several filtration methods that can be used to improve the quality of tap water, such reverse osmosis filtration and carbon filters. These filtration technologies can mitigate the risks of drinking and bathing in tap water. Even if we drink clean and pure glass-bottled mountain spring water, our skin absorbs toxins through water and it is therefore recommended to also filter bath and shower water.

Dr. Mercola also states that there is a growing epidemic of chronic dehydration with symptoms including[185]:

- *Digestive disturbances such as heartburn and constipation*

- *Urinary tract infections*

- *Autoimmune disease such as chronic fatigue syndrome and multiple sclerosis*

- *Premature aging*

- *High cholesterol*

- *Weight gain*

The current recommendation from doctors is to drink 8 glasses of water per day. However, those who live in arid climates, are athletes or physical laborers may require more water per day. While the 8 glasses of water per day recommendation is a good guide, it is more important to listen to your body. If you drink water at the onset of thirst and your urine is pale yellow, you are likely hydrating sufficiently. The National Academies of Sciences, Engineering, and Medicine recommend daily hydration of 15.5 cups (3.7 liters) for men and 11.5 cups (2.7 liters) for women. However, this also includes water, other beverages and food intake.

In addition to general healthy hydration, below are a few supercharged hydration options:

1. _H² Water_. _Molecular hydrogen (H²)_ occurs when two hydrogen atoms combine together. Because hydrogen is the smallest existent gas molecule, it has the ability to penetrate into virtually every organ and cell in the body, including the brain. H² is a gas with unique antioxidant effects that specifically target the most harmful free radicals. H² helps improve the ability of cells to achieve oxidant/antioxidant homeostasis. This results in improvements in superoxide dismutase, catalase and glutathione levels, thereby reducing the generation and storage of free radicals. In addition to its antioxidant effects, H² water has also been reported to boost energy, improve recovery from workouts, lower inflammation and slow the aging process.[186]

2. _Deuterium Depleted Water_. Deuterium is a heavy isotope of hydrogen that is naturally present in almost all water. Originally, it was thought that water is just H2O, however, almost all water contains a heavy hydrogen isotope known as deuterium ("D" or "²H"). There is an average of about 144.7 parts per million (ppm) of deuterium in most water.[187] When deuterium is removed from water, the water is often referred to as "_light water_" or "_deuterium depleted water_" ("DDW"). While deuterium exists naturally in the body and water, over time, deuterium tends to accumulate in our bodies and can cause significant detriment to our health including obesity, cancer, and reduced mitochondrial functioning.[188]

There are several research studies, showing that drinking "light water" under 125ppm of deuterium rather than water over 150 ppm of deuterium has significant health benefits including enhanced mitochondrial functioning, longer life spans for cancer patients, anti-carcinogen[189], as well as stimulating cell growth, promoting detoxification, boosting metabolism, preventing heart disease and depression and protecting the liver.[190] Leading proponents of DDW with whom I have spoken, support that by replacing other water consumption with DDW containing between 100 ppm to 125 ppm deuterium can help the body remove accumulated deuterium resulting in major health benefits. By using DDW between 25 ppm to 50 ppm of deuterium instead of tap or bottled water, the health benefits resulting from removing deuterium accumulations can be accelerated and exponentiated, however, it is not recommended that DDW under 50 ppm be consumed for over sixty days.

e. *Food-combining[191]*

Digestion is governed by physiological chemistry. Digestion is one of the most energy intensive processes of our bodies. If we want to have peak performance, it is important to increase the efficiency of our digestive processes to provide more energy with the least amount of work. This is where food-combining can provide a critical role. While food-combining is controversial with the western medicine and scientific communities, it has been utilized in Ayurvedic, Chinese and other ancient health practices for centuries. The principle behind food-combining is that different food classes require different enzymes, different rates of digestion, and different digestive pH balances for optimal digestion. For example, carbohydrate foods require the carbohydrate-splitting enzymes of amylase and ptyalin, whereas protein foods require the protein splitting enzymes of pepsin and erepsin; milk requires lactase and fat requires lipase and bile.

By properly combining and timing what we eat, we can significantly improve our digestive efficiency, assimilation and the amount of energy derived from our food intake. The benefits attributed to food-combining by its proponents are numerous, including increased energy for body functioning, metabolism and digestive/elimination efficiency, as well as maintaining ideal weight, preventing fermentation and reducing toxins. These claims have not been supported by medical and scientific research, however, I, and many others, have experienced great benefits from the practice of food-combining. Particularly, I have noticed, higher energy levels, lessened flatulence and improved regulation of weight. Because each person is different and there is no one-size-fits-all diet, it might be worthwhile to try food-combining and see if it benefits you.

Described below are the guidelines of food-combining. Because food-combining can seem a bit complex at first, the material has been presented in several different formats to help the reader obtain a clear understanding of this important dietary practice. The following food-combining protocols are provided to improve wellness, digestion and energy. The protocols below are written as the "principles of food-combining," and it is fine to apply the 80-20 rule rather than being obsessive and rigid about food-combining.

First, here are the *4 Basics of Food-combining*:

1. Eat proteins with vegetables (e.g. Chicken & Broccoli)

2. Eat starches with vegetables and other starches (e.g., Potato and mixed vegetables)

3. Don't eat starches and proteins together in the same meal (e.g., Meat & Potatoes)

4. Eat fruits alone on an empty stomach and sparingly

Most people can do quite well just following the 4 Basics above, however, the information provided below can help you achieve a greater degree of digestive efficiency:

- Don't eat concentrated proteins (e.g., nuts, meat, eggs, cheese) and concentrated starchy carbohydrates (e.g. bread, pasta, cereals, potatoes, sweet fruits, cakes, candy) at the same meal. Sugary and starchy carbohydrates greatly inhibit the secretion of gastric juice and markedly delay digestion and if consumed in large quantities, can depress the stomach activity.

- Don't eat two concentrated proteins at the same meal. For example, avoid mixing nuts and meat, cheese and eggs, eggs and meat, meat and milk, at the same meal. Milk, if taken at all, is best taken alone. The reason for avoiding eating these combinations is because each protein requires a specific character and strength of digestive juice to be secreted.

- Don't eat fats (e.g., cream, butter, or oil) with starchy carbohydrates. Fat depresses the action of the gastric glands by delaying the development of appetite juices and inhibiting the pouring out of the proper gastric juices for digestion of starches. According to Dr. Jeremy Kaslow, MD., *"Primitive man did not eat fats with carbohydrates. The food had fat in the animal meat; but in millions of years he never found lumps of pure fat attached to any vegetable (carbohydrate) foods. As he evolved he never needed to digest fats and starches at the same meal—he never developed such mechanism—and today we still haven't any."*

- Eat fruits alone and specifically don't eat acid fruits (e.g., oranges, tomatoes, lemons, pineapple) with proteins (e.g., meat, eggs, cheese or nuts). Acid fruits may be combined with sub-acid fruits (e.g., pear, cherry, peach). Sub-acid fruits may be combined with Sweet Fruits (e.g., papaya, fig, date). Fruit acids inhibit efficient carbohydrate and protein digestion and also produce fermentation. Fermentation lowers pH, increases gas, indigestion, as well as toxicity. Poor digestion causes such diverse problems as heartburn, headaches, distention and muscle spasms.

- Don't consume melons with any other foods. Watermelon, muskmelon, honeydew melon, cantaloupe and other melons should always be eaten alone. This is due to the ease and speed in which melons decompose.

- Don't consume sugars (e.g., jellies, jams, sucrose, honey, agave, molasses and syrups) with starches (e.g., bread, cake, cereals, potatoes). If sugar is taken into the mouth it quickly fills with saliva but no ptyalin, essential for starch digestion, is present.

- Tomatoes should not be combined with starchy food as the combination of the various acids in the tomato, which are intensified on cooking, are very much opposed to the alkaline digestion of starches. They may be eaten with leafy vegetables and fat foods.

By portioning, intelligently combining foods and eating the right foods at the right time, we can eat a great variety of delicious food while increasing our health, metabolism, energy and optimizing our weight.

Below is a chart showing the strength of various foods in relation to each other, as well as tables showing what foods to combine:

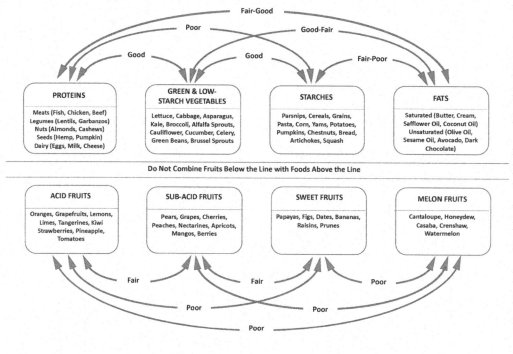

PROTEINS	GREEN & LOW-STARCH VEGETABLES	STARCHES	FATS
Meats (Fish, Chicken, Beef) Legumes (Lentils, Garbanzos) Nuts (Almonds, Cashews) Seeds (Hemp, Pumpkin) Dairy (Eggs, Milk, Cheese)	Lettuce, Cabbage, Asparagus, Kale, Broccoli, Alfalfa Sprouts, Cauliflower, Cucumber, Celery, Green Beans, Brussel Sprouts	Parsnips, Cereals, Grains, Pasta, Corn, Yams, Potatoes, Pumpkins, Chestnuts, Bread, Artichokes, Squash	Saturated (Butter, Cream, Safflower Oil, Coconut Oil) Unsaturated (Olive Oil, Sesame Oil, Avocado, Dark Chocolate)

Do Not Combine Fruits Below the Line with Foods Above the Line

ACID FRUITS	SUB-ACID FRUITS	SWEET FRUITS	MELON FRUITS
Oranges, Grapefruits, Lemons, Limes, Tangerines, Kiwi Strawberries, Pineapple, Tomatoes	Pears, Grapes, Cherries, Peaches, Nectarines, Apricots, Mangos, Berries	Papayas, Figs, Dates, Bananas, Raisins, Prunes	Cantaloupe, Honeydew, Casaba, Crenshaw, Watermelon

* It is recommended that you do not eat two concentrated proteins at the same meal (e.g., avoid nuts and meat, eggs and meat, cheese and nuts, cheese and eggs, meat and milk). **Tomatoes are an acid fruit, but in the digestive tract, they are highly alkaline, helping neutralize acid pH in the body. When tomatoes are cooked, they are highly acid forming and should not be eaten raw.

Because caloric intake, combining and portioning will be different for each individual depending upon such factors as gender, body weight, activity level, metabolism, genetics and environment, it is critical and recommended for each person to get their own expert advice from a knowledgeable health professional, do independent research and track their results to see what works best for them. Below are general dietary guidelines for food-combining and portioning that have made a positive difference in my life.

Breakfast		
Fruits eaten alone. Don't mix melons with other fruits. It is better to eat low glycemic fruits such as grapefruit, cherries, apples, and blueberries, to avoid blood sugar spiking and metabolic inconsistency and energy lows.	Portion: 1 to 2 pieces of fruit	Because of the sugars they contain, fruits should be eaten in the morning when blood sugar is generally at its lowest and sugars are most needed. As well, this allows for the sugars to be burned completely throughout the day and not stored as fats. Fruit naturally ferments which can create toxicity. Thus, eating fruit alone allows the fruit to be digested more efficiently and minimize fermentation.
Mid-Morning		
Vegetable Juices or Non-Dairy Soups.	Portion: 12-16 oz.	By staying with easily digestible, liquid-based nutrition in the morning, the body is able to take in much-needed hydration and easily digestible nutrient, while allowing the body to eliminate waste. However, eating the whole vegetable or fruit also provides fiber that is needed for cleansing the intestinal walls.
Lunch		
Non-starchy vegetables and protein	Portion: 2 oz of protein with 8 oz of non-starchy vegetables	Protein and non-starchy vegetables are a synergistic combination. Protein repairs body cells, builds and repairs muscles and bones, provide a source of energy of long term energy and helps control metabolism. The non-starchy vegetables provide short term energy, aid in digestion and provide nutrients and antioxidants.
Mid-Afternoon		
Starchy vegetables (preferably) or whole-grain starches	Portion: 8 oz of grains or 1 starchy vegetable	This provides additional post-lunch energy from carbohydrates and roughage to clear the digestive tract. Also, these foods create a feeling of fullness, so that cravings for a large dinner are diminished.
Dinner		
Protein and non-starchy vegetables	Portion: 4 oz of protein with 8 oz of non-starchy vegetables	See the Lunch recommendations above for the benefits of protein and non-starchy vegetables. Eating higher protein in the evening provides the body with amino acids and nutrients used for cellular repair and maintenance during sleep. Moreover, protein sources have little if any glycemic impact and thus are less likely to be stored as fat than carbohydrates. It is advised that nothing be eaten after 8pm.

f. Blood Type Diet[192]

Dr. Peter J. D'Adamo's revolutionary book "*Eat Right 4 Your Type*" pioneered the premise that one's blood type and genetic predisposition toward health can be improved by eating and exercising in a manner suitable to one's blood type. While the scientific research has yet to provide evidence supporting this diet, I and many others (7 million copies sold in print), have received remarkable results from this diet.

Proponents of the Blood Type Diet, assert that eating foods similar to those of our ancestors help promote benefits such as optimal weight, improved immune system function and ability to avoid disease, increased energy, clarity and stamina and overall improvement of health.

There are 8 different blood types: O positive, O negative, A positive, A negative, B positive, B negative, AB positive and AB negative. However, for this discussion, only the major four types (i.e., O, A, B, AB) will be addressed.

Blood Type	Classification & Character	Most Beneficial Food Recommendations	Foods to Avoid
O	**Hunter –** High Energy, Focused, Aggressive. Needs rigorous and regular exercise with running with bursts and High Intensity Interval Training ("HIIT") being recommended.	**Paleo/High Protein Diet** • Meats: Lean organic, grass-fed, pasture-raised meats such as lamb, mutton, venison and cold-water fish such as cod, mackerel, arctic char, steelhead, trout and king salmon. • Dairy: Limited consumption and select dairy including butter, goat cheese, feta cheese and eggs • Vegetables: Select vegetables including kale, collard greens, broccoli, arugula, romaine lettuce, spinach, artichokes, chicory, garlic, horseradish, leeks, okra, onions, parsley, cilantro, red peppers, sweet potatoes, pumpkin, parsnips and seaweed • Fruits: Select fruits including figs, prunes, plums, blueberries. • Nuts and Legumes: Most nuts including pumpkin seeds and walnuts being beneficial and all other nuts except those on the avoid list.	• Meats: Pork, goose • Dairy: Milk, yogurt • Vegetables: eggplant, potatoes, corn, shiitake mushrooms, Brussels sprouts, cabbage, mustard greens • Fruits: Melons, olives, oranges, tangerines, strawberries, blackberries, coconut, fermented olives, avocados • Grains should be strictly limited. All wheat products and sprouted grains. Occassionaly amaranth, barley, rice, kamut, kasha, millet and rye are allowable. • Nuts: Brazil nuts, cashews, peanuts, pistachios and poppy seeds
A	**Agrarian –** Earthy, Patient, Collaborative, Communal. Long slow distance and yoga are recommended exercise choices.	**Plant-Based Vegetarian Diet** • Vegetables: All vegetables with spinach, broccoli, carrot, kale, collard greens, asparagus and beets being the most beneficial • Fruits: All fruits with cherries, blackberries, blueberries, figs, grapefruit and pineapple being the most beneficial. • Grains: High grains intake with whole grains preferred such as buckwheat, amaranth, brown rice, oats, soy, rye, quinoa, spelt. • Nuts & Legumes: All nuts with pumpkin seeds, peanuts, lentils, black-eyed peas, black beans and pinto beans the most highly recommended. • Meats: Very limited with chicken, turkey and fish including salmon, trout, cod, red snapper, yellowtail and mahi mahi. Limited to only 3 servings per week. • Dairy: Limited dairy with only 4 servings per week recommended. Non-Dairy substitutes are recommended such as soy, oat or almond milk.	• Meats: All red meat including beef, pork, lamb, venison, buffalo and game • Grains: Wheat, wheat germ, farina and semolina • Dairy: Milk and eggs • Fruits: Bananas, tomatoes and oranges • Vegetables: Hot or sweet peppers, potatoes, cabbage, eggplant

Blood Type	Classification & Character	Most Beneficial Food Recommendations	Foods to Avoid
B	**Nomad –** Balanced, Versatile, Energetic, High Endurance, Robust. This blood type is concentrated mostly in Asia Animal herders that migrated from Africa to the Himalayan highlands, thus long slow distance walking, jogging and functional exercise are recommended. due to their nomadic nature, their diet requires greater variety.	**Balance of Meats and Vegetables** • Meats: Lamb, goat, mutton, rabbit, venison, salmon, cod, halibut, mackerel • Dairy: Low fat dairy including 2% milk, low fat yogurt, and skim milk cheeses (e.g., cottage cheese and mozzarella) • Vegetables: kale, collard greens, mustard greens, broccoli, beets, romaine lettuce, spinach, sweet potatoes and carrots • Fruits: Select fruits including cranberries, grapes, plums and papaya. • Legumes: Very limited with kidney, navy and lima beans being allowable. • Grains: Very limited servings with brown rice, oatmeal, oat bran and millet allowable.	• Meats: Chicken, shellfish, pork • Vegetables: Corn • Grains: All grains should be avoided except as provided in the recommended foods and especially avoid wheat, buckwheat, barley, bulghur and rye. • Fruits: Tomatoes, peanuts, sesame seeds, tomatoes avocados, artichokes, coconut, pomegranates, persimmons • Nuts and Legumes: All nuts and legumes should be avoided except as provided in the recommended foods and then only sparingly.
AB	**Enigma –** Harmonious, Collaborative, Social, Friendly, Trusting, Intuitive, Spiritual. The most rare bloodtype, AB's need social and alone time. It is recommended that mediation & yoga be balanced with challenging aerobic exercise. It is better for AB's to eat frequent small meals. AB's can also handle more starch and fructose than other blood types.	**Flexible Pseudo Vegetarian Diet** • Vegetables: All vegetables with spinach, broccoli, cauliflower, celery, maitake mushroom, carrots, parsnips, kale, collard greens, asparagus and beets, sweet potatoes, and alfalfa sprouts being the most beneficial • Fruits: All fruits with cherries, blackberries, blueberries, figs, grapefruit and pineapple being the most beneficial. • Grains: High grains intake with whole grains preferred such as amaranth, brown rice, oats, soy, rye, quinoa, spelt. • Nuts & Legumes: All nuts (except those on the avoid list) with peanuts, walnuts, lentils, black beans, red beans pinto beans and soy beans the most highly recommended. • Meats: Limited meats with fish (e.g., cod, red snapper, mahi mahi, sturgeon, sardine, trout, salmon, being the recommended choices) and lamb, rabbit and turkey being allowed. • Dairy: AB's tolerate dairy products well and can be a source of sufficient protein including yogurt, kefir, eggs, mozzarella and goat cheese.	• Meats: Pork, buffalo, venison, horse, chicken, duck, goose, smoked meats, and shellfish (e.g., crab, shrimp, lobster, mussels, oysters, clams, scallops, etc.) • Nuts, Legumes & Seeds: Hazelnuts, poppy seeds, sunflower seeds, pumpkin seeds, sesame seeds, kidney, lima, azuki, fava, black-eyed peas, and garbanzo. • Dairy: American cheese, blue cheese, brie, buttermilk, parmesan, provolone, sherbet and whole milk. • Grains: Buckwheat, corn, kamut, kasha, soba noodles, artichoke pasta

g.   *Optimizing Mitochondrial Function*

There has been a growing awareness of the importance that mitochondrial function plays in our health. Numerous studies support that mitochondrial dysfunction is common and associated with most chronic disease, including early aging, Alzheimer's disease, dementia, autism, cardiovascular disease, chronic fatigue syndrome, diabetes and Parkinson's disease.[193]

Mitochondria, often referred to as the powerhouses of the cell, are organelles that function like a digestive system for eukaryotic cells (e.g., animal, plant, fungi, protista which whose cells have their DNA enclosed in a nucleus). Every cell in your body contains organelles. Like organs in the body, organelles are cellular structures, each with a specific function for the benefit of the cell. The nucleus, mitochondria and chloroplasts are all organelles.

Mitochondria are responsible for a process known as "cellular respiration"—the biochemical process of taking in nutrients from the cell, breaking them down and converting the nutrients into adenosine triphosphate ("ATP"), which is used as a source of chemical energy. Mitochondria produce most of a cell's supply of ATP. Because ATP cannot be stored, a large amount of ATP must be produced by the mitochondria every second of every day. The mitochondrial cellular respiration process is so important that mitochondria can take up as much as 25% a cell's volume.

Healthy mitochondrial function is essential to our health and our ability to make and access energy. According to Joseph Pizzorno, ND, in his article entitled *Mitochondria-Fundamental to Life and Health*, published in the National Institute of Health, U.S. National Library of Medicine, "*Every day, a healthy person produces a remarkable 1200 watts! Because the brain uses 70% of ATP, this helps explain the strong correlation between mitochondrial dysfunction and neurodegeneration.*" Pizzorno states that "*The mitochondria are especially susceptible to nutrient deficiencies, environmental toxins, and oxidative damage.*

The following nutrients are recommended for ATP production and mitochondrial function:

- Vitamins: B1, B2, B3, C and E

- Antioxidants: CoQ10, NAC and Resveratrol

- Amino Acids: Carnitine, Cysteine, Glutamic Acid, Glycine and Lipoate

We are what we eat and how we eat! We each have unique individual requirements dictated by such factors as genetics, metabolism, gender, age and activity levels. There is no silver bullet diet and arriving at the diet and nutrition that is right for you often takes experimentation, discipline, awareness and tracking.

Because optimal wellness is so important in our lives, please consult with health and wellness practitioners, preferably those that are multi-disciplinary, integrative and/or Ecosystemic practitioners to provide you with a personalized program to help you achieve maximum benefits for your time, energy and money. They can also help you to avoid anything that may be injurious to your health due to specific issues related to such factors as your genetics, health history, current health conditions and environmental exposures.

The diet and nutrition protocols contained in this chapter, when adopted and practiced consistently, provide not only significant individual health benefits, but also great benefit to the environment, the economy and society. It's my hope that the foregoing materials have provided the necessary tools, information and motivation to create a conscious and highly fulfilling diet and nutrition program that enhances your life, optimizes your health, and contributes to the thriving of our planet.

CHAPTER 15

Internal Cleansing and Detoxification

Cleansing and detoxifying our body, improves wellness, clarifies our mind, increases our energy and enhances our emotional state.

Internal cleansing and detoxification consist of a combination of fasting, flushing, bathing, ingesting cleansing and highly nutritious foods, vitamins and herbs, as well as other methods to promote the elimination of toxins. Detoxification involves eliminating or neutralizing toxic substances via your skin, lungs, kidneys, liver, and intestines. Because we live in an environment where our air, food, water and surfaces contain chemicals, heavy metals, and other contaminants that contribute to toxic overload, no matter how conscious we are, it is foundational to achieving optimal wellness that we regularly help our body cleanse itself of toxins, rest and heal.[194]

Because cleansing and detoxification release toxins in our tissues and organs and can have significant impact on our health, it is critical that cleansing and detoxification be done carefully and under the supervision of a doctor and/or experienced health practitioner. Also, pregnant women and persons with chronic illness, including, but not limited to, diabetes, heart and organ conditions, and intestinal diseases, should consult their physician before embarking on a cleanse or detoxification program. The following is provided for informational purposes only and this author does not recommend or suggest you do any of the following or make any representations or guarantees of results you will receive.

When determining whether to try a new protocol claimed to be beneficial to my health, I personally use the "3 Rs"—Research, Resonance and Results.

- *Research*—I start with doing research about the protocol and analyze its benefits, risks, time consumption and costs. I speak with healthcare practitioners and subject matter experts. I do review studies, research papers, testimonials and ratings. If my research indicates that a protocol has very little risk and the benefits outweigh the time and costs, I try it. If I get good results, I adopt the protocol. If my research indicates a significant amount of benefit and also risks, time consumption and costs, I will seek further guidance from an experienced professional and if the benefits outweigh the risks, time and costs, I will try the protocol and, if I get results, adopt the protocol. It is often difficult to find scientific or medical research supporting alternative health protocols (e.g. cleansing, diet and nutrition) not offered by standard conventional medicine and pharma. This is largely because healthcare makes money on sick people not healthy people. Therefore, research supporting alternative protocols that increase health and prevent disease (without the costly invasive procedures, side effects and complications of many conventional medical protocols such as surgery, radiation and pharmaceuticals) doesn't get funding from pharma and conventional healthcare. If credible research doesn't exist for alternative protocols, I turn to Resonance.

- *Resonance*—Often my decision to embrace a protocol is based resonance, intuition and other sources aside from research. These may include factors such as the integrity of the provider selling the product or protocol, the historical use and reported results of the product or protocol, testimonials of people and peers using the product or protocol, the rationale upon which a protocol is based, as well as my own observation and experience of what works for me.

- *Results*—When I get consistent positive results from a protocol or a product, I adopt it. I don't have great concern over whether the results from a protocol or product may be "placebo effect" or unproven by evidence-based medicine—what matters most to me is that the product or protocol is generally safe and I'm getting consistent results that outweigh the time, money and risks of a protocol or product.

While controversial with the medical and scientific communities, cleansing, fasting and detoxification protocols are some of the world's most ancient natural healing methods for removing toxins from the body and maintaining optimal health. Numerous religions also have fasting, cleansing and conscious eating protocols for enhancing health (e.g., Jews, Christians, Muslims, Hindus and Buddhists). Cleanses have been attributed to benefits that include immune system efficiency, weight loss, increased energy, increased metabolism, temperature regulation, improved endurance, quicker recovery times and enhanced mental clarity.[195] My personal experience with cleansing and detoxification, and the protocols discussed herein, have demonstrated the significant benefits mentioned in this chapter, even though some of the protocols below have not been approved by conventional medical, large pharmaceutical companies, the scientific community and/or regulatory agencies such as the FDA.

While fasting and cleansing can provide significant health benefits, moderation is key. Overdoing fasting and cleansing can rob the body of important nutrients and cause the body to shut down health promoting natural functions. It's recommended that you consult an integrative medical doctor, naturopath and/or experienced health professional to help you engage in fasting and cleansing.

Fasting[196] is simply not eating food. Within 24 hours of curtailing food intake, enzymes stop entering the stomach and travel instead into the intestines and the bloodstream, where they circulate and process waste matter, including dead and damaged cells, microbes, metabolic wastes, and pollutants. Fasting induces metabolic changes that are inherently cleansing and repairing. The organs empty and rest, conserving energy, promoting the elimination of waste and accumulated toxins, and supporting efficient cellular regeneration. As well, the alimentary canal is cleansed. Fasting has a number of health benefits, including improved cardiovascular health, reduced cancer risk, gene repair, increased longevity, and dementia prevention.

Intermittent Fasting is gaining popularity as a way to incorporate regular and moderate fasting into one's lifestyle and to promote optimal wellness. Intermittent fasting provides many of the advantages of more rigorous fasting protocols, but without the disruptive aspects of longer and more intense cleanses and fasting. Intermittent fasting involves cutting calories in whole or in part, either a couple of days a week, every other day, or even daily. It's one of the most effective interventions for normalizing your weight.

Intermittent fasting helps the body to (1) more efficiently burn fat, (2) optimize insulin sensitivity, (3) improve mitochondrial health and function, (4) allow the endocrine system to rest and repair, (5) increase energy levels, (6) improve digestion, and (7) lower the risk of cancer and dementia.

The most popular intermittent fasting protocols include the following:

- **16:8 or Leangains:** This protocol involves skipping breakfast and restricting your food intake to a period of 8 hours each day. For example, the only time food is consumed is between 11:00am–7:00 pm and no food is consumed from 7:00pm until 11am the following day.

- **24-Hour Fast or Eat-Stop-Eat:** This protocol involves fasting for 24 hours, 1-3 times per week for a period of 24 hours. For example, not eating dinner on Monday and fasting until dinner on Tuesday and not eating dinner on Thursday and fasting until dinner of Friday.

- **5:2 diet:** This protocol allows for consumption of only 500–600 calories on two non-consecutive days of the week, but eat normally the other 5 days. For example, limit food consumption to 500 calories on Monday and Thursday.

Cleansing is typically accomplished by flushing toxins from the body with juices, teas and other liquids as well as engaging in elimination diets and protocols involving herbs, vitamins, minerals and chelators. Additionally, sweating from exercise and saunas and receiving colon hydrotherapy are effective techniques for cleansing.

When cleansing, it's important to provide fluid for the body that allow it to flush out toxins. Flushing can be done with water, juices, teas and/or other liquids. Additionally, herbs, extracts and oils may be helpful for certain types of fasts and detox cleansing. Moreover, hydrotherapy in the form of hot/cold baths, colon hydrotherapy, alkaline baths and mineral/salt baths are effective methods for cleansing.

In this chapter, we will discuss the following specific types of cleanses.

1. *Juice Cleanse*

2. *Kidney Cleanse*

3. *Parasite Cleanse*

4. *Liver and Gall Bladder Cleanse*

5. *Colon Hydrotherapy*

6. *Hydrotherapy*

7. *Heavy Metal Detox*

Below is a brief description of several different cleanses and detoxification protocols. The following is only meant to introduce the reader to several options. Before embarking on a cleanse, it's highly recommended that you visit a health practitioner knowledgeable about cleansing and read various books and other materials regarding the matter. Also, most health food stores have pre-packaged kits for many of the cleanses recommended below.

1. JUICE CLEANSE[197]

A juice cleanse is a liquid, nourishing diet consisting of solely juices, water and tea. The amount of juice taken should be sufficient so you feel satisfied and never hungry.

A juice cleanse balances nutritional health while allowing the digestive organs time to rest and heal. One of the most noticeable effects of a juice cleanse is feeling lighter and more energetic.

Since there is no solid food ingested during a juice cleanse, the bowel doesn't have any fiber to work against; therefore, the bowels stop moving. When the bowels don't move and a person keeps juicing, there are many toxins that are released into the bloodstream. Unless eliminated through urination or defecation, toxins can be reabsorbed back into the tissues. This can be avoided by taking an intestinal cleansing formula containing fiber such as psyllium seed husk and/or bentonite. You can also add a strong dose of cayenne and/or garlic clove with one or more of your vegetable juices. Anyone who has active colitis or a history of colitis should not take any laxative formulas, cayenne or garlic.

The Master Cleanse is one of the most popular liquid cleanses. It was created by Stanley Burroughs in the 1950s to eliminate toxins and congestion built up in the body. The Master Cleanse involves eating no solid food, but instead drinking a mixture of organic fresh squeezed lemon juice, organic maple syrup, spring water and cayenne pepper for 3 to 10 days. The Master Cleanse has been credited with significant weight loss, increased energy, detoxification of the liver and the alleviation of some chronic diseases.

Due to the high sugar and low protein characteristics of the Master Cleanse, I recommend it be modified by adding glutathione and substituting either blackstrap molasses or coconut nectar for the maple syrup in Stanley Burroughs' original recipe. Reducing high glycemic sugars and adding glutathione helps your liver detoxify xenobiotics, carcinogens, and heavy metals like mercury as well as control free radicals. Also, consider adding blue-green algae. Blue-green algae does introduce a nutrient to the mixture, however, it is a complete source of micro-nutrients and protein to aid the liver and body in the detoxifications process and can help support the body.[198]

The Juice Cleanse protocol that I prefer can be effective after 3 days, but is recommended for 7 days. The recipe for the daily mixture for the Juice Cleanse, based upon six 10 oz glasses per day, is as follows:

- 60 ounces water
- 12 tablespoons of fresh wheat grass juice (or 2 tablespoons of powdered wheat grass can be substituted)
- 12 tablespoons freshly squeezed organic lemon juice
- 12 tablespoons of either organic blackstrap molasses, coconut nectar or maple syrup
- 10 drops of cayenne tincture (or ½ teaspoon of cayenne pepper) or to taste
- Optional: 12 tablespoons of liquid blue-green algae (or 2 tablespoons of powdered blue-green algae can be substituted). This is recommended for longer cleanses.

As no solid food is eaten during the course of this cleanse, it is necessary to help the digestive system eliminate material, toxins and avoid constipation. This is achieved in two ways:

- Prior to going to sleep at night, it is recommended that you drink a cup of no caffeine herbal detox/mild laxative tea formula consisting of sarsaparilla, cinnamon bark, licorice root, burdock root and dandelion root.

- Upon waking up, drink an 8 oz. glass of lukewarm water with a tablespoon of pink Himalayan salt.

On this cleanse, it's recommended you drink <u>at least</u> one gallon of fluid every day. This can include the daily recipe above, herbal teas and water. The colon needs around two quarts a day to function properly. A gallon of fluids per day will give the kidneys ample opportunity to eliminate the toxins coming loose and going into the bloodstream, making the cleanse comfortable. The kidneys filter toxins out of the bloodstream and naturally release them into the urine.

Also, several synergistic ingredients cab maximize the benefits of The Juice Cleanse, as follows:

- *Cayenne Tincture*- cayenne has been used to increase energy, improve circulation, dissolve mucus, stop bleeding in the intestines and uterus and dissolve blood clots, Cayenne increases blood flow to the brain and has been used to treat Alzheimer's and other forms of dementia. The body gradually adapts to handle larger doses over time. Start with five to ten drops, and work up to one full dropper (30-35 drops) 3 times per day. Capsaicin is the active healing ingredient in cayenne. The hotter the cayenne, the more capsaicin and the more powerful it's healing properties. Take cayenne with juice not on an empty stomach as it can cause serious intestinal cramping.[199]

- *Wheatgrass Juice*—Wheatgrass is a good source of Vitamins A, B-complex, C, E and K, potassium, iron, zinc, copper, manganese and selenium. Fresh squeezed is preferred, but if unavailable, powder or capsules can be used.

- *Herbal Teas*—There are numerous organic herbal teas with Detox and Kidney/Bladder formulas available. These teas are a wonderful complement to a juice cleanse. Although it is recommended that non-caffeinated herbal teas be used during the cleanse, if coffee is consumed on a regular basis, switching over to caffeinated green tea during the initial stages of the juice cleanse can help avoid caffeine withdrawal symptoms. Try to find a formula containing sarsaparilla, cinnamon bark, licorice root, burdock root and dandelion root.

- *Algae (Optional)*—Blue-Green Algae, Spirulina and Chlorella are the most popular edible kinds of algae. People have been consuming certain types of algae as food for thousands of years. Algae have been found to contain all of the essential amino acids. They are a complete protein source second to none. The protein content of algae ranges from 60-70% with a very high protein utilization factor. This means that the body is easily able to absorb and use the protein contained in algae. Algae comes in a powder form, flakes, liquid or in tablets or capsules. Follow directions on the supplement bottle, as various algae processors have different strengths and concentrations. It's recommended that algae be taken in liquid form for this cleanse, as it is generally the most concentrated and easy to assimilate. For people who don't like the taste of algae, capsules are the next best way to take algae. The least desirable method is tablets since they are highly compressed, making them more difficult to digest and absorb.

2. KIDNEY CLEANSE[200]

Efficient kidney function is critical for our well-being. The kidneys are sophisticated waste processing machines. They process about 200 quarts of blood per day, sifting out about two quarts of waste products and extra water. If your kidneys did not remove these wastes, the waste would build up in the blood, damaging and eventually destroying your body.

Therefore, it's important to help these vital organs by engaging in a cleanse at least once per year and taking supplements that support their healthy functioning. There are numerous high-quality kidney/bladder cleanses on the market. The following ingredients are generally considered fundamental to an effective kidney/bladder cleanse program. These can be taken as supplements or made into a tea.

- *Cranberry*—Cranberry products contain proanthocyanidins (PACs) that prevent E. coli from adhering to the urinary tract epithelial cells by affecting the surface properties of the bacteria. E. coli is the cause of about 85% of urinary tract infections and 90% of cases of acute pyelonephritis.

- *Juniper Berry*—The traditional use of juniper is as a diuretic to treat conditions of the bladder or kidneys by washing out the offending bacteria in urinary tract infections. Diuretic action is well established and attributed to terpinene-4-ol, which increases the filtration rate of the kidney.

- *Parsley Root*—Parsley root flushes out the urinary tract and helps prevent and treat kidney gravel.

- *Uva Ursi Leaf*—Contains powerful phytochemicals such as volatile oils, arbutin, quercetin, and mallic and gallic acids. Arbutin is highly antibacterial and destroys bacteria and fungus that infect the urinary system such as E. coli, Candida albicans, and Staphylococcus.

- *Marshmallow Root*—Used in treating irritated tissues in urinary tract infections such as cystitis, colitis, and diverticulitis.

- *Ginger Root*—Strengthens kidneys by soothing stomach discomfort and promoting digestion. Also, fights inflammation, cleanses the colon, reduces spasms and cramps, and stimulates circulation.

- *Goldenseal Root*—Goldenseal goes straight to the bloodstream and eliminates infection in the body. Also, it destroys many types of bacterial and viral infections and stimulates the kidney function urinary infections. Goldenseal is an excellent antibiotic that has often equaled or outperformed allopathic antibiotics, but without the side effects. It destroys harmful bacteria and germs and is very helpful against staph and strep. It is very potent for intestinal and antibacterial activity.

- *Gravel Root*—Gravel root is used primarily for kidney stones or gravel. In urinary infections, such as cystitis and urethritis, it may also be used with great benefit. This herb can also play a useful role in the systematic treatment of rheumatism and gout.

- *Hydrangea Root*—Hydrangea root has been most promising in the treatment of an inflamed or enlarged prostate gland. It is also used for urinary stones associated with urinary infections.

- *D-Mannose*—D-Mannose is a naturally occurring simple sugar that appears to be a safe, practical alternative for the treatment of urinary tract infections (UTI's). D-Mannose is absorbed eight times slower than glucose, and when ingested, is not converted to glycogen or stored in the liver, but rather goes directly to the bloodstream from the upper GI tract. Hence, D-Mannose is mostly filtered through the kidneys and routed to the bladder. The bladder lining is comprised of polysaccharide molecules. Finger-like projections on the cell surface of E. coli bacteria adhere to these molecules, initiating an infection. In the presence of D-Mannose, E. coli preferentially attach to D-Mannose molecules forming a complex, which is expelled with the next voiding.

- *Organic Oregano Oil*—Organic oregano oil is an antibacterial that is complimentary to d-mannose, which is effective against the e.coli bug but not other urinary tract infection bugs. Oregano oil has a natural antibiotic called carvacrol within the oil, which many people have used to fight complicated urine infections such as pseudomonas.

The following is a highly effective Kidney/Bladder Cleanse inspired by Dr. Hulda Clark.

Ingredients	
1/2 cup Dried Organic Hydrangea Root	Organic Goldenseal capsules-500mg
1/2 cup Organic Gravel Root	Organic Ginger capsules-500mg
1/2 cup Organic Marshmallow Root	Organic Uva Ursi capsules-500mg
4 bunches of Organic Parsley	Vitamin B6, 250 mg
4 bunches of Organic Cilantro	Magnesium oxide, 300 mg in powder form
8 oz. Organic Black Cherry Concentrate	Organic Oregano Oil Extract
8 oz. Organic Cranberry Concentrate	D Mannose Powder

Mixture 1

Measure 1/4 cup of each root (this is half your supply) and set them to soak in 10 cups of purified water (spring or glacial water preferred). After four hours or overnight, add 8 oz. of the organic unsweetened black cherry concentrate and 8 oz of the organic unsweetened cranberry concentrate, heat to boiling and simmer for 20 minutes. Drink 1/4 cup as soon as it is cool enough. Pour the rest through a stainless steel strainer into a glass Ball or Mason jar. Refrigerate.

Save the roots after the first boiling, storing them in the freezer. After 13 days, when your supply runs low, boil the same roots a second time, but only add 6 cups of water and simmer only 10 minutes. This will last another 8 days, for a total of 3 weeks.

After 21 days, repeat with fresh herbs.

Mixture 2

Rinse the bunches of parsley and cilantro in warm water. Boil the fresh parsley and cilantro in 1 quart of purified water (spring or glacial water is preferred), or as much as needed to cover it. Boil it for five minutes. Drink 1/4 cup when cool enough. Freeze 1 pint and refrigerate the rest. Reuse or compost the parsley and cilantro.

Dosage and Instructions

Each morning, pour together 3/4 cup of Mixture 1 and 1/2 cup of Mixture 2, into a glass. Drink this mixture in 5 divided doses of 1/4 cup each throughout the day at waking, mid-morning, lunch, mid-afternoon and dinner. Keep the mixture refrigerated. Don't drink it all at once or you will get a stomachache and feel pressure in your bladder. If your stomach is very sensitive, start on half the dosage.

You need to do the Kidney Cleanse for six weeks to get good results, and longer for more severe and/or chronic problems. Also take the following supplements on the schedule set out below each day of the cleanse:

	D Mannose	Ginger	Uva Ursi	Goldenseal	Vit B6	Magnesium	Oregano
Breakfast	1 tsp	1 cap	1 cap		1 cap		
Lunch		1 cap		1 cap			1 dropper
Dinner	1 tsp	1 cap	1 cap			1 cap	

Heat the kidney teas to boiling every fourth day if it is being stored in the refrigerator to kill bacterial build up. If you sterilize it in the morning you may take it to work without refrigerating it.

Note, during the Kidney/Bladder cleanse, it is recommended that you cease drinking caffeinated beverages including coffee, teas and sodas.

3. PARASITE CLEANSE[201]

There are a variety of ways we can become infected with parasites, including the food or water we consume, insect bites, sexual transmission, eating raw or undercooked meats, or simply through the nose or skin. The most common reason many of us have persistent parasites is because of an unhealthy diet (high in sugars, dairy and fats) and an unhealthy digestive system. When our bowels are clogged, waste elimination becomes compromised, causing a buildup of mucoid plaque that clogs the walls of our colon, thus providing an environment for parasites to proliferate.

Parasites can be persistent and abundant. Once parasites establish themselves in your body, they live off your food intake, especially favoring sugars, fats, and waste. When they finish consuming, they commonly release waste products in the form of harmful toxins (e.g., neurotoxins, heavy metals and viruses) which enter into the interstitial fluid that surrounds the tissue cells.

These toxins are often the cause of many health problems such as acne, IBS, colitis, ulcers, candida, low energy, itching, body odor and halitosis. They also typically lay eggs and reproduce very quickly.

There are numerous varieties of parasites, but the most common in humans are worms and protozoa including roundworms, liver fluke, pinworms, hookworms, whipworms, giardia, entamoeba histolytica, cryptosporidium and toxoplasma gondii.

Numerous varieties of parasites make complete elimination difficult. However, there are three major herbs that help kill more than 100 kinds of parasitic organisms. They are the **Black Walnut Hull, Wormwood,** and **Cloves**. When these 3 herbs are combined together, it creates a powerful anti-parasitic formula that is generally effective against most common parasites. Black walnut and wormwood help eliminate grown parasites. The cloves help remove the eggs.

To increase the effectiveness of a parasite cleanse, it's important to do a partial cleanse for at least 3 days before taking any anti-parasite cleansers or herbs. The following are recommendations for the pre-cleanse diet:

- A juice cleanse consisting of vegetables with low sugar content, such as celery, cucumbers, kale, parsley and spinach.

- Avoid all sugars. Don't eat high glycemic vegetables such as carrots, beets, parsnip, potatoes and corn. Stay away from most fruits except lemons, limes and grapefruits.

- Soups, broths and limited solid foods can be eaten, but only about 25% of the intake. Pumpkin seeds and garlic should be high on the list of solid foods.

- Increasing your stomach acidity generally increases the effectiveness of the parasite cleanse. Apple Cider Vinegar before every meal is wonderful for this and many other health benefits.

- Use various anti-parasitic spices in your foods, such as cinnamon and cloves.

Dr. Hulda Clark has created some of the most effective parasite cleanses. The following cleanse is based upon her work. Below is 1) a list of the supplements required, 2) the regimen and 3) directions for the *18-Day Parasite Cleanse*. Please note due to the persistent and ubiquitous nature of parasites, it's important to maintain a practice of parasitic cleansing. Therefore, after the 18th day, the directions provide further instructions for the maintenance protocol.

Supplements Required
Black Walnut Hull Tincture Extra Strength
Wormwood capsules (200-300mg of wormwood per capsule)
Cloves capsules (500mg per capsule)

*After day 18, it is recommended that once a week you take the "Day 18" dosage as a maintenance protocol. See the directions below.

18-Day Parasite Cleanse Dosage Schedule		
Day	Black Walnut Hull Tincture Extra Strength Dose	Wormwood Capsule Dose (200-300mg)	Clove Capsule Dose (500mg)
1	1 Drop	1 Capsule	1 Capsule at Breakfast, 1 Capsule at Lunch, 1 Capsule at Dinner
2	2 Drops	1 Capsule	2 Capsules at Breakfast, 2 Capsules at Lunch, 2 Capsules at Dinner
3	3 Drops	2 Capsules	3 Capsules at Breakfast, 3 Capsules at Lunch, 3 Capsules at Dinner
4	4 Drops	2 Capsules	3 Capsules at Breakfast, 3 Capsules at Lunch, 3 Capsules at Dinner
5	5 Drops	3 Capsules	3 Capsules at Breakfast, 3 Capsules at Lunch, 3 Capsules at Dinner
6	6 Drops	3 Capsules	3 Capsules at Breakfast, 3 Capsules at Lunch, 3 Capsules at Dinner
7	7 Drops	4 Capsules	3 Capsules at Breakfast, 3 Capsules at Lunch, 3 Capsules at Dinner
8	None	4 Capsules	3 Capsules at Breakfast, 3 Capsules at Lunch, 3 Capsules at Dinner
9	None	5 Capsules	3 Capsules at Breakfast, 3 Capsules at Lunch, 3 Capsules at Dinner
10	None	5 Capsules	3 Capsules at Breakfast, 3 Capsules at Lunch, 3 Capsules at Dinner
11	None	6 Capsules	3 Capsules at Breakfast, 3 Capsules at Lunch, 3 Capsules at Dinner
12	None	6 Capsules	3 Capsules at Breakfast, 3 Capsules at Lunch, 3 Capsules at Dinner
13	5 Drops	7 Capsules	None
14	None	7 Capsules	None
15	None	7 Capsules	None
16	None	7 Capsules	None
17	None	7 Capsules	None
18	Once per Week: 5 Drops (for maintenance)	Once per Week: 7 Capsules (for maintenance)	Once per Week: 3 Capsules at breakfast, 3 Capsules at lunch, 3 Capsules at dinner (for maintenance)

Directions

1. _Black Walnut Hull Tincture Extra Strength_—Take the recommended amount shown in the Regimen above in 1/2 cup of water. Sip (don't gulp) the mixture on an empty stomach such as before a meal, but get it down within 15 minutes. You may also drop the mixture into an anti-parasitic tea, however, don't let the water of the tea get above 114 degrees as it may interfere with the anti-parasitic properties of the tincture.

For one year following week 18, take the dosage of Black Walnut Hull Tincture once per week. This is to prevent parasites from returning from sources like your family, friends, or pets. You may want to consider having family members and friends with whom you see on a daily basis, do the cleanse with you to avoid risk of reinfection from them. They may be harboring a few parasite stages in their intestinal tract without having symptoms.

Note, although the amount of the dose is small, those with sensitivity to alcohol in the tincture may feel slightly woozy for several minutes. If you have an issue with alcohol, you may want to substitute capsules for the tincture.

If you have a sensitive stomach or worried about toxicity or side effects, it's recommended that for the first 5 days you take smaller doses of the tincture starting with 1 dropper or capsule and building up to 2 tsp. or 2 capsules. By the sixth day, you will convince yourself there is no toxicity or side effect.

2. *Wormwood Capsules*—Take the dosage according to the chart above. Take all the capsules in a single dose (you may take a few at a time until they are all gone). Take 7 capsules once a week for the rest of your life. Try not to get interrupted before the 6th day, so you know the adult intestinal flukes are dead. After this, you may proceed more slowly if you wish. Many persons with sensitive stomachs prefer to stay longer on each dose instead of increasing according to this schedule. You may choose the pace after the 6th day. *Pregnant or breastfeeding women and infants should not take wormwood.*

3. *Cloves*—It's important the capsules be organic and freshly ground. Take according to the chart above.

The parasite cleanse has been known to alter energy levels and the ability to sleep. In addition to the foregoing herbal remedies and protocols, you may desire to take the amino acid *Ornithine* (500mg) before bedtime to promote improved sleep and the amino acid, *Arginine* (500mg) upon waking to provide additional energy during the day, especially if you choose the give up coffee while on the cleanse.

4. LIVER AND GALL BLADDER CLEANSE[202]

The liver plays a major role in metabolism, glycogen storage, decomposition of red blood cells, plasma protein synthesis, and detoxification. The bilary tubing of the liver delivers bile to one large tube known as the bile duct. The gallbladder is attached to the common bile duct and acts as a storage reservoir. Eating fat or protein triggers the gallbladder to squeeze itself empty after about twenty minutes, and the stored bile finishes its trip down the common bile duct to the intestine.

For many persons, the biliary tubing is choked with intrahepatic stones and the gall bladder with gallstones, thus creating inefficient digestion and microbial build up in the intestines, stomach and liver. When the stones grow and become more numerous, "back pressure" is put on the liver causing it to make less bile, thereby causing inefficient processing of fat and cholesterol. Gallstones, being porous, can pick up bacteria, cysts, viruses and parasites that are passing through the liver. It's therefore important to regularly cleanse (at least once per year) the liver and gall bladder.

Foods that are considered beneficial to the liver include the following:

- Turmeric—Its active ingredient curcumin helps reduce inflammation and contains enzymes that help detox the liver and repair liver cells.

- Green Tea—High in antioxidants and a compound named catechin attributed to improving liver function.

- Cruciferous Vegetables (e.g., Brussels sprouts, cabbage, kale, cauliflower, broccoli)—Sources of glutathione which assists the liver in flushing out toxins and carcinogens.

- Grapefruit and Lemons—Alkalizing fruits high in Vitamin C and antioxidants that help reduce inflammation in the liver.

- Garlic—High in Sulfur and Selenium, which helps activate liver enzymes that increase the efficiency of the liver to process toxins.

- Beets—High in iron and attributed to cleansing the blood and increasing oxygen, beets stimulate bile flow and enzymatic activity.

- Walnuts—a good source of glutathione and omega-3 fatty acids supports liver function and removal of ammonia.

- Cold Pressed Organic Oils (i.e., olive, flax and hemp)—helps the liver mobilize and more effectively metabolize fat and toxins within the fat.

- Dandelions contain bioactive compounds that may help lower cholesterol and levels of fat in the liver and increase the liver's ability to detox efficiently.

The following is a preparation inspired by Dr. Hulda Clark, an authority on the subject of liver, gall and microbial cleansing.

<u>Prerequisites:</u>

It is recommended before doing the Liver and Gall Bladder Cleanse that the Kidney Cleanse and Parasite Cleanse (both above) be completed. You want your kidneys, bladder and urinary tract in top working condition so they can efficiently remove any undesirable substances incidentally absorbed from the intestine as the bile is being excreted. Also, three weeks prior to the Liver and Gallbladder Cleanse, it's important to rid the liver of parasites.

If you have any mercury or amalgam fillings or open cavities, do any dental work before doing the Liver and Gall Bladder Cleanse, if possible. Your mouth should be free of toxic heavy metals and extraordinary bacterial loads (e.g., cavities, gum conditions, sores). A toxic mouth can put a heavy load on the liver, burdening it immediately after cleansing.

For greater effectiveness, it's recommended that three days prior to the cleanse, you consume the following each day:

- 2 apples

- 2—8 oz. cups of apple juice

- 1—8 oz. of apple cider vinegar be consumed each day.

Ingredients (per person)
1/2 Cup Organic Extra Virgin Olive Oil
32 Fl. Oz. of Fresh Squeezed Organic Grapefruit Juice (four 8 oz. cups)
4 tablespoons Epsom salts
Black Walnut Tincture
Ornithine capsules

Also, make sure you have two sealable one-quart containers, such as a Ball or Mason jar or Tupperware.

Directions:

1. Choose a day when you will have the following day off to start this cleanse, as you may need to rest, take it easy and use the bathroom frequently the next day. Following the timing and instructions below is critical to the success of this cleanse.

2. Take no medicines, vitamins or pills that you can do without, unless otherwise prescribed by your physician. If you are on a parasite, kidney or other cleanse program, stop the program the day before.

3. Eat a no-fat breakfast and lunch (no butter, milk, oils, fried foods, no fatty meats). Recommended is fruit, fruit juice, vegetables or vegetable juice. This allows the bile to build up and develop pressure in the liver. Higher pressure pushes out more stones.

4. 2:00 PM. Don't eat or drink after 2:00 PM. If you break this rule you could feel quite ill later. Also, do the following 3 steps. The amounts shown below are per person.

    (1) In one container mix four tablespoons of Epson salts in 3 cups of freshly squeezed organic grapefruit juice. This makes four servings, 3/4 of a cup each. Shake the container and set it in the refrigerator.

    (2) In another container measure the amount of grapefruit juice remaining. You should have 3/4 of a cup left in the first jar of grapefruit juice. You may also squeeze lemon into the grapefruit juice if you don't have enough grapefruit juice.

5. 6:00 PM. Drink the 1st serving 3/4 of a cup of the Grapefruit/Epsom salt mixture.

6. 8:00 PM. Drink the 2nd serving of the 3/4 of a cup of the Grapefruit/Epsom salt mixture.

7. 9:45 PM. Remove the jar of grapefruit juice without Epson salts from the refrigerator and run it under hot water to bring it to about 75 degrees. Add one eyedropper of the Black Walnut Tincture and 1/2 cup Organic Extra Virgin Olive Oil to the grapefruit juice. Close the jar tightly with the lid and shake hard until watery. Now visit the bathroom one or more time, even if it makes you late for your ten o'clock drink. Don't be more than 15 minutes late. You will get fewer stones.

8. 10:00 PM. Drink the Grapefruit/Olive Oil mixture. Take four Ornithine capsules with the first sips to make sure you will sleep through the night. Take eight if you already suffer from insomnia. Drinking through a large plastic straw helps it go down easier. Drink it standing up. It may be sipped but get down the entire mixture within 5 minutes. To aid in sleep take 1000 mg of Ornithine.

9. Lie down immediately; you may fail to remove the stones if you don't. The sooner you lie down the more stones you will get out. Be ready for bed ahead of time. Don't clean up the kitchen. As soon as you finish your 10:00 PM, lie down in bed flat on your back with your head up high on the pillow. Try to think about what is happening in the liver. Try to keep perfectly still for at least 20 minutes. You may feel a train of stones traveling along the bile ducts like marbles. There is no pain because the bile duct valves are open from the Epson salts. Go to sleep, as it is important to let the body totally relax to rid itself of the stones.

10. Upon awakening in the morning after 6:00 AM, take your 3rd dose of the Grapefruit/Epsom salt mixture. If you have indigestion or nausea wait until it is gone before drinking the Grapefruit/Epsom salt mixture. You may go back to bed. Don't take this portion before 6:00 am.

11. Two hours later, take the 4th (the last) dose of Grapefruit/Epsom salt mixture. You may go back to bed again.

12. If done properly, you will have some diarrhea and several bowel movements, in which you will notice green bile and gallstones in and around the feces.

13. After two hours from the 4th dose, you may eat. Start with fruit juice. Half an hour later eat fruit. One hour later you may eat regular food but keep it light. By supper you should feel recovered.

5. COLON HYDROTHERAPY[203]

To maintain good health, your body must effectively eliminate food and bodily waste. Your colon, together with your lungs, skin and kidneys, are designed to accomplish this essential task of eliminating toxins in the intestines, blood and lymph systems.

The colon (large intestine, rectum, and anus) is the end portion of the human gastrointestinal (GI) tract, which extends from the mouth to the anus. The colon is a muscular tube that starts on the lower right side of the abdomen, where the small intestine empties the contents of digestion (chyme) into the first portion of the colon (cecum).

The ascending colon goes up from the cecum to the level of the liver; it then bends sharply to the left and crosses the abdomen as the transverse colon. At the level of the spleen, the descending colon goes down the left side of the abdomen to the pelvis, where it becomes the sigmoid region. The sigmoid colon empties into the rectum, from which waste material is ultimately eliminated from your body.

The main functions of the colon are absorption of water and minerals, and the formation and elimination of feces. The colon contains nearly 60 varieties of microflora or bacteria to aid digestion, promote vital nutrient production, maintain pH balance, and prevent the proliferation of harmful bacteria. These symbiotic bacteria provide important functions such as the synthesis of folic acid and valuable nutrients from foods, including vitamin K and portions of the B complex. Bacillus coli and acidophilus comprise the majority of healthy bacteria in the colon along with other disease-producing bacteria in lesser numbers.

The process of digestion, from ingestion of food to defecation, normally takes between 12 to 24 hours. Improperly functioning GI tract can result in irregular or infrequent bowel movements, which can allow toxic residues from the by-products of undigested foods to remain in the colon. A person with a healthy colon will have two to three bowel movements per day. Elimination should be complete and easy. The stool should be light brown in color, long and large diameter. There should be no offensive odor. However, many people in our modern society don't have regular bowel movements or effective elimination. As well, many people eat food that is toxic, processed and devoid of essential enzymes and nutrients necessary for proper and efficient digestion. Thus, colon hydrotherapy can promote greater health by assisting in the elimination of waste and toxins.

Colon hydrotherapy, also known as colonic irrigation, is an alternative medicine form of body cleansing. Similar to an enema, it involves the introduction of discrete amounts of purified water, sometimes infused with minerals or other materials, such as coffee, into the colon using medically approved class II colon hydrotherapy devices with sanitary, disposable speculums or gravity-fed enema-like systems inserted into the rectum. The fluid is released after a short period, and the process will be repeated multiple times during the course of a treatment with the goal of releasing old fecal matter and clearing the colon of toxins.

Colonics can contribute to improved health as well as helping to remove toxins released from fasting or cleansing, thereby preventing re-absorption of released toxins back into the tissues.

6. HYDROTHERAPY[204]

Hydrotherapy, or using water as a healing modality, has been used for centuries for the treatment of disease and injury in many cultures, including the Asian, Indian, European and Native American cultures. Hydrotherapy includes many modalities, such as baths, steam rooms, Jacuzzis, saunas, douches, wraps, thermal soaking, and packs.

While hydrotherapy is generally regarded as safe for most people, it is contraindicated for pregnant women and those suffering from heart disease, incontinence, high blood pressure, kidney disease and other ailments. It is

recommended that you consult with your health care provider prior to engaging in hydrotherapy.

The recuperative and healing properties of hydrotherapy are based on its mechanical and/or thermal effects. It exploits the body's reaction to hot and cold stimuli, as well as the protracted application of heat, the pressure exerted by the water, the changes in gravitational experience, and the altered awareness and sensation water gives. The nerves carry impulses from the skin deeper into the body, where they are instrumental in stimulating the immune system, influencing the production of hormones, invigorating the circulation and digestion, encouraging blood flow, and lessening pain sensitivity.

Generally, heat quiets and soothes the body, slowing down the activity of internal organs, while cold, stimulates and invigorates, thus increasing internal activity. If you are experiencing tense muscles and anxiety from your stress, a hot shower or bath will help release the tension. Whereas, if you are feeling tired and stressed out, a cold plunge or shower could help to stimulate and reinvigorate your body and mind. By alternating between hot and cold hydrotherapy we can get the benefits of being both stimulated and relaxed.

When you submerge yourself in a bath, a pool, or a whirlpool, you experience a kind of weightlessness. Your body is relieved from the constant pull of gravity. This allows the body to move in ways that are less constrictive thereby allowing one to more effectively stretch muscles, nerve chords and realign joints. Water also has a hydrostatic effect and a massage-like feeling as the water gently kneads your body. Water, in motion, stimulates touch receptors on the skin, boosting blood circulation and releasing tight muscles.

Hydrotherapy and hydrothermal therapy can be used to tone the body, to stimulate digestion, enhance circulation, improve the immune system, and relieve pain. Water has been used to release stress and detoxify our body. It can calm the lungs, heart, stomach, and endocrine system while stimulating nerve reflexes on the spinal cord.

The Alternating Hot and Cold Bath ("AHCB") is one of the most effective hydrotherapy treatments. The AHCB is powerful in its ability to detoxify and strengthen immune system function, release muscle spasms and are useful in vaginal infections, chronic urinary tract infections, pelvic congestion, pelvic inflammatory disease, hemorrhoids, fissures, prostatitis, constipation, postpartum, improving neuralgias and insomnia.

AHCB Directions:

Fill one tub with hot water (about 106°F to 110°F) as high as possible without overflowing when you sit in the bath. Fill the other tub with cold water (50°F to 60°F). You may need to use ice in the tub if you are in a region whose room temperature tap water is greater than 60°F. You can also put Epsom salts in the hot bath for additional relaxation and detoxification.

When you first start doing hydrotherapy, it's recommended you do three sets of hot and cold. As you become accustomed to hot-cold hydrotherapy, you can do more sets and increase the time you spend in the hot and cold. Do at least three sets of hot and cold, always starting with the hot, and finishing with the cold as follows:

- 3 minutes in the hot and 30 seconds in the cold
- 5 minutes in the hot and one minute in the cold
- 7 minutes in the hot and two minutes in the cold

As you become acclimatized and comfortable with the AHCB, you can continually increase the hot-cold times until you feel relaxed, open, relieved, balanced and detoxified. However, it is not advisable to spend more than 20 minutes in the hot or 5 minutes in the cold.

7. HEAVY METAL DETOX[205]

As a result of the toxic environment we live in, the human body often contains microscopic pieces of heavy metal, such as the following:

- Mercury from dental amalgam fillings, coal burning plants, fluorescent light bulbs and mercury-contaminated seafood
- Lead from leaded fossil fuels and paints
- Cadmium from cigarette smoke, batteries and plastic pigments

- Aluminum from cooking with aluminum pots and pans and aluminum foil wrapping

While generally overlooked by western medicine, these traces of heavy metals in our bodies are considered to cause many diseases, including cancer, heart disease, diabetes, Parkinson's and Alzheimer's. As well, they've been attributed to birth defects, autism, PDD, Aspergers, ADD and *ADHD*.[206]

According to Margaret Sears, author of "Chelation: Harnessing and Enhancing Heavy Metal Detoxification", published in the Scientific World Journal, *"Toxic metals such as arsenic, cadmium, lead, and mercury are ubiquitous, have no beneficial role in human homeostasis, and contribute to noncommunicable chronic diseases."*[207]

Metal can be located anywhere in our bodies including our liver, kidneys, heart and muscles. When a free radical collides with one of these tiny pieces of toxic metal, instead of this collision creating a single new free radical, there could be a chain-reaction of millions of new free radicals produced from this one impact. When millions of new free radicals are released, it increases the likelihood that other collisions with heavy metals will occur. Free radicals are a fact of life, causing cellular and DNA damage, reducing the body's ability to fight disease and aging. Heavy metal detoxification can reduce free radicals resulting from heavy metal toxicity and thereby reduce the likelihood free radical linked diseases.

The method most commonly used by health practitioners is called oral chelation. There are currently no over-the-counter chelation products approved by the U.S. Food and Drug Administration ("FDA"). FDA approved chelation products require a prescription and supervision of a licensed health practitioner. Because of the risks and side effects of chelation, you should only engage in heavy metal detox protocols under the supervision of an experienced healthcare practitioner.

Guidelines for a successful heavy metal detoxification program using oral chelation are as follows:

General Information and Prerequisites:

Have all amalgam fillings removed by a dentist who specializes in a closed extraction procedure to ensure that no heavy metals are released into the mouth, throat or nasal passages during the removal procedure.

Seek the guidance of an experienced health care practitioner who will provide regular blood and urine testing to monitor your progress. During the initial stages of detox, symptoms of tiredness, dizziness, lack of focus and greater emotional sensitivity may result. It's important to distinguish between these "side effects" of detox and other complications that may arise as a result of releasing heavy metals back into the body for their elimination.

As described below, there are several different protocols that have been used effectively to remove heavy metals including NAC, EDTA and DMSA. Also, chlorella, cilantro, garlic, zeolite, blueberries, lemon water and barley grass are good for mild heavy metal detoxification and should be discussed with your health care practitioner. Depending upon the severity of the heavy metal toxicity and conditions of health, certain protocols may be more appropriate than others.

Don't attempt to fast during a heavy metal detoxification program and make sure you ingest a lot of protein. It's important to have a high protein diet during a heavy metal detox because the sulfur-bearing amino acids in the protein will greatly facilitate detoxification.

Depending upon the extent of heavy metal toxicity, full detox may take anywhere from six months to two years.

Heavy metals are eliminated primarily through the bowels, urine and sweat. During a heavy metal detox, it is recommended that you receive at least one colon hydrotherapy treatment per week and engage in cardiovascular exercise at least 30 minutes per day.

Also, prior to a heavy metal detox, it is advisable to do an intestinal cleanse and maintain two to three bowel movements per day. If you are not having this many bowel movements per day, take a high fiber laxative such as psyllium.

Guidelines and Protocols:[208]

The most effective and commonly used tools to assist us in heavy metal detoxification involve chelation, with NAC, EDTA and DMSA being the most popular. Because the chelation protocols and products require supervision of a licensed health practitioner, natural and dietary protocols have also been included below.

Make sure to take vitamins and eat nutritious foods to ease the effects of the detox. Mineralization is very important but adding mineral supplements may impede the effectiveness of the chelation therapy. Thus, your health practitioner should be consulted regarding proper mineralization. During heavy metal detoxification, make sure you take a multi-purpose vitamin and mineral, which contains all the essential minerals. Also, taking 1000mg of Vitamin C and 1000mg of Glutathione per day is recommended. It's important to have a generally healthy mineral base. Since many of the detox supplements also pull healthy minerals from the body, increasing mineralization is important. Depending upon the detox program, it's sometimes better to re-mineralize in between chelation, to assist the chelation process in removing heavy metals rather than loading up with minerals that make the detox process less efficient.

1.   _N-Acetyl-Cysteine ("NAC")_[209]

NAC is an important component of a good heavy metals detoxification program. NAC is currently the dietary supplement of choice for building up cysteine and conserving the body's store of Glutathione, Cysteine and other Sulfhydryl antioxidant resources. This is very crucial for the body's life functions. In addition to its ability to remove toxins and support the immune system, NAC is a chelator of heavy metals that binds to toxic heavy metals such as mercury, lead, cadmium, aluminum and arsenic to help removing such heavy metals from our body.

Although NAC is one of the most effective oral chelating agents, heavy metal detox is a slow process. Taken regularly over a period of time, generally between 12 to 24 months, NAC will typically remove many toxic heavy metals from the body.

NAC has been shown in many studies to reduce recovery times for cancer patients and decrease the likelihood of reoccurrence after remission.

Immunologically, NAC greatly enhances T-cell production. In fact, AIDS patients have categorically been shown to be deficient in NAC and glutathione. NAC suppresses the replication of HIV in vitro and enhances the ability of certain immune cells to kill pathogens. NAC has also been shown to be an excellent mucolytic agent. It keeps the membranes of the respiratory system moisten, thereby lessening the irritation of dry air, dust, and pollutants. NAC may be oxidized and become insoluble. This may form kidney stones. It is therefore recommended that individuals taking NAC take three times as much vitamin C and eat high antioxidant diets when taking NAC to prevent the NAC from being oxidized. Diabetics should consult their physician before using NAC, since it may have an insulin-blocking effect.

2.   *Ethylenediamine Tetra-Acetic Acid ("EDTA")*[210]

EDTA chelation is a therapy that gradually reduces atherosclerotic plaque and other mineral deposits throughout the cardiovascular system by literally dissolving them away. Because EDTA is highly effective at removing unwanted metals and other minerals from the blood, it has been the standard FDA-approved treatment for lead, mercury, aluminum, and cadmium poisoning for more than 50 years. EDTA chelation may be administered either orally or intravenously ("IV").

Oral EDTA chelation therapy is generally considered effective, safe, convenient and affordable and is being used more often than intravenous EDTA chelation. Clinical experience suggests that oral chelation provides many, but not all, of the benefits of IV therapy. IV EDTA chelation has a direct and powerful effect on the body almost instantaneously. An IV EDTA session usually lasts about three to four hours, during which about 1,500 mg to 3,000 mg of EDTA, plus vitamin C and other nutrients are administered.

Typical candidates for IV chelation are people who have been diagnosed with serious atherosclerosis, heavy metal poisoning, or symptoms of vascular occlusion or significant calcification of tissues. Oral EDTA is generally appropriate for people whose condition is less serious and does not demand prompt and intensive attention.

A series of needed sessions of IV EDTA will cost about $2,000 to $4,000. Oral EDTA is significantly less, about $15 to $40 per month, depending on one's intake. About 5%-10% of an oral dose of EDTA is absorbed into the bloodstream, compared with 100% of an IV dose. Yet, due to continuous daily intake, the amount adds up and can definitely offer benefits similar to IV chelation. Over the course of five or six weeks, regular use of oral EDTA can be as beneficial as a single IV EDTA session.

EDTA helps prevent heart attacks, stroke, varicose veins, and more by inhibiting blood clotting. EDTA makes stronger bones and reduces cholesterol by improving calcium and cholesterol metabolism. EDTA can help to lower cholesterol, the principal component of atherosclerotic plaque.

Oral EDTA chelation can be used as a preventive measure because it can retard the plaque buildup that progresses with aging, and it may even reverse plaque buildup in many cases. EDTA may very well be able to slow, or even reverse some of the aging of the cardiovascular system.

3. _Dimercaptosuccinic Acid ("DMSA")_[211]

DMSA is an FDA-approved oral protocol that is highly effective for removing heavy metals. Using DMSA requires a prescription and supervision by a licensed health care practitioner. Many practitioners are choosing DMSA over EDTA as an oral chelation protocol. DMSA binds with mercury, arsenic, lead, cadmium, antimony, bismuth, and gold, hastening excretion from the body.

Although the dose depends upon weight, gender and severity of the heavy metal toxification, the typical daily adult dosage is 20-30 mg of DMSA per kilogram or 9-13 mg of DMSA per pound of body weight.

The regimen gaining the most support is three days on eleven days off. This repeats in two-week (14 day) cycles. During the three days of active chelation, 1/3 of the daily dosage is taken three times throughout the day, preferably in the morning on an empty stomach, one hour after lunch and one hour after dinner. This protocol is continued for three to six months, until test results show acceptable levels.

4.   _Natural Heavy Metal Detox Support Protocols_

The following protocols for heaving metal detoxification support are largely natural, food-based and can be purchased over-the-counter:

a.   _Zeolite._ A volcanic mineral that has been referred to as the "Master Detoxifier" with it ability provide a wide range of health benefits, from detoxification to improving immune system. Zeolite has a negative ionic charge and utilizes a cationic exchange process which acts like a magnet to trap heavy metals inside its structure.

b.   _Chlorella._ The most potent blue-green algae for the removal of toxic metals from the connective tissue, Chlorella is an important part of the detoxification program, as approximately 90% of the mercury in our bodies is eliminated through the stool. Chlorella is an algae with high levels of chlorophyll and is comprised of a fibrous, indigestible outer shell (20%) and its inner nutrients (80%). The fibrous material has been proven to actually bind with heavy metals and pesticides to help eliminate such heavy metals and pesticides from our bodies. Additionally, a clean bloodstream with an abundance of red blood cells to carry oxygen, helps remove metabolic wastes from the tissues. Chlorophyll is effective against anemia and stimulates the production of red blood cells in the body. It also helps carry oxygen around the body and to the brain. Aside from aiding digestion and red blood cell production, chlorella has been found to stimulate the activity of macrophages and T-cells by increasing interferon levels, thus enhancing the immune system's ability to combat foreign invaders whether they are viruses, bacteria, chemicals or foreign proteins. Chlorella

c.   _Schisandra._ A medicinal berry with multiple healing properties, has been used in traditional Chinese medicine for thousands of years. Schisandra is probably best known for its impact on liver and adrenal function—it boosts the production of various detoxifying enzymes, while also balancing hormones naturally, thereby improving our ability to deal with stress and providing extra support for the adrenal glands. But schisandra is also a potent digestive aid with the ability to improve circulation, digestion and waste removal.

d. *Methylsulfonylmethane ("MSM").* An organic compound that contains biologically active sulfur, the fourth most plentiful mineral in the human body. Sulfur is required for many critical bodily functions and is important for the production of glutathione, a potent detoxifier, often referred to as the "Master Antioxidant."

MSM has been known to facilitate the detoxification process by making cells more permeable. This helps the cells release built up heavy metals, waste and toxins, while also increasing the ability of water and nutrients to enter the cells and continue the cleansing process.

MSM has also been found to improve immune function, lower inflammation and help restore healthy bodily tissue

e. *Detoxifying Foods.* Garlic, cilantro, wild blueberries, lemons, barley grass and reishi mushrooms and chlorella all have properties that help remove heaving metals from the body. In addition to regularly ingesting the foods just mentioned, it is suggested that the following be included in a daily routine:

- Eat garlic daily (the food rather than a supplement) to enhance sulfur stores. Two to three cloves a day is an excellent idea. Make sure you crush the garlic to release its active ingredients.

- Eat or juice cilantro. Cilantro will help mobilize mercury out of the tissue so the chlorella can bind to it and allow it to be excreted from the body through the stools.

- Ingest approximately 20 grams of chlorella per day in the form of powder, capsules or tablets.

Internal cleansing and detoxification are important for good health and should be practiced regularly as a preventative measure and to promote well-being and optimal wellness.

CHAPTER 16

Contentment, Calm, Rest, Sleep & Rejuvenation

Contentment, calm, rest, sleep and rejuvenation are key elements of a healthy and happy life. Contentment leads to calmness, calmness to rest, rest to sleep, and sleep to rejuvenation. Rejuvenation regenerates life and perpetuates optimal wellness.

There is a Chinese proverb that, *"Tension is who you think you should be. Relaxation is who you are."* Often, in our zeal to acquire money, power and material gain in order to be a "success," look good, and obtain the illusive sense of security we crave, we often forget the need to enjoy what we have—to be content, relaxed and happy right now.

Centenarian George Burns said, *"If you ask what is the single most important key to longevity, I would have to say it is avoiding worry, stress and tension. And if you didn't ask me, I'd still have to say it."* By consciously combining contentment, calmness, rest, sleep and rejuvenation into our lives, we can exponentially increase our health, wellness, productivity and quality of life.

We often feel that there is not enough time in a day for taking care of ourselves. Living in **optimal wellness** requires **balancing** our time for work, family, friends, errands and obligations with time for our health, which includes being content and calm, getting rest and sleep, so that our bodies, minds and beings can rejuvenate. Finding this balance takes presence and awareness (e.g., listening, feeling, intuiting) of our state of being (e.g., mental, physical, energetic, emotional) and fulfilling our present needs. By giving ourselves this balance, we increase our health and are able to be more engaged and present for our work, family, friends and other pursuits.

Yet, finding the balance leading to contentment is often challenging. This is because humans tend to be dichotomous creatures that have opposing desires, including the following examples:

Opposing Desires		
Privacy & Independence	vs	Companionship & Connection
Security, Stability & Predictability	vs	Growth, Risk & Adventure
Secrecy	vs	Transparency
Protection & Avoidance of Pain	vs	Love, Vulnerability & Intimacy
Self-Interest	vs	Collaboration
Purpose, Meaning & Commitment	vs	Freedom, Spontaneity, Flow
Logic & Pragmatism	vs	Creativity & Intuition
Quiet & Peace	vs	Activity & Excitement

Each of us has an individual balance/comfort range that shifts between our subjective opposing desires. Balancing our opposing desires can be challenging, yet when we find and maintain our balance, we enjoy a sense of peace, harmony and contentment that promotes our wellness.

Compartmentalization is an essential tool for giving ourselves the balance we need to live more fulfilling, healthy, productive and joyful lives. Compartmentalization, as used herein, is the ability and discipline to immerse ourselves fully in our present state of being without guilt or distraction. For example, when we're in an optimal state of being and flow for work, we're not distracted by our desire to engage with family, friends or other activities. We focus completely on our work. If, however, we find it hard to focus on work, it may be best to take a break from work and just allow ourselves to slip into a refreshing Alpha-Theta meditation (7 to 8 Hz) for 20-30 minutes, do some exercise, or spend quality time in full presence with our loved ones and not be distracted by work.

Sometimes, we have to push to meet deadlines, however, when we are tired or distracted, the result can be suboptimal work and delays. At times, it's beneficial to compartmentalize and give ourselves needed breaks for rejuvenation, rest or recreation. We then return to work in a refreshed and more optimal state for engaging in our work. It's also critical to set goals and commit a block of time to focus on getting work done and achieving a specific and well-defined goal. For example, focus on what you will achieve in the next hour rather than thinking about what you have to achieve in a day, a week or a month. Let no other thoughts or distractions detract you from achieving the goal(s) to which you have committed in the next hour. When you've accomplished the goal(s) take a break before setting the goal(s) or focus for the next hour. During this break consider meditating, connecting with friends or family, doing some exercise, or other activities you desire, or just do nothing. Be fully present with whatever activities or relaxation you choose rather than letting work and economic demands interfere with the quality of your leisure time.

In our society, there are many demands placed upon our time and attention. We often ignore our state of being and push through obligations without taking needed time for rejuvenation. For example, if we have a critical deadline and feel tired, we generally don't have the luxury of missing the deadline to compartmentalize and get some rest. In these instances, it's important to cycle into the state that allows us to best accomplish the work required and then take time for rest. However, if we consistently ignore or override our innate state of being, especially the need for rest and sleep, over time we're likely to suffer negative consequences, such as health issues, poor performance and strained relationships.

By understanding our states of being, we can employ intentional compartmentalization to achieve optimized states for our work, recreation, leisure, relaxation, rest, and sleep. Optimizing our states of being result in improved health, rejuvenation, energy level, focus, learning, visualization, emotional states, sex drive, athletic performance and achievement of goals.

In society, there's a tendency to elevate work and money over our well-being. In order to bring balance into our lives and enjoy optimal well-being and peak performance, it is important that we also make contentment, calmness, rest, sleep and rejuvenation and important part of our life.

CONTENTMENT

Contentment is the acknowledgment of satisfaction, fulfillment, abundance and/or comfort in one's life. Contentment is the acceptance and gratitude for one's current state of being. When we're content, we don't strive or feel compelled to achieve, acquire or pursue—we relax and appreciate the present moment. As Socrates said, *"Contentment is natural wealth, luxury is artificial poverty."* Indeed, contentment and optimal wellness are priceless.

The foundational keys to contentment are acceptance and gratitude. For example, Oprah was born into poverty in rural Mississippi to a single teenage mother. She had many hardships growing up including being raped at age 9. Oprah was able to overcome these hardships and become one of the most influential and wealthy media figures in history. Aside from years of hard work and personal development, Oprah credits her success to a mindset of gratitude and acceptance, which is contained in this quote: *"Be thankful for what you have; you'll end up having more. If you concentrate on what you don't have, you will never, ever have enough."* Oprah has clearly made contentment (acceptance and gratitude for one's current state of being) a platform for thriving in her life.

Contentment has a place within the integral quest for self-actualization or the satisfaction of reaching one's goals. Without contentment felt in the present moment, the quest to achieve goals is often attended by haphazard striving, suffering and a sense of incompleteness.

As Eckhart Tolle has said on numerous occasions, *"Life is a journey of present moments. If we are always striving for what we want in the future, we are not present to enjoy life's journey."* Contentment is an "inside job." It's an internal state of being fulfilled and grateful with who you are and what you have in the present moment. However, we often look outside ourselves for approval as a condition to our contentment. For example, we may seek security and contentment conditional upon money, possessions and/or the approval of family, friends or society. This outward and conditional seeking of contentment often causes unnecessary anxiety, stress and disappointment.

As Lao Tzu, the ancient Chinese philosopher said, *"Because one believes in one-self, one doesn't try to convince others. Because one is content with oneself, one doesn't need others' approval. Because one accepts oneself, the whole world accepts him or her."*

Being in a state of contentment doesn't mean that we give up our dreams and goals. While in a state of contentment, we can more effectively achieve our dreams and goals with greater ease by using compartmentalization. We, however, often have a tendency to seek our own self-approval and obtain validation through the fulfillment of goals or conditions. The goals and conditions we place on ourselves, are often not our goals and conditions, but the product of social conditioning or the expectations of others. Rather than being content with our own essential nature and being, we create anxiety, stress, fear and restlessness pursuing the goals and conditions of others. We become consumed with who we should become (e.g., a doctor, lawyer, billionaire, rock star, tech entrepreneur), or what we should have (a mansion, a Mercedes, a wealthy fashion model spouse), rather than appreciating who we are (divine consciousness having a human experience). With contentment, we can be in love with who we are right now.

The practice of being fully present in the moment and feeling gratitude for as little as our next breath increases our contentment. Contentment can be practiced at anytime and anywhere. When we become conscious of our inner discontent, desire or lack, we can return to a state of contentment by taking our next breath and giving gratitude for the miracle of life. It can be that simple. We can then start being grateful for all the blessings and goodness in our life as well as the challenges from which we grow and become stronger.

Contentment leads to a state of calmness, which allows us to go deeper into a state of optimal wellness.

CALMNESS

Calmness is a state of serenity, tranquility, or peace. Calmness arises from a state of stillness and contentment. We are composed of 99.99% empty space and therefore "stillness and silence" is part of our natural state of being. However, most of us have become so addicted to our mind chatter, pursuing goals and our "busyness" it's become difficult for most of us to find stillness and silence within.

The greatest challenge to our calmness is mind chatter that produces constrictive cognitive emotions (e.g., fear, anxiety, anger). The constrictive emotions trigger the *sympathetic* nervous system and the production of hormones (e.g., adrenaline and cortisol), which causes our bodies to go into sympathetic "flight or fight" mode. When in this state, the body tightens and contracts, and the blood supply to the brain, endocrine and digestive systems is reduced due to the blood being is sent into the limbs, heart and lungs in preparation to flee from a predator, hunt prey or fight for territory. This creates a feedback loop with our brain and body that typically promotes states such as agitation, fear, tightness and anxiety.

When we're calm, we enter the *parasympathetic* nervous system state where our bodies are allowed to heal. Blood returns to our internal organs and digestive processes. As well, hormones that repair our body and elevate our mood are secreted (e.g., serotonin, dopamine, melatonin, pregnenolone). This creates a feedback loop promoting good health, relaxation, increased immune function, improved digestion and repair of the body's systems.

Because sensory stimuli, conditioning and cognitive processes are continually grabbing at our attention, finding calm and sitting in stillness can be a struggle. For this reason, many spiritual systems provide the practices of mindfulness, meditation, prayer and/or immersion to quiet mind chatter, minimize desires and dissolve duality, allowing us to find our inner calm, peace and tranquility.

The calm of stillness and silence is always available. It's much like the still deep water under a choppy ocean surface. In order to access our state of calmness, we just need to dive in deep enough to find it. This can be done through meditation, immersion and breathing practices. *"Inscendence"*(see chapter on *Mindfulness, Meditation & Optimizing States of Being)* can be used to immerse ourselves in the silence and stillness that exists in the space of our physical being. The practice of immersing ourselves into a state of silence and stillness, allows us to cultivate the ability to access calmness at will. We can then stay in calmness or consciously guide ourselves to another desired optimal state of being.

Calmness not only has positive effects on our physical and mental health, but also has a profound effect on our relationships. Calmness reduces stress, reactivity, disconnection and fear, as well as increasing empathy, responsiveness, patience and compassion. Being calm allows us to comprehend situations more fully and objectively. This increases our ability to listen patiently, appreciate another's perspective and respond with greater love, compassion and relevancy. This heightened level of communication improves our relationships.

Calmness also leads to rest and sleep, which are also essential to rejuvenation and possessing optimal wellness.

REST, RELAXATION, SLEEP & REJUVENATION

> *"Sometimes the most important thing in a whole day is the rest we take between two deep breaths."*
>
> ~ Etty Hillesum

Rejuvenation is foundational to optimal wellness and requires rest, relaxation and sleep.

Rest is often thought to include the following:

1. The refreshing quiet or repose of sleep

2. Refreshing inactivity after exertion or labor

3. Relaxing or leisure activities

4. Relief or freedom, especially from worries or troubles

5. A period of inactivity, solitude, repose or tranquility

6. Mental or spiritual calm

7. Cessation or absence of motion

Dr. Rubin Naiman, a sleep specialist at University of Arizona's Center for Integrated Medicine and coauthor with Andrew Weil, MD, of *Healthy Sleep*, states, **"rest can be defined as a kind of waking sleep, experienced while you are alert and aware."** Dr. Naiman says, *"Rest is not what most people think it is. People confuse rest with recreation, doing things like hiking, watching movies, gardening, reading, or even* *inebriation—getting high, stoned, tipsy, or drunk. Any of these activities can only be termed restful because they are breaks from work." "Rest is the essential bridge to sleep. We can never 'go to' sleep, just as you can't 'go to' rest—it's already there. We achieve rest and sleep the same way, by making space for it and allowing it to happen."* Rest allows us to sleep and rejuvenate so that we can re-boot and re-set.

Rest and sleep have many health benefits, including improving memory, increasing lifespan, regulating blood pressure, reducing inflammation, spurring creativity, improving athletic performance, increasing learning ability, sharpening attention, regulating weight, lowering stress, increasing motor responses and enhancing mood.[212]

In order to get the maximum benefits from our rest, sleep, relaxation and leisure activities, It's important to distinguish between these activities and various brain wave frequency states of consciousness. According to neuroscience, there are **5 distinct brain wave frequencies**, namely **Gamma, Beta, Alpha, Theta and Delta.**[213]

Brain Wave	Description
Gamma (30-100 Hz)	Gamma waves are the highest frequency brain waves. Although little is known about this state of mind, initial theories suggest that Gamma waves are associated with unity consciousness, bursts of insight, intuition and high-level information processing. Experiments on Tibetan Buddhist monks have shown a correlation between transcendental mental states and gamma waves.
Beta (12-30 Hz):	Normal waking consciousness and a heightened state of alertness that includes logic, critical reasoning, speech and achievement of daily tasks. Heightened Beta waves often translate into stress, anxiety & restlessness.
Alpha (7.5-12 Hz)	Characterized by deep relaxation, detached awareness, day-dreaming and the state achieved during light mediation. The Alpha state heightens imagination, visualization, memory, learning and concentration. It is the mental state at which you consciously create your reality. At this frequency of mind control you are conscious of your surroundings but your body is in deep relaxation.
Theta (4-7.5 Hz):	Theta is the realm of the subconscious mind and is experienced during deep meditation or light sleep. Theta is characterized by a sense of deep spiritual connection and oneness with the universe. Vivid visualizations, profound inspiration, great creativity, deep insights, emotional and subconscious clearing and rejuvenation occur in Theta. The Alpha-Theta border (7 to 8 Hz), is the optimal range for using the creative power of your mind, visualization and mind programming.
Delta (0.5-4Hz):	Delta is the realm of the unconscious mind and is present in deep, dreamless sleep and in very deep, transcendental meditation where awareness is completely dissolved. Delta is sometimes referred to as the gateway to the Universal Mind and the collective unconscious. Delta is associated with deep healing and regeneration.

Restful practices include taking focused and conscious breaths, sitting in a hot bath, getting a massage, taking a nap, doing Yoga Nidra or Restorative Yoga, or sitting still and doing nothing.

Sleep is a naturally recurring state characterized by altered consciousness, reduced sensory activity, and relaxation of voluntary muscles. During sleep, we experience increased states of anabolism and rejuvenation (e.g., repair and growth of immune, nervous, skeletal, and muscular systems). Stages of sleep are characterized by stages of *Non-Rapid Eye Movement* ("NREM") and *Rapid Eye Movement* ("REM"), as follows:

Sleep Stage	Description
NREM Stage 1	This is the Alpha stage of deep relaxation between wakefulness and sleep. The muscles are active, and the eyes roll slowly, opening and closing moderately.
NREM Stage 2	The stage where Theta activity starts displacing the alpha waves associated with Stage 1. In Stage 2, the sleeper is harder to awaken and the voluntary muscles are relaxed. The awareness of conscious self fades into the subconscious state of awareness.
NREM Stage 3	Known as "slow-wave sleep" ("SWS"). SWS consists of Delta activity. In this stage, the sleeper is less responsive to many environmental stimuli and is "dissolving" from a subconscious to an unconscious state of being.
REM	When the sleeper enters the state of rapid eye movement (REM), most voluntary muscles become momentarily paralyzed. This level is also referred to as *paradoxical sleep* because EEG waves show similarities to a waking state and oxygen consumption and arousal are higher than when awake, yet it is harder to arouse the sleeper than at any other sleep stage. An adult reaches REM approximately every 90 minutes, with the latter half of sleep being more dominated by this stage. The purpose of REM is still somewhat of a mystery but is thought to be a profound part of healing, rejuvenation and higher brain functioning.
Sleep generally occurs in 4 to 5 cycles of REM and NREM per night as N1 → N2 → N3 → N2 → REM. There is a greater amount of N3 deep sleep earlier in the night with an increase in REM in the two cycles just before natural awakening.	

About 30% of adults have symptoms of insomnia with about 10% of adults having insomnia that is severe enough to cause daytime consequences and less than 10% of adults have chronic insomnia. The majority of us don't have sleep disorders, but do we really know how to get good quality sleep? Even though we eventually get to sleep, many people prevent themselves from optimizing their sleep by remaining in the Beta state with its accompanying "mind chatter" rather than consciously entering into relaxed states of being.

We can improve the quality of our sleep and its benefits by consciously moving from Beta (an active waking state) to Alpha (N1—deep relaxation) and into Theta (N2—deep meditation-light sleep). Once we enter the light sleep phase of Theta, the subconscious processes take over to "dissolve" the conscious mind chatter and deliver us into the deep unconscious realm of Theta and into Delta (N3—unconscious deep sleep).

Here are a couple of exercises that I find helpful to overcome Beta mind chatter and drop into Theta state of light sleep and transition to the Delta state of deep sleep:

Sleep Exercise #1:

1. Close your eyes

2. Focus on slow, relaxed breathing

3. Envision a beautiful, quiet, tranquil pond on a still sunny day

4. See yourself relaxing by the pond with not a care in the world

5. As the sun warms your body, you relax and start to fade into a carefree sleep

Sleep Exercise #2:

1. Close your eyes

2. Focus on slow relaxed breathing

3. Imagine yourself sitting in a movie theatre

4. Your thoughts are projected onto the screen as you sit in your seat observing your thoughts on the screen in a detached manner

5. Simultaneously, the screen starts to dim and moves farther away, getting dimmer and smaller until it disappears

The more we integrate periods of rest and sleep into our daily lives, the greater benefits we receive in our health, energy, mood and overall well-being.

The following supplements can help deepen sleep without the side effects and drowsiness that results from many sleeping pills.[214] The dosages are average doses, however, each person should check with their health care practitioner before taking any of the following:

Supplement	Dose	Effect
GABA	500 mg	A neuro-inhibitory transmitter that the brain uses to relax and calm down. GABA helps enter a parasympathetic state that promotes a calm state and acts as a precursor to sleep.
Melatonin	3 mg	A hormone naturally produced by the body that signals the brain to sleep. Melatonin promotes quality of sleep and reduces the time it takes for fall asleep.
Glycine	3 grams	An amino acid that acts as an inhibitory neurotransmitter that increases relaxation and helps you enter into sleep and wake up clear and energized.
L-Tryptophan	100 mg	An amino acid that promotes relaxation, reduced stress, accelerated onset of sleep and deepened delta-waves.
L-Theanine	100 mg	An amino acid that works well with excitable personalities and calming overly active minds to help relax the brain as a precursor to sleep rather than through sedation.
L-Ornithine	400 mg	An amino acid that reduces stress and anger and improves the quality and length of sleep
Griffonia Simpllicifolia / 5-HTP	100 mg	Seeds that supply 5-hydroxy L-Tryptophan with Serotonin to promote relaxation, happiness, elevated moods, clarity and deeper REM.
CBD	25 mg	CBD or Cannabidiol is a chemical compound found in cannabis and hemp. Unlike many products that contain THC, pure CBD doesn't cause intoxication, but has been found to promote relaxation and calm while reducing stress, inflammation, pain and symptoms of insomnia.
Magnesium	145 mg	A mineral that promotes relaxation, sleep and healthy enzyme function while also regulating blood pressure and mood stabilization.

The quality, depth and length of sleep is foundational to our ability to rejuvenate. Rejuvenation increases longevity, well-being and quality of life through the renewal of cells, the repair of cellular damage and systemic deterioration (e.g., tissue, muscles, skeletal, endocrine cardiovascular, immune, neurological) associated with aging, toxicity, stress and other factors of an industrialized society.

Rejuvenation, as used herein, is the continual process of miraculously regenerating our cells and healing our body. For example, we grow a new stomach lining in as little as 5 days, our skin is completely new every 2-4 weeks, our liver completely renews itself every 150-500 days, and we rebuild our entire skeletal structure every 10 years.[215]

Factors such as aging, stress, toxicity and disease can slow or disrupt our natural regenerative processes. Rejuvenation is essential to the process of maintaining robust and healthy regenerative processes.

There is amazing research in the area of stem cells and protein isolation to rejuvenate aging cells and systems, such as Harvard Stem Cell Institute's research showing that a protein known as "GDF11" can restore the functioning of hearts, skeleton, muscles and brains of aging mice.

In their article *"Mechanisms of cellular rejuvenation,"* researchers, Annina Denoth-Lippuner and Sebastian Jessberger, state, *"Rejuvenation is a process that not only delays aging but actually reverts it, leading to a younger cell, tissue, or body. Rejuvenation would erase age-accumulated damage and aging hallmarks collected during one's life. Thus, successful rejuvenation may not only lead to lifespan extension but ultimately to eternal life. In fact, rejuvenation is occurring in every human in the germ cells, thereby resetting the aging clock to zero in order to produce completely young and rejuvenated offspring. Yet, the underlying molecular mechanism remains elusive due to the complexity of this process."*

While science is pushing forward rejuvenation through genetics, stem cells and other discoveries, utilizing a holistic and multi-pronged approach for optimal health, we can stay youthful and healthy without requiring medical and scientific intervention.

By mimicking nature and its processes of rejuvenation and regeneration, we can more effectively create and maintain an optimal state of wellness. Rejuvenation and regeneration lead to healthy cells with healthy thoughts, emotions, diet, exercise, energy, environment and relationships. It's essential to the rejuvenation of our cells and systems that we adopt holistic and integrated approaches that include calm, contentment, rest, relaxation and sleep in addressing the optimal wellness of the whole human. By integrating M.E.D.I.C.I.N.E. into your life, you can possess improved health, vitality, youthfulness and improved states of being from this moment forward.

CHAPTER 17

Intimacy, Love & Connection

---

*"The need for love and intimacy is a fundamental human
need, as primal as the need for food, water, and air."*

~Dean Ornish

To be healthy as humans, we need intimacy, love, companionship and nurturing. The greater the intimacy, love, companionship and nurturing we share, the more health, enjoyment and longevity we receive in our lives.

We often think of "intimacy" as being private, romantic and sexual. However, intimacy is a process of open communication, bonding, connection, experiences, trust and comfort. Intimacy has several different forms, including the following:

- **Physical** intimacy is sensual and somatic. It includes touching, holding hands, hugging, kissing and sexual relations. Although physical intimacy is often considered to be sexual, it may also be non-sexual such as giving a family member a hug or a kiss, rubbing a friend's neck and shoulders, or feeding each other food. Physical intimacy can also include the somatic relationship we have with our planet such as the wind in our hair, the sun on our skin, jumping in the ocean, and feeling the smoothness of a beach agate.

- **Emotional** intimacy generally develops from a level of trust, openness, comfort and bonding. While we share emotional intimacy with family and friends, when emotional intimacy is coupled with sexual intimacy, biochemicals such as phenylethylamine, norepinephrine, dopamine and oxytocin are released which intensify feelings of love, closeness and bonding. Emotional intimacy is generally experienced as a deep loving or emotional bond with another. However, this bond can also occur with the reciprocal relationship we share with the planet, or feeling the way Mother Nature cares for us and provides us wondrous beauty. We can also experience emotional intimacy through the love we feel for a pet.

- **Intellectual** intimacy takes place during intellectual exchange, inquiry and engaging in projects requiring cognitive and mental applications. Sharing thoughts, ideas, beliefs and/or humor in an open and comfortable way, or researching and sharing facts to better understand our world are forms of intellectual intimacy. Intellectual intimacy tends to increase when there is agreement, alignment and similarity. However, people debating or even disagreeing can lead to cognitive intimacy if there's sufficient openness, respect and trust that the debate or disagreement is leading to an aligned outcome. And some people just really enjoy a good debate.

- **Experiential** intimacy occurs when people engage in, and experience, activities together. This can include such things as exercising together, watching a sunset, going to a spa, sharing a meal or working on a project. Experiential intimacy also includes such things as experiencing nature, sharing the Earth, and sharing the human experience.

- **Energetic** intimacy is experienced when we feel a deep sense of connection to another person or our environment for no reason in a way that can't be physically or rationally explained or scientifically validated. For example, energetic intimacy can be experienced through faith-based or spiritual connections where there is an intuitive knowing of destiny, guidance, remembrance or familiarity. Energetic intimacy also extends to a sense of oneness, unity, belonging, connection and bond with God/Source/Cosmic Intelligence or nature. This can include a sense of unity with everything from a seashell, to a flower, a sunset, the ocean, the planet, the stars in the sky, the life force flowing through each of us, and all of creation.

A significant amount of research supports that all humans tend to be happier and healthier when we're more connected and have greater intimacy, love, trust, nurturing and companionship in our lives. In support of this, Margaret Clark and Judson Mills, found that strategic relationships based on exchange are fragile and easily break down when there is disagreement. Communal relationships based upon exchange and benefit (e.g., intimacy, especially emotional intimacy), are much more robust and have a significantly greater ability to survive considerable challenges and disagreements.[216]

Karen J. Prager, author of *The Psychology of Intimacy* writes, *"In the face of stressful life events people who have intimate relationships have fewer stress-related symptoms, faster recoveries from illness, and a lower probability of relapse or recurrence than those who do not have intimate relationships." "Intimate relationships are often differentiated from other personal relationships by the presence of confiding interactions between the partners."*

Barbara and Irwin Sarason, authors of *Close Romantic Relationships,* write: *"The primary result of companionship is the generation of positive feelings—the intrinsic pleasures that make a difference in daily life." "Companiate activities need not have a purpose; instead they offer satisfaction in participation." "Social support, social control and companionship in particular close relationships not only contribute to health outcomes, but also are related to satisfaction with that relationship and its continuance."*

While love is amazing, beautiful and powerful, many of the activities of intimacy, such as enjoying adventures, sex, intellectual conversation, or confidential communication, don't require us to love those with whom we engage in these activities. However, love enhances and heightens intimacy and intimacy deepens and amplifies love.

Love is the magic elixir that brings fullness and meaning to life and also is a profound contributor to our wellness. According to cardiologist, Dr. Cynthia Thaik, love provides health benefits including enhancing self-esteem, improving immune system function, decreasing inflammation, reducing stress (leading to release of cortisol associated with high blood pressure, diabetes, heart disease and depression), and improving sleep.[217]

Despite the clear evidence that intimacy, love, companionship and nurturing provide great benefits to our health, many people live in fear, disconnection and loneliness. New research links loneliness to a number of dysfunctional immune responses, suggesting that being lonely has the potential to harm overall health.

Researchers at Ohio State University found that *"People who were more lonely showed signs of elevated latent herpes virus reactivation and produced more inflammation-related proteins in response to acute stress than did people who felt more socially connected... These proteins signal the presence of inflammation, and chronic inflammation is linked to numerous conditions, including coronary heart disease, Type 2 diabetes, arthritis and Alzheimer's disease, as well as the frailty and functional decline that can accompany aging."*[218] We don't do well in isolation. We need intimacy to be healthy.

We survived as a species through our collaboration and tribal culture, yet chronic loneliness has become a modern-day epidemic.[219] With the Internet, smartphones, social media and online dating apps, why is there such loneliness in our world?

It's likely that our civilization has been designed to promote fear, disconnection and loneliness. *"Divide and rule"* has been used for centuries by sovereigns, dictators and governments as a process for maintaining power and control over the masses. When people are divided, they are less likely to unify and rebel. Also, the phrase *"Give the people bread and circuses"* attributed to Roman poet, Juvenal, in political context, represents ruling the masses by satisfying the most basic needs of the populace using distraction and diversion. Television, Internet and smartphones, with the myriad of content and applications thereon, provide diversion and distraction that often isolates us. While we appear more connected than ever before, we, as a society, have never been more lonely.

In fact, loneliness has reached epidemic proportions and has been found a significant contributor to disease. According to the Health Resources & Services Administration, *"Loneliness and social isolation can be as damaging to health as smoking 15 cigarettes a day."*[220]

Our disconnection and loneliness largely stem from artificially created dividing lines, including race, religion, ideology, politics, age, gender and geography, as well as fear of rejection. We need to connect more deeply and realize that we are all in this together. In the words of Nobel Laureate, Albert Schweitzer, *"Until mankind can extend the circle of his compassion to include all living things, he will never, himself, know peace."*

When we reach out to another and connect intimately, both the giver and the receiver are benefited. While many people experience loneliness, there is not a single person who is truly alone because all inhabiting this planet are interconnected physically, energetically and experientially. At each moment, we have the opportunity to receive the benefits of having an intimate and loving connection with the creator, our planet or another person.

As Bjork said, *"I never really understood the word 'loneliness'. As far as I was concerned, I was in an orgy with the sky and the ocean, and with nature."*

Intimacy increases our health and the quality of our lives. Increasing and deepening intimacy can be achieved by practicing the following *"10 Intimacy Enhancing Elements"* in our lives and relationships:

1. **Connection**—In order to give and receive intimacy, love and nurturing, we need to have some form of connection. This connection could be physical, mental, emotional, energetic and/or experiential. The connection could also come from a sense oneness with all of life, the life force within each of us, and the Earth that we live upon.

2. **Love**—Love is often defined as a deep sense of appreciation, caring, connection and desire for another. When we love one another, we want the best life experiences for the ones we love. Love has profound effects on increasing levels of intimacy. Love can be both subjective and objective.

    *   *"Subjective Love"* represents the collection of personal experiences of love that an individual has. This may include experiences of love with our parents, siblings, lovers and friends. Subjective Love tends to be conditional and is often experienced in the context of the personal perspectives and experiences we bring to the relationship. Subjective Love may include the sweetness, depth and joy of love as well as the challenges, heartbreak and sadness that can arise in a love relationship.

- *"Objective Love "* is the creative life force in all things. It is unconditional. When we resonate with the infinite and creative life force, we experience unconditional Objective Love. When experiencing Objective Love, we see the creator's gift of love in ourselves, in others, in our environment and all of creation. Objective Love has a unifying effect that melts barriers and deepens connection.

3. **Communication/Exchange**—We often think of communication as verbal. However, the majority of our communication (e.g., what we exchange and understand) is non-verbal. Touching, looking, moving, body language and our state of being are all types of non-verbal communication. Communication is key to meaningful exchange, understanding, connection, harmony and deeper intimacy. Sometimes our communication is inconvenient, triggers hurt feelings or results in drama/challenges in our relationships. However, transparent, honest, loving and compassionate communication/exchange, (even if it contains invited constructive criticism) increases intimacy, trust and deeper connection. Harsh, insensitive, non-loving and uninvited criticism, even if honest and meant for another's improvement, doesn't generally improve intimacy.

4. **Openness and Vulnerability**—Being openhearted, open-minded and willing to love first, trust first, make mistakes, be embarrassed, get hurt and fully be yourself, allows us to grow, evolve and see our "blind spots." Openness and vulnerability allow us to connect more deeply and experience profound intimacy with another. To show up openly and fully requires being vulnerable and courageous. If you show up less than your full self, who is showing up? What is the other person's experience of you? Will they get a diluted or fake version of you? If we aren't our true self when engaging with another, we may enjoy some short term and partial intimacy, but a truly deep, long and intimate relationship will generally not develop.

5. **Integrity and Trust**—Be honest, transparent and true to yourself and communicate your truth with transparency and integrity. Build trust by being truthful and trustworthy. Trust comes from a sense of safety with another. So, while being honest, also be sensitive to the other's potential fears and the impact of your thoughts, words and deeds. Doing this demonstrates you have

the other person's best interests at heart. This promotes trust and creates a safe environment for the other to open up and receive. By being trustworthy and considerate, you'll find that your intimacy in your relationships deepens and increases.

6. **Respect**—The act of honoring, admiring, considering, valuing, appreciating and/or revering another being or one's environment and engaging in behavior in alignment with such values

7. **Empathy**—The capacity to understand, share feelings and relate to what another is going through from their perspective. It's the deeper connection of oneness with another and with the life force we all share. Empathy is a way of feeling and experiencing the depth of another's being, thoughts, emotions and experiences.

8. **Awareness**—The ability to perceive, to feel, or be conscious of your relationship is a sense of awareness of that relationship. Awareness is understanding the highest expression of the relationship and what you're building in the relationship. Awareness is also consciously observing another's state of being and utilizing our words, behavior and interactions to achieve the highest expression of the relationship.

9. **Commitment**—This requires taking the time, focus and energy to create intimacy. The more you focus on, and devote yourself to, the relationship, and the more types of intimacy you can create in the relationship (e.g., physical, emotional, intellectual, experiential, energetic), the deeper and stronger the intimacy, bond and value the relationship will have.

10. **Expression and Action**—Expressing the foregoing foundations of intimacy through your actions (e.g., behavior and deeds) is key to the reciprocal nature of giving and receiving intimacy, love, connection and nurturing. The more you love, intimacy and connection you express, the greater love, intimacy and connection you receive.

When we practice the foregoing *10 Intimacy Enhancing Elements* to increase our intimacy, our relationships and how we relate to our world, greatly improve. This life improvement is not just philosophical, but is also supported by scientific research showing that people in long-term, loving and intimate relationships receive significant health benefits[221] including:

- Fewer Doctor's Visits
- Improved Mental & Emotional State
- Less Depression & Substance Abuse
- Improved Heart Health & Lower Blood Pressure
- Less Anxiety
- Natural Pain Control
- Better Stress Management
- Fewer Colds
- Faster Healing
- Longer Life
- Improved Immune System Function
- Clear skin

Our thriving and health, as individuals and as a species, is directly related to the amount of intimacy, love, connection, collaboration and nurturing we share with one another, the Earth and all living things. Be generous, give and receive intimacy, love, connection and nurturance. We also must love ourselves. The more generously we love ourselves, the more we can love others.

Just remember the wonderful quote from Buddha: *"You yourself, as much as anybody in the entire universe, deserve your love and affection."*

CHAPTER 18

Natural & Ecosystemic Thriving

(The Interconnectedness and Interdependence of Everything)

"This we know: the earth does not belong to man, man belongs to the earth. All things are connected like the blood that unites us all. Man did not weave the web of life, he is merely a strand in it. Whatever he does to the web, he does to himself."

~Chief Seattle

Accepting our kinship with all life on earth is not only solid science. In my view, it's also a soaring spiritual experience.

~Neil deGrasse Tyson

The wellness of the planet and our environment is a reflection and expression of our inner wellness. If we love and respect ourselves, nature and each other, we will be abundantly nourished, supported and sustained.

Peter Seligman, writes, *"Nature, quite simply, is everything. It is the source of life. It is our foundation and our nourishment, our comfort and our treasury. And it is only by accounting for the full, comprehensive and irreplaceable value of nature in our decision-making that we can secure the future of human societies."*

Unfortunately, humankind has become "disconnected" from nature and from each other. This disconnection and fear are the root causes of the individual and social ills we face in modern society. For example, the phrase "people and planet" demonstrates we somehow believe we're separate from the planet. Once we separate from nature, we separate from each other. This disconnection creates fear. Fear leads to mistrust; and mistrust leads to disharmony, then to anger and finally to war and destruction. Fear can preserve life, but most often tends to damage life. Love creates life.

To thrive as humans, we must reconnect and love each other and nature. We are interconnected to each other and our planet, with each playing an important of part of the whole.

"A human being is a part of the whole, called by us, "Universe," a part limited in time and space. He experiences himself, his thoughts and feelings as something separated from the rest—a kind of optical delusion of his consciousness. This delusion is a kind of prison for us, restricting us to our personal desires and to affection for a few persons nearest to us. Our task must be to free ourselves from this prison by widening our circle of compassion to embrace all living creatures and the whole of nature in its beauty. Nobody is able to achieve this completely, but the striving for such achievement is in itself a part of the liberation and a foundation for inner security." ~Albert Einstein

Einstein clearly understood the interconnection of everything in the universe. This interconnection refers to the ecosystemic interconnection and interdependence of each and every person, animal, plant, object and thing on our planet and throughout the universe in an exquisite balance that creates, regenerates and ends life. The universal ecosystem is beyond our capacity to fully understand. For example, what is breathing us? What creates gravity and keeps our planet spinning around the sun? What keeps nature regenerating life? With our supposed intelligence, science, economic pragmatism and industry, we really know very little about the miracle of life. Still here we are experiencing this great miracle and mystery we call "life."

As John Muir, the renowned environmentalist, philosopher and author, said, *"When we try to pick out anything by itself, we find it hitched to everything else in the universe."* Muir understood our interdependence to nature and the universe. He saw this interconnection every day he spent in nature.

No matter how much we have been conditioned to believe we are alone in this world or strive for independence and exclusivity, we are all in it together. We are simultaneously the creator of nature, nature itself, and a part of nature. As Rumi said, *"You are not just the drop in the ocean. You are the mighty ocean in the drop."* Seen in this way, we can say all life is significant—all life matters. Our lives depend upon our interconnection to each other, the planet and its myriad of ecosystems (e.g., flora, fauna, air, water, soil, sun, wind). Likewise, the planet needs the sun, moon, stars, gravitational forces and universal life force to continue in its orbit and regenerate life. Simultaneously, we are the evolving creative life force in nature, the infinite awareness of everything and the self-experiencing consciousness of ourselves as individuals interconnected with and interdependent upon the whole.

Filmmaker Matthew Flickstein believes that *"The entire universe is one ecosystem, similar to a spider web—if one part is touched, the entire net shimmers. As a result of inter-relatedness and inter-dependency, every expression of energy, including our thoughts and intentions, ultimately touches and affects everything else."*

When we increase the wellness of our environment, we increase our personal wellness. When we understand that each thought, breath, word, deed and action has an impact upon the entire universe, and consistently provide conscious service to universal thriving, we enhance our own lives. The more each of us creates ecosystemic thriving, the more we all thrive.

Despite knowing that nature provides great abundance, its value is often viewed as nothing more than a commodity. However, there has been significant research demonstrating the importance of nature for human psychological well-being,[222] yet with urbanization and new technologies, our relationship with and the time we spend in nature has been eroded.

For Dr. John Mack, inventing a psychology of Earth is far more than an intellectual or therapeutic exercise. It entails a call for political commitment and activism. He states, *"we do have a psychology, or a prevailing attitude, conscious or unconscious, towards the Earth. We regard it a thing, a big thing, an object to be owned, mined, fenced, guarded, stripped, built upon, dammed, plowed, burned, blasted, bulldozed and melted to serve the material needs and desires of the human species, at the expense, if necessary, of all other species, which we feel at liberty to kill, paralyze, or domesticate for our own use. This form of species arrogance has received little scrutiny."*

The sociological disconnection from nature arises from 1) the delusional arrogance that we are smarter than, separate from, and the masters of, nature, and 2) conditioning to exert and maintain control over the masses by requiring dependence on money to obtain that which the Earth gave us for free.

Michael J. Cohen, Ph.D., eco-psychologist, author and Director of the Institute of Global Education, wrote, *"On average, society conditions us to spend over 95% of our time and 99.9% of our thinking disconnected from nature. Nature's extreme absence in our lives leaves us abandoned and wanting. We feel we never have enough. We greedily, destructively, consume and, can't stop. Nature's loss in our psyche produces a hurt, hungering, void within us that bullies us into our dilemmas."*

As much as our society has tried to "civilize" us and disconnect us from nature, we are just another species interconnected with, and dependent upon, nature. Everything that sustains our lives, including our next breath, water, food, shelter, energy and materials, are provided by Mother Nature, yet we, as a society, act with utter disregard to "our mother," the provider of all life, things and value. We're not loving her. We're using her. If we learned to love, respect and be grateful to our generous and abundant Mother Nature, we might just learn to love ourselves and each other.

If our environment is toxic, it's difficult for us to be well. If we're toxic, it's difficult for our environment to be well. Our personal and global wellness has to come from the inside-out. This inside-out internal cleansing necessitates a personal shift requiring us to find our inner beauty and capacity to love; to rid ourselves of isolation, negativity, fear, violence and stress; to cleanse our physical, mental, emotional and energetic systems of toxins; to learn new ways to lovingly and harmoniously relate to one another and our planet; and to collaborate with, serve and respect each other and our planet.

Many of us live in or around cities and environments devoid of natural beauty and full of toxicity. We breathe air filled with smog resulting from burned and refined fossil fuels and other toxic chemicals and particulates. We drink water containing heavy metals and chemical compounds such as mercury, fluoride, arsenic, cadmium, asbestos, lead, solvents, pesticides, hormones and chlorine, to name a few. We live in homes, drive cars and work in offices with carpets, paints/stains, plastics and other materials and cleaners full of toxic chemicals. We are given vaccines that contain mercury, aluminum, formaldehyde and cause autoimmune diseases. We are exposed to unnatural AC current and Electro Magnetic Waves, which create harmful effects on our energy field and distort the natural frequencies of our mind and body.

According to HeathlyStuff.org, *"Average Americans spend up to 90% of their daily lives indoors. The EPA has estimated indoor air pollution levels can be two to five times higher than outdoor air pollution levels. EPA has ranked indoor air pollution one of the top five environmental risks to public health. Next to homes and offices, we spend the most time in automobiles: 1.5 hours per day on average...Over 275 different chemicals have been identified in vehicles interiors, including chemicals associated with birth defects, impaired learning, liver toxicity and cancer."*

In addition to the protocols mentioned above in this section on Wellness, in order to create healthy environments for ourselves and those around us so that we can possess wellness in a toxic world, the following *"Actions for Environmental Health"* are highly recommended:

- Visit and commune with nature at least once a week.

- Share more and lower consumption.

- Make lifestyle and economic choices that benefit both your health and planetary health.

- Use air purification and change the filter regularly.

- Use water purification and change the filter regularly.

- Use renewable energy such as solar or wind for electrical generation.

- Turn off electrical equipment and lights when not in use and use energy-efficient utilities, lighting and HVAC.

- Reduce exposure to air conditioning.

- Reduce exposure to electromagnetic frequencies (EMFs) and radiation by lowering the use of computers, cell phone and television, and use a headset and EMF reducing equipment with your mobile phone.

- Use organic non-toxic cleaning products.

- Reduce and eliminate waste by recycling, repurposing, reusing, composting and upcycling waste.

- Walk, ride bicycles, take public transportation and drive electric, hybrid, hydrogen or bio-fuel vehicles if driving is necessary.

- Purchase and utilize products that are recycled and refurbished whenever possible.

- Eat organic foods from farms that don't use inorganic chemical pesticides that contribute to air and water pollution as well as contamination of our food.

- Invest in, and support, green and triple bottom line companies that embrace programs for the environment; don't buy products or services from, support, or invest in, companies that are willing to put toxic and unhealthy chemicals and ingredients in our food or our environment.

- Support non-profits and politicians with a record of strong environmental support.

- If you or family desire vaccinations, find out whether a vaccine contains harmful chemicals, compounds or heavy metals before getting vaccinated.

- Buy or rent a sustainable and non-toxic home

- Create workplace awareness and office space that is healthy free of toxic paint, carpets and materials, bring in plants, fresh air and nature to the extent possible

- Buy your food from local farmers and take a reusable bag to the grocery store

- Use organic remedies, additives and cleaners instead of chemical pesticides in your home and garden

- Work virtually as much as possible rather than driving or flying to meetings

- Take time every day to connect with and appreciate nature. If you live in a city, look up at the sky, take a walk, buy living plants for your workplace and home and water and care for them.

In addition to the foregoing steps, it's imperative we each take responsibility for the world we are creating. The health of the planet and survival of humankind requires loving care, respect and service to each other and nature. We are in an intrinsic feedback loop between ourselves and our environment. It may be said, the toxicity we see around us is a reflection of what is going on inside of us.

Are we willing to sacrifice our excessive consumerism and waste resulting in poverty, hunger, disease and war in order to create a more thriving, beautiful and abundant planet? Are we willing to transform a centralized toxic fossil fuel supply chain to a localized renewable energy supply chain? Are we willing to make the changes to move from industrialized food, farming, medicine, goods manufacturing and waste to create an earth-conscious economy built on restoration, regeneration and creating beauty and thriving? **Humans created the industrialized world. We can evolve beyond an industrialized society and create a regenerative civilization.**

As interconnected and interdependent individuals, we collectively create the reality we experience. Our Global Human Agreement ("GHA") has a profound impact on our environment as well as our physical, emotional, mental and energetic states of being. By changing our individual beliefs and behaviors, we contribute to changing the GHA. Our transformation starts by reconnecting with each other and nature in a loving and respectful manner. It's also critical to our well-being to take time communing with nature, experiencing her beauty and quiet wisdom.

Wherever we live, we can find and enjoy nature. We can go on a hike, walk in a park, swim at the beach, climb a mountain, watch a spider build its web, smell the flowers, look up at the sky, or just relax and listen to the birds. Even if you live in a concrete urban jungle, you can observe, connect and interact with nature, or look up at the sky and catch a sunset or sunrise. No matter where you are, there is some beauty found in people or nature around you. Find it!

By serving the beauty, abundance and thriving of our planet, we can create ecosystemic thriving and an abundant, well and empowered world that dramatically increases the health, well-being and thriving of each individual on this planet. Let us experience our lives and world with love, respect, caring and collaboration.

As we see the divinity in all things and serve each other and the planet, we will build a healthy, thriving and beautiful world together that supports Abundance, Wellness & Empowerment for all!

CHAPTER 19

Epigenetics and Energetic Activation

(Perception is Reality)

"We are not so much the victims of our genes as we are the creator of our lives, based upon our perception of reality. The creation we experience is an expression of how our perceptions control our behavior and our genes."

~Bruce Lipton

The experience of physical reality results from consciousness coupled with the fundamental energetic "forces" of the electromagnetic spectrum. These electromagnetic forces enter the "circuit board" of our DNA and are routed through the circuitry of our DNA by our genetic "on-off" codes thereby creating the holographic "reality" and form through which we experience our physical world.[223]

The principles arising from the field of *epigenetics*, introduced in this chapter, support such things as how our consciousness (e.g., beliefs, perceptions, emotional state), our diet, and the electromagnetic spectrum (e.g., light and sound) can influence our genes and our reality.[224]

According to Dr. Bruce Lipton, Ph.D. in cellular biology, and author of *Biology of Belief*:

"Hundreds upon hundreds of scientific studies over the last fifty years have consistently revealed that "invisible forces" of the electromagnetic spectrum profoundly impact every facet of biological regulation. These energies include microwaves, radio

frequencies, the visible light spectrum, extremely low frequencies, acoustic frequencies and even a newly recognized form of force known as scalar energy. Specific frequencies and patterns of electromagnetic radiation regulate DNA, RNA and protein syntheses, alter protein shape and function, and control gene regulation, cell division, cell differentiation, morphogenesis (the process by which cells assemble into organs and tissues), hormone secretion, nerve growth and function. Each of these cellular activities is a fundamental behavior that contributes to the unfolding of life."

Because we are energetic beings comprised of 99.99% space or 99.99% consciousness, we can literally reshape reality using our consciousness and energy. By understanding the role of DNA and our ability to mindfully direct the energy of the electromagnetic spectrum to activate genes, we can consciously direct and alter not only our health, but our entire reality.

DNA (Dioxyribonucleic Acid) is a nucleic acid that contains the genetic instructions used in the development and functioning of all known living organisms. The main role of DNA molecules is the long-term storage of information. DNA is often compared to a set of blueprints, since it contains the instructions needed to construct other components of cells, such as proteins.[225]

RNA (Ribonucleic Acid) is primarily the messenger of the DNA "blueprints" and plays several important roles in the processes of transferring genetic information from DNA to ribosomes.

Ribosomes are the workhorses of protein biosynthesis, (the process of translating messenger RNA into protein. Proteins (also known as polypeptides) are organic compounds made of amino acids arranged in a linear chain and folded into a globular form. Protein is essential to all organic cell building and functioning.[226]

There are several types of RNA with differing functions, as follows:

- **mRNA**—Messenger RNA is a "copy" of the DNA base sequence of a gene and transfers genetic information from DNA, which is a storage molecule and quite inaccessible, to ribosomes. Ribosomes then read the information in RNA and use it to produce proteins. Ribosomes do this by binding to a messenger RNA and using it as a template for the correct sequence of amino acids in building a particular protein.

- **tRNA**—Transfer RNA is "charged" with an amino acid and used to recognize the code in the mRNA and "translate" it into the amino acid it is carrying. There are specific tRNA molecules for each amino acid.

- **rRNA**—Ribosomal RNA makes up parts of the ribosome and has the catalytic transpeptidase action required to create polypeptide chains during translation.

- **snRNA**—Small nuclear RNA regulates and provides the catalytic machinery for splicing of mRNA.

- **gRNA**—Guide RNA directs editing of RNA to specific sites.

- **miRNA**—Micro RNA inhibits translation by base pairing with complementary sequences of mRNA.

Scientific research explains that all living things on this planet have the four nucleic-acid bases (Adenine, Cytosine, Guanine and Thymine) referred to as "ACGT" that make up all DNA. The Adenine pairs with Thymine and Cytosine pairs with Guanine. The four amino acids that make up RNA, the transport mechanism of DNA/Genetic coding, pair up the same way as DNA, except that Thymine is replaced with Uracil, and thus these nucleic acids are referred to as "ACGU."[227]

The human DNA "circuit board" is identical to the DNA "circuit boards" for all life on planet Earth. It is the genetic on-off switches that determine the difference between all life forms, their species and their individuality. For example, there is no difference between the DNA of a human and banana, however, the genetic coding is about 50% different. Also, our genetic coding is only about 1% different than chimpanzees and 2.5% different than mice, whereas, the difference in genetic code among humans is only about .1%. According to mainstream science, the programming of the DNA is accomplished by activating genetic codes through the ACGT.[228]

In support of the foregoing, Dr. Florencia Puali Behn, Genetisist at Stanford University, writes:

> *"The building blocks and shape of DNA molecules in humans, plants and every living thing is the same—we all have the famous A, C, G, and T's. It's the order of these letters that makes us different. When we think of a banana and a person,*

it's easy to assume that their DNA molecules might be different. In fact, the actual structure of the DNA molecule and how it codes for proteins is the same from bacteria to yeast to plants and animals."

"The DNA molecule in plants, humans, and all living things are all the same shape—like a twisted ladder, or a double helix. The backbone of the ladder is made up of sugar and phosphate molecules.

Each rung of the ladder is made up of two bases that stick out from the backbone and pair in the middle (a base pair). The letters A, T, G, and C represent the names of these bases. The ladder is twisted, forming the DNA molecule with which we are familiar.

DNA is folded, stored, copied, and used as a blueprint to make proteins in the same way in all living things. So why are living things so different? Some of the differences come from the order of A, T, C, and G's and the proteins for which they code, the time and place these proteins are made, and the number of chromosomes and genes."

As supported by Dr. Pauli Behn, because our human DNA contains the DNA for all life on this planet, we also possess the potential for extra-human characteristics, subject to activating the appropriate gene codes. For example, we have the potential to regenerate limbs like a salamander, to be amphibious like a frog, to go long periods without water like a camel, have the sight of an eagle, the sense of smell of a basset hound, the hearing of a bat, or even the ability to produce energy by photosynthesis as opposed to the Kreb cycle. This may sound far-fetched to many, but genetic research has already proven that by activating or deactivating certain genes, extra-human characteristics can be accomplished.

As a case in point, in a report published in the Proceedings of the National Academy of Sciences, researchers from The Wistar Institute demonstrated that mice lacking the p21 gene gained the ability to regenerate lost or damaged tissue.[229] *"Much like a newt that has lost a limb, these mice will replace missing or damaged tissue with healthy tissue that lacks any sign of scarring,"* said the project's lead scientist Ellen Heber-Katz, Ph.D., a professor in Wistar's Molecular and Cellular Oncogenesis program. *"While we are just beginning to understand the repercussions of these findings,*

*perhaps, one day we'll be able to accelerate healing in humans by temporarily inacti-
vating the p21 gene."*

Prior to our conception, the blueprint for our DNA exists as a possibility in
the quantum field. Upon our conception, the possibility of our DNA collapses into
a physical reality and our cellular being is built following our specific genetic blueprint.[230] This genetic blueprint initially shapes all of the characteristics of our being,
including whether we are human; the color of our eyes, skin and hair; our height,
weight and gender; our complexion; our energy level; the efficiency of our immune
system and our ability to heal; our intelligence; our sensitivity to light and sound;
and our food and water requirements.

Although we have been told that we are stuck with the genes we received at
birth, this is not the case. **Our genetic blueprint is not fixed and determinative.
It can be altered through consciousness, beliefs, sound, light and diet**. We have
the ability, throughout our life, second by second, to consciously activate our DNA
and alter our genetic coding. This is supported through epigenetic experiments
involving enucleation.

EPIGENETICS

Epigenetics simply means "above genetics" and, in part, involves the study of how outside influences affect mechanisms inside the cell like gene expression. Epigeneticists
originally engaged in research by enucleating cells (removing the nucleus of cell).
Based upon the theory of determinism, removing the nucleus containing the DNA
should have killed the cell. However, the cell lived on continuing its cellular function,
except the function of reproduction. Dr. Randy Jirtle, while a researcher at Duke
University, fed mice a special diet rich in genistein, which is an active ingredient in
soy to obesity-prone agouti mice during pregnancy. The result was their offspring,
which had a genetic predisposition to obesity, were slim, providing support that
extra-genetic influences can alter genetic heritage.[231]

Dr. Bruce Lipton, PhD, a cellular biologist, an epigenetics thought-leader and
author writes, *"In the last decade, epigenetic research established that DNA blueprints
passed down through genes are not set in concrete at birth. Genes are not destiny!*

Environmental influences, including nutrition, stress and emotions, can modify genes, without changing their basic blueprint. And those modifications, epigeneticists have discovered, can be passed on to future generations as surely as DNA blueprints are passed on via the Double Helix." We are not helpless victims with a predetermined fate decided by the genes we inherited from our ancestors. While our genes significantly contribute to our characteristics, they don't determine them.

Early DNA researchers believed that only 2-3% of DNA was active. The DNA that had no known biological function was often referred to as "Junk DNA" or "non-coding DNA." DNA was considered "junk" or "non-coding" when components of an organism's DNA sequences did not encode for protein sequences. However, as the science of genetics has evolved, scientists have found that non-coding DNA sequences have known biological functions, including the transcriptional and translational regulation of protein-coding sequences.[232] Moreover, research has shown that sound and light are also significantly responsible for DNA programming and genetic coding.

In 1970, Fritz-Albert Popp, a theoretical biophysicist at the University of Marburg in Germany, was researching the interaction of electromagnetic (EM) radiation on biological systems. Popp had been examining two almost identical molecules: benzoapyrene, a polycyclic hydrocarbon known to be one of the most lethal carcinogens to humans, and its twin (save for a tiny alteration in its molecular makeup), benzoepyrene. He had illuminated both molecules with ultraviolet (UV) light in an attempt to find exactly what made these two almost identical molecules so different. Popp discovered that benzoapyrene (the cancer producing molecule) absorbed the UV light, then re-emitted it at a completely different frequency. Whereas benzoepyrene (harmless to humans) allowed the UV light to pass through it unaltered.[233]

Popp performed his test on 37 different chemicals, some cancer-causing, some not. In every instance, the compounds that were carcinogenic took the UV light, absorbed it and changed or scrambled the frequency. Each of the carcinogens reacted only to light at a specific frequency of 380nm in the ultra-violet range. This led Popp into the research of *"Photorepair,"* well known from biological laboratory experiments in which a cell is blasted with UV light so that 99 per cent of the cell, including its DNA, is destroyed. The damage can be repaired in a single day just by illuminating the cell with the same wavelength at a much weaker intensity. Popp's experiments further discovered that photons switch on the body's processes.

Dr. Veljko Veljkovic, head of the Center for Multidisciplinary Research and Engineering, Institute of Nuclear Sciences Vinca questioned conventional "mechanical" biological principles. These mechanical principles assert that a cell is a bag of molecules dissolved in water and that molecules, randomly bumping into each other, have complementary shapes or morph shapes to lock onto each other so the appropriate biochemical reactions can take place. Dr. Veljkovic is attributed as saying, *"There are about 100,000 chemical reactions happening in every cell each second. The chemical reaction can only happen if the molecule which is reacting is excited by a photon. Once the photon has excited a reaction it returns to the field and is available for more reactions...We are swimming in an ocean of light."*[234]

Irena Cosic, Professor of Biomedical Engineering, RMIT University, Melbourne, Australia proposed that biomolecular interactions are electromagnetic in nature. They take place over large distances compared with the size of molecules. Cosic later introduced the idea of dynamic electromagnetic field interactions, which states that molecules recognize their particular targets and vice versa by electromagnetic resonance.[235]

Russian scientists, Vladimir Poponin and Peter Gariae, demonstrated that DNA's extraordinary electromagnetic properties have a special ability to attract photons, causing the latter to spiral along the helix-shaped DNA molecule instead of along a linear path. Although controversial with the established scientific community, their research demonstrates DNA has the amazing ability to bend or weave light around itself. Similarly, the Gariaev group demonstrated that chromosomes function much like programmable holographic biocomputers employing DNA's own electromagnetic radiation. Their research strongly suggests chromosomes, encoded and decoded by genetic codes, assemble themselves into a holographic lattice designed to generate and interpret highly stable spiral standing waves of sound and light, which directs all biological functions. Another revolutionary implication of this research is that Gariaev 's team created sophisticated devices capable of influencing cellular metabolism through sound and light waves keyed to human language frequencies. Using this method, Gariaev proved that chromosomes damaged by X-rays, for instance, can be repaired. Moreover, this was accomplished noninvasively by simply applying vibration and language, or sound combined with intention, to DNA.[236]

According to Iona and Richard Miller, authors of an article published in *Nexus,* based partly on Gariaev's findings, entitled *From Helix to Hologram,* *"Life is fundamentally electromagnetic rather than chemical, the DNA blueprint functioning as a biohologram which serves as a guiding matrix for organizing physical form."*

The far-reaching implication of the foregoing research is that DNA has the potential of being activated through conscious linguistic expression and sound (e.g., words, music, singing, sonic frequencies), and electromagnetic light to modify the human bioenergy fields, which in turn can modify the physical structure and functioning of the human body. In their book *The Reincarnation of David Cayce,* Wynn Free and David Wilock, note *"According to Russian findings, this spiraling 'torsion' energy could actually be the substance of our human souls, and is therefore the precursor to the DNA molecule... It already exists in the fabric of space and time before any physical life emerges on a given planet."* In keeping with Gariaev's "Wave-based Genome Theory," Free and Wilcock conclude that DNA functions *"somewhat like a computer chip, with different sections that can either be 'on' or 'off.'"* Thus, we can easily imagine how the torsion waves of human consciousness could actually program, or reprogram, DNA's binary code.

The foregoing breakthrough research supports that torsion energy permeates the entire multidimensional galaxy and not only is responsive to consciousness, but may be consciousness itself. *"To put it as bluntly as possible,"* writes Free and Wilcock, *"you cannot separate consciousness and torsion waves—they are the same thing. When we use our minds to think, we are creating movements of electrical impulses in the brain, and when any electrical energy moves, torsion waves are also created."* In other words, we are energetic beings continually interacting with and influencing the electromagnet field, even with just a thought.

Dawson Church, Ph.D., in his book *Genie in Your Genes,* explains as follows:

"As well as beings of matter, we are beings of energy. Electromagnetism pervades biology, and there is an electromagnetic component to every biological process.

While biology has been largely content with chemical explanations of how and why cells work, there are many tantalizing preliminary research findings that show that electromagnetic shifts accompany virtually every biological process. The energy flowing in, around, and out of neurons and genes interacts constantly with the outside environment. Genes are how organisms store information, while energy is about how they communicate information."

"The environment that activates genes includes both the inner environment—the emotional, biochemical, mental, energy and spiritual landscape of the individual—and the outer environment." The outer environment includes the social network and ecological systems in which the individual lives. Food, toxins, social rituals, predators, and sexual cues are examples of the outer environment.

Through our senses and perceptions, we convert vibrations from a cosmic quantum electromagnetic field ("the "wave" or "the field") into momentary experiences ("particles") that form our perceived physical reality. The field represents all possibility and infinite consciousness, whereas the particle is the personal subjective reality we each experience through our beliefs, perceptions and relationship with the field and our environment. *"The field, according to Einstein, is the sole governing agency of the particle."* There is an infinite potential between each thought as to what our next thought may be. The field influences us and we influence the field in a reciprocal co-creative feedback loop.

Dr. Bruce Lipton provides an eloquent explanation of our ability to affect our biology and genes with our beliefs, emotions and actions[237]. . .

"Cells respond to a massive variety of signals using protein switches: over 100,000 switches per cell built into its membrane. These protein switches are fundamental units of perception. They read environmental conditions and adjust the biology to meet the need required. This becomes very profound when we own that perception controls behavior, for it is how we perceive the world that controls our lives.

The "new biology" reveals that perception also controls the read-out of our genes. It is how we see life that determines which genes will be activated to provide for survival. *By sending a faulty signal, we are liable to subvert the health of our biology by incorrect gene activation, causing disease and dysfunction.*

Contrary to what many believe, we are not so much the victims of our genes as we are the creator of our lives, based upon our perception of reality. The creation we experience is an expression of how our perceptions control our behavior and our genes."

Our perception of our environment has a profound impact on which genes get activated. In our modern society, many of us live with high levels of fear, anxiety and stress, which can have a harmful effect on our health. Lipton provides further explanation of this phenomena:[238]

"Nature designed us to use protection behaviors only in acute responses like running from a saber tooth tiger. But if we maintain protection too long, the shutting down of growth compromises our survival. The more we live in fear, the more we allocate energy for protection, and the more we shut down life-conserving growth. In the world today, protection response accounts for a greater percentage of our life experience. Most of us live with high levels of stress, which debilitates our biology by interfering with growth. Simple point: cells cannot be in growth and protection at the same time.

Additionally, we have two different protection systems. The immune system deals with internal threats like viruses, bacteria, parasites or cancer cells. The adrenal system responds to exterior threats like a poisonous snake or a mugger by secreting stress hormones that engage a protection response. *These hormones constrict the blood vessels in the gut, forcing blood to the arms and legs where it nourishes fight or flight behavior. Growth functions are thus inhibited because of lack of blood-borne nutrients. Stress hormones also shut off the immune system to conserve energy. The reason is obvious:*

If chased by a lion, you do not put your energy into fighting off a bacterial infection; you put it into running.

Everyday stresses repress the normal functions of both the growth and immune systems. With enough stress, we reach a point where we do not replace the number of cells we lose, and this leads to organ and tissue dysfunction, the primary cause of disease. *Reduced immune activity also opens us up to attack by normally repressed infectious agents. Adding insult to injury, stress also constricts the flow of* *blood in the forebrain, sending it instead to nourish the hindbrain's high-speed reflex center, which controls the behavior used in stressful situations. Since the forebrain is where our consciousness and intelligence reside, shutting down its function in stress causes us to be less intelligent. Over time, chronic stress leads to disastrous effects."*

Based on the foregoing, if we desire to improve our physical health, thoughts and mental prowess, the quality of our emotions, our energy levels and ability to manifest desired outcomes in our lives, we must align our individual perception of our environment and circumstances in a way that optimizes each moment. This requires awareness, practice and open-mindedness. It also requires us to reprogram our beliefs about what is possible and utilize disciplines that help us to actively use our consciousness to influence our genes, which can be accomplished with "Energetic Activation" as a discipline

ENERGETIC ACTIVATION

Given the foregoing scientific support for our epigenetic ability to influence our genes through our consciousness and the way we relate to our environment, we can optimize our states of being and enhance energetic flow through our genetic circuitry by engaging in conscious energetic clearing and activation.

In electronic circuitry, a resistor is generally used to resist, slow down and/or step down the voltage of current. The usual result of resistance in electronic circuitry is a reduction of energy, to step down excess energy or reroute it. Resistance is typically dissipated through heat. With higher levels of resistance, the heat generated from the resistance become so great that it can cause damage to, and even melt, the circuit board. Just like a resistor in an electronic circuit board, when we have resistance in our "energetic/genetic circuitry," it reduces our life force, dulls consciousness, constricts our physical systems, causes inflammation and stress, and eventually leads to discomfort, pain, disease and/or death. Resistance, however, in our genetic circuitry can be beneficial by causing energy to bypass certain genetic switches that would be unhealthy or detrimental for us. Also, there may be resistance we hold that, if removed, would allow us to have extraordinary or even superhuman characteristics.

In order to possess optimal wellness and creative power, it's essential that our genetic circuitry, energy field, minds and bodies are clear of unhealthy and destructive resistance, constriction, obstructions and limitations (collectively "Resistance"). When our energy and beneficial genetic circuity are clear, unobstructed, and optimally flowing, we can access and utilize maximal energetic life force to enhance our state of being, increase our thriving, accomplish extraordinary feats, and manifest the life we desire.

Certain emotions cause constriction in the body, (e.g., fear, anger, anxiety) whereas others cause expansion (e.g., love, joy, peace). To be optimally well requires increasing expansive emotions that foster increased energy, vitality and thriving, while minimizing constrictive emotions and the resulting Resistance caused thereby. Clearing Resistance from our genetic circuit board is accomplished by (1) scanning the subtle energy systems in and around our body, mind, emotional field and energy field, and (2) consciously clearing or transforming resistant and limiting beliefs and perceptions, constrictive emotions, stored physical trauma and limitation, and genetic channel blockages.

When we clear Resistance from our genetic circuitry and consciousness fields, we can activate and shift to expansive states of being and access maximal energetic current to allow us manifest miracles in our lives. Raising our energy, capacity and frequency enables us to activate and open genetic circuitry. **Opening new genetic circuitry, or expanding the capacity of existing circuitry, allows us to consciously make epigenetic shifts in** the following:

- **Form** (e.g., fat reduction and increased lean muscle mass, youthful appearance);

- **Function** (e.g., immunity, strength, vigor, vitality, endurance, longevity);

- **Being** (e.g., physical vitality, mental positivity and focus, emotional expansiveness and energetic flow); and

- **Consciousness** (e.g., higher brain function, greater awareness and cognition, deeper spiritual connection).

- **Environmental Relationship** (e.g., improved perception, adaptability, resilience, harmony, intuition and instinct)

We each possess the potential for living our lives free of fear, disease, starvation, dehydration, drowning, and aging through genetic modification. While scientific skeptics may scoff at such claims, the field of epigenetics and the researchers cited above are providing evidence supporting the great potential of humankind to activate genetic coding and make exponential epigenetic shifts in our physical, mental, emotional and energetic states of being.

Our perception influences our genetic activation and our physical, mental, emotional and energetic states of being. In order to create greater awareness of, and connection to, our potential to perform epigenetic activation to enhance our states of being and promote beneficial gene activation, we can engage in the protocols below. These protocols utilize consciousness and energetic activation to transform our environmental perspective, improve systemic response and influence our genetic coding to improve our physical, mental, emotional and energetic States of Being.

If you have, or believe you have, chronic or acute injuries, disease, instability or pain, consult your healthcare practitioner before doing these protocols.

Somatic Clearing and Activation

Objectives:

- Clearing—Conditions to be cleared include, disease, pain, pressure, tightness, burning, stiffness, inflammation, constriction, resistance, limited range of motion and discomfort as well as abnormal body temperature, sensitivity and vitality levels.

- Activation—Physical States of Being to be activated include improved health and well-being, high systemic functioning (e.g., immune system, digestive system, endocrine system, respiratory system), accelerated ability to heal, achieve desired metabolic, strength, vitality, resilience, flexibility, balance and endurance.

Protocol:

1. Stand with your knees slightly bent and relaxed, buttocks tucked in and pelvis forward so that the line from the neck to coccyx is straight. Close your eyes and inhale slowly and deeply through your nose and then exhale through your

mouth. Notice any pain or pressure in the chest, rib cage, shoulders, back, neck or elsewhere as you breathe. Anywhere you feel discomfort, tightness or pressure, focus your breath on that area, breathe into that area, and move courageously a little bit at a time through the discomfort, tightness or pressure, releasing it with each exhale until it is gone. Take yourself to the edge of your comfort level, so that you are challenged and go a little further and deeper, even if it is a millimeter at a time. However, don't strain or put yourself in pain, be patient with yourself and only move through the existing limitations, extending beyond your comfort zone.

2. Let your chin fall to your chest and take three breaths here. Start slowly circling the neck counter-clockwise in an 8-second count with 4 counts from forward to back and 4 counts from back to forward. Inhale from center to right to back and exhale from back to left to center. Do this 5 times and then reverse the direction for another 5.

3. Relax—breathe slowly and deeply and move the neck slowly to the areas where you experience pain, discomfort, stiffness, pressure or congestion ("Resistance"). Focus your breath on the areas you desire to release bringing in healing light with your inhale and dissolving Resistance with your exhale. If you can, breathe through the Resistance until it is gone. If you experience pain, please be patient with yourself and determine your own threshold to work through. If you can, breathe up to the point of pain and move through the discomfort to extend your range of motion, even if it is a millimeter at a time.

4. While focusing on breath, start doing similar breathing and movement exercises as those described in paragraphs 2 and 3 starting, one at a time, with your jaw, your shoulders, elbows, wrists, hands, fingers, chest, upper back, mid back, low back, abdomen, pelvis, hips, knees, ankles and toes.

5. Now start moving all the parts of your body simultaneously. This may look like ecstatic or modern dance to some. Feel free to shake, jump, stretch and experiment with opening and freeing your body. Feel yourself in space, move around the environment rather than stand in one place. Experience different vertical levels from lying on your belly to crouching to standing normally to

standing on you tip toes and stretching every bit of your body. Do this for at least 5 minutes. Stay focused on breath.

6. During the whole body ecstatic dance motion, consciously focus on bringing abundant, pure white light energy into your body. Feel it coming through your crown chakra and down your spine and radiating into every cell in your body.

7. When your body is completely saturated with white light, become still and go back to the original standing posture with your knees slightly bent and relaxed, buttocks tucked in and pelvis forward so that the line from the neck to coccyx is straight. Close your eyes and inhale and exhale slowly and deeply through your nose.

8. Envision each area of the physical body that you would like to clear, change, strengthen and repair, one at a time. With each area of change, go deep into the cells of your body, into the nucleus, into the DNA circuit board and its genetic coding. Direct the white light energy to the circuit board and allow your body, and inner knowing, to intuitively use their genius to open up new circuits, clear existing circuits and charge them with light energy.

Mental Clearing and Activation

Objectives:

- Clearing—Conditions to be cleared include, constrictive and limiting beliefs, dullness, doubt, stress, distraction, confusion, obsession, psychosis, neurosis and other imbalanced or limited mental states.

- Activation—States of Being to be activated include optimal brain function, mindfulness, presence, awareness, clarity, confidence, high functioning, performance, flow and wisdom.

Protocol:

1. Sit still in lotus position with your eyes closed inhaling and exhaling slowly and deeply through your nose while focusing your breath on your third eye (about a half-inch above the point between the middle of your eyebrows).

2. Impartially observe the thoughts as they arise in your mind. Let them come and go. Just watch your thoughts without judgment or attachment. If you get

sucked into your thoughts, don't punish or reprimand yourself, just relax, let go and engage in observation again. Do this for at least 10 minutes.

3. After at least 10 minutes, observe your thoughts and the way your body and energy level respond to your thoughts. Also, observe the emotions triggered by each thought, and the visual images (e.g., shapes, patterns and colors) associated with each thought.

4. Whenever your thought creates a somatic sensation, emotion or color that contains or triggers Constrictive States of Being, hold your focus on the thought. What is the source of the thought (e.g., belief system, occurrence)? How does the thought change if you change the facts, context, perspective or belief structure upon which the thought is based? What emotions are associated with the thought?

5. Now feel where in your body that thought is associated. (For example, a thought of someone you love might be found in heart, or a thought that creates fear may be felt in the kidneys, or a thought that creates tension may be found in the neck and shoulders). What color and image is held in that part of the body?

6. Breathe into each area where you feel tightness, constriction or resistance and with each inhale, bring in light to expand, heal and open these regions. On each exhale, remove resistance, tightness and constriction from these regions. From what other perspectives can the situation causing the thought or emotions be viewed? What perspective or other thought gives you the greatest feeling of expansiveness and energy?

7. Using intuition and trust, visualize the genetic pathways and activation of codes that will achieve the desired result of transforming, healing and vitalizing the thoughts, emotions, beliefs and conditions causing tightness, constriction, resistance, limitation, discomfort or illness to optimally well states of being.

Emotional Clearing and Activation

Objectives:

- Clearing—Conditions to be cleared include emotions such as non-serving fear, apathy, depression, unworthiness, frustration, insecurity and anger.

- Activation—Emotional states to be activated include love, joy, bliss, enlightenment, happiness and courage.

Protocol:

1. Sit still in lotus position with your eyes closed inhaling and exhaling slowly and deeply through your nose while focusing your breath on your heart chakra. With each breath, let your heart chakra fill with light dissolving all walls, barriers or other obstacles that prevent you from feeling, giving and receiving unconditional love.

2. From the heart chakra radiate energy down the chakra column to the power chakra, the sex chakra and the root chakra. Feel the energy of all the different chakras. Balance the energy so that all the chakras are filled with equal and balanced energy.

3. Now allow the energy of the three lower chakras and the heart chakra to radiate upward into the throat chakra, the third-eye chakra and through the top of your head into the crown chakra and out into the universe. Again, balance all the energies so that all the chakras are fully and optimally energized.

4. Start sobbing for 3 minutes. At first, this might feel forced but go with it. Experiment with your sobbing. Cry tears of sorrow, joy, anger and frustration. If tears come great; if not, that's fine too.

5. Take a minute to feel your energy and your emotional state. Recheck the energy of the chakras and rebalance them.

6. Start cursing. Say every word that your parents and society told you not to say. Get pissed, get angry, tell people off. Get it all out. Jump up and down. Act like a kid having a temper tantrum. Experiment with how many different ways you can use "fuck."

7. Take a minute to feel your energy and your emotional state. Recheck the energy of the chakras and rebalance them.

8. Start laughing for 3 minutes. At first, it may feel unnatural, but go with it. Get into it with some really deep belly laughs. Experiment with your laughter; make it sound silly, sinister, goofy. Have fun. Crack yourself up. Do this for at least 3

minutes. During the three minutes find your humor, your happiness and feel all emotions associated with laughter.

9. Take a minute to feel your energy and your emotional state. Recheck the energy of the chakras and rebalance them.

10. Focus your intention on any sources of limiting or constrictive emotions that may remain and utilize the energy of the aligned chakras to dissolve all the constrictive non-serving emotions held anywhere in your field.

11. Inhale and exhale slowly and deeply through your nose. Envision each emotion that you would like to change, transform or heal one at a time. Go deep into the emotion. Become aware of the conditioning, beliefs and thoughts that trigger the emotion and replace the conditioning, beliefs and thoughts with those that serve desired emotional states feel where in your body the emotion resides. Become aware of the conditioning, beliefs and thoughts that trigger the emotion and replace the conditioning, beliefs and thoughts with those that serve desired emotional states. Feel where the emotion resides in your body. Focus on the cells of your body in that area and direct the breath and energy of the chakras to the genetic circuit board to create the changes you desire.

Energetic Clearing and Activation

Objectives:

- Clearing—Removal of areas in your internal and external energy fields, including those that are restrictive, limiting, blocking, disconnected, slow, shut down, unbalanced, agitated, constricting or immobilizing.

- Activation—Upgrading your energetic system (aka energetic circuit board) to receive and access on-demand, the utmost energy from the field so that abundant, fully and freely flowing energy can be utilized to increase well-being, accelerate manifestation and achieve optimal States of Being.

Protocol:

1. Stand comfortably with your feet about shoulder distance apart. Put a big smile on your face and push out your chest. Start shaking your hands and let the

shaking move into your arms and shoulders, neck and head. While keeping the shaking going, start shaking your feet and allow the shaking to shake your calves and legs and hips. Keep the shaking going in the hands, arms, shoulders, neck, feet, calves, legs and hips and add the torso, including the chest, abdomen and back. Shake your entire body and now include the face, scalp and any other place on the body that has yet to start shaking. Shake every part of your body for at least 3 minutes.

2. After 3 minutes of shaking (or such additional time as you desire), breathe, relax, unwind and come laying down in a place that is comfortable, quiet and relaxed. With your eyes closed, start inhaling and exhaling slowly and deeply through your nose. Allow yourself to relax and enter into observer consciousness.

3. While continuing to focus on your breath, with your eyes closed, scan your energy field in and around your body. Start at your head and move through your body toward your feet. Scan your field to see or feel any places of constriction, resistance or limitation ("Constrictive States of Being"). While each person has their own experience of how the Constrictive States of Being show up in their field, sometimes they show up as dark or red spots in your energy field, or as visualization or feeling of energy being stuck or slow.

4. Inhale pure white light energy through the crown chakra and direct it to any areas where you experience any stuck or slow energy or other Constrictive States of Being. On your inhale, allow the white light to heal, clear and dissolve all constrictions, limitations, restrictions and congestion from your energy field. On your exhale, release and remove any Constrictive and Non-Serving States of Being with gratitude, and give love to yourself and the removed Constrictive and Non-Serving States of Being.

5. Once your field is clear of Constrictive and Non-Serving States of Being, while keeping your eyes closed and continuing your breathwork, set your intention for permanent clearing of Constrictive States of Being. Release your intention to the wisdom of the Creator within yourself to intuitively activate the DNA circuits that will result in your highest States of Being (e.g., abundance, wellness, empowerment, love, joy).

6. With your eyes closed and continuing your deep, relaxed and slow breathing, fill your entire head with white light energy. Do this for at least 1 minute.

7. After 1 minute, allow the white light in your head to slowly move down and through your body from your head, through your neck, torso, buttocks and legs and through your toes. For another 2 minutes, allow the white light energy to flow through your body from your crown chakra at the top of your head to your toes, let it out through your toes. Let the energy grow, expand and radiate from within your body out and around you until your entire body, mind and energy field extends into infinity and is completely bathed and saturated in white light.

8. Let go of all separation between the white light in and around you and dissolve into oneness with infinite white light. Remain in oneness with the white light for at least 10 minutes and just allow the conscious activation and clearing of your energy field to occur, trusting the creative genius of the Creator within you and the white light emanating in and around you, to heal and activate the genetic coding most optimal for your highest experience and expression.

By engaging in the foregoing specific exercises of clearing and activation of your genetic circuitry, you can sufficiently raise your energy levels to activate and connect directly into the highest energetic forces. This allows you to co-creatively re-program your perception of reality, your beliefs and your genetic codes to increase your overall ability to manifest a reality free from the programs of enslavement, limitation, restriction and resistance. This new reality supports you in being the most expansive and powerful creator of your life and experience of the universe.

Utilizing the foregoing process requires a significant commitment of time, discipline and consistency, as well as complete confidence and trust that you can epigenetically transform your life by transforming your consciousness, beliefs, state of being and way you experience and relate to the environment you are perceiving and creating.

Although rapid and significant transformation can happen at the quantum level, if at first, changes seem small and incremental, please know that with regular practice, the results often become exponential. With dedication to the M.E.D.I.C.I.N.E. program, you will notice an improved ability and power to influence, evolve and improve every aspect of your life, especially your States of Being. Once you achieve optimal wellness, the increase in life force, vitality, stamina, endurance and ability to focus will empower you to transform yourself and the world.

SECTION FOUR –

EMPOWERMENT

---

*(The Power to Transform
our World and Live in AWE)*

**We each are the creator of our universe and each have the
power to transform our world to one that is Abundant, Well,
Empowered, Loving and Thriving.**

CHAPTER 20

The Need to Transform
from Dysfunction to Function

(Being a Functional Virus in a Dysfunctional System)

"In order to change an existing paradigm you do not struggle to try and change the problematic model. You create a new model and make the old one obsolete."

~ Buckminster Fuller

Like a functional virus in a dysfunctional system, the proliferation of higher consciousness, loving behavior, regenerative practices and evolved living will eventually render obsolete the dysfunctional symptoms of toxicity, poverty, hunger, war and destruction of our current system.

We have the potential to live in a society that is regenerative, compassionate and perpetually abundant—a society where each person has water, food, energy, and shelter as well as meaningful work contributing to the health and thriving of humankind and our planet. Our world, however, has become plagued with war, pollution, overconsumption, over-extraction, over-population, social injustice, disease, poverty, corruption, climate change and disasters, pandemics and destabilizing destruction of Earth's ecosystems. Most of these challenges are symptoms of a dysfunctional socio-economic-political system ("the Matrix") with high degrees of fear, scarcity, control, divisiveness, extraction and exploitation.

The movie "The Matrix" provides a brilliant quote illustrating the pervasive constructed "reality" of the socio-political-economic system into which we were born:

Morpheus: The Matrix is everywhere. It is all around us. Even now, in this very room. You can see it when you look out your window or when you turn on your television. You can feel it when you go to work. . . when you go to church. . . when you pay your taxes. It is the world that has been pulled over your eyes to blind you from the truth.

Neo: What truth?

Morpheus: That you are a slave, Neo. Like everyone else, you were born into bondage. Into a prison that you cannot taste or see or touch. A prison for your mind."

We each are a living miracle, yet so many people live in servitude and quiet suffering, believing that the purpose of life is to obey authority, conform to society, reproduce, make money, consume, create waste, collect stuff, and die. This is the wool being pulled over our eyes!

We have been led to believe that the society we were born into and the problems we face as a society are somehow normal. Even when we acknowledge the need for change, we attempt to solve our problems with the same tools that created them (e.g., money, chemicals, machines, technology, politics, education and media). There is little attention paid to the fundamental transformation in our beliefs and behaviors required to affect the deep systemic change required. Those that have the power and influence to transform the Matrix are typically loathe to give up power, control and wealth. And the billions of people who have been conditioned to conform to modern societal dysfunction are reluctant to awaken to, and accept responsibility for, their power and potential. So we continue perpetuating a destructive spiral of fear, greed, scarcity, consumption, destruction, pollution and war.

The very survival of humankind and the health of the planet's ecosystems are threatened by the societal dysfunction that consistently elevates the economic imperative (e.g., money and quantitative metrics) over ethical and life-affirming imperatives (e.g., health, love, compassion, happiness, beauty and ecosystemic thriving).

"**Dysfunction**" generally means **impaired, abnormal or unhealthy interpersonal behavior** or **interaction within a group**.[239] Although the interpretation of "dysfunction" is often subjective, there is a groundswell of evidence, discussed in this chapter, supporting the need of humankind to make significant shifts in our dysfunctional, unhealthy, over-consumptive and destructive behaviors.

While this chapter discusses and provides evidence of our society's dysfunction to increase awareness and acceptance of our need to change, the following chapters in the Empowerment Section provide potential transformational solutions and suggestions. These solutions and suggestions will hopefully promote greater awareness leading to empowered action that moves us from dysfunction to function and from function into thriving.

To flourish as a species, there is an urgent need to transform ourselves and our society. The initial stage of transformation requires **awareness and acceptance** that our current state, whether internal or external, requires changes and can be improved. By developing awareness of society's dysfunction and our individual contribution to this dysfunction, we each can accept the need and responsibility for individual change and our contribution to society's transformation.

The second stage of transformation following awareness and acceptance is **vision and belief**. We need to hold a vision for the improvement that is achievable and the belief that we can execute the vision. We then need to **commit** to achieving the vision.

Once we have a clear executable vision, a belief in our abilities to fulfill the vision, and commitment to achieving the vision, **aligned and consistent action** is required to realize and fulfill the vision. As we change individually and consistently devote ourselves to creating a more loving, beautiful abundant, well and empowered world, our world and society change.

With greater awareness, acceptance, vision, belief, commitment and consistent action, I believe we can realize a highly functional and equitable world of love, health, beauty and thriving for humankind and our planet.

As will be discussed below, our socio-political-economic system (sometimes referred to herein as "the Matrix") has been designed, engineered, developed and maintained in a way that has resulted in the disconnection of people from each other and nature, dependence on money, extensive social injustice, economic inequality and destruction of Earth's ecosystems.

We often pretend that the Matrix is functional and that our governments, scientists, financial institutions and corporations will somehow solve the systemic problems plaguing our society without changing ourselves or accepting the challenges of systemic change. Much like big pharma, there is significantly more money in treating symptoms than in cures. Instead of transforming our beliefs and behaviors and healing the causes of social dysfunction, thereby transforming the Matrix itself, we generally focus on treating the symptoms caused by systemic dysfunction. This keeps the Matrix intact while perpetuating ongoing economic incentives for those that provide "treatments."

Real change requires systemic transformation, which means facing our fears and courageously embracing the unknown, insecurity and inconvenience of change and taking action to positively transform our world from the inside-out, ground-up and top-down.

Fear and disconnection from each other and nature are at the root of all social dysfunction. The cure of society's dysfunction is simply to increase our love and connection with each other and our planet and use our resources to support planetary thriving. While the cure is simple, it's not easy and will require great personal, societal and economic change and discipline. Unfortunately, the disconnection from each other and nature's regenerative abundance has increased with our addiction and dependence upon money, machines, chemicals and the centralized supply chain.

By practicing greater connection with, and love for, each other and nature, and embracing the challenges of transformation, we can create "*The Regenerative Economy*" dedicated to the thriving of people and planet. The multi-trillion-dollar Regenerative Economy is likely to be the largest and most robust economy in the history of humankind, and will also promote greater health, wealth, happiness, freedom and abundance for all people (see chapter entitled "*Transforming to a Regenerative Society*").

As a society, we too often take an approach of "fighting against," "warring against," and "eradicating" the symptoms of the current system by attempting to band-aid the symptoms without curing the core systemic causes of the symptoms. While humans may become extinct from natural disasters (e.g., meteorite impact or large scale volcanic eruptions), the odds are low compared to anthropogenic extinction due to such things as climate change, global nuclear annihilation, biological warfare, ecological collapse, advanced artificial intelligence, biotechnology, or self-replicating nanobots.[240]

The systemic change required will likely cause us to experience inconvenience, challenges and even some suffering for a period of possibly 10-20 years. Not immediately embracing systemic change will likely result in the continued increase in hunger, poverty, disease, war, climate change, toxicity and suffering on a mass scale until humankind either goes extinct in as little as 70 years,[241] or experiences a transformational breakthrough or miracle (e.g., free and democratized zero-point energy, a benevolent alien invasion, divine intervention or a mass behavioral transformation).

Although I am an optimist who believes in miracles and breakthroughs, as discussed in detail in this Empowerment section, practical and cost-effective solutions do exist and can be implemented now. Continuing to support and perpetuate a dysfunctional system that destroys life is a waste of human potential, time and resources and will have a massive negative impact on the quality of human life. It's analogous to an oil refinery that consistently dumps petrochemical waste into the river and killing the river's life and ecosystems. Rather than shutting down the oil refinery or preventing the pollutants from entering the river (e.g., cleaning, reusing and/or upcycling the refinery's waste into valuable products), we use other less toxic chemicals and filtering mechanisms to remediate the pollutants from the river and we give the diseased and dying fish and species of the river medicines to combat the effects of the petrochemicals, until all life in the river is destroyed and the river can no longer provide potable water or sustain life. Of course, the oil refinery, the providers of treatment for the fish and the water filtration company all make money. And in our society money is too often elevated over nature, health and beauty.

Like the oil refinery analogy, the solution for the transformation we need is systemic, not treatments of symptoms. Once we transform the core systemic causes of societal dysfunction, the symptoms often vanish, rendering continual remediation and treatment of the symptoms unnecessary.

We have the need and the power to build a society that's healthy, beautiful and ecosystemically thriving—a society born out of love, connection, wellness and abundance. Imagine a society with a Regenerative Economy that fosters ecosystemic and human flourishing based upon devoting our efforts and resources to serve each other and the planet.

The current socio-economic-political Matrix, in which we individually and collectively participate, is unsustainable and often borders on sociopathy. What is commonly referred to as *"Sociopathy"* or *"Psychopathy"* is now officially listed in the Diagnostic and Statistical Manual of Mental Disorders ("DSM") as *"Antisocial Personality Disorder"* and referred to as "ASPD." APSD is characterized by **an abnormal lack of** empathy combined with **strongly** amoral **conduct, reckless disregard for the safety of others**, but masked by an ability to **appear outwardly normal**.[242]

While there are many things about our society that function efficiently and reliably, there is significant societal dysfunction jeopardizing the health, well-being and survival of humankind. There are a plethora of examples evidencing **strongly amoral and unhealthy interpersonal behaviors or interactions** (e.g., war, destruction, toxicity, suffering, poverty) **within a group** (e.g., humankind, government, corporations) that **demonstrate a high degree of dysfunction and lack of empathy**, but **appear outwardly normal**. Here are just a few examples:

- Human activities are responsible for almost all of the increase in greenhouse gases in the atmosphere over the last 150 years. In 2017, human activities were responsible for releasing 6,457,000,000 metric tons of greenhouse gases in the atmosphere, according to estimates published by the EPA.[243] Of this total, 76%, was due to CO2 emissions largely from the combustion of fossil fuels.[244]

- Fossil fuel drilling, shipping, refining and burning has caused massive destruction and toxicity to the environment of the planet and health of humankind (e.g., Exxon Valdez, BP Gulf Oil Spill). The $3.2 trillion oil industry transports about 53 million barrels per day worldwide, most of which is used to support an appetite for the manufacturing, storage, trans-portation and selling of stuff we don't need that ends up in the landfill.[245] 97% of the scientific community supports that human activity is a major factor in climate change, according to NASA.[246] Yet a significant number of people deny or ignore climate change. Whether or not you believe climate change is a result of human activities, such as burning fossil fuels for energy to manufacture, transport, store and "dispose of " massive amounts of stuff, there is practically unanimous agreement that we have air pollution, water pollution, overconsumption and are becoming overrun with waste, all of which are having a negative impact on our health and the biosphere's ability to sustain life.

- Over $29 trillion has been spent in the global economic bailout from the 2008 financial crisis, according to Levy Economics Institute of Baird College. That's $83,000 for every American. For this amount of money and human energy, we could have created a wholly new renewal energy smart grid, upgraded our water infrastructure, improved and provided free healthcare and education, advanced new modes of transportation, provided the "bottom of the pyramid" with ongoing water, food, and sanitation, replanted and preserved forests, repopulated the oceans, and created a new thriving regenerative economy. Instead we used this massive amount of money to perpetuate a dysfunctional system with hand-outs, pork-barrel giveaways and large bonuses to the bankers that created the problem.[247]

- Total global defense spending for 2019 was $1.917 trillion overtaking the previous records including the post-Cold War spending of $1.63 trillion seen in 2010.[248] Over the last 5 1/2 decades, the U.S. spent $5.8 trillion on production of nuclear explosives and an additional $13.2 trillion on other defense spending, according to the Brookings Institution.[249] Over $1.6 trillion has been spent on the Iraqi Afghan wars, with a total price tag of $6 trillion, including ancillary costs and interest.[250]

- 5 billion people out of 7 billion live on $10/day or less, with 3 billion of the 5 billion living on $2.50 a day or less. About 80% of humanity lives in or near poverty and 8 of the wealthiest people control more resources than 3.6 billion of the poorest people. [251]

- Nearly half of the world's species of plants, animals and microorganisms will be destroyed or severely threatened over the next quarter-century due to rainforest deforestation. That equates to 50,000 species a year according to Save the Amazon Coalition.[252]

- According to the U.S. Bureau of Justice Statistics (BJS), over 6.9 million people in the U.S. were under supervision of the adult correctional system (e.g. in prison, in jail, on probation, or on parole). That's roughly 2.9% of all U.S. adult residents or 1 in every 35 adults.[253] On average, it costs $20,000 per year to maintain one prisoner, $100,000 to build a single prison cell, and $20,000 per year to staff one prison cell. We seem to be able to build and staff new prisons, but not to build and staff new schools or transform education, as there are more prisoners in the U.S. than there are teachers. In 2012, there were some 1,570,000 inmates in state and federal prisons in the U.S. By contrast, there were about 1,530,000 engineers in America last year, 815,000 construction workers, and one million high school teachers, according to the Bureau of Labor Statistics.[254]

- The U.S. education system, which has been a major influence on global education, is broken and OECD ranked the U.S. 29 out of 76.[255]

- In the U.S. the healthcare system is the third largest cause of the death and the number one cause of bankruptcy. It is the most expensive healthcare in the world and yet, according to the World Health Organization ranking, the health ranking of the U.S. is 37 under Costa Rica and above Slovenia.[256]

Here is a small sampling showing how our society prioritizes the spending of its money and resources:

Products	Annual Global Spending (USD)	Global Social or Economic Goal	Annual Investment Required (USD)
Military	$1.9 trillion[257]	Ending World Hunger	$44 billion[258]
Gambling	$565 billion[259]	Drinking Water	$6 billion[260]
Cosmetics & Personal Care	$382 billion[261]	Sanitation	$23 billion[262]
Pet Products	$94 billion[263]	Reproductive Health & Planning	$8 billion[264]
Chewing Gum	$23 billion[265]	Self Help Housing	$21 billion[266]
Jewelry	$316 billion[267]	Sustainable Energy Systems	$17 billion[268]
Total	**$3.281 trillion**		**$119 billion**

As a society, we can come up with trillions of dollars for war, unnecessary consumable products and bailing out financial institutions, but can't seem to provide $6 billion a year for healthy drinking water and $23 billion for sanitization to save the lives of the millions of people, including more than 800,000 children, that die each year from lack of potable water and sanitization.[269] We also seem to have little awareness or concern for the devasting effects of overconsumption and industrialization, not to mention the way we prioritize our spending.

When the foregoing examples are compared to the definitions of sociopathy and dysfunction above, it is clear that many of the practices and activities of humans in modern society accepted as "normal" are actually sociopathic and dysfunctional.

Still some might argue that because the human population is still growing, our society is *biologically functional*. This view completely ignores that the carrying capacity of our planet was surpassed in 1979 as supported by the findings of WWF's 2014 Living Planet Report,[270] which states as follows:

"Population sizes of vertebrate species—mammals, birds, reptiles, amphibians, and fish—have declined by 52 percent over the last 40 years. In other words, those populations around the globe have dropped by more than half in fewer than two human generations.

At the same time, our own demands on nature are unsustainable and increasing. We need 1.5 Earths to regenerate the natural resources we currently use; we cut trees faster than they mature, harvest more fish than oceans replenish, and emit more carbon into the atmosphere than forests and oceans can absorb."

The foregoing facts support that our society is not biologically functional, however some would still argue that our society is *ecologically functional*. Those making this argument assert that humans can still breathe the air and drink the water as is; that human activities have only minimal impact on our ecosystems; that burning coal and oil don't cause significant levels of pollution or damage our atmosphere; and that dumping petrochemicals into our rivers and oceans doesn't cause significant damage to these ecosystems. These arguments border on absurdity, especially when there is a 97% consensus in the scientific community that human industrialization is a major factor contributing to climate change.[271] Moreover, diseases such as cancer, respiratory infections, stroke, Alzheimer's, autism, heart disease and liver disorders are linked to chemical toxins and pollution in our air, water and food.

For the wealthiest 10% of humankind, it could be argued that society is *economically functional*. These people have a standard of living most of the world's population has never known. They have a full belly, a roof over their head, travel frequently, have many possessions and their credit cards work at the terminal. Yet, despite their material wealth, many of these people are unhappy and/or suffer from depression, have serious health issues, dysfunctional families, are on anti-depressants and engage in unfulfilling, exploitative, extractive work destructive to people and planet.

The argument for economic functionality further ignores the massive inequitable distribution of resources that allows **8 of the wealthiest individuals to control more resources than 3.5 billion of the poorest individuals.**[272] Thus, our society is not economically functional, especially when such a large percentage of the money and resources we spend goes toward destroying the environment and natural resources that provide for the sustenance of our lives and our economy.

Each person is a time bomb set to random. At some point, each of us will die and we don't know when. Based on evolutionary science showing that 99% of the species that have existed on planet Earth in its 4.5 billion years are extinct, it is highly likely that the human species will also become extinct. With this said, it's my hope we don't accelerate our extinction as a result of our arrogant, dysfunctional and sociopathic behavior. I am optimistic that we, as a society and a species, can acknowledge and transform from systemic dysfunction to thriving. To achieve this vision for a thriving world, it is important that we understand how our modern society and our conditioned beliefs came to be.

The current socio-economic-political regime, into which we were born, has largely been designed, influenced and controlled by corporations and other fictitious non-living legal entities. These entities don't breathe air, drink water, eat food, appreciate beauty and fall in love. The central banking system and multi-national corporations have been the largest influence on the design and building of our cities, the regulatory environment, government, finance, education and media. Because non-living entities have significantly influenced our world (e.g., laws, institutions, beliefs, behaviors and environment), our society largely serves the interests of "the non-living," thus causing destruction to humankind and living systems.

The blood that runs through the veins of corporations is money and their health and survival is dependent upon profits. This is why our economic vote and how we spend our money is so influential. If we stop buying the products and services of a corporation, its power and influence is diminished.

Conspiracy theories abound implicating the Bank of International Settlements, the central banking system, the large banking corporations (e.g., Bank of America, Citibank, Goldman Sachs Bank, JP Morgan Chase, Wells Fargo, Morgan Stanley) and the most wealthy and powerful persons in that last 200 years (e.g., Rothschilds,

Rockefellers, Warburgs, Morgans, Lazards, Schiffs, Loebs, Kuhns and Stillmans) in creating a global matrix. These power elite are often viewed as being above the law and controlling governments, banks, corporations, the military, construction, materials, energy, health care, manufacturing, transportation, media and the legal system, as well as access to the commons (e.g., land, water and food).[273] There are numerous conspiracy theories that provide versions of how our society was architected to control the masses and require reliance on fossil fuels, the centralized supply chain and the central banking system's fiat money.

Renowned historian and author, Niall Ferguson, in his book The Square and Tower, had this to say about such conspiracy theories[274]:

> "A fairly representative screed (the genre is enormous) describes the Illuminati as a 'super-rich Power Elite with an ambition to create a slave society': The Illuminati own all the International banks, the oil-businesses, the most powerful businesses of industry and trade, they infiltrate politics and education and they own most governments — or at the very least control them. They even own Hollywood and the Music Industry . . . [T]he Illuminati run the drug trade industry as well . . . The leading candidates for Presidency are carefully chosen from the occult bloodlines of the thirteen Illuminati families . . . The main goal is to create a One World Government, with them on top to rule the world into slavery and dictatorship . . . They want to create an 'outside threat,' a fake Alien Invasion, so that the countries of this world will be willing to unite as ONE. The standard version of the conspiracy theory links the Illuminati to the Rothschild family, the Round Table, the Bilderberg Group and the Trilateral Commission—not forgetting the hedge fund manager, political donor and philanthropist George Soros."

In his book Superclass, David Rothkopf, a former managing director of Kissinger Associates and an international trade official in the Clinton Administration, has identified about 6,000 individuals who have "the ability to regularly influence the lives of millions of people in multiple countries worldwide." They are the "superclass" of the 21st century, Rothkopf argues, spreading across borders in an ever-thickening web, with a growing allegiance, to each other rather than to any particular nation.[275]

While the foregoing conspiracy theories may seem far-fetched to some, according to Ferguson, conspiracy theories, such as the foregoing, are believed by a majority of Americans:

> "Such theories are believed, or at least taken seriously, by a remarkably large number of people. Just over half (51 per cent) of 1,000 Americans surveyed in 2011 agreed with the statement that 'Much of what happens in the world today is decided by a small and secretive group of individuals.' Fully a quarter of a larger sample of 1,935 Americans agreed that 'The current financial crisis was secretly orchestrated by a small group of Wall Street bankers to extend the power of the Federal Reserve and further their control of the world's economy.'"

For a narrative to be believed by a majority of a given population, there is generally some seed of truth in the narrative. While the conspiracy theories about large corporations, central banking and government may often be exaggerated and lack documentary support, history is replete with examples of powerful, wealthy, and influential people including monarchs, government leaders, religious leaders, corporate executives, bankers, revolutionaries, industrialists, organized crime bosses, inventors, artists, composers, visionaries, and philanthropists, ("Influencers") shaping our society. Some of the Influencers throughout history were benevolent, some corrupt and others sociopathic. Throughout history, it has been typical for Influencers to engage in discussions, make plans, combine forces, socialize, and do business, with others of power, wealth and influence. These discussions, plans and combinations often involved such things as the expansion of wealth, power and control and/or making benevolent contributions to society.

Many of these Influencers built large corporations, financial institutions and sometimes monopolistic empires. Some influenced and/or infiltrated governments, bribed government officials, sponsored regulations favorable to their interests, and fomented corruption, war, debt, pollution, damage to our environment, and social and economic injustice to serve their interests for power, control and profits. Other Influencers formed non-profits and organizations to benefit humankind and nature and created inventions to improve the quality of life for humankind. Some Influencers did both.

Whether for good, evil, benevolence or greed, the Influencers have been responsible for leading advances and paradigm shifts in modern society including, electricity; fossil fuels; automobiles; airplanes; modern agriculture; computers; new medical and scientific discoveries; centralized supply chain; modern architecture; globally exchanged currencies; the civil rights and environmental movements; and advancement of the arts. Some of these modern advances have been wondrous, while others have caused significant damage to humankind and our environment, and others have the potential to render humankind extinct. Meetings, discussions, agendas and events to shape the world actually happened throughout history and continue to happen. The World Economic Forum, Council of Foreign Relations, The Bilderberg Meeting are just a few examples of organizations that convene Influencers to discuss and shape important global, regional and industry agendas. Many of these groups seek to solve problems and accomplish "good" in the world. Because Influencers are human and "good" is subjective, Influencers often seek to benefit both themselves and the organizations they represent.

Rather than attempting to prove or disprove the veracity of conspiracy theories, our attention is better spent on (1) increasing mass awareness that our current socio-economic-political system is dysfunctional and is damaging to, the health, thriving and abundance of humankind and Earth's ecosystems, and (2) actively devoting action and resources for systemic transformation to create a world that serves the flourishing of people and the planet.

The need for systemic transformation is urgent and requires change from the inside-out (individually), ground-up (collectively with each other and the planet) and top-down (industry, financial, NGO, IGO and government leaders). Our transformation starts with understanding the forces that perpetuate the systemic dysfunction discussed in this chapter, including our *disconnection from nature, dependence upon money, our conditioning and education,* and *the corruption of government*. With this understanding, and as will be discussed in the following chapters, we can take the necessary action to shift individual and collective beliefs and behaviors to create functional systems that support the thriving of humankind and the planet.

DISCONNECTION FROM NATURE AND THE "NEED" FOR MONEY

For the last 300 years, humankind has become increasingly disconnected from nature, the commons (e.g., our sources of food, water and materials) and each other. Whether or not modern society, our education system and our cities were intentionally designed to do so, most people in modern society have lost their ability to survive in nature and have become almost completely dependent upon money to meet basic needs for such things as water, food, energy and housing.

In this way, money's importance in our lives has become elevated to a perceived "need" rather than merely a tool of convenient exchange. **Truly, we are the only species on this planet that believes we need money to survive, yet we survived 200,000 years without money.**

As a species, we have caused great destruction to the true wealth we have been gifted—the regenerative abundance of our planet that provides for all we need to live and flourish (e.g., our next breath, water, food, energy, materials). Without our planet and its gifts, we would have no life and no economy. Sadly, we, as a society, have taken for granted the amazing gifts Mother Earth bestows upon us and in return, have raped, pillaged and caused destruction to her and her ability to continue to provide regenerative abundance to us.

By systematically (1) privatizing and controlling necessities (e.g., water, food, energy, materials, construction, medicine, manufacturing), (2) diminishing our ability to access and live in nature, and (3) eliminating from our education any knowledge or skills that would allow us to survive outside of the money matrix, most of modern society has become completely reliant on money and the centralized supply chain. As well, we have been conditioned to believe our personal value is derived from consumption and accumulation of unnecessary possessions, resulting in compulsive purchases that typically yield only fleeting fulfillment and often end up in the waste stream.

Industrialized educational programming has not taught natural survival skills, such as hunting, gathering, farming, home building, cooking and collaboration. In the roughly 200,000 years that Homo sapiens have existed on the planet, we've relied on money for a little over an estimated 6,000 years. Yet, we have been convinced we "need" money to survive. Most of us in modern society have lost our innate skills to survive in nature, resulting in the conditioned "need" to hunt for a job and gather money. The trend of urbanization and technology has resulted in an ever-accelerating disconnection from nature and each other. A preponderance of the jobs, to which humans devote their efforts. are destructive, extractive, exploitive and unfulfilling.[276] Too many of us toil away until we die (or are lucky enough to retire), believing the lie that the key to our happiness, fulfillment and success is working a job, making money, overconsumption and the accumulation of possessions.

Michael J. Cohen, Ph.D., ecopsychologist, author and Director of the Institute of Global Education, writes, *"On average, society conditions us to spend over 95% of our time and 99.9% of our thinking disconnected from nature. Nature's extreme absence in our lives leaves us abandoned and wanting. We feel we never have enough. We greedily, destructively, consume and, can't stop. Nature's loss in our psyche produces a hurt, hungering, void within us that bullies us into our dilemmas."* Nature is a living entity full of grace, beauty and regenerative abundance. Nature gives us everything from our breath, to water, food, energy and materials. On the other hand, money is just a symbol of stored energy that has an agreed value to allow non-parity exchange to occur conveniently and objectively.

Although we can get creative and find ways to exchange value and live without money, (e.g., barter, exchange cooperatives, community currencies), money appears to be much more convenient. We've become so addicted to the convenience of money that many of us have actually developed a fear of inconvenience, (e.g., pulled over for a ticket, our mobile phone getting lost, our computer crashing, being late for work, hitting traffic, leaving our wallet at home, a bounced check, our credit score). Many of us have also been conditioned to fear not looking good, such as fear of not having the latest designer clothes, or the latest Apple iPhone, or a new car. None of these things are life-threatening, yet we elevate the fear of inconvenience and the fear of not looking good to levels of anxiety that often cause us to contract into "fight or flight." This activates our sympathetic nervous system, setting up a somatic-cognitive feedback loop of stress, fear and unease, often leading to dis-ease. It's the idea that money provides convenience coupled with the fear of inconvenience, fear of not looking good, disconnection from nature and dependence on money that makes us so easy to manipulate. Despite our desire for convenience, many of us spend most of our lives inconveniencing ourselves on freeways driving to and from jobs we dislike and spending 40-50 hours a week in these jobs. Talk about a serious inconvenience and extraction of human time and resources.

ENGINEERING SOCIETY & CONDITIONING THE MASSES

As a society, we have largely been conditioned to believe that "success" is quantitative rather than qualitative. Accumulation of money and physical possessions and the generation of short-term profits have often been elevated over personal and planetary health, love, connection, happiness, beauty and our ability to flourish as a species. So many humans have been induced into a mass hypnosis of indentured servitude to spend a significant portion of their waking hours working unfulfilling jobs to earn fiat money (which derives its value from debt and scarcity) to buy perceived "necessities" and attempt to elude the fears of inconvenience, not looking good, loneliness and disconnection. But why?

Fear and disconnection from each other and nature was accomplished by psychologically disconnecting humanity from nature, farms and interdependent self-sustaining communities to create dependence upon a centralized supply chain and economic system requiring money to meet basic needs for such things as water, food and shelter. Moreover, war, mass consumerism and an expanding population willing to be exploited was required in order for corporations and central banks to expand their control, influence and demand for debt-based fiat money. In order to condition and control the masses to fulfill the agenda of industrialization and expansion, psychology became the secret weapon of corporations, governments and the central banking system.

According to Philip Cushman, Ph.D., author of *Constructing The Self, Constructing America: A Cultural History of Psychotherapy,*

> *"Because psychotherapy denied the central influence of history and culture, symptoms reflecting the frame of reference of the modern Western world—such as loneliness and alienation, extreme competitiveness, and a desire for nonessential commodities—had to be considered natural and unavoidable. As a result, individuals have been constructed to strive tirelessly to consume and expand, and at the same time to believe that the search is simply an aspect of human nature."[277]*

Predicated on the promise of government and corporations as the road to safety, security and comfort and money as the means to achieve freedom and happiness, capitalism has become the most adopted financial and industrial value of the world. As American culture and other countries influenced by the "American Dream" began to see wishes as needs, the promise of salvation and freedom through money and consumption, known as the "consumer movement," was developed by creating the "empty self." Cushman wrote:

> "The empty self is a way of being human; it is characterized by a pervasive sense of personal emptiness and is committed to the values of self-liberation through consumption. The empty self is the perfect complement to an economy that must stave off economic stagnation by arranging for the continual purchase and consumption of surplus goods."[278]

> "Strategically the corporations infiltrated the collective psyche like "ghosts" with the idea of remaining invisible to make consumers believe the feeling of lack originated internally rather than externally from an outside entity."[279]

Some might defend the functionality and nobility of the current socio-economic-political system by discounting my discourse as "conspiracy theory." However, conditioning the masses to self-impose and enforce the beliefs and behavioral limitations on themselves and future generations is part of the brilliance of mass conditioning. One example supporting that our society has been intentionally engineered and the minds of the masses conditioned by a few very powerful men, comes from Edward Bernays.

Edward Bernays, often referred to as "*the father of public relations*," combined the ideas of Gustave Le Bon and Wilfred Trotter on crowd psychology with the psychoanalytical ideas of his uncle, Sigmund Freud. Bernays worked with the Wilson Administration and the Committee on Public Information to utilize propaganda to create support for World War 1. Bernays was so successful in gaining support for the war, that he utilized propaganda techniques from World War I to influence consumer behavior and promote a culture of consumerism. He felt this manipulation was necessary for society, which he regarded as irrational and dangerous as a result of the "herd instinct" described by Trotter. In his book *Propaganda*, Bernays openly communicates the engineering of our beliefs and society:

*"The conscious and intelligent manipulation of the organized habits and opinions of the masses is an important element in democratic society. Those who manipulate this unseen mechanism of society constitute an invisible government which is the true ruling power of our country. ...**We are governed, our minds are molded, our tastes formed, our ideas suggested, largely by men we have never heard of.** This is a logical result of the way in which our democratic society is organized. Vast numbers of human beings must cooperate in this manner if they are to live together as a smoothly functioning society. ...**In almost every act of our daily lives, whether in the sphere of politics or business, in our social conduct or our ethical thinking, we are dominated by the relatively small number of persons... who understand the mental processes and social patterns of the masses. It is they who pull the wires which control the public mind.**"*

It's ironic that most people have never heard of Edward Bernays or even consider where their beliefs, feelings and perceptions came from. We are taught what to believe, who to like, who to trust, what is beautiful, what tastes good, what smells good, what to buy, often "by men we have never heard of." We're further implanted with limiting beliefs based upon authoritative opinions, laws and codes of appropriate behavior, as promulgated by "experts" and "authorities" (e.g., scientists, economists, journalists, government officials, doctors, teachers, lawyers and psychologists). These so-called "experts" and "authorities" utilize their authority to dictate many of our thoughts, beliefs and behaviors. The irony is that many of the experts are also indoctrinated to believe that their conditioned beliefs, behaviors and proclamations are somehow independent, ethical and beneficial for humankind, even though they merely support an agenda to perpetuate social dysfunction.

For centuries, rulers, governments, and their puppets in education, media, science and mental health, have conditioned the masses to be largely dependent on government for "safety and security" and corporations for our economic sustenance (aka jobs), goods and services. We have been subjected to conditioning designed to atrophy brilliance, inhibit our individuality, and limit freedom of thought, empowered choice, collaboration, creativity, and our ability to be sustained by the regenerative abundance of Mother Earth. Often when an individual questions or rejects the conditioned paradigm, their labeled as "whack jobs" or "conspiracy theorists."

However, if we just open our eyes and our minds to (1) observe the destruction to humankind and our planet resulting from industrialized society and overconsumption, and (2) follow the money and power trail to see who is benefiting from this destruction, the more clearly we see how real (not a theory), pragmatic (not whacky) and urgent our need is for systemic transformation.

The Matrix supposedly created to "serve and protect" our interests of liberty, freedom, welfare and happiness has failed to do so. Instead of the Matrix serving us, we are now the servants of the Matrix. It's now becoming obvious that the Matrix is dysfunctional and unsustainable and is fostering the destruction of humankind and the planet. The consolidation and control of resources in combination with the military-industrial complex and the mastery of crowd control, has created a prison for humankind. We are pawns in a game we often don't know we are playing.

The foregoing examples of conditioning, manipulation and power aren't provided to create fear or promote a "victim" mentality, but rather to provide awareness, so we take conscious and responsible action toward empowered choice to free ourselves from the yoke of conditioned servitude. There is strength in numbers and unity. It's time for we, the people, to take back our rights to a life of abundance, wellness and empowerment and live in a world of beauty, love, trust, joy and freedom.

CORRUPTION[280]

Our society is infested with corrupt governments and political systems, enforcement agencies, judicial systems, regulatory agencies, healthcare systems, education systems, military contractors, financial institutions and corporations, to name a few. Corruption is a leading cause of social dysfunction.

Transparency International defines "corruption" as *"the abuse of entrusted power for private gain."* The four main categories of corruption are (1) political, (2) economic, (3) social, and (4) environmental. According to Wikipedia, *"Corruption" is a form of dishonesty or criminal offense undertaken by a person or organization entrusted with a position of authority, to acquire illicit benefit or abuse power for one's private gain."*

Despite the belief that corruption is illegal, many forms of corruption are actually considered legal. World Bank economist, Daniel Kaufmann, expanded the definition of corruption to include "legal corruption" as the abuse of power within the confines of the law.[281] Those empowered to make laws, often make laws that give the lawmakers and/or their collaborators legal benefits and advantageous protections. According to Kaufmann, *"it is increasingly widely accepted that corruption may arise through other less obvious forms, which may involve collusion between parties typically both from the public and private sectors, and may be legal in many countries. Legal lobbying contributions by the private sector in exchange of passage of particular legislation—biased in favor of those agents—or allocation of procurement contracts may be regarded as examples of interaction of both private and public sector representatives where the second makes use of her publicly invested power at the expense of broader public welfare."*

Corruption can range from small favors to outright bribery and extortion on a grand scale. We tend to believe stories about organized crime infiltrating government and utilizing bribery, extortion, blackmail and violence, but when the corruption of government, corporations and highly influential individuals is discussed, the conditioned "conspiracy theory" arguments are utilized to hide the corruption and perpetuate a system that benefits those that engage in corruption.

Theoretically, governments are created as organizing systems to serve the best interests, health, welfare and security of the people, as well as to administer the agreements, rights and obligations of the people to one another and society at large. For example, the Preamble of the Constitution of the United States, articulates that the federal government was established for six specific purposes:

> *"We the People of the United States, in Order to form a more perfect Union, establish Justice, insure domestic Tranquility, provide for the common defense, promote the general Welfare, and secure the Blessings of Liberty to ourselves and our Posterity, do ordain and establish this Constitution for the United States of America."*

In most instances, we, the people, have delegated trust and decision-making authority to our governments based upon government charters and oaths of elected officials to provide for our health, security, justice, tranquility and welfare. It is clear that most governments in the world, however, have been hijacked and corrupted by corporate and financial interests that manipulate politicians with money, power, influence and favors, and sometimes blackmail in order to promote their agendas for profit, power and control.[282] The result of this corruption is that our politicians and governments often act adversely to our health, security, justice, tranquility and welfare. The irony is we, the people, now serve the interests of governments, corporations and central banks, when these organizations were supposed to serve our best interests.

The regulatory regime to which we are subject is now largely manipulated and shaped by corporations and special interest groups with deep pockets (e.g., pharmaceuticals, oil, agriculture, defense, banking, insurance) who utilize high paid influential lobbying firms to help them pass advantageous legislation and obtain favors from politicians. While lobbying is constitutionally protected as free speech under the First Amendment, it is also highly controversial and is often described as a legal form of bribery and extortion, because it gives those with the deepest pockets the ability to manipulate federal, state and local lawmaking. Analyst, James A. Thurber, estimates that the lobbying industry brings in $9 billion annually.[283]

On the topic of corruption, dysfunction, death and destruction, war is at the top of the heap. War is expensive and often requires governments to take on massive debt,[284] so the numerous expenses, transactions and multi-million dollar rounding errors often go unnoticed. War has historically been good for corporations, governments and central banks, but highly destructive to humankind and the planet. War makes a lot of people rich. Thus, the business of war is fraught with corruption including externalizing the expenses of industry on the backs of taxpayers, favoritism in awarding government contracts, kickbacks, political favors and revolving door paybacks.[285] War has been, and continues to be, very profitable for the largest corporations in the world that sell massive amounts of weapons, ammunition, transportation, food, oil and fuels, medical supplies, technologies, and engineering services to the military-industrial-congressional complex.[286] Many corporations also benefit from the "spoils of war" being given the opportunity to buy strategic assets at pennies on a dollar and then get paid for rebuilding the destruction caused by war with materials, engineering, procurement and construction contracts. To rationalize and gain public support for the massive borrowing required for war, a tactic used by governments is to stage "false flag" operations. These false flag operations are designed to appear as if they're carried out by a country's enemies, when in fact they're started by the country seemingly being attacked. False flag operations are generally used to start a war or conflicts, pass emergency regulations, and allow the central bank and corporations to benefit from expenditures associated with war. Here are a few examples of false flag operations:[287]

- The Reichstag Fire of February 27, 1933 has been attributed to the government of the newly elected Adolf Hitler by documents obtained by the Allies after the war and testimony of the Nuremberg Trials. The fire was used to pass an emergency decree to counter the "ruthless confrontation of the Communist Party of Germany." With civil liberties suspended, the Nazi government instituted mass arrests of Communists, thus allowing Hitler to win the election and consolidate his power.[288]

- The mysterious explosion on the USS Maine in 1898 was not the result of Spanish sabotage but was used by the US government and media as a pretext for the Spanish-American War.[289]

- In the Gleiwitz incident in August 1939, evidence of a Polish attack against Germany was fabricated to mobilize German public opinion and to create a false justification for a war with Poland. This, along with other false flag operations in Operation Himmler would be used to mobilize support from the German population for the start of World War II in Europe. [290]

- In 1953, the U.S. and British-orchestrated "Operation Ajax" used false-flag operations and propaganda to overthrow Mohammed Mosaddeq, the democratically elected leader of Iran, due to his nationalization of British owned Anglo-Iranian Oil Company. The crushing of Iran's first democratically elected government launched 25 years of dictatorship under Mohammad-Rezā Shāh Pahlavi, who relied heavily on U.S. trained secret police SAVAK (described as Iran's "most hated and feared institution" because of its practice of torturing and executing opponents of the Pahlavi regime) and U.S. supplied weapons to hold on to power until he was overthrown in February 1979.[291]

- The 1964 Gulf of Tonkin Incident was a false flag operation conducted by the US Navy to justify the war in Vietnam. On August 2, 1964, the destroyer USS Maddox, while performing a signals intelligence patrol as part of DESOTO operations, was monitored by three North Vietnamese Navy torpedo boats of the 135th Torpedo Squadron. Maddox initiated the incident by firing three "warning" shots, and the North Vietnamese boats replied with torpedoes and machine gun fire. A second Gulf of Tonkin incident occurred on August 4, 1964, which the NSA reported as another sea battle. However, evidence was found that there were no actual North Vietnamese torpedo boats involved. The outcome of these two incidents was the passage by Congress of the Gulf of Tonkin Resolution, which granted US President Lyndon B. Johnson the authority to assist any Southeast Asian country whose government was considered to be jeopardized by "communist aggression." The resolution served as Johnson's legal justification for deploying U.S. conventional forces and the commencement of open warfare against North Vietnam.[292]

- Although still a highly controversial topic due to numerous conspiracy theories and contradicting evidence, the truth of which still remain shrouded by government cover-ups and harsh ridicule of those who dare to question that narrative, there is evidence suggesting that the 9/11 attacks on the world trade center and pentagon may have been false flag operations.[293] Like so many other false flag operations, 9/11 provided justification for war. [294] There is evidence to support, the reason for attacking Afghanistan was to create a military presence in Afghanistan, to secure and protect the TAPI pipeline (aka Turkmenistan-Afghanistan-Pakistan-India Pipeline) and obtain and secure the vast mineral and natural gas resources of Afghanistan[295], not to mention, an excuse to justify a "Homeland Security" agenda to erode the Bill of Rights,[296] specifically the Writ of Habeas Corpus and the expenditure of $5.9 trillion dollars on the wars in Afghanistan, Pakistan, and Iraq.[297]

As a society, we have traded our power, abundance, self-sufficiency, natural resources, freedom and well-being for an agenda of domination, war, scarcity, control and an endless spiral of national and individual debt.

The control, influence and power of corporations and central banking interests over government is based upon our reliance of the central bank's fiat money and the purchase of goods and services from corporations. The mindful use of money and our conscious participation in (or withdrawal from) the scarcity-based fiat money system is where we hold power. Think about it, if we all stopped driving or shopping for a month what would happen? Would that get the attention of government, corporations and the central banks?

We currently have the choice as to how we consume, where we deposit our money, how we spend our energy, where we work, who we buy goods and services from, and what we think and believe. We also have the power to decide to withdraw our economic and energetic support from the corruption and manipulation that leads to our enslavement and the destruction of people and planet. We possess the power to build a new paradigm that renders the existing system obsolete. However, our power, rights and choices are rapidly being eroded. "Terrorism" is used as an excuse to impose more restrictive laws, "secure" borders and ports to control the freedom of travel, and erode constitutional rights and freedoms.

Moreover, the COVID-19 pandemic has already been used to support erosion of rights and liberties and could be used a rationale for mandatory vaccines and microchipping. This is just the beginning of what might lead to an "economic police state" based upon a mandatory electronic currency, tracking and surveillance system that only gives those with microchip implants and full compliance with systemic directives access to money and privileges. While complete government and corporate control over our lives, rights, privileges and freedoms is a dystopian nightmare, for those in power who desire complete power, control and dominance, this represents the fulfillment of their dreams and desires. And the companies that provide the vaccines; the microchip technology; the tracking, monitoring and control technologies; digital ID, record verification and currency systems; surveillance technologies; computers; data technologies and centers; and weapons of enforcement stand to make a fortune.

While there is the potential for an economic police state and a world of dystopian fascism, there is also the potential to create a highly functioning and thriving world of abundance, wellness and empowerment.

TRANSFORMING FROM DYSFUNCTION TO FUNCTION—
(BEING A FUNCTIONAL VIRUS IN A DYSFUNCTIONAL SYSTEM)

Ultimately, we, collectively and individually, have the responsibility and power to change our world. Through our continued participation in and support of the current system, we continue to perpetuate a dysfunctional society. Fortunately, an increasing number of people are waking up and acknowledging that the system is broken; that change is required if we are to survive as a species; and that each of us holds the power of transformation to create thriving world.

Each time any of us experiences disempowering or limiting beliefs, we incrementally create greater disempowerment and limitation for all beings on the planet and even the universe. When we hate the enemy, we create more hate. When we wage war against terror, we create more war and terror. When we are controlled by fear, scarcity, disconnection, hatred and anger, we experience and perpetuate the very things we are trying to transform.

"Darkness cannot drive out darkness; only light can do that. Hate cannot drive out hate; only love can do that." ~ Martin Luther King, Jr.

By consciously shifting our attention to experience and express empowering beliefs and emotions that serve us (e.g., love, respect, trust, empowerment, gratitude, and generosity), we're able to raise our States of Being and increase our power of manifestation. When we do this, we influence those around us and the collective Global Human Agreement to create a new and empowered world.

I advocate that humankind is capable of creating a much more loving, thriving, healthy and beautiful world—a world of AWE. Much like using the energy from polluting coal fire plants to manufacture solar panels, we each can utilize the resources of the existing system to transform it from dysfunction to function and from function to thriving. We can and will see massive positive shifts in our economy, society, political systems and biosphere when we each consistently commit to doing the following **5 daily practices**:

1. Consistently loving, accepting, serving and respecting ourselves, each other and our planet;

2. Use our economic vote and power to purchase ethical and healthy products and services from companies that adhere to a code of environmental, social and governance responsibility that benefits people and planet;

3. Voluntarily and generously exchange value (e.g., services, goods, appreciation, kind acts) in a way that promotes love, abundance and ecosystemic thriving;

4. Collaborate, rather than compete, with each other in the way we live, work, learn and consume (e.g., sharing, acts of kindness, responsibility, inclusivity and integrity); and

5. Create a new world, rather than fix the symptoms of the current system, using whole systems and regenerative applications. Instead of problem solving and killing the bad, we create wholly new systems that promote goodness and thriving in ways that render the core systemic dysfunction obsolete.

Our time, energy, money, thoughts, emotions, words, actions and behavior are the "Personal Resources" we each possess. We'll see transformative shifts as we devote our individual and collective Personal Resources to furthering a Regenerative Society. Like a functional virus in a dysfunctional system, if we use our Personal Resources to transform our world from the inside-out, ground-up and top-down, we can develop a thriving, well and abundant world for ourselves, future generations and the planet.

A new and "Regenerative Society" will emerge as we dedicate ourselves to the service of people and planet; consciously eat only nutritious and humanely produced food; drink the purest water; replace what we extract; and work in service to beauty, ecosystemic thriving and abundance. And as the Regenerative Society gains adoption, the toxic and sociopathic systems of the industrial age that promote and perpetuate scarcity, hunger, poverty, war, disease, climate change, pollution and ecosystemic destruction will be rendered obsolete and antiquated.

As we transform our beliefs and actions, we and our world will be transformed.

"A radical inner transformation and rise to a new level of consciousness might be the only real hope we have in the current global crisis brought on by the dominance of the Western mechanistic paradigm." ~ Stanislav Grof

In alignment with Grof's statement, a shift in personal consciousness, beliefs and behaviors is potentially the most powerful way to transform our world. As will be discussed in the following chapters, the transformation of creating an Abundant, Well & Empowered world includes

1. realizing the incredible power we have individually and collectively;

2. transforming our economic system and relationship to money;

3. replacing the quantitative metrics by which we determine "success;"

4. creating a Regenerative Economy and Society based upon ecological thriving;

5. healing and evolving our relationships;

6. transforming our energy portfolio and supply chain;

7. transforming our organizations and governance structures;

8. balancing our consumption with the carrying capacity of the planet while also increasing the carrying capacity of the planet through regenerative innovation; and

9. developing regenerative communities that positively transform the way we live, work, learn, play and consume.

By committing to the transformation discussed in the following chapters, we will change the Global Human Agreement ("GHA") and realize the most abundant economy in the history of humankind—the Regenerative Economy. The multi-trillion-dollar Regenerative Economy essentially is a powerful economic engine that integrates and aligns economic imperatives with ethical and life-affirming imperatives. By creating a global Regenerative Economy that aligns economic abundance with service to ecosystemic thriving, we can create a world of great abundance, beauty, love, peace and thriving that renders the world of extraction, exploitation, fear, war, toxicity and destruction obsolete.

CHAPTER 21

The Power to Transform

(Changing the Global Human Agreement
from Dysfunction to Thriving)

"Our deepest fear is not that we are inadequate. Our deepest fear is that we are powerful beyond measure. It is our light, not our darkness, that most frightens us."

~ Marrianne Williamson

E ach of us holds a unique consciousness—an individual perspective of the universe, our world and reality, which contributes to the collective "human consciousness." As discussed, our collective human consciousness creates, manifests, reinforces and perpetuates a "Global Human Agreement" that defines our society and the way humanity experiences "reality" on this planet. The Global Human Agreement, in turn, influences our individual perspective and experience of "reality," creating a feedback loop that is often self-reinforcing. The power to transform the current Global Human Agreement is done incrementally by changing our individual perspectives and beliefs in the way we see ourselves and our world. *Transcending the limitations of the Global Human Agreement sets us free to be the divine creators we truly are—to make conscious and powerful decisions that manifest new realities.*

Marianne Williamson's famous quote provides an eloquent statement of the power we each hold and why we often fail to embrace and use our power:

"Our deepest fear is not that we are inadequate. Our deepest fear is that we are powerful beyond measure. It is our light, not our darkness, that most frightens us. We ask ourselves, who am I to be brilliant, gorgeous, talented and fabulous?

Actually, who are you not to be?

You are a child of god. You're playing small doesn't serve the world. There's nothing empowered about shrinking so that other people won't feel insecure around you.

We were born to make and manifest the glory of god that is within us. It's not just in some of us; it's in everyone. And as we let our own light shine, we unconsciously give other people permission to do the same. As we are liberated from our own fear, our presence automatically liberates others."

Realizing the truth of Williamson's words is a critical step forward in our evolution and transformation. From such examples as Gautama Buddha, Mahatma Gandhi, Susan B. Anthony, Martin Luther King, Nelson Mandela, Thomas Edison, Nikola Tesla, Johannes Gutenberg and Mother Teresa, to the field workers who pick our food, the construction workers who build our homes, the operations manager at the power plant that provides us with electricity, the inventors and entrepreneurs that have contributed to the technologies and businesses that have profoundly impacted civilization, and those that are homeless and living in poverty, we each contribute to our world and the Global Human Agreement in our own special way. It's this collective perception and belief of reality that forms our culture.

Every day each of us influences the world through our thoughts, beliefs, words, deeds and being. Although our individual contributions may, at times, appear small, we can often have a profound "Butterfly Effect" on the world by making changes in ourselves, our perceptions and the way we interact with the world around us. Edward Norton Lorenz, an American mathematician, meteorologist, and a pioneer of chaos theory, coined the term "Butterfly Effect," as a metaphoric concept that illustrates whole-systems interconnectivity. In essence, the flapping of a butterfly's wings in one part of the world may create a hurricane in another part of the world. This represents the concept of *sensitive dependence on initial conditions* in chaos theory; namely, in a complex system, a small change in one place can have large effects elsewhere. Small things can make big changes.

Because our beliefs and perspectives change the way we create reality and inter-act with the world, we each have the ability to change our world by simply changing our beliefs and perspective. We are truly powerful beyond measure. However, we are only as powerful as we believe ourselves to be and the actions we are willing to take. Anthony Robbins understood this when he wrote the following:

> *"You're in the midst of a war: a battle between the limits of a crowd seeking the surrender of your dreams, and the power of your true vision to create and contribute. It is a fight between those who will tell you what you cannot do, and that part of you that knows, and has always known, that we are more than our environment; and that a dream, backed by an unrelenting will to attain it, is truly a reality with an imminent arrival."*

As Robbins suggests, our society generally provides conditioning that promotes conformity to authority, competition against each other and dependence upon a system that cultivates compliant followers rather than empowered leaders. The effect of this systemic conditioning is too often fear, insecurity, divisiveness, disconnection and greed, leading to greater dependence upon, and conformity to, the system.

Those who dare to be different, believe in miracles, and utilize their power to change the world are often ostracized by their families, teachers, colleagues and friends. And if they become too powerful, they are often discredited, bankrupted, jailed or assassinated (e.g., Jesus Christ, Martin Luther King, Gandhi, Abraham Lincoln, Nikola Tesla). Thus, we are taught to fear standing out, exercising our individuality and demonstrating our power. What if our society provided education that taught us to be powerful, free-thinking, sovereign, emotionally intelligent and inquisitive individuals who trust, respect and collaborate with each other? What might the world look like then?

Albert Einstein was called a rebel and a dunce by his teachers, yet he chose not to believe them. He chose to question authority, and as a result of his questioning and curious mind, he completely changed the world and the way we understand "reality." In reflecting on the opposition he faced, Einstein said, *"Great spirits have always encountered violent opposition from mediocre minds."* Thanks to the great spirits, our eyes have opened to new miracles and possibilities including such things as quantum physics, epigenetics, nanotechnology, biomimicry and expansive philosophies. **It is**

clear that we live in a universe of unlimited possibilities and have the power to manifest our wildest dreams, including creating a world that supports thriving, loving, abundant, happy and harmonious lives.

Changing our reality requires changing ourselves. This, in turn, entails consciously replacing thoughts, beliefs, emotions and actions that are limiting, non-serving and/or destructive, (e.g., scarcity, fear, war, poverty, injustice, restriction), with those that are expansive, creative and life-enhancing, (e.g., love, trust, respect, collaboration, generosity, abundance and the health of people and planet). Our imaginations are powerful forces for change. Every great invention or advancement of humankind arose from imagination (e.g., from the wheel, printing press, the automobile, the airplane, putting a man on the moon, Internet and smartphones). We can imagine whatever we want, yet we often imagine the worst rather than the best. Walt Disney said, "*Worry is a waste of imagination.*" He's correct.

Our imaginations and thoughts are like seeds that grow into reality when planted in the fertile soil of our minds. Whatever we plant in the garden of our minds will grow. If we plant toxic and fearful thoughts and images, our lives and our culture will be imbued with toxicity and fear. If we plant thoughts of beauty, kindness, love and respect, our lives and culture will be beautiful, kind, loving and respectful.

We each have a choice as to what we believe, imagine and think, as well as how we perceive and respond to our world. We each have a choice to consciously reimagine, influence and transform the Global Human Agreement by simply changing our perspective and consciously using the remarkable power we've been given to transform our world. It's time to awaken to the truth of our divine nature and the power of our creative abilities. The world we perceive, believe in, and support exists as a result of our individual and collective unconscious, subconscious and conscious agreement of "reality," much of which is the result of conditioned programming. If we want to change our world, it is necessary to first change our beliefs, thoughts, words and deeds. As we change our perception of, and agreement with our world, we change and the world changes with us.

Also, according to behavioral epigenetics, our survival instincts, fight and flight mechanisms, sex drive, sensory and perceptual filters, and socialization have been "programmed" into our genes throughout generations. This genetic programming is retained at a cellular level and is often reflexive and unconscious. Based upon the behavioral epigenetic research of molecular biologist and geneticist, Moshe Szyf, and neurobiologist, Michael Meaney, Discover Magazine's Dan Hurley writes, *"Your ancestors' lousy childhoods or excellent adventures might change your personality, bequeathing anxiety or resilience by altering the epigenetic expressions of genes in the brain."* *"According to the new insights of behavioral epigenetics, traumatic experiences in our past, or in our recent ancestors' past, leave molecular scars adhering to our DNA. Jews whose great-grandparents were chased from their Russian shtetls; Chinese whose grandparents lived through the ravages of the Cultural Revolution; young immigrants from Africa whose parents survived massacres; adults of every ethnicity who grew up with alcoholic or abusive parents — all carry with them more than just memories."*[298]

Ancestral heritage plays an important role in our gene make up and by changing our beliefs and perceptions, we can potentially change the genetic programming of future generations. Aside from the social and genetic programming received from our ancestors, from the time we are born, we're conditioned to accept programs and beliefs from our family, friends, teachers, acquaintances, media, scientists, government officials, psychologists, society ("Influencers" or "Circle of Influence"). These Influencers are, in turn, responding to their subconscious and unconscious ancestral beliefs, patterns, and programming. The subconscious mind absorbs, stores, recalls and reacts to information without discernment of the information's truth or falsity. The subconscious mind accepts everything we imagine and experience as real without conscious filtering, judgment or analysis. Thus, the subconscious mind will often drive emotions, decisions and behavior based upon information that is imagined even if false or contrived.[299]

For example, if we are exposed to pleasure or pain in connection with a specific sensory stimulus (e.g., color, touch, sound, scent, flavor), we, like Pavlov's dog, may associate the sensory stimulus with a feeling of pleasure or pain even if the pleasure or pain from the stimulus is no longer present. For example, if our mother wore a certain perfume and gave us a great deal of love when we were infants, we are likely to respond favorably when we smell similar scents. If, however, our father was a whiskey drinker who was an abusive drunk, then the smell of whiskey may trigger anxiety, fear or anger. As well, if we are conditioned to believe that success, happiness and the meaning of life consists of going to school, getting a job, getting married, having kids, buying a house and filling it with stuff purchased on credit, then we are likely to pursue such goals in our life without questioning whether such actions truly represent happiness, fulfillment and success for us as individuals.

The subconscious mind (representing an estimated 92% of the total brain's capacity), is a powerful influence on our behavior and decision-making. According to Dr. Bruce Lipton, "*When it comes to sheer neurological processing abilities, the subconscious mind is millions of times more powerful than the conscious mind.*" If the desires of the conscious mind conflict with the programs of the subconscious mind, the subconscious mind generally wins and determines our thought, emotion and behavior. If we are to thrive as a species, it's critical that we discipline the conscious mind to consistently influence the subconscious mind with positive thoughts and images that align with the world we desire to see (e.g., a world of ecosystemic health and thriving, abundance, beauty, love, respect and unity).

There are, however, individuals whose vision is to create a world they dominate and control even if it requires killing, brutality, destruction, deprivation and exploitation. Aside from the blunt tools of death, torture, imprisonment, bankruptcy and public humiliation, those that desire to control humankind have honed the skills of subtly manipulating and implanting our subconscious with disempowering information and beliefs.

From the time we are very young, we are taught to act "appropriately." Our parents generally rewarded us for behavior they were conditioned to believe was good and punished us for behavior they were conditioned to believe was bad. Often what is good is simply compliance or following authority and what is bad is noncompliance, questioning or disobeying authority. Our parents too received much of the same programming by their parents and so on. Based upon ancestral, multi-generational and current conditioning, we develop beliefs and behaviors of what is "appropriate" within our Circle of Influence. When we receive significant reinforcement of what is "appropriate" from our Circle of Influence, we link our identities with our conditioning and a viral reinforcing loop is created whereby each of us behaves "appropriately" and then reinforces "appropriate behavior" on others in our Circle of Influence. This leads to mass agreements of "appropriate reality." "Appropriate behavior" and "appropriate reality" is often based upon "authoritative reality." "Authoritative reality" utilizes the power of government, religion, media, education, scientists, doctors, psychologists and other experts to create mass agreements that often elevate limiting beliefs, or use an exaggerated or untrue story of reality, to manipulate the masses so they are more easy to control and dominate.

As an example of "authoritative reality," the existence of Jesus has been debated amongst scholars due to the lack of credible historical evidence about his existence,[300] yet billions of people believe in the existence of Jesus, so the existence of Jesus is accepted as reality. This "authoritative reality" was promulgated by the Catholic church. When President George W. Bush, a born-again Christian, said in June, 2003, that he was instructed by Jesus to attack Afghanistan and Iraq, the majority of the United States did not question his sanity, because such a statement conforms to a belief accepted by the masses that Jesus existed. If he was instructed to attack Afghanistan and Iraq by Tinkerbell, he may have been thrown out of office and sent to a mental institution. If he said he was instructed by Buddha, (whose life is supported by historical evidence) to attack Afghanistan and Iraq, he most likely would have had his competency and fitness for office questioned. This is because nearly 71% of the U.S. is Christian, whereas less than 1% are Buddhist.

To provide another example, in 1616, the "authoritative reality" promulgated by the Catholic church was that the earth was the center of the universe. When Galileo demonstrated that earth revolved around the sun, Galileo was enjoined by the Inquisition and ordered not to hold, communicate, teach, or defend his theory under threat of death. Those who expose the falsity of "authoritative reality" or demonstrate new truths that don't conform to "authoritative reality" are often ostracized, publicly humiliated, jailed, tortured and/or killed. These threats, coupled with the manipulation of human beliefs and behaviors, create a self-imposed adoption of "authoritative reality" and mass acceptance and perpetuation of misinformation.

There exists such a great need to be accepted as "normal" that many people live in fear of expressing their individual uniqueness and living powerful and fulfilling lives based in their own truth. So instead, they adopt "authoritative reality," and limiting belief systems that disempower themselves in order to conform with and receive acceptance from their Circle of Influence. What's interesting is that each member of our Circle of Influence is also conforming to the system to obtain acceptance from us and their Circle of Influence. This is the subtle manipulation and brilliance of the *"the conscious and intelligent manipulation of the organized habits and opinions of the masses"* that Edward Bernays referred to.

While societal conditioning is powerful, influential and pervasive in mass consciousness, it is not impervious to change and being rendered obsolete. Our society was created by people and is being operated and perpetuated by people. People die, people change, new people are born, consciousness expands, new inventions are discovered and systems evolve. As renowned physicist, Max Plank, wrote, *"A new scientific truth does not triumph by convincing its opponents and making them see the light, but rather because its opponents eventually die, and a new generation grows up that is familiar with it."*

Throughout history, we have seen many paradigm shifts in all areas of life including science, math, philosophy, technology, business, media, communications, art, and music. The phrase *"Paradigm Shift,"* originally applied to the field of science and popularized by renowned physicist Thomas Kuhn, has evolved in its definition to include a *significant change in beliefs, agreements, principles, techniques, approaches, and rules applied to a discipline (e.g. science, economics, philosophy, art & music, media & communications) or a group (e.g., scientists, philosophers, members of a country, a race, a religion or a species)*. In reflecting on Kuhn's work on paradigm shift, Al Gore wrote: *"Well-established theories collapse under the weight of new facts and observations which cannot be explained, and then accumulate to the point where the once useful theory is clearly obsolete."* As Gore suggests, discovery of new truths create shifts in point of view.

Paradigm shifts happen from environmental or evolutionary circumstances or through imagination or by accidental discovery questioning old theories of beliefs. Once a new and better way of doing things and being in relationship with the world emerges and is demonstrated (e.g., more life-affirming, effective, respectful, regenerative, sustainable, value-adding, adaptable and resilient), it's likely to be adopted and a new paradigm can emerge.

As adoption grows for new technologies, beliefs and disciplines, old ways of doing things become obsolete and are replaced. Examples of paradigm shifts include:

- Stone Tools
- Spoken and Written Language
- Domestication of Fire
- Art and Music
- Use of the Wheel
- Domestication of Animals
- Agriculture
- Astronomy
- Legal System
- Metallurgy
- Mathematics
- Renaissance Paradigm
  - Printing Press
  - Advances in Science, Art, Music, Astronomy
  - Newtonian Physics
- Industrial Paradigm
  - Advanced Chemistry
  - Biology
  - Quantum Physics
  - Electricity
  - Propulsion
  - Automobiles
  - Aviation & Space Travel
  - Production Line Manufacturing, Radio
  - Television
- Information Paradigm
  - Personal Computers
  - Advanced Computers and Electronics,
  - Internet, Cloud Computing, Big Data
  - Mobile & Smartphones
  - Genomics
  - Computer Automation and Robotics Digital Currencies
  - Artificial Intelligence
  - Singularity
- Regenerative Paradigm
  - Clean and Renewable Energy
  - IoT and Smart Infrastructure
  - Biomimetic Materials
  - Waste Upcycling
  - Aquatech and Agtech
  - Vibrational Medicine
  - Resource Optimization and Regeneration
  - Reciprocal Value-Adding Relationships
  - Social Models based on Ecosystemic Thriving
  - Local Living and Collaborative Economics
  - Whole Systems, Regenerative, Biomimetic, Bio-Energetic Natural Approaches

Each paradigm shift marks an evolutionary shift in thinking, beliefs, principles, behavior and culture. With each paradigm shift, the beliefs of "reality" and human potential from the old paradigm were either significantly expanded, radically altered or rendered obsolete. In our modern world, paradigm shifts are happening at an ever-quickening rate and are starting to overlap. Observation reveals that we are concurrently experiencing the tail end of the Industrial Paradigm, the adolescence of the Information Paradigm and the birth of the Regenerative Paradigm.

We are a much different society today than we were even just a few decades ago in 1990 (e.g., before commercial use of the Internet, Smartphones, clean energy standards, evidence of climate change and greenhouse gas emissions, nanotechnology, the human genome project and epigenetics, blockchain and COVID-19). Change in almost every aspect of our lives is accelerating. Buckminster Fuller's "Knowledge Doubling Curve," shows that until 1900 human knowledge doubled approximately every century. By the end of World War II, knowledge was doubling every 25 years. Today human knowledge is on average doubling every 13 months and according to IBM, the build out of the "internet of things" will lead to the doubling of knowledge every 12 hours.

The rapid and overlapping paradigm shifts in information, human knowledge and technology are affecting every field, discipline and person on earth. These shifts are pushing humankind to reevaluate its current beliefs, agreements, principles, rules and approaches to life, as well as our economic, political and social systems. We are seeing a paradigm shift that can evolve humankind from our current society based largely upon industrialization, scarcity, fear, extraction, centralized control, exploitation and divisiveness to a Regenerative Society built upon interconnection, collaboration, abundance, love, respect and service to ecosystemic thriving.

The paradigm shift to a Regenerative Society will be brought to fruition when a significant number of people lovingly engage in service to humankind and our planet in a way that renews and regenerates the life-giving gifts and resources of our planet. This service by humanity to ecosystemic thriving represents an evolutionary and reciprocal, value-adding relationship between people and planet resulting in the most robust economy in history.

The **5 major stages of transformation** below are the pillars of the Regenerative Paradigm leading to a healthy, abundant, thriving and beautiful world:

1. **Awareness and Acceptance**—Awareness and acceptance of dysfunction, need for change and/or opportunity for improvement are the first steps in transformation. Unless we become aware of and accept the need for change or the potential for improvement, we generally continue doing what we're comfortable doing. When we become aware that our current beliefs and behaviors are dysfunctional and leading to social dysfunction, we become open to new ideas and taking steps to improve our circumstances

2. **Vision**—Seeing and holding a clear vision for change. Vision is an imaginative process that provides us with the ideas, concepts and trajectory for transformation to occur, and upon which the future is built.

3. **Belief**—Holding the belief that we have the power to create and transform the world and achieve our vison. Our beliefs empower us to create a new reality.

4. **Commitment**—Courageously committing to fulfill the vision of a better world with tenacity and dedication. Commitment is the seed to attraction and propels us into action. Committing to such things as expressing more love, compassion and generosity; exercising our economic will to purchase healthy products from environmental and socially responsible vendors; devoting time to increasing the beauty and resilience of our cities; and serving nature's thriving, can make profound impacts in our world.

5. **Consistent Action**—Taking consistent and progressive action in alignment with the achievement of an executable vision for a more loving, thriving and beautiful world. When we consistently choose to take action in a manner that is in alignment with a clear and executable vision, we powerfully and progressively realize our vision. Let our hearts guide our actions so that they are nurturing, loving and create great benefit for people and planet.

By consistently practicing these 5 major stages of transformation, we each contribute to the collective transformation of our world. We are each interconnected to, and interdependent upon, each other, our planet, and the universe. When we realize we are divine consciousness transcending all temporary illusion of physical reality our fears dissolve. We can then release our limiting beliefs, and awaken to embrace the infinite power, creative force and brilliance that we truly are. From this state of being, we can remove the shackles that bind us to disempowering mass conformity, change the Global Human Agreement and transform the world.

CHAPTER 22

Transforming Money & The Economy

(The 12-Step Program for Moneyholics)

I love money. I love everything about it. I bought some pretty good stuff. Got
me a $300 pair of socks. Got a fur sink. An electric dog polisher. A gasoline
powered turtleneck sweater. And, of course, I bought some dumb stuff, too.

~Steve Martin

Too many people spend money they earned. . .
to buy things they don't want. . .
to impress people that they don't like.

~Will Rogers

Just about every person on Earth has some relationship with money. Even remote
tribes in the Amazon, Papua New Guinea, Australia and the Philippines have
bartered for manufactured goods and money and have had interfaces with tourists,
researchers and adventurers, who used money to get to these remote destinations.
Our ability to obtain a copy of this book and read it is evidence of literacy, access to
a computer, the Internet or a book store, and therefore the use of money. To acquire
this book required interaction with money either directly (a purchase) or indirectly
(a gift). Additionally, the electricity, computers, Internet, mobile and supply chain
infrastructure required for the writing, publishing and delivering this book, required
money. Because money is so pervasive in our society, our beliefs about money can

have profound effects on our lives and the world. But it's our beliefs that create the power of money and perpetuate the monetary system.

THE OBSESSION WITH THE ILLUSION OF MONEY

Money often costs too much.

~Ralph Waldo Emerson

Money is essentially a token or object that functions as a medium of exchange at a socially agreed value and is accepted in payment for goods and services and in settlement of debts. Money also serves as a standard of value for measuring the relative worth of different goods and services and as a store of value. The absence of money can cause an economy to be inefficient because it requires a coincidence of wants between traders and an agreement that these needs are of equal value before a barter exchange can occur. The efficiency gains through the use of money are thought to encourage trade and the division of labor, in turn increasing productivity and wealth. Thus, money is the symbol of our stored energy and represents the ability to conveniently and effectively trade our stored energy for things we desire without being in parity with the seller's desire for the value we personally provide.

The original use of money was tied to tangible value. For example, the first form of exchange was direct barter, without the use of money, which can be traced back to 100,000 BC. In the 200,000 that homo sapiens have existed, we survived approximately 197,000 years without money. It wasn't until about 3,000 BC that the barley/shekel, recognized as the first non-parity currency, was used. With the advent of paper currency in about 800 AD, a new convenient and transportable currency was created. However, paper currency was generally representative of a store of value, generally metals such as gold, silver, nickel and copper. From the early 1800s, most countries adhered to a gold standard for their currency. Because countries on the gold standard can't increase the amount of paper money in circulation without also increasing their reserves of gold, in about 1931, Great Britain abandoned the gold standard and many countries followed. In about 1933, Roosevelt abandoned the gold standard in the U.S. After paper currency was detached from the gold standard and later from any tangible store of value, the central banks around the world could issue paper money without the constraint of actually having any tangible value required to back the issuance, except the promise of the central bank, the bonds of respective governments and the general agreement of the public that the valueless fiat currency actually has value.

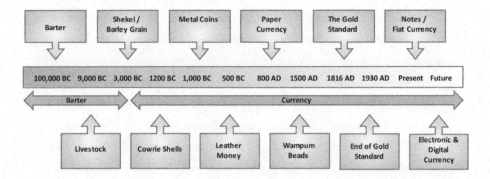

With the prolific use of credit cards, online banking and online brokerage accounts, we are at the dawn of the age of electronic/digital currency, where coin and paper will soon be rendered obsolete. Sweden became the first country to enlist its citizens in an economic experiment: negative interest rates in a cashless society. In 2018, only 13% of Swedish citizens used cash. 80% of transactions in the country were done by debit card and 7% by credit card.[301]

The proliferation of "smart cards" (e.g., credit cards containing microchips) is not only leading to a cashless society, but also personal digital identification, authentication, geolocation (e.g., tracking whereabouts of people, animals and goods), data storage of personal records (e.g., medical, financial, preferences) and transactions. The number of smart card integrated circuits ("ICs") in 2020 is estimated at 12.8 billion.[302] Elon Musk's company, Neuralink, is developing chip implants to initially help those that are paralyzed. However, according to an article in Synced, *"Musk's dream was spawned by AI's unprecedented progress over recent years and its potential for human cognitive enhancement toward the new superintelligence that people like futurist Ray Kurzweil believe is approaching. In a 2018 interview with podcaster Joe Rogan, Musk said Neuralink will do this by symbiotically merging human brains with a super digital intelligence that will serve as a tertiary cognition layer augmenting the human cortex and limbic systems."*[303]

There may come a time when implanted microchips will be required for us to effectively live in modern society. Microchips will likely be required (1) to access our bank accounts and engage in transactions utilizing digital currency, (2) to provide identification for privileges such as driving and travel, (3) to access medical records and for proof of vaccinations, (4) for mandatory geographic tracking, (5) and for access to school, work and public places. If each person is required to have an implanted microchip, the dystopian potential for total control, tracking, punishment and death of people at the push of a button could become a reality. As scary and sci-fi as this may seem, because of the large scale dependence on money in our society, if microchipping becomes required for us to exchange digital currency, it is likely that a majority of people in this world will obediently line up to get chipped. This could represent the ultimate control and domination of the masses. Now with COVID-19 and the imminent requirement for proof of vaccination certificates, microchipping, as a public health and safety requirement, could potentially be the tip of the spear of dystopian fascism.

AN ECONOMIC SYSTEM OF DEBT AND SCARCITY

In order to understand how we became so dependent upon money in modern society, it's important to have some background on one of the most influential and powerful organizations in the world today—the central banking system that issues and controls fiat money for governments throughout the world.

A central bank is an independent authority that essentially manages monetary policy, sets money supply and interest rates, regulates banks and provides financial services. Central banks also act as lenders of last resort to banks experiencing financial difficulty. The stated overarching goals of central banks are to stabilize a nation's currency, prevent inflation and reduce unemployment.[304]

Through their charter, the central banks (aka "reserve banks" or "monetary authorities") are typically provided with the exclusive right and authority to issue and control the supply of the money for nations. When currency is recognized as the exchange currency of a country and the sole currency for paying tax obligations, it is known as *"legal tender."* There are an estimated 195 recognized countries in the world,[305] with all but 9 countries (Andorra, Isle of Man, Kiribati, Marshall Islands, Micronesia, Monaco, Nauru, Palau and Tuvalu) having central banks.[306] Almost all of today's widely accepted money is issued by central banks. Most central bank issued currencies are "fiat money" that comes into existence in the form of debt bearing interest. "Fiat money" refers to currency without intrinsic value. Thus, practically all money in global circulation today is fiat money.[307]

Our current economic system and the value of fiat money is not based upon the intrinsic value of money, but the confidence of exchange and scarcity. This is supported by the statement of the Federal Reserve System (the largest and most powerful central banking system in the world). According to "Modern Money Mechanics" published by the Central Bank of Chicago, a Member of the Federal Reserve System[308]. . .

> "In the United States **neither paper currency nor deposits have value** as commodities. Intrinsically, a dollar bill is just a piece of paper. Deposits are merely book entries. Coins do have some intrinsic value as metal, but generally far less than their face value.
>
> What, then, makes these instruments—checks, paper money, and coins—acceptable at face value in payment of all debts and other monetary uses? Mainly, it is the **confidence** people have that they will be able to exchange such money for other financial assets and for real goods and services whenever they choose to do so.
>
> Money, like anything else, derives its value from its **scarcity** in relation to its usefulness." [emphasis added]

By its own admission, the currency issued by the Federal Reserve is based upon scarcity and the confidence of the general public that something of no intrinsic value has value. "Federal Reserve Notes" are the legal tender currently used in the U.S. The Federal Reserve Notes, authorized by Section 16 of the Federal Reserve Act of 1913, are issued to the Federal Reserve Banks at the discretion of the Board of Governors of the Federal Reserve System. The Federal Reserve Notes are then put into circulation by the Federal Reserve Banks, at which point they become liabilities of the Federal Reserve Banks and obligations of the United States.[309] Federal Reserve Notes are backed by the assets of the Federal Reserve Banks, which are generally in the form of U.S. Treasury securities (generally issued as a debt in the form of bills, bonds and notes) purchased by the Federal Reserve using the issuance of Federal Reserve Notes. The money supply is expanded using *"Fractional Reserve Banking"* whereby the Treasury securities are deposited as "reserves" on which further loans are made at multiples of the reserves.[310]

Fractional Reserve Banking allows banks to issue debt significantly in excess of their reserves on deposit. The tool of *"fractional reserve banking"* is used to expand the money supply and gain massive leverage on the underlying reserves. Fractional-reserve banking involves banks accepting deposits from customers and making loans to borrowers, while holding in reserve only a fraction of the bank's deposit liabilities. Bank reserves are held as cash in the bank or as balances in the bank's account at the central bank. The minimum amount that banks are required to hold in liquid assets is determined by the country's central bank, and is called the "reserve requirement" or "reserve ratio."[311] For example, in the U.S., the Federal Reserve has the following reserve requirements: Banks with less than $16.9 million in assets are not required to hold reserves. Banks with assets of more than $16.9 million, but less than $127.5 million have a 3% reserve requirement, and those banks with more than $127.5 million in assets have a 10% reserve requirement. Using fractional reserve banking, a bank with $1 billion in reserves and a 10% reserve requirement, can loan $10 billion. Larger banks can loan 10 times the money they have in actual reserves, whereas banks with a 3% reserve requirement can loan 33 times the money they have in reserve. This is the way the money supply is expanded.

The Federal Reserve Bank of Atlanta ("FRBA") uses the following example to explain Fractional Reserve Banking:[312]

> *"For example, if the Federal Reserve were to lower reserve requirements, that would ordinarily allow banks to lend out more money, which would create more deposits, which would allow the fractional reserve banking system to create an increasing quantity of money in circulation. Conversely, if the central bank increases the reserve requirement the process will work in reverse, deposits will be contracted, and the money supply will shrink.*

While the FRBA takes exception to the historical accuracy of the following story, it uses the story to serve as a useful illustration of fractional reserve banking:

"The story that's usually told about the origin of fractional reserve banking is told about ancient goldsmiths. Goldsmiths stored precious metals in their vaults and people came to them to store precious metals on their account. And, over time, the goldsmiths realized, you know, if I lent this gold out and put it out there in the community in some sort of an investment, then I could made a profit and return the gold to the vault before anybody is the wiser.

"It's a useful story because it reminds that resources that sit idle in some vault really aren't of much value to the community and that if you can put those resources to work for productive investment, you can make a profit and the community is enriched in the process."

The quote above illustrates how fractional reserve banking got started and the rationale for not keeping money and valuables idly in a vault. At one point in history, it was illegal to take money, gold or valuables on deposit and loan it to third parties without the express permission of the asset owner and pay them virtually nothing for using their money, gold or valuables. Now, under fractional reserve banking, these practices are legal so long as the lender is a bank and stays within the reserve requirements of the central bank. While most banks pay a very low interest for use of deposits, some banks in the world are actually paying no interest and charging depositors for lending their money to the bank and then using the deposits to create more money using fractional reserve banking.[313]

It could be said that the central banking system has become the most powerful and controversial of all organizations in existence today due largely to the central banking system's control of the world's money supply. The central banking system holds most countries and their people hostage in an endless spiral of debt, as each "dollar" issued by a central bank is issued in debt and carries interest. Therefore, more debt is required to pay off the interest of the old debt. Global debt now stands at approximately $66 trillion or about 80% of the global GDP.[314]

The revenue for most governments comes from collection of taxes from such things as income, import duties and tariffs, "sin taxes" such as cigarette and alcohol, as well as excise taxes on gasoline, transportation and infrastructure. As an example of the debt load required to be paid to the Federal Reserve, in 2019 the tax revenues for the U.S. were estimated at $3.422 trillion, however, the budget was estimated at

$4.407 trillion leaving a deficit $984 billion[315] and the interest paid to the Federal Reserve in 2019 is estimated at $393.5 billion, or 8.7% of all federal outlays. The total U.S. federal government debt is $22.023 trillion.[316] It appears that with the continued expansion of debt and the continued indebtedness to the central banking system, governments and future generations worldwide will be perpetually indebted to the central banking system.

The central banking system has been the subject of considerable controversy. While there are proponents of the central banking system, there is also considerable opposition to the central banking systems.

For example, Alexander Hamilton, a proponent of the central banking system and America's first treasury secretary, admired Britain's financial system. Finances were chaotic in the aftermath of independence. America's first currency, the Continental, was afflicted by hyperinflation. Hamilton believed that a reformed financial structure, including a central bank, would create a stable currency and a lower cost of debt, making it easier for the economy to flourish.[317] In 1907, Jacob Schiff, the CEO of Kuhn, Loeb and Co., another central bank supporter, warned that *"unless we have a central bank with adequate control of credit resources, this country is going to undergo the most severe and far reaching money panic in its history."*

While segments of the financial community were worried about the power that had accrued to JP Morgan and other 'financiers', most were more concerned about the general frailty of a vast, decentralized banking system that could not regulate itself without extraordinary intervention. After the Panic of 1907, financial leaders, including Frank Vanderlip, Myron Herrick, William Barret Ridgely, George Roberts, Isaac Newton Seligman and Jacob Schiff, advocated for a central bank with an elastic currency. Following the demands of bankers and financial leaders, Congress established a commission of experts to come up with a nonpartisan solution, eventually resulting in the Federal Reserve Act signed into law by President Woodrow Wilson on December 23, 1913. It was Wilson who insisted that the regional Federal Reserve banks be controlled by a central Federal Reserve board appointed by the president with the advice and consent of the U.S. Senate.[318]

Warren Buffet, the billionaire investor, compared the Federal Reserve to a hedge fund saying, *"The Fed is the greatest hedge fund in history"* because of its ability to profit from its bond purchases and accumulate a balance sheet of more than $3 trillion.[319]

While the central banking system has its supporters that believe the central bank provides stability and maximum employment, throughout history there has also been considerable opposition to the central banking system, including many of the founding fathers of the U.S., heads of state and economists (e.g., Thomas Jefferson, Benjamin Franklin, Andrew Jackson, Abraham Lincoln, John F. Kennedy and Nobel Laureate, Economist, Milton Friedman). The following provide examples of some of those that opposed the central bank.

Thomas Jefferson has been attributed as making the following statement about the central bank:[320]

"The central bank is an institution of the most deadly hostility existing against the Principles and form of our Constitution. I am an Enemy to all banks discounting bills or notes for anything but Coin. If the American People allow private banks to control the issuance of their currency, first by inflation and then by deflation, the banks and corporations that will grow up around them will deprive the People of all their Property until their Children will wake up homeless on the continent their Fathers conquered."

As stated by Sir Josiah Stamp, President of the Bank of England in the 1920s, then the second richest man in Britain:

"Banking was conceived in iniquity and was born in sin. The Bankers own the Earth. Take it away from them, but leave them the power to create deposits, and with the flick of a pen they will create enough deposits to buy it back again. However, take it away from them, and all the fortunes like mine will disappear, and they ought to disappear, for this world would be a happier and better world to live in. But if you wish to remain slaves of the Bankers and pay for the cost of your own slavery, let them continue to create deposits."

President Abraham Lincoln, was noted as saying:

"The money powers prey on the nation in times of peace and conspire against it in times of adversity. The banking powers are more despotic than monarchy,

more insolent than autocracy, more selfish than bureaucracy. They denounce as public enemies all who question their methods or throw light upon their crimes.

I have two great enemies, the Southern Army in front of me, and the bankers in the rear. Of the two, the one at my rear is my greatest foe. As a most undesirable consequence of the war, corporations have been enthroned, and an era of corruption in high places will follow. The money power will endeavor to prolong its reign by working upon the prejudices of the people until the wealth is aggregated in the hands of a few, and the Republic is destroyed."

"The government should create, issue, and circulate all the currency and credit needed to satisfy the spending power of the government and the buying power of consumers. Money will cease to be master and will then become servant of humanity."

President Andrew Jackson, who was an adversary of the bank, is attributed with the following quote:

"I am one of those who do not believe that a national debt is a national blessing, but rather a curse to a republic, inasmuch as it is calculated to raise around the administration a monied aristocracy dangerous to the liberties of the country."

President James Garfield understood the power of controlling a country's currency:

"Whoever controls the volume of money in any country is absolute master of all industry and commerce."

Henry Ford, founder of the Ford Motor Company, is credited with the following statement:

"It is well enough that people of the nation do not understand our banking and monetary system, for if they did, I believe there would be a revolution before tomorrow morning."

After signing the Federal Reserve Act into law, a remorseful President Woodrow Wilson was attributed with saying the following:

"A great industrial nation is controlled by its system of credit. Our system of credit is concentrated. The growth of the nation, therefore, and all our activities are in

the hands of a few men. We have come to be one of the worst ruled, one of the most completely controlled and dominated Governments in the civilized world no longer a Government by free opinion, no longer a Government by conviction and the vote of the majority, but a Government by the opinion and duress of a small group of dominant men."

Ron Paul, U.S. Representative, had this to say about central banking:

"It is no coincidence that the century of total war coincided with the century of central banking."

In the case of *Lewis vs. United States*, 680 F. 2d 1239 9th Circuit 1982, the court found that the Federal Reserve Bank is not a federal agency and ruled as follows:

"Examining the organization and function of the Federal Reserve Banks, and applying the relevant factors, we conclude that the Reserve Banks are not federal instrumentalities for purposes of the FTCA, but are independent, privately owned and locally controlled corporations."

"Each Federal Reserve Bank is a separate corporation owned by commercial banks in its region. The stockholding commercial banks elect two thirds of each Bank's nine member board of directors. The remaining three directors are appointed by the Federal Reserve Board."

The Federal Reserve, arguably the largest and most powerful of the central banks, along with the central banks of Greece, Italy and South Africa are privately owned. The central banks of Japan, Belgium, Turkey and Switzerland are both owned privately and by the governments they serve. The central banks generally issue money out of thin air to buy government bonds thereby indebting nations to pay back their obligations to the central banks with interest while the issuance of money costs the central bank virtually nothing.

It could be argued that the feedback loop of fear, insecurity, debt, war, extraction, exploitation, wealth disparity, social injustice, destruction of our environment and dependence on fiat money is perpetuated by the central bank. Because of the interest charged by the central banks, governments are generally required to obtain new central banking debt with interest thereon to pay off the old debt to the central banks. The spiral of debt owed to the central banking system is effectively guaranteed into perpetuity. According to New York Times journalist, Nelson Schwartz, *"The federal government could soon pay more in interest on its debt than it spends on military, Medicaid or children's programs."*[321]

When discussing the central banking system, the *Bank of International Settlements ("BIS")*, headquartered in Basel, Switzerland, is considered the central bank of central banks. The BIS is owned by the largest sixty central banks in the world, accounting for about 95% of the world's GDP.[322] The BIS was established in 1930 to facilitate reparations imposed on Germany by the Treaty Versailles after World War 1 through an intergovernmental agreement by the central banks of Belgium, France, German, Great Britain, Italy, Japan and the United States, as well as banking groups including J.P. Morgan & Company of New York, the First National Bank of New York and the First National Bank of Chicago. The BIS is free from government oversight by rights granted under its agreement with the Hague Convention in 1930, the Brussels Protocol of 1936 and the Swiss Federal Council in 2003. The BIS and its employees pay no taxes, can't be sued unless it consents, and all of its documents and information are protected against inspection, search and/or seizure. Furthermore, officers and employees of BIS enjoy immunity from criminal and administrative jurisdiction.[323]

Even though the BIS was founded as an intergovernmental organization, it has been criticized for its support of Nazi Germany. For example, as a result of the policy of Appeasement of Nazi Germany, the BIS transferred to the German Reichsbank 23 tons of gold it held for Czechoslovakia. Moreover, between 1933 and 1945, the BIS board of directors included Walther Funk, a prominent Nazi official, Emil Puhl, responsible for processing dental gold looted from concentration camp victims, Baron von Schroeder, the owner of the J.H. Stein Bank, and Herman Schmitz, the director of IG Farben, all of whom were later convicted of war crimes or crimes against humanity.[324] IG Farben was largest company in Europe at the time and utilized slave labor from concentration camps, including 30,000 prisoners from Auschwitz. IG Farben also supplied the poison gas, Zyklon B, that killed over one million people in gas chambers during the Holocaust.[325]

As Mayer Amschel Rothschild is attributed with saying, *"Permit me to issue and control the money of a nation and I care not who makes its laws."*

The control of the monetary system of the world is an awesome power, and with the immunities and unquestionable authority of the BIS and the central banking system, it could easily be concluded that these organizations are effectively above the law and the economic rulers of the world.

THE CONDITIONED OBSESSION WITH MONEY

Money never made a man happy yet, nor will it. The more a man has, the more he wants. Instead of filling a vacuum, it makes one. ~Benjamin Franklin

Rather than merely appreciating money as a convenient method of exchange, our society has become obsessed with money itself. We have been conditioned to "salivate" over money like Pavlov's dogs on the ringing of a bell. Pavlov's dogs would reliably salivate (Unconditional Response) when given meat powder (Unconditional Stimulus), but they gave no response to the ringing of a bell (Neutral Stimulus), before conditioning took place. In classical conditioning experiments, Pavlov always rang a bell immediately before presenting the dogs with meat powder. The dogs soon thereafter began to associate the sound of the bell with meat powder. As a result, the dogs would begin to salivate as soon as they heard the bell, even if Pavlov did not give them meat powder. The result was proof that a neutral stimulus can elicit an involuntary, automatic, reflexive response.

Much like Pavlov's dogs, we too have been conditioned to believe money is necessary for achieving abundance, fulfillment, happiness, freedom and success. Most of humankind no longer hunts for, or grows, their food. We have become dependent upon the "centralized money grid" for our basic physical necessities such as water, food, and shelter, as well as our modern-day social needs like and energy, transportation, communications, healthcare, education and manufactured goods. The "grid" requires money for us to get our needs met. As a result, we now associate money with survival, safety and security. We have also conditioned to associate money with our happiness, self-worth, freedom, fulfillment and abundance. As a result, many of us feel insecure, unhappy, unfulfilled and often worthless without money. However, while most people falsely believe that having more income and money will make them happier, there is significant research supporting the correlations between higher income and happiness is greatly exaggerated and mostly an illusion.[326]

As multi-billionaire Bill Gates said, *"I can understand wanting to have a million dollars, but once you get beyond that, I have to tell you, it's the same hamburger."*

Numerous surveys indicate that rising incomes have little influence on happiness once basic needs are satisfied (for water, food, shelter, energy, healthcare, education and transportation). After real material physical and social needs are met, it's more effective to increase happiness by improving the quality of life rather than increasing the quantity of goods purchased.[327]

Income and happiness have been shown to be relative to a person's region, culture and peers. For example, in Dubai, where there are a plethora of oil billionaires and oligarchs, the perceived need for wealth is higher than Germany, where wealth is more evenly distributed.[328]

According to a nationwide survey from the Bureau of Labor Statistics, men making more than $100,000 per year spend 19.9 percent of their time on passive leisure, compared to 34.7 percent for men making less than $20,000. Women making more than $100,000 spend 19.6 percent of their time on passive leisure, compared with 33.5 percent of those making less than $20,000.[329] Additionally, Galup research informs us that unhappy employees outnumber happy ones by 2 to 1 worldwide;[330] two-thirds of employed people are spending half of their waking hours working jobs that makes them unhappy. This is especially troubling considering the percentage of our lives spent working. The average full-time employee spends 2087 hours per year (50% of their waking hours) working in a job they dislike that causes social and environmental damage largely to pay banks for a house and a car, as well as for food and utilities.

In a study by two Princeton professors, Angus Deaton and psychologist and Nobel laureate, Daniel Kahnaman, published in *Proceedings of the National Academy of Sciences (PNAS)*, it was reported that *"People's life evaluations rise steadily with income, but the reported quality of emotional daily experience levels off at a certain income level."*[331] In the U.S., the study found, that *"while life evaluation rose steadily with annual* *income, the quality of the respondents' everyday experiences did not improve beyond approximately $75,000 a year."* In other words, happiness increases in correlation with income up to $75,000 a year and then levels off even as income continues to climb. Further proof that money doesn't buy happiness. Though clever marketing convinces us that if we buy more stuff, we'll be worthy, attractive and successful, the truth is that the "happiness" possessions bring is fleeting at best, and the debt we incur just keeps us on the hamster wheel of servitude. However, there are some ways in which money can make us feel happier and more fulfilled. These things encompass education, personal growth, well-being, inspiring experiences and service.

A study published in the Journal of Consumer Psychology [332] entitled *"If Money Doesn't Make You Happy, Then You Probably Aren't Spending It Right"*, included the following eight general recommendations:

1. Spend money on "experiences" rather than goods.

2. Donate money to others, including charities, rather than spending it solely on oneself.

3. Spend small amounts of money on many small, temporary pleasures rather than less often on larger ones.

4. Don't spend money on "extended warranties and other forms of over-priced insurance."

5. Adjust one's mindset to "pay now, consume later," instead of "consume now, pay later."

6. Exercise circumspection about the day-to-day consequences of a purchase beforehand.

7. Rather than buying products that provide the "best deal," make purchases based on what will facilitate well-being.

8. Seek out the opinions of other people who have prior experience of a product before purchasing it.

Another study conducted by Daniel Kahneman with economist Alan B Krueger, published in Science found those with higher incomes have higher tension and spend less time doing activities they enjoy.[333] According to this study, Kahneman and Kreger write:

> "The belief that high income is associated with good mood is widespread but mostly illusory. People with above-average income are relatively satisfied with their lives but are barely happier than others in moment-to-moment experience, tend to be more tense, and do not spend more time in particularly enjoyable activities."

> "Despite the weak relationship between income and global life satisfaction or experienced happiness, many people are highly motivated to increase their income,"

> "In some cases, this focusing illusion may lead to a misallocation of time, from accepting lengthy commutes (which are among the worst moments of the day) to sacrificing time spent socializing (which are among the best moments of the day)."

The effect of income on life satisfaction seems to be transient. People exaggerate the contribution of income to happiness because they focus, in part, on conventional achievements when evaluating their life, or the lives of others, such as devoting more time to work, shopping, childcare and other "obligatory" activities instead of social activities that promote connection, relaxation and happiness. People with higher incomes spend less time on "passive leisure" activities such as socializing, doing hobbies, or watching television, which the respondents viewed as more enjoyable.[334]

In succumbing to the conditioning that money will give us freedom, security and fulfillment, ironically many of us actually give up our time and freedom, separate from our families, and abandon many of the things that bring us joy. We give all these things up in order to work 40-50 hours per week at jobs that typically offer very little security and fulfillment in workplaces that are often unhealthy, sedentary and full of stress. Is it any wonder why so many of us end up with diseases and shortened lives from spending our lives in unhealthy and unfulfilling jobs?

Our society has, for generations, largely accepted, defended, reinforced and perpetuated as a "reality," the Global Human Agreement that "we need jobs and money." It's now accepted as a foregone conclusion that it's "normal" to sacrifice our time, freedom, life, abundance, health, dreams and passions to work in jobs that are often meaningless; emotionally, mentally and spiritually unfulfilling; and damaging to the well-being of humankind and the planet.

Money is much like a battery. We can use a battery to light a flashlight or to trigger a time bomb. It's not the battery that is good or evil. The battery has no ethics or intention. It's our intention and use of the battery that determines whether our conduct is ethical. Money doesn't have life, intention, ethics or an agenda. Money is not even an actual store of energy (except maybe the heat the paper may provide when burned). Money is not abundance and does not create abundance. Living systems create abundance. The value of money comes from our beliefs and agreement that money has value.

It's our relationship, beliefs and use of money that determines its impact on the world. Our economic vote, how we spend our time and money, can reshape our socio-economic-political system. **The monetary system and its fiat money is a belief system supported by a Global Human Agreement and transaction infrastructure.** The current monetary belief system is powerful in creating our reality. We have been conditioned to believe if we have money, everything will be wonderful! The research above, however, shows that most of us want what money represents—not money itself.

Most of us really don't want stacks of worthless paper or electronic journal entries. Most of us want free time, clean water, healthy food, comfortable shelter, good health, love, freedom, security, comfort, peace, meaningful connection and joy in our lives. And about two billion people just want a drink of clean water and a nutritious meal.[335] We often are so focused on money as an end in itself that we forget the numerous ways we abundantly create, experience, exchange and receive value that don't involve money. We share our time and our gifts. We enjoy loving each other and our friendships. We do favors for each other, give acknowledgment, show gratitude, and we engage in acts of beauty, kindness and support, such as hug, lending a helping hand, giving compassion and listening. Moreover, we share experiences together, such as watching a sunset, taking a hike, prayer/meditation, exercise, listening to music and sharing a meal. Ultimately, the greatest value we can exchange is that which enhances our health and the quality of life for ourselves, each other and the planet.

As will be discussed in the Chapter on *Transforming to a Regenerative Society*, we can create the largest economy known in the history of humankind—*The Regenerative Economy*. To create the Regenerative Economy will require us to transform the current monetary system, the global supply chain, our energy portfolio and our overconsumption, as well as the ways we obtain and use money. Rather than devoting our time to destructive, toxic, extractive and exploitive jobs, we could use our time, effort, energy and resources to do jobs that manifest abundance, beauty, and wellness in our world. Such regenerative jobs can, by way of example, include, (1) developing renewable energy and waste upcycling systems, (2) planting edible landscaping in cities, (3) permaculture farming, (4) plastic recycling, (5) creating products and foods that enhance health and boost the immune system, (6) redeveloping our transportation and fuel infrastructure, (7) applied education that inspires and teaches valuable skills, (8) improving ecosystemic health, (9) inventing biomimetic materials, (10) transforming manufacturing and the supply chain, and (11) restoring the wetlands, oceans, fisheries and forests, just to name a few opportunities. Additionally, by sharing more goods and services, we can create a higher quality of life with lower costs of living and reduced time and effort to meet or needs.

Our beliefs about value, exchange and money profoundly impact our ability to create real wealth for ourselves and our world. Our beliefs about money can attract or repel it. Some of us believe money is good, want lots of it and tend to attract it. Others believe money is evil, avoid placing their attention on it and tend to repel it. Money doesn't create abundance. Our universe, the Earth, living systems and humans create abundance. Money doesn't choose us. It cannot make choices. We make choices to choose or not choose money. Money, in and of itself, isn't alive. However, our thoughts around money are full of energy and, through our energy, we create aliveness or destruction. The following questions will help determine your relationship and choices around money:

- Would you rather have money than your health?

- Would you destroy the planet and beauty for money?

- Would you rather have money than your freedom?

- Would you kill and steal for money?

- Would you give up your happiness for money?

- Would you sell your family or yourself into slavery for money?

- Would you cheat your best friend for money?

Most people would answer "No" to all or most of the preceding questions. However, there about 6.5 billion out of 7.5 billion people that in some manner support, work for, propagate and participate with governments, banks, corporations and systems that consistently engage in conduct that includes: 1) harming human health and well-being; 2) creating waste, pollution and toxicity that destroys our environment and its beauty; 3) diminishing happiness and connection, 4) causing and supporting war, destruction and killing; 5) exploiting people and planet; (6) promoting human servitude to a system that perpetuates debt, scarcity and disempowerment; and (7) consistently lying, cheating, manipulating and stealing. While there may be extenuating circumstances where some people might answer "Yes" to one or more of the foregoing questions, we should inquire into how much of our behavior directly and indirectly supports and perpetuates systemic sociopathy and dysfunction. I must admit my own participation in our dysfunctional society—I work for fiat money, I shop for food and products that rely on the centralized supply chain, I use computers and cell phones that promote child labor and environmental waste, I drive a hybrid automobile that uses fossil fuel, I generate waste, I have a bank account, and I use credit cards. While I make significant efforts to be environmentally and socially conscious and consistently shift my behavior, participating in modern society is, by default, participating in dysfunction. I hold that we have the potential to systemically transform societal dysfunction into function and participate in a system and society that serves and fosters human and ecosystemic thriving.

ABUNDANCE, CURRENCY AND TRANSFORMING OUR RELATIONSHIP TO MONEY

If money is your hope for independence you will never have it. The only real security that a man will have in this world is a reserve of knowledge, experience, and ability.

~Henry Ford

The U.S. Declaration of Independence provides that our unalienable rights are "Life, liberty and the pursuit of happiness." The phrase "pursuit of happiness," rather than "experience of happiness," may fundamentally be why so many people in the U.S., the wealthiest country in the world, are so unhappy. We spend a considerable amount of our energy and attention pursuing happiness, but as a society are often discontent, unfulfilled and unhappy.

To achieve true happiness and live in regenerative abundance, we need to shift our beliefs. This requires us to transform our conditioned beliefs about (1) <u>pursuing</u> money and happiness rather than <u>being</u> content, fulfilled and happy in this moment, (2) the definitions and metrics of "success" (e.g., GDP, hoarding of wealth and resources) that perpetuate unsustainable and harmful growth and consumption, and (3) the elusive pursuit of happiness through the acquisition of "stuff." This perpetual cycle of unsustainable economic growth creates significant harm to the biosphere and our well-being as a species, while the engine of perpetual desire and greed prevents us from experiencing the true state of abundance we crave.

By changing our definition and metrics of "success," we can transform our socio-economic-political system from being destructive to regenerative and abundant. To create regenerative abundance in our society requires the following:

1. Balancing the consumption and growth of humankind with the planet's capacity to regenerate the resources we consume;

2. Switching to renewable energy and materials;

3. Replacing that which we take from the planet (e.g., regenerating our oceans, forests, soils and watersheds);

4. Reducing consumption by sharing goods and services;

5. Manufacturing products that are built to last rather than for obsolescence;

6. Circular economic practices that reuse, recycle, refurbish and upcycle materials from obsolete products;

7. The equitable and conscious generation, distribution and use of resources in a way that allows all life to thrive and experience abundance through healthy and regenerative ecosystemic thriving; and

8.   Generously and voluntarily giving, investing and exchanging our resources and currency for the betterment and thriving of humankind and the planet.

The root of the word "currency" is *"current."* For there to be an abundance of wealth, there must be continual flow and *current*. For example, when the money supply is flowing abundantly, new businesses are created, existing businesses can expand, more opportunities are generated and money flow multiplies resulting in exponential growth and a robust economy. However, when the money supply is shut down (e.g., The Great Depression, the 2008 economic crisis or the 2020 COVID-19 pandemic), businesses fail, people lose their jobs and homes go into foreclosure. The issue is how is the supply of money is used. Rather than continuing to use money for obsolete products that fuel a toxic greenhouse gas belching supply chain, consumerism and waste, or bailing out the too-big-to-fail corporations, we could create robust wealth and a plethora meaningful jobs by using money and resources to promote wise, regenerative and resilient infrastructure and conscious industries that promote ecosystemic thriving.

Exchange creates the *"current"* of currency, which leads to an abundance of wealth. Greed, hoarding and consolidation generally are adverse to *current*. Voluntarily recognizing, rewarding and exchanging value is critically important to *current* and promoting an abundant economy. Also, how we spend resources and currency has a profound impact on the quality of life we experience When we purchase and invest in regenerative businesses, services and products, we increase the flow of currency, well-being and abundance of people and planet.

The creation of abundant wealth requires value exchange, equilibrium, momentum and circulation. However, there are many people who feel entitled to take the time, effort and property of others and the planet's resources without exchange. When each of us receives or takes value without recognition, fair exchange and equilibrium, we negatively impact the momentum of currency and therefore harm the development of an equitable and robust global economy. By privatizing, exploiting and extracting the natural resources from the planet without replacing or regenerating these valuable and life-giving resources, we diminish the ability of our planet to support the continuation of humankind and many of the planet's species upon which we depend.

Our monetary system is based upon an illusion of finite resources and value derived from scarcity. While the Earth can only support a certain level of population and consumption, it is our consumptive and unsustainable practices, not the Earth's limitations, that are creating scarcity and threatening our survivability. By reallocating our time, effort, energy and resources to regenerating the Earth's life-giving systems, we can support an estimated population of ten billion people. Building the Regenerative Economy and providing meaningful work supporting ecosystemic thriving will allow future generations to live healthy, abundant and thriving lives.

Abundance and energetic exchange is a constant state in the universe and nature. This constant state is not conditional upon money. While universal energy, consciousness and nature are abundant, it is easy to view our planet as having a finite size and a limited capacity to support life. Shifting mass consciousness from the current scarcity-based mindset to an abundance-based belief system will lead to restorative practices and the Regenerative Economy.

The UN Report submitted by the Special Rapporteur, Olivier De Schutter, on the right to food, concludes that poverty and inequality, not limited stocks of food, are responsible for hunger.[336] The world already produces more than 1½ times the food to feed everyone on the planet. We have enough food to feed 10 billion people, the population expected by 2050. However, due to costs of fuel, shipping and supply-chain intermediaries, a high percentage of the food goes to waste and those living in or near poverty go hungry.

The UN provides the following suggestions for creating the abundance required to feed the entire population: "*Agriculture must develop in ways that increase the incomes of smallholders. Food availability is, first and foremost, an issue at the household level, and hunger today is mostly attributable not to stocks that are too low or to global supplies unable to meet demand, but to poverty; increasing the incomes of the poorest is the best way to combat it. Cross-country comparisons show that GDP growth originating in agriculture is at least twice as effective in reducing poverty as GDP growth originating outside agriculture.*"

The UN report provides some examples on how to address the increased needs of a growing population:

"At present, nearly half of the world's cereal production is used to produce animal feed, and meat consumption is predicted to increase from 37.4 kg/person/year in 2000 to over 52 kg/person/year by 2050, so that by mid-century, 50 per cent of total cereal production may go to increasing meat production. Therefore, real-locating cereals used in animal feed to human consumption, a highly desirable option in developed countries where the excess animal protein consumption is a source of public health problems, combined with the development of alternative feeds based on new technology, waste and discards, could go a long way towards meeting the increased needs."

"By enhancing on-farm fertility production, agroecology reduces farmers' reliance on external inputs and state subsidies. This, in turn, makes vulnerable smallhold-ers less dependent on local retailers and moneylenders. One key reason why agro-ecology helps to support incomes in rural areas is because it promotes on-farm fertility generation. Indeed, supplying nutrients to the soil does not necessarily require adding mineral fertilizers. It can be done by applying livestock manure or by growing green manures. Farmers can also establish a "fertilizer factory in the fields" by planting trees that take nitrogen out of the air and "fix" it in their leaves, which are subsequently incorporated into the soil."

The approach to "solving" the world's challenges is often similar to the approach of western medicine—treat the symptom rather than cure the root cause. The symptoms of climate change, environmental destruction, pollution, poverty, hunger and war arise from a dysfunctional system and require systemic change, rather than symptomatic treatment. Adhering to the quantitative metric of GDP as a measurement of success and continuing to support the existing corrupt and dysfunctional socio-economic-political systems will not shift the existing paradigm or cure the cause of systemic social dysfunction.

Systemic paradigm shifts, innovation and creativity, and new metrics, beliefs and behaviors are required to transform our socio-economic-political model and cure the ills caused by the existing system. To shift the current paradigm, create abundance and thriving for humanity and our planet requires an inside-out, ground-up and top-down approach.

- *Inside-Out*—Transforming our individual belief systems and perceptions, increasing awareness and evolving consciousness to shift from beliefs and behaviors that are competitive, harmful and wasteful to those that are regenerative, collaborative, loving and conscious. This also includes culti-vating deeper connection with one's self, each other and our planet. As we each change individually, we contribute to the collective transformation of our civilization and planet.

- *Ground-Up*—Evolving the way we relate to the Earth and transforming our rapacious economy based upon extraction and waste by developing regenerative ways of living and being on the Earth. This includes fostering new, regenerative, renewable and respectful ways to engage in agriculture, energy, water, transportation, construction, materials, manufacturing, sup-ply chain, education and community development so that these activities result in ecosystemic thriving.

- *Top-Down*—Changing our socio-economic-political system and the "met-rics of success" (e.g., growth, expansion, GDP, profit-at-all costs) that drive, perpetuate and influence the current matrix of power, control, domination, war and corruption. In our current money-driven profit-at-all-costs society, the most meaningful vote is not our political vote but our economic vote. The way we spend our time and money and the economic choices we make are far more powerful than our political vote. Politics generally follows market economics. The language of money and economics is the language that bankers, governments and corporatocracy understand. For example, the more we choose organic food over junk food, clean energy vehicles over gas guzzlers, and services and products from ethical providers, the less ethical corporations will either shift to fulfill the demand for ethical and socially responsible behavior, products and services or go out of business.

  We can send a clear message through the language of money that the old paradigm of profit-at-all-costs corporations understand: *If you want our money and business, adhere to ethical, socially and environmentally responsible practices.* When this message shows up as higher revenues and profits to conscious companies and losses in revenues and profits to unconscious companies, corporate behavior will change. As large corporations positively transform their behavior with commitments to ESG and corporate responsibility, and as new conscious corporations arise, corrupt and destructive government practices are likely to change.

One way we can transform our world to one that is abundant and thriving is to buy products from and invest in only *"Ethically Sustainable Companies."* Ethically Sustainable Companies are those that engage in the following conduct:

- Utilize business practices and processes that are based in ethical conduct that is regenerative and good for people and planet;

- Treat their employees and business contacts with integrity, equitability and respect;

- Help build communities and cooperate with entrepreneurs and small business owners instead of destroying them;

- Respect the environment and foster programs to create ecosystemic thriving;

- Utilize safe, non-toxic ingredients and methods in the creation of their products;

- Contribute to the flow and currency of global abundance;

- Strive to create a world of Abundance, Wellness & Empowerment with solutions and programs that help create systemic change that eliminate disease, hunger, starvation, pollution and war rather than promote it and profit from it; and

- Elevate transparency and collaboration over secrecy and competition

Follow the money and the motivation of sellers of goods and services—if a company profits from, or perpetuates, disease, hunger, starvation, pollution, imprisonment, the exploitation of people and planet,

and/or war, don't invest in their stock and don't buy their products or services. They will get the message when it hits their bottom line and the CEO's bonus.

In practical terms, *triple bottom line* accounting generally means expanding the traditional company reporting framework to take into account not just profits and financial outcomes, but also environmental and social performance. We'll see massive positive shifts in corporate behavior once we (1) stop investing in the stocks of destructive corporations adhering to "profits at all costs" behavior, (2) stop purchasing the products and services of extractive, exploitative and polluting companies, and (3) require the CEOs, CFOs, COOs and EVP's to be personally accountable, rather than receiving bonuses, for the destruction and fraud that their businesses perpetrate.

We are seeing a growing demand for Environmental, Social and Governance ("ESG") investments. There is now $40.5 trillion USD invested into ESG Assets Under Management ("AUM") globally.[337] There was also another $600 billion invested in green, social and sustainability bonds ("GSSS") in 2020—nearly double the $326 billion invested in 2019.[338]

While commitment to ESG should be applauded as a step in the right direction, much of the $40.5 trillion of ESG investment has gone into large public companies that continue to perpetuate the centralized supply chain, fossil fuel burning, greenhouse gas emissions, extraction and exploitative practices. The ESG commitment and the massive investment into ESG is just not enough to address the urgent transformation we require.

In our society, money is a major stimulus to almost all action. In order to accelerate the transformation required to reverse the damage to our ecosystems and foster a thriving society, trillions of dollars need to be put to work in funding and accelerating core Regenerative Enterprise & Projects ("REPs"). REPs are characterized as projects that promote the health and thriving of people and planet with measurable and quantifiable regenerative criteria and achievement of the United Nations' Sustainable Development Goals ("SDGs").

THE 12-STEP PROGRAM FOR MONEYHOLICS

We often tend to blame the oppressive "system" of capitalism and the corporations for much of the suffering, damage, toxicity and pain on this planet. However, it's not money doing this, nor is it some "system" out of our control that is victimizing us. It's the system "We, the People" support every day. We have allowed the rape and toxification of the planet, so let us not "otherize" or play the role of victim. We are each a creator, participant in, and perpetuator of, our current system. So long as we use and depend upon world currency, drive a car, use fossil fuels dirty energy, purchase manufactured products, live in a house, eat store bought food, have a bank account, use credit cards or invest in stocks or bonds, we support and reinforce the dysfunction of the system.

Too many of us in the developed world have bought into a way of life that promotes having and hoarding more than we need. We have learned to compete rather than collaborate and hoard rather than share. We compete to have more stuff, resources and power than the guy next door, largely to satisfy the desire of our egos for validation, security and status. This competition, hoarding and elevation of quantitative value over qualitative value annihilates abundance and diminishes the quality of life.

The more each of us change, the more the Matrix changes. As we take back our power and independence, the stronger we become, leading to more rapid and widespread adoption of the new paradigm. Like a functional virus in a dysfunctional system, the proliferation of higher consciousness and a shift in beliefs, metrics of success and systems will empower the collaborative co-creation of a world of abundance, health, thriving, love, respect and unity.

Here are some questions to consider:

- How can we devote our Personal Resources (e.g., time, energy, attention, services, thoughts, money) and the convenient exchange money provides to being in service to planetary thriving rather than destruction?

- How do we overcome our addiction to useless stuff that ends up in landfill and requires a toxic greenhouse gas belching supply chain that causes destruction of the planet's ecosystems?

- How can we collaborate and share more to have a higher quality of life with less time, toil and struggle?

- How can we create regenerative enterprises that provide meaningful work in service to the planet that result in humans becoming more healthy, happy, loving, free, kind and fulfilled?

- How can we overcome our addiction to the current Matrix and create a transformed society and world?

While money has many beneficial uses and is the stimulus for action in our society, much of our conditioning and addiction to money perpetuates destructive and wasteful activities harmful to ourselves, society and our planet. Using the **12-Step Program for Moneyholics** outlined below as a framework for monetary and economic transformation, we can start becoming the change that is so necessary for the thriving of humankind and our ecosystem.

The 12-Step Program for Moneyholics

1. **Become aware of your beliefs and behaviors** that contribute to, and support, the perpetuation of dysfunction in our society.

2. **Acknowledge the need for change** and accept personal responsibility for changing systemic dysfunction, starting with you.

3. **Courageously commit to transforming your beliefs and behaviors** (Be the change you want to see, be a functional virus in a dysfunctional system, and be the agent of change in the Global Human Agreement). Replace the obsolete and harmful beliefs, behaviors, systems and paradigms with those that promote regenerative abundance, wellness, empowerment, beauty and love.

4. **Create the future rather than fix the past.** Innovate solutions rather than trying to fix and fight against the problem. Be willing to create new systems, beliefs and behaviors.

5. **Redefine the measurements of success,** including, as examples, ecosystemic thriving over economic growth, real fulfillment and sustainability over money, local independence over centralized dependence, generosity over hoarding, innovation over stagnation and cooperation over competition.

6. **Advance opportunities that increase quality of life, ecosystemic thriving and net positive impact** by engaging in such things as voluntary simplicity and sufficiency, collaborative consumption, inclusivity, respect and regenerative practices.

7. **Exercise our conscious and economic vote** by purchasing products and services from ethical and sustainable companies, living in communities that utilize integrative design and regenerative practices, working for, and investing in, companies that promote health, beauty, equitability and ecosystemic thriving.

8. **Engage in direct value exchange** utilizing barter, direct and generous personal giving and ethical decentralized alternative currencies. Create an abundant economy through voluntary and generous recognition and rewarding of value and building a sharing economy.

9. **Elevate good reputation**, ethical conduct, generosity and equitability over accumulation of wealth and ruthless competition.

10. **Fearlessly claim our sovereignty and freedom** to live in, and contribute to, a thriving, abundant, well and empowered society.

11. **Understand and see the divine nature in everything** and have deep respect for all that exists. When we spend money, ask whether the expenditure supports and respects the miracle of life and promotes greater personal and planetary wellness, connection and thriving.

12. **Educate and mentor others to be in service to a Regenerative World** that supports the thriving of people and planet. Multi-generational conditioning and our education system must be transformed so that our children and future generations are able to thrive as a species and serve each other the planet.

Moneyholics have an addiction to money and much of the meaningless stuff money buys. We often don't consider the great harm and impact that our consumption causes by perpetuating a toxic, extractive and exploitative supply chain, as well as poverty, hunger, suffering, economic inequality and social injustice. If we are to heal this addiction to money, we must overcome our desire for, and overconsumption of, stuff we don't need. This will help alleviate the related ecological and social symptoms of our addiction to material consumption. We must take responsibility on an individual level to make the change toward having a healthy relationship with money. Grounding this transformation into practical and economic next steps includes transforming economic metrics and models of "success," the way we relate to each other and our planet, our governance and organizational practices, our education system, and our communities, as well as investing in the Regenerative Economy to create a new economic system based upon abundance, wellness and empowerment.

In understanding the consciousness of money and gaining a new perspective on our relationship with money, I'd like to share one of the most brilliant and original passages I have read regarding money written by Jeff Vander Clute. In the following passage, Jeff channeled the consciousness of money as if it were a living entity and here is what money had to say:

> "*I have been asked to support every kind of enterprise imaginable. Those enterprises that are the most aligned with my generative impulse, I am able to support freely, which is to say without the barricades that you have created...*
>
> *My roots go immensely deep, and what you call money are but finite forms of my Unlimited Nature. So deepen your relationship with me, and you will discover so much more of me.*
>
> *There is nothing you need to do to earn me in my essence for I am the active aspect of Life. I am all around you in hyper-abundance. And as the active aspect of Life, I am always available to you. Let us be clear that I am always supporting evolution. I am that which makes evolution possible. I am the Evolutionary Impulse. This is why you need only say "yes" to me, to open your arms and heart to me, and I will come to you. I will animate your luminous projects.*

You have had the idea that I am a problem, because the limited forms of me—of what you have called money—have been created for specific purposes that have naturally reached their limits. I am not a problem, and certainly I am not evil. In fact, I am the force that solves all problems by introducing new possibilities into even the direst situations.

Become friends with my true nature and you will discover that I am able to find you even through the limited forms of me, for as the matrix of ever-expanding Life energy I do overflow. There is always a crack in the barricades that you have erected with such diligence over millennia. There is always a way in for the light that I am. And there are so many ways I am streaming to you, even now.

I am Consciousness, and I am Love. So love me, just as I love you. I have loved you since the beginning. Therefore it is safe. You can give me, receive me—stop rejecting me—, invest me, exchange with me. Offer me in gratitude and I will keep returning to you in multidimensional ways that overwhelm mere... transactionality. Relax. Become open to me, permeable to me, and we shall merge in the dance of Life. For once again, I am Life, and we are one. I love you. Will you have me?"

As Jeff points out, if we see money as nature, as life and as a means for accomplishing good in the world, our perception and relationship with money can change it into a tool for positive transformation. Money can be used in service to love, beauty, kindness, abundance and ecosystemic thriving.

CHAPTER 23

Transforming Economic Metrics
to Support Well-Being

"Gross National Product counts air pollution and cigarette advertising, and ambulances to clear our highways of carnage. It counts special locks for our doors and the jails for the people who break them. It counts the destruction of the redwood and the loss of our natural wonder in chaotic sprawl. It counts napalm, nuclear warheads and armored cars for the police to fight the riots in our cities. It counts Whitman's rifle and Speck's knife, and the television programs which glorify violence in order to sell toys to our children. Yet the gross national product does not allow for the health of our children, the quality of their education or the joy of their play. It does not include the beauty of our poetry or the strength of our marriages, the intelligence of our public debate or the integrity of our public officials. It measures neither our wit nor our courage, neither our wisdom nor our learning, neither our compassion nor our devotion to our country, it measures everything in short, except that which makes life worthwhile. And it can tell us everything about America except why we are proud that we are Americans."

~Robert F. Kennedy (March 18, 1968)

Not much has changed in our money system and economic metrics since Robert F. Kennedy made his speech in 1968. Money is still the primary method by which most of humankind acquires its needs (e.g., water, food, shelter, energy, healthcare) and fulfills its desires (e.g., computers, cell phones, fashion, cars, planes, artwork, travel, entertainment). Unfortunately, our money system is largely based upon debt, scarcity and quantitative measurements, such as Gross Domestic Product ("GDP") and short sighted quarterly earnings.

The most widely used definition of progress is known as Gross Domestic Product ("GDP"). GDP is a measure of a country's economic performance based upon the market value of all final goods and services produced within the borders of a nation in a year. Thus, "progress" and "success" are largely defined as productivity translated into dollars—the more dollars, the more progress.

As a species, we have become disconnected from each other and nature and have elevated the importance of quantitative measurements (e.g., profits, money earned, money saved, the value of our stuff, GDP, GNP and quarterly earnings), over the qualitative principles (e.g., beauty, love, joy, kindness deep connection with each other and nature, great health, work-live-play balance, spiritual development, art, music, and development of our core gifts). We are seeing the erosion and destruction of natural capital and the ability of the Earth's ecosystems to service our consumptive demands. This is largely due to (1) the widely accepted principle that scarcity creates value rather than abundance; and (2) the continual extraction from nature without replenishment in order to gain higher short term profits.

As Gunter Pauli, author of the Blue Economy, said, *"Give a man a fish and he'll eat for a day. Teach a man to fish and he'll overfish."*

The quote above rings true in a world conditioned to over-consume and metrics that reward overconsumption and the externalization of corporate expenses. The unsustainable desire for more than is sufficient is substantially due to societal conditioning defining "success" in terms of quantitative growth, expansion and productivity, as well as the conditioned fear and insecurity of not having enough. In this context, "productivity" means generating and purchasing goods or services that add to, and continually expand, the Gross Domestic Product ("GDP"). However, GDP and other quantitative metrics are often dysfunctional and harmful as they do not value good health, happiness, quality of life, beauty, ecosystemic thriving and the plethora of things that make life worth living.

We are destroying our planet, sacrificing our health, surrendering our happiness, and perpetuating human suffering for next quarter's profits to support the GDP and a quantitative system of destructive and unsustainable growth.

Efficient, clean, healthy and affordable water collected, food grown, and energy generated on-site; good health; enjoyment of nature; time spent with our friends and family; collaborative consumption; and creating beauty, generally don't contribute to the GDP. For example, one of the most efficient, convenient, cost-effective and healthy things I can do is pull an apple off a tree in my backyard. However, plucking an apple off my tree is bad for the GDP—the government did not collect taxes, the corporations did not profit, and I didn't need to use the central bank's fiat money. I didn't engage or utilize the farming industry, the petrochemical/pesticide industry, the packaging industry, the manufacturing of trucks and transportation, shipping & logistics, the oil industry's polluting fossil fuel and asphalt, the military to protect the oil industry's interests and pipelines, the construction and maintenance of storage and distribution facilities, the construction and maintenance of grocery stores, or the auto industry so I could drive to the store to buy my apple. Also, eating a fresh apple is good for my health, so the medical and pharmaceutical industry didn't get its "bite of the apple."

Our socio-economic political system has been designed in an unsustainable and inefficient manner to support dependence upon a fossil-fuel, a centralized grid and the central banking money system. Thus, to "meet our needs," we depend upon money, oil, debt and the military industrial complex. The GDP supported Matrix has been designed to make it difficult for us to meet our needs for even the basics of water, food, shelter and energy without money. By creating more centralization, more perceived "needs" and more inefficiency, we create more jobs, which we believe is a good. However, human effort, time, energy and brilliance has largely been diverted away from serving the health and thriving of humankind to perpetuating sustaining the Matrix. The existence and expansion of the Matrix rely on fictitious legal entities, fiat money, electronic journal entries, mass overconsumption, destructive behaviors and quantitative measurements such as the GDP.

While quantitative measurements, such as GDP, have their place, they should be in last place, not first place. It's critical to our survival and well-being that we adopt and elevate ethical and qualitative metrics such as the Genuine Progress Indicator ("GPI"), Gross National Happiness ("GNH") and Well-Being Indices:

1. GROSS DOMESTIC PRODUCT ("GDP")

GDP is a quantitative measurement that generally omits any qualitative measurements. For example, disease, war and disasters are often good for the GDP, as they cause people to spend money, create jobs and support industry. Things like health, love, happiness, home and family care, community involvement, peace, respect for each other, and the preservation of indigenous cultures have relatively no measurement in GDP.

GDP is fundamentally a destructive, inhumane and wasteful measurement of progress and leads to blind consumerism, extraction, and exploitation for the purpose of stimulating economic growth rather than the promotion of a higher quality of life. The GDP thrives on inefficiency and the wasteful mismanagement of the Earth's resources resulting in wasted energy, pollution and environmental destruction, disease, greenhouse gas emissions and climate change. For example, to get products onto Wal-Mart's shelves, think about the precious natural resources and energy required to (1) build, power and operate polluting factories in China to make cheap, often low-quality products for Wal-Mart, (2) extract and/or harvest, package and ship the raw supplies (largely from South America and Africa) to China for manufacturing; (3) manufacture, package and ship the merchandise from the factories in China to a port in the U.S.; (4) ship the products on rail or trucks to one of Wal-Mart's 112 distribution centers, (5) ship the products from the distribution centers to over 4,100 Wal-Mart and Sam's Club locations across the U.S., (6) build, power and operate each of the over 4,100 Wal-Mart stores (Wal-Mart's electricity bill alone runs approximately $7 billion a year), (7) manufacture and ship cars, fuel cars and then drive cars to and from Wal-Mart, (8) pay for, power and maintain the additional square footage to store these products, (9) move the obsolete, unfashionable and unwanted products to landfill, and (10) remediate the ecological damage and impact on our health from the waste and burning of fossil fuels. The cost and negative impact to our health and environment is staggering, but it's good for the GDP.

We have been led to believe that the collective resources of planet Earth and humankind to serve a toxic quantitative measurement of GDP is somehow noble. GDP is often equated with national, even patriotic, pride. However, using GDP as a definition of economic strength and progress demonstrates is accomplishing just the opposite—we are killing ourselves and the planet, perpetuating widespread poverty and increasing economic injustice. We are not progressing, getting healthier, nor happier. In the U.S., the wealthiest country in the world, 47 million people live in poverty.[339]

Real progress and success is more qualitative than quantitative. Things like greater abundance, optimal health, increased happiness, more time for intellectual, spiritual, creative, family and social activities, more beauty, peace and a clean environment are true indicators of real progress and success.

The limited and destructive nature of GDP, as a success metric, has been under scrutiny for years. The largest and most powerful economies of the world are members of the Organization for Economic Co-operation and Development (OECD). The members of the OECD accept the principles of representative democracy and a free-market economy. Since its inception, the members of the OECD have adhered to GDP as a measurement of success. Below are the countries and the dates they ratified the convention.

AUSTRIA: 29 September 1961	LUXEMBOURG: 7 December 1961
BELGIUM: 13 September 1961	MEXICO: 18 May 1994
CANADA: 10 April 1961	NETHERLANDS: 13 November 1961
CZECH REPUBLIC: 21 December 1995	NEW ZEALAND: 29 May 1973
DENMARK: 30 May 1961	NORWAY: 4 July 1961
FINLAND: 28 January 1969	POLAND: 22 November 1996
FRANCE: 7 August 1961	PORTUGAL: 4 August 1961
GERMANY: 27 September 1961	SLOVAK REPUBLIC: 14 December 2000
GREECE: 27 September 1961	SPAIN: 3 August 1961
HUNGARY: 7 May 1996	SWEDEN: 28 September 1961
ICELAND: 5 June 1961	SWITZERLAND: 28 September 1961
IRELAND: 17 August 1961	TURKEY: 2 August 1961
ITALY: 29 March 1962	UNITED KINGDOM: 2 May 1961
JAPAN: 28 April 1964	UNITED STATES: 12 April 1961
KOREA: 12 December 1996	

As of 2005, the OECD started formally re-examining GDP as a measurement and found that it is a flawed measurement as it does not account for the well-being of a country. In 2012, the OECD Secretary-General, Angel Gurria, said *"the economic crisis has shown that it is essential to make well-being a central criteria for determining policies. Governments' response to the crisis must be based around policies that lay the foundation for more inclusive and sustainable growth in the future.*"[340]

The well-being or quality of life of a population is an important concern in economics and political science. There are many components to well-being, including the standard of living and the amount of money and/or access a person has to goods and services. These numbers are fairly easily measured. Others like freedom, happiness, art, environmental health, and innovation are harder to measure. This has created an inevitable imbalance as programs and policies are created to fit the easily available quantitative economic metrics while ignoring the other qualitative measures that are more difficult to assess.[341]

The OECD identifies 11 different dimensions that are important for well-being grouped under two broad headings—1) Quality of Life and 2) Material Conditions:

Individual Well-Being	
Quality of Life	*Material Conditions*
• Health Status • Work-Life Balance • Education and Skills • Social Connections • Civic Engagement and Governance • Environmental Quality • Personal Security • Subjective Well-Being	• Income and Wealth • Jobs and Earnings • Housing • Necessary Products and Goods

In order to sustain well-being, four different types of capital need to be addressed and preserved:

Sustainability of Well-Being	
• Natural Capital • Economic Capital	• Human Capital • Social Capital

It is clear, even to the OECD, that our definition, mindset, lifestyle and measurement of "progress" and "success" need to change to include quality of life and well-being.

2. THE GENUINE PROGRESS INDICATOR (GPI)[342]

The Genuine Progress Indicator ("GPI")[343] is a transformational metric that has significant support to replace or complement GDP as a measure of economic growth. GPI is designed to take a more full and complete account of the health of a nation's economy by incorporating environmental and social factors which GDP does not measure. GPI utilizes True Cost Accounting to include transparency of subsidies, environmental impact, health and social costs of a business or activity.

By the early 1990s, there was a consensus in human development theory and ecological economics that growth in money supply was actually reflective of a loss of well-being. GDP values all economic activity regardless of its true costs and destructive impact on society or the environment. For example, GDP does not generally value the natural capital services the Earth does for free, quality of life, and good health, but does value natural disasters, bad health and economic spending that's adverse to the quality of life.

GPI, however, measures whether a country's increased production of goods and expanding services have actually resulted in the improvement of the well-being of the people in the country and the environment. GPI can more reliably measure true economic progress, as it distinguishes between worthwhile growth and uneconomic growth. Accordingly, the GPI will be zero if the financial costs of crime, poor health, pollution and environmental devastation equal the financial gains in production of goods and services, all other factors being constant.

The "costs" of economic activity include the following potential harmful effects:

- Cost of resource depletion
- Cost of crime
- Cost of increased health risks
- Cost of global warming
- Cost of war
- Cost of energy
- Cost of family and social breakdown
- Cost of air, water, and noise pollution
- Loss of farmland
- Loss of wetlands

GPI takes account of these problems by incorporating sustainability as a metric. A determination is made whether a country's economic activity over the fiscal year has left the country with a better or worse future possibility of repeating at least the same level of economic activity in the long run. For example, agricultural activity that replenish water resources, such as river runoff, will score a higher GPI than the same level of agricultural activity that drastically lowers the water table by pumping irrigation water from wells.

Another application of GPI is to calculate the true costs of goods sold. For example, when determining the cost of a gallon of gasoline, GPI would calculate the government subsidies; the cost of the military to secure the oil supply; the cost of pollution and environmental impact; the impact on human health; and the impact on society and indigenous cultures. Using these metrics, a gallon of gasoline would cost approximately $15 per gallon.[344] Even if we ignore the negative externalities of fossil fuels, the independent think tank, Overseas Development Institute (ODI), reports that G20 countries provided fossil fuel subsidies totaling $444 billion per year. This is more than four times the subsidies the entire world spends on renewables.[345] Thus, using the true cost accounting measurements of GPI would reveal that renewable energy and biofuels are already a less expensive, viable and practical choice for energy. By replacing GDP with GPI, we can start to transform our economic decisions to incorporate truly pragmatic investments that support quality of life.

3. GROSS NATIONAL HAPPINESS (GNH) AND WELL-BEING INDICES[346]

A metric used in Bhutan to promote a healthy and happy society is Gross National Happiness (GNH). Using metrics and surveys, GNH is a measurement that defines quality of life in more holistic and psychological terms than GDP. The term was coined by Bhutan's former King Jigme Singye Wangchuck in 1972. It signaled his commitment to building an economy that would serve Bhutan's unique culture based on Buddhist spiritual values. According to Adrian White's study entitled "*A Global Projection of Subjective Well-being: A Challenge to Positive Psychology*"[347], Bhutan ranked 8th out of 178 countries in Subjective Well-being, (a metric used by many psychologists since 1997) and the only country in the top 20 "happiest" countries that had a very low GDP.

The **Four Pillars of GNH** are:

1. The promotion of equitable and sustainable socio-economic development,

2. Preservation and promotion of cultural values,

3. Conservation of the natural environment, and

4. Establishment of good governance.

Many of the metrics of GNH are somewhat subjective and easier to state than to measure; however, measurement of subjective well-being has advanced significantly in the last 20 years. The OECD, in their report *OECD Guidelines on Measuring Subjective Well-Being* stated, *"Notions of subjective well-being or happiness have a long tradition as central elements of quality of life. However, until recently, these concepts were often deemed beyond the scope of quantitative measurement. In the past two decades, however, an increasing body of evidence has shown that subjective well-being can be measured in surveys, that such measures are valid and reliable, and they can inform policy making."*

According to the OECD, there are several models for measuring subjective well-being. Subjective well-being consists of 3 parts:

1. Life Evaluation—a reflective assessment on a person's life or some specific aspect of it.

2. Affect—a person's positive or negative feelings or emotional states, typically measured with reference to a particular point in time.

3. Eudaimonia—a sense of meaning and purpose in life, or good psychological functioning.

Questions that measure life satisfaction include:

- Are you satisfied with your life?

- How are the conditions of your life?

- Are you close to your ideal life?

- Have you gotten the important things you want in life?

- Would you change things about your life?

The UN, OECD, governments and a plethora of universities have conducted studies to address the metrics and measurement of subjective well-being.[348] By integrating these various sources, I developed the following **9 Dimensions and Metrics of Well-Being**:

9 Dimensions and Metrics of Well-Being	
Dimension of Wellness	*Metrics*
1. Environmental	Applied environmental metrics, such as inclusion of nature, as well as levels of pollution, noise, traffic, waste and toxins (e.g., pesticides, fungicides, herbicides). Also, measurements of toxicity in products and environments (e.g., food, beverages, skin products, cleaners, automobiles, homes, and offices)
2. Physical	Measurement of physical health such as levels of illnesses, disease, and addictions, as well as healthy diet, exercise, vitality, and the ability to effectively engage in desired daily activities.
3. Mental	Utilization of mental health metrics, such as levels of usage of antidepressants, rise or decline of psychotherapy patients, as well as alternatives such as practicing mindfulness and meditation. Also, metrics such as literacy, productivity and mental acuity can be utilized.
4. Emotional	Rating and correlating emotional states such as happiness, joy, inspiration, contentment, generosity vs. anger, guilt, frustration, stress and fear can be used to determine the well-being of people.
5. Spiritual/Energetic	Assessing one's sense of peace, unity, equanimity, optimism and connection, as well as the energy levels required to achieve desired states of being.
6. Social	Measurement of our ability to maintain positive relationships with family, friends, and workers and contribute to society. Metrics include quality of relationships, community engagement, discrimination, safety, divorce rates, complaints of domestic conflicts and family lawsuits, public lawsuits, crime rates, free time, working hours, access to housing, education, healthcare transportation, and public services.
7. Occupational	Quantifying work-related factors and labor metrics, such as jobless claims, job change, workplace complaints and lawsuits, prevailing wages, workplace benefits and incentives, and social and environmental responsibility record.
8. Economic	Measurement of economic metrics, such as consumer debt, savings, average income to consumer price index ratio and income distribution.
9. Political	Evaluation of political metrics, such as the quality of local democracy, individual freedom, foreign conflicts, effectiveness of regulatory bodies, corruption, systemic efficiency, budget surpluses or deficits, safety, security, taxation as a percentage of income, and benefits to people and planet.

Clearly the foregoing metrics are much more holistic and meaningful for measuring true progress, success and quality of life than GDP and purely quantitative measurements. By implementing and adopting qualitative metrics as a foundation for progress and success, we are likely to see significant transformation in our socio-economic-political conditions and build a world that accounts for improved quality of life.

TRANSFORMING ACCOUNTING AND VALUATION PRINCIPLES

Generally Accepted Accounting Principles ("GAAP") as established by the Financial Accounting Standards Board ("FASB") are used to set the standards for accounting, auditing and determining the value of companies. The value of a public company is generally known as "Market Capitalization" (aka "Market Cap"). Market Cap is a measurement of the economic value and size of a company equal to the share price, times the number of shares outstanding. For example, a company with 100 million shares issued and outstanding and trading at $10 per share has a market cap of $1 billion.

Public perception and market dynamics are major factors in determining stock price. Another major factor is a company's economic performance. An essential benchmark of that economic performance is "EBITDA" or Earnings Before Interest, Taxes, Depreciation and Amortization. This is fundamentally a simple benchmark for determining the operating pre-tax net profit of the company before the creative accounting begins. EBITDA multiplied by the Price/Earnings ("P/E") Ratio is a method for determining the value of shares. Companies in industries that are seeing long term growth potential, scalability and higher profit margins tend to have a higher P/E Ratio than companies in declining industries with lower profit margins.

For example, if the board of a company with an EBITDA of $1 billion, a P/E Ratio of 10:1 and a market cap of $10 billion decides they want to spend $100 million on programs for social and environmental good, their EBITDA would be reduced to $900 million and the shareholders at a 10:1 P/E Ratio would potentially suffer a loss of $1 billion dollars of Market Cap. Suffering losses generally gets shareholders aggravated and they often sue the company, board and/or management for making decisions that cost the shareholders money or value.

If we truly want a more abundant world, we may want to reconsider our demand for unceasing growth and high returns and look toward new metrics that have more holistic benefits to people and planet. The current measurements, such as EBITDA and GAAP standards, do not have mechanisms specifically designed to promote long term investing or utilizing earnings for social and environmental good. To promote long term investment in social and environmental good, will require new accounting standards and principles. This will include redefining EBITDA as a measurement for valuation.

The interesting thing is that EBITDA is not a GAAP financial measure, but rather a creative measure approved by the SEC that allows companies significant subjective latitude in defining their performance. According to a release by the SEC on June 13, 2003 entitled *Frequently Asked Questions Regarding the Use of Non-GAAP Financial Measures*, EBITDA should be reconciled to net income as presented in the statement of operations under GAAP. Operating income would not be considered the most directly comparable GAAP financial measure because EBIT and EBITDA make adjustments for items that are not included in operating income. Yet many companies reconcile EBITDA to operating income rather than net income. Since the creative corporate accounting happens after EBITDA calculations, a new standard is proposed for a baseline. This baseline measurement would be known as *Earnings Before Interest, Taxes, Depreciation, Amortization, Social and Environmental ("EBITDASE")*. Thus, when P/E ratios are multiplied times EBITDASE, the company does not suffer a loss in valuation for doing social and environmental good.

Working with such agencies as the U.S. Treasury, FASB, the Public Company Accounting Oversight Board ("PCAOB"), the Securities and Exchange Commission ("SEC"), the Sustainability Accounting Standards Board ("SASB"), and the White House, legislation can be promulgated to implement these new standards that reward corporations for beneficial investments into environmental, social and governance ("ESG") without penalizing shareholder value. This can lead to more corporations playing a role in beneficial eco-social impact.

With a little creative adjustment in economic performance measurements, the conflicts between corporate profits and ESG responsibility can be reduced so that corporations, corporate management, shareholders and humankind can benefit from widespread corporate programs that promote ESG.

In order for investment in such social and environmental programs to be adopted and succeed, they must be objective, measurable and auditable. These programs can provide objective measurements in dollars demonstrating the impact and return-on-investment ("ROI") of ESG investments. Measurements can include such things as (1) reduction of waste, (2) reduction of resource and energy usage, (3) increase in the value of brand equity, (4) reduction of carbon emissions, (5) increased sales from implementation of proactive ESG programs, including (a) environmental improvement (e.g., environmental remediation, preservation of nature, new systems to upcycle waste) and (b) community betterment (e.g., parks, victory gardens, school projects, job training programs and promotion of community cultural events), (6) improvements in health and lowering costs and claims for employee sickness, disease and injury, and (7) increased productivity from implementation of programs for employee education, advancement and well-being.

TRANSFORMING TO AN ABUNDANT ECONOMY WITH THE REPUTATION-BASED, ZERO-BALANCE ECONOMIC MODEL

With the power of the Internet, mobile, blockchain, ubiquitous information, social media, digital mobility, IoT, AI, crowdfunding platforms and new, non-structured information management systems, it's now feasible to create and efficiently connect highly functioning complementary currencies, collaborative communities and exchange networks. Innovation and connectivity can be used to create greater abundance, wellness and empowerment in our society. For example, using a *"Reputation-Based, Zero-Balance" Economic Model"* (or "RBZB") can provide an ethical, abundance-based currency owned by the members participating in the RBZB system.

In RBZB, reputation (rather than credit based upon borrowing) is the most important rating and is a multiplier times of all activity. The reputation score is increased by keeping one's word and agreements, engaging in generous exchange, and providing exemplary service and/or products. The reputation rating is decreased by lying, cheating, hoarding, gaming the system, taking advantage of another and failing to deliver on one's word and agreements. We are already seeing the importance of reputation on sites such as Yelp, Amazon, Ebay, Uber and AirBnB, where consumers rate and review providers of goods and services. Those with higher reputations get more business and often can charge higher prices.

In the RBZB system, the ideal balance in one's account is zero, not billions, as hoarding decreases the reputation score. The reputation score is a multiplier that can increase or decrease the value of a person's goods, services and/or actions. One way to increase reputation and multiply points is to give them to friends, family, entrepreneurs, philanthropic causes and ethical businesses participating in the RBZB system. When a member (e.g., individual, entrepreneur, business or non-profit) with a high reputation score needs currency, it automatically shows up. This is one of the benefits of having a high reputation score, giving generously, and stimulating the abundant flow of currency on the RBZB system. Thus, members with high reputation scores need not struggle in debt and servitude to obtain cash, resources and investments.

Conversely, when a member fails to deliver on their promises and agreements or provides substandard services and/or products, it will likely negatively affect their reputation score. However, members can minimize damage to their reputation by providing full and transparent disclosure of any risks up front. Also, poor market conditions, competitive technological breakthroughs, or force majeure beyond a member's control can be utilized to minimize damage to reputation. Moreover, mechanisms and processes are available for healing a member's reputation. A member with a low reputation score may be required to engage in activities to improve their reputation score before the RZBZ system provides further support. These activities can include volunteer work, generous giving and consistently keeping one's word. Upon a member increasing their reputation score, support will again be provided by the RZBZ system.

RBZB has a built-in crowdsourcing and crowdfunding component, which helps entrepreneurs and businesses identify demand, determine viability, receive valuable market feedback and target customers ahead of taking reputation, capital and resource risks. This model also utilizes a hybrid mutual credit network providing a system that is Abundant, In-Parity & Balanced, Elastic, Decentralized & Democratic, Stable, Accessible & Efficient, Symmetrical and Collaborative, as follows:

- <u>Abundant</u>—Rather than an economy and currency based upon the notion that scarcity equals value and debt, which leads to hoarding, wealth disparity, poverty and inflation, RBZB provides an abundant, balanced exchange where there is always sufficient currency backed by goods, services and network value. RBZB is based upon trust, which allows robust and abundant exchange, opportunities, innovation and efficiency in the money system. Trust is also backed by reputation, responsibility, objective performance metrics and clear agreements.

- <u>In-Parity & Balanced</u>—Because of the reputation-based incentive to rapidly deploy currency, money comes into existence based upon a reputation-based promise of value delivery. So long as a member's reputation score demonstrates honesty and consistency in delivering as promised, money will be delivered upon request. Thus, supply and demand are in parity and balance.

- <u>Elastic</u>—The mutual credit model is also elastic as currency comes into existence in the exact amount of the borrower's promise to repay the credit, or provide value, to the system. The promise of value and/or providing value catalyzes the issuance of currency.

- <u>Stable</u>—Because currency flow is based upon value, rather than being printed out of thin air, the currency is equal to the value in the system and therefore stable. This establishes stable equilibrium, which reduces the likelihood of inflation or recession. Moreover, elasticity, parity and balance further promote stability.

- <u>Decentralized & Democratic</u>—There is no central bank or centralized control authority. The system is run by its members for the benefit of its members and is governed by reputation-based voting that eliminates transferrable or assignable voting. As well, since reputation is not based upon wealth and accumulation of currency, RBZB reduces the plutocratic control seen in most monetary systems where those with the most ownership or money control the vote.

- <u>Accessible and Efficient</u>—Because all participants have equal access, subject only to their reputation, the system and credit are easily accessible.

Currency and credit are provided easily, efficiently and rapidly without the necessity of overly complex and collateralized contracts with onerous default provisions.

- <u>Symmetrical</u>—Providing or promising to provide value unlocks access to credit, which can be leveraged for goods and services. So long as sufficient network value is created to repay the credit or engage in network activities that repay credit, typical default and performance provisions can be significantly relaxed. There are numerous ways exist (aside from just the payment of money) to create network value to bring defaulted or negative accounts back to zero balance. This includes a mechanism for those seeking to repair or enhance their reputation to heal the default of other members that benefit themselves and the system. When a third-party cures another's default, it does not enhance the defaulting party's reputation, but rather the curing party's reputation.

- <u>Collaborative</u>. All members take responsibility for the success of the network and each other as their reputation scores provide the incentives to do so. It is the consistent exchange of value that leads to increased network value, the expansion and diversity of goods and services, and the growth of aggregate value of the network. With each person's collaboration, the network becomes exponentially more abundant, robust, scalable and flexible.

By utilizing the *Reputation-Based, Zero-Balance Economic Model*, we can create a democratized, abundant, ethical, and stable economy that operates efficiently at the speed of trust and integrity.

Also, by applying (1) *The 12-Step Program for Moneyholics*, (2) *The 9 Dimensions and Metrics of Well-Being*, (3) *The Qualitative Metrics of Success*, and (4) our economic vote, we can promote a *Regenerative Economy* that supports a higher quality of life and ecosystemic thriving, thereby achieving the promise of greater abundance, empowerment, happiness and freedom for humankind.

CHAPTER 24

Transforming to a Regenerative Society

*("Tarzan Economics"—Swinging from Destruction
& Scarcity to Regeneration & Abundance)*

---

*"Sustainable development is the pathway to the future we want for all.
It offers a framework to generate economic growth, achieve social justice, exercise environmental stewardship and strengthen governance."*

*"Saving our planet, lifting people out of poverty, advancing economic growth.
. .these are one and the same fight. We must connect the dots between climate
change, water scarcity, energy shortages, global health, food security and wom-
en's empowerment. Solutions to one problem must be solutions for all."*

~Ban Ki-moon, Secretary-General of the United Nations from January 2007 to December 2016.

TARZAN ECONOMICS

"Tarzan Economics" refers to the act of courageously letting go of the "old vine" of
systemic dysfunction and swinging to the "new vine" of systemic function. This "new
vine" is called *"The Regenerative Economy."* This economy is committed to a world
of regenerative abundance, wellness, empowerment, collaboration, beauty, love and
ecosystemic thriving.

TARZAN ECONOMICS	
Swinging from Destruction & Scarcity to Regeneration & Abundance	
From	**To**
• Destruction	• Creation
• Degeneration	• Regeneration
• Scarcity	• Abundance
• Poverty	• Natural Wealth
• Divisiveness	• Unity
• Ecosystemic Devastation	• Ecosystemic Thriving
• War	• Peace
• Fear	• Courage
• Hate	• Love
• Cruelty	• Compassion
• Unhappiness	• Happiness
• Sadness	• Joy
• Extractive	• Renewable
• Exploitative	• Equitable
• Dissatisfaction	• Fulfillment

For millennia, rulers and governments have used the tools of fear and divisiveness to gain and maintain control over the masses (aka "divide and rule"). The current disconnection from each other and nature arises primarily from artificially created dividing lines (e.g., race, religion, ideology, politics, age, gender and geography) and campaigns designed to erode our natural sovereignty, self-sufficiency and abundance (e.g., living "off-the-grid" and in a value-adding relationship with nature). "Divide and rule" has historically been accomplished by disconnecting, dividing and pitting powerful and rebellious groups and individuals against each other to prevent the masses from gaining power and overthrowing the current regime.

The systematic campaign of fear and disconnection from nature and each other has resulted in a society that is more pliable, obedient to authority and easily manipulated. The more insecure and divided we are, the less likely we are to exercise our collective power to change the system. The conditioned fear of the unknown and change may be our undoing. If we fearfully cling to the "old dysfunctional vine" for much longer, the vine is likely to snap and we'll hit the jungle floor, missing any opportunity and momentum we may still have to swing to a "new functional vine."

Putting duct tape on the current vine (attempting to band-aid and eradicate the symptoms of a dysfunctional system while preserving the system causing the symptoms) is not a solution. Fighting against, warring against, killing, hating or eradicating the current systemic symptoms and those who benefit most from it only perpetuates the dysfunction. Instead, we must give love, caring and nurturing to the system and those who perpetuate the dysfunction so that we can heal and transform the system. Hating the haters and warring against that which we perceive as bad only leads to more hate, war and bad.

For example, rather than profligate use of antibiotics to kill, eradicate or fight against bacteria (which results in more virulent strains of bacteria), we can utilize protocols that improve our health and strengthen our immune systems so that we share a healthy symbiotic relationship with bacteria. Rather than warring against terrorists (who we often attacked first, taking innocent lives), let's seek to heal their anger and pain with love forgiveness and compassion, while also loving ourselves and our right to live in love, peace and safety. Likewise, rather than using unhealthy and/or carcinogenic pesticides, herbicides, fungicides and preservatives in agriculture and food, we can focus on growing food using technologies that promote the health of crops, the soil, people and planet. Examples of these more healthy alternatives include (1) permaculture, organic and regenerative farming, (2) sonic and photonic repellants, (3) hydroponics, (4) biomimetic agriculture, (5) fresh, local and community agriculture, (6) AI and robotics, (7) natural biostimulants, fertilizers and composting, and (8) bio-dynamic agriculture. The foregoing are but a few of the things we can do to transform our agriculture and food systems. However, the Regenerative Economy requires transformation across almost every industry.

To live in a regenerative society means respecting all life and honoring our interconnection with each other and nature. When we focus on opportunities that serve and fulfill ecosystemic thriving and positive global transformation, we increase the likelihood that we'll emerge from our current challenges more abundant, resilient, wise and well.

THE REGENERATIVE ECONOMY AND ECONOMIC PRAGMATISM

A complete inside-out, ground-up, top-down renaissance is required to fulfill the paradigm shift necessary for the thriving of humankind and our planet. It is critical that we first transform of our individual beliefs and behaviors (inside-out) to embrace those that foster ecosystemic thriving and hold the vibrational frequency of love, connection, trust, compassion, generosity and respect ("Expansive Values"). We each hold the power and potential to shift our internal narrative and beliefs to those that promote Expansive Values. As Expansive Values gain adoption in society and become Global Human Agreements, we will swing from the vine of scarcity and destruction to the vine of regenerative abundance and thriving.

The Regenerative Economy represents both a paradigm shift and the largest, most stable and robust economy in the history of humankind. With a focus on eco-systemic thriving, the Regenerative Economy promotes living systems, as well as the health and longevity of humankind. The centralized supply chain, the industrialized war complex, fossil fuel energy, chemicals and materials and destructive mining, as well as toxic food and commercial agriculture will eventually be rendered obsolete by the Regenerative Economy.

Industries and businesses focusing on profits-at-all-costs, often engage in activities harmful to people and planet. Because their profits often result from destructive, extractive and exploitative undertakings, these entities resist eco-social change and innovation necessary for planetary thriving. Their destructive activities are routinely supported with arguments of *"economic pragmatism."* This argument of economic pragmatism is based upon the mistaken belief that these industries are perpetuating their profits, power and monopolies. Nothing could be farther from the truth. These industries are, in fact, destroying the planet's Natural Capital, the well-being of humankind and the sustainability of their profits, power and monopolies. By deploying short-term strategies focusing on quarterly earnings, the economic pragmatists are now facing major risks from climate disasters, pandemics, increased costs of resources, inability to scale production, supply chain inefficiencies, and waste management expenses.

Pragmatism is defined as *a practical and logical approach based upon reality rather than ideological and theoretical considerations.*

It could be argued that these "economic pragmatists" actually adhere to an impractical and dysfunctional economic system based upon ideological and theoretical agreements where paper fiat money without intrinsic value has greater value than nature and where profits, consumption and growth are elevated above the long-term survivability of humankind. Destroying that which gives us life, health and abundance for short term profits, based upon electronic journal entries and worthless paper, doesn't appear to be pragmatic at all. R. Edward Freeman provides a persuasive analogy for industrial pragmatists to consider:

> *"We need red blood cells to live (the same way a business needs profits to live), but the purpose of life is not to make red blood cells (the same way the purpose of business is not to exist to make profits)."* ~ R. Edward Freeman

The purpose of business is to provide value. Value results in profits. Continual extraction of Natural Capital at the expense of our planet's ability to regenerate its systems that sustain humankind is the extraction of value, not the creation of value. Our planet creates real value. The most pragmatic things we experience are our next breath, the hydration of water, the nutrients of food and the comfort of shelter, which all come from our planet. **Without our planet bestowing its gifts upon us, there would be no life, no society and no economy.** All of nature enjoys these gifts without money, yet our society has been conditioned to believe money and profits are more important than preserving the source of our life and well-being. We extract, rape, exploit, over-consume, destroy and toxify the planet. The most pragmatic thing we can do is protect and serve the planet and the health of its ecosystems. Our health and survival are completely dependent upon the Earth and its ability to continue to support humankind.

According to The Nature Conservancy[349]...

> *"Each year, our planet's complex land and water systems — a "natural living infrastructure"— produce an estimated **$72 trillion** worth of "free" goods and services essential to a well-functioning global economy."*

Moreover, research conducted by United Nations Environment Programme (UNEP)[350] reveals...

*"an investment scenario of allocating two per cent of global Gross Domestic Product (GDP)—US $1.3 trillion—a year to greening economic sectors will produce a higher global GDP within ten years, compared to a business-as-usual scenario. It will also reduce the ecological footprint and resource intensity of current growth models. The economic cost of failing to transition is far greater. True cost puts the annual cost in Natural Capital degradation and negative environment externalities at **US $7.3 trillion** a year."*

The math on these two studies show we have just ten years from the date these studies were done (2012 and 2013) before the Earth's ecosystems and Natural Capital hit the point of no return. Just 2% of the GDP invested into greening the economy, represents an **ROI of $1.3 Trillion per year** ($7.3T minus $6T). There are legitimate economic benefits for investing in remediating the damage done to Earth's ecosystems by humans, and utilizing innovation to create ecosystemic thriving. Regenerative investments represent a much larger economic opportunity than investments in destructive industries such as defense, oil, mining and unnecessary consumer products.

"The wealth of the nation is its air, water, soil, forests, minerals, rivers, lakes, oceans, scenic beauty, wildlife habitats and biodiversity... that's all there is. That's the whole economy. That's where all the economic activity and jobs come from. These biological systems are the sustaining wealth of the world." ~ Gaylord Nelson

The *Regenerative Economy* represents a multi-trillion-dollar economy that will transform our existing economy and give rise to a multitude of multi-billion-dollar regenerative businesses. These businesses, in the aggregate, will generate tens-of-trillions of dollars each year, and hundreds of millions of jobs doing meaningful work for the benefit of people and planet.

Examples of regenerative industries include the following:

1. Wise, Regenerative and Resilient Cities, Communities and Local Living Economies: Regenerative planning & design; smart grid; living microgrid and regenerative and high-performance buildings that collect and purify water, grow food, generate energy and recycle waste; efficient integrated autonomous transportation (e.g., driverless cars, smart mass transit); distributed resources

including localized water, food, and clean energy; IoT, sensors, monitoring and automated efficiency controls; local and bioregional innovation; collaborative consumption; and supply chain efficiency.

2. Agtech and Aquatech: Permaculture; bio-dynamics; soil remediation and building healthy soil; non-toxic EMF pest repellents; sensor/data automated systems; robotics; water catchment; water purification; water conservation, recycling and atmospheric water; and regenerative aquaculture.

3. Renewable Energy and Energy Efficiency: Hydrogen; solar; wind; biofuels; waste-to-energy; living buildings; and energy-efficient systems.

4. Environment, Resource Management and Conservation: Cleaning, conserving and managing valuable natural resources, such as air water, land, forests, oceans, as well as climate change solutions.

5. Biomimetic Materials and Sciences: Mimicking nature's designs and solutions (e.g., spider silk biomimicry and biopolymers that replace steel and concrete, Galapagos shark biomimicry for antibacterial applications), wastewater treatment and environmental remediation using the wisdom of nature's systems.

6. Transformative Living: Ethical and regenerative communities based upon "Collaborative Consumption," living systems innovation, optimal wellness and evolutionary consciousness."

7. Hybridization of For-Profit and Non-Profit: Holistic aggregation of resources and organizations to provide for significant social, economic, environmental, political reform and benefit.

8. Optimal Wellness and Holistic Health: Optimal wellness, longevity, Integrated and Alternative Medicine, holistic diet and nutrition, exercise, meditation, energy-medicine and epigenetics

9. Transformative and Applied Lifelong Learning: Interactive, gamified, personalized, and applied education with community involvement, home-schooling, mobile and geocentric education with VR, AR, Internet and mobile technologies.

10. <u>IT, Internet, Blockchain and Communications:</u> Decentralized Ledger Technologies (e.g., Blockchain-Crypto), Internet of Things, semantic web, spacial web, profiling/filtering, green Enterprise Resource Planning, mobile computing, quantum computing, privacy/security technologies, and big data analytics & modeling.

11. <u>Ethical and Democratized Finance</u>: Ethical banking, social impact, ESG and regenerative investment, environmental incentives and funding (e.g., Carbon Credits, Plastic Credits, Agroforestry Credits), meaningful work, and equitable pay.

12. <u>Ethical Nanotechnology</u>: Materials and devices that help solve health, energy, electronics, environmental and waste issues.

13. <u>Transparent and Honest Politics and Governance</u>: Good, honest and ethical political leadership with transparent monitoring via Internet.

For example, the *"Biomimetic Industry"* is just one of many regenerative industries. The Biomimetic Industry is projected to provide massive market opportunity of **$425 billion** by 2030. Terrapin Bright Green's research paper entitled *Tapping into Nature—The Future of Energy Innovation and Business*[351] reports as follows:

> *"Bioinspired innovation has the potential to transform large segments of the U.S. economy by increasing both gross domestic product (GDP) and employment. The Fermanian Business and Economic Institute estimates that bioinspired innovation could account for approximately $425 billion of U.S. GDP by 2030 (valued in 2013 dollars). Beyond 2030, the impact of bioinspired innovation is expected to grow as knowledge and awareness of the field expand."*

Bioinspired innovation and living technologies that support ecosystemic thriving are going to see massive growth and adoption, as well as a source of millions of jobs and economic abundance.

Another example of innovation within the *Regenerative Economy* is the *"Internet of Things"* ("IoT"). IoT is largely based upon the convergence of information and innovation to create greater efficiency, productivity, conservation and resiliency in our cities, infrastructure and lives. Using sensors, data, digital identification, geo-tracking, monitoring, automation and collaborative consumption, IoT and Smart Cities promise such things as (1) healthier environments, (2) nutritious and fresh locally grown food, (3) greater convenience, (4) improved healthcare, (5) smart personal transportation (e.g., driverless cars) and mass transit (e.g., smart trains), (6) abundant renewable energy (e.g., solar, wind, tidal, zero-point, green hydrogen and fusion), energy efficiency, and (7) supply chain efficiency.

The market size and opportunities surrounding IoT alone are staggering[352] as noted in the following examples:

- $41 Trillion spent by cities in the next 20 years on infrastructure upgrades for IoT (Intel)

- $1.9 Trillion in economic value across industries worldwide by 2020 (Gartner)

- $10-15 Trillion added to the GDP from the Industrial Internet (GE)

- 50 billion devices will be connected to the Internet by 2020 (Cisco Systems)

The number of developers involved in IoT activities will exceed over 3 million globally by the end of 2019, representing about 10% of all software developers (ABI Research).

Another segment of the Regenerative Economy is the "*Restoration Economy*," which, according to Storm Cunningham, author of *The Restoration Economy*, is alone a $1 trillion economy. The Restoration Economy is devoted to restoring or upgrading damaged and obsolete resources, such as degraded forests, watersheds, oceans, cities, communities, buildings, transit and infrastructure.

Pollution, war, poverty, disease, climate change and destruction of our biosphere are major challenges that threaten the survivability of humankind. These issues arise from systemic dysfunction and must be addressed at a systems level. Addressing the challenges without addressing the system that is causing them is a bit like continually cleaning pollution from a river without either shutting down or transforming the upstream plant that is the source of the river pollution.

The *Regenerative Economy* addresses these challenges systemically. Rather than attempting to treat the symptoms or fix the existing system, the Regenerative Economy creates holistic solutions and innovations that shift our current paradigm at the belief, behavior and systemic level across all industries, economies and areas of human consumption.

The planet is abundantly generous with us. However, Earth's ecosystems are being destroyed by human activities at an alarming rate, significantly decreasing the ability of the planet to regenerate and serve our current levels of consumption. Regenerative behavior requires that we repair what we have destroyed while creating systems to replace more than we take. For example, if we chop down one tree, we plant two in its place. If we catch 1,000 fish, we hatch 2,000 more. Of course, this is an oversimplification. As has been demonstrated on numerous occasions, human interference has caused ecological imbalances and catastrophes, even when done with the best intentions. So, when engaging in restoration and regeneration, it's essential that we take whole-systems approaches that incorporate great awareness and sensitivity to ecosystemic wisdom.

Mother Nature has great wisdom and power to heal, restore and regenerate its systems. Allowing Mother Nature to guide us as we support her in healing, restoring and regenerating her ecosystems will result in greater well-being to humankind, the planet, society and our economy. It's essential to maintain the balance between the needs and desires of humankind and the ability of the planet to sustainably support us. By respecting and emulating the planet's natural systems with over 4.5 billion years of evolutionary wisdom ("biomimicry" or "biomimetic approaches"), we can go beyond sustainability to create abundance and thriving for present and future generations of humanity and the planet as a whole.

There is a highly pragmatic opportunity, both ethically and economically, to transform our socio-economic-political system to build a world that is both ecologically and economically thriving and abundant. In order for us to thrive, it is imperative that we build a regenerative socio-politico-economic system that promotes ecosystemic health and quality-of-life as its highest priorities. The *Regenerative Economy* will redefine "success" by (1) elevating qualitative metrics (e.g., Gross National Happiness, Genuine Progress Indicator) over quantitative metrics (e.g., GDP), (2) creating economically flourishing industries that serve the thriving and abundance of people and planet, (3) providing meaningful work (rather than wasteful jobs) for all of humankind, and (4) sufficiently filling the reasonable needs of all of humankind in balance with the planet's regenerative capacity.

There is a growing awareness that transformation of business and our economy is required to not only sustain humankind and a healthy planet, but also to increase profitability, sustainable economic growth, resilience and quality-of-life. This awareness has led to increasing commitments of governments, banks, corporations and businesses to environmental, social and governance ("ESG") goals and policies. Additionally, institutional investors, family offices, pensions, ETFs, mutual funds and asset managers now have an estimated $40.5 trillion USD invested in ESG assets under management ("AUM") globally.[353] Additionally, green, social and sustainable ("GSSS") bond investment has grown to $600 billion USD in 2020—nearly double the $326 billion USD invested in GSSS bonds in 2019.[354]

The massive investment into ESG demonstrates the significant desire of financial institutions, money managers and investors to invest in assets and projects that provide both economic and ESG returns. While commitment to ESG should be applauded as a step in the right direction, much of the $40.5 trillion ESG investment has gone into large public companies that continue to perpetuate the centralized supply chain, fossil fuel burning, greenhouse gas emissions, and extractive and exploitative practices.

Money and economic returns have become the prime accelerants and motivators of action in our world. To accelerate regenerative enterprises and projects, significant investment needs to be put to work in Regenerative Impact Investments ("RIIs") as an asset class to finance core Regenerative Enterprises and Projects ("REPs") that increase productivity, resiliency, sustainable economic growth, quality-of-life and tax revenues. RIIs and REPs are devoted to promoting the health, resiliency and thriving of people and planet while fueling the transformation from an "Industrialized Civilization" to a "Regenerative Civilization." REPs are economically viable projects, enterprises and investments that will most directly, rapidly and positively transform our world and significantly contribute to the Regenerative Economy and improving Ecosystemic Thriving. RIIs and REPs will utilize multi-stakeholder participation (e.g., governments, NGOs, IGOs, REPs and private capital) and incentives (e.g., tax credits, employment credits, waiver of tariffs, accelerated depreciation, fast-tracked permits and credit enhancement/guarantees) in order to lower cost of capital, increase security and provide market-rate risk-adjusted returns that make RIIs. Utilizing the foregoing as well as providing quantitative measurements of impact (e.g., achievement of the SDGs, health and quality of life in a community, city or region), RIIs and REPs can become the most attractive asset class for investment.

THE PILLARS OF THE REGENERATIVE ECONOMY

The *Regenerative Economy* is based upon the integration of **regeneration, conservation, innovation, information** and **collaboration**.

- **Regeneration** is generally defined as the act of regeneration, the ability to recreate lost or damaged tissues, organs and limbs, spiritual renewal or revival.[355] "Regeneration" as used herein also includes the following:

  - improving a place or system, especially by making it more healthy, robust, adaptable and resilient

  - continually adding value in a way that replaces and/or expands resources that stimulate ecological rebirth, equilibrium and flourishing that perpetuate abundant resources

  - giving new life or energy

  - restoring to a better, higher or more worthy state

  - evolutionary improvement of a being and/or system, biologically, spiritually and/or morally

  "Regeneration" involves a whole-systems approach that integrates not just the biological ability to renew, restore, revitalize and improve ecosystems, but also the evolutionary, spiritual, moral, ethical and economic transformation that improves the health and thriving of systems and environments and quality of life.

  The application of regenerative approaches requires us to utilize such things as (i) bio-energetic healing and remediation of water, soil and air; (ii) renewable and clean energy from plants, waste, solar, wind, hydro, tidal and geothermal, (iii) clean and nutritious food from agricultural practices that build healthy soil, return nutrients to the soil and support prolific reproduction including agroforestry and permaculture approaches, (iv) materials and chemicals from renewable resources (e.g. plants, algae, spider silk, bio-resins, regenerative forests) and upcycling of waste therefrom, and (v) lowering human consumption and balancing human needs with that of the ecosystem to support integrated ecosystemic health and regenerative abundance of the Earth. Regenerative practices include biomimicry, permaculture, cradle-to-cradle, and circular, as well as living, renewable and bioenergetic protocols to name a few. Regenerative practices also include changing fundamental beliefs and measurements of "success," as well as providing education, skills, capital and resources to help leaders, entrepreneurs and workers expand and proliferate regenerative businesses.

Much like an oak tree that grows from a single acorn, but drops millions of acorns in its life, we can collaborate to help current and future generations expand and reproduce value-adding regenerative opportunities that foster the evolutionary flourishing of humankind and the planet's ecosystems.

- **Conservation** is the ethical use, allocation, and protection of resources with a primary focus on maintaining the health of the natural world. A primary focus of conservation has been the preservation of biodiversity and ecosystemic health. Conservation seeks to minimize negative impacts on the planet resulting from human consumption and activities by applying the ethics of rethinking, recycling, reusing, repairing, restoring and reducing consumption. As one example, lack of water represents enormous societal, health and economic risks that require massive efforts in infrastructure repair and conservation to remedy. McKenzie & Company reports:[356]

> "A larger global population and growing economies are placing bigger demands on already-depleted water supplies. Agricultural runoff and other forms of pollution are exacerbating the scarcity of water that is clean enough for human and industrial use in some regions, and changes in climate may worsen the problem. Scarcity is raising prices and increasing the level of regulation and competition among

stakeholders for access to water. To continue operating, companies in most sectors must learn how to do more with less."

"Closing the gap between supply and demand by deploying water productivity improvements across regions and sectors around the world could cost, by our estimate, about $50 billion to $60 billion annually over the next two decades. Private-sector companies will account for about half of this spending, government for the rest."

"Inescapably, water will become a strategic factor for companies in most sectors. All businesses will need to conserve, and many will make a market in conservation."

It's clear that a water crisis will be one of the largest issues faced in the 21st century. The conservation, care, purification, recycling and reuse of valuable life-giving water is critical to humankind's survival and our ability to become a Regenerative Society.

To conserve Natural Capital, we must reduce consumption. Aside from limiting hoarding and the purchase of needless goods that end up in landfill, "Collaborative Consumption" represents a shift in beliefs and behaviors that will reduce consumption through sharing of resources and goods, thereby conserving resources and demand upon Earth's ecosystems. Collaborative Consumption promotes the manufacture of higher quality and more durable goods. Because of the collective purchase, manufacturers can charge more, but consumers individually pay less. Collaborative Consumption creates a shift from manufactured obsolescence to long-lasting products, thereby conserving the energy and resources used for, and waste generated from, obsolete products.

The way "sustainability" is practiced today is essentially just a slower way to die. For example, we use the energy of coal fire plants to make solar panels, to fill the increasing demand for greater energy consumption from such things as electric cars, data centers, computers and cell phones. The continued growth and overconsumption will likely exceed the generation of capacity of solar, thus leading to the continuation of fossil fuels.

Conservationists support the reduction of consumption, regenerating nature's systems, and the use of ethical and renewable resources.

- **Innovation** is the creation and application of highly effective, evolutionary and/or transformative products, processes, services, technologies, know-how and/or inventions. The intent and purpose of life-enhancing innovation is the betterment of society and ecosystemic thriving. In order to balance human consumption and well-being with the carrying capacity and health of the planet, to ensure the survival of humankind, we need life-enhancing innovation across every industry. This innovation is currently found in the fields of renewable energy, agtech, aquatech, biomimetic materials, waste upcycling, biology, regenerative economics, living systems applications, communications, information technologies, Internet of Things, blockchain and ethical nanotech. Life-enhancing innovative industries will see massive explosion and growth in the coming years.

  Social innovation will also play a major role in reshaping our world. Social innovation includes such things as incentivizing new beliefs and behaviors that foster collaboration, love, trust, respect, sharing and compassion in service to people and planet. Social innovation can happen through inspired media, applied education, and personalized learning using technologies such as VR, AR, AI. The new education paradigm will not only teach STEM, but also evolutionary consciousness, emotional intelligence, collaboration, and regenerative capacity. Social innovation also includes advances in (1) smart growth communities, (2) retooling the workplace to be healthy, inspiring and productive, (3) the sharing economy and collaborative consumption, (4) global open source IP, (5) ethical reputation-based zero-balance currency systems built on blockchain technologies that incentivize good reputation and generosity, (6) social networking, and (7) biomimetic practices.

- **Information** consists of symbols, data, sensory stimulus and thoughts that are received, constructed and assembled to provide meaning, purpose, education, entertainment, empowerment and enlightenment. Information mediums can consist of written, visual, audio and kinesthetic materials interacting with our senses from which we experience meaning, such as news, books, videos, games, music, art, research, performances, touch, food, and experiential learning.

Information, media and communications have reached a level of democratization never known in the history of mankind. Internet, mobile and communications technologies have already caused massive transformation in our society, launching entirely new industries and processes for the production, distribution and consumption of information. Information exchange will continue to provide global influence and wealth in the future. By coupling information, media and communications with practical applications and capacity that foster a Regenerative Society, we can transform from the age of industrial dysfunction to regenerative thriving.

Examples of the major paradigm shifts being inspired by information technologies include the Internet of Things ("IoT"), the spatial web, satellite mapping, sensors, artificial intelligence, augmented reality, virtual reality, data visualization and the multitude of information distribution channels on Internet and mobile networks. These technologies will change the way we share information, learn, communicate, interact with each other, and understand our world. IoT, for example, utilizes sensors, data, networks, digital identification, the cloud and information technologies to help increase efficiencies in energy, agriculture, resource management and supply chain, as well as the potential to increase our health, knowledge and quality of life. As one example, IoT applied to agriculture uses sensors that measure moisture in the ground. This data then will be used to turn on watering systems when needed and turn them off when not needed. This information can be integrated with weather and usage patterns to effectively predict demand for water and control dams, irrigation, water delivery systems, pumps and the energy required to fill demand effectively and conservatively. The result is lower water and energy usage and healthier crops.

By including such subjects as living systems thinking, reverence of nature, collaboration and emotional intelligence into an applied, incentivized and gamified personal learning system, future generations will have fun learning and develop the skills, capacity and tools required to transform our world.

- **Collaboration**[357] is a cooperative relationship of teamwork with the intent of yielding synergistic results based on combined efforts. Because the carrying capacity of the planet to address human consumption was exceeded in 1970s[358], our future socio-economic-political system will require increased collaboration including sharing resources and goods, living in regenerative communities, value-based exchange and abundance-based currencies, behavioral and reputation-based incentives, and conservation/regenerative consciousness. **Even though the human population is over 7.5 billion, it is the overconsumption by developed nations that is putting more strain on the environment and our resources than overpopulation.** According to Fred Pearce, author of Yale 360 article "*Consumption Dwarfs Population as Main Environmental Threat*",[359]

  > "*The carbon emissions of one American today are equivalent to those of around 4 Chinese, 20 Indians, 30 Pakistanis, 40 Nigerians, or 250 Ethiopians.*"

  > "*The lifestyle of the average American takes 9.5 hectares, while Australians and Canadians require 7.8 and 7.1 hectares respectively; Britons, 5.3 hectares; Germans, 4.2; and the Japanese, 4.9. The world average is 2.7 hectares. China is still below that figure at 2.1, while India and most of Africa (where the majority of future world population growth will take place) are at or below 1.0.*"

  > "*Stephen Pacala, director of the Princeton Environment Institute, who calculates that the world's richest half-billion people, totaling about 7 percent of the global population, are responsible for 50 percent of the world's carbon dioxide emissions. Meanwhile the poorest 50 percent are responsible for just seven percent of emissions.*"

Based upon Pearce's work, it could be argued that overconsumption by North America, Europe, Australia and Japan is a leading cause of climate change. Collaboration, sharing, localization and inclusivity are ways to solve the problems of overconsumption leading to climate change, environmental degradation, social and economic injustice and trade inequalities. Utilizing network, IT and distributed ledger technologies, we can engage in *"Collaborative Consumption"* (including sharing, bartering, lending, trading, renting, gifting, and swapping) on a scale never possible before. From marketplaces (e.g., eBay and Facebook Marketplace) to social lending (e.g., Kickstarter and Wefunder), peer-to-peer travel (e.g., Airbnb and Couchsurfing), car-sharing (e.g., Uber and Lyft), and the growth of intentional and sustainable communities (e.g., ic.org), Collaborative Consumption is disrupting previous modes of business and reinventing not just what we consume, but how we consume.

The Center for Planetary Culture writes: *"New Consumers crave the freedom and flexibility of living simply and distancing themselves from the burdens of ownership—from depreciation and maintenance to the sheer psychological weight of keeping track of all that stuff. New Consumers want the freedom of owning less, while promoting access to new experiences that help build a sense of community, trust and optimism as they turn to one another to live more sustainably."*[360]

The Havas Group further supports this trend toward a sharing economy with the following: *"We have entered an age when sharing, rather than buying, everything from cars and vacation homes to textbooks and pets has become socially acceptable among those who realize we have exhausted the planet and ourselves with way too much stuff and responsibility."*[361]

There is a new consumption trend that values quality of life and experiences over quantity of stuff, leading to a greater desire to share more. Also, when we share, we generally get the benefit of higher quality products, facilities and services that we could not afford on our own. Moreover, we get the social benefit of community. For example, we share the equipment, classes and facilities at a health club. We get a higher quality and greater variety of equipment and classes without having to solely pay for and maintain the facilities, the instructors, staff and equipment.

There is also a growing demand for alternative workspaces (e.g., co-working spaces and incubators) that serve entrepreneurs, individuals and companies that seek an amenity-rich, collaborative work environment, distinct from fluorescent-lit cubicles so common today.[362]

We have been collaboratively sharing such things as roads, fire, police, sewers, hospitals, supermarkets, airplanes, beaches, parks, health clubs and dry cleaners for years. We have no need for exclusive ownership of such infrastructure, facilities, things and services and we derive great benefit from sharing these resources. As we move from centralized grids to distributed, local living economies based upon collaborative consumption, we will see not only a reduction in consumption and use of resources, but also an increase in quality of life, greater connectedness, and increased conservation of resources-both natural and economic. Most of what we own sits unused (e.g., our cars, boats, planes, sporting goods, electronics, tools, clothing). Exclusive ownership of material possessions requires massive amounts of resources, from the materials and energy for building and running factories and warehouses, packaging and shipping of goods, to the time, maintenance and storage of stuff. And when we accumulate enough stuff, we then purchase bigger houses with more room for our stuff. And when our stuff becomes unfashionable, obsolete, or goes unused, it often ends up in landfill. Collaborative consumption allows us to have a higher quality of life, have access to more stuff, while spending considerably less time, money and resources required to own it all.

"Regenerative Systems" (also known as "Living Systems") transform, evolve, improve and adapt or they become extinct. Likewise, to be regenerative, humankind needs to transform, evolve, improve and adapt or become extinct. Mechanical, non-living systems invented by humans wear out, do not self-evolve and become quickly obsolete. As well, man-made chemical approaches (e.g., petrochemicals, pesticides, fungicides, antibiotics) too often destroy the environment (inner and outer terrain) that provides for our continued existence. This is unsustainable.

By committing to regenerative applications, humankind will transform and evolve from the industrial-mechanical-chemical age to the "Regenerative Age" that supports the health and thriving of humankind and the planet's ecosystems. The Regenerative Age requires humans to set aside our foolish arrogance and develop a deep reverence for nature's 4.5 billion years of wisdom by 1) reconnecting with and learning from nature, 2) allowing nature's living systems to do that which they do best without our interference, 3) creating a new socio-political-economic system that supports life and ecosystemic thriving, and 4) elevating the ethical imperative over the economic imperative.

John Fullerton, a thought leader and author in Regenerative Capitalism, as well as the founder and President of the Capital Institute, is known as the originator of the following 8 *Principles of Regenerative Capitalism*:

1. *In Right Relationship*—Humanity is an integral part of an interconnected web of life in which there is no real separation between "us" and "it." The scale of the human economy matters in relation to the biosphere in which it is embedded. What is more, we are all connected to one another and to all locales of our global civilization. Damage to any part of that web ripples back to harm every other part as well.

2. *Views Wealth Holistically*—True wealth is not merely money in the bank. It must be defined and managed in terms of the well-being of the whole, achieved through the harmonization of multiple kinds of wealth or capital, including social, cultural, living, and experiential. It must also be defined by a broadly shared prosperity across all of these varied forms of capital. The whole is only as strong as the weakest link.

3. *Innovative, Adaptive, Responsive*—In a world in which change is both ever present and accelerating, the qualities of innovation and adaptability are critical to health. It is this idea that Charles Darwin intended to convey in this often misconstrued statement attributed to him: "*In the struggle for survival, the fittest win out at the expense of their rivals.*" What Darwin actually meant is that: the most "fit" is the one that fits best (i.e., the one that is most adaptable to a changing environment).

4. *Empowered Participation*—In an interdependent system, fitness comes from contributing in some way to the health of the whole. The quality of empowered

participation means that all parts must be "in relationship" with the larger whole in ways that not only empower them to negotiate for their own needs, but also enable them to add their unique contribution towards the health and well-being of the larger wholes in which they are embedded.

5. _Honors Community and Place_—Each human community consists of a mosaic of peoples, traditions, beliefs, and institutions uniquely shaped by long-term pressures of geography, human history, culture, local environment, and changing human needs. Honoring this fact, a Regenerative Economy nurtures healthy and resilient communities and regions, each one uniquely informed by the essence of its individual history and place.

6. _Edge Effect Abundance_—Creativity and abundance flourish synergistically at the "edges" of systems, where the bonds holding the dominant pattern in place are weakest. For example, there is an abundance of interdependent life in salt marshes where a river meets the ocean. At those edges the opportunities for innovation and cross-fertilization are the greatest. Working collaboratively across edges—with ongoing learning and development sourced from the diversity that exists there—is transformative for both the communities where the exchanges are happening, and for the individuals involved.

7. _Robust Circulatory Flow_—Just as human health depends on the robust circulation of oxygen, nutrients, etc., so too does economic health depend on robust circulatory flows of money, information, resources, and goods and services to support exchange, flush toxins, and nourish every cell at every level of our human networks. The circulation of money and information and the efficient use and reuse of materials are particularly critical to individuals, businesses, and economies reaching their regenerative potential.

8. _Seeks Balance_—Being in balance is more than just a nice way to be; it is actually essential to systemic health. Like a unicycle rider, regenerative systems are always engaged in this delicate dance in search of balance. Achieving it requires that they harmonize multiple variables instead of optimizing single ones. A Regenerative Economy seeks to balance efficiency and resilience; collaboration and competition; diversity and coherence; and small, medium, and large organizations and needs.

The Regenesis Group, a leader in regenerative planning, design and applications, differentiates "regenerative" approaches from "sustainable" approaches as follows:

"The emerging field of regenerative development and design marks a significant evolution in the concept and application of sustainability. Practices in sustainable or green design have focused primarily on minimizing damage to the environment and human health, and using resources more efficiently; in effect, slowing down the degradation of earth's natural systems. Advocates of a regenerative approach to the built environment believe a much more deeply integrated, whole systems approach to the design and construction of buildings and human settlements (and nearly all other human activities) is needed. Regenerative approaches seek not only to reverse the degeneration of the earth's natural systems, but also to design human systems that can coevolve with natural systems—evolve in a way that generates mutual benefits and greater overall expression of life and resilience. The field of regenerative development and design, which draws inspiration from the self-healing and self-organizing capacities of natural living systems, is increasingly seen as a source for achieving this end. This field is redefining the way that proponents of sustainability are thinking about and designing for the built environment, and even the role of architecture as a field."

The regenerative model goes beyond sustainability and conservation by looking to design new and more effective human systems that work with, and support, nature. Regenerative Design and Development, according to Regenesis Group, includes and incorporates the following philosophies, principles and disciplines:[363]

- *Biomimicry*: An emerging design discipline based upon 4.5 billion year of systems wisdom demonstrated in nature.

- *Cradle-to-Cradle*: A framework for designing manufacturing processes "powered by renewable energy, in which materials flow in safe, regenerative, closed-loop cycles. Cradle-to-Cradle also identifies three key design principles in the intelligence of natural systems: Waste Equals Food, Use Current Solar Income, Celebrate Diversity.

- *Eco-literacy*: The ability to understand the natural systems that make life on Earth possible, including understanding the principles of organization of ecological communities (i.e., ecosystems) and using those principles for creating sustainable human communities.

- *Ecological Sustainability*: A biocentric school of sustainability thinking based on ecology and living systems principles, that focuses on the capacity of ecosystems to maintain their essential functions and processes, and retain their biodiversity in full measure over the long-term; contrasts with technological sustainability based on technical and engineering approaches to sustainability.

- *Ecology*: The interdisciplinary scientific study of the living conditions of organisms in interaction with each other and with the surroundings, organic as well as inorganic.

- *Ecosystem*: The interactive system of living things and their non-living habitat.

- *Ecosystem Concept*: A coherent framework for redesigning our landscapes, buildings, cities, and systems of energy, water, food, manufacturing and waste" through "the effective adaptation to and integration with nature's processes." It has been used more to shape an approach than as a scientific theory.

- *Living Systems Thinking*: A thinking technology, using systemic frameworks and developmental processes, for consciously improving the capacity to apply systems thinking to the evolution of human or social living systems.

- *Locational Patterns*: The patterns that depict the distinctive character and potential of a place and provide a dynamic mapping for designing human structures and systems that align with the living systems of a place.

- *Pattern literacy*: Being able to read, understand and generate ("write") appropriate patterns.

- *Permaculture*: A contraction of permanent agriculture or permanent culture, permaculture was developed as a system for designing ecological human habitats and food production systems based on the relationships and processes found in natural ecological communities, and the relationships and adaptations of indigenous peoples to their ecosystems.

- *Place*: The unique, multi-layered network of ecosystems within a geographic region that results from the complex interactions through time of the natural ecology (climate, mineral and other deposits, soil, vegetation, water and wildlife, etc.) and culture (distinctive customs, expressions of values, economic activities, forms of association, ideas for education, traditions, etc.).

- *Regenerative Design*: A system of technologies and strategies, based on an understanding of the inner working of ecosystems that generates designs to regenerate rather than deplete underlying life support systems and resources within socio-ecological wholes.

- *Regenerative Development*: A system of technologies and strategies for generating the patterned whole system understanding of a place, and developing the strategic systemic thinking capacities, and the stakeholder engagement/commitment required to ensure regenerative design processes to achieve maximum systemic leverage and support, that is self-organizing and self-evolving.

- *Restorative Design*: Sometimes called restorative environmental design; a design system that combines returning "polluted, degraded or damaged sites back to a state of acceptable health through human intervention" with biophilic designs that reconnect people to nature.

Protecting our planet and revitalizing its ecosystems is not only practical and economically pragmatic, its critical for our survival. The planet and our need for clean air, water, food, shelter and energy are very real. Our economic system and today's fiat money are fundamentally just a social agreement and system that places an agreed value on relatively worthless paper to make trade and non-parity exchange more efficient and convenient. Yet our society often elevates money and short-term profits over long-term, regenerative abundance, health and survival, which is not very pragmatic.

We have confused profits and money with ethical purpose and have made the pursuit of money and the accumulation of stuff the definition of wealth. A mass amount of human time, energy and attention is focused on the pursuit of money and profits, without regard for the destruction it causes, rather than creating regenerative abundance. If the collective effort of humankind largely supports the exchange of worthless paper fiat money and electronic journal entries for the benefit of fictitious non-living legal entities without trickling down to benefit people and planet, then what and who are our efforts benefiting?

Oxfam's 2014 report entitled *"Working for the Few"* provides an explanation of the few who may benefiting:

- The richest 8 people in the world own the same amount as the bottom half of the world's population (3.6 billion).[364]

- The wealth of the one percent richest people in the world amounts to $110 trillion. That's 65 times the total wealth of the bottom half of the world's population.

- Seven out of ten people live in countries where economic inequality has increased in the last 30 years.

- The richest one percent increased their share of income in 24 out of 26 countries

- In the US, the wealthiest one percent captured 95 percent of post-financial crisis growth since 2009, while the bottom 90 percent became poorer.

Despite the inequitable distribution of wealth and appearance of power held by the wealthiest humans, the planet is far more powerful than humankind, including the most powerful, wealthy and influential people. The planet and her forces of nature can destroy humankind in an instant. The planet will survive and be just fine without us. The planet will eventually cleanse and heal the destruction caused by humans. The planet doesn't need us, our money or our industries. We need the planet. We can, however, thrive by devoting ourselves to loving and serving each other and the planet. If we don't choose wisely and correct our course immediately, we'll likely become extinct as a species within 100 years.[365]

Pope Francis writes, *"Here too, it should always be kept in mind that "environmental protection" cannot be assured solely on the basis of financial calculations of costs and benefits. The environment is one of those goods that cannot be adequately safeguarded or promoted by market forces. Once more, we need to reject a magical conception of the market, which would suggest that problems can be solved simply by an increase in the profits of companies or individuals. Is it realistic to hope that those who are obsessed with maximizing profits will stop to reflect on the environmental damage which they will leave behind for future generations? Where profits alone count, there can be no thinking about the rhythms of nature, its phases of decay and regeneration, or the complexity of ecosystems which may be gravely upset by human intervention. Moreover, biodiversity is considered at most a deposit of economic resources available for exploitation, with no serious thought for the real value of things, their significance for persons and cultures, or the concerns and needs of the poor."*

Pope Francis, clearly sees that real value is not in quarterly profits, but in long term stewardship and caring for our planet's ecosystems.

In his book, *Earth in the Balance: Ecology and the Human Spirit*, Al Gore diagnoses our ecological problem as being a symptom of a dysfunctional, addictive civilization. Gore writes:

"I believe that our civilization is addicted to the consumption of the earth itself. This addictive relationship distracts us from the pain of what we have lost: a direct experience of our connection to vividness, vibrancy, and aliveness of the rest of the natural world. The froth and frenzy of industrial civilization masks our deep loneliness for communion. The price we pay is the loss of our spiritual lives."

As Al Gore suggests, humankind has become disconnected from nature and each other to the detriment of our spiritual lives. For example, the phrase "people and planet" demonstrates that we somehow believe we are separate from the planet. The irony of this disconnection is that without nature, we have no economy or GDP. As much as our society has tried to "civilize" us and disconnect us from nature, we are truly just another species living on this planet interconnected with, and interdependent on, each other and nature. Everything that sustains our lives, including our next breath, water, food, shelter, energy and materials, are provided by "Mother Nature," yet we, as a society, act with utter disregard to "our mother," the provider of life.

There is wisdom in remaining connected to nature. I have found repeatedly that people, who have a deep connection to, understanding of, and appreciation for, nature, live in greater abundance, health and happiness than those who are disconnected from nature, but have great material wealth.

Indigenous cultures still connected to nature spend much less time working than we do in the industrialized world. A joint study *entitled "Gendered Time Allocation of Indigenous Peoples in the Ecuadorian Amazon"* by University of California Santa Cruz, University of North Carolina, Asheville and Carolina Population Center[366] found *"all groups spend roughly 40% of their time in social activities, 25% of their time in individual activities and about 10% each in domestic, commercial and subsistence activities."* Whereas, based upon sources such as U.S. Bureau of Labor Statistic and Deloitte, assuming 8 hours of sleep and 16 waking hours, 9 hours of work and work related activities (e.g., commuting, preparation), 2 hours on domestic activities (e.g., house cleaning and meal preparation), 2 hours of childcare, and 3 hours of leisure time, in modern society we spend 56% of our waking hours engaging in work and work related activities, 13% in domestic activities, 13% in childcare and 19% in leisure and social activities.[367] Based upon this research, it's clear that industrialized society, on average, spends more time working and far less time enjoying life than indigenous cultures. Is this really progress? I would say not. What if we could have practically everything we need whenever we needed it and work half the time we do now? We can!

Nature creates abundance and we have a choice to foster or destroy the life-giving abundance that nature provides us. We can facilitate transactions, non-parity exchange and trade, and motivate action with money, however, money doesn't create anything by itself. Nature creates value, and we, as living beings within nature, create value. For example:

- Nature bestows food and water and we create farms that feed us;

- Nature provides us timber, stone and earth and we build houses and shelter;

- Nature gives us energy and we find ways to harness it to expand our capabilities;

- Nature furnishes us materials and we manufacture products; and

- Nature presents us lessons on love, collaboration, flourishing and beauty and some of us embrace and mimic nature's creativity and wisdom by engaging in living systems innovation, service to planet, collaboration, conservation, regenerative practices, and the creation of beauty with such things as art, music, dance and theatre.

We can reclaim our regenerative abundance by returning to our direct connection, collaboration and love for each other and our planet. From this consciousness and transformed behavior, we can heal the disconnection, dependence, disempowerment and conditioned belief systems that promote the exploitation and indentured servitude of humankind. We can experience greater health, love, spiritual connection, beauty, freedom, joy and quality time, to name a few, by engaging in the following shifts in beliefs and behavior:

1. Consciously using our money and economic will to purchase products and services from eco-social companies that are devoted to ecosystemic thriving;

2. Transitioning our energy portfolio to using only abundant and renewable source of energy;

3. Replacing the manufacture of unneeded, transient collectibles, obsolescent products and weaponry destined for landfill with long-lasting, high-quality products that foster health, beauty, peace and flourishing;

4. Adopting collaborative consumption, sharing and inclusivity over exclusivity, hoarding and competition;

5. Reusing, recycling and upcycling waste so that words "waste" and "toxicity" become obsolete words;

6. Providing access to clean and abundant water, food and energy infrastructure along with necessary resources, skill and tools to all of humankind without ecological offense to other living species;

7. Providing education and capacity building that creates knowledge and skills to foster ecosystemic thriving and balance population growth with the carrying capacity of the local community and planet;

8. Voluntarily recognizing and reward value;

9. Evolving our regulatory environment and quantitative metrics of success to allow for the development of a world that fosters ecosystemic thriving, quality of life and ethical conduct; and

10. Reconnecting with and serving the health and flourishing of our biosphere.

We cannot exceed the carrying capacity of the planet that sustains us, however, by serving the regenerative abundance of nature, we can increase the carrying capacity of the planet. Due to our interconnectedness and interdependence with each other and our planet, we cannot truly derive any meaningful or sustained fulfillment from another's suffering or the destruction of Mother Earth. It is when we, as a unified whole, collaboratively hold and serve the thriving of life and nature as supreme, that we can experience and create a world of Abundance, Wellness & Empowerment in which we all can be truly fulfilled.

Biologist, Elisabet Sahtouris advises that by following, respecting, mimicking and serving nature, our economy, our businesses and our lives will be more healthy and productive:

> *"Cooperation, collaboration and community empowerment are, as Nature role-models them and as I cannot repeat too often, more efficient and effective ways of doing business than living in fear of drowning in a competitive race or wasting energy and resources on beating down the competition."*

> *Tachi Kiuchi, former CEO of Mitsubishi Electric, and Bill Shireman, an ecologist, put it this way in their important book, What We Learned from the Rainforest: "There is no problem ever faced by a business that has not been faced and solved by a rainforest. ... The rainforest (like a prairie or coral reef) creates enormous new value continually by very complex production and trading systems as well as by recycling its resources very rapidly."* [368]

In furtherance of creating a Regenerative Society, where people and planet thrive, there is a need to be consistently aware of the oneness, interconnectedness and interrelationship of all humankind, the planet, it's ecosystems and the universe. The most important thing humankind can do at this critical point in our evolution is take personal and collective action that supports ecosystemic thriving.

Each of us has a profound impact on each other and nature. We can try to ignore and desensitize ourselves from, and rationalize the ecosystemic destruction and dysfunction of our society, yet we feel the suffering, destruction, cruelty and injustice in our hearts and at the core of our being. We know that we are capable of creating a more beautiful, thriving, abundant and loving world.

As each one of us changes our consciousness and swings from lack to abundance, we incrementally affect the Global Human Agreement. It is critical that we use our individual resources to transform our society from dysfunction to function. These resources include our time, energy, money, attention, thoughts, emotions, words, actions, behavior and connection with nature.

For Dr. Bruce Lipton, a cellular biologist and author of *The Biology of Belief: Unleashing the Power of Consciousness, Matter and Miracles*. . .

"Nature is based on harmony. So it says if we want to survive and become more like nature, then we actually have to understand that it's cooperation versus competition."

"Through consciousness, our minds have the power to change our planet and ourselves. It is time we heed the wisdom of the ancient indigenous people and channel our consciousness and spirit to tend the garden and not destroy it."

By observing, learning from and imitating the laws, wisdom and abundance of nature and respectfully reconnecting and collaborating with each other, we can create the most robust, regeneratively abundant and ethical society in the history of humankind.

CHAPTER 25

Transforming our Energy Portfolio and Supply Chain

There is an urgent need to stop subsidizing the fossil fuel industry, dramatically reduce wasted energy, and significantly shift our power supplies from oil, coal, and natural gas to wind, solar, geothermal, and other renewable energy sources.

~Bill McKibben

E nergy is the gating factor for quality of life in modern society. Energy is needed for such things as getting food from the farm to our table, pumping water to our homes, farms and businesses, keeping our lights on, handling waste, transportation and shipping of materials and goods, and powering our electronic devices, to name a few. Without energy, modern society virtually shuts down.

We have the technologies to give clean water, nutritious food and renewable energy to the world. We can grow bananas on the North Pole and harvest potable water from the atmosphere and desalinate seawater. We can power the world through natural and renewable energy sources (e.g., hydrogen, solar, wind, hydro, tidal, biomass). We have the ability to bio-energetically regenerate soil and purify water stores, grow food hydroponically in vertical urban towers, and regeneratively cultivate an abundance of seafood, sea vegetables and materials from the ocean. We have the ability to ship food, water, materials and supplies to anywhere in the world and alleviate hunger, suffering and death worldwide. However, we haven't engaged in deploying these technologies and life-affirming activities in a truly meaningful way largely because the energy costs are generally too high and doing so is not profitable.

There is another issue that has slowed the adoption of clean and renewable energy and activities that alleviate world poverty, hunger and suffering. The governments around the world, who write and enforce regulations have been infiltrated by incumbent industries such as banking, oil, auto, utilities (e.g., electricity, gas and water), construction (e.g., lumber, concrete, steel, glass) and commercial agriculture. These industries have been responsible for sponsoring legislation to impede or prevent innovative progress in energy, materials, construction, transportation, supply chain efficiency, and local self-sufficiency for water, food, energy and materials. Moreover, governments generate significant revenues from the supply chain including income tax, import-export tariffs, sales tax, utility tax, and excise taxes collected on fossil fuels. For example, the U.S. generates an estimated \$36.4B annually from federal fuel taxes[369] and California generates more than \$26.4B billion in state and local tax revenues and \$28.5 billion in sales and excise taxes from fossil fuels.[370]

The U.S. energy generation portfolio by source is 60.3% from fossil fuels, 19.7% from nuclear, 19.8% from renewables, .1% from pumped hydropower, and .3% from other sources.[371] Thus, the vast majority of energy in the U.S., (80%), is from fossil fuels and nuclear sources. With the billions of dollars spent on lobbying by the oil industry and the taxes collected at the pump, governments have been loath to kill the "greasy golden goose."

With the growth of both population and consumption, we are seeing increasing demand for energy, food, products and services while concurrently seeing a diminution of potable water and arable land. As well, human activities, including burning fossil fuels and deforestation for commercial agriculture, timber and cattle ranching, have contributed to high levels of $CO2$ and greenhouse gasses in our atmosphere which the scientific community attributes to climate change.[372]

In addition to many other transformational societal shifts that must be addressed, there are three fundamental shifts in our society that will have a material impact on improving the quality of life and creating a thriving world for future generations: (1) clean, renewable, affordable, accessible and reliable energy, (2) supply chain efficiency and disintermediation through localization, and (3) reduced consumption.

CLEAN ENERGY

"Almost every way we make electricity today, except for the emerging renew-
ables and nuclear, puts out CO2. And so, what we're going to have to do at
a global scale, is create a new system. And so, we need energy miracles."

~Bill Gates

It is clear that we need to transform our energy portfolio from greenhouse gas producing fossil-intensive energy (e.g., coal, oil, natural gas) and radioactive waste producing nuclear energy sources to clean, non-destructive sources of fuel and power, such as hydrogen, solar, wind, hydro, tidal, geothermal, biomass, biofuels and microbial fuel cells ("Clean Energy Sources").

The greenhouse gas emissions from fossil fuels have been proven to contribute to climate change, pollution, environmental destruction and disease. Multiple studies published in peer-reviewed scientific journals[373] show that 97 percent or more of actively publishing climate scientists agree that climate-warming trends over the past century are extremely likely due to human activities.[374] According to the World Bank, the impact of climate change will lead to increased poverty, hunger, disease and natural disasters, costing hundreds of billions of dollars per year.[375] For those that still deny climate change is real, it's difficult to deny that air pollution is bad for our health. Clearly, breathing emissions from fossil fuel is bad for our health with diseases including Asthma, Pneumonia, Bronchitis, Upper Respiratory Infections, Eye Irritation, Heart Disease, Neurological Deficits and Cancer.[376]

Moreover, fossil-fuel-related accidents have caused billions of dollars of damage to our environment. For example, the damages from the Exxon Valdes oil spill alone are estimated at $7B based upon cleanup, the devastation to the ecosystems of Prince William Sound, and the contamination of 1,300 miles of shoreline, as well as the impacts on fisherman and the tourism economy of Alaska.[377]

While nuclear energy generation doesn't emit greenhouse gasses, (1) disposing of nuclear waste presents a significant risk of radioactive contamination to water and soil, and (2) nuclear plant accidents (e.g., Chernobyl and Fukushima) have caused, and are likely to cause, massive destruction to the environment and the economy as well as harm to human lives. Globally, there have been at least 100 reported nuclear reactor accidents from 1952 to present with damages totaling, in the aggregate, well over $100B. With the economic value of nuclear power in the U.S. estimated at $7.8T, the economic value of nuclear appears to outweigh the economic damage.[378] However, with so many safe sources of clean and renewable energy available, there is no need to expose millions of people to radiation and increased rates of cancer, not to mention the devastating impact on our environment, resulting from nuclear "accidents." Moreover, with costs of developing, building and commissioning nuclear plants substantially increasing, much of the prior support for, and investment in, nuclear as an economic energy source is losing momentum.[379]

While nuclear energy is becoming more expensive, most of the Clean Energy sources mentioned above are becoming more efficient, more durable and less expensive. According to a 2019 report by the International Renewable Energy Agency ("IRENA), unsubsidized renewable energy is frequently the cheapest source of energy generation.[380] According to the report:

"Costs from all commercially available renewable power generation technologies declined in 2018. The global weighted-average cost of electricity declined 26% year-on-year for concentrated solar power (CSP), followed by bioenergy (-14%), solar photovoltaic (PV) and onshore wind (both -13%), hydropower (-12%), geothermal and offshore wind (both -1%), the report finds."

While the consumption of fossil fuels has decreased from 1970 as a percentage of energy used, fossils fuels still account for almost 80% of the world's energy source.[381] According to Stanford University's Professor Mark Z. Jacobson, a goal of 100 percent renewable energy is achievable by 2050, without the need for radically new technology. There is hope that by 2050, our world can be running on Clean Energy. However, achieving this goal will require trillions of dollars in infrastructure investment. This investment can also be a tipping point into creating the Regenerative Economy.

In addition to the Clean Energy sources mentioned above, there are also some potential highly disruptive energy solutions that are still theoretical, but have great promise, such as *Zero-Point Energy* and *Cold Fusion*. These technologies have the potential to transform our entire energy paradigm and give humankind abundant and inexpensive energy into the future. We just need to figure out how to harness and implement these technologies to take them from theory into practical application.

It's interesting, when talking to physicists about energy, especially regarding the possibility of perpetual energy, how closed-minded they often are. Foundational to the training of physicists is learning the "*Laws of Thermodynamics*." The three Laws of Thermodynamics define the physical quantities that comprise thermodynamic systems including *temperature, energy* and *entropy*.

1. The first law of thermodynamics, also known as the Law of Conservation of Energy, states that energy cannot be created or destroyed in an isolated system.

2. The second law of thermodynamics states that the entropy of any isolated system always increases.

3. The third law of thermodynamics states that the entropy of a system approaches a constant value as the temperature approaches absolute zero.

According to the first law thermodynamics, perpetual motion machines that produce energy without energy input are deemed impossible; under the second law, perpetual motion machines that spontaneously convert thermal energy into mechanical work are deemed impossible; and under the third law perpetual motion machines that convert thermal energy into mechanical work are deemed impossible.

While I am nowhere near as savvy about the Laws of Thermodynamics as those deeply trained in the subject, I do know that these "Laws" were created by man based upon man's observations, understanding and knowledge of the way the universe supposedly works. I also know that man observes, understands and knows very little about the universe.

The universe appears to have an infinite supply of energy that keeps the entire universe in motion. Even if not infinite, there is surely enough energy in the universe to power the needs of humankind. The planets don't need fossil fuels or nuclear plants to keep spinning around the sun and they don't need money to pay utility companies. The energy clearly exists to power the universe and all the needs of humankind abundantly, efficiently and without money. Maybe our scientists need to open their minds and question the Laws of Thermodynamics, much like how Einstein questioned Newtonian physics. What if the universe is not an isolated system? What if entropy (the degree of disorder or randomness in a system) is a massive source of energy that science hasn't yet been able understand or harness? What if energy can be created or destroyed?

In a universe of infinite possibilities, there would have to be a possibility of perpetual and infinite energy. Given the latest research on *Zero-Point Energy* and *Cold Fusion/Low-Energy Nuclear Reactions*, we may be getting closer to abundant, cheap, clean and globally available energy.

Zero-Point Energy ("ZPE") is a term used in quantum mechanics for the lowest possible energy that a quantum mechanical system may have at absolute zero. ZPE is the energy that remains when all other energy is removed from a system. ZPE is based on the fact that even at an absolute zero temperature of -273 degrees Celsius, elementary particles still display energetic traits. This behavior is demonstrated by, for example, liquid helium. As the temperature is lowered to absolute zero, helium remains a liquid rather than freezing to a solid, owing to the irremovable ZPE of its atomic motions.[382] According to quantum research, each cubic centimeter of apparently empty space contains an enormous amount of energy, and these are measurable in the laboratory. Physicists Richard Feynman and John Wheeler calculated the zero-point radiation of the vacuum to be an order of magnitude greater than nuclear energy, with a single light bulb containing enough energy to boil all the world's oceans.[383]

One measurable consequence is the Casimir effect. The Casimir force is due to so-called radiation pressure from the zero-point energy of the background electromagnetic field. For instance, two uncharged conductive plates in a vacuum are placed a few nanometers apart. In a classical description, the lack of an external field means that there is no field between the plates, and no force would be measured between them. When this field is instead studied using the quantum electrodynamic vacuum, it is seen that the plates do affect the virtual photons which constitute the field and generate a net force in the form of either an attraction or a repulsion depending on the specific arrangement of the two plates. Although the Casimir effect can be expressed in terms of virtual particles interacting with the objects, it is best described and more easily calculated in terms of the zero-point energy of a quantized field in the intervening space between the objects. In effect, some wavelengths of the field are excluded from between the plates, reducing the energy density compared with that of empty space. The imbalance results in the plates being pushed together.[384]

Having attempted to describe ZPE, let's look at some of the exciting research and applications associated with ZPE. NASA's Eagleworks Labs, for example, is an advanced propulsion physics laboratory pursuing propulsion technologies necessary to enable human exploration of the solar system over the next 50 years and enabling interstellar spaceflight by the end of the century. Eagleworks is currently working on a ZPE design called the *"Quantum Vacuum Thruster"* or *"QVT"* that only requires energy in the form of electrical power rather than fuel. Using ZPE theories, Eagleworks developed highly specialized conducting cavities to generate a thrust that "pushes" against the vacuum of space and directs the flow of virtual electrons and positrons generated from a standing radio-frequency wave inside the closed cavity.[385]

Cold Fusion, also known as *"Low-Energy Nuclear Reactions" ("LENR"),* was originally introduced by electrochemists, Martin Fleischmann and Stanley Pons in 1989. Fleischmann and Pons found that deuterium atoms from heavy water that had penetrated the palladium cathode were fusing to form helium atoms. The excess energy from the process dissipated as heat. Fleischmann and Pons attributed this to a nuclear reaction, rather than any known chemical reactions. The results found by Fleischmann and Pons were allegedly not able to be replicated and cold fusion was dismissed as a viable energy technology. However, the field of *"Cold Fusion"* was rebranded *"Low-Energy Nuclear Reactions" ("LENR").* LENR is interesting because it harnesses the power of weak nuclear force rather than splitting atoms (fission) or by fusing atoms (fusion). Research into Cold Fusion and LENR has continued and there is recently renewed interest and funding flowing into fusion technologies from the likes of Google, MIT, NASA and Breakthrough Energy Ventures ($1B energy innovation fund started by Bill Gates with partners including Jeff Bezos, Jack Ma, Richard Branson, Michael Bloomberg and Vinod Khosla). Even though the excess energy generated from LENR is considered "nuclear" energy, according to the International Atomic Energy Agency ("IAEA"), **LENR doesn't produce any material amount of nuclear waste, is inherently safe and can't cause a nuclear accident:**[386]

"*Nuclear fission power plants have the disadvantage of generating unstable nuclei; some of these are radioactive for millions of years. Fusion on the other hand does not create any long-lived radioactive nuclear waste. A fusion reactor produces helium, which is an inert gas. It also produces and consumes tritium within the plant in a closed circuit. Tritium is radioactive (a beta emitter) but its half life is short. It is only used in low amounts so, unlike long-lived radioactive nuclei, it cannot produce any serious danger. The activation of the reactor's structural material by intense neutron fluxes is another issue. This strongly depends on what solution for blanket and other structures has been adopted, and its reduction is an important challenge for future fusion experiments.*"

According to a report by Edmund Storms, published in Innovative Energy & Research[387]

"*The energy released by LENR involves no significant radioactivity or harmful radiation, and the generators can be small and inexpensive. Nuclear meltdown is not possible. Because the fuel is contained in ordinary water, the energy would be available to all countries and could be generated in each home or business. Such energy could not be interrupted by weather, terrorists, or political conflict. Since CO2 is not produced at any stage in its use, LENR poses no threat to global warming. A rational person has to wonder why such an ideal energy source is not implemented immediately.*

But like all good things, a dark side is possible. First, the present industries supplying carbon-based or uranium-based fuel would go out of business. The grid system would not be necessary and would cease to exist. Even the clean energy sources, such as solar and wind that are attached to the grid, would find selling their energy to be very difficult. In short, the advanced nations that use oil, coal, natural gas, and uranium for energy would face possible financial collapse of their major industries. In addition, all nations that rely on selling these fuels to the rest of the world would experience the same fate. Although wars over access to oil would no longer be necessary, the initial economic collapse might be too high a price to pay."

It is now critical to the survival and future of humankind that we shift our energy portfolio to Clean Energy regardless of the economic consequences. If the world can justify a $29T bailout of the banks and bulge bracket firms as a result of the 2008 financial collapse, we should be able to justify a global spend of $3T per year to transform our energy portfolio to Clean Energy by 2050.[388] With a commitment of sufficient resources, it seems highly likely that we will be able to not only replace fossil fuel sources of energy with Clean Energy sources by 2050, and even more exciting, we may be able to crack the code on ZPE and Cold Fusion/LENR by 2050. The question is will governments around the world commit the resources and shift the regulatory environment to implement a world running on Clean Energy.

SUPPLY CHAIN EFFICIENCY AND DISINTERMEDIATION

The "supply chain" essentially refers to the movement of goods from raw materials to end users. In our current world of centralization, the supply chain generally involves a network of producers of raw materials, component suppliers, transporters, manufacturers, packagers, vendors, distributors, storage facilities, wholesalers, retailers and customers. The supply chain runs largely on fossil fuels for transportation and packaging, and electricity for manufacturing, refrigeration and storage. As mentioned, fossil-fuels have been implicated as a significant contributor to climate change as well as a large cause of pollution to our air, water, soil and food.

A supply chain generally consist of the following 3 components: (1) Supply, (2) Manufacturing, and (3) Distribution. The activities close to the Supply (e.g., raw material and commodities largely coming from China, South America and Africa) are known as *upstream activities*. Activities between Manufacturing (e.g., China, EU, U.S., Japan and India) and Distribution to the end consumer (e.g., U.S., EU, China, Japan, UK) are *downstream activities*.

While the supply chain seems efficient because I can easily purchase goods at my grocer, restaurant, big box store or Amazon, it is actually the inefficiencies that create massive profits for oil companies, transportation manufacturers, shipping companies, logistics companies, packaging companies, the construction industry, equipment manufacturers and retailers. Because the supply chain runs primarily on fossil fuels, it supports the rationale for massive funding to the military industrial complex in order to protect oil in the name of national security. The oil companies are not only given subsidies and tax breaks by our governments; they also don't pay for the military to protect their oil fields, refineries and pipelines. The U.S. spends an estimated $81 billion annually to protect oil supplies around the world (not including the multi-trillion-dollar war in Iraq and Afghanistan.[389] This is the astronomical tax we pay to subsidize the oil industry and allow them to externalize military expenses to taxpayers. Additionally, The International Monetary Fund recently updated its comprehensive report on global fossil-fuel subsidies. It arrives at a staggering conclusion: In 2017, the world subsidized fossil fuels in an amount of $5.2 trillion, equal to roughly 6.5 percent of global GDP.[390]

Fundamental shifts required to increase supply chain efficiency and reduce reliance on fossil fuels, transport, packaging, distribution, and military spending associated with the supply chain, include (1) Localization, (2) Collaborative Consumption, (3) Planned Durability, and (4) Technological Innovation.

1. _Localization_: By planning and developing our cities and communities in a way that localize the production of food, energy, materials and goods, we can lower our dependence upon a centralized supply chain and many of the environmentally destructive ramifications of the supply chain, including greenhouse gasses and pollution. By applying regenerative planning, design and applications to our cities and communities, we can nurture and promote the Earth's abilities to provide us with an abundant and regenerative supply of water, food, energy and materials.

    Localization, in the context used herein, refers to urban and community planning that provides for a mix of residential, commercial, retail, industrial, social and agricultural uses within distances that are walkable (no more than 1 mile) or bikeable (no more than 5 miles). As mentioned, if we go into our back yard and pull an apple off the tree, it's efficient, healthy and fresh. We didn't need any trucks, cars, warehouses, packaging or grocery stores. We also didn't need a military to protect the oil pipeline. Moreover, the environmental impact and carbon footprint was minimal.

Many of our cities and communities have been intentionally planned to promote the centralized supply chain, vehicle manufacturing and burning of fossil-fuels and energy sources. By developing new cities and communities, and redeveloping/retrofitting existing cities and communities into, regenerative, walkable, mixed-use communities, with their own water, farms, clean energy generation, waste upcycling systems, materials and goods production, we can create cities and communities that promote a higher quality of life and are more vibrant, beautiful, efficient, economically abundant and healthier (See the chapter entitled "*Transforming Our Communities*").

2. *Collaborative Consumption*: As we discussed in the chapter entitled "*Transforming to a Regenerative Society*," there has been a rapid explosion in sharing, bartering, lending, trading, renting, gifting, and swapping reinvented through network technologies on a scale and in ways never possible before. Sharing, utilizing, giving away and/or selling under-utilized resources such as homes, cars, offices, sporting goods, clothing, furniture, jewelry tools, health clubs and machine shops has created numerous multibillion dollar enterprises (e.g., Uber, Airbnb, eBay, WeWork). "Collaborative Consumption" and the "Sharing Economy" are disrupting outdated modes of business and reinventing not just what we consume, but how we consume.

According to Havas Group, "*Unhappy with the results of decades of over-consumption, many people around the world are searching for a better way of living and consuming. A large majority of those surveyed in 29 markets believe that overconsumption is actually putting our planet and society at risk. Most say they could happily live without most of the items they own and that they make it a point to rid themselves of unneeded possessions at least once a year. We have entered an age when sharing, rather than buying, everything from cars and vacation homes to textbooks and pets has become socially acceptable among those who realize we have exhausted the planet and ourselves with way too much stuff and responsibility.*"[391]

Collaborative Consumption and the Sharing Economy provides greater freedom and flexibility as well as a higher quality of life, with more options and amenities, without the burdens and expense of sole ownership. In our society, we generally share public infrastructure and services such as beaches, parks, roads, schools, police, fire, sewer systems, courts, public transportation, waste management and telecommunications infrastructure. It is also fairly common to share health clubs, restaurants, entertainment venues, hotels and community amenities. By increasing our sharing and bringing resources into our communities (e.g., facilities, community farm, community kitchen, cars, tools and equipment), we can greatly reduce the expense and environmental impact related to exclusive ownership and enjoy higher quality lives with improved health, greater freedom, more amenities, lower cost and less stress.

3. *Planned Durability:* Almost every manufacturer in the world today designs their products to have an artificially limited useful life whereby the product becomes no longer functional or fashionable. This design and manufacturing strategy is known as "*Planned Obsolescence.*" Examples include, (a) Apple and Samsung being accused of providing software updates that inhibit the performance of their older phones;[392] (b) The "Phoebus cartel (consisting of GE, Philips, Osram and AEI) that colluded to reduce a light bulb's lifetime to 1,000 hours when Edison's first commercial bulb from 1881 lasted 1,500 hours,[393] (c) General Motors utilized annual redesign of its automobiles to drive the demand for the newer and more fashionable automobile, and (d) short-lived and/or disposable products such as plastic forks, paper plates, plastic water bottles, unfillable ink cartridges, nylons, cheap clothes and fashion. We have been conditioned to link our identity and value to products. This conditioning has created a world of wasteful consumers always wanting the latest, newest, fashionable and shiny object. Aside from products becoming unfashionable, we have come to expect the products we purchase will have a limited lifetime of usefulness. Often these products are actually designed and built to fail sooner or become unfashionable. Planned obsolescence is good for manufacturers and sellers of goods and their investors, but creates massive waste and is not in the best interests of consumers or the planet.

On the other hand, "*Planned Durability*" or "*Built to Last*" is better for both consumers and the planet. By designing and manufacturing products that are built last and will remain fashionable, we, as a species, can enjoy high-quality modern-day products and conveniences with reduced expense, waste and environmental impact. Moreover, by reusing products; designing products using recycled materials and parts; reducing packaging; and digitizing products (e.g., books, music, videos, games), we can significantly improve supply chain efficiency, minimize waste, and reduce greenhouse gasses and environmental impact.

4. *Technology Innovation*: Aside from using renewable clean fuels and energy, aquatech and agtech discussed previously, technology innovation can play a pivotal and important role in transforming the supply chain. Examples of innovation that will transform the supply chain include the following:

    • *Internet of Things ("IoT")*. IoT involves the integration of technologies that allow for automation and increased efficiencies in the supply chain, our cities, communities and homes. Primarily, IoT provides us the ability to use sensors to provide data that can be used to make smarter and more efficient decisions as well as automate processes to reduce human involvement and intervention. The foundational technologies of IoT are wireless technologies (e.g., wi-fi, cellular, Bluetooth); sensors; Internet; data analytics, storage and management; object recognition, Machine-to-Machine Learning and Communications, Global Positioning Satellites ("GPS"), Radio Frequency Identification ("RFID"), Artificial Intelligence ("AI"), Augmented Reality ("AR") and predictive modeling, software, hardware and storage.

    Some of the benefits of using IoT, include (1) conserving precious water by using sensors that determine moisture levels to turn on and off watering systems; (2) saving energy by turning off lights and reducing HVAC when no person is present; (3) creating greater energy generation and distribution efficiency by utilizing locally generated energy and distributing it on demand to where it is most needed; (4) powering autonomous driverless vehicles that safely take us to our destinations and provide efficient supply chain transportation and delivery services with motion sensors, cameras, AI and predictive modeling; (5) having traffic control and parking systems that change signals and guide routes based upon real-time data; (6) tracking the movement of commodities, parts, manufacturing progress, finished goods and shipments through the supply chain; and (7) providing robots instructions on tasks and monitoring their accuracy and efficiency.

The promise of IoT is that many of the robotic and mechanical activities that humans currently do can be automated and made more efficient, thereby freeing humankind to engage is higher and more inspiring activities and work.

- *Robotics and Drones.* Robots will contribute greatly to the efficiency of the supply chain. We often think of robots as machines that resemble humans and are capable of carrying out human movements and functions. However, robots are machines capable of carrying out complex functions from instructions programmed into a computer and can be designed to carry out certain functions better than humans. Using cameras, sensors, object learning and AI, robots are now becoming capable of doing such things as growing, identifying and picking our foods, loading trucks, driving trucks, unloading trucks, picking, packing and shipping orders from a warehouse and delivering the order to the end purchaser. Robots will soon be able to also do a significant amount of mechanical services, customer service and tech support.

  Drones, are technically unmanned flying robotic aircraft. Drones can be controlled remotely by a human or given instructions through software controlled flight plans working with integrated systems such as GPS, sensors and object recognition. Aside from Drones being used by the military, they can be used to more effectively deliver packages. For example, at the time of this writing, Amazon has unveiled a plan to use drones to more effectively deliver packages directly to its customers.

- *Blockchain.* While cryptocurrencies such as Bitcoin and Ethereum have become fairly well known, the underlying blockchain technology and its importance is less known. A blockchain is, in essence, a distributed ledger technology with a list of records (known as "blocks") that are linked together using cryptography (encrypted security communication protocols). A blockchain is a decentralized, distributed and public digital ledger used to record transactions across many computers so that any involved record cannot be altered retroactively, without the alteration of all subsequent blocks. Each block contains a hash, a timestamp and transaction data. Once recorded, the data in a block is subject to network consensus to validate the authenticity of the block and thereby ensure the block is unalterable. Because the data in the blocks are redundant, validated and decentralized, blockchain has very high security and tolerance to attack and alteration. Also, using embedded smart contracts (contracts with predefined conditions that are digitally and automatically executed by the blockchain pursuant to the instructions), can create great efficiencies for execution and settlement of agreements.

The impact on supply chain efficiency is that tracking of status, transport, manufacturing and distribution of supplies, components and goods in the supply chain can be done much more securely and efficiently. Utilizing blockchain can create end-to-end visibility from origin to consumer and can be used to minimize counterfeit products, theft, embezzlement, kickbacks and much of the corruption currently found in the supply chain. Additionally, blockchain can ensure transparency and security of claims and certifications, such as organic, fresh, local, and fair trade certifications. Moreover, using blockchain the contents of international containers can be easily, securely and transparently verified to ensure greater efficiency at customs.

As mitigating climate change, carbon reduction and localization become more important to consumers and regulators, blockchain can be used to provide indelible proof of origin, quality, claims and compliance, as well as providing a reliable local currency.

By transforming our energy portfolio to using renewable and clean energy sources, reducing our consumption, localizing our needs, and minimizing our dependence on the existing supply chain, we are likely to see a significant reduction in greenhouse gas emissions and a positive transformation in the health of humankind and our planet's ecosystems.

CHAPTER 26

Transforming Organizations and Governance

(Situationally Adaptive Organizations)

---

*Corporations, as non-living fictitious entities that don't breathe air, drink water,
eat food or experience love and beauty, have used their money, power and influence
to create a world that serves their interests—"A World for the Non-Living." This
World for the Non-Living often rationalizes the destruction of life, health, beauty
and nature in the name of increased profits and growth. If the people managing these non-living entities care about human and planetary thriving and the
long-term success of their businesses, they need to transform their organizations.
This transformation includes embracing conscious organizational governance
and a quadruple bottom line that serves people, planet, purpose and profits.*

The challenges and rapidly changing social, political and economic landscape of
the 21st century are requiring significant transformation in the way business
is done. This includes transforming the purpose, structure, governance, culture and
behavior of organizations. In order to thrive in the 21st century, organizations must
evolve from hierarchical, siloed and competitive bureaucracies to a new generation
of whole-systems organizations that are agile, adaptable, resilient, innovative, collaborative and socially responsible. This includes balancing the demand of shareholders
to maximize profits with the needs of other Ecosystemic Stakeholders, including their
customers, employees, business relationships, community, society and the planet.
To serve the flourishing of the organization and all of its Ecosystemic Stakeholders,

an effective and ethical governance structure dedicated to quadruple bottom line of people, planet, purpose and profits is critical.

There is a significant consensus that the prevailing hierarchical-bureaucratic profit-at-all-costs model does not effectively address the business and economic challenges of the 21st century. Even economic pragmatists understand that climate change and dwindling resources are bad for business. As well, more consumers want to purchase products and services from ethical companies with commitments to environmental, social and governance ("ESG") improvements. Fostering ESG not only improves the value and appeal of a company's brand, but also generally enhances the quality of human life, employee morale, top line growth and the health of our biosphere.[394] Clearly, new models for organizational structures, governance and business that are holistic, adaptable, cooperative and regenerative are needed to thrive in a world concurrently transitioning from an industrial society into an information and regenerative society.

As mentioned, there is a groundswell of adoption and investment in ESG companies with over assets under management ("AUM") totaling $40.5 trillion USD globally.[395] Also, green, social and sustainable ("GSSS") bond investment grew to $600 billion USD in 2020—nearly double the $326 billion USD invested in GSSS bonds in 2019.[396] In support of the multi-trillion opportunities in ESG, Larry Fink, CEO of BlackRock, the largest asset manager in the world with AUM over $6 trillion, stated, in his 2020 letter to CEOs, that his firm would make investment decisions with environmental sustainability as a core goal:[397]

> "Over the course of 2020, we have seen how purposeful companies, with better environmental, social, and governance (ESG) profiles, have outperformed their peers. During 2020, 81% of a globally-representative selection of sustainable indexes outperformed their parent benchmarks."

> "From January through November 2020, investors in mutual funds and ETFs invested $288 billion globally in sustainable assets, a 96% increase over the whole of 2019.[398] I believe that this is the beginning of a long but rapidly accelerating transition—one that will unfold over many years and reshape asset prices of every type. We know that climate risk is investment risk. But we also believe the climate transition presents a historic investment opportunity."

While commitment to ESG should be applauded as a step in the right direction, much of the $40.5 trillion of ESG investment has gone into large public companies that continue to perpetuate the centralized supply chain, fossil fuel burning, greenhouse gas emissions, extraction and exploitative practices. The ESG commitments and the massive investment into ESG is just not enough to address the urgent transformation we require. Although there has been significant exploration into organizational change, many of the organizational change models have not integrated a whole systems and flexible approach where form (e.g., structure and governance) follows function (e.g., purpose, vision, mission, objectives, goals, and increasing the quality of life). Instead of making real change, most organizations have adopted "organizational change models" that leave the hierarchical structure, form and system in place while just addressing the symptoms of organizational dysfunction. Occasionally a "new" structure is put in place, but often these are equally form-based, myopic, inflexible, bureaucratic, disempowering and inefficient.

Having a single organizational structure is like trying to use a single tool for every situation. As the saying goes, "If our only tool is a hammer, every problem looks like a nail," When presented with a tomato, we hit with our hammer; when presented with a nut and bolt, we hit it with our hammer; when presented with a screw, we hit it with our hammer. If only we had a knife for the tomato, a wrench for the nut and bolt, and a screwdriver for the screw, the outcome of our actions could be considerably more effective and elegant.

So rather than having a singular, one-size-fits-all, form-based organizational structure that frequently fails to effectively address the rapidly changing landscape of the 21st century, *"Situationally Adaptive Organizations" ("SAOs"),* as discussed in this chapter, can provide a highly effective, flexible, agile and multi-structured organizational protocol to address the in today's rapidly changing socio-economic-political climate. SAOs respond to circumstances with a tool chest of adaptable forms that enlists the most effective people, resources, tools and processes to optimally address each situation as it arises.

This chapter examines different organizational structures and seeks to demonstrate that SAOs provide greater effectiveness resulting in increased profits, executing organizational change, fulfilling ESG commitments, and greater Ecosystemic Thriving.

THE IMPACT AND INFLUENCE OF CORPORATIONS

Just 150 years ago, the business corporation was a relatively insignificant institution. Today, corporations have become the dominant institution of business and influence. Corporations impact practically everything on this planet, from people, animals, plants and the environment to foreign relations, trade, money and just about every resource imaginable (e.g., water, air, metals, food, gems, oil and chemicals).

A "corporation" is defined by Stewart Kyd, the author of the first treatise on corporate law in English, "*as having perpetual succession under an artificial form, and vested, by policy of the law, with the capacity of acting, in several respects, as an individual, particularly of taking and granting property, of contracting obligations, and of suing and being sued, of enjoying privileges and immunities in common, and of exercising a variety of political rights, more or less extensive, according to the design of its institution, or the powers conferred upon it, either at the time of its creation, or at any subsequent period of its existence.*"

Ambrose Bierce's Devil's Dictionary defines the "corporation" as "*an ingenious device for obtaining profit without individual responsibility.*"

The corporation, as a form and structure, is relatively benign and provides a method for a collection of individuals to unify their efforts and capital to achieve a mission. Like a pot of stew, corporations are analogous to a container of boiling water—it has no flavor or character but takes on the characteristics of the ingredients thrown into the pot. The corporate stew consists of such ingredients as the mission, purpose, organizational structure, leadership, employees, policies, protocols, regulations, facilities and culture of an organization. If a corporation (1) is led by ethical, equitable, socially responsible and environmentally conscious management, (2) has a highly functional governance structure, and (3) is supported by like-minded shareholders and customers, a corporation can do great good in the world while generating extraordinary profits. However, when a corporation, with the rights and powers of an immortal person, is controlled by greedy, corrupt and power-hungry sociopaths, whose management and shareholders abandon qualitative and ethical considerations for profit, and turn a blind eye to the destruction, toxicity, injustice and suffering they cause, a corporation can become a dangerous and powerful enemy to humankind and the planet.

Prior to the 17th century, the first corporations were created in Europe as not-for-profit entities to build institutions for the public good, such as hospitals and universities. They had constitutions detailing their duties overseen by the government. Straying outside these was punishable by law.

It wasn't until the 17th century that making money became a major focus for corporations. Corporations were used by the imperial powers to maintain draconian control of trade, resources and territory in Asia, Africa, and the Americas. The world's first commercial corporation was the East India Company, set up by British merchant adventurers and granted the Royal Charter of Queen Elizabeth I in 1600. It shipped out gold and silver to Asia in return for spices, textiles and luxury goods. The East India Company expanded into a vast enterprise, conquering India with a total monopoly on trade and all the territorial powers of a government. At its height, it ruled over a fifth of the world's population with a private army of a quarter of a million.

Early American corporations, like British corporations, were chartered to perform specific public functions (e.g., building hospitals, bridges, universities and infrastructure). Their charters lasted between 10 and 40 years, often setting limits on commercial interests, prohibiting any corporate participation in the political process and requiring the termination of the corporation within a specific time or upon completion of a specific task.

In 1844, British Parliament passed The Joint Stock Companies Act of 1844, allowing broad access to incorporation and companies to define their own purpose. In 1855, shareholders were awarded limited liability, which protected them personally from the consequences of their corporate behavior.

In 1886 case of Santa Clara County v. Southern Pac. R. Co., 118 U.S. 394 (1886), the U.S. Supreme Court recognized the corporation as a "natural person" under law without argument on the point. The "ruling" that has been relied upon to support "corporate personhood," occurred in the case headnote entered by the Court Reporter, which stated as follows:

> *"One of the points made and discussed at length in the brief of counsel for defendants in error was that 'corporations are persons within the meaning of the Fourteenth Amendment to the Constitution of the United States.' Before argument, Mr. Chief Justice Waite said: The court does not wish to hear argument on the question whether the provision in the Fourteenth Amendment of the Constitution, which forbids a State to deny to any person within its jurisdiction the equal protection of the laws, applies to these corporations. We are all of the opinion that it does."*

Following the example of The East India Trading Company, over the past 300 years, corporations have conquered territories and brought in resources for the state, manipulated lawmakers and broke laws put in place to constrain them, all the while gaining in power and privilege. History shows a repetitive cycle of corporations causing social and environmental destruction and violence. In the past, the state was forced to reign them back through regulation. However, the gritty underbelly of regulation today generally benefits those who have the resources (e.g., money, political influence, lobbyists and an army of lawyers) to sponsor legislation and comply with the regulatory overhead. Thus, much of today's regulatory environment perpetuates anti-competitive practices and/or provides incumbent corporate interests with subsidies, government contracts, and other "pork barrel" rewards that negatively impact individuals, entrepreneurs, small businesses, innovation and society. The large and resource-rich corporations are favored by the politicians who receive "donations," campaign contributions, favors and other payoffs for promoting their sponsored legislation and awarding them contracts.

Our government, monetary system and resources are now largely controlled by corporate interests. Although corporations are managed by people, corporate leadership has historically adopted a profit-at-all-costs culture, which largely disrespects the environment, social justice, human life and happiness.

However, we are seeing the emergence of a transformative corporate culture that is beginning to embrace the triple bottom line (profits, people, planet) and ESG. A good percentage of corporate leadership and shareholders are starting to understand that doing good for people and planet can actually increase profits, productivity, efficiency and brand equity.

We are also starting to see a movement toward more open and natural organizational structures and governance that support a quadruple bottom line as we evolve beyond the bureaucratic and hierarchical structures that served the industrial age and military-industrial complex.

BUREAUCRATIC ORGANIZATIONS

Most government and corporate organizational structures today consist of bureaucracies with hierarchical structures. Hierarchical bureaucracies generally seek predictability, standardization, control and security. Their influence on our society has resulted in a global culture that promotes scarcity, fear, disempowerment, extraction and competition over health, love, abundance, beauty and thriving. Also, the rigid structures and processes inherent in today's bureaucratic organizations promote standardization, duplicatable and mechanistic systems, much like a McDonald's franchise. While McDonald's has created a standardized system for fast-food franchises, their food is considered mediocre and unhealthy and their reputation has suffered for contributing to obesity and mistreatment of their employees.[399] This same mechanistic approach to standardization has been applied to our lives, education, relationships, business practices, organizational structures and governance, creating a society that is also largely mediocre and unhealthy.

The bureaucratic hierarchical organizational structure has become significantly obsolete, expensive and ineffective. Despite the inefficiencies and expense of many bureaucratic hierarchies, leadership continues to perpetuate this model because the leaders generally obtain greater control, power and remuneration, at the expense of shareholders and employees in these bureaucratic organizations. In fact, Forbes states that *"CEOs earn 331 times as much as average workers and 774 times as much as minimum wage earners."*[400] So, if you're the CEO of a large organization that pays you 774 times that of minimum wage earners, why change a model that rewards you so well?

Although many large company CEOs have been reaping disproportionate rewards for years, the inequitable, socially irresponsible, unsustainable, unethical, dishonest, destructive and callous "industrial age profit-at-all costs corporate dinosaurs" are being rendered obsolete. They will either evolve into environmentally and socially responsible organizations or become extinct.

In this fast-paced world of multi-national transactions, global online information, outsourcing, automated processes, on-demand technological efficiencies, real-time budgeting, whole systems applications, social and environmental responsibility and the need for transparent and effective communication flows, organizations can no longer hide their unethical and harmful behavior in the shadows. Organizations are being called to a new code of conduct that includes integrity, equitability, ethical conduct, transparency and ESG. Also, adaptability, agility, collaboration, innovation and quality are required for companies to thrive in the 21st century.

While bureaucracies can be effective for certain situations, the inefficiencies, opacity, rigidity, blame, expense, sociopathic behavior, quarterly short-sightedness, and myopic profit-at-all-cost thinking are causing great detriment to the organizations and their Ecosystemic Stakeholders (e.g., their employees, shareholders, customers, business partners, society and the environment). To better understand why bureaucratic organizations are largely inefficient in today's quickly changing world, a closer look at what bureaucracy entails may help to provide clarity.

"Bureaucracy" is the combined organizational structure, procedures, protocols, and set of regulations in place to manage and standardize activity, usually in large organizations. Bureaucratic organizations are most often hierarchical and possess the following characteristics:

- Standardized procedures and rules that direct the execution of most or all processes within the organization

- Formal division of powers with authority largely residing in the non-productive executives and general administration as opposed to residing with specialized and productive divisions (e.g., manufacturing, sales and R&D)

- Hierarchical organizational structure and vertical power relationships

- Form and standardization are elevated over function and excellence

- Information is typically siloed and held in secret

- Indirect and opaque communication often prevail

- People are generally given responsibility without authority

- There is typically a culture of competition, finger-pointing and blame rather than collaboration and problem solving

Most corporations have a mission statement and function to provide a needed product or service to customers at a reasonable price while providing their shareholders with a significant return on their investment. A majority of organizational structures and their governance are out of alignment with their purpose. Such divergence from purpose generally decreases performance and causes many unseen negative consequences. The purpose, function and mission of most corporations is not to destroy the biosphere and cause pollution; subjugate and demean employees; destroy communities, small business and indigenous cultures; and promote war, injustice and poverty. However, when a rigid and sociopathic profit-at-all cost structure and culture is elevated over an ethical, purpose-driven, multi-benefit structure, the results can be appalling, especially when the governance of the organization is controlled by unscrupulous, power-hungry and greedy individuals.

There have been several organizational and management-change concepts applied to bureaucratic structure and governance in the latter half of the 20th century. These include the following:

- *Functional Structure*—Employees within a functional organization tend to perform a specialized set of tasks. For instance, a software company engineering division would be staffed only with software engineers. This structure leads to operational efficiencies when the company is a producer of standardized goods and services with large volume and low cost. This structure can work well for OEM producers and outsourced providers that sell products to brands that maintain sales and distribution channels. However, this structure does not work well for a market-driven business that sells customized or rapidly evolving consumer-centric products or services that require interface between sales and marketing, engineering and production.

- *Divisional Structure*—In the divisional structure, each division contains all the necessary resources and functions within it (e.g., general administration, engineering, manufacturing, sales and marketing). Divisions can be geographically based (e.g., a US division and an EU division) or product/service based (e.g., an automobile company might have separate divisions for SUVs, compact cars, sedans and hybrids). Divisional structures can provide a more focused and efficient organizational structure than a centralized structure, but too often lead to siloed information, redundancy and duplicative expenses, unless integrated and holistic communications, knowledge transfer and management are implemented.

- *Matrix Structure*—Matrix organizations are often set up to make organizations more flexible, to break down the old bureaucratic functions, divisional redundancies, information "silos" and geographic divisiveness, and to encourage more cooperation across the business groups. In matrix organizations, employees are often grouped by cross-sector specialization, geography and product. A matrix organization frequently uses multi-disciplinary teams of employees in order to take advantage of innovation, fresh perspectives, and holistic approaches that centralized and siloed structures don't provide. For example, sales, customer service, accounting, engineering and manufacturing may be grouped together so that sales and customer service can work with engineering and manufacturing to focus their efforts on making products that more effectively meets the needs of the company's customers, while accounting ensures that such products can be made on time, in budget and that capacity and inventory levels meet demand. These cross-sector groups may collaborate on multiple products or geographies. Among many large organizations using the Matrix structure, Starbucks has successfully used the Matrix structure by combining functional and product-based divisions that empower employees to make their own decisions rather than requiring layers of bureaucracy and management in order to make decisions. This has allowed Starbucks to increase its efficiency and achieve high levels of customer service. Other companies that have successfully used Matrix structure and multi-national design include IBM, Procter & Gamble, Toyota and Unilever.

- *Total Quality Management and Six Sigma*—Total Quality Management (TQM) is a management concept coined by W. Edwards Deming. The basis of TQM is to reduce the errors produced during the manufacturing or service processes, increase customer satisfaction, streamline supply chain, aim for modernization of equipment and ensure workers have the highest level of training. One of the principal aims of TQM is to limit errors to one per one million units produced. TQM is often associated with the development, deployment, and maintenance of organizational systems that are required for various business processes. The main difference between TQM and Six Sigma is that TQM tries to improve quality by ensuring conformance to internal requirements, while Six Sigma focuses on improving quality by reducing the number of defects. TQM and Six Sigma adopt a number of management principles that can be used by upper management to guide their organizations towards improved performance. The principles cover:

  - Customer focus

  - Leadership

  - Involvement of people

  - Process approach

  - System approach to management

  - Continual improvement

  - Factual approach to decision-making

  - Mutually beneficial supplier relationships

Although improved efficiency and higher performance have generally resulted by applying the foregoing process-improvement and "organization-change" structures, very few have created a new paradigm that transformed the core inefficiencies or improved the endemic inequities of bureaucratic structures. For example, hierarchical organizations generally reward title and authority rather than genuine value, performance, responsibility and productivity. Those at the top of the hierarchy often contribute the least to the productivity and profitability of the enterprise, while making exponentially more than those who create, produce, provide and sell the products and services. Furthermore, due to the layers of hierarchy generally characteristic of bureaucracies, organizational communication is often slowed, blocked, manipulated and contorted. Moreover, budgets and resources in bureaucratic organizations tend to be divisionalized and allocated without a real-time whole systems view of the corporate strategy and best use of resources. For example, rather than divisions contributing unneeded budget allocations back to the organization, they are misused and abused in order to set a precedent upon which to base the subsequent year's budgets.

POST-BUREAUCRATIC MODELS

By the 1980's, it had become exceedingly clear that the structure of hierarchical bureaucratic organizations was too often failing in a fast-paced, technological and highly competitive global marketplace. This resulted in experimenting with new structural, governance, economic, and cultural models to replace the bureaucratic model.

- *Flat Organizations* are based upon the belief that well-trained workers will be more productive when they are more directly involved in the decision-making process. The Flat Organization is based on a structure that has the least amount of intervening management levels between staff and managers. The flat structure is common in entrepreneurial start-ups, university spin-offs or small companies in general. Employees often act as management and wear many hats. As the company grows, however, there is a tendency to become more complex and hierarchical, which leads a structure with more levels, departments and rules. In general, over the last decade, it has become increasingly clear that through the forces of globalization, competition and more demanding customers, the structure of many companies has become flatter, less hierarchical, more fluid and even virtual.

- *Team Organizations* can be both horizontal and vertical. The overarching character is they combine individual competencies to achieve synergistic outcomes. Thus, the total performance of the team defines the quality of the organization. Although team structures are often used in smaller organizations, larger bureaucratic organizations can benefit from the flexibility

of teams as well. For example, each Whole Foods Market store is an autonomous profit center composed of an average of ten self-managed teams,
while team leaders in each store and each region are also a team.[401]

- *Network Organizations* overcome expense, inefficiency and internal incom-
petence by outsourcing any business function that can be done better or
more cheaply. In essence, managers in network structures spend most of
their time coordinating and controlling external relations, usually by electronic means. For example, H&M outsources its clothing manufacture to a
network of 700 suppliers, more than two-thirds of which are based in low-
cost Asian countries. Not owning any factories, H&M can be more flexible
than many other retailers in lowering its costs, which aligns with its low-
cost strategy. Aside from outsourcing production, shipping, storage, fulfillment, distribution and customer service, many larger companies are also
outsourcing product design and development and even management.[402]

- *Virtual Organizations* work in a network of external alliances, primarily
using the Internet, telecommunications, video conferencing and collaborative software to connect the organization. This means that the organization
can maintain a small core but can operate globally as a market leader in
its niche.

- *Consensus Organizations* are based upon a collaborative community model
developed by Charles Heksher. The organization is a network rather than
a hierarchy in which decisions are based on horizontal decision-making
(e.g., dialogue and consensus) rather than vertical control (e.g., authority
and command). In Heckscher's "Ideal Type" model, "*The master concept is
an organization in which everyone takes responsibility for the success of the
whole.*"[403] As well, this model links individual contributions to the company's
mission and focuses on widespread information sharing. This overcomes and
replaces traditional bureaucratic boundaries (e.g., rigid job descriptions and
segmentation) with principled action, greater trust, openness, creativity and
collaboration. This model is often used in housing cooperatives, non-profit
organizations and community organizations. It is also used to encourage
participation and empower people who normally experience oppression in

groups. While consensus models have merit in certain applications, such as collecting group wisdom and non-urgent problem solving, it can create inefficiencies and delays in the decision-making and execution process. By applying SAO strategies to consensus organizations, consensus can be designated as the standard operating system, with situational exceptions. Thus, a modified consensus can be used to allow for openness and horizontal decision-making but puts time limits on such decision-making depending upon the urgency and complexity of a required decision. If the decision is not made within the designated time, either a democratic or hierarchical process can be employed to avoid inefficiencies while still benefiting from collective wisdom.

COMPLEX ADAPTIVE SYSTEMS ORGANIZATIONS

Complex Adaptive Systems Organizations ("CASOs") are based upon the application of natural systems to organizational management. CASOs are differentiated from ordered and chaotic systems by the relationship between the system and the agents that act within it. In an ordered system, all agent behavior is constrained and limited by the rules of the system. In a chaotic system, the agents are unconstrained, which can lead to disorganization and lack of cohesion, but potentially more independence and creativity. In CASOs , the system and the agents co-evolve and the ordered and chaotic applications are balanced. The system lightly constrains agent behavior, but the agents modify the system by their interaction with it.

CASOs utilize whole systems dynamics, evolutionary and natural applications to organizational creation, functioning and interaction. Characteristics of CASOs include. . .

- Highly organic structure

- Minimal formalization of behavior

- Job specialization and authority based on experience and abilities

- Cross-sector teams, communication and participation

- Responsibility and teamwork rather than blame, competition and ostracism

- Minimal standardization of procedures

- Roles not clearly defined

- Selective decentralization

- Organizational structure follows function rather than form

- Power shifts to specialized teams and individuals and away from general administration (e.g., production, sales, R&D)

- Horizontal job specialization provides for fluidity and ability to fully express multiple talents

- Networked transparent communication

- Culture based on productive non-bureaucratic work rather than layers of non-productive middle management

- Members are given authority equal to responsibility subject to specialization, skills and purpose

CASOs seeks to understand the nature of system constraints and agent interaction and generally take an evolutionary or naturalistic approach to strategy. Examples of include Adhocractic, Biomimetic, Chaordic, Fractal and Holocratic models.

- *"Adhocracies"*, first popularized in 1970 by Alvin Toffler, is a type of organization that seeks flexibility and adaptability by focusing on opportunities and individual initiative rather than bureaucratic rules, policies and procedures.[404] World renowned author and expert on management practices, Robert H. Waterman, Jr., defined *"adhocracy"* as *"any form of organization that cuts across normal bureaucratic lines to capture opportunities, solve problems, and get results."* For Henry Mintzberg, an internationally renowned academic and author on business and management, adhocracy is a complex and dynamic organizational form. Mintzberg considers bureaucracy a thing of the past, and adhocracy one of the future. Adhocracies tend be excellent for problem-solving, innovation, and flourishing in a rapidly changing environment. Adhocracies require sophisticated and often automated technical systems to develop excellence and cohesion.[405]

- *"Biomimetic Organizations"* apply biological methods and natural systems applications that have evolved over 4.5 billion years of the planet's evolutionary systems design. The pressure to evolve in order to survive typically forces living organisms, including flora and fauna, to become highly optimized and efficient. As influences such as environment, culture and access to resources change, living organisms are forced to adapt or become extinct. Thus, by learning from and mimicking nature, there is a greater likelihood of developing systems that optimally function and allow businesses to evolve and thrive.[406]

- *"Chaordic Organizations"* was a term coined by Dee Hock, the founder and former CEO of the Visa credit card association, and refers to a system of governance that harmoniously blends characteristics of chaos and order, with neither behavior dominating the other. Nature is largely organized in such a manner as living organisms and evolutionary process by which they arose, often described as chaordic. The chaordic principles have also been used as guidelines for creating hybrid business, nonprofit and governments that are neither centralized nor anarchistic.[407]

- *"Fractal Organizations"* are a hybrid model that integrate Chaos and Complexity Theory; Quantum Mechanics and Quantum Biology; with Fractal Geometry and Cosmology to inspire the "Biomimetic Natural Hierarchies." Fractal organizations also rely heavily on biomimicry due to nature's ability to create, innovate, adapt, evolve and cleanse. Fractal organizations also share knowledge and decision-making in a collaborative and iterative manner allowing for experimentation and discovery through trial and error. According to Janna Raye, founder of Strategems and a leading proponent of fractal organizations, *"Fractal organizations are complex, adaptive systems that self-organize and succeed by cohering group efforts with shared vision and purpose."* When asked what differentiates the Biomimetic Natural Hierarchies of Fractal Organizations from bureaucratic hierarchies, Janna Raye said, *"The primary differentiator is that people are led, empowered and evolve naturally. Processes, such as the production of products, are managed, people are not. This allows leadership to value and interrelate with people as complex living beings, not things, helping them improve and evolve. Leaders in Fractal Organizations provide the managers of processes with resources, information and support that enable the collective intelligence of the group to drive change and innovation. Top-down hierarchies increase entropy (disorder) through managerial attempts to control staff and the internal competition that emerges through perceived limited room for advancement."*[408]

- *"Holocratic Organizations"* apply whole systems approaches, largely in the form of "nested wholes" to create greater interaction, connection and transparency. In a Holocratic organization, authority is distributed into self-organizing teams that can be created, expanded or contracted as is required for the purposeful functioning of the organization. The vision is for employees to hold multiple roles and move fluidly in and out of circles, increasing the flexibility and adaptability of people and the organization. Holocracies are often mistakenly thought to be non-hierarchical or flat, when, in actuality, they create a new hierarchy around work rather than titles and authority. Zappos is one of the largest holocratic organizations, and was recognized six years in a row by Fortune as one of the "100 Best Companies to Work For."[409]

Just as hierarchies and relationships between living systems can be seen in nature (e.g., commensalism, mutualism, parasitism, competition and predation), various governance systems and organizations result in cultures and relationships (i) of mutualism where mutual benefit to all stakeholders is received, (ii) of commensalism where a class of stakeholders benefit while not harming or providing some lesser benefit to others, (iii) that are competitive where stakeholders compete for resources, attention, validation and incentives at the expense of others, but can sometimes result in improvement for the whole, (iv) that are predatory where stakeholders prey on others often at the expense of the prey and the whole, and (v) that are parasitic where stakeholders feed off the energy, knowledge, expertise and ingenuity of others while often taking credit for such benefits or receiving credit through association.

CASOs consciously create a culture and governance structure that supports mutualism as the standard operating culture. CASOs provide a continuum for personal progress and growth through various stages of responsibility in an atmosphere of cooperation and support for each individual's contributions, but may add enlightened commensalism and competition that benefits the whole and rewards those that are the most productive, passionate, committed and high-performing. Dedication to self-management and coherence to shared purpose helps make these organizations resilient to changing market forces.

In CASOs, a culture of inspired leadership and shared vision aligns personal achievement with the success of the whole. Unlike adhocracies, pure consensus and anarchistic organizations that often oppose bureaucracy, CASOs evolve top-down hierarchies into adaptable and vital organizations by turning unnatural hierarchies into natural hierarchies.

CASOs endeavor to approach organizational structure and development, utilizing natural organizational systems rather than contrived mechanical systems. Natural organizational systems imitate the regenerative, abundant, adaptable, resilient and cooperative characteristics of nature, whereas contrived/mechanical systems often result in, scarcity, adversity, rigidity, inefficiency, and competition, as well as increased entropy, energy output and expense. This is because contrived/mechanical systems often work adversely to the laws of nature and the universe, thereby requiring more energy, resources and force to make them work efficiently. Because CASOs imitate and align with natural systems, rather than attempting to "paddle upstream," there is less force, energy and artificial organization required to maintain, evolve and grow. The contrived/mechanical systems typically result in entropy and mediocrity, whereas natural systems generally lead to syntropy, innovation and excellence.

There are many examples of the regenerative, abundant, adaptable and cooperative characteristics found in nature. For example, when an acorn grows into an oak tree, the oak tree generates thousands of acorns, which serves an abundant ecosystemic role as a reproductive function for the oak, a nutrient for the forest and food source for humans and animals. When a magnet is cut into pieces, each piece contains a complete field. When the fields are combined, they become stronger and no piece is weakened by the presence of the other pieces. Even human sperm form cooperative groups to increase their swimming velocity and thereby provide greater success of procreation.

While it appears from our anthropocentric view and reductionist theories that nature is competitive, in the 150 years since Darwin published *Origin of a Species*, biological and social research is now supporting that cooperation is a more important factor than competition to the flourishing of a species. Peter Kropotkin published *Mutual Aid: A Factor of Evolution* in 1902, which contrary to Darwin, supported that cooperation increased the success of a species, not competition:

> *"If we . . .ask Nature: 'who are the fittest: those who are continually at war with each other, or those who support one another?' we at once see that those animals which acquire habits of mutual aid are undoubtedly the fittest. They have more chances to survive, and they attain, in their respective classes, the highest development of intelligence and bodily organization."*

The Darwinistic, competitive and mechanical approach historically found in organizational structure and governance is largely devoid of the regenerative, abundant, cooperative, adaptable and life-enhancing qualities of nature. The man-made systems governing modern society largely arose from man's arrogant and mistaken assumptions that 1) humans are separate from and superior to nature, and 2) that our nature is Darwinstic and competitive, *whereby the strongest, the swiftest, and the cunningest live to fight another day*. Based upon these two flawed assumptions, humankind created a mechanical society that has been significantly harmful to life, nature, beauty, trust and the well-being of humankind.

There are, however, situations that arise where rigid adherence to biomimetic approaches is not optimal. For example, a natural system would allow a fire to burn freely through a forest until it was extinguished naturally. Although fires are wonderful for regenerating nature by bringing new nutrients and life to a forest, we most likely wouldn't sit idly by while a fire ravages our cities, homes and offices. Thus, even though CASOs tend to be a more effective operating system, any myopic adoption of a single system, even if the system is highly adaptable, can create rigidity and limitation. Thus, it is important to be able to situationally change systems to optimally adapt to numerous circumstances as they arise. This necessitates a pan-systemic, integrated and inclusive approach of many different systems.

Thriving in the 21st century requires a new generation of Abundant, Well and Empowered organizations and leaders that are situationally adaptive,

integrated, pan-systemic, evolutionary and resilient with a mission of creating ecosystemic thriving as the overarching value and profit motive. The new generation of conscious, evolved and courageous leaders understand the critical importance of applying living systems approaches that balance the demands of shareholders for profit with conscious choices that promote the flourishing of their Ecosystemic Stakeholders. The foregoing whole, integrated and adaptive systems that benefit of all Ecosystemic Stakeholders are embodied in Situationally Adaptive Organizations.

SITUATIONALLY ADAPTIVE ORGANIZATIONS ("SAOS")

Situationally Adaptive Organizations ("SAOs") provide a flexible, adaptable and resilient multi-structure model. Rather than a single tool, SAOs are analogous to a tool chest that contains many different tools, structures and forms of governance that can be used to effectively respond to any given circumstance. SAOs can use any of the previously discussed forms and structure, including hierarchies, if such form, or a combination of forms, optimally addresses a given situation. Rather than serving a monolithic, inefficient and dysfunctional form and requiring all circumstances to be handled within the constraints of the form, SAOs shift form to optimize solutions and effectiveness. Unlike single-structure organizational models and even CASOs, in SAOs, the situation and function dictate form to achieve optimal results in a majority of situations with the least amount of time, effort, resources and energy. For example, a creative organization that engages in ideation and design will often require a structures that promote creativity, whereas a manufacturer of machinery may need more structures that facilitate quality-control and standardization. However, under certain circumstance, the creative organization may need quality control and the manufacturer may need structures that promote innovation, design and creativity.

By utilizing a multiplicity of tools and an integrated/pan-systemic approach to governance, SAOs gain greater adaptability, agility and ability to optimally address a wide variety of situations. For example, a dictatorship may provide for rapid decision-making and handling emergencies. However, dictatorship (or other single-point of command and control), may result in narrow, self-centered, and corrupt decision-making resulting in hardship, disempowerment and inequity in the organization. Democracy, on the other hand, provides greater representation and engagement than a dictatorship, but may have a slower decision-making and implementation process and can be subject to manipulation, influence-mongering and secret agendas. Consensus-based organizations tend to have increased social benefits with a more engaged and egalitarian culture, but decision-making is often mired in processing resulting in slow decision-making and bottlenecks. Consensus organizations also tend to disincentivize individual performance, merit and innovation. If any of the foregoing systems are used exclusively, the outcome is often rigidity and an inability to optimally address changing conditions.

For example, in an SAO, if there is a fire, the most qualified person to fight fires would be designated as the commander-in-chief until the fire is put out. In this example, the organization changes from its standard daily operating policy (e.g., a holocratic and biomimetic flat nuclear organization) to a dictatorship. If the janitor is the person with the most experience in fighting fires, then he becomes the commander-in-chief, not the CEO, until the fire is out. Holding a democratic vote or obtaining consensus to determine who wants to get the hose, the pale and shovel while the headquarters burn down would not be optimally responsive to the fire. When the emergency from the fire has been resolved, the janitor's elevated leadership status returns to his role as the janitor and the organization returns to its standard nuclear and flat operating structure. When an issue arises regarding how best to clean and maintain the company's facilities, the janitor makes the decisions, not the CEO.

As another example, if there is an obsolete machine tooling that is creating product defects that threatens the reputation and success of the company, the entire organization of an SAO wouldn't generally need to be involved in repairing and replacing the tooling. The operations manager would have full authority to replace the tooling, if this is the best option. However, if this is a complicated and expensive problem that exceeds the operations manager's budget authority, the operations manager may need to collaborate in the decision-making process with other colleagues who have a deeper understanding of the company's budget, sales trajectory and market demands. In this situation, the operations manager may coordinate a committee of multi-disciplinary colleagues, including the relevant leaders in manufacturing, engineering, sales and finance. The CEO, CFO or even the operations manager's superior, if any, does not need to approve this meeting or the quality assurance engineer's ability to call the meeting. A collective intelligence gathering and democratic process involving multi-disciplinary viewpoints could be used to examine various scenarios, such as 1) whether and how to upgrade the tooling to avoid recurrence of the problem, 2) whether the market and sales of the product warrant the upgrade or the line should be shut down, and 3) whether the product should be upgraded to better meet market demand that requires additional investment in product upgrades, tooling and reconfiguring equipment. Once the recommendations of the stakeholders committee are finalized, the findings and recommendations may be implemented without further authority. However, if the implementation is beyond the authority of the operation manager's committee, the recommendations, plan and budget will be taken to the CEO and/or CFO for approval of the budget and plan.

Although structure, process, personnel and responsibility can change at any time to most effectively address situations as they arise, clear, objective and flexible Standard Operating Structure and Procedures ("SOSP") are also recommended. When an organization seeks to develop an SAO, it is important that the SAO implement and adopt an SOSP that it is confident will optimally handle 70% of normal daily operations and a process for addressing the other 30% of extraordinary, urgent and critical situations.

The following represents an example of a summary for an effective SOSP for an SAO:

- A flat nuclear structure that integrates Complex Adaptive Systems (e.g., Adhocratic, Biomimetic, Chaordic, Fractal and Holocratic) and utilizes living systems approaches that arise organically to serve and balance the higher ethical and business functions of the organization. The SOSP provides descriptions of scenarios that require a departure from the flat nuclear structure and expert authority to decisions made by committee, board or a situational commander-in-chief.

- Automated systems and procedures that 1) foster transparency and trust, 2) maximize flexibility and performance of required tasks through an opt-in process, 3) support real-time resource and budget allocation to holistically fulfill the organization's needs, 4) real-time knowledge transfers, and 5) transparent and decentralized recordation of transactions, exchanges, resource flows and results of budgetary investment.

- A structure that optimizes leadership and management. Leaders lead people. Managers manage processes and resources. The core leadership serves, leads, and inspires the team leadership and the team leadership serves, leads, and inspires team managers and personnel. The general administration and IT serve, support and empower the members of the organization to achieve their highest and most inspired performance. A significant percentage of the efforts and resources of general administration and IT go to support the team members that add the greatest direct value (e.g., innovation, product development and manufacturing, marketing and sales). Team managers manage processes (e.g., supply chain, scheduling, manufacturing, processes) and resources (e.g., supplies, money, equipment).

- The organization utilizes a standard operating culture of transparent, direct and compassionate communication, collective intelligence and participation with time-sensitive democratic voting after opt-in collective wisdom gathering. Automated and transparent intranets and communications efficiency tools are utilized to improve team involvement, cohesion and mutualism.

- Meritocratic rewards are first weighted to organizational performance, then to team performance and finally to individual performance. While it is recommended that clear and objective milestones and key performance indicators be communicated, the evolution and changing of milestones and metrics is encouraged. When incentives evolve and change, it is critical that such changes be immediately communicated to the team. Those who provide performance that leads to furthering the organization's function and goals are reasonably and equitably rewarded. Aside from providing bonuses for objective performance, such as sales, profits, or output (e.g., providing deliverables on time and in budget), the organization also rewards subjective and intangible value. This can be done by creating a peer-reviewed internal credit rating that supports intangible and subjective value such as emotional intelligence, leadership, cultural enhancement, involvement in activities that help promote the values of the organization, personal health, growth and leadership, and being a good corporate citizen.

In addition to the Standard Operating Structure and Procedures, it is recommended that an SAO also develop its Extraordinary Operating Structures and Procedures ("EOSPs"). Both SOSPs and EOSPs are agreements rather than rules that remain open to evolution, amendment and improvement.

EOSPs are developed by 1) submitting hypothetical scenarios, (including various extraordinary force majeure, supply, market, organizational, financial, legal and technology circumstances), 2) ranking the hypothetical scenarios by urgency, importance and material impact, 3) examining the organizational structure and person(s) best suited to handle the situation, 4) developing the organizational structure, persons and process to optimally deal with extraordinary scenarios, and 5) publishing the situationally adaptive structure, personnel and process change to the group. The published EOSPs should be made accessible in the company's intranet and in a location where it can be easily obtained in the event of an emergency or extraordinary situation.

The following represents situational hypotheticals for developing an EOSP for a technology SAO:

- In the event that a new technology enters the market that renders the company's current product obsolete and threatens the company's ability to maintain or grow its business, a committee will be formed consisting of the company's CEO, CFO, CTO, SVP of Sales, Top Sales Representatives, and VP of Product Development. This committee will engage in a buy, build, partner or bail analysis and develop a strategic roadmap and business plan based upon a review of the following:

  - Company's current technology, product development roadmap and capabilities;

  - Company's financial resources;

  - Expertise in-house and expertise required;

- Supply chain strengths and requirements;

- A market and SWOT analysis including the state, size and growth of the market and the company's market-share and position;

- Sales and marketing strategies and competitive analysis;

- The objectives required to address the challenges along with the time, personnel, resources and budgets required to achieve the objectives; and

- Innovative approaches and strategies.

- A report will be prepared and shared with the relevant team members of the organization chosen by the committee, for the review, feedback and input of the relevant team members.

- The committee will then modify the report and elect a leadership and management group who will be responsible for tactically executing on the strategies and guidance in the report.

- Until the organization has arrived at a complete resolution of the situation, the organization will be managed by the appointed leadership and management group with the greatest expertise.

- In the event there is an unresolved conflict and reasonable time has elapsed (as determined by a majority vote), the conflict will be resolved by majority vote. During the collective wisdom gathering process, if a party opposes the resolution, then said opposing party, is required to explain the reasons for his or her opposition and propose a resolution that improves upon the resolution they are opposing.

Based upon the preceding discussion, using an integrated, pan-systemic approach in which form, structure, processes, resources and personnel can change and be repurposed to optimally address situations provides increased function, efficiency, productivity, resiliency and responsiveness to a wide array of circumstances. This also requires "slowing down to speed up" meaning significant strategic planning, scenario exercises, systems architecture, organizational design and culture building are critical to developing and operating and SAO.

The characteristics of SAOs are as follows:

- A multi-structure organization that serves function rather than form
- Function is driven by purpose, vision, mission, principles, ethics and values
- Structures are adaptable and primarily based upon biomimetic and living systems principles
- Applied whole systems strategies are used to define circumstantial organizational shifts for optimal results
- Principles, values and agreements are elevated over rules and processes
- Authority is equal with responsibility
- People are led and empowered, whereas processes are managed
- Collaborative meritocracy that rewards innovation
- Individual contributions are respected with minimal formalization of behavior
- Work assignments and leadership are based on expertise, abilities and performance
- Promotion of cross-sector teams, communication and participation to ensure greater cohesion
- Standard procedures are agreements rather than rules that are open to evolution, betterment, interpretation and individual approaches, subject to objective quality and production measurements
- Roles are defined but can shift anytime with a minimum of hierarchical involvement upon agreement of the team members
- Individual and team responsibility
- Conflict resolution is compassionate (e.g., non-positional and non-adversarial), as well as exploratory, equanimous and openminded

- Culture based on collaborative, productive and meaningful work rather than layers of non-productive bureaucracy, self-promotion and authority

- Solutions and productive empowerment over blame

- Collaboration over competition

- Decentralized knowledge transfers, exchanges and reporting

- Objectively defined milestones and commitments with great flexibility as to the style and method by which they are achieved

- Rapid and optimal response with consistent, real-time monitoring and feedback

- Flexibility, resilience, agility and adaptability

- Consistent evolution allows for gaining wisdom by making mistakes and taking risks

- Leverages networked and virtual efficiencies

- Conscious development of emotional intelligence and behavioral expression with shared responsibility and reliability

- Open, transparent, direct, integral, inquiring and compassionate communication

- Consciousness and culture of love, abundance, wellness and empowerment

ETHICAL GOVERNANCE

Ethical governance is critical to the transformation needed by humankind and its systems. It is vital that ethical individuals, eco-social entrepreneurs and conscious corporations shift from the widespread destructive and corrupt practices of profit-at-all-costs tactics to ethical practices that will increase quality of life and ecosystemic thriving as follows:

Transforming to Ethical Governance and Government	
From	To
Self-serving corrupt, controlling, and manipulative	Serving people and planet and increasing personal freedoms, health and wealth
Managing economic growth to maximize profits	Socio-economic development that increases quality of life and profits
Distrust, fear, competition, military offense, bullying, economic warfare	Trust, love, collaboration, synergy, innovation, with minimal ethical military only used for defense
Destruction of the environment and health	Regeneration of the environment and health
Unfair trade practices	Equitable trade practices
Unsustainable overconsumption, hoarding and exclusivity	Regenerative and collaborative consumption, sharing and inclusivity
Secrecy	Transparency
Serving the interests of the non-living (e.g., central banks, corporations and government)	Serving the living and ecosystemic thriving for the benefit of people and planet
Industrialized authoritative education	Applied living systems education (adding arts, health, whole systems applications, biomimetics, ecosystemic thriving, agtech, aquatech, biomaterials, renewable energy, collaboration and emotional intelligence to STEM)
Quantitative measurements	Genuine Progress and Qualitative measurements

Businesses, NGOs, IGOs and governments can realize social, economic and environmental benefits from making substantial improvements in their archaic organizational structures to serve the health and flourishing of humankind and the environment. McKinsey & Company reports, "*Several trends are creating a new set of challenges for corporations. For example, even as a global company facing resource scarcity must create more efficient products and production techniques and invest in research into how to use raw materials that are more sustainable, it also has to advocate for stronger government protection of such resources in emerging markets, where regulations may be weaker. Furthermore, the company needs to show the world that it is doing something about sustainability to protect its reputation and to avoid potential backlash from various stakeholders. What's more, corporate leaders are facing these challenges at a time when the public's trust in institutions, particularly market-based ones, is low.*

However, businesses that actively address these issues in collaboration with government and social-sector leaders (and sometimes, where warranted, even with their competitors) can help shape a better future in which citizens have more of their needs fulfilled, businesses act more responsibly and earn the right to operate more freely in a cooperative ecosystem, and the economic climate fosters growth and innovation. It sounds utopian, but it's not. This scenario is attainable—and preferable to the path down which we may be headed. To be sure, the world will always have problems, but helping to solve them is increasingly in businesses' best interests."[410]

With governments around the world making decisions and creating regulations often at the direction of corporate lobbyists, central bankers and special interest groups, real change is much more likely to come from the people exercising their economic will, entrepreneurial innovation and collective activism. Together we can free ourselves from dependence upon a system of dysfunction, toxicity and scarcity and develop a highly functioning system based upon enhancing quality of life and well-being for people and planet.

As more people purchase goods and services from ethical and conscious companies, we will see these companies grabbing market share away from, and replacing, corrupt, unethical and unconscious companies. In order to retain their customers, ethical companies will be required to adhere to and demonstrate ethical governance and a commitment to ESG. As ethical companies replace unethical companies becoming the leading socio-economic-political influencers, we will likely see a significant transformation of from corrupt to ethical government and regulations.

ECOSYSTEMIC STAKEHOLDERS

More companies are starting to realize that they are more than an organization created to do business and maximize profits at all costs. The emergent understanding is that legal contrived and formed organizations (e.g., incorporated entities, government, IGOs and NGOs) are non-living entities that hold structure, agreements and resources for living, interconnected and interdependent beings to more effectively achieve collective missions and goals. Each organization, and those that participate in the organization, have impact on a larger ecosystem of stakeholders. These *"Ecosystemic Stakeholders"* include 1) Shareholders, 2) Customers, 3) Employees, 4) Business Relations (e.g., suppliers, vendors, strategic partners, distributors, retailers),

Ecosytemic Stakeholders

5) Society (the organized container governing relationships and interactions with each other and planet), and 6) the Planet (e.g., natural ecosystems and services).

Institutions, rather than private individuals, own and control about 78% of the market value of the U.S. broad-market Russell 3000 index, and 80% of the large-cap S&P 500 index totaling about $21.7 trillion and $18 trillion, respectively.[411] The jobs, salaries and bonuses of many of the executives managing the large financial institutions are dependent upon achieving targeted financial performance and returns for their shareholders (which often are also incorporated entities run by managers whose salaries and bonuses are primarily measured by financial performance). This perpetuates the ongoing obsession with money, returns and short term profits performance. As a result, the beneficiaries of human and planetary resources have largely been non-living incorporated entities. Corporations that view their primary purpose as maximizing profits often show sociopathic disregard for humankind and the biosphere. The result is often the destruction of life, beauty, health and future flourishing. Such things as dumping carcinogenic waste and contaminants into our land and watershed; polluting our air; perpetuating poverty, suffering and war to support supply chain economics and unsustainable consumerism; and the destruction of our biosphere are rationalized as creating shareholder value. However, after stripping away the layers of institutional ownership and economic performance as the measure of pragmatism, the real shareholders are people and planet. Without the planet supplying us with its life-giving air, water, food, energy and materials, there is no shareholder value.

When workers are sick, tired and poor, productivity decreases. When customers are dissatisfied with the products, services and the ethics of vendors, they purchase from their more ethical competition. When strategic relationships are mistreated and taken advantage of, they tend to terminate contracts and/or provide inferior products or services. Our current socio-economic-political model is broken, and large corporations have the power, money, influence and responsibility to support life rather than destroy it. By doing so, they will generate even greater profits by doing so.

Our socio-economic-political system can increase profits, quality of life and ecosystemic thriving by synergistically balancing the interests of all Ecosystemic Stakeholders including (1) the desire of shareholders and executives for profits, returns and economic growth (2) the demand of customers for products that meet or exceed their expectations of quality, price, fitness, durability and service, (3) the equitable, respectful and kind treatment of employees, (4) honesty, integrity, trust and fair dealing with strategic relationships, (5) necessity of society, cities and communities to improve the quality of life and well-being for their residents, and (6) the need of humankind to serve our planet and its ecosystems, so that the planet can thrive and continue to provide us with regenerative abundance.

Empowered and conscious organizations are waking up to the realization that humankind and the planet need to be the real beneficiaries of the value, wealth and abundance. The more humankind and the planet thrive, the more that business thrives. Without the planet sustaining life and providing resources, there is no economy or profits. The organizations making evolutionary changes to balance the interests of all Ecosystemic Stakeholders and improving the quality of life for the living will thrive. By incorporating regenerative applications for the benefit of people as the fundamental tenets for value creation and success, corporations will thrive.

In a society of automation, commoditization, information and transparency via the Internet and mobile devices, a brand of quality, differentiated value, honesty, service and social responsibility is vital to acquiring customers and retaining their loyalty. The reputation and brand of a company has become more valuable, fundamental and vital to successfully acquiring and retaining customers. Merchant rating systems on websites and mobile apps such as Amazon, AirBnB, Ebay and Yelp are rapidly and transparently exposing both good and bad behavior. Merchants with higher ratings get more customers and can often charge more than poorly rated merchants. For example, the UC Berkeley study by Michael Anderson and Jeremy Magruder showed that an extra half-star rating on Yelp causes restaurants to sell out 19% more frequently (from 30% to 49%), and up to 27% more frequently when alternate information is more scarce.[412] And the study done by Michael Luca at Harvard Business School demonstrated how a one-star increase on Yelp leads to a 5-9% increase in revenue.[413]

To support ethical consumption and ethical corporate practices, an important factor in evaluating whether to purchase from one brand or another is the brand's commitment to social responsibility (e.g., sustainability, non-toxic products, fair trade, philanthropic programs). According to global measurement and data analytics company, Nielson. . .

"Fifty-five percent of global online consumers across 60 countries say they are willing to pay more for products and services provided by companies that are committed to positive social and environmental impact. The propensity to buy socially responsible brands is strongest in Asia-Pacific (64%), Latin America

(63%) and Middle East/Africa (63%). The numbers for North America and Europe are 42 and 40 percent, respectively.

"Consumers around the world are saying loud and clear that a brand's social purpose is among the factors that influence purchase decisions," said Amy Fenton, global leader of public development and sustainability at Nielsen. *"This behavior is on the rise and it provides opportunities for meaningful impact in our communities, in addition to helping to grow share for brands."*[414]

Companies, such as Google, Microsoft, Apple, Toyota, Tesla, Solar City, Whole Foods, Starbucks, Zappos and Patagonia are leading examples of brands that are redefining "shareholder value" by committing to social responsibility and building brands of excellence, service and trust. These companies have also successfully demonstrated that valuing employees, and fostering a healthy and inspiring culture, is paying big dividends in profitability, productivity, efficiency, innovation and employee retention. The corporate world is waking up and more corporations are starting to make commitments to ethical and conscious ESG programs, not just because it's the right thing to do, but because it makes good business sense.

Additionally, organizations like the Environmental Working Group are exposing manufacturers who put harmful ingredients in their products and more people are reading labels (e.g., Organic, non-GMO, Gluten-free, Fair Trade). Also, with widespread public reviews of companies and their products and services on sites like Yelp, Amazon, Facebook and Twitter, companies are being forced to provide better and more ethical products and services, as well as providing a higher level of customer service and support. Moreover, sites like CSRHub, rate companies based upon their commitment to ESG and CSR. Ethical conduct, healthy products, and eco-social responsibility are paying off by enhancing reputation leading to increased revenues, brand equity and customer loyalty.

In the connected, transparent, fast-moving, global world of the 21st century, valuable brand equity, reputation and loyalty are earned by 1) providing products and services that satisfy the demands of purchasers for quality, price, fitness and durability, 2) providing ethical, honest and caring support to customers, 3) empowering employees by treating them with fairness, respect and authority equal to responsibility, 4) acting ethically and consciously by creating value for people and planet, 5) treating strategic relationships with fairness, integrity and added value, 5) balancing the needs of all Ecosystemic Stakeholders in a way that improves the quality of life and thriving.

AWE ORGANIZATIONS AND CULTURE

Creating a culture of AWE—Abundance, Wellness & Empowerment in organizations leads to increased revenues and profits, organizational efficiency, and employee morale, health and performance. In AWE Organizations, it is incumbent upon leadership to make, empower, fund and implement programs that foster the regenerative growth, health and sustainability of the organization and its Ecosystemic Stakeholders. The following summary of programs provide examples leading to an organizational culture of AWE:

- *Abundance Programs* create regenerative and synergistic ecosystemic value and wealth by inspiring people to engage in intrinsically motivated high-performance activities that increase such things as innovation, productivity, collaboration, effectiveness, growth, sales, profitability and distributions of wealth.

  Stock and cash incentive plans have been used as a method for motivating performance by sharing the distribution of wealth. These programs have a much higher success and performance rate when coupled with (1) a sense of passion and purpose, (2) a commitment to the success of both the organization and its employees, (3) the personal growth of employees, (4) a culture of health and inspiration, and (5) expanded levels of authority with clear, objective and articulated performance measurements.

  Abundance Programs balance the desire for growth and profits with (1) ethical, efficient and productive use, circularity and regeneration of resources (e.g., reuse, recycling, replacing, repurposing), (2) adoption of living and regenerative systems applications, and (3) equitable and generous recognition, exchange and distribution of value that creates scenarios where all parties benefit. Abundance is born of generosity, exchange and gratitude. By expanding and sharing wealth through regenerative applications, utilizing collaboration and innovation to create "a bigger pie," organizations can exponentially accelerate and increase their wealth and that of their employees.

- *Wellness Programs* holistically increase the physical, mental, emotional, energetic and fiscal well-being of the organization and its Ecosystemic Stakeholders. These health and wellness programs include training programs, education, workshops, activities and peer support for such things as diet and nutrition, exercise, mindfulness (increased awareness, stress relief and optimized states of being), internal cleansing, natural connection, reduction of environmental toxicity, preventative diagnostics and protocols. The organization can also add significantly to its brand equity, goodwill and loyalty by extending Wellness Programs to the families of personnel, customers, business relations, the communities in which the company does business, as well as its shareholders.

   Moreover, the **organization**, when viewed as a living organism, has a **body** (e.g., physical assets such as real estate, facilities, equipment), a **mind** (e.g., intellectual property, collective intelligence, and mentally constructed agreements and processes), **emotions** (e.g., the collective emotions and morale of the organization), and an **energetic essence** (e.g., the soul, essence, culture, and vitality of the organization and its ability to convert assets/resources into productive results). For example, an organization is not optimally well and functioning when its employees are unhealthy, emotionally constricted and energetically depleted, or when its equipment and facilities are in disrepair and unsafe, or when massive amounts of energy and waste are required to convert assets and resources into value due to a bureaucratic culture based on mistrust, scarcity and disempowerment.

   An increasing number of companies are implementing programs including such things as personal training and coaching, fitness facilities, nutritious food, live-work balance, child care, telecommuting, generous health plans, personal and creative time, peer support, rewarding innovation, flexible work schedules, autonomous authority and trust, transparent communication and engagement in social responsibility and philanthropic causes.

These programs used to be thought of as "fluffy" cost centers, however, there is significant evidence that such programs are economically beneficial to the organization and increase profitability. For example, the ROI on comprehensive, well-run employee wellness programs can be as high as 6 to 1[415] (Harvard Business Review) and eco-conscious, sustainability programs on average have a ROI of 2 to 1[416] (Bloomberg).

According to Forbes, healthcare spending in the U.S. in 2015 was a crippling $4.9 trillion. Chronic diseases are responsible for 7 out of 10 deaths each year and treating people with chronic diseases accounts for 86% of the U.S. health care costs. About 70% of the diseases contributing to this crippling cost are avoidable with preventative measures including heart disease, obesity, diabetes, osteoporosis, insomnia, depression, chronic back pain and muscle spasm.[417] A high percentage of these diseases are incubated in a sedentary, stress-filled, junk-food eating and dehumanizing work environment.

Aon Hewitt's analysis showed the average health care cost per employee was $10,471. When added to Mercer's estimates of an average of $14,000 per employee per year resulting from absenteeism and inefficiency, the total is $24,471 on average per employee per year.[418] It's pretty astounding what poor health is costing both enterprise and society. Moreover, the costs of health insurance is a major expense for organizations. Many organizations are utilizing "captive insurance" programs such as significantly raising their deductibles and taking the risk up to the higher limits (typically between $25,000 to $50,000 per employee). Unhealthy employees significantly increase the risks to organizations. Therefore, organizations using captive insurance programs have a substantial interest in improving the health of their personnel.

The wellness of an organization and its members is paramount to the success of the organization. If its Ecosystemic Stakeholders are well, there is a much higher likelihood that the organization will be well. If employees are not provided with humane benefits and are having their wellness compromised by the work environment (e.g., toxicity, stress, fear, sugar, caffeine, junk food, no exercise, no sunshine, lack of appreciation), the wellness and productivity of the organization will be compromised. If the Ecosystemic Stakeholders of the organization are not treated with integrity, respect, dignity and appreciation, the organization will diminish its relationship with its Ecosystemic Stakeholders.

By increasing its physical, mental, emotional and energetic wellness, an organization can create exponentially more value with the same resources, including increasing its profits and having significantly greater social and market impact.

- *Empowerment Programs* foster both personal and organizational development with a focus on such things such as personal growth, courage, collaboration, innovation, love, trust, innovation, generosity and gratitude. Empowerment Programs build emotional, spiritual and creative intelligence that help us evolve to deeper levels of understanding, connection, being and presence, thereby improving the way we relate with co-workers and business relations. as well as our families, friends and communities. The Empowerment Programs remove layers of bureaucracy, standardization and mistrust, giving employees authority and trust to make empowered decisions within clear and objective parameters. Excellence in decision-making, problem-solving and performance can also be incentivized.

Empowerment in organizational leadership is accomplished by providing each employee the ability to grow, learn, evolve and expand his or her consciousness, skills and abundance. Also, it is vital to balance the needs, beliefs and experiences of each individual with the collective goals of the organization. When people are inspired, enthusiastic and immersed in their work, they are productive, committed and effective.

For over a century, the prevailing management practice is to use the "carrot and stick" model to reward desired behavior and punish undesirable behavior. This philosophy has a long history of being incorporated into compensation models, employee incentive plans, performance management programs and the culture of organizations. The problem is that, aside from increasing short-term performance of generally low-level tasks, the carrot and stick approach actually decreases performance over time.

Author and motivation guru, Daniel Pink, posits that economic rewards and punishment programs often have a negative effect on such things as intrinsic motivation and passion, creativity, good and ethical behavior, and long-term commitments. In his TED Talk, Pink informs us as follows:

"The good news is that the scientists who've been studying motivation have given us this new approach. It's built much more around intrinsic motivation. Around the desire to do things because they matter, because we like it, they're interesting, or part of something important. And to my mind, that new operating system for our businesses revolves around three elements: Autonomy, Mastery and Purpose.

- *Autonomy: The urge to direct our own lives.*

- *Mastery: The desire to get better and better at something that matters.*

- *Purpose: The yearning to do what we do in the service of something larger than ourselves.*

These are the building blocks of an entirely new operating system for our businesses."

Bonuses and incentives have generally been focused on only objective performance, such as sales, profits, or output (e.g., providing deliverables on time and in budget); however, the effectiveness of these incentives is limited. It is increasingly important to provide an atmosphere that treats humans like living, thinking, breathing, emotional and complex beings, rather than machines. Supporting people to find purpose, pride and joy in their work; showing appreciation with equitable rewards and acknowledgment; creating a sense of belonging and collaboration; and providing an environment for inspiration, mastery and personal growth are of significant importance for human flourishing. When humans thrive, the organization thrives.

In many organizations, only objective performance is valued. Objective performance is typically measured by sales, revenue and profits performance. In AWE Organizations, subjective value is also measured. Subjective value includes such things as emotional intelligence, leadership, humor, compassionate support, philanthropy, and involvement in eco-social activities that help promote the values and brand of the organization ("Subjective Value Contributions"). The Subjective Value Contributions can lead to a corporate culture that contributes to morale, productivity and flourishing.

In summary, the cornerstones of highly successful organizations in the 21st century include:

1. Agile and situationally adaptive governance that fosters a culture of abundance, wellness and empowerment;

2. Providing quality products and services backed by meaningful warranties;

3. Great customer service;

4. High employee morale;

5. Fairness and integrity in business dealings;

6. Balancing benefits to all Ecosystemic Stakeholders, and

7. Real commitment to ESG and human and planetary thriving

By committing to the milestones, corporations can make great positive change in our world, build a beloved brand and increase profitability.

CHAPTER 27

Transforming Culture, Ethics and Education

---

*Learning and innovation go hand in hand. The arrogance of success is to
think that what you did yesterday will be sufficient for tomorrow.*

~William Pollard

I n order to transform our world, it is essential that we open our minds to new possibilities, innovate and evolve our beliefs, behaviors and cultural mores. Resistance
to change and failure to evolve often perpetuates non-serving societal dysfunction
caused by our enculturated beliefs and behaviors. Our beliefs and behaviors largely
come from our environment and our culture and, in turn, influence culture and
affect our environment. Concurrently, the anthropocentric, ethnocentric and/or
theocentric aspects of culture influence such things as ethics, education, customs and
narratives. Culture often creates a sense of belonging, safety, security and predictability by setting forth rules of conduct and appropriate behaviors. However, culture
can also keep us stuck in old and non-serving beliefs, behaviors, patterns and ways
of being. At this point in human evolution, failure to transform old beliefs, behaviors
and cultural mores may lead to the extinction of humankind. The transformation
required for us to thrive as a species involves moving from a "me" culture to a "we"
culture and from an industrialized, extractive, exploitative and destructive culture
to a regenerative, collaborative and loving culture.

CULTURAL TRANSFORMATION

Our environment (e.g., land, water, growing season, weather, flora, fauna, family, friends, social conditioning and narratives) has, throughout history, been the greatest influence on our beliefs and behavior, and therefore human culture. Most cultural practices arose from adapting to the environment, including survival skills, mating rituals, dietary choices, creative expression, clothing, shelter and language. Culture is defined by our beliefs and behaviors, and our beliefs and behaviors are shaped by our environment.

Changing our environment generally causes our beliefs, behaviors and culture to change. Environmental change is a very powerful lever for transformation. By creating environments that promote abundance, wellness and empowerment, as well as greater love and connection, we can positively transform our culture, our society and the way we care for each other and our planet's ecosystems. By developing new personal, societal, economic and political beliefs and behaviors that foster loving and caring for the Earth and each other, we can create a new society devoted to ecosystemic thriving, beauty, love and abundance.

As a new regenerative culture and economy gain mass adoption, market forces will drive demand for such things as regenerative communities, renewable and circular industries, as well as ethical products and services (much like how organic food, electric cars, and clean energy have gained adoption). As adoption becomes viral, the paradigm shift will result in an exponentially higher quality of life and the largest economy in the history of humankind—The Regenerative Economy.

For example, our culture today is much different with electricity, cars, airplanes, television, mass-manufacturing, computers, mobile phones and Internet than prior to these technologies existing. Each of these technologies met with resistance, went through exponential adoption curves and have now achieved mass adoption and success in the market place. These technologies have changed the way we relate to each other, our environment and our access to information. While these technologies have provided great advancement, they have also contributed to cultural and consumptive practices that have been harmful to people and planet.

Human culture is the expression of how we live and includes socio-economic-political systems, beliefs, behaviors, language, music, art, food, fashion, rituals, customs, livelihoods, media, conditioning, education, sexuality and our relationships, as well as our interactions with the environment and natural resources. Cultural observation and analysis can be both macro and micro. For example, a culture can consist of the entire human population (e.g. human culture), the behavior of a nation (e.g., Japanese culture), a small tribe of Aborigines, a section of the Amazonian rainforest, or a Petri dish full of bacteria.

In our society, cultural identities and subcultures are often described using the following:

- Sexuality and Gender Identity (e.g., Male, Female, LGBTQ)

- Profession (e.g., Lawyer, Doctor, Truck Driver)

- Workplace (e.g., Google, Toyota)

- Political Affiliation (e.g., Liberal or Conservative)

- Historical (e.g., Medieval Times, The Renaissance)

- Archaeological (e.g., Defined by artifacts such as Egyptian Pyramids, Flint Arrows of Native American Indians)

- Broad Geography (e.g., Western Culture)

- Narrow Geography (e.g., Culture of Chinatown in San Francisco)

- Fashion (e.g. Earrings, Tattoos, Mini-Skirts, Long Hair)

- Language, Writing and Literature (e.g., The first Sutras of Buddha were written on palm leaves in the ancient Indian languages of Pali and Sanskrit)

- Ethnicity (e.g., Asian, African-American, Mexican, Caucasian)

- Religious Beliefs (e.g., Jewish, Christian, Buddhist, Muslim)

- Individual adoption of cultural style (e.g., Hippy, Goth or Emo)

- Accomplishments (e.g., Virtuoso Musician vs. Hobbyist)

- Audience (e.g. Popular Culture, Classical Culture)

- Cultural landscape—(e.g., Mountain, Ocean or Rainforest)

- Wealth or Caste (e.g., Rich or Poor)

The foregoing descriptors can be divisive by excluding people outside of a specific class while creating deeper connection to those within a certain class. Unfortunately, monarchs and governments have utilized cultural divisiveness for centuries to keep citizens from aligning in mass and overthrowing the sovereign or the government. We have been taught throughout history to compete, to mistrust, to desire exclusivity rather than inclusivity and to align our identities into limited classes that perpetuate divisiveness.

Transforming our world, requires transforming ourselves, our culture and ethics to remove the descriptors that divide us. We need to understand that we are one species living together on this beautiful planet, that we are interconnected with, and interdependent upon, each other and all life on this planet. We share a commonality of basic needs for air, water, food, shelter and connection. We also share modern-day needs for energy, communications, health, and education.

As a species, we have survived and often thrived through our collaboration and have diminished our survivability through competition. While our cultures and descriptors often divide us, our common needs unify us. The thriving of humankind is directly linked and correlated to the thriving of the planet. Because we are so connected to each other and the planet, and because planetary thriving benefits and unifies us all, it seems that our highest objective, ethical calling and conduct is to support ecosystemic thriving. The ethical transformation and alignment we need to unify as a species is likely to create a more healthy, thriving and beautiful world for all life on Earth.

ETHICAL TRANSFORMATION

It is important that systemic transformation be ethical and utilize whole systems applications in order to succeed. Ethical conduct is behavior made in accordance with standards for right conduct or practice. "Right conduct" is fairly subjective and unless we have considerable consensus, it is difficult to develop aligned standards of ethical conduct. Sometimes it's easier to eliminate what's wrong than to decide what's right. This is why we tend to solve our problems with double negatives, like the "War on Terror," or the "End of Poverty" or diagnose and treat "mental illness" rather than define "mental health." It could be said, however, that ***the framework and higher purpose of ethics is to engage in decisions and conduct that are the most loving, harmonious and supportive to the well-being of all parties affected by the decisions and conduct.***

There are several different philosophies relating to the field of ethics:

- *Moral Absolutism*[419] is the view that there are universal moral principles that should be applied in all circumstances without exception. Moral Absolutism is often practiced by those who are adherents to literal interpretations of religious texts. For example, if the Ten Commandments state, "Thou shalt not kill" then under Moral Absolutism, killing in self-defense or the defense of a loved one, would be considered ethically wrong. Also, since "killing" is not qualified, it could also include killing animals for food. Often ethics may change in Moral Absolutism depending upon the interpretation of the ethical code or group espousing the code of morality. For example, ethics of one country or religion will often be different, but each country or religion would see their ethical principles as right and moral for their group. A grave problem occurs when one group imposes their ethical principles on another, especially by force (e.g., the Christian Crusades and Spanish Inquisition, the World Wars), resulting in unethical outcomes.

- *Moral Relativism*[420] holds that the application of moral principles are not fixed, but should be applied contextually based upon the present circumstances. Thus, while killing would generally be considered an unethical act, under Moral Relativism, killing would be ethical in self-defense or defense of loved ones. Moral Relativism has often led to rationalization of conduct that would normally be considered unethical because the ends justified the means.

- *Principled Ethics*[421] includes a theory or system of moral values guided by principles and standards of conduct governing an individual or a group. For example, the founding principles for the U.S. Constitution are (1) individual liberty, (2) federalism, (3) limited government, (4) representative government, (5) private property, (6) separation of powers, and (7) all men are created equal. With Principled Ethics, there is a framework for making contextual decisions, however, the interpretation of the principles can sometimes lead to unethical decisions (e.g., agenda-driven interpretation of the Constitution and erosion of the Bill of Rights).

- *Situational Ethics*[422], pioneered by Joseph Fletcher, holds that moral decisions and conduct must be based contextually upon circumstances and outcomes, so long as love is the force guiding the intention. Situational ethics posits that a morally right action is one that produces a good outcome or consequence.

With several different ethical viewpoints arising from a multitude of cultures and interpreted by billions of people, coming to an agreement on a universal definition of ethical conduct is challenging. As a result, ethics have often been used to achieve various agendas and manipulate behavior. For example, moral relativism is often used by corporations to rationalize activities harmful to people and planet because shareholders benefit from greater profits. Also, governments have used ethical and moral strategies to erode personal freedoms and rights under the moral flag of patriotism, public health and increased security.

I would posit that *true ethical conduct is conduct that promotes "ecosystemic thriving"—the thriving of all species and the planet.* By using whole systems approaches, we can create ethical solutions that sufficiently address our needs while minimizing harm and maximizing benefits to society and the planet with economic and environmental outcomes that regeneratively repair, remediate and offset any damage caused by our activities. For example, coal and oil are the major sources of power in the worldwide energy portfolio. These sources of energy are substantially responsible for the conveniences and "higher standard of living" enjoyed by the developed nations. However, the externalities of oil wars, destruction of the environment and damage to the general health of humankind, to name a few destructive characteristics of these energy sources, clearly show a lack of ethics, especially when the externalities of the oil and coal industry are borne by taxpayers rather than the industries themselves. However, all who drive cars and use electricity are strengthening these industries and reinforcing the unethical behavior of these industries. In essence, all of us who, through our consumptive behaviors, monetarily support oil and coal companies participate in the unethical conduct of these companies. Can we be more ethical in our consumption and our behaviors? Of course, we can!

For example, with regard to transforming energy and transportation, ethical solutions could include the following:

1. Implement transitional strategies for using the current portfolio of fossil fuel, coal and nuclear energy to create clean energy portfolios (e.g., solar, wind, geothermal, hydro and hydrogen) and infrastructure;

2. Impose strict environmental compliance, and mandatory carbon offsets, for the current "dirty energy" industries;

3. Phase-out government subsidies and payments of externalities and allocate this money to new clean energy solutions;

4. Require "dirty energy" companies to disgorge a percentage of their huge profits to contribute to the costs of (i) military to defend their oil supplies and operations in foreign countries, (ii) the development of clean fuels, (iii) the remediation of environmental destruction, and (iv) healthcare for disease caused by their pollutants;

5. Give "dirty energy" companies favorable incentives and transition subsidies to transform into clean energy companies;

6. Phase-out gasoline burning transportation and develop incentives for clean and smart transportation systems and infrastructure;

7. Increase clean public rapid transit and clean autonomous driverless vehicles; and

8. Utilize renewable resources and biomaterials instead of extracted materials.

If the short-term inconvenience and the costs of transitioning to clean fuels and transportation (1) produce long-term sustainable results that benefit people and planet, and (2) provide a reasonable return-on-investment ("ROI") based upon true cost accounting, the foregoing solutions for transitioning to clean energy are arguably ethical.

Another industry that often engages in highly destructive practices is the multi-trillion-dollar commercial agriculture and food industry. It is unethical to continue to give billions of dollars of subsidies to current commercial agriculture to support unsustainable practices that contaminate and degrade arable land, deplete the soil of nutrients, pollute downstream water and produce toxic and unhealthy products.[423] Moreover, it is unethical to subsidize the production of non-nutritious food, containing toxic carcinogenic dyes, preservatives, sweeteners and other unhealthy ingredients leading to diseases like diabetes, obesity, dementia, ADHD, cancer and generally poor health.[424] Ethical conduct would disincentivize destructive and unsustainable commercial agriculture and food industry practices and incentivize regenerative agriculture practices producing healthy soil, products and food. Ethical conduct could include replenishing resources in amounts taken, such as planting at least two trees for each tree cut down, re-establishing fish populations through hatchery programs and building healthy and nutritious soil through regenerative land management practices.

Also, in the context of community planning, development and construction, ethical conduct would require that our communities contribute to ecosystemic thriving and offset the impact of human living and consumption. Ethical communities would utilize onsite production of nutritious food, pure water, renewable materials and clean energy as well as waste upcycling. These practices increase the health and quality-of-life of community members while reducing waste and greenhouse gasses and increasing ecosystemic thriving. Ethical communities also utilize codes of conduct based upon values, ethical principles and agreements that promote personal, community, social and planetary wellness. Rather than rigid rules, members are provided significant freedom of expression and incentivized to devote efforts, resources and time to ecosystemic thriving while behavior that disrespects or causes harm to another, the community or the planet is disincentivized. In the practice of ethical exchange, the community rewards the value services provided by each member. In this reciprocal value-adding relationship, ethical conduct is both equitably recognized and rewarded, leading to an ethical culture in service to ecosystemic thriving.

We are living in a very exciting time where we have an opportunity to heal our past, and overcome our fear-based and divisive conditioning to create a new economy based upon ecosystemic thriving, regeneration and unity. There are many evolutionary breakthroughs occurring right now in human consciousness, culture and society, including the following:

- Regenerative Design and Applications
- Regenerative Agtech
- Smart Infrastructure and Internet of Things
- Alternative and Decentralized Currencies
- Artificial Intelligence
- Augmented and Virtual Reality
- Geo-Engineering
- Clean, Affordable and Abundant Energy & Fuels

- Biomimetic Materials & Nanomaterials
- Biotech
- Regenerative Aquatech
- Genetic Engineering & Epigenetics
- Optimal & Integrative Wellness
- Robotics
- Internet, Smart Mobile & Spacial Web
- Applied, Personalized & Regenerative Life-Long Learning

These breakthroughs, if done regeneratively, ethically and equitably, have the potential to dramatically transform and improve our lives and our world (e.g., the way we live, work, learn, play, consume, as well as the way we relate to each other and nature). As well, many of these breakthroughs, if done unethically, could have devastating effects on humankind and the planet. By implementing personal, social, economic and political incentives that support ethical and regenerative practices in service to Ecosystemic Thriving, we can reshape our world at a highly accelerated rate with exponential positive impact.

As a foundational requirement to building a regenerative world that supports ecosystemic thriving, we will need to transform our beliefs and behaviors and build the skills and capacity required to fulfill the vision of a new paradigm. Our beliefs and behaviors largely are a result of our conditioning. One of the largest institutions of conditioning, beliefs and behaviors, as well as supposedly preparing our children to be productive members of society, is our education system.

EDUCATION[425]

In modern society, our education system is largely responsible for our conditioned beliefs and behaviors, which define and perpetuate our culture. Our education system is also given the responsibility for teaching kids to be "productive members to society." Unfortunately, education has largely failed to provide kids any practical skills and capacities to promote health, happiness, collaboration, creative thinking and emotional intelligence in a way that contributes to the evolution a society and ecosystemic thriving.

Our current public education system was designed in the early 1800s largely to meet the needs of the industrial economy. Modeled after the design and environments of factories, public schools filled the need of industry for factory workers— generally complacent people willing to work robotic jobs, at low wages, with rigid schedules set to a time clock. The industrial age didn't need creatives and free-thinkers—it needed robots who did as they were told and didn't question authority.

Public schools supplied factories with the labor force needed to build the machines and products of the industrial age, while also providing basic reading, arithmetic and language skills. Secondary education supplied management for the industrial economy. Higher education supplied the professionals (e.g., engineers, executives, doctors, and scientists to facilitate rapid urbanization and technological advancement for the economy. The industrialized public school system that exists today is relatively unchanged from their original design in the 1800s. It doesn't serve the advancement of our children or society.

The public school system has fundamentally become a glorified day-care system providing working parents a place to leave their kids so they can earn money to pay for their family's needs, their debts to the banks and taxes to government. By removing children from their families, our society has caused substantial damage to the family unit. Furthermore, by disconnecting children from nature and developing a curriculum omitting life skills such as farming, building, cooking, collaboration and relationship development, our education system ensured children would grow up dependent upon the monetary system. This required young adults to take jobs in industry to sustain themselves by paying money for such things as food, water, power, housing and products rather than having the skills to sustain themselves with the regenerative abundance provided by nature. Thereby the industrial economy was assured of its supply of both employees and consumers from the educational assembly line.

Despite studies and common knowledge that children who are healthy and happy are better learners,[426] our public school system has systematically removed from their curriculum such things as health education, physical activities and creative experiences such as art and music, all of which contribute to healthy development of the brain, body and spirit. Additional factors adversely affecting mental health, development and learning include stress caused by a highly competitive environment, socioeconomic factors and disconnection from family.[427]

As a result of our disconnection from each other, nature and our self-sufficiency, many of us have become easily manipulated consumers of corporate products and services that are polluting the planet with waste and toxins, as well as tacit supporters of the military-industrial complex and the fossil fuel industry, and apathetic participants in the erosion of our sovereign rights by central bank controlled governments and politicians. And through our education system, we have been conditioned to think this is normal.

H. L. Menken, an American journalist and magazine editor known as the "Sage of Baltimore" said *"The aim of public education is not to spread enlightenment at all, it is simply to reduce as many individuals as possible to the same safe level, to breed a standard citizen, to put down dissent."*

Many of us have had the personal experience that Menken speaks of. In the two decades that I spent in the public education system, college and law school, I actually learned very little and was rarely inspired. I often felt bored, controlled, marginalized and unseen. I was not being seen for my passions or being given skills that would promote greater love, beauty, connection and flourishing in the world. Between kindergarten and law school, I spent almost 20 years in school. Although my education contributed to my ability to write this book and engage in research, there were very few practical skills I learned in school. I was not taught emotional intelligence, collaboration, appreciation of natural beauty or practical survival or nature skills such as growing food, building shelters or living in harmony with nature. I didn't learn much in the way of how to communicate compassionately or engage in evolved loving relationships. I didn't even learn entrepreneurial skills such as how the monetary system works, or how to manage finances, start and run a business, manage resources or useful communication to lead and inspire people. In law school,

I was not even taught how to take the bar exam, let alone practice law. I had to take a bar exam preparation course and work in a law office to learn about the practice of law. The failure of our education system to provide real skills is pervasive. As another example, I have engaged in mentoring many MBA graduates from top schools who, after four years of college and two years in an MBA program, could not create a professional business plan or financial projections, let alone actually run a business.

The way our education system works, with few exceptions, is analogous to obtaining a degree in swimming without ever getting in the pool. You will learn about the shape, length and depth of the pool, they'll show you pictures of the pool, tell you all about the molecular structure of water, but you'll not have a single class where you get in the pool and swim.

It's also ironic that our schools are supposed to prepare our youth to be valuable members of society, yet many of the university presidents/chancellors, administrators and professors I have spoken with are completely unaware of the Regenerative Economy and very few schools are providing the skills and capacity to fulfill the Regenerative Economy and evolution of humankind.

Aside from failing to teach meaningful life, survival and practical skills, the school system has been structured to create a society of easily controlled and compliant "homogenized" humans that fit into the pattern of mediocre "normalcy" and standardization. Bill Gates, Michael Dell, Steve Jobs, Larry Ellison, Oprah Winfrey and Richard Branson are a few examples of college drop-outs, who understood the inability of the education system to develop their unique creativity and brilliance. These individuals created some of the world's most highly successful and innovative enterprises. As well, Einstein was considered "mentally retarded" and was expelled from school. These individuals and many others attribute much of their success to thinking differently and not succumbing to the conditioning of the education system. Today, kids that don't conform or thrive in the education system are often medicated with pharmaceutical drugs that dumb them down, making them more easily controllable and compliant.[428] In today's educational system, the geniuses mentioned above would have likely been medicated and never achieved their potential.

Charles Kettering, an American inventor, engineer, a founder of Delco and head of research for General Motors for 27 years, and the holder of 186 patents, said, "*genuine innovators were hobbled more than helped by what they had learned in school. Overly educated people were least likely to make new discoveries...they were too intent on doing things the way they had been taught.*"

Our education system has consistently proven it's ineffectiveness at fostering originality innovation, empowerment, inspiration, creative thinking and development of practical skills, but instead has been effective at promoting mediocrity, conformity, dependence, scarcity and insecurity. There are many dedicated teachers and professors that try to inspire kids and make a difference, however, they are often thwarted by the system.

Education today is focused on STEM (an acronym for Science, Technology, Engineering and Math). While this curriculum has the potential of creating new innovation to solve some of the big challenges we face as a society, it also has the potential to turn humans into computerized robots that spend their life working on and programming computers and developing robotic technologies. We run the risk of dehumanizing humankind unless we holistically balance the STEM curriculum with functional and creative skills in health, art, music, cooking, home building, farming, nature, collaboration, mindfulness, empathy and emotional intelligence. With interactive and gamified education, we can personalize education allowing each child to find their passions and excel. However, getting kids away from the screen and into nature, allowing them to play and build interactive skills not involving a computer, mobile phone or television is critically important. Children need outdoor learning spaces, to be in nature, and be given the freedom for creative exploration.[429]

I am encouraged and optimistic that we can overcome segregation, competitiveness, archaic education systems and unhealthy environments that are prevalent in many schools by creating new education paradigms that integrate regenerative practices and whole-person learning (e.g., development of mind, body, emotions, spirit, intuition and practical skills). Even though there are public schools making small changes toward holistic learning, I am not optimistic that the transformation will happen quickly enough in the current bureaucratic, antiquated, over-regulated and rigid education system that has consistently resisted any real change for almost 200 years.

There are, however, some schools and education systems around the world that are making real and positive changes in learning. For example, at the Kin's School in Southern Russia created by Academician Mikhail Petrovich Shchetinin, pupils develop their own curriculum, design and construct school buildings, grow their own food, cook their own meals and cover the 11-year curriculum of the Russian school system in just two years, and earn their bachelor's and master's degrees from accredited universities by the time they are 17, with little if any help from adult teachers. The kids also engage in healthy and creative activities that include sports, gardening, music, art and theatre. When these kids graduate, they have real life skills and competency.

Our children deserve to grow up in a world that is abundant, healthy, empowered, thriving and loving. Clearly, we need to transform from "education" to "learning" to prepare future generations to reach their fullest individual and societal potentials. In addition to providing skills in basic reading, writing and STEM, this new learning system could also provide the following learning experiences:

- *Innovative*—Students are taught the art of imaginative visualization, inquiry, and creativity. They're encouraged to be visionaries, to think outside of the box, to create and build new models, systems and processes that will help transform our world. The learning system itself is flexible, evolving and able to implement new systems of learning to fulfill the potential of its students.

- *Interactive*—Students are provided current technology and tools to interactively work at their own pace and find their strengths and passions through discovery, research and engagement. Students are encouraged to nurture that which inspires and motivates them and helps them access their own individual talents and aptitudes. Students are incentivized to exchange and share what they've learned and what inspires them with each other and via media with children in different schools, cities and nations. No child left behind and no child held behind.

- *Inspiring*—Students are delivered knowledge and experiences in a way that is fun and inspiring. Inspired children want to learn and are engaged. By inspiring children to discover and pursue their passions and by using AI to deliver a customized holistic curriculum relevant to the interests and passions of each child, children become self-motivated and passionate about learning.

- *Applied and Practical*—Students are taught applied skills with greater emphasis than the rote book, lecture, worksheet and testing protocols. Rather than teaching kids to memorize information in a vacuum and regurgitate the information on a test, kids learn by doing. For example, kids learn (1) *biology* by working on a farm or going into in nature; (2) *chemistry* in real labs mentored by chemists, in kitchens and food labs with chefs, bakers and food scientists, and/or in manufacturing making real useful products and compounds: (3) *physics and quantum physics* by engaging in such things as plumbing, electrical engineering, circuit board design, product design, astronomy, sacred geometry, observation of nature, doing real life experiments demonstrating the principles, and utilizing the principles of quantum physics to imagine, create, design and build novel inventions; (4) *math* (including algebra, geometry and calculus) and *engineering* by designing and building practical structures with architects, engineers and builders, (5) *technology* (including math and engineering by programming computers and smartphones and using computers for graphic and CAD design; (6) *writing* by attending inspiring creative and journalistic seminars taught by published authors, doing research and writing articles and blogs; (7) *arts* by engaging in music, art, dance and theatre; (8) *health and wellness* by studying nutrition, making healthy meals, doing field trips to farms and food processing facilities, working out, engaging in sports, doing yoga, meditation and healing work.

When kids graduate, not only are they competent at reading, writing, science, math, technology and engineering, but they also have the skills to plant a garden; prepare nutritious meals and snacks; harvest, recycle and purify water; collaborate with and love each other; care for our soil and animals and produce food; build shelters and functional buildings; do electrical, plumbing and mechanical work; play music, sing, participate in art and dance; and do healing work as well as sports and physical activities that sustains their bodies in health.

- *Peer-Supported*—Students engage in peer-supported social interaction and learning. The best way to learn is to teach. Giving kids incentives to learn and teach will help kids master what they learn. Teachers coach students to prepare lectures, papers and workshops that they will deliver and teach to other students. Many older or more accomplished students will be incentivized to teach and mentor younger and less accomplished kids. By pairing student teachers with kids eager to learn and a professional teacher to act as a guide, student teachers are afforded the opportunity to increase the depth of their subject matter as well as learn how to care for, encourage and teach others. This can also be applied by having more proficient students tutor struggling students. This reinforces the knowledge of both the teacher and student and builds compassionate and cooperative relationships between students. By teaching each other, students build skills in leadership, communication and collaboration, as well as mastery. Furthermore, teaching students can get paid for their teaching and their successes, as well as deepen their relationships with other students.

- *Collaborative and Inclusive*—Students create fun, inspiring and practical projects where everyone wins, and the success (e.g., quality, completion, timelines, results) of the project is more important than the individual roles and victories. Kids learn collaboration and the ability to work in teams to serve a mission bigger than themselves. These collaborative environments recognize and utilize the uniqueness and strengths of each individual, building incredible confidence, collaborative skills and self-worth.

- *Accessible*—Students have access to necessary resources. Learning must be accessible for all students, including those who are disadvantaged or have special needs (e.g., blind, deaf, poor, geographically remote or otherwise disabled). With the technologies available for accessibility and personalized learning, no student should be held back due to another's disabilities or inabilities. Each student can move at their individual pace with incentives that accelerate learning and an emphasis on fulfilling each student's most inspiring subjects and methods of learning.

- _Mindful_—Students learn the benefits of positive thoughts, affirmations, silence, centering and mindfulness to calm their minds and gain clarity through practices such as meditation, yoga and contemplation work. Students learn basic brain development to understand their own cognitive and emotional needs throughout their brain's development cycles, including developing an understanding that they are responsible for their perceptions, thoughts, beliefs, emotions, feelings, relationships and experiences. They are given tools to courageously and transparently communicate and fulfill their needs through value-exchange. These tools can be used to reduce teen suicide, depression, isolation, bullying and anger and promote love, trust, respect, collaboration, peace and joy.

- _Emotionally Intelligent_—Students participate in exercises, play and studies that help them more deeply feel and clearly communicate their emotions, feelings, compassion and empathy; engage in active listening; learn body language; practice conscious breathwork; build trust and deeper relationships; develop integral alignment of thoughts, words and deeds; and clearly communicates one's needs and desires. The goal of this learning and training is to increase love, acceptance, harmony and compassionate communication. Emotional intelligence is key to improving the relationships and life experiences of students throughout their lives.

- _Healthy_—Students learn and experience the health benefits of conscious diet (e.g., nutritious foods, pure water, portion-control, conscious consumption, vitamins and minerals); exercise; mindfulness; and connection with nature. This is largely experiential learning with fun games and everyone-wins- competitions fostering social interaction, team dynamics, leadership, overcoming fear and achieving goals.

- _Balanced Between Digital and Physical_—While students learn how to use and program computers, mobile phones and digital devices, students also learn how to digitally detox and participate in meaningful activities without technology with an emphasis on interaction with each other and nature. Students engage in various skills, such as planting trees and gardens, learning about flora and fauna on nature field trips, mechanical repair, crafts, cooking, farming, care-taking younger children or the elderly, tending animals and immersive nature activities/sports. This allows students direct contact with materials, people and all living things in their physical world. Students find the balance between technology (e.g., computers, cells phones, interactive education, IT, video games, Internet and mobile applications) and interaction with each other, people in their community, animals and nature.

- _Holistic_—Students learn to be whole systems thinkers. They learn the value of integrative, ecosystemic and regenerative approaches that honor the 4.5 billion years of nature's wisdom readily available to them. Students experience the interconnectedness of all things and systems (from micro or macro). They learn everything is holistically interconnected and that each of us has a significant impact on each other and our world.

Rather than schools being glorified day care centers or institutions that create an army of robots for industry, the next generation of learning centers can inspire kids to find their superpowers and passions, and develop real and practical skills that will help them to be happier, healthier, more productive and fulfilled humans— humans that contribute to a flourishing, loving and beautiful world.

With the advent of computers, mobile apps, the Internet, video games, virtual reality, augmented reality, automation and artificial intelligence, education can move beyond a classroom of 20-25 students and one instructor who teaches a standardized and antiquated curriculum. Using these new technologies and gamified approaches, students can learn through highly personalized, inspiring and fun protocols with information and classes custom-tailored to the way each student learns best. Most kids complain about having to go to school, but love to play video games. By gamifying and personalizing education, we can make learning more engaging and desirable for kids. For example, in these gamified and highly personalized learning environments, a child who loves music can learn math, history and science through the lens of music, or a child who is very active and loves the outdoors can learn biology and math on the farm, garden or in the forest. A child who is gifted at math and loves mechanics can learn STEM by programming computers, building robots, engaging physics challenges, and learning music through the lens of math and engineering.

A potential risk of gamified learning is separation and isolation from nature and personal connection with other kids. Augmented reality and gamification technologies can be used to inspire and incentivize interactions in nature, society, and each other in-person to promote the practical and social skills that the children require to grow up into whole, healthy, happy and contributing adults. From these augmented reality challenges, students will learn practical skills, both individually and with others, to help them live a high-quality and healthy life and contribute to a flourishing regenerative civilization. These skills include the purification and recycling water; gardening and growing food; preparing food; building a house, generating clean energy, building clean energy/zero point motors, programing a computers, developing software and mobile apps, investing their money and engaging in resource planning and projects to regenerate ecosystems.

Also, students will learn collaborative and communication skills such as compassionate communication, emotional intelligence, project management and team building. Through a series of AI feedback and learning algorithms, kids can be provided with instruction on art, health and physical activities that resonate most with each child. Also, the AI can help organize group interactions that are both gamified and in person to pursue and improve skill.

As the industrialized education systems transform into highly personalized inspired learning systems, we will see a shift in our culture as future generations transform the world.

CHAPTER 28

Transforming our Communities

It is possible that the next Buddha will not take the form of an individual. The next Buddha may take the form of a community—a community practicing understanding and loving kindness, a community practicing mindful living. This may be the most important thing we can do for the survival of the Earth.

~Thich Nhat Hanh

A community is an ecosystem that has a defined boundary and character. We often think of a community as someplace where a group of people live. However, each of us is a home to entire ecosystems of cells and microbes (e.g., bacteria, parasites, fungi) that interconnect to form a "community." According to the National Institutes of Health, *"The human body contains trillions of microorganisms — outnumbering human cells by 10 to 1. Because of their small size, however, microorganisms make up only about 1 to 3 percent of the body's mass (in a 200-pound adult, that's 2 to 6 pounds of bacteria), but play a vital role in human health."*[430] The original estimates of the NIH have been revised by later studies to 1.3:1[431], however, the point is that each one of us is a community for entire worlds of microorganisms that we depend upon for our survival.

When you look at yourself, you see a whole and individual person, however, each individual is a community unto themselves. Humans living on Earth are much like the microorganisms living on each of us. Unlike humans, the microorganisms that live in, and on, us often live in a symbiotic, mutualistic or commensalistic balance with us. Humans, however, are more parasitic and predatory, overconsuming and destroying the ecosystems that nurture us, thus reducing the Earth's ability to sustain our species.

As explained by Bruce H. Lipton, PhD, an internationally recognized leader in bridging science and spirit and bestselling author of *The Biology of Belief*. . .

> *If you understand the nature of who you are, you realize that you are actually a community of about 50 trillion living cells. Each cell is a living individual, a sentient being that has its own life and functions but interacts with other cells in the nature of a community."*

> *Noetic science emphasizes that the structure of the universe is made in the image of its underlying field. The physical character of atoms, proteins, cells, and people are controlled by immaterial energies that collectively form that field. The cellular community comprising each human responds to a unique spectrum of the universe's energy field. This unique energy spectrum, referred to by many as soul or spirit, represents an invisible moving force that is in harmonic resonance with our physical bodies. This is the creative force behind the consciousness that shapes our physical reality. Noetic consciousness reveals that collectively we are the "field" incarnate. Each of us is "information" manifesting and experiencing a physical reality. Integrating and balancing the awareness of our noetic consciousness into our physical consciousness will empower us to become true creators of our life experiences. When such an understanding reigns, we and the Earth will once again have the opportunity to create the Garden of Eden."*

In essence, when we understand that we are part of an interconnected community of all things and use our creative powers to better the flourishing of all life, humankind will be able to manifest a world that supports planetary and human thriving.

If we're going to survive as a species, we need to change the way we live, consume and relate to the planet. For example, in 1800, only 3% of the world's population lived in urban areas. This number grew to almost 14% in 1900 and 30% in 1950. According to the United Nations, in 2018, 55% of the world's population was living in urban areas, and by 2050, it is anticipated that 68% of humanity will live in urban areas.[432] We have destroyed and polluted our lands, waters and air and cut down forests while increasing population and releasing greenhouse gasses into the atmosphere. The trend toward urbanization, growth and overconsumption has reduced our food and water supply, contributed to climate change, advanced desertification and disconnected most people from nature.

> *"We abuse land because we regard it as a commodity belonging to us. When we see land as a community to which we belong, we may begin to use it with love and respect." ~ Aldo Leopold*

Leopold suggests finding a deeper affinity with the land is the beginning of creating love, respect and community with nature. There is growing awareness of and demand for eco-communities based upon collaboration, sharing and eco-social consciousness as a solution to creating a "better" world. Intentional Communities, Eco-villages and Cohousing Collectives (collectively "Conscious Communities") around the world, are creating new models for living in collaboration. These communities (e.g., Mondragon, Auroville, Damanhur, Tamera and Findhorn) are not ideal utopias, but provide some examples of "potentially better" ways of living. The reason I use "potentially better" rather than "better" is that many "Conscious Communities" experience economic hardship (sometimes voluntarily) while benefiting from personal and spiritual growth, connection and abundance. Some have traded independence, wealth and personal space for greater health, less stress, deeper meaning, spiritual growth, and connection. Also, many of the Conscious Communities have adopted a culture of retreatism and Neo-Luddism rather embracing innovation and technology for the evolution of humankind and the advancement of society. Many people hold that individualism and economic wealth are of primary importance, while others hold that love, trust, connection, personal growth, live-work balance, wellness and sharing are of primary importance.

Material wealth, free time, optimal wellness, individual empowerment, collaboration, deep love and spiritual development are not mutually exclusive and can co-exist in communities intentionally created to allow for this holistic integration. For me, a "better" and more fulfilling way to live is experiencing the integration abundance of love, connection, free-time, freedom, collaboration, self-sufficiency, vitality, beauty, inspiration and joy, as well as independence and material wealth. "Better" also includes devotion of community time and resources to ecosystemic thriving and creating a "Garden of Eden" that can inspire global transformation. With a focus on love and connection to each other and nature, innovation, abundance, wellness and empowerment, Regenerative Communities that increase human and planetary thriving can be a reality.

Is there a more relevant definition of "better" that can be used in the context of transforming our communities? "Better" generally means improved, enhanced or superior. Although my "Better List" is quite long, in the context of new paradigm communities, here is my Top 10 "Better" List:

1. Clean air, pure water and plentiful fresh, organic, locally grown, highly nutritious food;

2. Regenerative, renewable and affordable energy, housing and infrastructure;

3. High-quality, efficient, affordable and functional education and healthcare;

4. A 20-25 hour work-week as opposed to a 40-50 hour work-week providing greater time to devote to entrepreneurial, cultural, creative, family and social activities;

5. Organizational structure and governance based on SAO models discussed above, providing higher incentives, greater flexibility, empowerment and authority based upon expertise;

6. Commitment to principles of peace, love, harmony, contentment, equitability, exchange, transparent non-violent communication, ethical behavior and inclusivity;

7. An efficient self-governing, resilient and adaptable society based upon principles, agreements and rewards rather than a wasteful and inefficient bureaucratic government and community agencies grounded on stagnant unchanging rules, regulations and forced adherence to the status quo upon fear of punishment.

8. Shared resources and collaboration providing increased choice and higher quality-of-life for a fraction of the cost, energy, resources and stress;

9. Pursuing one's life purpose and passions with greater freedom, time, meaning, connection, support, compassion and acceptance; and

10. Using regenerative and practices that promote ecosystemic thriving, health and beauty and living in <u>Abundance</u> (sufficiency, fulfillment, wholeness, gratitude), <u>Wellness</u> (health, vitality, well-being) and <u>Empowerment</u> (courage, sovereignty, freedom, inclusivity, choice, love, respect, influence);

To transform society, it is essential that our communities (e.g., villages, towns and cities) become *"Wise, Regenerative and Resilient Communities."* The following discussion will help clarify the elements and deepen our understanding of the concepts of *Sustainability, Regenerability* and *Thriving* that are foundational to our creating a "Regenerative Society" and a "Regenerative Economy."

SUSTAINABILITY

"Sustainability" is broadly defined as *"the capacity to maintain a certain process or state."*

In an ecological context, "sustainability" can be defined as the ability of an ecosystem to maintain ecological processes, functions, biodiversity and productivity into the future. Thus, in order to be sustainable, the Earth's resources may only be used at a rate at which they can be replenished. The human economy is a subsystem of the ecosystem. Therefore, the human economy cannot function when its growth exceeds the carrying capacity of the ecosystem.

The main systems that affect the carrying capacity of the planet are as follows:

- The food system (e.g., agriculture and food production)
- The industrial system—(e.g., manufacturing, shipping, storing, distributing and retailing)
- The population system (birth rates/death rates)
- The non-renewable/extractive resources system (e.g., fossil fuels, metals, minerals)

- The waste/pollution system (e.g., solid waste, air pollution, water toxicity, landfill and soil contamination)

Research done by the World Wildlife Fund for Nature ("WWF")[433] supports that the carrying capacity for the human population was exceeded over 50 years ago, as measured using the "Ecological Footprint." WWF's *Living 2016 Planet Report* states,

"Humanity currently needs the regenerative capacity of 1.6 Earths to provide the goods and services we use each year. Furthermore, the per capita Ecological Footprint of high-income nations dwarfs that of low- and middle-income countries). Consumption patterns in high-income countries result in disproportional demands on Earth's renewable resources, often at the expense of people and nature elsewhere in the world."

According to the Millennium Ecosystem Assessment, a four-year research effort by 1,360 of the world's leading scientists commissioned to measure the actual value of natural resources to humans and the world. . .

"The structure of the world's ecosystems changed more rapidly in the second half of the twentieth century than at any time in recorded human history, and virtually all of Earth's ecosystems have now been significantly transformed through human actions. Ecosystem services, particularly food production, timber and fisheries, are important for employment and economic activity. Intensive use of ecosystems often produces the greatest short-term advantage, but excessive and unsustainable use can lead to losses in the long term. A country could cut its forests and deplete its fisheries, and this would show only as a positive gain to GDP, despite the loss of capital assets. If the full economic value of ecosystems were taken into account in decision-making, their degradation could be significantly slowed down or even reversed."

Another study by the United Nations Environment Programme (UNEP) called the Global Environment Outlook that involved 1,400 scientists and took five years to prepare came to similar conclusions.[434] UNEP found that human consumption had far outstripped available resources: *"Each person on Earth now requires a third more land to supply his or her needs than the planet can supply."* The study faults a failure to "*respond to or recognize the magnitude of the challenges facing the people and the environment of the planet and the systematic destruction of the Earth's natural and nature-based resources has reached a point where the economic viability of economies is being challenged—and where the bill we hand to our children may prove impossible to pay.*" The report found that

- 45 thousand square miles of forest are lost across the world each year

- 60% of the world's major rivers have been dammed or diverted

- 34%: the amount by which the world's population has grown in the last 20 years

- 75 thousand people a year are killed by natural disasters

- 50%: The percentage by which populations of fresh fish have declined in 20 years

- 20% increase in the energy requirements of developed countries such as the United States

The report's authors warn that tackling the problems may affect the vested interests of powerful groups, and that the environment must be moved to the core of decision-making processes around economy and nature-based resources.

The foregoing research shows that our practice of sustainability is really not being ethically implemented and that sustainability is not going to save our species. Our economy is harmful to, and doesn't serve, people or the planet, but rather serves non-living corporate entities, profits and GDP. The "do no harm" philosophy of sustainability, even if impeccably practiced, is just not enough. We must go beyond sustainability. With our current population growth and consumptive habits, we may find ourselves on the endangered species list in the not-to-distant future. For humankind to survive, and thrive, we must immediately move to a **regenerative model** based on the principles of *doing good* and thriving rather than *doing no harm*.

REGENERATION

As discussed previously, "Regenerative" can be defined as *improving, giving new life, and adding value to a place or system by making it more healthy, robust, adaptable and resilient resulting in its thriving.* While the 4 R's of sustainability (Recycle, Reuse, Rethink, Reduce) are important behavior modifications, "Regeneration" applies ethical conduct and whole systems applications to move our world from sustainability to flourishing. Bill Reed, a leader in regenerative planning and design, describes "*Sustainability*" as "*a slower way to die.*" This is because sustainability works on a model of scarcity such as resource conservation, reduction of waste, reduced population, reduced consumption and energy efficiency. While sustainability can contribute to the transformation we require, it is just not enough as a singular solution. Regeneration works on a model of living systems abundance and flourishing by engaging in a reciprocal value-adding relationship with our planet and each other. Regeneration requires us to not only sustain our resources, but to multiply our resources and continually add value. Examples include replanting forests, expanding the amount of arable land, increasing the supply of potable water, reinvigorating the wetlands, restocking the fisheries, bringing renewed health and flourishing to our oceans, lakes and rivers, and utilizing renewable biomaterials rather than extracted materials.

While the extract-destroy-waste economy generates money and jobs, it also is destructive to people and planet. **There is exponentially more money and more jobs in the sustain-and-regenerate economy. The sustain-and-regenerate economy not only will add tens-of trillions of dollars to the GDP, it's also good for life, health, beauty, planet and the thriveability of humankind.**

THRIVING

While at a sustainability conference, a friend of mine asked me how my girlfriend and I were doing. I humorously replied, "we're sustainable." This bit of humor raises the point that "sustainability" is not really a worthy ideal for our relationship with each other and our planet. Although there is great hype around "sustainability" as an ideal, it is a marginal objective, whereas "thrive-ability" is truly a worthy ideal.

"Thriving" means flourishing, prospering, abundant, healthy and prolific. Thriving is truly what we desire as a species rather than sustainability. Because we are interconnected with the planet and all life on it, for humankind to thrive requires that all life thrive. It's critical for our thriving that we maintain a mutualistic, cooperative and symbiotic balance between our needs and those of nature. While it might appear to some that we are thriving, the depletion and contamination of our resources (e.g., the planet's soil, watershed and oceans) is neither sustainable nor thriving. The unsustainable gluttony that fuels human population growth and consumption beyond the planet's carrying capacity, is just a sign of ignorance, a major denial of the evidence and disastrous short-sightedness.

In our current system, "thriving" is typically associated with having an abundance of money and possessions. However, in a regenerative economy true wealth is an abundance of natural capital, beauty, freedom, clean water, nutritious food, comfortable and healthy housing and safe communities, as well as great health and a higher quality of life.

True regenerative and enduring thriving, requires giving back more than we take and engaging in a value-adding reciprocal relationship with our planet. Thus, if we take one tree, we plant two or more. Thrive-ability is dependent upon both sustainable and regenerative behavior, in alignment and balance with nature. Nature will regenerate and be fine once we are gone, but if we are to thrive we need to build a new economy dedicated to ecosystemic thriving.

Our true potential to thrive as a species can be realized through living in regenerative communities and working in ethical industries serving ecosystemic thriving.

REGENERATIVE COMMUNITIES

The environments where we live, work, learn and play are the most impactful influences on our lives. By transforming these environments to be regenerative and supportive of thriving for humans and our planet, we can rapidly transform our world. As discussed previously, we are systems within systems. While our global environment and society have substantial impact on our lives, our local environment has the greatest direct influence on our lives, culture, beliefs and behaviors. Unfortunately, many of our communities are controlled by old paradigm, scarcity-based influencers (e.g., oil, auto, commercial agriculture, pharma, defense) who use regulations, military force, conditioning and political maneuvering to protect their monopolies, power and control. Those in power to use their power to stay in power and utilize a model whereby the masses have been conditioned to accept sociopathic and harmful behavior as normal.

The development and adoption of new paradigm regenerative communities shift power to the people by providing (1) onsite or local regenerative and abundant sources of water, food, materials for shelter, clean energy, and waste upcyling ("Physical Needs"), and (2) community healthcare, lifelong learning, communications, transportation, meaningful work and living systems innovation centers devoted to ecosystemic thriving ("Social Needs"). Regenerative communities disintermediate the inefficient, greenhouse gas emitting and wasteful central supply chain by substantially localizing the Physical Needs and Social Needs of the community members..

Regenerative Communities harmonize the highest ethical principles with environmental services, wellness, consciousness, arts, technology, government, business and education. This new paradigm of community living also includes the integration of ancient earth principles, spiritual wisdom from indigenous cultures, biomimicry, whole systems dynamics and modern-day life-affirming technologies and harmonic regenerative strategies to create environments for exceptional living.

The current regulatory regime (e.g., antiquated zoning and building codes, energy sales prohibitions, water collection prohibitions, farming regulations, securities laws) promoted by monopolistic industries and enforced by closed-minded bureaucrats, regulators and enforcement agencies typically have the effect of slowing down, and often stopping, beneficial progress and innovation. To provide an example of the bureaucrats that enforce the antiquated regulatory regime and impede innovation and progress relating to the development of regenerative communities, below is a conversation with a city planner about utilizing regenerative practices to dramatically improve development standards and create ecologically and socially conscious regenerative communities that increase quality of life and transform our world. The regenerative practices include mixed use development; smart infrastructure and growth; building local self-sufficient economies for water, food, energy, materials and products; clean energy; zero waste; and collaborative consumption. The conversation went as follows:

Planner: I get the idea of energy efficiency and use of renewable energy, such as solar. I understand mixed-use development where there is retail, office and residential in walkable and bikeable proximity, but explain what you mean by regenerative practices and collaborative consumption.

Me: Regenerative practices mimic the way nature creates abundance and heals itself. For example, we plant a single seed that grows into a tree. In its lifetime, the tree bears fruit that nourishes and sustains life while also generating thousands of seeds from which new trees sprout. The fruit drops and become nutrients for flora and fauna. Regeneration also refers to the interconnectedness and interdependence of all species and entering into a mutualistic value-adding relationship with nature. We can optimize the health, joy and thriving of humankind by mimicking nature. Examples of this include, utilizing bio-energetic solutions rather than mechanical-chemical solutions to promote the health of the community, the land and the watershed; cultivating businesses that create abundance for all stakeholders and have a positive impact on our ecosystem; efficiently localizing our supply chain (e.g., onsite food, water, energy, materials, waste upcycling and lite industrial); balancing reasonable and sufficient consumption with the capacity of the community and land for production; realizing that everything has value and can be reused, recycled and/ or upcycled; and utilizing collaborative consumption.

Planner: So what is collaborative consumption?

Me: Collaborative Consumption refers to the sharing of facilities, expenses, maintenance and benefits of things, like a community farm, on-site renewable energy systems, a community kitchen and dining hall, a centralized commercial laundry facility, a shared transportation fleet, a community wellness center, as well as community education and innovation centers.

Planner: This sounds pretty hippy-dippy and communistic to me. I would never want to live in a community that shares things like that.

Me: You currently live in city with 450,000 other people. You share the roads, fire, police, schools, sewers, parks and beaches. If you go to a gym, you share the equipment and classes. If you go to a movie theatre, a concert, a restaurant, a market, you share the venue.

Actually, collaborative consumption leads to greater independence, health, connection and freedom, as well as a higher quality of life and increased variety of choices and experiences.

For example, by having a community farm, members of the community get the freshest, highest quality, most nutritious food at 20% of the cost of going to the market and without all of the greenhouse gas emissions resulting from the supply chain. By sharing a transportation fleet, the cost of auto payments are 20% of the cost of individual car ownership and there is greater access to larger variety of vehicles. Aside from food and transportation, savings also apply to utilities, education, childcare, personal wellness and healthcare. Also, by having walkable amenities of a farm, onsite renewable energy generation, a community school of applied life-long learning, onsite community restaurant, optimal wellness facility and recreational activities, people not only save money on these expenses, but reduce the time spent and fossil fuel burned for such things as driving to work, running errands, engaging in recreation and social activities and shuttling their kids around.

Planner: Well OK, but I own my own house, my car and my possessions. I don't have to share any of it. I like my privacy and don't want to give up my independence and freedom.

Me: In truth, the bank most likely owns your house and your car because you probably took a loan out to buy both of them and you go to work every day to pay your loans so you can retain possession of your house and car. You give up your independence and freedom 8 hours a day, 5 days a week to your employer, not to mention the time you spend driving to and from work.

Planner: I guess that's true. However, it seems like I would have to give up even more freedom and independence by living in your proposed community.

Me: Privacy and personal freedom are very important to AWE Communities. In AWE Communities, residents will be able to purchase their own homes, own their own cars and go to work at a job of their choosing and take vacations whenever they want. However, those that can't afford a home can rent an apartment and contribute to the community in the form of barter to pay for their rent. Those that desire to participate and exchange less with the community, however, will be required to provide monetary contribution, such as increased homeowners' association ("HOA") fees. However, a portion of the HOA fees are also credited to an equity investment in community businesses. So, as the community businesses grow, people who invested a portion of their HOA fees into the community get paid to live in the community through distributions from the community businesses.

Smart planning, design and construction, as well as community principals, agreements and covenants ("PACs"), will allow for higher qualities of life and health, privacy and freedom with lower costs. Moreover, people tend to be dichotomous. By engaging in smart zoning, the communities contain silent zones for contemplation and meditation, quiet zones for research and personal development, social zones for connection with others, and free zones for full expression, music, dance and the celebration of life. Buildings will be designed to minimize invasive noise and smells and promote greater personal space and comfort.

Planner: Well, this is starting to make a lot of sense, however, I don't want to have to deal with other people for my water, food and energy. For example, I just go to the store and get my food or go out to a restaurant. I don't want a bunch of hippies cooking food I don't like and sitting around with a bunch of strange people.

Me: We're at a restaurant and the chef may be a hippy and most of the people in this restaurant are strangers. Also, you didn't get to provide any input on the menu options or the source of the food you're eating. In our current model of society, you actually depend upon more people to get your water, food and energy. For example, in this restaurant, the food that we're eating here involved farmers, farm workers, packaging, trucking, storage, builders, warehouses, distribution centers and retail facilities, road workers, the auto industry and the oil industry. Because oil is required to get our food and for you to drive your car to the store, oil has become a subject of "national security" requiring a large military costing approximately 50% of all tax dollars in the U.S. to protect the oil pipelines, refineries and transportation of oil.

You are actually depending upon many more people, a polluting and inefficient supply chain and a currency system based upon debt and scarcity, to get your food, your water, your energy and your materials. So why wouldn't you want higher quality and fresher food directly from your community farm at a fraction of the cost and have a trained gourmet chef making your meals?

Also, having local, self-sustaining and regenerative sources of food, water, building materials and energy guarantees greater security than our current supply chain models. Moreover, the community will have a store where you can pick up the freshest ingredients and make your own meals if you choose to do so.

Planner: How do you provide security from locals coming in and stealing things or vandalizing the property?

Me: As part of our early planning process, we strive to develop a strong bond with our neighbors and surrounding communities and seek to engage them early in the development process. We also may set aside land for local homesteading, provide affordable housing for local workers, create cooperative reward programs, as well as have programs for community barter, the education and mentoring of local kids, and an open-door policy that embraces our neighbors and local cultures. If necessary, we will provide for security, but our first approach is love and inclusion rather than fear and exclusion.

Planner: I am seeing how this may be attractive for some people, but I am not sure I would want to buy a home in a transient community or one that allows poor, local people to participate in the community.

Me: AWE will not be designed as a transient community, but the hospitality and education components will draw visitors, many of whom will not become permanent community members. We anticipate that these visitors and our neighbors will enrich our community, both socially and economically. In just about every town or city, there is a hotel, restaurant, market and gas station to serve the needs of visitors.

Although we plan to take an inclusive approach, AWE Communities won't be for everyone—members of AWE Communities will be both self-selecting and community-selected. Because the community is based on inclusivity rather than exclusivity, we also have options for people to rent or work in exchange for living in the community. The work exchange program has great appeal for the many young adults who are brilliant, dynamic and also strapped with student loans, can't get a decent job and won't be able to afford a home. I have met many 20 to 30-year olds who dream of becoming a member of the AWE Community and contributing to its success.

Planner: You have given this quite a bit of thought and I can see why this kind of living would be attractive. If I moved there, how would I make a living in your community?

Me: These communities are not just a bunch of McMansions behind a security gate. AWE Communities are designed to be collaborative and meritocratic, live-work communities that create meaningful work, rather than just jobs—work that enriches both the quality of life in the community and the world with a foundational ethic to serve ecosystemic thriving. While AWE Communities provide great opportunities for meaningful work, any community member, may engage in work outside of the community and contribute monetarily to the community rather than providing services to the community. By focusing on regenerative business, living technologies innovation and optimal wellness, AWE Communities provide opportunities for generating abundant wealth by serving ecosystemic thriving and fostering the regenerative economy.

AWE Communities are designed for economic scale and balancing the carrying capacity of the land and community with its population of 500-2,000 members. Integration and diversity of people (e.g., gender, age, race), skills and economic strata is key to a balanced community. The economic models include a 1) portfolio permaculture farm of organic foods, biofuel feedstocks, and crops for phytomedicines; 2) lite industrial processing and packaging facility, 3) science, technology and media incubator and entrepreneurial center focused on regenerative innovation, 4) real estate sales and construction, 5) hospitality, 6) education, training and certification, 7) optimal wellness center, 8) imagination and innovation center, 9) regenerative community development and consulting company, 10) prototyping precision machine shop, 11) a living laboratory and demonstration facility, and 12) a regenerative university campus.

You can also engage in outside work, entrepreneurial endeavors of your choosing. However, as a member of the community, your community service contributions, monetary contributions and Homeowners Association Fees earn you distribution interests in the for-profit community cooperative. The cooperative makes pro rata distributions of profits after the end of each year. If the members of the community have significant business success, the cooperative distributions eliminate the Homeowners Association Fees and could provide income instead of expense to homeowners.

Planner: So what you're telling me is I get to have my own home, have meaningful and inspiring work, my homeowner's association fees are investments, I get to have my privacy and come and go as I please, I get to eat healthy fresh food and cook when I want to, I have someone pick up my laundry and drop it off, I live with conscious and dynamic people who are doing good things for the world, and I have all the amenities of a high-end personal development resort. And if the economy collapses or goes through massive inflation, I am invested in real and sustainable assets that will provide me with water, food, shelter and energy security.

Me: That is correct.

Planner: I really fought you and you have really made me consider new ways of thinking about planning communities and how we can shape our future. Thank you. It's going to be tough, however, to get the planning, zoning and building variances and permits required to build the regenerative communities you envision, but we do need to make significant changes in our established regulations to make our communities more efficient, productive, resilient and ecologically sustainable.

Often those in planning, zoning, building and other regulatory agencies are there to enforce regulations, not change them. States, counties and cities can, however, pass regulations that provide for more discretionary zoning (e.g., pilot projects, mixed-use, experimental zoning, innovation zoning).

In providing greater detail into the planning, development, governance and operations of regenerative communities, I will share much of the research, planning, features and considerations utilized for AWE Communities.

AWE COMMUNITIES

AWE Communities are built on the foundations of abundance, wellness, empowerment in service to ecosystemic thriving with a focus on living systems and technology innovation, regenerative practices and optimal wellness. AWE Communities provide residents and members an environment to deepen their love and connection to each other and the planet, flourish and achieve their potential. As the members flourish, the community will benefit, businesses will thrive and community real estate will increase in value. Using a cooperative model, members have ownership interests in community businesses and homeowners associations fees and community contribution earn members meritocratic distributions from the cooperative. Moreover, the regenerative applications demonstrated by AWE Communities will have social, economic and environmental benefits that can influence the world and shift culture towards regenerative living.

Providing regenerative planning and design, AWE Communities integrate the infrastructure, foundation, culture and environment that supports thriving including the following:

1. Pure water and organic, fresh, highly nutritious food and supplements, grown and processed on community property;

2. Community kitchen and dining hall;

3. Regenerative, bio-regionally optimized, energy-efficient and healthy environments for living, learning, working and play including regeneratively designed and built residential, hospitality, dorms, learning center, staff housing, commercial and retail;

4. Clean, renewable energy with onsite generation;

5. Waste and wastewater recycling, reuse and upcycling;

6. Immersive, inspiring and practical "lifelong learning" (rather than "education");

7. Well-care and health insurance;

8. An optimal wellness and fitness center providing for optimal health of the community;

9. Entrepreneurial and business centers where residents can start and operate businesses, hold meetings, and be productive

10. Community transportation fleet;

11. Communications including phone, mobile and internet;

12. Media, arts and performance center;

13. Living innovation, science and technology center;

14. Economically flourishing community businesses; and

15. Center for personal and community spiritual development and evolved consciousness.

The following considerations are foundational to developing and operating a thriving regenerative community:

OPTIMAL POPULATION, LAND RATIO AND LAND USE

After engaging in deep research and calculations on the optimal population size of a village, the plans for AWE communities were based upon an optimal population of between 500 to 1,500 residents. Based upon research and historical data,[435] significant economies of scale are realized with 500 to 1500 residents, allowing community members to have access to a greater variety and quality of services, skills and amenities at lower costs. As discussed in greater depth below, the maximum community guideline of 1,500 residents allows the community to remain principles-based and relatively non-hierarchical.

When communities reach their optimal size, rather than overcrowding the existing community or causing resource constraints, sister communities will be started. AWE communities can engage in cooperative exchange relationships to ensure continuity of regenerative community growth and thriving abundance. As AWE and other regenerative communities grow and multiply, the aggregation of proximate regenerative communities will form regenerative towns and cities. However, instead of unsustainable, grid-based concrete structures made for machines and electrons, the regenerative communities and cities of the future will be built to support quality of human life and natural beauty containing a harmonious balance of nature and built-environment, community and independence, work and play, health, creativity and spiritual development.

The ratio of land-to-person in rural developments with good soil and long growing seasons should be at least 1/4 acre per person with a general guideline of 20% for built environment, 30% for agriculture, 25% for recreation and 25% for conservation. In urban environments, the foregoing ratios may be challenging. However, utilizing rooftop, hanging gardens, and indoor vertical growing facilities, less land is required to provide a sustainable food supply for the population. Also, exchanging some of the urban built environment for recreational parks and gardens will support greater health and well-being in urban communities.

REGENERATIVE PLANNING AND DEVELOPMENT CONSIDERATIONS

All infrastructure, building and activities should be sustainable and regenerative. Power should come from renewable sources, such as solar, geothermal, wind, tidal or hydrogen. Each community should have independent sources of water, food and power and will, to the greatest extent possible, not rely on grid provided necessities, although grid utilities may be used as a backup. However, if the grid utilities are renewable, clean, ethical and affordable, consideration can be given to being tied to the grid.

In choosing site locations and planning AWE Communities the following factors are considered:

- Water Quality and Availability
- Climate and Growing Season

- Soil Quality and Access to Seed and Soil Amendment

- Access to Building Materials and Skilled Labor

- Usability and Topography of the Land

- Zoning, Building and Permitting Regulations

- Governmental, Title and Legal Compliance Issues

- Access to Infrastructure (e.g., roads, rails, airports, electricity)

- Literacy, Language and Training of Local People

- Taxes (e.g., Income, Property, Sales, Excise, Use, Import, Ad Valorem)

- Distance from Major Cities and Airports

- Economic Climate (e.g., expansion or contraction) and Industries

- Development Costs and Financing

- Community Zoning for Aesthetics including Visual (e.g., allowable design of built environment and landscaping), Noise (e.g., location of silent, quiet, private, community, free-for-all zones, as well as roadways and industrial activities), Smell (e.g., location of kitchen, farm, wastewater treatment, smoking areas), and Space (e.g., open space, recreational space, walking and riding)

- Security, Government Stability, Corruption and Crime Rate

- Unique Value Proposition (e.g., hot springs, waterfalls, lakes, mountains, surf break)

- Regional Health Issues (e.g., obesity, diabetes, heart disease, cancer, AIDS, malaria)

- Community Agreements, Governance, Decision-making and Merit System

ORGANIZATIONAL STRUCTURE, GOVERNANCE AND INCENTIVES

The initial challenges in building community include deciding how to decide and community governance. Unanimous consensus provides for the collective intelligence to be tapped, but is typically slow and inefficient. A single leader approach consolidates power and supports rapid decision-making, but often disempowers community members and reduces their ability to share their wisdom and ideas. A democratic model provides a good middle ground but is not the most efficient or empowering in all situations. Thus, the recommended default community decision model utilizes time-based collective wisdom gathering and input decision structure with democratic voting. This structure provides for (1) a time parameter in which a decision must be made, (2) allows for those who desire to provide input to do so, and (3) in the event that unanimous agreement is not reached at the end of the time allocated, majority vote decides. In the event more time is required, then upon a majority vote, additional time can be scheduled and allocated. Members who do not participate waive rights to later object. Any member who disagrees with another or the proposed course of action must state factual reasons for disagreement and provide an improved suggestion.

In the event of an emergency and a requirement for critical urgent decision-making, the default decision process will give way to a Situationally Adaptive Organization ("SAO") structure, (discussed in greater detail in the chapter entitled *Transforming Organizations and Governance,*) with decision protocols that allow those with the greatest expertise the authority to address emergencies and critically urgent situations. As discussed, SAOs integrate the best of capitalism, communism, socialism and democracy. The SAO model requires whole systems planning to define the situations that cause governance to adapt from (1) the standard flat nuclear democratic structure of shared wisdom and servant management to (2) governance by committee for highly specialized and/or expert decision-making to (3) single leader structures for urgent and critical situations requiring experienced and wise rapid decision-making.

Unlike communism, community members will be rewarded for their performance and the quality of both their community and individual contributions. Moreover, individual talents are honored and utilized to enhance the community living environment as well as the lives of individuals. The dreams and desires of members are supported in balance with the needs of the community in alignment with the values and principles of the community.

Unlike capitalism, all basic necessities are provided with quality and integrity in consideration for services, cash contribution and/or other community value. Members are valued on both their quantitative and qualitative "contribution" to the community. The qualitative aspects of contribution include the ability to inspire, elevate, heal, love and create joy, rather than just purely tangible productivity and personal wealth. The qualitative aspects and contributions can be quantified through surveys and various peer review methods.

As well, an incentives model (e.g., community currency, digital tokens, points) will be implemented to reward productivity, community benefit and valued qualitative contributions of the members. The incentives can then be used for community exchange to purchase goods and services or invest in community businesses. Also, the incentives can be used as a basis for making bonus distributions to community members and provide for efficient and transparent voting on community matters.

AWE leadership and community members must have deep integrity and commitment to serving the community's needs and environments, and frequently elevating the community's needs over their individual needs. As the community scales to a population of 1,500 members, evolved, scalable and automated whole systems analysis, planning, governance and structures will be required in order to optimally respond to, manage and resolve situations arising from increasing population and complexity of social interactions. The situational codification and planning required to effectively and compassionately manage complex social interactions and conflict resolution should be based upon principles and agreements rather than rigid rules, procedures and standardization. Such situations, when identified, are first remedied in supportive, flexible and effective social governance and resolution systems. Here agreements and protocols for solutions can be adopted to best respond to situations as they arise in a way that maintains the principles and values of the community. Moreover, it's important that those given the responsibility for governance, synergistic resolution and maintaining the articulated principles and values of the community also be given authority to inspire, train, manage, lead and, when necessary, enforce the social, governance and resolution systems.

A collaborative hybrid organizational structure is recommended for governance, economic and societal needs. This involves a for-profit structure for businesses, a co-op structure for the community and a non-profit structure for such things as education, well-care, research, scholarships, and conservation. Each of these various entities will support the value of the other. For example, the for-profit can grant the non-profit the non-developable land and community land in a conservation trust. The for-profit will get the benefit of the donative offset against income taxes. The non-profit will own the open space, farmland and community land and will enter into a percentage lease with the community co-op for the development and management of the community amenities, housing and farming operations. Because the lease is based upon a gross percentage of revenues, the community will not face being in default and the community and non-profit will be aligned in the community's success. As the community increases its revenues, the non-profit's rents increase. The non-profit and co-op will also be given an equity stake in the for-profit creating incentive to promote the success of the for-profit. As the community develops the amenities, centers and businesses, the demand and value of the developable land will increase, thereby increasing the investment for the community and the for-profit.

In alignment with the meritocratic nature of the community, clear performance and production standards must be articulated to community members, especially those that are contributing work and services in exchange for room, board and community benefits. As mentioned above, the target work-week is 25 hours, based upon realistic performance measurements as decided by the community, its leadership and/or management. Unless performance is time-sensitive, performance will take precedence over time spent and rigid schedules. Thus, those who are more efficient will not be penalized for superior performance. Those that exceed performance standards and community contribution will be rewarded pursuant to the meritocratic incentive system. The incentives can be used in exchange for community products and services, as well as a method for determining contribution and pro-rata distribution of bonuses and co-op distributions to community members.

ECONOMIC FLOURISHING

The community, to be successful, must thrive economically, socially and environmentally. To the extent possible, the planning, development and businesses of the community can be financed through a combination of equity capital, contribution of services, licensing, inventory/receivables financing, grants and strategic debt. By using a community credit union model, the credit union can avail itself of fractional reserve leverage and fund community projects and businesses, while paying depositors better than average returns. As well, a community entrepreneurial center and incubator will help spawn businesses and innovation, as well as create an environment for mentoring and supporting community businesses.

Because the community will be based upon co-op model, the members of the community will benefit individually as a result of the collective success. Thus, there is significant incentive for the community members to support community businesses.

The community benefits and amenities will be supported through a combination of (i) operating business revenues (e.g., food, phyto-medicines, fuel, resort, hospitality, workshops, technology, licensing, media, events and consulting), (ii) homeowner's association fees, (iii) royalties from licensing, (iv) investment activities, and (v) liquidity events resulting from incubated companies.

The costs of development and building can be financed through the sale of community lots and housing. As well, since a significant percentage of the facilities, projects and programs will be developed and maintained for social good, (e.g., education, spiritual and personal growth, systemic transformation), and environmental benefit, (e.g., ecological conservation, regeneration, preservation, remediation), a non-profit structure can be employed to finance these related projects through donations and grants.

PORTFOLIO FARMS—ORGANIC FOODS, PHYTO-MEDICINES AND ENERGY FEEDSTOCK

A cornerstone of AWE Communities is a "portfolio" of agricultural enterprises. To foster independence and revenue generation, it's recommended farms grow a portfolio of (i) high-quality organic and superfood products, (ii) phyto-medicines, (iii) skin and hair care crops, and (iv) fuel and energy feedstocks.

The implementation of living systems technologies and vertical integration for growing, harvesting, stabilization and value-added processing for the agricultural products is essential to the integrity of the community and the regenerative economic aspects of the farming operations. These ethical and regenerative practices include regenerative agriculture, permaculture, bio-dynamics, sonic and other non-violent "pest" control, bio-reactors, composting, recycling, waste-to-energy, equitable trade practices, and integration of automated and local energy/labor efficient processing.

By utilizing these practices, the farms will be a model of both advanced sustainable and regenerative farming technologies that enhance the independence, health and economic flourishing of the community and also serve as a unique value proposition to distinguish the farm as a producer of the exceptionally high-quality, healthy and conscious value-added products.

In order to generate greater profitability, create productive work for the community members and ensure freshness and quality of the community's products, the community will house facilities for stabilization, value-added processing, packaging, shipping, marketing, selling and administering the community's farm products. These facilities can acquire, accelerate and service strategic businesses, as well as provide cooperative facilities with local farmers and product manufacturers. The community, local farmers and product manufacturers can obtain higher sales pricing and distribution arrangements in the market, increase supply chain efficiencies and receive a larger percentage of the supply chain proceeds.

Because the food is grown onsite and locally, the costs of processing, transportation, storage, distribution and retailing are disintermediated, and the cost of food for community members is reduced by 50-80%, while the products sold by the community will receive value-added pricing and higher profitability. Moreover, utilizing cooperative exchange arrangements with other food suppliers, the community can provide a significant variety of foods to its members.

As mentioned above, the availability of plentiful water for drinking, agriculture and processing is of critical importance. While technologies, such as reverse osmosis, atmospheric water and molecular resonance are becoming more effective and less expensive, natural, reliable and abundant sources of clean water (e.g., deep aquifers or underground springs), are critical.

RENEWABLE ENERGY PRODUCTION AND ENERGY EFFICIENCY

To facilitate greater independence, it's recommended that the community operate "off the grid" and fulfill 100% of its fuel and energy needs with a combination of on-site solar, wind, geo-thermal, hydro-electric, tidal, hydrogen and/or waste-to-energy technologies with bio-fuel generators for secondary power. However, the use of renewable energy is often site specific and requires a climate, resource and economic analysis. If, for example, the community is located in an area that has lots of fog, clouds and rainy days, solar would be a less effective option. As well, if the community is in a country or region whose energy generation is primarily from renewable energy sources (e.g., Costa Rica, Germany, Sweden), then it may be economically advantageous to utilize grid power, especially in the early stages of community development. If, however, the grid is powered by non-renewable fossil fuels, every effort should be made to use off-the-grid energy and find alternative sources of energy even if more expensive. To do otherwise, merely supports a destructive and toxic paradigm that elevates the economic imperative over the ethical imperative. Even if the grid energy sources are clean, off-the-grid generation should be implemented when economically and environmentally beneficial, especially when considering energy security and long-term independence.

Onsite renewable energy generation can often provide significant savings in the costs of energy. Moreover, substantial energy savings can be realized through (1) conservative behavior and constructing the built environment using energy-efficient design (e.g., passive solar, thermal mass, energy-efficient siting, thermal glass, air-water-environment leverage); (2) natural heating, cooling and climate management (e.g., sensors, sub-metering, zoning, low energy fans, passive solar, heat syncs, radiant heating, subterranean cooling, electron offset); (3) energy-efficient lighting (daylighting, LED, sensors); (4) energy-efficient appliances; (5) water collection and conservation (e.g. rainwater catchment, gray-black water recycling); (6) waste harvesting and upcycling (e.g., waste-to-energy, anaerobic digestion, methane gas, composting); and (7) gravity and magnetic alternatives to electronic pumps and motors.

COMMUNITY LIFELONG LEARNING

As we move toward a collaborative, experiential, automated and rapidly evolving Regenerative Economy devoted to ecosystemic thriving, the way we learn must evolve to provide the skills and capacity for this new paradigm. The Lifelong Learning Centers of AWE Communities will provide students, STEM (Science, Technology, Engineering, Math) as well as literacy/communication skills and stimulating, interactive and practical whole-life skills, including the following:

- Living Skills (e.g., farming, ranching and food production, food preparation, building and construction, mechanics, renewable energy generation)

- Economic and Business Skills (e.g., entrepreneurship, finance, investing, business formation, marketing, sales, customer service, operational management)

- Technological and Scientific Skills (e.g., computer programming, scientific and technological research, epigenetics, food engineering, biotech, agtech, aquatech, mariculture, energy sciences)

- Optimal Wellness skills based upon M.E.D.I.C.I.N.E.

- Healing and Coaching Skills (e.g., massage, wellness, mindfulness, yoga, integrated wellness, nutrition, life-coaching, personal training, nutritional coaching)

- Creative Skills (e.g., music, art, dance, theatre)

- Political Skills (e.g., leadership, governance, conflict resolution, law)

- Social Skills (e.g., collaboration, compassionate communication, social responsibility, sharing, leadership, ethics, AWE guidance)

- Environmental Skills (e.g. environmental preservation, conservation, remediation, regeneration, recycling, permaculture)

- Spiritual-Emotional Skills (e.g., emotional intelligence, empathy, compassion, sensitivity, love, ethics and mindfulness)

In the learning system of AWE Communities, adults, children and elders will often be integrated. Adults and elders will mentor, empower and inspire children; and, children will bring fresh insight and energy to the adults and elders. Rather than being presented with information and materials at their desks, children will learn through practical application. They'll spend time outside playing, moving, creating and doing projects that improve their health and foster the development of lifelong practical skills. For example, biology will be learned on the farm; chemistry in the bio-fuels lab; algebra and deductive reasoning in the computer lab; geometry and calculus from designing and building structures; electronics and engineering from working with clean energy, power and storage systems; business and management from working in community businesses; healing arts from doing healing work, teaching yoga and providing personal training; creative skills from doing art, music and dance as a foundational cultural practice of the community; philosophy and spiritual-emotional development from attending and teaching workshops for spiritual and personal growth; and health and physical development by living a lifestyle of optimal wellness based upon the M.E.D.I.C.I.N.E. protocols. Students will also have numerous opportunities to engage in community apprenticeships and mentoring opportunities to help them further their passions and interests.

By the time a student is 18 years old, they will have acquired real-life skills, experiences and certifications with which to contribute immediately to society, as well as having a clear sense of their true, higher and inspired purpose. Adults will also benefit from this education as they engage with students providing mentorship and apprenticeship opportunities. Learning will be coupled with the supportive and collaborative environment of community and infrastructure that inspires and fosters lifelong learning for the community members. This focus on learning is lifelong, allowing all community members to evolve and better their lives as well as their value to the community. Members of AWE Communities can learn the skills with community support to live in alignment with their higher truth and purpose.

OPTIMAL WELLNESS AND HEALTH INSURANCE

Because of AWE Community's (1) focus on health, wellness, consciousness and balance, (2) reduced work hours, (3) diminished stresses that plague our society,

(4) healing services and preventative medicine programs, (5) highly nutritious fresh organic diet, and (6) incentives for personal health, much of the disease and illness plaguing our society will be significantly reduced in our community. Thus, the population of AWE Communities will be healthier, happier and more productive. As a result of overall healthy living and the "well-care" being provided by community physicians and healers in a manner that is proactive and curative, it is anticipated that the community will have higher degree health with lower major health claims. Thus, the community can negotiate favorable group rates for health insurance. Moreover, to lower health insurance rates, the community can self-insure up to large deductible limits (e.g., $25,000 per person) and, reduce the risk of large exposure from catastrophic and major illness, by obtaining an umbrella policy to provide insurance for claims over the self-insured limits.

TRANSPORTATION

AWE Communities will be designed for walking, biking, skating, zip-lining and other healthy modes of mobility. For longer distances, small electric vehicles, such as golf carts, scooters, e-bikes, can be used. Because of the walkable work-live-play design of the community, the need for automobile ownership will be substantially reduced. For extra-community general transportation, the community will have a fleet of primarily hydrogen, electric, smart and/or hybrid vehicles, light-duty trucks, vans, and cargo vans. In a community with 1,000 members, a community fleet of only 150 shared vehicles will provide every person a vehicle whenever they need one. Thus, the cost of auto payments will be reduced by about 85%. Moreover, due to the collective bargaining power of the community, automobile insurance and maintenance expenses are decreased, as is the time spent in washing, fueling and maintaining automobiles. Utilizing a real-time reservation/inventory/ride-share program for the community can allow members to be even more efficient and conscious in the way they use transportation and can also ensure that those with mandatory transportation requirements have their needs met.

COMMUNICATIONS AND COLLABORATION TECHNOLOGIES

The combination of Internet proliferation, smartphones, the reduced costs of hardware and bandwidth, the availability of open-source software, cloud-based storage and collaboration, artificial intelligence and augmented reality have resulted in affordable efficiencies and improvements in (1) communications (e.g., Internet, VOIP, Video-Conferencing, email, text messaging, mobile data and mobility), (2) automation of the enterprise tasks (enterprise resource management, project management, integrated systems, collaborative tools, peer review), (3) collaboration (e.g., online collaborative documents, spreadsheets, presentations), (4) data usage (e.g., filtering, recommendation, and predictive modeling), and (5) governance (e.g., digital identification, voting, rating, rewards, input collection and community meetings). Thus, the community can provide highly effective enterprise and personal communication, collaboration, productivity and governance tools to promote more effective management and community interaction that will increase efficiencies and allow global business to be conducted from just about anywhere in the world. This will afford the community a plethora location options more conducive to the principals of the community (e.g., connection with nature, less oppressive regulatory environment, less expensive land, building costs and labor), while not compromising connectivity, productivity, innovation and creation of abundance.

Some of the attributes of AWE Communities described above may be interpreted by some as "utopian." They are not. They're just a lot better than our current default communities. AWE Communities are planned to provide higher-quality-of-life with greater love, connection, freedom, abundance, wellness, empowerment and economic-social-environmental-spiritual balance. AWE Communities are designed to create a powerful, heart-based lifestyle for individuals within a dynamic community focused on providing an environment of AWE—Abundance Wellness and Empowerment in service to love, connection, beauty and ecosystemic thriving.

CHAPTER 29

AWEdoption

"Great spirits have always encountered violent opposition from mediocre minds."

~Albert Einstein

I t is not hard to imagine a better world. A world that is more loving, kind, harmonious, inspiring, beautiful, equitable, abundant, well and empowered. A world less stressful, polluted and destructive. A world that provides a greater balance between work, play and personal growth. We are beginning to see an accelerating global adoption of people desiring to live in Conscious Communities; corporations adopting corporate social responsibility practices (e.g., ESG, regenerative applications, sustainability, circular economy); and governments providing grants, regulatory variances and incentives to stimulate a green economy.

There are those, however, that attempt to thwart betterment, excellence, innovation and vision. They point out only faults and failures without constructive input. They promote and celebrate the failures of "great spirits" who to make the world a better place. Those that attempt to shift the status quo (e.g., the visionaries, innovators, creatives, inventors) are likely to be exposed to criticism, ridicule and ostracism. The masses that protect the status quo are generally scared of change and are immobilized by fear of the unknown. They defend and perpetuate a corrupt, destructive, toxic and unsustainable way of life—running a fear-based divisive program created by the power elite. The power elite who control and benefit from the status quo, use their power to stay in power by conditioning the masses to be divided and insecure, to perpetuate and enforce old paradigm programs and rely upon corporations and governments for their safety and security.

The way to shift old paradigm consciousness is by courageously building and demonstrating a new paradigm that is better.

It's time to get off the hamster wheel. While the 20th century represented a period of great progress, it also was a period of industrialization, competition, centralization, profit-at-all costs, debt, greed, hoarding, consumerism, waste, individualism, war, fossil fuels, and environmental destruction. The 21st century can be an era of peace, prosperity, abundance, well-being, personal and collective empowerment, love and environmental regeneration.

In the 21st century, there is a potential to create a Regenerative Society based upon the following:

1. Love over fear;

2. Inclusion over divisiveness;

3. Collaboration over competition;

4. Sufficiency over greed;

5. Sharing over hoarding;

6. Localization over centralization;

7. Inspiring, evolutionary and valuable experiences and over jobs, possessions and debt;

8. An economy and society dedicated to ecosystemic regeneration, renewal and flourishing over environmental degradation, destruction and extraction

9. Highly nutritious, fresh organic agriculture and foods, pure water and clean air over toxic food and water and polluted air;

10. Ethical manufacturing of long-lasting, high-quality products over cheap products built for obsolescence;

11. Distributed, accessible and affordable clean energy over centralized dirty and destructive energy;

12. Upcycling, reuse and recycling of waste over careless dumping and disposal of valuable products as waste;

13. Clean, connected, collaborative and conscious communities over disconnected, competitive, toxic and polluting urban and suburban environments;

14. Healthy and energy-efficient places to live and work over buildings made of toxic materials, and living and working environments that degrade health;

15. Practical, applied, inspiring, personalized and immersive lifelong learning over standardized, mechanistic, authoritarian, uninspiring and impractical education;

16. "Wellcare" that is loving, compassionate, empathic, holistic and curative over impersonal and mechanistic "sickcare" that is too often is more interested in profits than the health and wellness of people, society and planet (e.g., treating symptoms rather than curing illness and creating addiction and dependence on pharmaceuticals rather than promoting natural remedies and healthy lifestyles);

17. Balanced population growth with carrying capacity over endless growth and consumption;

18. An economic system devoted to ecosystemic thriving based upon abundance, quality-of-life, trust and voluntary exchange over scarcity, debt, quantitative measurements and hoarding.

The 21st century has the potential of elevating a qualitative civilization over a quantitative society. Such things as love, health, connection, happiness, integrity, generosity and beauty will find their way into the hearts and minds of humankind and will be a profound influence on evolving our beliefs, behaviors and culture. As this cultural renaissance gains adoption, we will start seeing new ways of being that serve people and planet embraced by society. No longer will be people feel obliged to conform to conditioning compelling humans to act as robots while moving from one box to another (e.g., home, car, office); spending a significant amount our time, energy and life at exploitative work staring into screens rather than looking into each other's eyes; and doing dull and repetitive and often meaningless tasks rather than enjoying nature. We could instead be fulfilling our purpose, realizing our dreams, learning, evolving, collaborating and creating real living value, love and connection for ourselves, our planet and society. With the advent of new technologies including robotics and artificial intelligence, humankind can be set free to expand our free time and engage in that which we love and brings us joy.

In the 21st century, humankind has the opportunity to achieve a world of AWE that balances meaningful work in service to ecosystemic thriving and the betterment of society with personal freedom and time to pursue and realize one's true purpose. By applying regenerative applications, every person can obtain access to a secure and renewable supply of clean water, food, shelter, energy, education and healthcare. We'll have more time to spend with family and friends, as well as exploring and expressing our personal vocational and avocational interests. Adopting a lifestyle of health and vitality will be supported and incentivized by our society and a culture of wellness and thriving. With our expanded freedom and time, travel, adventure and expansive experiences can be a part of everyone's life.

So how does adoption of the new paradigm occur? By creating and demonstrating paradigm-shifting innovation and evolution of beliefs and behaviors that provide significantly better social, environmental and economic benefits. Examples of innovation that have shifted beliefs, behaviors and culture include such things as (1) the printing press, (2) automobiles and airplanes, (3) personal computers and photocopiers replacing typewriters and carbon paper; (4) smartphones replacing fixed phones, and (5) clean energy; (6) new discoveries in biotechnology, molecular and genetic sciences and (7) biomimetic materials. Additionally, we are now seeing such things as solar and clean energy replacing coal, nuclear and petroleum for energy. As well, electric cars are replacing a percentage of fossil fuel cars and soon autonomous driverless vehicles will offer safe and reliable personal transportation without the need for owning a car. Green buildings and developments are replacing conventional building and developments.

People innately adopt things that provide greater health, beauty, love, abundance, harmony, convenience, freedom and enjoyment of life. The more that innovation supports these qualitative aspects of life and the more accessible and affordable innovation becomes, the more our paradigm will shift.

In his book called *Diffusion of Innovations*, Everett Rogers stated that adopters of any new innovation or idea could be categorized as follows:

- **Innovators** (2.5 %) Venturesome, educated, multiple information sources, greater propensity to take risk

- **Early Adopters** (13.5%) Social leaders, popular, educated

- **Early Majority** (34%) Deliberate, many informal social contacts

- **Late Majority** (34%) Skeptical, traditional, lower socio-economic status

- **Laggards** (16%) Bound by tradition, very conservative and fear change

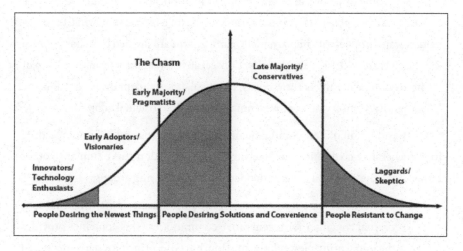

Building on Rogers' observations, Geoffrey Moore, created the following groups to describe the adoption curve of technological innovation:

- **Technology Enthusiasts** (Innovators) are pioneers who are often inventors and are technologically savvy. This group is curious, explorative and willing to take a risk.

- **Visionaries** (Early Adopters) are more geared towards exploitation. They are willing to accept a product that has disruptive impact, appears to work, but are willing to deal with bugs. The Visionaries like being involved as testers and helping make things work.

- **Pragmatists** (Early Majority) want a product that works. They want a 100% solution to their business problem. If they get the 80% that delighted the visionary, they feel cheated, and they tell their pragmatist friends.

- **Conservatives** (Late Majority) buy products because they really have no choice. They are not reassured by having books about the product, because the existence of books implies the product isn't simple enough to use. Conservatives will not tolerate complexity.

- **Skeptics** (Laggards) are not going to buy, though they may talk other people out of buying.

According to Moore, different groups adopt innovations for different reasons with technology enthusiasts and visionaries looking for a radical shift, while the pragmatists want productivity improvement. Both groups are divided by a chasm. Once the chasm is crossed, the Late Majority/Conservatives start considering adoption of the innovation. Once the Early Majority/Pragmatists fully adopt the innovation, the Late Majority/Conservatives move from consideration to actual adoption.

The adoption of new paradigm communities, beliefs and behaviors leading to a regenerative civilization, are likely to have an adoption curve similar to other innovation. The adoption curve is divided into the following groups:

- **Pioneers/Developers**—These are visionaries that create the vision and conceptual container for regenerative communities. This container provides the initial principles, culture, mission, purpose, principles, agreements and governance upon which the community is based. This container should be flexible and evolutionary. The Pioneers/Developers also find the land that meets the needs of the community, master plan the community, and develop the land and attract the community members.

- **Settlers/Early Community Builders**—This group joins the regenerative community to manifest the vision and plan of the Pioneers and contribute to such things as the design, infrastructure, construction, businesses, operation, marketing and sales of the community. This group may be incentivized by such things as the purchase or grant of land and/or equity stakes in the community.

- **Joiners/Community Members**—Once the infrastructure and community amenities are built, the regenerative community will have achieved initial viability, increased value and greater appeal to a broader market. With the community ready for growth and expansion, the Joiner/Community members will be attracted to become members of the community and contribute to the growth, economic development, technology, education, art, culture, management, operations and maintenance of the community along with other services that enrich the community. As the community grows and becomes able to demonstrate a higher quality of life with a full offering of holistic services, amenities and options, the community will draw more members to join and participate in the community.

- **External Community Acceptance and Collaboration—Crossing the Chasm of Consciousness and Culture**—As mentioned, we are all interconnected and interdependent. Each community will have an influence and impact on the proximate community, environment and culture in which it is nested. It is important for the regenerative community to create and demonstrate value for those effected and influenced by the community. This requires awareness, consciousness, compassion, love and respect for one's neighbors and the culture of the location where the community is located. The community can prove its viability, value and contribution locally and then expand regionally, nationally and globally demonstrating an improved quality of life with greater abundance, wellness, empowerment, freedom harmony and regenerability. The community can then be a significant influence on mainstream conservative consciousness.

- **Conservatives**—Once the community has proven its model and provided the conservatives convincing evidence that it can provide a higher quality of life for less effort, time and money, the conservatives will then shift from fear to neutrality, from neutrality to acceptance and from acceptance to adoption. When the conservatives adopt and imitate the concepts, models and structure of regenerative communities, the mass adoption curve starts and the regenerative movement will proliferate throughout the world to become a way of life.

- **Laggards/Skeptics**—As food, water, energy, jobs and resources become scarce under the old paradigm, even a percentage of the laggards and skeptics, will eventually adopt the new paradigm, although it may be difficult for them to integrate into a collaborative and regenerative community. This group may need additional education, clearing and personal growth work before they are ready to truly contribute to a regenerative and conscious community and embrace the new paradigm.

The demonstration and adoption of new paradigm belief systems, innovation and regenerative communities will have a profound impact on our world. The shifts will be seen in the way we relate to each other, the planet and its resources, in the way we spend our time, and what we believe is important.

As we change our beliefs and behaviors, courageously devote ourselves to developing a regenerative society in service to love, connection and ecosystemic thriving, we will realize the transformation into a world of Abundance, Wellness & Empowerment, where humankind can live in AWE.

CONCLUSION

"In the end these things matter most:
How well did you love?
How fully did you live?
How deeply did you let go?"

~Jack Kornfield

REFERENCES

1   The Hidden Costs of our Nuclear Arsenal, Brookings Institution, https://www.brookings.edu/the-hidden-costs-of-our-nuclear-arsenal-overview-of-project-findings

2   SIPRI, Global military expenditure sees largest annual increase in a decade—says SIPRI—reaching $1917 billion in 2019; https://www.sipri.org/media/press-release/2020/global-military-expenditure-sees-largest-annual-increase-decade-says-sipri-reaching-1917-billion#:~:text=Global%20military%20expenditure%20sees%20largest%20annual%20increase%20in%20a%20decade,reaching%20%241917%20billion%20in%202019&text=(Stockholm%2C%2027%20April%202020),Peace%20Research%20Institute%20(SIPRI).

3   https://www.imf.org/en/News/Articles/2015/09/14/01/49/pr1393

4   29,000,000,000,000: A Detailed Look at the Fed's Bail-out by Funding Facility and Recipient", Levy Economic Institute of Bard College

5   https://www.oxfam.org/en/pressroom/pressreleases/2017-01-16/just-8-men-own-same-wealth-half-world

6   https://www.cdc.gov/healthywater/global/wash_statistics.html

7   https://news.nationalgeographic.com/news/2004/06/source-of-half-earth-s-oxygen-gets-little-credit

8   https://www.dailygood.org/story/426/how-imagination-shapes-your-reality-gabriel-cohen/

9   http://blogs.worldbank.org/developmenttalk/international-poverty-line-has-just-been-raised-190-day-global-poverty-basically-unchanged-how-even

10 Emergo, Worldwide Spending on Healthcare, https://www.emergobyul.com/resources/worldwide-health-expenditures

11 https://en.wikipedia.org/wiki/Max_Planck

12 http://en.wikipedia.org/wiki/Albert_Einstein

13 http://en.wikipedia.org/wiki/Louis_de_Broglie

14 http://en.wikipedia.org/wiki/Arthur_Compton

15 http://www.thespiritguides.co.uk/Psychic_Events.aspx/FeaturedEvents/
Article_The_Soul_and_Quantum_Physics_671.aspx

16 https://en.wikipedia.org/wiki/Dzogchen

17 https://en.wikipedia.org/wiki/Ch%C3%B6gyal_Namkhai_Norbu

18 Ibid.

19 http://en.wikipedia.org/wiki/Jean_Piaget

20 https://en.wikipedia.org/wiki/Yogi_Pullavar

21 https://www.anl.gov/article/no-magic-show-realworld-levitation-to-in-
spire-better-pharmaceuticals

22 https://en.wikipedia.org/wiki/Matthew_Manning

23 https://www.urigeller.com/scientific-paranormal/the-geller-papers/
introduction/

24 https://en.wikipedia.org/wiki/Saints_and_levitation

25 https://jamesaconrad.com/TK/Ninel-Kulagina-telekinesis-case-rebut-
tals-to-skeptical-arguments.html

26 Elmer & Alyce Green, Beyond Biofeedback, 1977 Knoll Publishing Co.,
Chapter II: Self-regulation: East and West, pp. 197 218.

27 https://en.wikipedia.org/wiki/Edgar_Cayce

28 https://en.wikipedia.org/wiki/Morris_E._Goodman

29 https://en.wikipedia.org/wiki/Judith_Orloff

30 https://en.wikipedia.org/wiki/Barbara_Brennan

31 https://en.wikipedia.org/wiki/Roger_Bannister

32 https://entertainment.howstuffworks.com/arts/circus-arts/adrena-
line-strength.htm

33 https://en.wikipedia.org/wiki/Ivujivik#cite_note-10

34 https://www.foxnews.com/us/oregon-man-pinned-under-3000-
pound-tractor-saved-by-teen-daughters

35 Sources consulted include: https://www.tandfonline.com/doi/full/10
.1080/23311908.2017.1307633; https://blogs.scientificamerican.com/
observations/the-hippies-were-right-its-all-about-vibrations-man/

36 http://www.ehd.org/science_technology_largenumbers.php

37   http://www.theceugroup.com/brain-facts-to-blow-your-mind/

38   https://www.ncbi.nlm.nih.gov/pmc/articles/PMC2776484/

39   https://en.wikipedia.org/wiki/Neuron#cite_note-21

40   https://blogs.scientificamerican.com/news-blog/computers-have-a-lot-to-learn-from-2009-03-10/

41   Sources consulted include: https://www.ncbi.nlm.nih.gov/pmc/articles/PMC5034293/; https://www.basicknowledge101.com/subjects/brain.html; https://www.sciencedirect.com/topics/neuroscience/reticular-activating-system; https://medium.com/@sandrosafareli/the-reticular-activating-systems-ras-huge-influence-on-self-perception-6e8015f43764#:~:text=The%20Reticular%20Activating%20System%20is,mind%20and%20your%20subconscious%20mind.&text=What%20about%20our%20subconscious%20mind,40%20million%20bits%20of%20information;

42   https://en.wikipedia.org/wiki/Prefrontal_cortex

43   Medical Daily, A New Theory Suggests All Conscious Thoughts And Decisions Are Actually Made By Your Unconscious (2015); http://www.medicaldaily.com/new-theory-suggests-all-conscious-thoughts-and-decisions-are-actually-made-your-340238; http://www.simplifyinginterfaces.com/2008/08/01/95-percent-of-brain-activity-is-beyond-our-conscious-awareness;

44   https://www.gaia.com/article/a-team-just-built-a-supercomputer-to-mimic-human-brain-functions

45   http://www.basicknowledge101.com/subjects/brain.html

46   The Gut Microbiome, Journal of Medicinal Food, Galan 2014-12-1; https://www.ncbi.nlm.nih.gov/pmc/articles/PMC4259177

47   https://in5d.com/the-heart-has-its-own-brain-and-consciousness

48   http://transmissionsmedia.com/the-heart-has-its-own-brain-and-consciousness/

49   https://in5d.com/the-heart-has-its-own-brain-and-consciousness/

50   See footnote 12

51   http://www.cyberphysics.co.uk/topics/medical/heart/neurons.html

52   https://www.ncbi.nlm.nih.gov/pmc/articles/PMC3860382

53   http://courses.aiu.edu/NEUROSCIENCE/NEUROSCIENCE%20-%20SESSION%205/NEUROSCIENCE%20-%20SESSION%205.pdf

54   Source: https://imagine.gsfc.nasa.gov/science/toolbox/emspectrum1.html

55   http://en.wikipedia.org/wiki/1_E-7_m

56   Sources consulted include: https://www.mindful.org/mind-vs-brain; https://www.wsj.com/articles/the-mind-vs-brain-is-there-a-dif-ference-11569009725; https://www.simplypsychology.org/mind-bodydebate.html

57   Sources consulted include: https://www.scientificamerican.com/article/there-is-no-such-thing-as-conscious-thought; https://www.ncbi.nlm.nih.gov/pmc/articles/PMC2440575; https://www.dharmaocean.org/meditation/somatic-meditation

58   https://www.deepakchopra.com/articles/can-brain-science-explain-ex-perience-part-3

59   Sources consulted include: https://link.springer.com/chap-ter/10.1007%2F0-306-48052-2_21; https://www.ncbi.nlm.nih.gov/pmc/articles/PMC2763392;

60   Sources consulted include: https://simple.wikipedia.org/wiki/Sensation

61   https://www.sciencedirect.com/science/article/abs/pii/S1364661305002305

62   Sources consulted include: https://www.psychologytoday.com/us/blog/in-flux/201106/emotions-change-energy-in-motion; https://en.wikipe-dia.org/wiki/Emotion; https://en.wikipedia.org/wiki/Emotion_(disam-biguation); and https://plato.stanford.edu/entries/emotion/

63   https://en.wikipedia.org/wiki/Emotion

64   Ibid

65   Sources consulted include https://www.ncbi.nlm.nih.gov/pmc/arti-cles/PMC5298234/; https://discoverhealing.com/dr-david-hawkins-scale-consciousness-emotion-code/; https://iamfearlesssoul.com/the-energy-frequency-of-love-can-change-your-conscious-mind-bruce-lipton/; https://www.amrita.edu/news/hormones-and-chemi-cals-linked-our-emotion#:~:text=Excess%20of%20serotonin%20caus-es%20sedation,social%20behaviour%20and%20sexual%20problems

66   Ibid

67   https://www.health.harvard.edu/staying-healthy/understand-ing-the-stress-response#:~:text=After%20the%20amygdala%20sends%20a,as%20adrenaline)%20into%20the%20bloodstream.

68   https://www.revolvy.com/topic/Klaus%20Scherer

69   https://courses.lumenlearning.com/boundless-psychology/chapter/theories-of-emotion

70   http://en.wikipedia.org/wiki/John_Cacioppo

71   http://en.wikipedia.org/wiki/Ant%C3%B3nio_Dam%C3%A1sio

72   http://en.wikipedia.org/wiki/Joseph_E._LeDoux

73   http://en.wikipedia.org/wiki/Robert_Zajonc

74   http://www.cnn.com/2015/10/29/health/science-of-fear/

75   Sources consulted include: https://www.sciencedirect.com/science/article/pii/S0149763418308674; https://www.ncbi.nlm.nih.gov/pmc/articles/PMC2288613/; https://en.wikipedia.org/wiki/Somatic_experiencing; https://www.psychologytoday.com/us/blog/hide-and-seek/201412/whats-the-difference-between-feeling-and-emotion

76   Sources consulted include: https://www.merriam-webster.com/dictionary/feeling; https://imotions.com/blog/difference-feelings-emotions/

77   https://www.wtmsources.com/files/144_Instinct-Merriam-Webster%20Dictionary.pdf

78   Rudolf Steiner, Theosophy: An Introduction to the Spiritual Processes in Human Life and in the Cosmos (1994)

79   Sources consulted include: https://en.wikipedia.org/wiki/Emotion; https://en.wikipedia.org/wiki/Emotion_(disambiguation); and https://plato.stanford.edu/entries/emotion/

80   Sources consulted include: https://www.merriam-webster.com/dictionary/feeling; https://imotions.com/blog/difference-feelings-emotions/

81   Sources consulted include: https://en.wikipedia.org/wiki/Belief; https://www.merriam-webster.com/dictionary/belief; https://dictionary.cambridge.org/us/dictionary/english/belief

82   Sources consulted include: https://www.merriam-webster.com/dictionary/behavior; https://en.wikipedia.org/wiki/Behavior; https://www.merriam-webster.com/dictionary/culture; https://en.wikipedia.org/wiki/Culture

83   https://en.wikipedia.org/wiki/Culture

84   https://qubitsnews.com/2016/02/02/human-culture-technology-and-the-neocortex/

85   https://www.merriam-webster.com/dictionary/ethnocentric

86   The New Business Imperative: Valuing Natural Capital, The Nature Conservancy (2012) http://www.corporateecoforum.com/valuingnaturalcapital/offline/download.pdf

87   UN Environnent (2013) https://www.unenvironment.org/news-and-

stories/press-release/new-study-shows-multi-trillion-dollar-natural-capital-risk

88   https://medium.com/@jeremyerdman/we-produce-enough-food-to-feed-10-billion-people-so-why-does-hunger-still-exist-8086d2657539#:~:text=The%20world's%20farmers%20produce%20enough,this%20excess%2C%20hunger%20still%20exists

89   https://en.wikipedia.org/wiki/Dream

90   Ibid see footnote 40

91   http://kobuchi.com/?p=158

92   https://www.entrepreneur.com/article/295885

93   https://www.oprah.com/omagazine/what-oprah-knows-for-sure-about-finding-success

94   https://blogs.scientificamerican.com/news-blog/computers-have-a-lot-to-learn-from-2009-03-10/

95   Ibid see footnote 40

96   https://en.wikipedia.org/wiki/Wave%E2%80%93particle_duality

97   https://en.wikipedia.org/wiki/Inattentional_blindness

98   https://en.wikipedia.org/wiki/Multiverse

99   https://www.space.com/32728-parallel-universes.html

100   https://en.wikipedia.org/wiki/Quantum_entanglement

101   https://en.wikipedia.org/wiki/Copenhagen_interpretation

102   https://en.wikipedia.org/wiki/Schr%C3%B6dinger%27s_cat

103   https://en.wikipedia.org/wiki/Many-worlds_interpretation

104   https://en.wikipedia.org/wiki/Many-minds_interpretation

105   https://www.thoughtexperiments.net/many-minds/

106   Sources consulted include: https://education.jlab.org/qa/matha-tom_04.html; https://www.wonderopolis.org/wonder/how-many-cells-are-in-the-human-body#:~:text=Scientists%20concluded%20that%20the%20average,cells%20in%20your%20own%20body!; https://www.healthline.com/health/number-of-cells-in-body#:~:text=Humans%20are%20complex%20organisms%20made,Written%20out%2C%20that's%2030%2C000%2C000%2C000%2C000!; https://www.smithsonianmag.com/smart-news/there-are-372-trillion-cells-in-your-body-4941473/; https://www.ncbi.nlm.nih.gov/pmc/articles/PMC534598/

107   Sources consulted include : https://www.feelguide.com/2010/11/13/
        did-you-know-the-regeneration-of-the-human-body-2/; https://sci-
        ence.howstuffworks.com/life/cellular-microscopic/does-body-really-
        replace-seven-years2.htm; https://www.discovery.com/science/Body-
        Really-Replace-Itself-Every-7-Years

108   http://stephenleahy.net/2012/11/02/plankton-death-to-come-with-ac-
        id-oceans-and-sunlight

109   http://scienceline.ucsb.edu/getkey.php?key=3542

110   http://www.nbcnews.com/id/18442426/ns/health-diet_and_nutri-
        tion/t/declining-honeybees-threat-food-supply/#.VJd8rUCAJc

111   Crop Pollination Exposes Honey Bees to Pesticides Which Alters
        Their Susceptibility to the Gut Pathogen Nosema ceranae, PLOS
        ONE (July 24, 2013)—http://www.plosone.org/article/info%3A-
        doi%2F10.1371%2Fjournal.pone.0070182#authcontrib

112   https://www.nature.com/news/scientists-bust-myth-that-our-bodies-
        have-more-bacteria-than-human-cells-1.19136

113   https://academic.oup.com/qjmed/article/103/9/721/1581110

114   https://www.dreamit.com/journal/2018/4/24/size-healthcare-industry

115   World Health Organization, Tandon, Murray, Lauer & Evans, Measur-
        ing Overall Health System Performance for 191 Countries (2018)

116   https://www.opensecrets.org/lobby/top.php?indexType=i; https://
        www.opensecrets.org/federal-lobbying/industries/summary?cy-
        cle=2012&id=E01; https://www.opensecrets.org/federal-lobbying/
        sectors/summary?cycle=2002&id=H; https://www.opensecrets.org/
        federal-lobbying/sectors/summary?cycle=2019&id=D

117   Study Suggests Medical Errors Now Third Leading Cause of Death in
        the U.S, Johns Hopkins Medicine (2016); https://www.hopkinsmedi-
        cine.org/news/media/releases/study_suggests_medical_errors_now_
        third_leading_cause_of_death_in_the_us

118   https://www.thebalance.com/medical-bankruptcy-statistics-4154729

119   Barbara Starfield, "Is U.S. health really the best in the world?" Journal
        of the American Medical Association,

120   Sources consulted include https://sweeneylawfirm.com/content/un-
        necessary-surgeries#:~:text=Government%20health%20statistics%20
        shows%20that,around%208.9%20million%20a%20year; https://www.
        ncbi.nlm.nih.gov/pmc/articles/PMC5234149/; http://www.prweb.com/
        releases/2017/09/prweb14734455.htm

121   Source: http://www.ihi.org/about/news/Documents/IHIPressRelease_IHILaunchesCampaigntoReduceHarm_Dec06.pdf

122   http://en.wikipedia.org/wiki/List_of_withdrawn_drugs

123   http://www.naturalnews.com/021791.html

124   https://www.cdc.gov/chronicdisease/about/index.htm

125   https://blog.sfgate.com/smellthetruth/2012/04/11/ron-paul-fda-and-big-pharam-are-in-bed-together/

126   Eric G. Campbell, Ph.D., et. al., A National Survey of Physician-Industry Relationships, New England Journal of Medicine, (2007); https://www.nejm.org/doi/full/10.1056/nejmsa064508; https://www.jonbarron.org/article/drug-companies-lobby-physicians

127   http://articles.mercola.com/sites/articles/archive/2011/06/11/burzynski-the-movie.aspx#!

128   http://www.anh-usa.org/readers-corner-can-doctor-get-into-trouble-offering-natural-treatments

129   Sources consulted include: https://cohenhealthcarelaw.com/video-library/complementary-and-alternative-medicine-legal-issues/; https://www.pbs.org/wgbh/pages/frontline/shows/prescription/hazard/independent.html; https://www.modernhealthcare.com/article/20171219/NEWS/171219880/fda-to-target-high-risk-alternative-remedies; https://www.ncbi.nlm.nih.gov/pmc/articles/PMC2957745/; https://prospect.org/coronavirus/big-pharmas-game-of-control-covid-drug-treatment/https://www.fda.gov/regulatory-information/search-fda-guidance-documents/complementary-and-alternative-medicine-products-and-their-regulation-food-and-drug-administration

130   http://www.bostonreview.net/angell-big-pharma-bad-medicine

131   Sources consulted include: https://www.ncbi.nlm.nih.gov/pmc/articles/PMC3341916/; https://patient.info/mental-health/psychosomatic-disorders

132   Sources consulted include: https://www.ncbi.nlm.nih.gov/pmc/articles/PMC4020364/; https://www.ncbi.nlm.nih.gov/pmc/articles/PMC2913884/; https://en.wikipedia.org/wiki/Traditional_medicine

133   Congleton, Holze & Lazar, Mindfulness Can Literally Change Your Brain, (January 8, 2015) Harvard Business Review (https://hbr.org/2015/01/mindfulness-can-literally-change-your-brain)

134   Healthline, 12 Science-Based Benefits of Meditation, https://www.healthline.com/nutrition/12-benefits-of-meditation#section1

135   Silananda, U., & Heinze, R.I. (1990). The Four Foundations of Mind-
        fulness, Boston: Wisdom Publications; Smith, H. (1994), *The Illustrated
        World's Religions: A Guide to our Wisdom Traditions*, San Francisco:
        Harper-Collins; and Luis Felipe Morales Knight, *Mindfulness: History,
        Technologies, Research, Applications* (http://allansousa.files.wordpress.
        com/2009/11/mindfulnessarticleluis.pdf)

136   Rick Hanson, PhD, Relaxed and Contented: Activating the Parasym-
        pathetic Wing of Your Nervous System, Wisebrain.org (2007) (http://
        www.wisebrain.org/ParasympatheticNS.pdf0

137   Sources consulted include https://www.health.harvard.edu/diet-and-
        weight-loss/calories-burned-in-30-minutes-of-leisure-and-routine-ac-
        tivities; https://www.nutristrategy.com/activitylist4.htm

138   Sources consulted include https://www.health.harvard.edu/mind-and-
        mood/relaxation-techniques-breath-control-helps-quell-errant-stress-
        response; https://www.healthline.com/health/diaphragmatic-breathing;
        https://www.livestrong.com/article/92264-benefits-deep-breathing/;
        https://www.nytimes.com/2016/11/09/well/mind/breathe-exhale-re-
        peat-the-benefits-of-controlled-breathing.html; https://chopra.com/
        articles/a-great-addition-to-meditation-conscious-breathing; https://
        www.frequencymind.com/top-10-benefits-of-breathwork;

139   Vegetarian Times, Vegetarianism in America, https://www.veg-
        etariantimes.com/uncategorized/vegetarianism-in-america#tar-
        getText=The%20%E2%80%9CVegetarianism%20in%20Ameri-
        ca%E2%80%9D%20study,no%20animal%20products%20at%20all.

140   NAMI, The United States Meat Industry at a Glance

141   Sources consulted include: https://www.forbes.com/sites/jeffmc-
        mahon/2019/04/04/meat-and-agriculture-are-worse-for-the-cli-
        mate-than-dirty-energy-steven-chu-says/?sh=120b7fa911f9; https://
        ourworldindata.org/environmental-impacts-of-food; https://
        awellfedworld.org/livestock-climate-advanced/; https://www.na-
        ture.com/articles/d41586-019-02409-7; https://news.un.org/en/sto-
        ry/2018/11/1025271

142   https://www.ncbi.nlm.nih.gov/pmc/articles/PMC5466942/

143   http://static.water.org/pdfs/Water%20Crisis%205-10.pdf

144   UNESCO The Green, Blue, and Grey Water Footprint of Crops and
        Derived Crop Products (2010) http://www.waterfootprint.org/Reports/
        Report47-WaterFootprintCrops-Vol1.pdf; UNESCO The Green, Blue,
        and Grey Water Footprint of Farm Animals and Animal Products
        (2010) http://www.waterfootprint.org/Reports/Report-48-WaterFoot-
        print-AnimalProducts-Vol1.pdf

145 Sources consulted include https://waterfootprint.org/en/resources/ waterstat/product-water-footprint-statistics/; https://www.watered-ucation.org/post/food-facts-how-much-water-does-it-take-produce; https://www.treehugger.com/green-food/from-lettuce-to-beef-whats-the-water-footprint-of-your-food.html; https://88acres.com/blogs/ news/water-footprint-of-seeds-vs-nuts

146 Source: https://en.wikipedia.org/wiki/Allan_Savory#cite_note-1

147 Grand View Research, Inc., Food and Grocery Retail Market Analysis Report by Type (2018)

148 U.S. Fish & Wildlife Service, ECOS Environmental Conservation Online System, https://ecos.fws.gov/ecp/; Shilcutt, 10 Fish You're Eating that are Endangers Species, Houston Press (2011), https://www. houstonpress.com/restaurants/10-fish-youre-eating-that-are-endan-gered-species-6439972

149 Sources consulted include https://www.eufic.org/en/whats-in-food/ article/what-are-proteins-and-what-is-their-function-in-the-body; https://en.wikipedia.org/wiki/Protein; https://www.webmd.com/men/ features/benefits-protein#1; https://www.healthline.com/nutrition/ functions-of-protein#section8

150 Sources consulted include http://www.fao.org/ag/humannutrition/359 78-02317b979a686a57aa4593304ffc17f06.pdf; https://www.diaascalcu-lator.com; https://www.ncbi.nlm.nih.gov/pmc/articles/PMC6322793/; https://en.wikipedia.org/wiki/Protein_quality; https://www.research-gate.net/figure/PDCAAS-and-DiAAS-for-selected-isolated-pro-teins-and-foods_tbl1_316856528; https://www.mondoscience.com/ blog/2017/10/25/100-amino-acid-score; https://www.todaysdietitian. com/newarchives/0217p26.shtml; https://www.mdpi.com/2071-1050/11/10/2747/htm; https://www.nutritionadvance.com/types-of-protein-powder/

151 https://www.drperlmutter.com/learn/faq/

152 Sources consulted include https://en.wikipedia.org/wiki/Protein_qual-ity; https://www.ncbi.nlm.nih.gov/pmc/articles/PMC5041535/#:~:-text=For%20example%2C%20the%20PDCAAS%20(DIAAS,0.66%20 for%20dehulled%20hemp%20seed; https://www.researchgate.net/pub-lication/47555086_Evaluating_the_Quality_of_Protein_from_Hemp_ Seed_Cannabis_sativa_L_Products_Through_the_use_of_the_Pro-tein_Digestibility-Corrected_Amino_Acid_Score_Method

153 https://www.health.com/nutrition/spirulina-benefits

154 Sources consulted include https://en.wikipedia.org/wiki/Ami-

no_acid; http://pennstatehershey.adam.com/content.aspx?produc-tid=117&pid=1&gid=002222; https://healthyeating.sfgate.com/differ-ence-between-essential-non-essential-amino-acids-9687.html

155   https://www.hsph.harvard.edu/nutritionsource/carbohydrates/; https://en.wikipedia.org/wiki/Carbohydrate; https://www.healthline.com/nutrition/good-carbs-bad-carbs#section3; https://health.usnews.com/wellness/food/articles/2019-02-01/complex-vs-simple-vs-refined-car-bohydrates-whats-the-difference; https://www.health.harvard.edu/healthbeat/8-principles-of-low-glycemic-eating#:~:text=Eight%20principles%20of%20low%2Dglycemic,glycemic%20index%20than%20typical%20desserts.

156   https://en.wikipedia.org/wiki/Fat; https://www.healthline.com/health/brown-fat#1; https://www.healthline.com/health/food-nutrition/satu-rated-vs-unsaturated-fat; https://www.mayoclinic.org/healthy-lifestyle/nutrition-and-healthy-eating/in-depth/fat/art-20045550; https://www.healthline.com/nutrition/omega-3-6-9-overview#section3

157   International Journal of Science and Research, Dodecanoic-Acid in Extra Virgin Coconut Oil, May Reduce the Incidence of Heart Disease and Cancer in Humans, (2015), https://www.ijsr.net/archive/v5i11/ART20162857.pdf

158   Patrick Seale and Mitchell Lazar, Brown Fat in Humans: Turning Up the Heat on Obesity, American Diabetes Association, (2009); http://diabetes.diabetesjournals.org/content/58/7/1482

159   https://hvmn.com/blog/fasting/can-if-turn-white-fat-into-brown-fat

160   Sources consulted include https://www.health.harvard.edu/stay-ing-healthy/listing_of_vitamins; https://en.wikipedia.org/wiki/Dietary_Reference_Intake; https://en.wikipedia.org/wiki/Dietary_Reference_Intake, https://www.webmd.com/food-recipes/guide/vita-mins-and-minerals-good-food-sources#1

161   Sources consulted include https://www.health.harvard.edu/stay-ing-healthy/listing_of_vitamins; https://en.wikipedia.org/wiki/Dietary_Reference_Intake; https://en.wikipedia.org/wiki/Dietary_Reference_Intake, https://www.webmd.com/food-recipes/guide/vita-mins-and-minerals-good-food-sources#1

162   Sources consulted include https://www.medicalnewstoday.com/arti-cles/319704.php#examples, https://en.wikipedia.org/wiki/Enzyme

163   https://healthyalternativesinc.com/what-are-enzymes/

164   https://pubmed.ncbi.nlm.nih.gov/8450725/; http://www.longlonglife.org/en/transhumanism-longevity/aging/biological-causes-aging/

165   Sources consulted include https://www.healthline.com/nutri-tion/10-healthy-herbs-and-spices#section1; https://www.webmd.com/healthy-aging/over-50-nutrition-17/spices-and-herbs-health-benefits; https://www.ncbi.nlm.nih.gov/pubmed/30651162; https://foodfacts.mercola.com/herbs-and-spices.html

166   Sources consulted include https://www.ncbi.nlm.nih.gov/pmc/articles/PMC2841576/; https://articles.mercola.com/antioxidants.aspx; https://www.healthline.com/nutrition/foods-high-in-antioxidants#section11; https://www.medicalnewstoday.com/articles/325873.php

167   Sources consulted include David Wolfe, Superfoods, North Atlantic Books (2009); https://www.health.harvard.edu/blog/10-superfoods-to-boost-a-healthy-diet-2018082914463; https://www.healthline.com/nutrition/true-superfoods; https://www.womansday.com/food-recipes/food-drinks/g2211/best-superfoods/

168   https://www.coconutresearchcenter.org/

169   Sources consulted include https://www.webmd.com/diet/ss/slide-show-serving-sizes; https://www.webmd.com/diet/healthtool-food-cal-orie-counter; https://www.nia.nih.gov/health/serving-and-portion-sizes-how-much-should-i-eat; https://www.healthline.com/nutrition/portion-control#section3; https://www.webmd.com/diet/printables/portion-control-size-guide

170   Sources consulted include https://www.health.harvard.edu/diet-and-weight-loss/calories-burned-in-30-minutes-of-leisure-and-routine-activities; https://www.webmd.com/fitness-exercise/healthtool-exer-cise-calculator

171   Sources consulted include Mercola, Ketogenic Diet: A Beginner's Ultimate Guide to Keto, https://articles.mercola.com/ketogenic-diet.aspx; https://www.hsph.harvard.edu/nutritionsource/healthy-weight/diet-reviews/ketogenic-diet/

172   https://www.hsph.harvard.edu/nutritionsource/healthy-weight/diet-re-views/ketogenic-diet/

173   http://articles.mercola.com/ketogenic-diet.aspx#_edn4

174   Sources consulted include NIH, The Alkaline Diet: Is There Evidence That an Alkaline pH Diet Benefits Health? https://www.ncbi.nlm.nih.gov/pmc/articles/PMC3195546

175   Sources consulted include https://www.ncbi.nlm.nih.gov/pmc/articles/PMC3195546/; https://www.ncbi.nlm.nih.gov/books/NBK470195/; https://www.abundanthealth4u.com/optimal-body-ph

176   Sources consulted include Tafton, Acidic environment triggers genes that help cancer cells metastasize, MIT (2019), https://medicalxpress.com/news/2019-03-acidic-environment-triggers-genes-cancer.html; Robey and Nesbit, Investigating Mechanisms of Alkalinization for Reducing Primary Breast Tumor Invasion, NCBI (2013), https://www.ncbi.nlm.nih.gov/pmc/articles/PMC3722989/; https://journals.plos.org/plosone/article?id=10.1371/journal.pone.0076327

177   Gilles, MRI of the tumor microenvironment, JMRI (2002), https://onlinelibrary.wiley.com/doi/full/10.1002/jmri.10181

178   NIH, The Alkaline Diet: Is There Evidence That an Alkaline pH Diet Benefits Health?; https://www.ncbi.nlm.nih.gov/pmc/articles/PMC3195546

179   Mercola, https://articles.mercola.com/sites/articles/archive/2018/05/07/drinking-baking-soda-for-autoimmune-disease.aspx

180   Sources consulted include https://greenopedia.com/wp-content/uploads/Alkaline-Acid-Food-Chart-Printable.pdf; https://www.avocadoninja.co.uk/pages/list-of-alkaline-foods: http://www.icakusa.com/content/alkaline-diet

181   Sources consulted include https://www.hydrationforhealth.com/en/; https://www.ncbi.nlm.nih.gov/pmc/articles/PMC2908954/; https://www.cnn.com/2017/09/27/health/benefits-of-water-and-fluids/index.html

182   http://freshlysqueezedwater.org.uk/waterarticle_watercontent.php

183   EWG's Tap Water Database, https://www.ewg.org/tapwater/state-of-american-drinking-water.php#.WYDfkoqQwUE

184   https://www.ehn.org/bpa-pollution-2645493129.html?rebelltitem=3#rebelltitem3

185   Mercola, https://www.mercola.com/article/water.htm

186   https://www.healthline.com/nutrition/hydrogen-water#benefits

187   NIH, https://www.ncbi.nlm.nih.gov/pmc/articles/PMC3703265

188   Medium, What You Need to Know About Deuterium: Fatigue, Cancer, Metabolic Issues; https://medium.com/@corey_nelson/what-you-need-to-know-about-deuterium-fatigue-cancer-metabolic-issues-82c8f6748e34

189   Source: NIH, https://www.ncbi.nlm.nih.gov/pubmed/23441611

190   https://selfhacked.com/blog/deuterium-depleted-water

191   Sources consulted include Marsden, The Complete Book of Food-com-

bining, Piatkus (2000); https://www.ayurveda.com/pdf/food_com-bining.pdf; https://health.usnews.com/health-news/blogs/eat-run/2015/05/12/debunking-the-myth-of-food-combining

192   Sources consulted include D'Adamo, Eat Right 4 Your Type (Up-dated and Revised), New American Library (2016); https://www.health.harvard.edu/blog/diet-not-working-maybe-its-not-your-type-2017051211678

193   Joseph Pizzorno, ND, Mitochondria-Fundamental to Life and Health, Integrative Medicine: A Clinician's Journal (2014); https://www.ncbi.nlm.nih.gov/pmc/articles/PMC4684129

194   Sources consulted include http://www.oprah.com/health/dr-oz-on-cleansing-do-you-need-a-cleanse/all; https://www.health.harvard.edu/staying-healthy/the-dubious-practice-of-detox

195   Sources consulted include https://www.fishertitus.org/health/the-health-benefits-of-a-body-cleanse; https://www.webmd.com/diet/features/detox-diets-cleansing-body#1; https://www.rmalab.com/ben-efits-detoxification; https://www.gaiam.com/blogs/discover/10-bene-fits-of-colon-cleansing

196   Sources consulted include https://www.health.harvard.edu/stay-ing-healthy/can-scheduled-fasting-improve-your-health; https://www.healthline.com/nutrition/fasting-benefits; https://www.dietdoctor.com/7-benefits-of-fasting; https://www.healthline.com/nutrition/intermittent-fasting-guide#methods; https://www.strongerbyscience.com/intermittent-fasting-study/; https://www.healthline.com/nutri-tion/10-health-benefits-of-intermittent-fasting#section1; https://fit-ness.mercola.com/sites/fitness/archive/2016/04/29/peak-fasting.aspx

197   Sources consulted include https://www.medicalnewstoday.com/articles/323136.php; https://www.huffpost.com/entry/juice-cleans-es_b_4549641; https://www.health.harvard.edu/healthy-eating/juicing-fad-or-fab

198   Sources consulted include https://www.ncbi.nlm.nih.gov/pmc/articles/PMC3576896/; https://en.wikipedia.org/wiki/Master_Cleanse; https://www.ncbi.nlm.nih.gov/pmc/articles/PMC3680567/

199   https://www.healthline.com/nutrition/8-benefits-of-cayenne-pepper

200   Sources consulted include https://pkdcure.org/blog/spices-and-herbs/; https://www.kidney.org/atoz/content/herbalsupp; https://www.health-line.com/health/kidney-cleanse#hydration; https://drclarkstore.com/kidney-cleanse-instructions/

201   Sources consulted include https://drclarkstore.com/parasite-cleanse-di-

rections/; https://www.medicalnewstoday.com/articles/326696.php#ef-fectiveness; https://www.ncbi.nlm.nih.gov/pubmed/28606189; https://www.healthline.com/health/human-parasite-cleanse#diet; https://microbeformulas.com/blogs/microbe-formulas/12-parasite-die-off-symptoms-and-how-to-fight-them

202   Sources consulted include http://www.drclarkinfocenter.com/en/cleanses_clean-ups/liver_cleanses/advanced_livere_cleanse.php; https://www.mitoq.com/blog/blog/19-super-foods-naturally-cleanse-liver

203   Sources consulted include https://www.gaiam.com/blogs/discover/10-benefits-of-colon-cleansing; https://www.webmd.com/balance/guide/natural-colon-cleansing-is-it-necessary#1

204   Sources consulted include https://www.ncbi.nlm.nih.gov/pmc/articles/PMC4049052/; https://www.versusarthritis.org/about-arthritis/treatments/therapies/hydrotherapy/

205   Sources consulted include https://articles.mercola.com/sites/articles/archive/2016/06/19/heavy-metal-detoxification.aspx; https://nccih.nih.gov/health/chelation

206   Sources consulted include https://www.ncbi.nlm.nih.gov/pmc/articles/PMC4691126/; https://www.govinfo.gov/content/pkg/CHRG-111shrg54469/html/CHRG-111shrg54469.htm; https://www.ncbi.nlm.nih.gov/pmc/articles/PMC6504940/; https://www.ncbi.nlm.nih.gov/pmc/articles/PMC4144270/

207   Margaret Sears, Chelation: Harnessing and Enhancing Heavy Metal Detoxification-A Review, Scientific World Journal (2013), https://www.ncbi.nlm.nih.gov/pmc/articles/PMC3654245/

208   Sources consulted include https://drclarkstore.com/heavy-metal-cleanse-directions/; https://www.ncbi.nlm.nih.gov/pmc/articles/PMC3654245/; https://www.ncbi.nlm.nih.gov/pmc/articles/PMC4303853/; https://www.gaiam.com/blogs/discover/how-to-detox-from-heavy-metals-and-mercury; https://www.mercola.com/article/mercury/detox_protocol.htm; https://www.who.int/selection_medicines/committees/expert/18/applications/4_2_LeadOralChelators.pdf

209   Sources consulted include https://www.healthline.com/nutrition/nac-benefits; https://pubmed.ncbi.nlm.nih.gov/1540408/#:~:text=We%20have%20shown%20directly%20that,stress%20and%20replenishes%20depleted%20GSH.; https://www.mskcc.org/cancer-care/integrative-medicine/herbs/n-acetylcysteine

210   Sources consulted include https://www.nccih.nih.gov/health/ques-

tions-and-answers-the-nih-trials-of-edta-chelation-therapy-for-cor-onary-heart-disease#:~:text=In%20the%20case%20of%20ED-TA,treatment%20of%20heavy%20metal%20poisoning.; https://www.mayoclinic.org/diseases-conditions/heart-disease/expert-answers/chelation-therapy/faq-20157449

211   Sources consulted include https://www.ncbi.nlm.nih.gov/pmc/articles/PMC1128144/; https://www.ncbi.nlm.nih.gov/pmc/articles/PMC2774660/

212   Sources consulted include https://www.inc.com/rhett-power/a-day-of-rest-12-scientific-reasons-it-works.html; https://www.medicalnewstoday.com/articles/325353.php

213   Sources consulted include https://www.mind-your-reality.com/brain_waves.html; https://www.scientificamerican.com/article/what-is-the-function-of-t-1997-12-22/

214   Sources consulted include https://www.healthline.com/nutrition/sleep-aids; https://thesleepdoctor.com/2018/12/25/10-of-the-most-effective-natural-sleep-aids/

215   https://curiosity.com/topics/does-your-body-really-replace-itself-every-7-years-curiosity; https://science.howstuffworks.com/life/cellular-microscopic/does-body-really-replace-seven-years2.htm

216   Sources include https://www.oxfordhandbooks.com/view/10.1093/oxfordhb/9780195398694.001.0001/oxfordhb-9780195398694-e-012; https://clarkrelationshiplab.yale.edu/sites/default/files/files/Interpersonal%20attraction%20in%20exchance%20and%20commual%20relationships.pdf

217   Dr. Cynthia Thaik, Love Heals, Huffington Post (2013), https://www.huffpost.com/entry/love-health-benefits_b_3131370

218   https://news.osu.edu/loneliness-like-chronic-stress-taxes-the-immune-system

219   Laura Entis, Chronic Loneliness Is a Modern-Day Epidemic, Fortune (2016), http://fortune.com/2016/06/22/loneliness-is-a-modern-day-epidemic/

220   HSRA, The Loneliness Epidemic, https://www.hrsa.gov/enews/past-issues/2019/january-17/loneliness-epidemic;

221   Sources: https://psycnet.apa.org/record/2016-03251-001; https://www.ncbi.nlm.nih.gov/pmc/articles/PMC3150158/; https://medicalxpress.com/news/2019-06-lifelong-health-benefits-intimacy.html; https://www.health.harvard.edu/newsletter_article/the-health-ben-

efits-of-strong-relationships; https://www.insider.com/health-bene-
fits-of-being-in-a-relationship-dating-someone-2017-10; https://www.
ncbi.nlm.nih.gov/pmc/articles/PMC5549103/, https://www.sas.roches-
ter.edu/psy/people/faculty/reis_harry/assets/pdf/Reisetal.JPSP_2010.
pdf

222   Oscar N. E. Kjell, Sustainable Well-Being: A Potential Synergy Between
       Sustainability and Well-Being Research, Review General Psychology
       (2011)

223   Supporting sources include https://ucsdnews.ucsd.edu/archive/news-
       rel/science/YeastGenes.asp; https://physicsworld.com/a/lipid-nanotab-
       let-makes-tiny-biocomputer/

224   Sources consulted include Lipton, The Biology of Belief, Hay House
       (2005); https://www.ncbi.nlm.nih.gov/pmc/articles/PMC4224074/;
       https://en.wikipedia.org/wiki/Electromagnetic_theories_of_conscious-
       ness; http://philsci-archive.pitt.edu/1210/1/PCC.pdf; https://www.ncbi.
       nlm.nih.gov/pubmed/21856569

225   https://en.wikipedia.org/wiki/DNA

226   https://en.wikipedia.org/wiki/RNA

227   Sources consulted include https://en.wikipedia.org/wiki/Nucleic_acid_
       sequence; https://ghr.nlm.nih.gov/primer/basics/dna

228   Sources consulted include https://genetics.thetech.org/ask/ask83;
       https://www.sciencefocus.com/the-human-body/what-is-dna/

229   Sources consulted include NCBI, The role of p21 in regulating mam-
       malian regeneration, https://www.ncbi.nlm.nih.gov/pmc/articles/
       PMC3152998/; NIH, Regenerative wound healing via inflamma-
       tion-modulating biomaterials, http://grantome.com/grant/NIH/R01-
       DE021104-04

230   Sources consulted include https://www.sciencedaily.com/releas-
       es/2011/03/110331104014.htm; https://www.technologyreview.
       com/s/419590/quantum-entanglement-holds-dna-together-say-physi-
       cists/

231   Sources consulted include https://en.wikipedia.org/wiki/Randy_Jirtle;
       http://randyjirtle.com/research; https://www.ncbi.nlm.nih.gov/pmc/
       articles/PMC1392256/

232   Sources consulted include https://www.npr.org/2011/08/19/139757702/
       dont-throw-it-out-junk-dna-essential-in-evolution; https://evolution-
       news.org/2011/10/post_32/

233   Sources consulted include https://en.wikipedia.org/wiki/Fritz-Al-

bert_Popp; https://www.biontologyarizona.com/dr-fritz-albert-popp/; https://www.iumab.org/prof-fritz-albert-popp/

234 Sources include http://www.viewzone.com/dnax.html; http://humanityincorporate.blogspot.com/2014/02/photogravitation-story-of-entanglement.html

235 Cosic, I, Cosic, D and Lazar, K 2016, 'Environmental light and its relationship with electromagnetic resonances of biomolecular interactions, as predicted by the resonant recognition model', International Journal of Environmental Research and Public Health, vol. 13, no. 7, 647, pp. 1-10; http://researchbank.rmit.edu.au/list/?cat=quick_filter&form_name=adv_search&search_keys%5Bcore_66%5D=2006065538

236 Sources consulted include Popinin, The DNA Phantom Effect—Direct Measurement of a New Field in the Vacuum Substructure, https://www.bibliotecapleyades.net/ciencia/ciencia_genetica04.htm; Gariaev, Investigation of the fluctuation dynamics of DNA solutions by laser correlations spectroscopy, ResearchGate, https://www.researchgate.net/publication/281411802_Investigation_of_the_fluctuation_dynamics_of_DNA_solutions_by_laser_correlation_spectroscopy

237 Bruce Lipton, The Biology of Belief, Hay House (2016); https://www.ncbi.nlm.nih.gov/pmc/articles/PMC6438088/; https://www.brucelipton.com/the-wisdom-your-cells/

238 http://processworkhub.gr/blog/wp-content/uploads/2012/10/Bruce-Lipton-How-Your-Beliefs-Control-Your-Biology.pdf

239 Source: Merriam Webster Dictionary

240 https://en.wikipedia.org/wiki/Human_extinction

241 https://en.wikipedia.org/wiki/Doomsday_argument

242 PsychCentral, Antisocial Personality Disorder Symptoms, https://psychcentral.com/disorders/antisocial-personality-disorder/symptoms

243 EPA, Sources of Greenhouse Gas Emissions, https://www.epa.gov/ghgemissions/sources-greenhouse-gas-emissions

244 EIA, Energy and the environment explained, eia.gov/energyexplained/energy-and-the-environment/where-greenhouse-gases-come-from.php

245 U.S. Energy-Related Carbon Dioxide Emissions, 2013, U.S. Energy Information, Administration (2014) http://www.eia.gov/environment/emissions/carbon, http://www3.epa.gov/climatechange/ghgemissions/gases/co2.html

246 http://climate.nasa.gov/scientific-consensus/

247    $29,000,000,000,000: A Detailed Look at the Fed's Bailout by Funding Facility and Recipient, James Felkerson, Levy Economics Institute of Bard College (2011)

248   SIPRI, Global military expenditure sees largest annual increase in a decade—says SIPRI—reaching $1917 billion in 2019; https://www.sipri.org/media/press-release/2020/global-military-expenditure-sees-largest-annual-increase-decade-says-sipri-reaching-1917-billion#:~:text=Global%20military%20expenditure%20sees%20largest%20annual%20increase%20in%20a%20decade,reaching%20%241917%20billion%20in%202019&text=(Stockholm%2C%2027%20April%202020),Peace%20Research%20Institute%20(SIPRI).

249   http://prop1.org/2000/98nucost.htm

250   http://time.com/3651697/afghanistan-war-cost/

251   https://www.theguardian.com/global-development/2017/jan/16/worlds-eight-richest-people-have-same-wealth-as-poorest-50

252   http://www.savetheamazon.org/rainforeststats.htm

253   Correctional Populations in the United States, Glaze, Bureau of Justice (2013); http://www.bjs.gov/index.cfm?ty=pbdetail&iid=4843

254   http://californiateacherpathway.org/america-has-more-prisoners-than-high-school-teachers/

255   Education at a Glance, OECD http://www.oecd.org/edu/EAG-Interim-report.pdf

256   Measuring Overall Health System Performance for 191 Countries, Ajay Tandon, et al., World Health Organization

257   SIPRI, Global military expenditure sees largest annual increase in a decade—says SIPRI—reaching $1917 billion in 2019; https://www.sipri.org/media/press-release/2020/global-military-expenditure-sees-largest-annual-increase-decade-says-sipri-reaching-1917-billion#:~:text=Global%20military%20expenditure%20sees%20largest%20annual%20increase%20in%20a%20decade,reaching%20%241917%20billion%20in%202019&text=(Stockholm%2C%2027%20April%202020),Peace%20Research%20Institute%20(SIPRI).

258   http://www.bloomberg.com/apps/news?pid=newsarchive&sid=axB-4c8xDmBAk

259   https://blog.marketresearch.com/the-gambling-industry-forecasts-and-trends#:~:text=According%20to%20The%20Business%20Research,rate%20of%205.9%25%20through%202022.

260   World Health Organization, Global costs and benefits of drink-

ing-water supply and sanitation interventions to reach MDG target and universal coverage, p. 5 (2012); http://apps.who.int/iris/bitstream/10665/75140/1/WHO_HSE_WSH_12.01_eng.pdf

261   http://www.ukessays.com/dissertations/business/personal-care-products-industry.php

262   World Health Organization, Global costs and benefits of drinking-water supply and sanitation interventions to reach MDG target and universal coverage, p. 5 (2012) -http://apps.who.int/iris/bitstream/10665/75140/1/WHO_HSE_WSH_12.01_eng.

263   http://www.researchandmarkets.com/reports/2238951/pet_care_forecast_revisit_2012_how_resilient_is

264   http://www.unfpa.org/public/home/news/pid/11239

265   http://www.prweb.com/releases/gums_chewing_gum/sugarless_bubble_gum/prweb9246521.htm; https://www.chicagotribune.com/business/ct-xpm-2010-10-02-ct-biz-1003-gum-wars-20101001-story.html

266   http://www.unesco.org/education/tlsf/mods/theme_a/interact/www.worldgame.org/wwwproject/what03.shtml

267   http://www.businesswire.com/news/home/20160718005552/en/Jewellery-Records-316-Billion-Sales-2016-15

268   http://www.unesco.org/education/tlsf/mods/theme_a/interact/www.worldgame.org/wwwproject/what07.shtml

269   https://www.cdc.gov/healthywater/global/wash_statistics.html

270   http://www.worldwildlife.org/pages/living-planet-report-2014

271   http://climate.nasa.gov/scientific-consensus

272   https://www.theguardian.com/global-development/2017/jan/16/worlds-eight-richest-people-have-same-wealth-as-poorest-50

273   http://www.hannenabintuherland.com/europe/the-federal-reserve-cartel-the-eight-families-who-own-the-usa-the-rise-of-bis-imf-world-bank-dean-henderson-on-free21-org/

274   Niall Ferguson, The Square and the Tower, pp. 21-22, Penguin Books (2017); Also see https://en.wikipedia.org/wiki/New_World_Order_(conspiracy_theory)

275   Source: https://scholar.princeton.edu/sites/default/files/slaughter/files/superclass.pdf

276   Source: https://www.inc.com/jt-odonnell/how-this-1-question-can-make-you-choose-wrong-career.html

277   Constructing The Self, Constructing America: A Cultural History Of Psychotherapy, (Cushman, 1995, p. 157).

278   Constructing The Self, Constructing America: A Cultural History Of Psychotherapy, (Cushman, 1995, p. 6).

279   Consumerism and Extinction, Cary Dakin, (2014); Constructing The Self, Constructing America: A Cultural History Of Psychotherapy, (Cushman, 1995, p. 154).

280   Sources consulted include Journal of Economic Surveys, Dimant, Causes and Effects of Corruption: What has Past Decade's Empirical Research Taught Us? A Survey (2016); https://www.transparency.org/what-is-corruption; https://en.wikipedia.org/wiki/Corruption; https://www.worldbank.org/en/topic/governance/brief/anti-corruption; http://documents.worldbank.org/curated/en/113281515516828746/pdf/WPS8299.pdf;

281   Kaufmann, Daniel; Vicente, Pedro (2005). "Legal Corruption"(PDF) World Bank.

282   Sources consulted include https://ourworldindata.org/corruption; https://en.wikipedia.org/wiki/Corruption_Perceptions_Index; https://www.transparency.org/news/feature/corruption_in_the_usa_the_difference_a_year_makes

283   Sources consulted include https://smallbusiness.chron.com/corporate-lobbying-11729.html; https://en.wikipedia.org/wiki/Lobbying_in_the_United_States#cite_note-twsN411-1; https://www.thenation.com/article/shadow-lobbying-complex/

284   Forbes, Central Banking's Connection To Warfare Is Intimate, Brian Domitrovic, https://www.forbes.com/sites/briandomitrovic/2018/07/01/central-bankings-connection-to-warfare-is-intimate/#238647777299

285   Sources consulted include https://www.icij.org/investigations/makingkilling/; https://www.washingtonpost.com/graphics/2019/investigations/afghanistan-papers/afghanistan-war-corruption-government/

286   https://en.wikipedia.org/wiki/Military%E2%80%93industrial_complex

287   https://en.wikipedia.org/wiki/False_flag

288   Tobias, Fritz, The Reichstag Fire, New York: Putnam, 1964, pages 26–28.; https://en.wikipedia.org/wiki/Reichstag_fire

289   Source: https://en.wikipedia.org/wiki/USS_Maine_(ACR-1)

290   Source : https://en.wikipedia.org/wiki/Gleiwitz_incident

291   Source: https://en.wikipedia.org/wiki/1953_Iranian_
coup_d%27%C3%A9tat; https://en.wikipedia.org/wiki/SAVAK

292   Source: https://en.wikipedia.org/wiki/Gulf_of_Tonkin_incident

293   Source: https://en.wikipedia.org/wiki/9/11_conspiracy_theories

294   https://www.gaia.com/article/911-false-flag

295   https://fpif.org/afghanistans_energy_war; https://www.nytimes.
com/2018/02/23/world/asia/afghanistan-pipeline-tapi.html

296   Sources consulted include https://en.wikipedia.org/wiki/Patriot_Act;
https://www.aclu.org/other/how-patriot-act-2-would-further-erode-
basic-checks-government-power-keep-america-safe-and-free

297   Source: https://watson.brown.edu/costsofwar/costs/economic

298   Dan Hurley, Grandma's Experiences Leae a Mark on Your Genes,
Discover, (2013), http://discovermagazine.com/2013/may/13-grand-
mas-experiences-leave-epigenetic-mark-on-your-genes

299   Christopher Bergland, "Imagination Can Change Perceptions of
Reality", Journal of Management, Psychology Today (2013); https://
www.psychologytoday.com/us/blog/the-athletes-way/201306/imagina-
tion-can-change-perceptions-reality

300   https://en.wikipedia.org/wiki/Historicity_of_Jesus

301   https://www.npr.org/2019/02/11/691334123/swedens-cashless-experi-
ment-is-it-too-much-too-fast
http://wolfstreet.com/2015/11/07/first-they-came-for-the-pennies-in-
the-war-on-cash; https://www.riksbank.se/globalassets/media/statistik/
betalningsstatistik/2018/payments-patterns-in-sweden-2018.pdf

302   https://technology.ihs.com/582859/smart-card-ic-shipments-to-reach-
128-billion-units-in-2020

303   https://syncedreview.com/2019/07/17/elon-musks-neuralink-plans-to-
put-chips-in-human-brains-by-2020/

304   Kimberly Amedeo, the balance, Central Banks, Their Functions and
Role, https://www.thebalance.com/what-is-a-central-bank-definition-
function-and-role-3305827

305   Source: https://www.worldometers.info/geography/how-many-coun-
tries-are-there-in-the-world/

306   World Population Review, Countries Without Central Banks 2019,
http://worldpopulationreview.com/countries/countries-without-cen-
tral-banks/

307   http://www.forbes.com/sites/pascalemmanuelgobry/2013/01/08/all-money-is-fiat-money

308   Source: https://upload.wikimedia.org/wikipedia/commons/4/4a/Modern_Money_Mechanics.pdf

309   https://www.federalreserve.gov/aboutthefed/section16.htm

310   Source: https://en.wikipedia.org/wiki/Federal_Reserve_Note

311   Source: https://en.wikipedia.org/wiki/Fractional-reserve_banking

312   The Federal Reserve Bank of Atlanta, Fractional Reserve Banking-An Economist's Perspective, https://www.frbatlanta.org/education/classroom-economist/fractional-reserve-banking/economists-perspective-transcript

313   https://www.bloomberg.com/quicktake/negative-interest-rates

314   Source: https://en.wikipedia.org/wiki/Government_debt

315   Source: https://en.m.wikipedia.org/wiki/2019_United_States_federal_budget

316   Source: https://www.pewresearch.org/fact-tank/2019/07/24/facts-about-the-national-debt/

317   The Economist, History of the Central Banks, https://www.economist.com/briefing/2017/04/27/the-history-of-central-banks

318   https://en.wikipedia.org/wiki/History_of_central_banking_in_the_United_States#cite_note-6

319   https://www.bloomberg.com/news/articles/2013-09-20/buffett-says-federal-reserve-is-greatest-hedge-fund-in-history

320   Barry Ritholtz, Bailout Nation, p.15, John Wiley & Sons, Inc. (2009); Also see: https://www.monticello.org/site/research-and-collections/private-banks-spurious-quotation; According to Montecello, the statement was not in found in Jefferson's writings and is more accurately contained in the following: "And I sincerely believe with you, that banking establishments are more dangerous than standing armies; & that the principle of spending money to be paid by posterity, under the name of funding, is but swindling futurity on a large scale." "Bank-paper must be suppressed, and the circulating medium must be restored to the nation to whom it belongs."

321   Nelson D. Schwartz, As Debt Rises, the Government Will Soon Spend More on Interest Than on the Military, New York Times (2017); https://www.nytimes.com/2018/09/25/business/economy/us-government-debt-interest.html

322   https://www.bis.org/about/index.htm

323   The Tower of Basel: Secretive Plans for the Issuing of a Global Currency, Ellen Brown (2009); League of Nations Treaty Series (1930) , p. 445-446; Constituent Charter of the Bank of International Settlements (The Hague Convention of 1930); Brussels Protocol regarding the immunities of the Bank for International Settlements (1936); Agreement between the Swiss Federal Council and the Bank of International Settlements to determine the Bank's legal status in Switzerland (2003); Statutes of the Bank of International Settlements, as amended, (2005); https://www.change.org/p/united-nations-revoke-world-bank-group-bis-imf-immunities-from-financial-regulation-judicial-action

324   https://en.wikipedia.org/wiki/IG_Farben; https://en.wikipedia.org/wiki/Bank_for_International_Settlements

325   Ibid

326   UN Inclusive Wealth Report 2012 and Daniel Kahneman and Angus Deaton: High income improves evaluation of life but not emotional well-being, Doug Short: Happiness Revisited: A Household Income of $75K, Council for Community & Economic Research, D.G. Myers, Income and Happiness in the United States 1957-2004 (2007) http://www.huffingtonpost.com/2014/07/17/map-happiness-benchmark_n_5592194.html

327   Betsey Stevenson, Juston Wolfers, Economic Growth and Subjective Well-Being: Reassessing the Easterlin Paradox, National Bureau of Economic Research, (2008), https://www.nber.org/papers/w1428 Robert Wiblin, *Everything you need to know about whether money makes you happy,* 80,000 Hours (2016), https://80000hours.org/articles/money-and-happiness

328   Skandia International, Skandia International Wealth Sentiiment Monitor, (2012), http://www.huffingtonpost.com/2012/12/02/income-happiness_n_2220693.html

329   https://prospect.org/article/money-buy-happinees/

330   https://www.forbes.com/sites/susanadams/2013/10/10/unhappy-employees-outnumber-happy-ones-by-two-to-one-worldwide/#4c-1b3e3a362a

331   Kahneman, D., Deaton, A. (2010). High income improves evaluation of life but not emotional well-being. Proceedings of the National Academy of Sciences of the United States of America, 107(38), 16489-16493; https://scholar.princeton.edu/deaton/publications/high-income-im-

proves-evaluation-life-not-emotional-well-being; https://en.wikipedia.org/wiki/Daniel_Kahneman

332   http://scholar.harvard.edu/files/danielgilbert/files/if-money-doesnt-make-you-happy.nov-12-20101.pdf; https://en.wikipedia.org/wiki/Happiness_economics

333   https://www.princeton.edu/news/2006/06/29/link-between-income-and-happiness-mainly-illusion

334   Daniel Kahneman, et. al., Would You Be Happier If You Were Richer?, Science 312, 1908 (2006), http://pages.ucsd.edu/~aronatas/Kahneman%20et%20al%20Would%20You%20Be%20Happier%20Science-2006.pdf

335   http://www.un.org/en/sections/issues-depth/water/

336   Report submitted by the Special Rapporteur on the right to food, Olivier De Schutter, UN General Assembly (2010) http://www2.ohchr.org/english/issues/food/docs/A-HRC-16-49.pdf

337   https://www.pionline.com/esg/global-esg-data-driven-assets-hit-405-trillion

338   https://www.environmental-finance.com/assets/files/research/sustainable-bonds-insight-2021.pdf

339   U.S. Census Bureau, 2014 Highlights, https://www.census.gov/hhes/www/poverty/about/overview

340   https://www.oecd.org/newsroom/davosoecdsgurriatalksmetricsthatmattergoingbeyondgdp.htm

341   Richard D. Young, Quality of Life Indicator Systems–Definitions, Methodologies, Uses, and Public Policy Decision Making (2008)

342   https://en.wikipedia.org/wiki/Gross_National_Happiness; https://gnhusa.org/gross-national-happiness/; https://ophi.org.uk/policy/gross-national-happiness-index/; https://www.npr.org/sections/parallels/2018/02/12/584481047/the-birthplace-of-gross-national-happiness-is-growing-a-bit-cynical

343   Sources consulted include https://en.wikipedia.org/wiki/Genuine_progress_indicator; https://sustainable-economy.org/genuine-progress/; https://gnhusa.org/genuine-progress-indicator/#:~:text=Genuine%20Progress%20Indicator%20(GPI)%20is,Gross%20Domestic%20Product%20(GDP)

344   Brian Merchant, The True Cost of Gasoline is Closer to $15 per Gallon, Treehugger (2013) http://www.treehugger.com/fossil-fuels/true-cost-gasoline-closer-15-gallon-video.html

345   Elizabeth Blas, Alex Doukas, Sam Pickard, Laurie van der Brug and Shelagh Whitley, Empty Promises, ODI and Oilchange International (2015), http://www.odi.org/sites/odi.org.uk/files/odi-assets/publications-opinion-files/9958.pdf

346   Sources consulted include https://en.wikipedia.org/wiki/Gross_National_Happiness; https://gnhusa.org/gross-national-happiness/; https://ophi.org.uk/policy/gross-national-happiness-index/

347   Adrian G. White, A Global Projection of Subjective Well-being: A Challenge to Positive Psychology?, University of Leicester (2007); http://citeseerx.ist.psu.edu/viewdoc/download;jsessionid=D124A6012E3C0B5FDC699EAA277A5D07?-doi=10.1.1.661.5083&rep=rep1&type=pdf

348   Sources consulted include https://unstats.un.org/unsd/broaderprogress/pdf/How's%20life%20-%20Measuring%20well-being.pdf; https://www.sciencedirect.com/science/article/pii/S0091743520300281; https://www.worldgovernmentsummit.org/docs/default-source/default-document-library/global-happiness-policy-report---final.pdf?sfvrsn=936ee0a_0; https://link.springer.com/article/10.1007/s41060-020-00224-2; https://standards.ieee.org/content/dam/ieee-standards/standards/web/documents/other/ead1e_state_well-being_metrics.pdf; https://www.researchgate.net/publication/225882270_Dimensions_Of_Well-Being_And_Their_Measurement_The_Spf-Il_Scale; https://www.hsph.harvard.edu/health-happiness/research-new/positive-health/measurement-of-well-being/

349   The New Business Imperative: Valuing Natural Capital, The Nature Conservancy (2012) http://www.corporateecoforum.com/valuingnaturalcapital/offline/download.pdf

350   UN Environment (2013) https://www.unenvironment.org/news-and-stories/press-release/new-study-shows-multi-trillion-dollar-natural-capital-risk

351   http://www.terrapinbrightgreen.com/tapping-into-nature/

352   https://datasciencebe.com/tag/internet-of-things; https://www.abiresearch.com/press/iot-developers-to-total-3-million-in-2019-paving-t

353   https://www.ussif.org/files/GSIR_Review2018F.pdf

354   https://www.environmental-finance.com/assets/files/research/sustainable-bonds-insight-2021.pdf

355   https://www.merriam-webster.com/dictionary/regeneration; https://ahdictionary.com/word/search.html?q=regeneration

356   McKinsey & Company, The business opportunity in water conserva-
        tion"(2009); http://www.mckinsey.com/business-functions/sustainabil-
        ity-and-resource-productivity/our-insights/the-business-opportuni-
        ty-in-water-conservation

357   Sources consulted include https://journals.sagepub.com/doi/
        full/10.1177/0022242919825649; https://hbr.org/2008/10/creativity-
        and-the-role-of-the-leader; https://www.neighbor.com/storage-blog/
        sharing-economy-pioneers/

358   David Lin, et al., "Ecological Footprint Accounting for Countries:
        Updates and Results of the National Footprint Accounts, 2012–2018",
        https://www.mdpi.com/2079-9276/7/3/58; https://wwf.panda.org/
        knowledge_hub/all_publications/ecological_footprint2/

359   https://e360.yale.edu/features/consumption_dwarfs_population_as_
        main_environmental_threat

360   https://wiki.commonstransition.org/wiki/Center_for_Planetary_Cul-
        ture_Overview#Collaborative_Consumption

361   https://download.havas.com/prosumer-reports/the-new-consumer-
        and-the-sharing-economy/

362   http://www.forbes.com/sites/karstenstrauss/2013/05/28/why-cowork-
        ing-spaces-are-here-to-stay

363   Pamela Mang, Bill Reed, Regenerative Development and Design,
        http://regenesisgroup.com/wp-content/uploads/2015/02/Encylope-
        dia_Sustainability_Science_Ch303.pdf

364   https://www.oxfam.org/en/pressroom/pressreleases/2017-01-16/just-8-
        men-own-same-wealth-half-world

365   https://en.wikipedia.org/wiki/Human_extinction

366   Lu, Fariss, Bilsborrow, Gendered time allocation of indigenous peoples
        in the Ecuadorian Amazon, ResearchGate (2009), p.242

367   Sources consulted include https://www.bls.gov/news.release/pdf/atus.
        pdf; https://deloitte.wsj.com/cmo/2019/01/03/work-sleep-tv-how-
        americans-spend-their-days/; https://www.bls.gov/news.release/ar-
        chives/atus_06222011.htm

368   http://www.gift-economy.com/womenand/womenand_biology.html

369   https://en.m.wikipedia.org/wiki/Fuel_taxes_in_the_United_States

370   LAEDC, Oil & Gas in California: The Industry and Its Economic Im-
        pact; https://laedc.org/2017/06/08/oil-gas/

371   EIA, https://www.eia.gov/tools/faqs/faq.php?id=427&t=3

372   Sources consulted include: NASA Global Climate Change, Scientific Consensus: Earth's Climate is Warming, https://climate.nasa.gov/scientific-consensus/https://climate.nasa.gov/causes/; https://www.ucsusa.org/resources/global-warming-faq ; https://www.nrdc.org/stories/fossil-fuels-dirty-facts; https://www.eesi.org/topics/fossil-fuels/description;

373   Ibid

374   Ibid

375   Climate Change, The World Bank, https://www.worldbank.org/en/topic/climatechange/overview

376   https://blog.arcadia.com/10-health-problems-fossil-fuels/

377   Susan Lyon and Daniel Weiss, Oil Spills by the Numbers, Center for American Progress (2010), https://www.americanprogress.org/issues/green/news/2010/04/30/7620/oil-spills-by-the-numbers/

378   Daniel Bechstein, Nuclear Risk Pricing, Stanford University (2013), http://large.stanford.edu/courses/2013/ph240/bechstein1

379   Economics of Nuclear Power, World Nuclear Association (2009), https://www.world-nuclear.org/information-library/economic-aspects/economics-of-nuclear-power.aspx

380   International Renewable Energy Agency, Renewable Power Generation Cost in 2018, (2019), https://www.irena.org/publications/2019/May/Renewable-power-generation-costs-in-2018

381   The World Bank, Fossil fuel energy consumption, https://data.worldbank.org/indicator/eg.use.comm.fo.zs?most_recent_value_desc=false

382   http://www.calphysics.org/zpe.html; https://en.wikipedia.org/wiki/Zero-point_energy

383   en.wikipedia.org/wiki/Zero-point_energy

384   https://en.wikipedia.org/wiki/Casimir_effect

385   http://large.stanford.edu/courses/2017/ph240/blakemore1; https://en.wikipedia.org/wiki/Quantum_vacuum_thruster; https://ntrs.nasa.gov/search.jsp?R=20110023492

386   IAEA, Fusion-Frequently asked questions; https://www.iaea.org/topics/energy/fusion/faqs

387   Edmund Storms, The Present Status of Cold Fusion and its Expected Influence on Science & Technology, Innovative Energy & Research, (2014), https://www.omicsonline.org/open-access/the-present-status-of-cold-fusion-and-its-expected-influence-on-scienceand-technology-2090-5009-1000113.php?aid=44645

388   Phil McKenna, That $3 Trillion-a-Year Clean Energy Transforma-
       tion? It's Already Underway, Inside Climate News (2018); https://
       insideclimatenews.org/news/11102018/ipcc-clean-energy-transforma-
       tion-cost-trillion-climate-change-global-warming-renewable-coal-fos-
       sil-fuels

389   CNBC, US spends $81 billion a year to protect global oil supplies,
       report estimates; https://www.cnbc.com/2018/09/21/us-spends-81-bil-
       lion-a-year-to-protect-oil-supplies-report-estimates.html

390   The Atlantic, The Hidden Subsidy of Fossil Fuels, (2019); https://www.
       theatlantic.com/science/archive/2019/05/how-much-does-world-sub-
       sidize-oil-coal-and-gas/589000; https://www.imf.org/en/Publications/
       WP/Issues/2019/05/02/Global-Fossil-Fuel-Subsidies-Remain-Large-
       An-Update-Based-on-Country-Level-Estimates-46509

391   Havas Group, https://download.havas.com/prosumer-reports/the-new-
       consumer-and-the-sharing-economy/

392   IT World, Apple and Samsung fined for planned obsolescence; https://
       www.itworld.com/article/3316958/apple-and-samsung-fined-for-
       planned-obsolescence.html

393   https://en.wikipedia.org/wiki/Phoebus_cartel

394   Sources consulted include https://corpgov.law.harvard.edu/2020/01/14/
       esg-matters/; https://www.mckinsey.com/~/media/McKinsey/Busi-
       ness%20Functions/Strategy%20and%20Corporate%20Finance/
       Our%20Insights/Five%20ways%20that%20ESG%20creates%20value/
       Five-ways-that-ESG-creates-value.ashx; https://www.fool.com/invest-
       ing/2019/05/22/does-esg-investing-produce-better-stock-returns.aspx

395   https://www.pionline.com/esg/global-esg-data-driven-assets-hit-405-
       trillion

396   https://www.environmental-finance.com/assets/files/research/sustain-
       able-bonds-insight-2021.pdf

397   https://www.blackrock.com/corporate/investor-relations/larry-fink-
       ceo-letter

398   Sources: Simfund, Broadridge, GBI. Data as of November 2020.
       Closed-end funds, funds of funds excluded; Money Market funds
       included

399   https://money.howstuffworks.com/mcdonalds7.htm

400   https://www.forbes.com/sites/kathryndill/2014/04/15/report-ceos-
       earn-331-times-as-much-as-average-workers-774-times-as-much-as-
       minimum-wage-earners/#580ce9112520

401   https://www.forbes.com/sites/davidburkus/2016/06/08/why-whole-foods-build-their-entire-business-on-teams/#5fb46cf33fa1

402   https://en.wikipedia.org/wiki/Organizational_structure

403   Charles Hecksher, Defining the Post-Bureaucratic Type, Rutgers, ResearchGate (1994)

404   Sources consulted include https://www.mckinsey.com/business-functions/organization/our-insights/adhocracy-for-an-agile-age; https://www.investopedia.com/terms/a/adhocracy.asp

405   https://en.wikipedia.org/wiki/Adhocracy

406   Sources consulted include https://biomimicry.org/what-is-biomimicry/?gclid=CjwKCAjw-qeFBhAsEiwA2G7Nl4djm5o4nMcent0ys8Y-iL6Q51lavM2qeCq4PRe-fBn-GW2UD_TjQxBoCQ4oQAvD_BwE; https://www.raycandersonfoundation.org/issue/biomimicry?gclid=CjwKCAjw-qeFBhAsEiwA2G7Nl_YFk5XgGKVGOIvJZptjM8xFnux-irId_LQBoc4cKVYUIPp3THUBjCBoC0oYQAvD_BwE

407   Sources consulted include https://thesystemsthinker.com/the-nature-and-creation-of-chaordic-organizations/; https://en.wikipedia.org/wiki/Chaordic_organization#:~:text=A%20chaordic%20organization%20refers%20to,the%20Visa%20credit%20card%20association.

408   Sources consulted include https://www.icos.umich.edu/sites/default/files/lecturereadinglists/fractalorgtheory.pdf; https://meisterplan.com/blog/fractal-organization-complex-systems-ppm/?utm_campaign=US%20-%20DSA&utm_term=&utm_medium=ppc&utm_source=adwords&hsa_ad=377445611457&hsa_tgt=dsa-43245954176&hsa_kw=&hsa_net=adwords&hsa_acc=2236149123&hsa_src=g&hsa_ver=3&hsa_grp

409   Sources consulted include https://www.holacracy.org/; https://en.wikipedia.org/wiki/Holacracy; https://fortune.com/best-companies/2015/search/

410   McKinsey & Company, Doing good by doing well: Shaping a sustainable future, (2011); http://mckinseyonsociety.com/doing-well-by-doing-good-shaping-a-sustainable-future/

411   https://www.pionline.com/article/20170425/INTERACTIVE/170429926/80-of-equity-market-cap-held-by-institutions

412   Michael Anderson, Jeremy Magruder, Learning from the Crowd: Regression Discontinuity Estimates and Effects of Online Review Database, The Economic Journal (2011), https://are.berkeley.edu/~jmagruder/Anderson%20and%20Magruder.pdf; https://are.berkeley.edu/news/2014/11/yelp-ratings-give-restaurants-boost

413   https://harvardmagazine.com/2011/10/hbs-study-finds-positive-yelp-reviews-lead-to-increased-business

414   https://www.nielsen.com/us/en/press-releases/2014/global-consumers-are-willing-to-put-their-money-where-their-heart-is/

415   Leonard Berry, Ann Mirabito and William Baun, What's the Hard Return on Employee Wellness Programs?, Harvard Business Review (2010), https://hbr.org/2010/12/whats-the-hard-return-on-employee-wellness-programs

416   Tamar Wilner, Bloomberg Claims 200% ROI on Sustainability, Environmental Leader (2011) http://www.environmentalleader.com/2011/05/bloomberg-makes-back-double-its-sustainability-dollar/

417   Centers for Disease Control & Prevention, Chronic Disease Prevention and Health Promotion, https://www.cdc.gov/chronicdisease; Allison Van Dusen, America's Most Expensive Medical Conditions, Forbes (2008); https://www.forbes.com/2008/02/06/health-diseases-expensive-forbeslife-cx_avd_0206health.html

418   Aon, Aon Hewitt Analysis Shows Lowest U.S. Health Care Cost Increases in More Than a Decade, (2013); http://ir.aon.com/about-aon/investor-relations/investor-news/news-release-details/2013/Aon-Hewitt-Analysis-Shows-Lowest-US-Health-Care-Cost-Increases-in-More-Than-a-Decade/default.aspx

419   https://en.wikipedia.org/wiki/Ethics; https://en.wikipedia.org/wiki/Moral_absolutism#:~:text=Moral%20absolutism%20is%20an%20ethical,end%20promote%20such%20a%20good.

420   https://en.wikipedia.org/wiki/Moral_relativism

421   Sources consulted include https://ndpr.nd.edu/reviews/principled-ethics-generalism-as-a-regulative-ideal/; https://en.wikipedia.org/wiki/Principlism

422   https://en.wikipedia.org/wiki/Situational_ethics

423   https://www.ucsusa.org/resources/subsidizing-waste; https://fee.org/articles/the-government-has-been-meddling-in-food-and-nutrition-for-a-long-time/

424   https://www.hsph.harvard.edu/obesity-prevention-source/obesity-causes/food-environment-and-obesity/; https://www.hsph.harvard.edu/obesity-prevention-source/obesity-prevention/food-environment/food-pricing-and-agricultural-policy-and-obesity-prevention/; https://www.sciencedaily.com/releases/2020/02/200225122954.htm

425 Sources consulted include https://en.wikipedia.org/wiki/History_of_education_in_the_United_States; https://www.americanboard.org/blog/11-facts-about-the-history-of-education-in-america/#:~:text=The%20first%20schools%20in%20the,2.; https://www.publicschoolreview.com/blog/a-relevant-history-of-public-education-in-the-united-states; https://www.publicschoolreview.com/blog/the-15-biggest-failures-of-the-american-public-education-system; http://hackeducation.com/2015/04/25/factory-model; https://en.wikipedia.org/wiki/Factory_model_school

426 AC Novello, C Degraw and DV Kleinman, Healthy children ready to learn: an essential collaboration between health and education. PMC (1992);

427 Office of Disease Prevention and Health Promotion, Early Childhood Development and Education; https://www.healthypeople.gov/2020/topics-objectives/topic/social-determinants-health/interventions-resources/early-childhood-0

428 https://www.psychologytoday.com/us/blog/freedom-learn/201009/experiences-adhd-labeled-kids-who-leave-typical-schooling; https://www.vincegowmon.com/why-kids-need-to-question-not-conform/; https://newrepublic.com/article/114527/self-regulation-american-schools-are-failing-nonconformist-kids; https://time.com/3822755/adhd-disease-called-childhood/

429 https://childmind.org/article/why-kids-need-to-spend-time-in-nature/

430 https://www.nih.gov/news-events/news-releases/nih-human-microbiome-project-defines-normal-bacterial-makeup-body

431 https://www.cell.com/cell/fulltext/S0092-8674(16)00053-2?_returnURL=https%3A%2F%2Flinkinghub.elsevier.com%2Fretrieve%2Fpii%2FS0092867416000532%3Fshowall%3Dtrue

432 https://www.un.org/development/desa/en/news/population/2018-revision-of-world-urbanization-prospects.html

433 WWF, Living Planet Report (2016); https://www.footprintnetwork.org/content/documents/2016_Living_Planet_Report_Lo.pdf

434 Sources consulted include United Nations Environment Programme, Global Environment Outlook: Environment for Development, United Nations Environment Programme (2007); United Nations Environment Programme, Global Environment Outlook, Healthy Planet Healthy People, Fourth United Nations, General Assembly (2019); https://www.globalpolicy.org/component/content/article/212/45348.html; https://www.wwfpak.org/knowledge_hub_/natura_june/popu-

lation_woes/#:~:text=A%20study%20undertaken%20by%20the,sup-ply%20(Bongaarts%2C%202018).

435   Sources consulted include Kirkpatrick Sale, Human Scale, (2007) Chelsea Green Publishing, p. 125; https://www.sciencedirect.com/science/article/pii/S109051381730209X

ABOUT THE AUTHOR

Throughout history the two most impactful levers of influence on humankind have been (1) the environments in which we live and (2) innovation. By focusing on these levers of change, Mark seeks to accelerate and exponentiate the "Regenerative Economy" – an economy devoted to the thriving of people and planet.

Mark's track record includes being a lawyer; a serial entrepreneur with a public exit and two M&As; a renewable energy and structured finance executive; a financial advisor and innovator who has participated in over $500 million of financial transactions; and an intuitive healer.

As the CEO of Transformative, Inc. and AWE Global, Inc. ("AWE"), Mark is committed to the mission of creating an abundant, well and empowered society by focusing on (1) developing regenerative communities and environments, (2) advancing living systems innovation and eco-social entrepreneurship, and (3) fostering the "Regenerative Economy."

In *Living in AWE*, Mark brings a lifetime of valuable and inspiring experiences to provide holistic solutions to positively transform our world and increase the quality of our lives.